# COLLECTED WORKS OF ERASMUS

## VOLUME 37

# COLLECTED WORKS OF
# ERASMUS

APOPHTHEGMATA

translated and annotated by
Betty I. Knott and Elaine Fantham

edited by Betty I. Knott

University of Toronto Press

Toronto / Buffalo / London

The research and publication costs of the
Collected Works of Erasmus are supported by
University of Toronto Press.

© University of Toronto Press 2014
Toronto / Buffalo / London
Printed in the U.S.A.

ISBN 978-1-4426-4166-2

Printed on acid-free paper

**Library and Archives Canada Cataloguing in Publication**

Erasmus, Desiderius, –1536
[Works. English]
Collected works of Erasmus.

Includes bibliographical references and indexes.
Contents: v. 37–8. Apophthegmata
ISBN 978-1-4426-4166-2 (v. 37–38)

I. Title.

PA8500 1974        199'.492        C740-06326x

University of Toronto Press acknowledges the financial assistance
to its publishing program of the Canada Council for the Arts
and the Ontario Arts Council, an agency of the Government of Ontario.

 **Canada Council    Conseil des Arts**
**for the Arts      du Canada**

University of Toronto Press acknowledges the financial support
of the Government of Canada through the Canada Book Fund
for its publishing activities.

# Collected Works of Erasmus

The aim of the Collected Works of Erasmus
is to make available an accurate, readable English text
of Erasmus' correspondence and his
other principal writings. The edition is planned
and directed by an Editorial Board, an Executive Committee,
and an Advisory Committee.

These volumes, the last in the Collected Works of Erasmus series
to grow from their inception to publication under his supervi-
sion, are dedicated to the series originator, mover, and champion,
Ron Schoeffel.

# Contents

Book 8
866

# Introduction

Erasmus' *Apophthegmata*, 'things well said,' was dedicated to the fifteen-year old Prince William of Cleves, and Erasmus makes it clear in his letter of dedication that his primary purpose was to provide something of an edifying nature for the moral instruction of young boys in general, and in particular of a young prince destined to rule. This educational function of the text explains the nature of the material that immediately confronts the reader: a succession of sayings many of which exemplify, either directly or by contrast, the virtues of the good ruler and high standards of personal integrity. These potentially instructive sayings are presented individually in short free-standing paragraphs that Erasmus presumably thought would be easily grasped by a young mind and painlessly absorbed without undue boredom. This format was taken from Erasmus' primary source, the Greek *Apophthegmata* of Plutarch and was maintained by Erasmus throughout his own collection of *Apophthegmata* as it grew from a modest two books to eight, drawing on a wide variety of other sources. Much of the content of Erasmus' collection is unoriginal in so far as the anecdotes are either translated from a Greek source or adapted from a Latin one, with varying degrees of freedom. Erasmus' own contribution is to be found in miscellaneous comments and explicatory material which he adds to many of them. In the early books these are mostly intended to reinforce the moral message.

Erasmus believed that the early years of any educational programme should, with adaptation to the learners' capacities, inculcate virtue and the abhorrence of vice, a theme he had emphasized years before in a similar work, *The Education of a Christian Prince* of 1516, dedicated to another young prince, the one born to be the Emperor Charles v. In that treatise, Erasmus in passing (CWE 27 251) specifically recommends Plutarch's *Apophthegmata* as conducive to the proper training of the young princely mind, and now, 15 years later in 1531, seeking something to dedicate to young Prince William, he offers this collection of sayings and anecdotes which draws in the first instance on that collection of Plutarch.[1]

He takes from it the sayings of Spartans with which the work opens. These, by the living word, give vividness to the qualities of the ideal ruler set out at length in that earlier treatise. (For the importance of speech for the revelation of character, see eg dedicatory epistle 5–6, and 3.70 with n1 242 below). These include qualities such as self-discipline, putting country before personal advantage, tireless vigilance, considered decisions, dispassionate judgment, magnanimity, firmness without cruelty, absolute integrity, and above all being impervious to flattery. Erasmus had long seen this as the bane of rulers' courts (see General Index: flattery). He often quotes in his *Apophthegmata* from Plutarch's essay *How to tell a flatterer from a friend* (*Moralia* 48E–74E), which he had chosen to translate in England in 1513, saying (Ep 271) that he liked it best of all Plutarch's treatises, and he had sent the Latin translation of the essay in manuscript to the young Henry VIII of England. It was published with the first edition of *The Education of a Christian Prince*.

Erasmus also believed that the learning experience should be pleasurable to be effective, so, as the work grew, he included with his 'worthy' sayings all kinds of puns and witty retorts, even those emanating from the mouths of parasites and prostitutes. Whatever philosophical justifications he may offer for such inclusions,[2] the primary purpose seems to be light relief and entertainment.

We should also take into account the role Erasmus intended for his text in language teaching. Not that young William still needed instruction in basic Latin grammar. Erasmus wanted to set before him a model of good writing in Latin and to increase his *copia* in vocabulary, versatility in grammatical construction, fluency, and supply of illustrative examples (see Introduction xxv–xxvi below). This last was particularly important for the wider audience Erasmus had in mind beyond his dedicatee, for the work, especially in its final form, provides an abundance of quotable anecdote and glimpses of life in the classical world, assembled in one place from a wide variety of sources to most of which his readers would probably not have ready access. It did indeed find a wide readership. It was reprinted three times in 1531 and Erasmus was encouraged by its popularity to produce two subsequent editions in 1532 and 1535, the first of which was enlarged by two new books, 7 and 8, and this last edition was frequently reprinted before the end of the century (see 764 below).

* * * * *

1 See dedicatory epistle 7 n19 below.
2 See dedicatory epistle 14–17 below.

Book 1 of Erasmus' *Apophthegmata*, and most of book 2, are essentially translations from the Greek of the sayings collected in Plutarch's *Moralia* 208B–242D – in book 1 *Sayings of Spartans* (*Moralia* 208B–232D); in book 2 *Sayings of unnamed Spartans* (*Moralia* 232D–236E), *Early Spartan customs* (*Moralia* 236F–240B), and *Sayings of Spartan women* (*Moralia* 240C–242D), supplemented from other sources. The sayings of the Spartan Chilon with which book 2 concludes are translated from Diogenes Laertius *Lives of the Philosophers*, again supplemented from elsewhere.

For Plutarch, Erasmus had available the important *editio princeps* of the *Moralia* (Venice: Aldus et Andreas Asulanus 1509). He had witnessed the preparation of this when he was staying at the house of Aldus in Venice in 1507–8. Armed with this, Erasmus was able to use Plutarch as a major source for the revised *Adages* and for *Parabolae* of 1514, and to translate various treatises from *Moralia* in 1512–14 (and again in 1525–6). In fact, Plutarch becomes his third most-quoted author after Homer and Cicero, and he can never praise him too highly (see dedicatory epistle 6 and 9 below). Erasmus does not seem to have worked specifically on Plutarch's collection of sayings before embarking on this present work, though his use of it in *Lingua* of 1525 and the addition of a number of extracts from *Sayings of Spartans* to the *Adages* in 1526 show his thoughts turning towards it. Erasmus was, however, unhappy with the quality of Aldus' printed text of *Moralia* (for an early complaint in 1513 about its corruptions, see Ep 268:18, also 1.331n 147 below) and he made numerous marginal emendations in his copy. (For details relating to this text, see ter Meere's edition of *Apophthegmata* I–IV, ASD IV-4 Introduction 13.) In preparing his own *Apophthegmata*, for the early books Erasmus was also able to use the Latin translations from Plutarch of Francesco Filelfo and Raffaele Regio (see dedicatory epistle 7–8 and nn20 and 21). Latin translations were an important factor in the transmission and interpretation of Greek texts both before and after the texts themselves became available in the original Greek. In later books, Erasmus will use Traversari's translation of Diogenes Laertius, Giorgio Merula's Latin version of Dio Cassius for his citations from that author, and Angelus Cospus for Diodorus Siculus. (See Introduction xvi–xvii and xx, dedicatory epistle 6 n17.)

The texts translated in books 1 and 2 (like those in books 4 and 5 from *Sayings of kings and commanders* and Romans) contain much material which is also to be found incorporated into various of Plutarch's *Lives* of famous men and also into other parts of the *Moralia*. A comparison of the *Apophthegmata* with these other texts often reveals discrepancies of fact or interpretation. Erasmus clearly consulted them as he, in places, made silent adjustments to his translation or added explanatory details (see, for example, 1.13, 1.16–17, 1.77). Nonetheless, in spite of his censures of the author, whoever he was,[3] Erasmus mostly accepts the text in front of him and in spite of the freedom which he claims in approaching his sources[4] does in these books at least provide a Latin version which for the most part follows the Greek text fairly closely. It has not been judged necessary to analyze comparable passages in the *Lives* and supply cross-references on every occasion, but only where this seems relevant to Erasmus' treatment of the section. If the reader wishes to pursue this matter however, the footnotes in, for example, the Loeb text of Plutarch *Moralia* III will provide the necessary information.

Modern scholarship is divided on the question of the authenticity of Plutarch's *Apophthegmata Laconica* (translated in books 1 and 2) and *Dicta regum et imperatorum* (translated in books 4 and 5). There is as has been said a certain amount of overlap in the content of these and Plutarch's *Lives*. It is possible that, as the Preface to *Dicta regum* claims, Plutarch himself extracted that group of sayings from the *Lives* and offered them to the Emperor Trajan as a separate work and Erasmus accepts this view.[5] As for *Apophthegmata Laconica*, it could represent a collection of Spartan sayings (in alphabetical order for reference purposes) made by Plutarch himself for use in his other works. Plutarch could, however, have used an already existing collection – he refers in more than one place to collections of sayings attributed to various persons, and the appearance in Greek literature of Spartan sayings not included here indicates a wider tradition. The view that *Apophthegmata Laconica* is independent of Plutarch is supported not only by the historical errors it contains, not repeated by Plutarch elsewhere, but by its more uncritical pro-Spartan tone compared with corresponding passages in the *Lives*. *Apophthegmata Laconica* is listed as number 169 in the 'Lamprias' catalogue of Plutarch's works, but not all the works listed there are genuine.[6] Erasmus too thinks that this work is not genuine Plutarch (dedicatory epistle 9 below), but he translates it nonetheless. In fact, although *Sayings of kings and commanders* actually comes first in Plutarch's collection of sayings, Erasmus has put the *Apophthegmata Laconica* first because the Spartans 'win first prize in apophthegms' (end of book 3, 334 below). Possibly his doubts about its genuineness developed only as he worked on it.

\* \* \* \* \*

3 See dedicatory epistle 9 below.
4 See dedicatory epistle 8 below.
5 See dedicatory epistle 5.
6 See *Detti dei Lacedemoni*, introduzione, testo critico, traduzione e commento a cura di Carlo Santaniello (Naples 1995).

These Spartan sayings are predominantly noble, admirable, and meant to inspire, but the Spartans also come across as self-righteous, priggish, and the product of a blinkered world-view. The cumulative effect on the reader combined with Ersamus' insistent moralizing is tedium and exasperation, and one wonders how this first part of the work was received by its young dedicatee, but presumably it was meant to be read only in short bursts.

After the somewhat daunting austerity and high-mindedness of Sparta and its warriors and its women, Erasmus has a change of tone, topic, and source, and in book 3 moves to philosophers, starting with the most famous of all, Socrates. This excursus in justified by his idea that Socrates was 'very like the Spartans.'[7] Socrates brings in his train two highly-contrasted philosophers from the next generation: the worldly and pleasure-loving Aristippus from the Greek city of Cyrene in Libya, and the famous Diogenes from Sinope, on the south coast of the Black Sea, the isolationist and often outrageous founder of the Cynic school.[8] Socrates himself wrote nothing (see 3.88 and 8.112 below) and is reported by Plato as believing, like Diogenes (see 3.257 below) that written texts were an untrustworthy source for philosophical thinking, but the tradition was rich in anecdote of his spoken word. Diogenes Laertius' *Lives of the Philosophers* is Erasmus' main source in this book, and this was written about five hundred years after Socrates and the others, but Erasmus' other two main sources were contemporary with Socrates: Plato's dialogues with their vivid portrayal of Socrates' philosophical method (see 3.130, 8.198 below) and his character (he was known as 'the buffoon of Athens,' see dedicatory epistle 17 below), and Xenophon's *Memorabilia*, memoirs of conversations which he, like Plato, had personally heard conducted by Socrates. Xenophon, like Plato, wrote a version of Socrates' defence against the death sentence for corrupting the young, also a dramatic scene set at a banquet (but not the same *symposium* that Plato reports). Erasmus will quote from all these together with Plutarch's *Moralia* (Plutarch has no collected sayings of Socrates).

Diogenes, like Socrates, probably wrote nothing, but his personality too attracted a plethora of anecdotes, many of them demonstrating both his austerity and his disregard of normal conventions, or telling how he confronted and impressed Alexander the Great, so many, indeed, that once Erasmus has adapted the many tales found in Diogenes Laertius, he can still find

* * * * *

7 See note at beginning of book 3, 221 below.
8 For testimonia and fragments of Aristippus and Diogenes see *Socraticorum Reliquiae* ed Gabriele Giannantoni (Rome 1983) 2.185-285 (reference supplied by a University of Toronto Press reader).

new ones in other classical authors. Many of the Cynic Diogenes' sayings are similar to apophthegms of Socrates and a number of sayings are attributed to both in the tradition.

In contrast to both Socrates and Diogenes, Aristippus cultivated a life of leisured comfort as the guest of wealthy men and despots. The tradition left a number of stories describing how Aristippus sparred with Plato when both were at the court of Dionysius I, despot of Syracuse. Some readers may regret that we get fewer than seventy stories of the hedonist Aristippus as opposed to two hundred and twenty-five stories about the admirable but harsh Diogenes, though many of the anecdotes show Diogenes to have had a ready if brutal wit.[9] The whole book is much less earnest than the previous two, but many of the sayings of Socrates and Diogenes still implicitly convey a moral message.

Erasmus did not at first have access to Diogenes Laertius in Greek for this book. For the first edition of *Apophthegmata* he was dependent for his extracts on the Latin translation originating with Ambrogio Traversari, a straightforward version following the Greek text faithfully as far as possible, even though the translator is often puzzled by its corruptions. Erasmus paraphrased this translation more or less freely. (In the earlier editions of *Adages* too quotations from Laertius are given in Latin from the same source.)

Ambrogio Traversari (c. 1386–1439) was a Greek scholar and theologian, Minister General of the Camaldoese Order, possibly a pupil of Chrysoloras, the pioneer teacher of Greek in Florence at the end of the fourteenth century. He dedicated his Latin translation of Diogenes Laertius to Cosimo de' Medici in 1433, after about ten years' work consulting a number of manuscripts in the hope of elucidating the problematic text. It was printed in 1473 (Rome, Georgius Laver, ed Elius Franciscus Marchisius) and again in 1475 (Venice, per Nicolaum Jenson, ed Benedictus Brognolus) and frequently reprinted thereafter, sometimes in corrected or expanded form, for example in 1524 by Valentinus Curio (see below xvii). Froben's *editio princeps* of Diogenes Laertius appeared in 1533, based on a Greek manuscript which he acquired in 1532 and which was made available to Erasmus in time for

* * * * *

9 On Diogenes and his image and legend as reported by the Cynics, see the general introduction to R. Bracht Branham and Marie Odile Goulet Cazé eds *The Cynics: the Cynic Movement in Antiquity and it Legacy* (Berkeley 1997) and A.A. Long 'The Socratic tradition: Diogenes, Crates and Hellenistic Ethics' 28–46 in the same volume.

the second edition of *Apophthegmata*. This edition contained the new book 7, largely made up of extracts from Laertius. Though Erasmus was now able to translate directly from the Greek, he continued to refer to the Latin translation, especially when faced with the many problems of text or interpretation. There are a number of places where he refers to 'the translator' (unnamed) or offers an alternative version which on investigation is seen to be suggested by Traversari's text. In other places he has been silently influenced by Traversari who sometimes leads him astray.[10] The title page of this second edition specifically says that Traversari has been corrected on the basis of the manuscript.

The preface to the Greek text of Laertius, written by Froben and Nicolaus Episcopius, comments that the Latin translation had long been available, though they question its accuracy. They also comment on the fact that Traversari did not translate into Latin the numerous extracts from the Greek poets which Laertius recorded the philosophers as quoting to reinforce their message. Traversari asked Filelfo (see dedicatory epistle 7 n20 below) for verse translations, but he did not oblige. In any case, in his own preface Traversari says he omitted many quotations where this did not destroy the sense, as being 'not sufficiently serious.' As Erasmus quotes these in Greek (and translates them into Latin verse), it is clear he is using not the 1475 edition of Traversari but one which added the verse quotations in Greek, and this appears to be the 1524 edition by Valentinus Curio (ter Meere, Introduction 17). Erasmus' version also includes a number of Greek words and phrases not dependent on Curio. For proverbial phrases in Greek he could use his knowledge of the *Corpus paroemiographorum* which he had drawn on for *Adagia*. Other words are his own insertions, Greek translations of a Latin term, all part of 'making the work his own' (see dedicatory epistle 8 and 10 below).

Though Latin texts had their problems, the texts of all Greek authors were particularly susceptible to corruption through misreading and misunderstanding, as Erasmus himself comments (see dedicatory epistle 8 below). It is clear from his Latin translations from Greek in all the books that his Greek text, whether manuscript or printed, frequently offered unsatisfactory

* * * * *

10 For references to Traversari see Index of Mediaeval and Renaissance Persons. Not every case of influence by Traversari has been recorded in our annotations. For full details of Erasmus' use of Traversari in book 3 and in the sayings of Chilon taken from Diogenes Laertius at 2.161–87 (208–216 below) see the commentary of ter Meere ASD IV-4 16–17 and book 3 passim.

readings that have been eliminated from modern editions. There are numerous places throughout the *Apophthegmata* where Erasmus discusses a reading and emends the text, both in Greek and Latin. If such textual *cruces* significantly affect the understanding of the extract they are commented on in the footnotes.

To balance the three Greek philosophers in book 3, Erasmus now has the thought of selecting in book 4 three Greek military commanders: the two kings, Philip of Macedon and his son Alexander, and Antigonus I. These are followed by three parallel figures from Roman history, Augustus, Julius Caesar, and Pompey. He then thinks of including three great orators (see 4.256): Phocion, Cicero, and Demosthenes. The bulk of his anecdotes are again extracted from Plutarch's *Apophthegmata* (the so far untapped parts of *Sayings of kings and commanders* and also *Sayings of Romans*). Plutarch's *Life of Augustus* was lost, and Erasmus has converted the mere fifteen stories from Plutarch's collection of sayings into more than sixty (4.133–199) from his knowledge of Suetonius' *Augustus*, Macrobius, and other Latin sources. The twenty-one anecdotes about Cicero have become seventy, drawing on the collections of Cicero's witticisms in Macrobius and Quintilian, supplemented by Aulus Gellius and Plutarch's *Life of Cicero*. The Demosthenes anecdotes come from Plutarch's *Life* of the orator, from various essays in *Moralia*, and from elsewhere.

Erasmus originally intended to stop at the end of book 4, but he could not resist the temptation to go on (see his comment at the beginning of book 5, 493 below), so in book 5 he returns to Plutarch's collection and translates the remaining *Sayings of kings and commanders* and *Romans* that he had not used in book 4. As usual, when he has exhausted Plutarch's supply of anecdotes, he supplements from his wide reading (for example, Plutarch's *Lives*, Nepos, Valerius Maximus). When he comes to the Roman heroes, Erasmus justifiably inserts between Fabius Maximus and Scipio Africanus a collection of deeds and sayings of their great opponent, the Carthaginian commander Hannibal. These have no parallel in Plutarch; Erasmus must rely on Nepos' *Life of Hannibal* and Livy's continuous historical narrative from book 21 to Hannibal's death in book 39 (see 5.270n and 5.281n below). At the end of the book, we have a small selection of anecdotes about various later historical personages of considerable significance (Marius, Sulla, Lucullus, Crassus, Antony), but because Erasmus has already covered Caesar, Pompey, and Cicero in book 4, there is a thinness and scrappiness in his material from the last generation of the republic.

It is worth noting his impatience with Plutarch for including anecdotes that did not contain 'sayings,' but were 'stratagems,' that is, effective military tactics not accompanied by speech, but he cannot bear to leave them out, nor the anecdotes describing a silent message by demonstration (as, for example, performed by Heraclitus or Alexander) or indeed describing nothing more than plain actions.[11]

Erasmus gets fresh inspiration in book 6. Continuing the historical sequence from Roman republic to Roman empire in the first part of the book, apophthegms from Roman emperors (including usurpers) from Tiberius to Bonosus (that is, from the first to the third century AD) are assembled. Julius Caesar and Augustus, the first two emperors, are omitted as they had already figured in book 4. Here Erasmus is drawing primarily on Latin sources: Suetonius' *Lives of the Caesars*, Tacitus, and the lives of later emperors (Hadrian onwards) recorded in the *Historia Augusta*. Here he could use his own emended texts: he had supplied an edition of Suetonius together with the *Historia Augusta* for Froben's *Historiae Augustae scriptores* of 1518 (Basel, Froben, reprinted 1533; see the dedicatory epistle to that edition, Ep 586). Two years previously in 1516 Battista Egnazio had produced an edition of Suetonius for the Aldine firm. This edition of Suetonius reached Erasmus too late for him to take account of it in establishing his own text, as he explained in a second preface to his edition (Ep 648). Froben's 1518 edition did however incorporate a list of Egnazio's emendations to Suetonius, as well as his texts of Eutropius and Aurelius Victor,[12] also texts of Paulus Diaconus and Ammianus Marcellinus, and a list of unusual expressions and Greek words in Suetonius compiled by Erasmus. (Aurelius Victor, Eutropius, and Ammianus are sources Erasmus draws on occasionally in *Apophthegmata*.)

Six writers were accredited at the time with the authorship of the *Historia Augusta*: Aelius Spartianus, Julius Capitolinus, Aelius Lampridius, Vulcatius Gallicanus, Trebellius Pollio, and Flavius Vopiscus, names nowadays considered spurious. Erasmus does not question their authenticity, though elsewhere he, like many others, with good reason censures their Latinity.[13]

Erasmus also draws indirectly on Dio Cassius. The text of Dio Cassius' eighty-book history of Rome exists in a fragmentary state, mainly books

* * * * *

11 For references to stratagems, see General Index: stratagems. For Heraclitus see 8.188 below, for Alexander 4.49 below, and for other 'actions' see eg 1.43, 4.120, 4.243, 4.300. See also dedicatory epistle 9 n26 below and General Index: wordless sayings.

12 For Aurelius Victor, see 6.81 n2 (Vespasian) below.

13 See *Ciceronianus* CWE 28 410 / LB 1 1006D. The 'six authors' were criticized on grounds of style, accuracy, and credulity for centuries, but were not finally discredited and seen as the work of a single forger until H. Dessau's article 'Über Zeit und Persönlichkeit der scriptores historiae Augustae' in *Hermes* 24 (1889) 338–92.

36–60, the rest being reconstructed from excerpts and the twelfth-century epitomes of Zonaras and Xiphilinus. The first attempt at an edition was not made until Robert Stephanus published books 23 and 36–58 in Greek from a single manuscript in 1548 (Lutetia Parisiorum: R. Stephanus), so Erasmus is unlikely to have any direct knowledge of Dio in Greek. However, Giorgio Merula (1430–94) had translated into Latin Xiphilinus' epitome covering the reigns of Nerva, Trajan, and Hadrian (Venice: Bernardino dei Vitali 1500). The *Historia Augusta* has no account of Nerva or Trajan, but begins with the Emperor Hadrian. Erasmus draws on Merula for Nerva and Trajan and also to supplement *HA*'s account of Hadrian. (Modern references to Dio Cassius are given only for the reader's convenience.) A text of Merula may be found eg in Baptista Egnazius' *De Caesaribus* (Florence: 1519, *Per haeredes Philippi Iuntae*). Erasmus speaks well of him as a translator from Greek in *Ciceronianus* of 1528 (CWE 28 417), no doubt on the basis of this text, but Merula does not appear to have translated anything else.

These emperors in book 6, good and bad (but, as he remarks, mostly bad) gave Erasmus ample scope for illustrating, sometimes with brief comments to make sure the young prince did not miss the point, behaviour to be emulated or shunned in a ruler.

In the second half of book six however his aim seems to be pure entertainment, and he raids several explicit and well-known ancient joke collections: the excursus on jokes in Cicero *De oratore* 2.240–289, Quintilian's chapter 6.3 on Wit, and Macrobius' collection of jokes in *Saturnalia* 2.2–5 (already drawn on for Cicero in book 4). These are topped up with all kinds of witty and satirical remarks, puns, and smart ripostes assembled from all kinds of people and from a variety of sources – in Latin, Aulus Gellius, Tacitus, Livy, Valerius Maximus, Frontinus, Quintus Curtius, the Elder Pliny - very often with quite a run from the same author. In Greek, he draws above all on his favourite and much admired Plutarch, using both the *Lives* and the *Moralia*, supplemented with extracts from Herodotus, Aristotle, Lucian, Aelian,[14] Philostratus, Diogenes Laertius, and Stobaeus (for whom see below xxi). The amusing collection of witticisms attributed to the citharist

* * * * *

14 Thirteen sayings in books 4, 6, and 8 seem to be derived from Aelian *Varia historia* books 2 and 9, but Erasmus could not have had a printed text of this as the Greek text first appeared in 1545 (Rome, ed Camillo Peruschi) and it was not translated into Latin until 1558 by Vulteius Wetteranus. Stobaeus quoted a number of extracts but they are on the whole not the ones quoted by Erasmus. Aelian's *Historia animalium*, which was more popular, had been translated into Latin by Pierre Gilles (Lyon 1533) and Erasmus owned this text; see CEBR 2 98.

Stratonicus (6.445–488) is lifted almost entirely from Athenaeus (see below
xx), who in turn was drawing on ready-made collections by Machon and
Clearchus.[15] Athenaeus also supplied many of the amusing tales about notorious courtesans which Erasmus incorporates, regardless of their doubtful
moral implications. Erasmus here, as indeed elsewhere on occasion, seems
to lose sight of his young dedicatee in his zeal for collecting anecdotes.

For his citations from Athenaeus, Erasmus uses the publication of
1514 edited by Manutius and Musurus (Venice, apud Aldum et Andream
socerum, Aug. 1514). His annotated copy is in the Bodleian Library, Oxford. The first complete translation of Athenaeus into Latin was made by
Natale de' Conti in 1556 (Venice, A. Arrivabene).[16] Erasmus however deserves credit for his pioneering work in translating and explaining Athenaeus. He had been using Athenaeus as a source for *Adages* since 1509, first
from a manuscript source, and then from the 1514 publication.[17] A modern
reader, equipped with a better text and various aids to understanding, can
fault Erasmus' interpretation in many places (see footnotes passim), but his
achievement was considerable, since he was wrestling with a text that was
physically difficult to read in Aldus' complicated Greek font, confusingly
presented, and still corrupt in many places in its printed form, in spite of
the great insights brought by Musurus. It was also full of strange vocabulary, and stuffed with literary allusions and unfamiliar quotations from
otherwise unknown Greek literature. There were no aids to the reader and
no index. Yet the way he uses the material shows his control of this very
sizable work.

Like Athenaeus' discursive text, Stobaeus' *Florilegium*, a vast anthology
of extracts from Greek literature, offers a useful assemblage of miscellaneous sayings and anecdotes, but in this case handily arranged by subject
under 126 headings. The complete version of this text was not published
till February 1535 (Venice, Bartholomaeus Zanetti, ed Victor Trincavallus),
though books 3 and 4 appeared in 1525/6. It is clear however that Erasmus knew of Stobaeus long before that, from manuscript and other sources.
He mentions Stobaeus in passing in the first edition of *De copia* (1508; see
CWE 24 626) and in the first edition of *Adagia* (also 1508) in the introduction
(CWE 31 8) and in *Adagia* I vi 1, where he says that he found a collection of

* * * * *

15 See 6.445 n1 below.
16 For this see Rosemary Bancroft-Marcus 'A Dainty Dish to Set before a King,
   Natale de' Conti's Translation of Athenaeus' *Deipnosophistae*' in D. Braund and
   J. Wilkins eds *Athenaeus and His World* (Exeter 2000).
17 See *Adages* II i 1: *Festina Lente* CWE 33 14, also 400 82n.

anecdotes, not attributed to any author, which he surmises (correctly) are from Stobaeus. Books 3 and 4 are quoted sixty times in the *Adagia*. As this was the first section to be printed it was presumably the most readily available in manuscript. Aldus, in the preface to his edition of Lucretius (1500), said that he planned to publish the fragments of Empedocles out of Stobaeus.[18] Presumably he had the use of a manuscript of Stobaeus which Erasmus could have seen at the time of his stay in Venice with Aldus (1507–8), though he does not mention a Stobaeus in the list of manuscripts to which he says he had access there (*Adagia* II i 1 CWE 33 14). Thomas Gaisford, in his edition of Stobaeus (Clarendon, Oxford 1822, Praefatio III) quotes Conrad Gesner (bilingual edition of Stobaeus, 1543) to the effect that a good number of extracts from Stobaeus were incorporated by Raffaele Maffei of Volterra in his *Commentaria Urbana* (1506). According to CEBR (s.v. Raffaele Maffei), Erasmus was familiar with this work, so this provides another possible source. Froben also included in an edition of Callimachus' hymns of 1532 some Stobaeus extracts on which Erasmus drew for *Adagia* (see *Adagia* I vi 1 5n CWE 32 283). There are numerous places where the translators have posited Stobaeus as a source, but this is often in default of any other traceable source and may give an overgenerous impression of Erasmus' use of this collection.

In book 7, added like book 8 in 1532, Erasmus returns to straightforward translation of a Greek source, taking up those anecdotes in Diogenes Laertius' *Lives of Eminent Philosophers* which he had not used in book 3, with occasional supplements as usual from his other sources: Plutarch, Cicero, Herodotus, Valerius Maximus, Athenaeus, and Xenophon. (As mentioned previously, xvii above, he now has both a manuscript of Laertius' text in Greek and Froben's edition, but continues to refer to Traversari's version.)

For the last book of his collection, Erasmus declares he will pass from 'horses to asses,' that is, from philosophers to sophists, those rhetoricians of the late first and second century AD for whom in general he has nothing but contempt. Here Erasmus seems to be hunting for material and the book turns out to be rather a rag-bag as he seeks to make up his quota – whatever his goal was, he eventually achieves 3080 apophthegms. He opens with a run of fifty-three anecdotes taken from a new Greek source, *The Lives of the Sophists*, of the second century AD Lucius Flavius Philostratus, and he has another long run of thirty-five sayings from another new Greek source, Lucian's probably fictional biography (second century AD) of the Cynic De-

* * * * *

18  A. Firmin-Didot *Alde Manuce et l'Hellénism à Venise* (Paris 1875) 146

monax. This is followed in 1532 only by sixteen sayings (transmitted in Latin) of a modern personage, King Alfonso v of Aragon (i of Naples). See the dedicatory epistle (11–12 below) for Erasmus' original intention to confine himself to classical sources. The rest of the book is a miscellaneous collection of sayings drawn rather haphazardly from various sources, some familiar but worth trawling again for anything missed, but also some other new ones, such as the letters of the younger Pliny, and the late third to fourth century ecclesiastical historians, both Latin and Greek. For his possible use of Aelian see n14 above.

From all this, it will be seen that Erasmus' working method in *Apophthegmata* is to follow one particular source, working through it rather mechanically, and, when he has taken all it has to offer, to supplement it with miscellaneous material from elsewhere.

With major sources used *in extenso,* Erasmus presumably has the text in front of him. Incidental single insertions and short clusters of anecdotes about the same person but from different sources are more likely to come from Erasmus' notebooks, where, according to contemporary practice, he had jotted down under useful headings miscellaneous material gleaned from a lifetime's reading in classical literature. The inadequacy or illegibility of his notes probably accounts for some of the features one can fault in his version when compared with the source, such as hasty misreading of text, excessively truncated or muddled account, anecdote attributed to the wrong speaker, etc (see notes passim).

Not that one would gather from Erasmus' text what sources he is using. The dedicatory epistle informs the reader only that much of what is to come is derived from Plutarch's vast output. Even the much-used Diogenes Laertius is only occasionally mentioned by name (see Index of Classical Persons). Probably Erasmus did not pause to consider whether information about sources other than Plutarch was necessary. The whole work is in some ways a superficial production (as he himself seems to suspect, dedicatory epistle 10–11 below), one not planned but developing in an unsystematic way as he wrote it and one which the numerous mistakes and careless errors suggest was written at speed.

There are in the text a number of vague attributions to source provided for individual anecdotes in a haphazard way: 'this comes from St Augustine,' 'from Livy's third decade,' 'from Plutarch's *Life of Aemilius Paulus,*' 'Cornelius Nepos says,' 'the line in comedy,' 'Philostratus tells the story quite differently in his *Sophists,*' 'Herodotus in book 3,' 'Cicero in the first book of the *Tusculan Disputations.*' More precise references in the modern style where not of course possible. Erasmus was dependent on what his texts offered. Like the manuscripts from which they were printed, prose texts were at first presented continuously without chapter divisions within the separate books and this continued for some time. This makes it difficult to locate individual passages within the solid text, hence the dependence on extracts in note books. Possibly Erasmus did not usually record even the author there. Such references as occur seem from their casual tone to be passing thoughts based on memory. A striking more precise reference occurs at 7.287: Gellius, book seventeen, chapter nineteen. Joannes Andreas, the editor of the *editio princeps* of Gellius' *Noctes Atticae* (Rome 1469, Conradus Sweynheym and Arnoldus Pannartz) boasts in his preface that he has marked separate chapters with rubrication, and this was continued in Aldus' edition of 1515, which is probably the text Erasmus had. Erasmus' memory was indeed prodigious, but was not infallible. For example, in book 8 there are three stories (8.115–17) attributed to Eutropius, where they are not to be found. At 6.532 an anecdote is attributed to Valerius Maximus but it seems to be from Plutarch. Some whole anecdotes similarly seem to be written up from memory rather than reflecting a specific source.

One wonders if Erasmus' adult readers would have wished for some more generous indication of author, especially if they were going to re-use the anecdote. Lycosthenes, who re-arranged Erasmus' anecdotes with those of others under commonplace headings in his own *Apophthegmata* of 1577, thought it desirable to add author and work where he could.

Many of these apophthegms of Erasmus are related to the *chreiae* or 'useful sayings' discussed in handbooks of rhetoric by authors such as Theon, Hermogenes, and Aphthonius. In fact, a number of the Greek ones occur as demonstration examples, either quoted in the rhetoricians or identified as such elsewhere.[19] Erasmus could have read the Greek rhetoricians in Greek in Aldus' *editio princeps* of *Rhetores antiqui Graeci* (Venice 1508–9), but he may well have known them in a Latin version also (see 3.386 n1 below).

The *chreia* was originally nothing more than the concise reporting of a noteworthy saying or action (or a combination of saying and action), prompted by some occurrence and attributed usually to some well-known figure, such as Alexander the Great and especially Diogenes the Cynic. It could also be ascribed to a less specific but typical figure, such as 'a slave,' 'a Spartan.' (Erasmus gives a series of sayings of unnamed Spartans in book 2.) A typical *chreia* takes the form, 'On seeing so and so' or 'On being asked such and such, X said/did ...' (Quintilian 1.9.4). A simple *chreia* of this

* * * * *

19 For references to *chreiae* see General Index: chreia; and to the Greek rhetoricians Theon, Hermogenes, and Aphthonius see Index of Classical Persons. Texts are cited from Leonhard Spengel ed *Rhetores Graeci* (Leipzig 1854).

standard type may be found at 1.29 (Agesilaus): 'When someone asked him how far Spartan dominion extended, he brandished his lance and said, 'As far as this can reach' (Plutarch *Moralia* 210E).

Such sayings were recorded frequently in Greek literature, especially in lives, such as Plutarch's *Lives of Famous Greeks and Romans*. They also pervade Plutarch's *Moralia* as illustrative examples. Various persons made separate collections of them, as Plutarch says he did himself (*Moralia* 457D–E). Their popularity in literature can be gauged from the wide variety of sources on which Erasmus is able to draw in these eight books.

The *chreia* was however taken up by the teachers of rhetoric and made the basis of a series of exercises designed to train the young pupil in the first stages of rhetoric, teaching him the fundamental techniques of first expressing the basic material in a variety of linguistic forms, and then developing it imaginatively. Different teachers put forward slightly different schemes with different emphases. The student might first learn to manipulate the anecdote at the verbal level, for example, by the use of different grammatical cases (many of the anecdotes reported by Erasmus are given in the form 'to one who asked him X replied') or by substituting different vocabulary or by paraphrase or by casting it in a different form, such as a question. The student would eventually proceed to the elaboration (ἐργασία), employing a set series of procedures, such as brief single-sentence comment (labelling it 'noble, unworthy' etc); expansion and condensation; explanation and justification of the remark; refutation (as, for example, implausible, shameful, a bad example); and finally confirmation, that is, a development by such means as praise of the speaker, historical parallels, digressions, explanations, and reinforcement by quotations from literature, all of which could develop into a short essay.[20]

Erasmus does not specifically mention the *chreia* anywhere in this work, but the whole exercise seems to be in the back of his mind as he writes up these sayings, especially in the earlier books. In the dedicatory epistle (14–16 below), he speaks of what happens *tractando* 'in the handling' of sayings, a word which probably corresponds to the ἐργασία of the rhetoricians, and goes on to give two extended examples employing the various rhetorical procedures. He then speaks of the value of worthwhile sayings as material for school-boy exercises. On the educative value of apophthegms in general, see *De recta pronuntiatione* (LB I 930C / CWE 26 402): *In hunc usum vale-*

* * * * *

20 See Ronald F. Hock and Edward N. O'Neil *The Chreia in Ancient Rhetoric* 1 *The Progymnasmata* (Atlanta GA 1986). See also Erasmus' treatment of examples at *De copia* CWE 24 606–20.

*bunt celebrium virorum apophthegmata, exquisitae brevesque sententiae, proverbia ac lepide dicta, cuiusmodi suppellex ad omnem dicendi facultatem plurimum habet momenti* 'The sayings of famous men, good, pithy aphorisms, proverbs, *bon mots*, all these server the purpose [ie of giving children worthwhile material] and moreover provide extremely useful ammunition for the future speaker on all sorts of occasions.' Cf Seneca *Epistles* 33.17: *ideo pueris et sententias edis-cendas damus et has quas Graeci chrias vocant, quia complecti illas puerilis animus potest, qui plus adhuc non capit* 'We give schoolboys sententious sayings to learn by heart and also what the Greeks call *chreiae*, because the mind of the child, which cannot as yet take in more than this, can grasp these.'

The earlier apophthegms in book 1 offer worked-out examples of how to develop a saying by means of mini-essays according to a selection of the precepts of the rhetoricians. The very first one, for example, concerning Aga-sicles, king of Sparta, has both an introductory and a closing paragraph. We find there reasons why such a remark should be made, confirmation from a parallel example (Rome), contrast with an opposite example (Athens), and an explanation of the implied meaning of the not immediately obvious re-mark (this meaning being that teachers are more important than parents, which is a *chreia* in its own right, attributed to Isocrates; Theon *Progymnas-mata* 5.207, Spengel 2.99). This in its turn is expanded with both positive and negative arguments. (See also 1.108 or the second paragraph of 1.12.)

For practical reasons, Erasmus could not continue to develop each apophthegm at such length, and thereafter the scale of comment varies greatly. A good many sayings still give rise to short paragraphs in which Erasmus rewrites the saying in other words or explicates its import (fre-quently, 'He meant by this . . .,' 'This means . . .'); for a few examples out of many, see 1.257, 5.141, 5.196, 5.339, 8.93. Many of his comments are, how-ever, brief and perfunctory, as if Erasmus felt that he must write something. More positively, the saying may, as in the rhetoricians, be identified as cruel or witty or a joke, especially one dependent on an unexpected retort.[21] Eras-mus also added in the margin similar one- or two-word characterizations of the majority of his extracts, as witty, cunning, trenchant, cruel, merciful, and so on, which also links them to the contemporary practice of keeping notebooks where examples were assembled from one's reading under com-monplace headings. In many cases any 'moral' explication is replaced by a brief account of Greek or Roman practices, a correction on a point of fact, or a discussion of the reading in the text. Many apophthegms are left with no added comment at all.

\* \* \* \* \*

21 For examples, see General Index: replies, unexpected.

One of the things Erasmus remarks on in his dedicatory epistle (12–13 below) is that these sayings were attributed now to this person and now to that; many such duplicate attributions are pointed out in the translators' footnotes, and Erasmus himself also points out some of them. This is really an essential feature of the *chreia*. According to the etymology given by the Greeks, it must not be a trivial remark but useful (*chreiodes*) for life, because of its wit or wisdom or striking (or even shocking) nature. Therefore it does not really matter who said it, provided it is appropriate to the character of the person uttering it (a commander, a philosopher, a courtesan, etc). This is why so many of these apophthegms, even if attributed, came to Erasmus in a chronological limbo. In one sense, the exact historical situation is unimportant, so long as the anecdote carries its essential message, for example, the admirable character of the Spartans, the quick wit of the philosopher, and many of the sayings throughout the whole work are self-explanatory. Some background knowledge would however be necessary if the *chreia* is to be developed with appropriate detail. Perhaps Erasmus expected a teacher or tutor to supply this along with his other expository material (see dedicatory epistle 8 below). Many sayings, however, do require a context, social or historical, for the real import of the remark to be appreciated, or to be even comprehensible, especially to the modern reader who is not as familiar with the main events and main names of Greek and Roman history as the original (ancient) readership. Historical notes have therefore been supplied throughout by the translators as an extension of Erasmus' own practice and as an aid to modern readers. In book 1, for example, where the various Spartan kings have been identified and given their dates, this is justified by the fact that Erasmus himself, speaking of book 1 in the dedicatory epistle (10 below), comments that the arrangement of the speakers in alphabetical order has destroyed any sense of historical relationship and so made it impossible for the reader to get the added bonus of learning some history, a subject which he considered of great educative value.

'Sayings' may also be unclear because of the truncated form in which they are presented. The words in themselves without a further clue supplied by a context could be interpreted in more than one way and there are numerous places where it is easy to 'miss the point' – Erasmus, being human, seems to have done so on occasion, as he was well aware (see the dedicatory epistle 8 below). The jokes especially very often need the original context to be comprehensible and to enable one to tease out the reason why this particular saying was thought memorable and worth recording. Those apophthegms that depend on ambiguity, punning, and wordplay, especially in Greek, where they may also give rise to textual problems, are particularly difficult to grasp. Many jokes, even if the point is grasped, are untranslatable into Latin (or English) and Erasmus gives up, though conscientiously explicating the mechanics of the wordplay.[22] There are many places where Erasmus seems merely to have translated the unadorned saying automatically without questioning its meaning. Where he does attempt to explicate a joke, his heavy-handed explanation often succeeds in killing it.

## MAIN EDITIONS

A    1531 *editio princeps* Basel: Froben (books 1–6). It was reprinted in Venice, Paris, and Lyons in the same year.

B    1532 Basel: Froben (revised and improved, and enlarged with the addition of books 7 and 8)

C    1535 Basel: Froben (as 1532, with corrections and some omissions and additions, especially 8.306–319)

D    1538–9 Basel: Froben (a reprint of C, with minor alterations and miscorrections)

E    1550 Basel: Froben (a reprint of D)

BAS    *Omnia opera* Basel: Hier. Froben et Nicholas Episcopius, 1540, t. IV

LB    *Opera omnia* ed P. vander Aa, Lugduni Batavorum 1703–6. t. IV 85–380

The translators were able to use a text of *Apophthegmata* I–VIII prepared many years ago by Professor Sir Roger Mynors, which largely agrees with the definitive edition of *Apophthegmata* I–IV by Dr. Tineke ter Meer, ASD IV-4 (2010). For books V–VIII, Mynors' text was generally preferred to that of LB, which often has inferior readings and seems to go back to D. Variations among the different editions are annotated only if they seem significant for Erasmus' practices.

### EDITORIAL PRACTICES

For the benefit of the modern reader, in all eight books the translators have, as far as possible, indicated in the source note (an unnumbered note for each apophthegm) the source apparently being used. Erasmus' additional comments and explanations have usually been set out as a separate paragraph. It is hoped that this will make it easier to see what sources Erasmus was drawing on ultimately and how he employed and adapted them.

The Loeb edition index (volume 16) to Plutarch's vast corpus of *Moralia*, on which Erasmus draws constantly, has been particularly helpful in identifying sources, also the index to the Teubner text of the *Lives*. However, there remain a number of anecdotes from sources other than Plutarch where the

* * * * *

22 Eg 1.222, 3.280, 6.19, 6.33, 6.563, 6.456, 7.137.

translators, in spite of much searching, have not been able to identify the precise source. Well known stories appear in several places and Erasmus may well in these cases have written his own free version of the incident.

The apophthegms have been numbered continuously throughout each book, in order to facilitate cross-referencing and indexing, rather than following LB's numeration by successive hundreds or smaller units. The LB numbering is given in Roman numerals at the beginning of the source note for each item. Erasmus' marginal notes (see xxvi above) also appear in the source note.

Erasmus' Latin text of *Apophthegmata* is full of Greek words and quotations. It was felt to be inappropriate to preserve the Greek in its entirety in a translation designed for a readership of whom many would have no Greek. Accordingly, as much Greek as possible has been removed from the translation itself, even if this gives a false impression of Erasmus' actual practice. (A definitive text such as ASD reveals the extent to which Erasmus without question interweaves the two languages.) Extensive quotations have been translated in the text and the original Greek relegated to a footnote. Individual words and brief phrases have been omitted without comment where this can be done without detriment to the meaning. Where Erasmus discusses the reading of his Greek text or tries to explain a Greek joke or pun, the Greek words are an integral part of what Erasmus writes and these have been preserved and/or represented in transliteration according to context.

In books 1 and 2, made up of sayings of Spartans mostly translated from Greek texts, Erasmus uses several Latin words for 'Spartan,' his choice being determined by what the Greek text offers. By far the commonest word, as in the Greek original, is *Lacedaemonii*. This means all the free inhabitants of Laconia, the geographical area round the River Eurotas in the south-east Peloponnese immediately controlled by the city of Sparta. As a political entity, this was known as Lacedaemon. The term included the inhabitants of the city of Sparta and also those of various subject communities at some distance from Sparta, known as *perioikoi* 'dwellers round about.' These *perioikoi* were obliged to provide military contingents when ordered to do so. Consequently, in many of these apophthegms, which occur in a military context, *Lacedaemonii* refers to the whole military force led by Sparta. An individual 'Spartan,' especially in book 2, may be *Lacedaemonius, Lacon, Laconicus,* or for a woman, *Lacaena*. All of these have been translated, according to convention, by 'Spartan / Spartans.'

The inhabitants of the actual city of Sparta and its immediate environs were the 'true Spartans,' an élite, politically and economically privileged class, whose origins went back to the early days of the city (according to tradition, 9000 in number). It was these who conformed their lives to the famous all-embracing, all-demanding Spartan social and military discipline (described 1.258–87 below under Lycurgus and 2.83–119 in book 2 Early Spartan Customs). They were called, among other things, *Spartiatai*, and this term occurs at appropriate points in the text of Plutarch. Erasmus sometimes represents this by *Spartiatae*, but mostly by *Spartani*, a term he also employs where the dwellers in the actual city of Sparta are indicated by the context. He inserts the word *Spartanus* where an anonymous saying seems to belong naturally in the mouth of a true Spartiate.

To maintain the distinction from 'Spartan' in general, *Spartiates* is translated by 'Spartiate' where Erasmus employs this term. Otherwise *Spartani* and *Spartanus/Spartana* are represented by such terms as 'warrior class,' 'Spartan élite,' 'true/traditional Spartan,' or finally, where appropriate, 'inhabitants of Sparta.'

ACKNOWLEDGMENTS
The translators wish to acknowledge the contribution of the two readers, Professor William Barker and Dr Tineke ter Meer, who read the whole work at an advanced stage and made many useful suggestions which led to its improvement, both in detail and in general. Dr ter Meer also generously made available in advance the Latin text with extensive and learned commentary prepared for her edition of *Apophthegmata* books 1 to 4, ASD IV-4 (Amsterdam 2010). This provided additional information on many points of detail and a deeper understanding of the development of Erasmus' text, especially Erasmus' use of translations of Greek authors by earlier scholars. The translators are grateful for her free permission to make use of this material for the betterment of their own work. We also wish to thank the anonymous reader who at an early stage made us aware of the relevance to the *Apophthegmata* of the ancient rhetorical exercise of the *chreia*. Its importance can be seen from the many references to *chreiae* now supplied in the footnotes.

Especial thanks are due to Philippa Matheson who has meticulously copy-edited this lengthy text and its annotations, identifying obscurities, removing redundancies and inconsistencies, and generally improving the economy of the whole work. That in itself is no small contribution, but her valuable suggestions as to procedure and her enthusiastic collaboration throughout have played an inestimable part in producing the final result. Also at the University of Toronto Press, Lynn Browne prepared the manuscript, then deciphered, typed, and coded for typesetting a much corrected text, with extraordinary patience, care, and attention to detail.

Such errors and inadequacies as remain are the responsibility of the editor.

We also wish to pay tribute to the late Ron Schoeffel for his guidance and for the kind words and unfailing encouragement and optimism at all times over many years which did so much to re-invigorate endeavour in the face of what often seemed a daunting task. We are honoured that this volume is dedicated to his memory.

BIK

# APOPHTHEGMATA

THE APOPHTHEGMS AND AGREEABLE SAYINGS
OF RULERS, PHILOSOPHERS,
AND MEN OF DIVERSE KINDS
SELECTED FROM GREEK AND LATIN AUTHORS
AND SUPPLIED WITH A HANDY COMMENTARY
EXPLICATING THE NICETIES OF THE SAYING
BY
DESIDERIUS ERASMUS
OF ROTTERDAM

# DEDICATORY EPISTLE

TO THE ILLUSTRIOUS PRINCE WILLIAM THE YOUNGER,
DUKE OF CLEVES-JÜLICH-BERG,
COUNT OF MARK AND RAVENSBERG, ETC
FROM D. ERASMUS OF ROTTERDAM,
GREETING

Your royal highness, the gracious reception accorded by yourself together with your illustrious parents[1] to the modest volumes which I sent you earlier as a token, however humble, of my esteem,[2] made me desirous of presenting to you another work, more appropriate to your noble rank and more beneficial, I trust, to your studies. I have therefore made a collection, drawn from all the best authors, of what the Greeks call *apophthegmata*, ie 'things well said,' as this seemed to me the most appropriate subject for a book offered to a prince, especially one still young.

It is of course good to know what the philosophers have written about how to conduct oneself, how to govern, and how to wage war. But few men, even those without public responsibilities, have sufficient time to unravel the labyrinthine twists and turns of Socrates' methods of argument, his manner of feigning ignorance, his ways of leading into the subject,[3] as depicted for us by Plato. Aristotle had much to say on the subject of ethics, but he wrote for philosophers, not for a prince. His works on

* * * * *

1 Duke John III of Cleves and Maria of Juliers.
2 Ie *De pueris instituendis*, published in 1529, when William was thirteen, which included Ambrose's *Apologia David* and *De David interpellatione* (Epp 2189, 2190). Now, at the time of this second dedication in 1531, the young duke was fifteen. He succeeded his father as duke 8 years later in 1539, and ruled until his death in 1592, though his powers were impaired after a stroke in 1566. He endeavoured to improve the educational and legal systems in his territories and in religious matters was in favour of moderate reform (see CEBR 1 316). Erasmus had a long-standing association with the Duchy. His ideas on Church reform and education had found their way to the ducal court via Erasmus' friend John Vlatten, who was counsellor from 1530 and influential in forming the educational and religious policies of both the older and younger duke (see CEBR 3 414–6).
3 See 3.36, 3.130, 8.198 below.

economics[4] and politics are easier to understand, but whatever his subject, he demands of the reader both concentration and plenty of time. Besides, his dispassionate style has nothing to grip the attention of a mind taken up with all the concerns proper to a prince. In the philosophical works, as in Cicero's writings on philosophical subjects, there is much of such a sort that it does not matter a great deal whether a prince knows it or not; for example, their discussions on 'the bounds of ultimate good and evil,'[5] which are ingenious but of no practical benefit. These are fine for people who spend their lives debating right conduct but go no further. A man born to exercise authority needs to put virtue into immediate practice, not debate it at leisure.

As for history, this presents us with a vivid tableau wherein we can observe with pleasure the representation of things nobly or ill done. Consequently it might be thought more congenial to persons in high places, but even if a prince had time to turn the pages of the vast number of books on the subject, who could possibly remember it all?

Wrestlers have in their repertoire specific sequences of moves which enable them to grip their opponent or escape his grip in turn. Likewise, those wrestling with the problems of peace and war need to have to hand specific thoughts which will help them to decide what is the appropriate course of action in the circumstances and what is not. In this we see that learned men have endeavoured to use their skills to lighten the prince's burden of care. Some, like Theognis[6] and Isocrates,[7] wrote books of maxims; others collected

\* \* \* \* \*

4 The *Oeconomica* is now considered spurious. The other writings of Aristotle here referred to are chiefly the *Nicomachean Ethics* and the *Politics*, published by Aldus Manutius in Venice 1495–8. In 1531 Johann Bebel produced a new edition of Aristotle (ed S. Grynaeus) for which Erasmus wrote the preface (Ep 2432). This task had required much reading in Aristotle. Consequently Aristotle was still much in his mind as he wrote this dedicatory epistle in the same month as that preface.

5 Ie *De finibus bonorum et malorum*, the title of a five-volume work by Cicero. For the term *finis*, see Cicero *De finibus* 3.26, 5.23.

6 Theognis was a Greek poet of the sixth century BC. The work going under his name contains elegiac verses which give moral advice and exhortation of a sententious nature. Numerous extracts are quoted by Stobaeus (for whom see Introduction xxi–xxii above).

7 Isocrates was a fifth- to fourth-century BC Athenian teacher of rhetoric and a political and educational theorist. Erasmus is here thinking of Isocrates' *De institutione principis ad Nicoclem*. Erasmus' translation of this work was published with his own *Institutio principis Christiani* in 1516. (It was a favourite subject for translation.) Both were works dedicated to a young ruler and consist largely

the stratagems and apophthegms of distinguished men, writers such as Valerius Maximus[8] and Sextus Iulius Frontinus.[9] Frontinus tells us that several other people had done the same thing.

It takes a great deal of time to hunt for gold in ore-bearing veins or search for gemstones on the beach or in the sea. A man does great service to a busy ruler when he presents him with the gold ready refined and shaped, who offers him gems already selected,[10] cleaned and mounted in gold or set in goblets. Many have sought to do this service but no one in my opinion performed it better than Plutarch. After publishing that very useful work of his on the lives of eminent men,[11] where their words and deeds are recorded all interlaced together, he made and dedicated to Trajan,[12] the best loved of the Roman emperors, a separate collection of the striking sayings of the various individuals, his reason being that sayings let us see the mind of the

* * * * *

of a series of precepts loosely grouped under different heads. In paragraph 43, Isocrates recommends the gnomic poets Hesiod, Theognis (see previous note), and Phocylides as wise teachers for human conduct. Much that Erasmus says in this part of the dedicatory epistle echoes Isocrates' sentiments. This seems to be the work of Isocrates that Erasmus is most familiar with. He rarely quotes Isocrates in *Adagia*, and his criticisms of Isocrates' excessively smooth and polished style in *Ciceronianus* (CWE 28 377–8) and elsewhere seem to be derived from Cicero *Orator* 151, 174– 6 and Quintilian 10.1.79.

8 Valerius Maximus, a Roman historian of the first century AD, author of *Factorum et dictorum memorabilium libri XI*, a convenient collection of illustrative examples derived from earlier writers and organized according to subject matter on which Erasmus drew for the *Apophthegmata*.

9 Sextus Iulius Frontinus, a Roman general of the second century AD. Of his several practical writings, only *De aquis urbis Romanae* (on aqueducts) and the *Strategemata* in four books have survived. This last is a collection of examples taken from Greek and Roman history, illustrating various types of military stratagem used by great commanders, for the information of officers. Other similar works are mentioned in his preface to book 1. See p9 and n26 below.

10 See Quintilian 5.10.121 on the usefulness of ready-made collections of examples.

11 Ie Plutarch's *Parallel Lives* of distinguished Greeks and Romans. These and also the considerable corpus of the *Moralia* had long been a favourite source for Erasmus; see Introduction xi–xiv above. In fact, Plutarch is the third most common source in the *Adagia* after Cicero and Homer. For Erasmus' use of him in *Apophthegmata*, see n19 below.

12 Trajan, Roman emperor AD 98–117, was the second of the 'Five Good Emperors.' For the dedication, see the preface to Plutarch's *Sayings of kings and commanders* (*Moralia* 172B–E), a work which Erasmus accepts as genuine. Although he does not translate this preface, Erasmus uses material from it in this paragraph and elsewhere in the dedicatory epistle. See Introduction xiv.

person truly reflected.[13] In deeds on the other hand, while a good part of the credit goes to the counsellor, the leader or the soldier, most of it goes to fortune. Fortune sees to it that sometimes the best laid plans end in disaster, while unthinking folly has a successful outcome. The Persian Siramnes (a general, I think) was asked why events did not correspond to his noble words. 'I can control what I say,' he replied, 'but what happens lies in the hand of Fortune and the king.'[14] Not that honourable purposes are for that reason robbed of the approbation they deserve.

Plutarch is superior to the other writers not only in what he chooses for inclusion but in the way he presents it. Apophthegms have a special property and character of their own: they provide a brief, sharp, witty, amusing revelation of character. Just as individual persons have their own traits of character, so do individual nations. One way of going about things fits Alexander, another Philip or Antigonus, another Phocion, another Alcibiades.[15] One form of behaviour characterizes a Spartan, another a Scythian or Thracian, yet another an Athenian or Roman.[16] Xenophon's representation of this seems to me rather undifferentiated, Herodotus is flat, Diodorus[17]

* * * * *

13 See 3.70 n1 (Socrates) below.
14 An apophthegm quoted in Plutarch's preface (see n12)
15 Ie Alexander the Great, his father Philip II of Macedon, Antigonus I (one of Alexander's generals and successors), and two contrasting Athenian characters, the upright Phocion and the rakish Alcibiades. All of these are represented in Plutarch's *Sayings of kings and commanders*, translated by Erasmus in books 4 and 5 below.
16 Erasmus has a number of *Adages* illustrating the accepted stereotypes of various nations, ancient and modern, which he does not question, eg Greeks (duplicitous: I vii 95), Thracians (drunkards: II iii 17, IV ix 58), Thessalians (fraudulent: I iii 10–12), Cretans (liars: I ii 29), Carthaginians (treacherous: I viii 28), Scythians (cruel, boorish: II iii 35), Germans (arrogant, overbearing, drunkards: I ix 44), Dutch (unsophisticated and uncultured: IV vi 35).
17 See 4.97–9 below. It is doubtful whether Erasmus was familiar with the Greek text of Diodorus Siculus, a contemporary of Caesar and Augustus. Of his forty book compendium ('too wordy') of world history only books 1 to 5 (prehistory) and 11 to 20 (covering the period from the second Persian War to the death of Alexander) were extant, the rest being fragmentary. There was no edition of the Greek text until books 16 to 20 appeared in 1539 (Basel per Joannem Oporinum). There were however numerous MS copies of the extant sections in Italy and various sections had been translated into Latin over the years. Poggio, for example, translated books 1–5 (prehistory); Angelus Cospus translated books 16–17 (Vienna 1516, repr Froben, Basel 1532); in the Preface to Aldus' *Greek Grammar*, published posthumously in 1515, the editor, Musurus,

and Quintus Curtius[18] too wordy, to say nothing of the rest. Plutarch satisfies on every count, so above them all I have chosen him as my guide.

Consequently, you will find in this work everything that is included in his *Apophthegmata*.[19] This has been twice translated into Latin, first by Francesco Filelfo,[20] and then by Raffaele Regio, with whom I was acquainted

* * * * *

says that Andreas Asolanus intends to carry out various of Aldus' unfinished projects, including an edition of Diodorus Siculus, whether in Latin or Greek is not clear. In 1525 (see Allen VII p547) Erasmus ordered a number of books including a Diodorus. Perhaps he had wind of a projected edition, but as the title is listed after Cicero's *Letters to Atticus* and the *Historia Augusta*, he may have assumed it would be in Latin.

18 Quintus Curtius (first century AD) wrote a ten-book history of Alexander the Great, of which the first two are missing with gaps elsewhere. It may be padded out with rhetorical speeches and moralizing comments, but the vivid circumstantial narrative is fast-paced and gripping. It is not, however, a quick source for the apophthegms, the point being made here. Erasmus had published an edition in 1518 (Strasburg: Matthias Schürer); see Ep 704.

19 Ep 2261 (1530) and the dedicatory epistle (see 10–11 below) suggest that Erasmus' first plan for *Apophthegmata* was to present his personalized version only of some of the sayings recorded in Plutarch's collection, a plan which was modified as the work developed over the three editions. However much he intended to include at first, he does eventually finish up by translating it all somewhere: *Sayings of kings and commanders* in books 4 and 5, *Sayings of Romans* in book 5, *Sayings of Spartans* in book 1, *Sayings of unnamed Spartans*, *Early Spartan customs*, and *Sayings of Spartan women* in book 2, with two extracts from *The bravery of women* inserted at the end of book 6, and as an afterthought, 8.207. This is why he devotes so much of this dedicatory epistle to discussing Plutarch.

20 Francesco Filelfo (1398–1481) was a distinguished if turbulent scholar, teacher, and writer, especially and with justification proud of his expertise in classical Greek, which he acquired in Constantinople, and which enabled him to become a pioneer in the art of composing Greek verse in classical metres. He was intensely interested in Greek philosophy and admired especially Plutarch's *Moralia*. His translations into Latin from Greek literature include the *Dicta regum et imperatorum* and *Apophthegmata Laconica*. Erasmus uses these translations; for references see Index of Mediaeval and Renaissance Persons: Filelfo. Filelfo also translated Xenophon's *Agesilaus* and *De republica Laconica*, which are related in subject matter. *Dicta regum* was complete in 1437, *Apophthegmata Laconica* in 1454; both translations were printed in 1471 (Venice: Vendelino da Spira). Erasmus considered Filelfo of sufficient importance as a Latinist to merit inclusion in the list of notable writers in Latin given in *Ciceronianus*. He also acknowledged his achievement, in spite of errors, as an early translator of Greek literature into Latin. See *Ciceronianus*

in Padua.[21] Filelfo made a number of errors which Raffaele corrected, but he in turn made shipwreck elsewhere; they were, after all, both human. Neither of them intended to do anything more than produce a straight translation, whereas my own policy has been, for several reasons, to take my cue from Plutarch rather than translate him, to expand the text rather than simply convert it into Latin.[22] For one thing, the Latin version can be clearer if it is not closely tied to the words of the Greek original. After all, this book is not intended for Trajan, who was well read in both Greek and Latin literature and a man moreover of long experience. It is for a young prince, and – through your royal highness – for all those of school or student age who are engaged in liberal studies. Nor is it written for an age when such words and deeds were the subject of common talk in the baths,[23] at social gatherings, and in town squares.

Next, I wanted to be free to clarify the point of a saying if it was not immediately obvious. Many of these sayings are puzzling not only to inexperienced readers but even to persons of some scholarship. I certainly had to rack my brains to tease out the meaning in many places, and I suspect I sometimes did not get it right even then.

There were besides many places where I had to wrestle with a faulty text,[24] where the translators too had met problems. You would hardly believe what licence copyists or rather, persons of half-baked knowledge, have allowed themselves in ill-treating the text of this author, who deserves to be

\* \* \* \* \*

CWE 28 415 / LB I 1008 ff; also Ep 2422 11.62–5, where he says he had no predecessor.
Filelfo, like Raffaele (see next note), would be translating from manuscript copies with all their textual problems (see 8–9 below). There were several fifteenth-century manuscripts of Plutarch which included the *Apophthegmata*, as well as many earlier ones.

21 Raffaele Regio (ca 1440–1520) a scholar whose publications were mainly in the field of Latin literature. He crossed swords with Filelfo on points of classical scholarship. His translation of Plutarch's *Dicta regum et imperatorum* and *Apophthegmata Laconica* appeared in 1508 (Venice: G. dei Rusconi) and again in 1510 (Paris: Crispinus). Erasmus met him in Padua in 1508. For Erasmus' use of his translations, see Index of Mediaeval and Renaissance Persons: Regio.

22 See Introduction xi and xiii–xiv above and 10 below.

23 Public baths in the Roman world were, like gymnasia, cultural and social centres.

24 See Introduction xvii–xviii above. There are many places where Erasmus' Latin version reveals an inferior reading in the Greek text available to him. For some examples, see eg book 1.9, 23, 47, 151, 312, 328; book 2.40; book 3.335; book 6.447, 461, 502, 513, 527, 575; book 7.74, 192, 212.

regarded with a kind of religious awe. Of all the Greek writers, Plutarch is the most saintly and the most worth reading, especially in the area of moral instruction. The very thing that should have made them fear to touch invited these hankerers after fame and fortune to corrupt, to put in, to take out. It is of course the most admired and famous authors that are most subjected to this treatment, all for the sake of gain.

This is demonstrated by the variations one finds in different manuscript copies of a Greek work. Saying nothing of others, I shall illustrate this only from the work we are concerned with at the moment. Filelfo has some things which do not appear in Raffaele, and vice versa. Plutarch tells us in his preface[25] that in the *Lives* he reported the words of his famous men all mixed up together with their deeds, but here, in order to produce something more compact, he strung together the apophthegms by themselves. Yet we find a lot of things included which are stratagems, not apophthegms.[26] Moreover, the many repetitions of the same anecdote that we find here surely cry aloud that the body of the text has been tampered with by some other person.

We can forgive the fact that an apophthegm is reported under the name of the person *to* whom it is said, not *by* whom it is said (as with Lysimachus and Philippides: in Plutarch's own collection, Philippides' reply to Lysimachus is given under Lysimachus).[27] It was more highhanded to make two books out of one.[28] Because Plutarch had used only some of the many sayings attributed to Spartans in the tradition (quite enough, in his opinion, for a busy emperor), this fellow, whoever he was (if indeed there was only one), created a separate book for 'sayings of Spartans,'[29] and, what's more, arranged the speakers alphabetically according to the order of the letters in Greek. (Raffaele changed this to Latin alphabetical order in his translation.)

This alphabetical order was absolutely the worst of three possible ways of arranging the material. Valerius and Frontinus organize their maxims into groups based on what the sayings illustrate: patriotism, loyalty, bravery, justice, and so on, distributing each under its proper head. The arrangement that Plutarch followed is the one requiring the greatest understanding of the

\* \* \* \* \*

25 Plutarch *Moralia* 172E.
26 See 11 n40 below. Erasmus quotes them nonetheless, though always with a disclaimer.
27 For the wrong attribution, see Erasmus' comment in 5.111 (Lysimachus) below (Plutarch *Moralia* 183E), and also 6.408 below where the remark is correctly attributed to Philippides; see also 5.272–3.
28 See Introduction xiii–xiv above.
29 See Introduction xiv above.

subject matter:[30] he works methodically through a list of countries and king-
doms, and puts individuals into correct temporal sequence. After each king
he puts his generals, and after each general his colleagues. From the Persians he moves to the Egyptians, from the Egyptians to the Thracians, from
the Thracians to the Scythians, from the Scythians to the Sicilians, from the
Sicilians to the Macedonians, from there to the Athenians and on from them
to the Spartans (where he has the individual persons in chronological, not
alphabetical, order); from the Spartans to the Thebans, from the Thebans to
the Romans; with the result that the reader gets an idea of the whole course
of history from these sayings of a few individuals. Any such historical sequence was thrown into wretched confusion by the person who made that
separate book of Spartan sayings – in which, incidentally, he repeated ones
Plutarch had put in his collection for Trajan. There are repetitions within
each book, but there are so many places where this second book of Spartan sayings repeats the other one that one cannot attribute such an oversight
to Plutarch, who was a most meticulous writer. Moreover, this second book
has no preface, and the dedication to Trajan which precedes the first is not
applicable to both of them.

I am not going to say anything at the moment about the debt of gratitude we owe to persons who interfere with the works of great authors in
this way; to me it seems a form of sacrilege. All the same, except for a few
Spartan sayings, all of them repeated in the other series,[31] I have omitted
nothing that passes under Plutarch's name, for two reasons: the avid reader
(if not the discriminating one) will not feel that he has been deprived of
something; also I saw nothing there that was not worth the knowing, even
if it was not in the right place.

The whole work however I have made to some extent my own, as I have
expanded the Greek text by inserting additional information from other authors and including a good deal of material which was not in Plutarch's text
at all. I have also added notes explaining the meaning of a saying or its application, at least in places where some light on the subject was required,
but only brief ones, as I did not want to spoil things by getting away from
the essential nature of an apophthegm.

\* \* \* \* \*

30 The rest of this paragraph describes the organization of Plutarch's two books
of *Sayings of kings and commanders* and *Sayings of Romans* (*Moralia* 172B–194E),
translated by Erasmus in books 4 and 5.
31 A number of sayings are recorded in both *Sayings of Spartans* (book 1) and
*Sayings of kings and commanders* (book 4), eg those attributed to Brasidas, Agis
I, Lysander, Eudamidas, Antiochus the ephor. Erasmus occasionally omits a
repeated anecdote. See 1.329n, 2.1, and 2.3 below.

My arrangement is even more confused than the one I found in the text, because my first intention was to go over just a few individuals, distinguished ones of course, but as I warmed to the task I got carried away and went on and on instead of stopping.[32] There would have been no end to it if the vastness of the sea of material presenting itself to my eyes[33] had not forced me to sound the retreat. According to Quintilian,[34] one of the marks of a good teacher is not to know some things; with a subject like this, a thoughtful treatment means leaving out some parts of it.

So I decided to be a civilized host and not an embarrassing one, especially as anything not included in this meal can be served at another one, when all this has been digested.[35] In any case, there is an index to make up for the lack of order.[36]

As for the general title, the name of the book does not matter particularly, since Plutarch's collection of sayings, which he called *Apophthegmata*, includes many examples that other people might well wish to classify as *skommata*, 'jibes,' *loidoriai*, 'raillery,' *asteia*, 'witticisms,' *eutrapela*, 'repartees' or *geloia*, 'jokes.' Cicero laboured to no avail[37] trying to distinguish between different types of humorous remark; the efforts of the learned Marsus did not satisfy Quintilian.[38] For that matter, Quintilian, who was a better scholar than Marsus, did not satisfy himself. So I did not think it worth while to devote thought and effort to the problem of distinguishing one from another, but contented myself with pointing out now and again in passing what sort of saying or joke we have.[39]

In my own additions to the work, I was very careful not to confuse stratagems with apophthegms,[40] nor did I add anything at all that was not taken

* * * * *

32 The work is confused because of the way it developed. Erasmus' first intention seems to have been to use just Plutarch's *Apophthegmata Laconica* and outstanding characters from *Dicta regum* (books 1, 2, and 4), but he decided to change subject and source and insert book 3, concerning just three philosophers. He probably then meant to stop at the end of book 4, but instead used the rest of *Dicta regum* to make book 5.

33 This metaphor was probably suggested to Erasmus by Livy's remarks in the Preface to book 31 of his history (31.1.5) where he says he finds himself getting into ever deeper water as he wades into his subject.

34 Quintilian 1.8.21

35 See 2.193 n1 below.

36 Erasmus provided indexes of persons and of things and *loci communes*.

37 Cicero *De oratore* 2.253–89

38 See Quintilian 6.3.102ff.

39 For example, 'jokes depending on the unexpectedness of the reply'; see General Index: replies, unexpected.

40 See 5 n9, 9 n26 above.

from standard classical authors, either Greek or Latin. I know, of course, that recent writers have contributed many witty and amusing sayings, but things that come to us with all the venerability of antiquity carry more weight. In any case, I had to draw the line somewhere.[41]

We find the same remark attributed to different speakers[42] in different authorities, but this should not worry anyone. What was said is more important than who said it, even if sayings do come with authority and find ready acceptance when they originate with somebody famous and well-liked. This happens so often it doesn't need demonstrating with examples. Sometimes, of course, it is due to a lapse of memory (a very human failing!), but there is no reason why the same sentiment should not have been expressed by more than one person, whether in deliberate imitation or purely by chance. It is agreed[43] that the line 'Rulers learn wisdom by consorting with the wise'[44] comes from Sophocles,[45] but Plato cites it[46] from Euripides. Sophocles' *Philoctetes*[47] has the line 'I shall guide you, one old man leading another.' It occurs in Euripides' *Bacchae*[48] as well. Likewise the line 'Keeping silent where silence needful is and in due season speaking timely words,' comes from Aeschylus' *Prometheus*,[49] but we find it in Euripides with the small change to 'To keep silent ... to speak.'[50]

\* \* \* \* \*

41 Nonetheless, Erasmus did, when running out of material, include in book 8, which was added in 1532, some sayings of the near contemporary King Alfonso I of Naples (8.288–8.304).

42 See eg 1.102, 1.297, 1.298, 1.332 below. Many such items are pointed out in the notes passim.

43 The whole section from here to the end of the paragraph follows closely Aulus Gellius *Noctes Atticae* 13.19.

44 See *Adagia* III vi 97: *Sapientes tyranni sapientum congressu* 'Kings become wise through association with the wise.' See also Plutarch's essay *Maxime cum principibus philosopho esse disserendum* (*Moralia* 776A–778B).

45 According to Aulus Gellius this comes from the (now lost) *Ajax Locrus* (fr 13 Nauck²).

46 According to Aulus Gellius, Plato cites this in his *Theaetetus*, but actually at *Theages* 6.

47 According to Aulus Gellius, not from *Philoctetes* but the (now lost) *Phthiotides* (fr 633 Nauck²). There is however a textual problem here in Aulus Gellius. Aldus' 1515 edition of Gellius reads *Philoctetes*.

48 Euripides *Bacchae* 193, again quoted from Aulus Gellius.

49 Not from *Prometheus Vinctus* but the (now lost) *Prometheus Pyrphoros* (fr 208 Nauck²), as Aulus Gellius says.

50 Euripides *Ino* (fr 413 Nauck²). The line as quoted by Aulus Gellius is actually more divergent in form than Erasmus suggests ('to speak what is sure.' So in Aldus' 1515 text). Erasmus' is possibly misremembering and confusing it

Sometimes the sources differ not only over the speaker but over the content of the saying. For example, Fabius Maximus was taunted by a certain person who said it was thanks to himself that Fabius had recaptured Tarentum. For Cicero that person is Livius Salinator,[51] for Livy Marcus Livius,[52] for Plutarch Marcus Lucius (or as the Greek manuscripts have it, Markios Leukios).[53] Again, Fabius Philostratus has the story that the Athenian assembly all laughed at the sophist Leon because he was enormously fat;[54] Plutarch says it was because he was a tiny man. [55] What differences there are in the accounts of the quarrel between Gnaeus Domitius and Lucius Crassus in Valerius Maximus[56] and Pliny![57]

The least convincing sayings are those put into the mouths of characters from literature. The sophist Philostratus for example makes up anything he pleases for Palamedes, Ulysses and so forth.[58] These become twice as feeble once you start handling them.[59] I have included absolutely nothing of this sort. Close behind these come sayings attributed to characters in the sort of dialogue that makes no claim to verisimilitude but is devised simply to provide recreation. Sayings extracted from comedy or tragedy have more life, in fact they can be very satisfactory used in the right place, even if they can't be called apophthegms, except when some great writer adapts them to his present purpose – they become more pleasing if they are given a new twist and made to imply something slightly different. For example, Aristotle cautioned Callisthenes when he was more outspoken with Alexander than was wise,[60] quoting the line from Homer, 'Doomed to an early death shalt thou be, my son, with such words upon thy lips.'[61]

\* \* \* \* \*

with Aeschylus *Choephori* 582, which does simply show the small change from participle to infinitive.

51 Cicero *De oratore* 2.273; *De senectute* 11.

52 Livy 27.25.3; see 5.276 below.

53 Plutarch *Life of Fabius Maximus* 23.3. Modern texts give the name as Marcus Livius.

54 Philostratus *Vitae sophistarum* 1.2, the same author as the one referred to in n58 below.

55 Plutarch *Moralia* 804A (*Precepts of statecraft*). See 6.414n and 8.1 below.

56 Valerius Maximus 9.1.4

57 Pliny *Naturalis historia* 17.1.2–4. See 6.329 below.

58 The sophist Favius (sic) Philostratus in *Heroicos*, a dialogue on the heroes of the Trojan War, 3.25, 11.2, 19.5.

59 Presumably developing them in the various exercises prescribed for *chreiae* (see Introduction xxv above).

60 See Plutarch *Life of Alexander* 54.1. Callisthenes was notorious for his bluntness and lack of tact or moderation. The incident will be used in 7.220 below.

61 Homer *Iliad* 18.95

I felt no inclination to include many of Herodotus' apophthegms, because most of them seem to be entirely the product of the author's imagi-
nation. Of the same stamp[62] are sayings found in the speeches which historians invent, according to their ability, for the characters in their narrative,
though even such sayings have their uses in developing the critical faculty
and fluency of style.

The best type of apophthegm is one which in a few words suggests
rather than spells out some out-of-the-ordinary thought, such that no one
could deliberately invent it, and which becomes more and more satisfactory
the more closely you study it.

Everything included under proverbs, maxims, striking sayings, striking actions, is particularly relevant to men in positions of authority, who
are so busy with the practicalities of government that they cannot devote
much of their lives to books. But the things I have listed are learned with
enjoyment and easily take root in the mind, and actually contain more deep
teaching than appears at first sight. We are told that whenever Caesar Augustus came across any of these instructive items, he made sure to have
them copied and sent out to various places.[63]

It was the policy of those wise men of old to use the bait of pleasure to introduce into young minds things worth knowing, so that children
while still unformed and not yet ready for serious moral instruction should
learn in play what would stand them in good stead all their lives. In line
with this theory, they sprinkled their cosmology, astronomy, music, natural and moral philosophy with cleverly thought up stories and fables. It will
be observed that my collection contains some items that do nothing to teach
morals but simply raise a laugh. Not that I should be censured for that –
laughter relaxes tired spirits, provided the joke shows some wit and is not
offensive. This sort of thing cheers and enlivens the minds of the young,
makes life more civilized, our speaking more attractive.[64] What does more
to sweeten Cicero's style than his constant seasoning of it with bon-mots of
this sort? What are Plutarch's moral writings if not tapestries embroidered
with such colours?

Indeed, things that seem to be quite ridiculous become serious once
you start handling them. What could be more ridiculous than Diogenes

* * * * *

62 *Adagia* iii v 44: *Nostrae farinae* 'Same flour as we are'
63 Suetonius *Augustus* 89.2
64 Erasmus believed in the need for interspersing hard work with lighter pursuits. See *Adagia* iv viii 39: *Iocandum ut seria agas* 'Play in order to be serious.'
   Cf Aristotle *Nicomachean Ethics* 10.6 (1176b33–5).

going about with a lantern in broad daylight in the crowded city centre and saying over and again that he was looking for a man?[65] We laugh, but at the same time we learn that what looks like a man is not necessarily a man – after all, statues look like a man. To find a man, you have to look into the mind. If the mind is guided by reason rather than feelings, then you have at last found a man. Then what about that ridiculous thing Phryne did? At a banquet, she got all the other women to agree to copy whatever she did. She then twice dipped her hand in water and laid it on her brow. By this trick, to everyone's amusement, she revealed that all the others were wearing cosmetics, while she herself appeared even more lovely.[66] From this amusing incident we learn the same moral lesson as we do from Socrates when he remarked, in a serious context, that we should endeavour to be in reality the kind of people we want others to think we are.[67] Otherwise, once our pretence is stripped off, our ill-based repute will be replaced by humiliation. We also learn not to depend on external impermanent advantages, which all kinds of mishap can take away from us, but to provide ourselves with the true riches of the mind, over which fortune has no jurisdiction. All this serious moral teaching is to be found in an amusing thing done by a mere woman, and one of easy virtue at that.

Similarly, although the régime which Lycurgus devised for the citizens of Sparta was generally speaking a harsh one, he not only allowed but positively enjoined decent, healthy humour. He established an activity which he called *leschai*.[68] The older men, who were retired from serving the state, met for that purpose and happily passed the time in pleasant chat and jocular conversation free from vulgarity, praising the good and censuring the bad.

\* \* \* \* \*

65  See Diogenes Laertius 6.41 (3.226 below). This is quoted as a *chreia* in the rhetoricians (see Hock and O'Neill 321; Introduction xxiv n19 above).
66  Phryne was a courtesan famed for her beauty which needed no enhancement. She was used as a model by the painter Apelles for his Venus Anadyomene and the sculptor Praxiteles for his Cnidian Venus. For the incident, see Galen *Protrepticus* 10.26. There are anecdotes about her in 6.575–581 below, where this story is repeated.
67  Xenophon *Memorabilia* 1.7.1; 2.6.39; Cicero *De officiis* 2.12.43.
68  See Plutarch *Lycurgus* 25.2–3. When writing *Adagia* II ii 3 'Nightingales perching on trifles' Erasmus thought λέσχαι meant 'trifles.' He later discovered the true meaning 'public benches' from Harpocration and in 1533 rather grudgingly added this as a possible meaning to *Adagia* IV vi 36. (Harpocration *Lexicon in decem oratores Atticos* [Aldus 1503] was a source which Erasmus used extensively for the 1533 additions to *Adagia*.) Here however he interprets it as a light-hearted form of relaxation in which retired gentlemen indulged in witty conversation.

He even dedicated a statue to Gelos, the god of laughter[69] as he thought it a good thing to restore jaded spirits with clean humour and so make them alert and ready again for worthwhile labours. Truly in the affairs of men, 'Nothing can last that knows not rest in turn.'[70] Cleomenes was so strict that he would not allow into the country actors or female performers on the lyre or pipers, yet even he allowed the citizens to bandy about decent jokes and wisecracks.[71] If we have some free time or if we find ourselves in a situation where some merriment is appropriate, it is far more decent to have fun with this kind of talk than to find pleasure in vulgar, ignorant, obscene stories.

It seems to me much more sensible to give schoolboys practice with items of this sort rather than the ones in common use, which are not only pathetically unappealing in content but don't reveal the mysteries of the Latin language either. The teacher must, of course, point out the various ways of expanding what has been said concisely and of adapting to serious use what has been said in jest. I would also say this: while it is probably not right to mingle human jest with divine scripture in sermons, there would be more excuse for putting in this sort of thing to wake the sleepers up[72] than the old wives' tales picked out of the gutter which some preachers drag in for no apparent reason.

In the midst of all his civil and military preoccupations, Julius Caesar used to dispel the weariness brought on by burden of care by reading witty remarks, which he enjoyed so much he appreciated even ones directed at himself, provided they were clever.[73] None of the emperors was more to be revered, or more devoted to his task than Augustus, yet none could surpass him in the polished urbanity of his witticisms.[74] Cicero I shall ignore, as some people think he paid no attention to either moderation or decency in making his wisecracks.[75] The philosopher Xenocrates was a great man, but marred by his dour disposition – Plato was constantly telling him to offer

* * * * *

69 See Plutarch *Life of Lycurgus* 25.4.
70 Ovid *Heroides* 4.89
71 This is Cleomenes III, king of Sparta 236–2 22 BC. See Plutarch *Life of Agis and Cleomenes* 33.
72 See Erasmus *Ecclesiastes* 2 / LB V 860 / ASD V-4 276, lines 640–71.
73 See Cicero *Ad familiares* 9.16.4; Suetonius *Julius Caesar* 73.
74 See Macrobius *Saturnalia* 2.3.13. A selection of Augustus' witticisms is given there at 2.4. See 4.133–199 below.
75 See Quintilian *Institutio oratoria* 6.2.3– 6; Macrobius *Saturnalia* 2.3.13; Erasmus *Ciceronianus* CWE 24 358 / LB I 980D. See some of these quoted at 4.280–350 below.

some sacrifice to the Graces.[76] Zeno was the complete Stoic and used to call Socrates 'the buffoon of Athens,'[77] because of his constant flow of amusing talk. Yet everyone would agree that Socrates is more to be revered than either of them. I need not remind you that the most celebrated sayings are those salted with clever wit. Socrates, Diogenes, and Aristippus would have more to contribute to the education of children than Xenocrates or Zeno.[78]

If wise men were right in using things that appeal to children in order to draw them on gradually to enjoy instruction that is harder and more demanding, this approach is even more appropriate in the case of a student somewhat older and a prince as well. A prince needs to be alert, he must never be depressed or send anyone away depressed.[79] The mind that has enjoyed what it has learnt has more resilience in the face of any problems, is more able to be genial whatever company he finds himself in.

I could defend myself with arguments such as these if my collection were entirely made up of humorous items. As it is, humorous items are combined with serious ones, acting like seasoning in a dinner. If I learn that you have enjoyed a book like this, I shall not regret writing such a work, even if some people maybe will think it rather elementary. Others may well produce works for students at a more advanced stage: we are providing milk for a prince of tender years. If however this is not advanced enough for you (and I should be pleased if that were so), I know that you will be happy if, through you, this attempt at something useful becomes available to help all young persons in their studies. Maybe we will give you something harder one day, once you have got this by heart – for it all needs to be learnt, so that it can all be ready to hand.

Though you have no need of anything I can offer, since you have Conrad Heresbach[80] living with you, a man thoroughly versed in every literary discipline and so affectionate towards you that, like every good tutor, he is more delighted with the advances and successes of his pupil than with

* * * * *

76 See Plutarch *Life of Marius* 2.3; *Moralia* 769D (*On love*); *Moralia* 141F (*Advice to bride and groom*); Diogenes Laertius 4.6; also 6.581 and n1 below. This is briefly referred to in *Adagia* II vi 18: Ἄμουσοι 'Strangers to the Muses.'

77 See Cicero *De natura deorum* 1.93.

78 These are the three philosophers whom Erasmus singles out for inclusion in book 3. Zeno here seems to be the abusive Epicurean, Zeno of Sidon, not the famous Zeno of Citium.

79 See 6.84 (Titus) below.

80 It was due to the recommendations of Erasmus and John Vlatten (see n2 above) that Heresbach was appointed tutor to the prince in September 1523. See Ep 1316 introduction.

his own. He has shaped your childhood with his lessons; he will be able to assist your maturer years with loyal and wise counsel. I too feel honoured as well as pleased that my efforts have been able to contribute in however small a capacity to the advancement of your gifts of intellect. It remains only to pray almighty God that he may graciously preserve, protect, and increase the gifts which he has bestowed upon you in such rich measure. Then you will fulfil all the hopes that your honoured parents cherish for you, grow up worthy of your long line of distinguished ancestors, and be equal to ruling the glorious realm to which you have been born and for which you are destined.

One more thing and I have done: when you study this book, remember you are reading the apophthegms not of Christians but of pagans, in other words, read critically.

Freiburg im Breisgau, 26 February 1531

# BOOK I

## SAYINGS OF SPARTANS
## ARRANGED IN ORDER
## ACCORDING TO
## THE GREEK ALPHABET

**Agasicles**
The Spartans were markedly strict and their morals particularly uncorrupted. Their chief concern was military glory. Consequently they despised all arts which in their view made the minds of the citizenry soft and drew them away from true worth to idle ostentation.[1] Rome too, at the time when she was still breathing that spirit of austerity with which she began, drove from the city those pestilential Greeks.[2] No part of Greece was more corrupted by such intellectual pursuits than Athens, where Gorgias, Lysias, Isocrates, Prodicus and innumerable other sophists[3] performed their patter to the plaudits of the people – and considerable financial reward.

\* \* \* \* \*

1 On Erasmus' translation of words for 'Sparta' and 'Spartan' see Introduction xxix–xxx above. For the Spartan attitude to music, see General Index: trivial pursuits.
2 This refers to the year 155 BC, when the Greek states sent to the Roman senate an embassy consisting of the philosophers Diogenes the Stoic, Carneades the Academic, and Critolaus the Peripatetic. While in Rome, they took the opportunity of lecturing on philosophical topics, and Carneades in particular made a great impression by his eloquent demonstration of the opposing theses that justice is a/ natural, b/ merely conventional. Cato the Censor, famed for his strict, old-fashioned views, accordingly took steps to have them hurried from the city as a dangerous influence. See Plutarch *Cato maior* 22; Aulus Gellius *Noctes Atticae* 6.14.
   Erasmus employs the term *Graeculi*, a disparaging diminutive form, used by the Romans (first century BC onwards) to refer to contemporary Greeks, whom they considered clever, unprincipled, and lacking in seriousness. See eg Juvenal 3.78; *Adagia* I vii 95: *Da mihi mutuum testimonium* 'Lend me your evidence.'
3 These were itinerant Greek teachers who charged fees for public lectures and courses of instruction in various subjects including the art of public speaking. Given the nature of contemporary Greek society, this skill was expected to ensure success in life. Students were taught, among other things,

1 So when somebody remarked to Agasicles, king of Sparta, that he was surprised that he, Agasicles, being so fond of learning things, did not invite the
sophist Philophanes[1] to join his retinue, he with true kingly dignity replied,
'I desire to be the pupil of those whose son I also am.'[2]

By this he meant that it is equally important whom you get as parents and whom you engage as teachers. As family characteristics reappear
in later generations, so the faults of teachers are transmitted to their pupils.
Where honourable living is the subject of instruction, the teachers must be
those who have demonstrated virtue in their actions, not those who prate
about virtue in stylish rhetoric. But nowadays, good God, what sort of men
are entrusted with the formation and education from their earliest years
of those who will one day be rulers of the whole world! Yet for a prince
it is just as harmful, just as improper, to be educated by persons of unworthy character as to be born of them. Moreover, a prince should not
learn any and every art, but only those which teach the principles of good
government.

* * * * *

how to argue effectively for any point of view, irrespective of truth or personal conviction. The most famous sophists amassed large fortunes as their
courses were immensely popular, especially in cities such as Athens. Gorgias, Lysias, Isocrates, and Prodicus were some of the most famous, working in the period fifth to fourth century BC. To some extent their teaching
overlapped with that of contemporary philosophers. In the hands of lesser
men, the teaching concentrated on self-advancement at the expense of truth
and integrity and gave rise to the bad name that sophistry eventually acquired. A later generation of sophists flourished in the first to second centuries AD (the 'Second Sophistic') concentrating on rhetoric. Erasmus will
record sayings of both early and later sophists in 8.1–52 below. See the Preface to book 8 for Erasmus' views on sophists, which are no doubt influenced by Plutarch's low opinion of them. See also 1.88, 2.17 n2, and 3.36
below.

1   (1) Plutarch *Moralia* 208B (*Apophthegmata Laconica*). In margin 'noble'
Agasicles was king of Sparta, c. 575–550 BC. Information about the various
kings of Sparta and other Spartan persons whose sayings will be recorded
in *Apophthegmata* is to be found in Paul Poralla and Alfred S. Bradford *A
Prosopography of Lacedaemonians from the Earliest Times to the Death of Alexander
the Great (X–323 B.C.)* 2nd ed (Chicago 1985).
1 For the sixth century BC, the word 'sophist,' which Erasmus has taken from
the Greek text of Plutarch, is an anachronism. When it first came into use in
the fifth century it had no pejorative overtones and meant simply a wise or
skilled man, which is presumably what it means here.
2 A better version of Plutarch's Greek text here gives the meaning, 'whose son
I would also wish to be.'

2 On another occasion someone asked Agasicles how any ruler could be safe without a bodyguard. He replied, 'If he rules his people as a father rules his children.'

No one ever said more in so few words. It is only masters who are feared, and that by slaves: it is fear of punishment that restrains those who are not kept from wrongdoing by a sense of decency. Since a father is concerned for his children rather than for himself, their love for him combines reverence with an acknowledgement of his authority. There is no need of a bodyguard to protect from these – their attendance on him is in fact the most reliable form of bodyguard. If a king wins over the affections of the citizens by benevolence and well-doing, he will have no need of foreign mercenaries to guard him. His own citizens, towards whom he will feel as a father feels, will be the surest possible protectors of his person. There is a well-known quotation: 'Let them hate as long as they fear.'[1] Those who approve of such a sentiment find in the very people they should be trusting their chief objects of suspicion, and anyone feared by many must needs fear many in turn.

### Agesilaus

3 Agesilaus, the famous king of Sparta, was once at a drinking party, and after lots had been cast in the customary fashion, was appointed master of ceremonies. (The duty of the master of ceremonies was to prescribe the amount each person should drink.) When the butler asked him how much wine he should pour each person, he replied, 'If there is plenty of wine provided, give each as much as he asks for; if there isn't enough, divide it equally among them all.'

This clever solution made sure that in case of plenty, there would be no shortage for those who liked to drink deeply, while the abstemious would not be compelled to drink. On the other hand, if supplies were limited, by treating all equally he removed any occasion for resentment. As an equal

\* \* \* \* \*

2 (II) Plutarch *Moralia* 208B. In margin 'weighty, forbearing'
  1 A famous line from the early Roman tragedian Accius, a fragment quoted by Cicero *Philippics* 1.14.34. See also Seneca *De clementia* 2.2.2; *Adagia* II ix 62. See the anecdote about Caligula (6.21 below).

3 (III) Plutarch *Moralia* 208B–C. In margin 'ingenious'
  Agesilaus II, king of Sparta 400–360 BC, was one of the most famous of Spartan kings and the city's foremost general. He was promoted to the kingship only in 400 BC, after the Peloponnesian War. Many of the sayings here quoted belong to the time when he was general but not yet king, though Erasmus often calls him 'King.' See 1.242 n1 below. In Plutarch's *Parallel Lives* he is compared with the Roman military leader Pompey the Great.

amount of wine was served to each person, those who usually drank with moderation had plenty; and those who were intending to drink more deeply had enough to satisfy normal physical needs and could not complain if their greed went unsatisfied, since no one in the whole company had more or less than the rest. So even those who normally liked to indulge settled without ill-humour for moderation. The Spartans indeed approved of frugal living more than the rest of the Greeks.

4 When it was reported to Agesilaus that a certain criminal had withstood torture with fortitude, he said, 'A man who applies his powers of endurance and tolerance of suffering to wicked and disgraceful ends is truly wretched.'

Among the Spartans endurance of suffering was considered admirable. If suffering is accepted for honourable ends, it merits high praise; but if for evil ends, the person concerned does not deserve praise for fortitude; in fact, the more resolute he shows himself, the more to be pitied and the more reprehensible he is. (I give these two meanings because the Greek word *ponēros* means either 'wicked' or, with a different accent, 'distressed' or 'unfortunate.')[1]

The general was very sorry that so much strength of mind and body had been expended on an unworthy end. If the person had employed it on honourable ends, he could have served his country well.

5 Someone else was praising a rhetorician for his amazing development of a slight subject. Agesilaus remarked, 'I wouldn't consider even a shoemaker good, if he fitted big shoes on a small foot.'[1]

\* \* \* \* \*

4   (iv) Plutarch *Moralia* 208c. In margin 'weighty'
  1 Erasmus' comment does not make it clear that the word πονηρός [*ponerós*] oc-
    curs in the Greek text of the apophthegm, where he has opted (line 3) for the
    Latin translation *miser*, ie 'wretched, unfortunate.' This distinction between
    πόνηρος [*pónēros*] 'suffering, unfortunate,' and πονηρός [*ponērós*] 'wicked, evil'
    is propounded in Byzantine etymological compilations: Hesychius' *Lexicon* of
    fifth to sixth century AD (M. Musurus, Venice 1514), the Suda of the tenth cen-
    tury (Demetrios Chalcondyles, Milan 1499), and the *Etymologicum Magnum* of
    the twelfth century (Zacharias Callierges, Venice 1499). Only the accentuation
    πονηρός is recognized nowadays for all meanings.

5   (v) Plutarch *Moralia* 208c. In margin 'witty'
  1 For the sentiment, 1.230 and 2.115 below; *Adagia* III vi 67: *Herculis cothurnos
    aptare infanti* 'To put Hercules' boots on a baby'

Sincerity is highly desirable in oratory,[2] and the best speaker is one whose speech fits his subject;[3] the style of the speech must derive from the subject matter, not from the speaker's artistry.

6 A certain person kept badgering Agesilaus, relentlessly pursuing him with some petition and saying, 'You promised,' over and over again, as if that constituted some moral obligation not to deny the request. 'Quite right,' said Agesilaus. 'If what you ask is justified, I did promise; if it is not, then I spoke but I didn't promise.' (By these words he cut the ground from under the importunate fellow's feet.) He however was still not prepared to desist and brought in a new argument: 'All the same, kings should honour anything "to which they give their royal nod."'[1] 'And petitioners to kings,' said Agesilaus, 'should just as much come with justifiable requests and legitimate appeals, choosing the right moment and bearing in mind what is right and proper for kings to grant.'

Some people spring on kings out of ambush, as it were, and demand something unjustifiable of them when they have been drinking or when they are busy with something else, and so cannot consider properly what kind of request is being put to them. It is quite right to go back on a promise made to such people, and wrong of them, when refused, to demand that the promiser keep faith, since they did not remember their own obligations when making their requests.

7 Whenever he heard people being praised or blamed, it was his view that one should look into the character of the speakers as much as the character of those they were speaking of.

Being a very sensible man, he realized that those who are only too ready to disparage others betray their own diseased minds more than they expose other people's failings. Those who applaud dishonourable conduct

* * * * *

2 On the need for a speaker to generate trust in his hearers, especially by avoidance of obvious artifice, see *Ad Herennium* 1.10.17; Cicero *De inventione* 1.25; *De oratore* 2.156, 177; Quintilian *Institutio oratoria* 12.9.5.
3 See Cicero *De oratore* 3.210; *Orator* 123; Erasmus *Ciceronianus* CWE 28 380 / LB I 991A / ASD I-2.634.

6 (VI) Plutarch *Moralia* 208C–D. In margin 'just and courteous'
1 Based on Homer *Iliad* 1.527.

7 (VII) Plutarch *Moralia* 208D. In margin 'sensible'

in others or censure admirable behaviour demonstrate their own stupidity and inverted standards.

8 While Agesilaus was still a boy, the annual boys' athletics demonstration was taking place, and the organizer assigned him to a not very prominent position.[1] He accepted this, although he was already king designate, saying, 'That's fine by me. I shall show that position does not bring distinction to men, but men give distinction to position.'

These words demonstrate the boy's remarkable nobility of mind combined with self-control. It is persons like this who are best fitted to rule a kingdom.

A similar story is told of Aristippus.[2]

9 A doctor once prescribed him an elaborate form of treatment, by no means the simple sort the Spartans normally employ. 'By the Twin Gods,'[1] he said. 'I will take your prescription, if indeed it's my fate not to live, even if I don't take it all.'[2]

He meant that treatment of that sort was more likely to hasten death than ward off disease, and that such powerful drugs should only be taken by someone set on dying. The Spartans approved of frugality and simplicity in every sphere.

* * * * *

8  (VIII) Plutarch *Moralia* 208D–E. In margin 'noble'
  1 This was no doubt because of his lameness and small stature, which disqualified him for the kingship. He was appointed to the office unexpectedly only in 400 BC.
  2 See Diogenes Laertius 2.73: Aristippus was sent to the bottom of the table after he had offended Dionysius I, ruler of Syracuse. Aristippus remarked, 'You must have wanted to confer distinction on the last place.' It was a popular story: see 1.163 below, where it is told of Damonidas, and Plutarch *Moralia* 149A (*Dinner of the seven wise men*), where it is told of an unknown Spartan. Cf *Adagia* I x 76: *Magistratus virum indicat* ''Tis the place that shows the man.' For Aristippus see 3.102–63 below.

9  (IX) Plutarch *Moralia* 208E. In margin 'shrewd'
  1 Ie Castor and Pollux, the Heavenly Twins. This oath was characteristic of the Spartans. Cf 2.17 below.
  2 Erasmus was puzzled by the inferior reading offered by his text of Plutarch, and has inserted *Sumam quae praescribis* 'I will take your prescription,' for which there is nothing corresponding in the Greek. A better text supplies the meaning: 'I don't have to live at any cost, and I don't put up with everything.'

**10** Once when Agesilaus was standing at the altar of Pallas (called *Chalkioikos* among the inhabitants of Sparta because of her temple of bronze)[1] preparing to offer a heifer in sacrifice, he was bitten by a louse. He did not turn away, but in full view of everyone caught and killed it, saying, 'By the Gods, so much for the lurking foe, even on the very altar.'

He thus demonstrated a mind free from foolish shame and from superstition and also indicated by implication that no altar or place of refuge should be safe for conspirators.

**11** He once watched a boy pulling a mouse he had caught out of a hole. The mouse turned, bit the hand of its captor, and escaped. Agesilaus drew the attention of his companions to this and said, 'Since a little tiny creature avenges itself like that on those who injure it, just think what men should do.'

The general, a brave man himself, used to find opportunities in all kinds of circumstance to fire the spirits of his men and make them bolder in the face of the enemy.

The incident however serves better to show that no one, however powerful, should provoke some one weaker than himself by ill-treatment. For it often happens, as Horace says, that he who 'sinks his teeth into something soft, strikes on something hard.'[1]

**12** When he was considering launching a war against the Persian king with a view to liberating the Greeks living in Asia,[1] Agesilaus consulted the oracle

* * * * *

**10**  (x) Plutarch *Moralia* 208F. In margin 'unaffected'
  1 'She of the House of Bronze,' a cult title of Pallas Athene at Sparta, so well known that the name of the goddess could be omitted, as in the Greek text Erasmus is translating. He inserts the name Pallas and explains the title. See also 1.145 and 1.263 below.

**11**  (XI) Plutarch *Moralia* 208E
  1 Horace *Satires* 2.1.77–8. Cf *Adagia* III vii 1: *Scarabaeus aquilam quaerit* 'A dung-beetle hunting an eagle' for the moral that one should not despise weak opponents.

**12**  (XII) Plutarch *Moralia* 208F–209A. In margin 'reverent'
  1 The Greeks living in Asia were inhabitants of Greek cities originally founded by colonists from the mainland in the coastal regions of Asia Minor (modern Turkey) and now subject to the kings of Persia, to whom they paid tribute. Several attempts were made to assert their independence. Agesilaus' campaign, launched in 396 BC, was attended with considerable success at first.

of Jove at Dodona. (The Spartans used to follow in most things the advice given by oracles of the gods.)[2] Jove directed him to commence hostilities as he thought fit, and he reported the god's answer to the ephors.[3] (These were five judges, to whose authority even the kings had to submit.) They urged him to go to Delphi and make the same enquiry of the oracle there. So he went and put his question in this form: 'Apollo, do you take the same view as your father?' Apollo confirmed the reply of Jove, and only then was Agesilaus appointed commander-in-chief and able to proceed with the war.

By this one incident, Agesilaus teaches us several things: first, inner control, since, though king, he was prepared to obey the ephors' superfluous instruction; second, that war should not be embarked upon thoughtlessly. For them, the oracle of Jove was not sufficient, whereas princes today often rush into hostilities without consulting, or indeed in opposition to, the will of the leading men and the cities. Finally, he demonstrated a genuinely religious attitude to the gods, since, if the gods disagree with each other, they are not gods.[4] In this he censured by implication the tales of Homer, who depicts violent quarrels between the gods and goddesses and ascribes to his divine powers behaviour that would be shocking in princes and magistrates.

13 The Persian general Tissaphernes[1] had concluded a treaty with Agesilaus not out of genuine desire but from fear. Under its terms, he was to allow the Greek city states autonomy under their own laws. Before long however, he sent to his king for huge reinforcements, and when they arrived he

* * * * *

2 See Cicero *De divinatione* 1.95: '(The Spartans) always used to seek an oracle from Delphi or Ammon or Dodona on all important matters.'

3 This is the first occurrence in this text of these important Spartan officials. They were first appointed in the seventh century BC in the reign of Theompompus (see 1.198 n1 below) and were elected to hold office for one year. There were three at first, five later. From the beginning they were intended to act as a check on the autocratic power of the kings, but their powers grew until they eventually controlled the kings. See eg 1.39, 1.107, 1.121 below; also General Index: ephors. Cleomenes III (236–222 BC) executed the ephors and abolished the office.

4 See Aristotle *Rhetoric* 1398b–1399a, where Hegesippus, an Athenian statesman, likewise consults Zeus and Apollo, and Aristotle suggests it would be improper for the gods to contradict each other.

13 (XIII) Plutarch *Moralia* 209A–B. Erasmus has extended this apophthegm and 1.14 with material from Plutarch's *Life of Agesilaus* 9. In margin 'equitable'

1 Erasmus seems to have been careless here in translating the Greek ἐν ἀρχῇ μέν, meaning 'at the outset,' not 'at the head, in command,' ie 'the general.'

informed Agesilaus that it would be war if he did not withdraw from Asia. Agesilaus gladly seized on this violation of the treaty, and with a pleased smile told the delegation that he was very grateful to Tissaphernes for antagonizing both gods and men by his perjury and so causing them to favour the other side. (He was well aware that nothing can be brought about in the affairs of men without God's providence, and that one should put one's confidence in divine favour rather than human counsel or strength.) He then manoeuvred his forces to give the impression that he was about to make a thrust into Caria. Tissaphernes, taken in by this stratagem, deployed his troops in that area, while Agesilaus made a sudden move against Phrygia. There he captured a considerable number of cities and carried off a large amount of money, and he said to his friends, 'To violate treaties without cause is wicked, but tricking the enemy is both justifiable and laudable – it's also satisfying and profitable.'

Although he loved fighting, nevertheless he always shrank from an unjust war, and tried not to provide others with any pretext for starting hostilities; but he happily seized on any pretext offered to himself, and thought it quite moral to use deceit against anyone who violated treaty obligations and broke the word he had sworn before gods and men.

14 Finding himself deficient in cavalry, Agesilaus withdrew to Ephesus and announced to the rich citizens that anyone who supplied a man and a horse to take his own place would be exempt from military service. This move enabled him to assemble quickly a force of horses and men both vigorous and fit for fighting, in place of cowardly, frightened, rich men. He used to say that in this he was following the example of Agamemnon, who took a mare of good stock and in return released from service a rich but ignoble fellow.

The reference is to Homer *Iliad* 23:[1] the mare

> Which Echepolus, son of Anchises, gave Agamemnon,
> Atreus' son, a gift to save him from going
> With the army to Troy, the windy town on the hill,
> But let him instead stay at home and there enjoy himself.
> For the thunder-wielding father had bestowed vast wealth on him.
> Indeed he dwelt in Sicyon with its spacious meadows.

\* \* \* \* \*

14   (xIV) Plutarch *Moralia* 209B–C. In margin 'ingenious'
  1 Homer *Iliad* 23.296–9. Erasmus supplies the passage in Greek (which is not in Plutarch) and appends his own Latin verse translation. The practice of the translators in such cases is to translate only Erasmus' Latin version.

Such skills befit a good prince. They enable him to acquire what is necessary for maintaining the state's position and safety, not by violent requisitions which cause antagonism, but by skilfully extracting it in a manner which places no burdens on humble folk and even makes the richer classes feel grateful to him.

15 When Agesilaus had decreed that the captives[1] should be sold unclothed, the *laphyropolae* (these were the people whose function it was to auction off the spoils of war) arranged the sale on that basis. Many came forward to purchase the clothes (for, as is the custom with barbarians, these were splendid and worth a great deal of money). The bodies of the prisoners however were pale, soft, and pampered, showing no sign of manliness, having been reared in idleness and pleasure, spending most of their time indoors. Far from desiring to buy them, everybody jeered at the merchandise thus offered as useless and of no value whatsoever. Agesilaus, who was presiding over the auction, (deciding to turn this chance event into yet another object lesson in bravery for his soldiers and pointing to the captives' fine clothes) said, 'These are what you are fighting for,' and (indicating the prisoners' naked bodies) 'These are what you are fighting against.'

He thus gave them a double incentive to bravery – eager anticipation of material reward and total contempt for the unwarlike foe.

16 When Agesilaus had put Tissaphernes to flight in Lydia, had killed large numbers of men, and had actually made an incursion into the royal domains, the Persian king sent an embassy headed by Titraustes[1] with an enormous sum of money, begging him to desist from the war. Agesilaus rejected the money and replied that in time of peace the authority of the state was paramount,[2] and the state accordingly had the right of determining what course of action seemed best suited to maintaining the country in

* * * * *

15  (xv) Plutarch *Moralia* 209C. In margin 'clever'
 1 Ie prisoners of war of various Asiatic nationalities serving in the Persian armies.

16  (xvi) Plutarch *Moralia* 209D. In margin 'spirited, generous'
 1 Information added from Plutarch *Agesilaus* 10.4.
 2 The Greek appears to mean 'it was the state that had the authority to make peace.' Erasmus seems to have misunderstood this and added the explanatory section 'and the state accordingly ... in time of war it was not so.' Agesilaus could not make peace on his own initiative but had to consult the authorities in Sparta.

a peaceable condition. In time of war it was not so. He personally would get more pleasure from enriching his troops than from becoming rich himself. Besides, he thought it was a good thing for Greeks to take spoils off the enemy by fighting, not to accept gifts from them.

What a splendid attitude this reveals! He sought no other reward for courage than glory, and would not sell peace to the enemy at the expense of his troops.

17 Megabates, son of Spithridates,[1] a very good looking youth, once went up to Agesilaus to greet him and, after the Persian custom, made to give him a kiss, being under the impression that Agesilaus was very fond of him; but he shrank from the kiss and turned his face away. The lad blushed, feeling he had been humiliated, and thereafter greeted him from a distance. This made the king regret avoiding the kiss, and he pretended to wonder what had happened to Megabates that he didn't greet him with a kiss any more. His attendants replied, 'The fault is yours, your majesty. You did not draw him close when he approached you, but shrank from letting such a handsome lad kiss you. Even so, he could still be persuaded to come and kiss you, only be sure not to draw back.' Agesilaus considered this in silence for some time, and then said, 'There is no need to persuade him to come back. I feel I would rather get the upper hand in a thing of this sort than take by force an enemy city garrisoned with brave men. I consider it a better thing for a man to preserve his own liberty than to take others' liberty from them.'

Now this was a man clearly fit to bear rule over others, since he could rule his own desires. And how surprising to find in a military man such

\* \* \* \* \*

17  (xvii) Plutarch *Moralia* 209D. In margin 'self-controlled'
  1 Spithridates was a Persian commander who had defected to Agesilaus with his children, his treasures, and two hundred cavalry. Erasmus' version of this incident has been influenced by the accounts of it in Plutarch *Agesilaus* 11.7 and Xenophon *Agesilaus* 5.4–5, but it still follows in the main the text of Plutarch's *Apophthegmata Laconica*, which, with its moralizing approach, does not make the point sufficiently clear. Also the Greek text appears to be at fault. In its context, the story lays more emphasis on Agesilaus' passionate attachment to the boy. Xenophon tells us that it was the custom among the Persians to kiss those they honoured and the boy was mortified at having his kiss of courtesy refused. Agesilaus was of course afraid of the effect of accepting his kiss and so felt it necessary to resist his inclination, even if this meant denying himself the pleasure of the boy's proximity. Plutarch uses the incident again as an example of resisting temptation in *Moralia* 31C (*How to study poetry*) and 81A (*On progress in virtue*).

a philosophical opinion! He understood that no one is free who is a slave to desire; he understood that the most impressive form of dominion is dominion over one's own inclinations. This example of self-control appears all the more admirable when one considers that Greek law allowed the love of handsome boys, though excluding vileness or coercion.

Plutarch records this apophthegm rather differently in his *Lives*: 'For myself,' he said, 'I would rather fight that fight about the kiss all over again than have everything before my eyes turn to gold.' The more conscious this great man was of the pangs of desire, the more convinced he was of the virtue of resisting.

18 Generally speaking, Agesilaus was rather inflexible and a stickler for justice and legality, but where his friends' affairs were concerned, he thought an overstrict application of the law in their case was just an excuse for inhumanity and cruelty.[1] This is borne out by a very brief letter written, as the story goes, to Hidrieus the Carian. In it he asks for mercy for a friend in these words: 'If Nicias has done nothing wrong, let him go; if he has done wrong, let him go for my sake; but in any case, let him go.'[2]

It is wicked to punish an innocent man, but occasionally to condone a guilty act as a favour to a respected person who speaks up for the accused is to show decent human feeling. Justice should always be tempered with clemency, but when a person of standing interposes, there is less resentment, more approval.

So this is how Agesilaus behaved with regard to his friends' affairs most of the time. On occasion though he acted as the interests of the state required instead of giving way to his feelings for his friends.

19 For example, one day camp had to be broken amidst considerable confusion, and he was leaving behind sick a young man of whom he was extremely fond. When the young man tried with tears and soft entreaties to keep him from going, he turned to his entourage and said, 'How difficult it is to feel sorry for someone and be sensible at the same time!'

\* \* \* \* \*

18   (XVIII) Plutarch *Moralia* 209E and F. In margin 'merciful'
  1 The words 'for inhumanity and cruelty' were added by Erasmus to elucidate the not very clear meaning of the Greek.
  2 The anecdote is repeated at Plutarch *Agesilaus* 13.5, 603B, *Moralia* 191B (*Sayings of kings and commanders*) and *Moralia* 807F (*Precepts of statecraft*).

19   (XIX) Plutarch *Moralia* 209F. In margin 'controlled and wise'

He preferred to follow the course of action that was right in the circumstances rather than do what his affection for his friend dictated. Such mental gifts made Agesilaus superior to others.

20 His physical régime was in no way superior to that of his companions, except that he totally abstained from over-eating and over-drinking. His sleep pattern did not dictate his activities but was subservient to them. He was so immune to cold and heat that he wore only the one set of clothing all year round.[1] When encamped in the midst of his troops he slept on a pallet bed just like everyone else's, as if he were any rank and file soldier. He was constantly saying, 'The mark of a prince is to excel ordinary men not in luxury and self-gratification but in self-control and fortitude.'

A remark truly worthy of a king, if he had added 'wisdom,' for that word sums up all the virtues of a prince.

21 When someone asked what benefit the laws of Lycurgus[1] had brought to Sparta, he replied, 'Contempt for pleasure.'

He thus implied that the chief source of corruption in a nation is self-indulgence.

22 To another who expressed surprise that Agesilaus and the other Spartans were so abstemious with regard to food and dress, he replied, 'My friend, in return for this abstinence we reap the rich harvest of liberty.'

He thus gave him a wise reminder that no pleasure is sweeter to freeborn men than liberty, and that liberty cannot exist long where self-indulgence reigns.

23 When someone was urging him to relax his rigorous way of life to some extent, reinforcing his words with the argument that life is so uncertain

\* \* \* \* \*

20 (xx) Plutarch *Moralia* 209F–210A. In margin 'controlled, weighty'
1 Modern texts of Plutarch offer a meaning 'he was the only one able to make good use of all the seasons.' Cf 1.24 below.

21 (xxi) Plutarch *Moralia* 210A. In margin 'controlled'
1 See 1.258–287 below.

22 (xxii) Plutarch *Moralia* 210A. In margin 'wise'

23 (xxiii) Plutarch *Moralia* 210B. In margin 'controlled and resolute'

that time itself could impose another manner of living, he replied, 'But I so condition myself as to seek no change personally, whatever change of fortune may befall.'[1]

What wonderful discipline of mind – in an austere lifestyle not to feel any need of luxuries and amidst luxuries to be incapable of being corrupted by them.

24 Not even in old age did Agesilaus introduce any relaxation in his manner of life, his diet, or his physical activities. When someone asked him why a man of such advanced years was walking about in the depths of winter wearing only a cloak and no tunic,[1] he replied, 'So that the young may copy this way of life, when they have as their example a man who is not only very old but also a prince.'

These words are a wise reminder that old men should so live as to display before the young a practical example of good living; also that common men copy with the greatest enthusiasm what they see important people doing.

25 The inhabitants of Thasos enjoyed an abundance of material things, being especially famous for their outstanding wine,[1] and were accordingly rather addicted to self-indulgence. When Agesilaus was passing through their territory with his army, the Thasians as a mark of respect sent him cereals, geese, sweetmeats, spiced honey-cakes, and all sorts of other luxurious things to

* * * * *

1 Modern texts of Plutarch offer a meaning 'to find a change in no change.' Erasmus' Greek text may have offered, with the negative placed earlier, 'to find no change in change.' He has endeavoured to elucidate this by expanding it slightly.

24 (xxiv) Plutarch *Moralia* 210B. In margin 'weighty'
 1 See 2.87 below.

25 (xxv) Plutarch *Moralia* 210C. The story as told in Plutarch *Life of Agesilaus* 36 and Nepos *Agesilaus* 8.3–4 is set in Egypt, whither Agesilaus had gone to serve as a mercenary under King Tachos (or Thacos; see 1.74 below). Agesilaus' attitude arouses the contempt of the Egyptians. Agesilaus on his way home from his campaigns in Asia passed through Thrace (see 1.41 below), and Thasos is an island off the coast of Thrace. Perhaps there has been confusion in the tradition between Thacos and Thasos. The island of Thasos became a proverbial example of abundance of good things: *Adagia* I iii 34: *Thasos bonorum* 'A Thasos of good things.' In margin 'temperate'
 1 Information from Pliny *Naturalis historia* 14.9.

eat and drink. He would accept none of this apart from the cereals, and ordered the bearers to take the rest home again as being of no use whatsoever to himself and his men. When they pressed him most insistently to accept it as a gift of friendship, he ordered it to be distributed among the Helots (they were a sort of slave the Spartans had).[2] When asked his reason for acting thus, he replied, 'It is not fitting for men who are motivated by a passion for virtue and courage to accept delicacies and tit-bits like these. This kind of thing has its attraction for those born with a slave mentality – it should be totally alien from men of free birth.'

In saying this he censured the Thasian way of life. Being slaves to pleasure they were not free, nor had they the mind of genuinely free men. He also indicated that spending one's life in thrall to the appetites and the pleasures of the belly is totally servile and abject.

26 That was an example of a heart undefiled when confronted by pleasure. The incident I shall now relate shows him equally invincible in face of vainglory.

The people of Thasos realized that Agesilaus had done much that deserved their gratitude, so they conferred on him temples and divine honours and sent a delegation to inform him of this. When he had read over the honours which the delegation had come to offer, he asked them whether their country had the power to turn men into gods. They replied that it had, so he said, 'Right, turn yourselves into gods first; if you manage that, then I will believe you when you say you can make me a god too.'

Which quality deserves our admiration more here? Is it the high principle of a mind which showed such contempt for apotheosis when it was handed to him? Yet apotheosis was a prize for which Empedocles the philosopher[1] threw himself into the crater of Etna, and so many educated

* * * * *

2 The Helots, who will appear frequently in these apophthegms of Spartans, were the serfs of the Spartiates. They worked the land for their masters, supplying them with a stipulated amount of produce and other services, thus freeing them from the need to work themselves and making possible the peculiar Spartiate social and military system (described below 1.258–87 under *Lycurgus*). As well as Laconian Helots, there was also a Helot population of Messenia, a territory in the western Peloponnese taken over by military force in the eighth century BC and kept in subjugation, in spite of attempts to regain their freedom, until 370 BC.

26  (xxvi) Plutarch *Moralia* 210D. In margin 'frank and earnest'
 1 See Diogenes Laertius 8.67 67–72 for various accounts of the death of Empedocles (ca 493–492 BC). He had always sought adulation and, according to one

princes have manoeuvred with ingenuity and expenditure to win it. Or is it the cleverness which forcibly opened the eyes of the Thasians to their supreme stupidity – or their abject flattery?

**27** We have a comparable demonstration of nobility of mind in the following incident.

The people who inhabited Greece[1] at that time decreed that statues should be erected in his honour in all the chief cities, but he wrote back: 'There is to be no representation of my person either painted or modelled or produced by any other technique.'[2]

The general run of rulers was of the opinion that this kind of honour put them on a level with the gods, and considered it the supreme reward for their achieveents. Agesilaus was content with honour itself and scorned such flatteries, for such they were, not real occasions of glory. He preferred to have his image carved on the hearts of wise and good men, rather than stand fashioned in bronze or gold in their public places. There is a special honour that naturally follows in the train of outstanding virtue. No statue can be as impressive as the admiring recollection of a life well lived.

**28** When he was in Asia, Agesilaus saw a house which had a roof constructed with squared timbers. He asked the owner whether trees grew square in their country. When he replied that they didn't grow like that, but that the round logs were processed to make them square, 'Oh,' he said, 'if they grew square would you make them round?'[1]

What a difference between that king's attitude and the elaboration of

\* \* \* \* \*

account, leapt into the crate of Etna in order that his unexplained disappearance might lend credence to a report that he had become a god. See 7.360 and 7.365, but the anecdotes in Erasmus' *Apophthegmata* do not touch on his philosophy: four basic elements governed by the opposing forces of love and strife, repeated world cycles and reincarnation.

**27** (xxvii) Plutarch *Moralia* 210D. In margin 'high-minded'
  1 A mistake for Asia.
  2 According to Plutarch *Agesilaus* 2.2, his reluctance to be portrayed was due to his lameness and unimposing presence, features which almost cost him the kingship.

**28** (xxviii) Plutarch *Moralia* 210E. In margin 'frugal'
  1 For the saying, cf 1.235 and 1.265 below.

our buildings, where nothing pleases unless imported from the far corners of the world or interfered with by artifice.

29 When someone asked Agesilaus how far Spartan dominion extended, he brandished his lance and said, 'As far as this can reach.'[1]

That was a reply worthy of a great general who embarked on no war but a just one and maintained by bravery an empire won by bravery.

30 When another person asked him why the city of Sparta had no walls,[1] he pointed to the armed citizens and said, 'These are the walls of the Spartan state.'

This indicates that the safest defence of a country is the courage of its citizens.

31 Similarly, when someone else asked the same question, he replied that a city should not be fortified by stones and beams. Instead of ramparts and walls, it is the noble qualities of its inhabitants that keep it safe.[1]

If they are linked by concord, they are more impregnable than any wall.

32 Agesilaus used to warn his friends against the desire for money, a vice which most people suffer from, urging them to strive to be rich not in money but in bravery and virtue.

* * * * *

29 (XXIX) Plutarch *Moralia* 210E. In margin 'resolute'
  1 For the saying, cf 1.149 below. It is identified as a *chreia* 'one combining speech and action' in Theon *Progymnasmata* 5.206 (Spengel II 99). See Introduction xxiv n19 above.

30 (XXX) Plutarch *Moralia* 210E. In margin 'resolute'
  1 Sparta was exceptional among ancient cities for not being walled, a fact of which the Spartans were inordinately proud, causing them to affect to despise other conventionally walled cities. Their military reputation in fact kept invaders at bay for 600 years, making walls unnecessary, until the occasion in 370 BC during the conflict with Thebes, recorded below at 1.82. For other relevant apophthegms, see General Index: Sparta.

31 (XXXI) Plutarch *Moralia* 210E–F. In margin 'wise'
  1 Cf 1.30 n1 above.

32 (XXXII) Plutarch *Moralia* 210F. In margin 'wise'

It is pointless for a man to lay up riches if he is destitute of the real wealth of the mind.

33 If there was any task he wanted the soldiers to perform quickly, Agesilaus was the first to tackle the job himself in front of them all.

This was to shame them into making an effort. It is a very effective form of exhortation if the ruler does himself what he wants to be done by others.

34 He used to congratulate himself particularly on the fact that, although he was king and had to look to the future and take counsel for all the rest, he was second to none in taking on hard physical labour; and he thought it a finer thing that he could command himself and was, so to speak, king over himself than that he held sway over others.

35 Someone saw a lame Spartan going off to war and tried to get him a horse on the grounds that a cripple needed one, but Agesilaus said, 'Don't you realize that war needs people who stay at their post, not people who flee?'[1]

This means that the soldiers really valuable in war are the ones who have made up their minds to find either victory in the battle or death.

36 When someone asked how he could win himself great glory,[1] he replied, 'By scorning death.'

A man whose mind is preoccupied with the fear of death will perform no great exploit in war. This same fear holds people back[2] from noble deeds in every sphere of human life.

* * * * *

33  (xxxiii) Plutarch *Moralia* 210F. In margin 'energetic'

34  (xxxiv) Plutarch *Moralia* 210F. Erasmus has expanded the brief original. In margin 'weighty'

35  (xxxv) Plutarch *Moralia* 210F. In margin 'apt'
  1 Cf the incident at 1.122 below.

36  (xxxvi) Plutarch *Moralia* 210F. In margin 'weighty, disregard for life'
  1 This should be 'asked how Agesilaus had achieved his great glory.'
  2 Cf 2.189 below.

37 When someone enquired why the Spartan warriors deployed into battle positions to the music of pipes,[1] Agesilaus replied, 'So that, when they march
in time with the music, it may be obvious who are the fearful and who the
brave.'

The anapaestic rhythm[2] would rouse the ardour of the bold, while striking the terrified with trembling and pallor. The cowards' weakness was betrayed by their inability to keep time with the music. It is vital for a general
to be thoroughly acquainted with the minds of his soldiers, so that he knows
who should be withdrawn from the battle and who should be stationed in
which section.

Valerius Maximus in book 2[3] expresses the opinion that pipes were
used to rouse the soldiers' ardour; Thucydides on the other hand, as we read
in Aulus Gellius,[4] tells us that the Spartans used pipes for battle, instead of
trumpets and horns, in order to moderate[5] the soldiers' force and impetuos-
ity, so that they did not rush upon the enemy in a ragged and straggling mob,
but advanced in disciplined formation, each keeping to his line. The records
tell us that the Cretans[6] used to march into battle to the music of the lyre.

38 When someone was commenting admiringly in his hearing on the good fortune of the Persian king, to be so prosperous and so young, he replied, 'Not
even Priam was unfortunate at that age.'

He was saying that no one should be called happy unless he had
reached the last day of his life – neither Priam[1] nor Croesus[2] died happy.

* * * * *

37  (xxxvii) Plutarch *Moralia* 210F–211A. In margin 'sagacious'
  1 'Pipes' translates Greek *aulos*, Latin *tibia*. This was a reeded instrument and
    with its sharp sound was more akin to the modern oboe than the flute, fife, or
    recorder, names which give the wrong impression.
  2 'The anapaestic rhythm' is added from Cicero *Tusculan Disputations* 2.37 and
    Valerius Maximus 2.6.2. This rhythm was a recurrent pattern of two light
    syllables followed by a heavy one ($\smile \smile -$ in traditional notation).
  3 Valerius Maximus 2.6.2.
  4 Aulus Gellius 1.11.5, referring to Thucydides 5.70.
  5 Cf 2.97 below.
  6 See Aulus Gellius 1.11.6. The whole chapter is relevant.

38  (xxxviii) Plutarch *Moralia* 211A. In margin 'shrewd'
  1 The aged king of the flourishing city of Troy who eventually, at the end of
    the Trojan War, saw his family murdered and his city sacked by the victorious
    Greeks and was himself slain.
  2 The king of Lydia in the sixth century BC who became a byword for wealth

39 When he had subjugated most of Asia by arms, Agesilaus decided to advance on the king of Persia himself, in order to put a stop to his activities, since the king was so little affected by the war personally that he was
meantime sending money to bribe the Greek leaders. Agesilaus was however summoned home by the ephors on account of Sparta's now being surrounded by hostile Greek states, which is what the Persian king had brought
about by his bribes. He obeyed, saying that a good commander should obey
the commands of the law, and without delay sailed from Asia, to the great
regret of the Greeks living there.[1]

His scheme had a good chance of success and the enthusiasm of the
Greeks invited him to proceed with it. This king, however, had nothing to do with tyranny and considered the authority of the law to be
paramount.

40 Persian coinage bore the image of an archer, so when he was leaving Asia he
used to say that the king was driving him out of Asia with 33,000 archers.
By sending that number of gold darics[1] to Athens and Thebes and distributing them to those who controlled the mob, Timocrates had roused in
the people there a belligerent attitude towards the army.[2] However, Agesilaus wrote to the ephors in these terms: 'Greetings from Agesilaus to
the ephors. We have subjugated a large part of Asia, driven out the barbarians, and fought many engagements in Ionia; but since in virtue of the
authority of your office you bid me present myself before you by an appointed day, I shall follow close on this letter of mine, or possibly arrive
before it. I do not bear rule for my own benefit, but for the state and the

* * * * *

and prosperity until he was defeated and captured by Cyrus, king of the Persians. See the famous story of Croesus and the sage Solon in Herodotus 1.30–
43 – Solon warns Croesus that no man may be called happy until his life
has concluded still in happiness (7.22 below). This was a commonly voiced
sentiment: see eg Epaminondas at 5.243 below.

39 (xxxix) Plutarch *Moralia* 211A–B. This paragraph and 40 should be read together. In margin 'controlled'
   1 One of Agesilaus' aims in attacking the Persian empire was to liberate from
   Persian overlordship the Greek cities along the coast of Asia Minor. See 1.12
   above. He had had a number of military successes before he was recalled.

40 (xl) Plutarch *Moralia* 211B–C. In margin 'witty, controlled'
   1 Ie Daric staters, the gold coinage issued by the Persian kings and named from
   King Darius of Persia. Timocrates of Rhodes was the agent of the Persians.
   2 A better reading in the Greek text gives 'towards the Spartiates.'

allies and friends of the state. A man who exercises authority only uses that authority truly and legitimately when he himself submits to the authority of the law and the ephors, or whoever it may be who bears office in the state.'

What could be more controlled than the attitude of this king? Yet what more splendid?

41 Then, after crossing the Hellespont, when Agesilaus was making his way through Thrace, he did not request any of the barbarians to grant him passage, but sent messengers to the various tribes to ask whether he was passing through hostile or friendly territory. All the others received him in friendly fashion when he arrived and gave him an escort out of their territories, but the people called Troades, to whom Xerxes, according to the story, had given gifts and so purchased permission for himself to pass through, demanded from Agesilaus as the price of passage[1] one hundred talents of silver and one hundred women. He laughed at them and asked why they hadn't come at once to collect what they were demanding. He moved his army up close and falling upon them as they stood in battle formation barring his path, slaughtered a large number and put them to flight. Thus he opened up a path with his sword.

42 Similarly, he sent messengers to the Macedonian king[1] to ask whether they would pass over enemy or friendly soil. When the king replied that he would take counsel, Agesilaus said, 'Do so then; in the meantime we will go on our way.' The king was amazed at the man's boldness, and fearing for himself decided it was better to receive him as a friend.

43 Agesilaus ravaged the territory of the Thessalians, who had given aid to the enemy.

His bravery was so tempered with justice that he neither hurt friends nor spared enemies if chance gave him the opportunity of taking revenge.

* * * * *

41 (XLI) Plutarch *Moralia* 211C–D. In margin 'confident, spirited'
   1 Erasmus seems to have translated twice the Greek words meaning 'the price of passage.'

42 (XLII) Plutarch *Moralia* 211D. In margin 'fearless'
   1 This was probably Amyntas III. The Macedonian kings had in recent years constantly switched their support between Sparta and Athens.

43 (XLIII) Plutarch *Moralia* 211E. In margin 'uncompromising'

This is not an apophthegm, and was added in mutilated form by some ignorant fellow.[1]

**44** The people of Larissa,[1] however, had not assisted the enemy, and he sent Xenocles and Scythes to them as ambassadors to establish friendly relations. When the Larissaeans seized the two men and kept them in custody, the others took great exception to it and proposed that Agesilaus should move up his troops and invest the city. He, however, said that he was not prepared to take even Thessaly in its entirety if it meant losing either of the two men he had sent, and he would lose both if he provoked the inhabitants of the city with hostile moves. Accordingly he offered terms and so freed and recovered the captives.

He overlooked such a gross injury to ensure the safety of his two friends, though generally speaking he did not put up with slights. You could say he had his feelings under control.

**45** A successful battle had been fought outside Corinth.[1] Agesilaus was informed that only a few of the Spartan élite had been lost in the fight, whereas a huge number of Corinthians had perished, as also of Athenians and men from other allied cities. Far from rejoicing and feeling elation at the victory, he sighed deeply and lamented the fate of Greece. 'Poor Greece,' he said, 'she has lost enough men in civil conflict to defeat the whole barbarian world.'

To this noble-souled man victory was a desirable thing, but the safety of his companions in arms was more important. How would he have felt if the victory had cost the lives of large numbers of Spartan citizens? Such an attitude deserved high praise when seen in a Spartan general of bellicose character, and a pagan at that. To a christian prince every victory should be an occasion for sorrow when it involves the destruction of many men, even if they are enemies.

* * * * *

1 'This is . . . ignorant fellow' was added in C. See the dedicatory epistle 9 above.

**44** (XLIV) Plutarch *Moralia* 211E. In margin 'controlled, affectionate'
1 Larissa was the chief town of Thessaly. Cf 1.43 above.

**45** (XLV) Plutarch *Moralia* 211F. In margin 'merciful'
1 Sparta's combined enemies had assembled at Corinth, where they were defeated. Agesilaus at this point was still in northern Greece and was not involved in the battle.

**46** When the people of Pharsalus[1] kept making annoying raids on his forces, he put them to flight with six hundred cavalry,[2] and set up a trophy in the territory of the Narthacii.[3] He was more pleased about this victory than any other, because he himself at the head of a small cavalry unit without the support of any other forces had defeated a people who prided themselves particularly on their horsemanship.

It is satisfying to defeat those who attack you, especially when you deploy the very resources on which the foe congratulates himself.

**47** Here are two examples of moderation provided by this leader, in spite of his passion for glory.

Diphridas brought Agesilaus a message from his home country that he was to abandon his current activities and immediately invade Boeotia.[1] He had in fact determined to do precisely that later on, when he had assembled greater resources. Nonetheless in obedience to the magistrates, he summoned 20,000 of the troops who were serving in the Corinth area and invaded Boeotia. Close to Coronea he joined battle with the Thebans, Athenians, Argives, and Corinthians, and defeated both battle lines,[2] although he himself was in a poor physical state because of the many wounds he had received. This battle was the greatest of all his exploits, according to Xenophon.[3] Yet when he got back to Sparta he made no alteration to his long established way of life or to his modest standard of living, in spite of all his great successes and many victories.

Far more deserving of a triumph was the victory by which this great man first gave the authority of the law precedence over his own designs and then remained completely unaffected by all his mighty deeds.

* * * * *

**46** (XLVI) Plutarch *Moralia* 211F. For the moral, cf 1.160 below. In margin 'successful'
1 Pharsalus was a town in Thessaly.
2 A mistake for five hundred. The Thessalian cavalry were second to none.
3 Possibly this should be 'at Mount Narthecium,' a mountain a few miles south of Pharsalus.

**47** (XLVII) Plutarch *Moralia* 212A. In margin 'modest'
1 Boeotia lay some distance to the south of Thessaly and shared its southern border with Athenian territory. It lay across Agesilaus' homeward route to Sparta. Sparta's combined enemies met him in Boeotia at Coronea (394 BC).
2 Modern texts of Plutarch give 'engaged in battle the Thebans and the two Locrian peoples' (ie contingents from the two separate parts of Locris).
3 Xenophon was present at the battle (see 1.49 below) and he describes it in *Agesilaus* 2.9–16.

48 Observing some citizens who were looked up to by others and also had high opinions of themselves because they kept racing stables, Agesilaus persuaded his sister Cynisca to mount a chariot and take part in the race at the Olympic Games,[1] hoping thereby to show the Greeks that that kind of exercise required no real valour, but merely involved the display of wealth and the spending of it.

For that reason it was more fit for women than men.

49 He had in his company the famous philosopher Xenophon.[1] He thought so highly of him that he asked him to send for his sons to come to Sparta, where they would be instructed in the fairest art of all, that is, the art of both wielding authority and of submitting to it.

Every kind of liberal discipline flourished at Athens,[2] but Agesilaus was of the opinion that this subject, the noblest of them all, could be studied nowhere better than among the Spartans, where people did not talk about good government but provided a living example of the splendid thing in the conduct of its citizens. At the same time he demonstrated that those who did not know how to submit to the laws and to the authority of office were not fit to hold office themselves.[3]

50 When someone asked him why the traditional Spartan state was so success-

\* \* \* \* \*

48 (xlviii) Plutarch *Moralia* 212B. In margin 'amusing'
   1 Erasmus' Greek text seems to have read καθίσασαν from καθίζω 'sit' rather than καθεῖσαν from καθίημι 'enter (for a race),' as in Plutarch *Agesilaus* 20.1, hence his idea that Cynisca drove the chariot herself. Not even wealthy men drove their own chariots but employed professionals. Cynisca's chariot was victorious in 396 and again in 392 BC.

49 (xxlix) Plutarch *Moralia* 212B. In margin 'earnest'
   1 Xenophon is best known for his historical writings, especially the famous *Anabasis*, but he wrote on numerous topics, including memoirs of Socrates and other writings touching on Socrates' teaching and character. Primarily an experienced soldier, he has been described as 'an amateur philosopher, historian, and economist' (*OCD*), and would not today be considered a serious philosopher. He wrote an encomium of Agesilaus, who was his hero. He is considered a philosopher by Quintilian (10.1.75 and 82), and Plutarch, like Quintilian, links him with Plato (*Moralia* 79D)
   2 Xenophon was an Athenian.
   3 The Spartans prided themselves on their unquestioning obedience. See eg 1.39, 1.47, 1.88, 1.195, and 2.70 below.

50 (l) Plutarch *Moralia* 212C. In margin 'civic discipline'

ful compared with others, he replied, 'Because they endeavour more than others to know both how to command and how to obey.'

These two things exclude sedition from the citizen-body and preserve concord.

51 After Lysander's death, Agesilaus discovered the existence of a large group of supporters whom Lysander had organized immediately after returning from Asia[1] to use against Agesilaus. Incensed by this, Agesilaus determined to make known to everyone the kind of citizen Lysander had been while he was alive. He also found and read a speech of which Lysander had left a copy among his papers. It had been composed by Creon of Halicarnassus[2] for Lysander to learn by heart and deliver before the general populace, and its subject was of a revolutionary nature, advocating constitutional change. Agesilaus wanted to publish this, since it indicated that Lysander had been disruptive and seditious, but when an old man (who happened to be an ephor) had read it, he was alarmed lest the forcefulness and vehemence of the language even when read, might incite many to revolutionary fervour. Accordingly he advised Agesilaus not to raise Lysander from his grave but to suppress the speech. Agesilaus took the old man's advice and gave up his plan.

He was schooled to obey not only public laws and bearers of office but also advice given by an old man in a private capacity. Being a man of noble spirit, he was happy to let the public good carry more weight with him than his personal grudge. He also realized that it was undignified to carry on a quarrel with the dead and buried.[3] This self-control was displayed in relation to one who had been a manifest enemy.

\* \* \* \* \*

51  (LI) Plutarch *Moralia* 212C–D. In margin 'controlled'
    This is the first mention of Lysander, an influential Spartan politician and general at the time of the long Peloponnesian War between Athens and Sparta (431–404 BC). Lysander set up an alliance with the younger Cyrus, a Persian prince, and using Persian money defeated the Athenians decisively at sea and eventually reduced the city by blockade. He supported Agesilaus and helped to secure his unexpected election to the kingship in 400 BC. He had high political ambitions, perhaps hoping to be elected king himself (see 1.302 n1 below), and his establishment of a personal faction caused a certain rift with Agesilaus. He died in 394 BC.
  1 He returned from Asia (ie the area covered by modern Turkey) at the end of the Peloponnesian War in 404/3.
  2 It was customary to commission speeches to deliver oneself, especially in a law-suit, from professional teachers of rhetoric. The name should probably be Cleon, but nothing more seems to be known of him.
  3 See *Adagia* I ii 53: *Cum larvis luctari* 'To wrestle with ghosts.'

**52** He never did anything openly to make trouble for his secret opponents, but arranged for them to accompany him on military service. Quite a number of these he promoted to the rank of officers and magistrates. After they had behaved dishonestly and greedily when holding their public positions and were called to account and in trouble, Agesilaus now spoke up for them and took their side, and so transformed them from stealthy opponents into supporters and won them over to himself. And so eventually he had no one opposing him.

This wise behaviour was extremely civic-minded, in that he preferred to reform the malicious rather than punish them.

**53** A certain person asked Agesilaus to write a letter of recommendation for him to the people in Asia with whom Agesilaus had ties of friendship and hospitality, so that he would receive from them what was right. Agesilaus replied that there was no need of a commendatory letter. 'My hosts,' he said, 'do what is right of themselves, without my writing to them.'

With good men and a good cause commendation is superfluous, for in such circumstances the favourable response which entreaties might extort is granted as a matter of course.

This fine general had formed ties of hospitality only with persons like himself.

**54** Somebody was once showing him the well-fortified and strongly built walls of a certain city, and asked him whether he thought them a fine sight. 'By Jove,' he said, 'very nice indeed, but they seem to have been built for a population of women rather than men.'

He believed that the most appropriate defence for a city was its brave citizens.[1]

**55** An inhabitant of Megara[1] was boasting to Agesilaus with youthful cocksure-

* * * * *

52    (LII) Plutarch *Moralia* 212D. In margin 'ingenious, controlled'

53    (LIII) Plutarch *Moralia* 212E. In margin 'honourable, civilized'

54    (LIV) Plutarch *Moralia* 212E. In margin 'earnest'
    1 See 1.30 above.

55    (LV) Plutarch *Moralia* 212E. In margin 'forbearing'
    1 See 1.86 below.

ness about his native city. 'Young man,' said Agesilaus, 'your talk requires
great strength.'

He meant that it is inappropriate for anyone to talk big unless he has
the power to match his words.

56 Our wise hero was so far from sharing the opinions of the crowd that he
did not merely despise things he saw others admiring but was so indifferent
to them as to seem unaware of their existence. Take for example what happened with Callipides.[1] He was a tragic actor of great renown, far-famed
among the Greeks and highly esteemed by all. This man first of all came up
to Agesilaus and spoke to him; then he brazenly joined the group of people
walking with the king and drew attention to himself, thinking that the king
would make the first move and welcome him with a gracious and friendly
gesture. When this did not happen, eventually he said, 'Do you not recognize me, your majesty? Or haven't you heard who I am?' Agesilaus peered
at him and said, 'Aren't you that mummer fellow?' He used the word *dikelik-
tas*, which in the Spartan dialect means *mimus*,[2] that is, a 'mimic' or 'copier';
*deikelon* means a likeness or statue in Spartan speech.[3]

He wisely measured everything by its value to the state, and accordingly paid no honour to an actor, however distinguished he was, since his art
served no purpose but pleasure and was more likely to corrupt the morals
of the citizens than edify them.[4]

57 There was a similar incident when he was asked to listen to someone who
could do a life-like imitation of a nightingale. He refused, saying, 'I've heard
real nightingales often enough.'

He meant that it's a foolish pleasure to take more delight in the imitation than in the real thing.[1]

* * * * *

56  (LVI) Plutarch *Moralia* 212F. In margin 'serious'
 1 See *Adagia* I vi 43: *Callipides*.
 2 An actor in a vulgar, farcical type of popular entertainment called a mime –
   not a mime in the modern sense, but with speaking accompaniment. Athenaeus
   *Deipnosophistae* 14.621 describes the kind of performance given by a *deikeliktas*.
 3 Information possibly derived by Erasmus from the Suda δείκελον, δίκελον. (See
   1.4 n1 above.)
 4 For the Spartan attitude to expertise in the fine arts, especially in music, see
   General Index: trivial pursuits.

57  (LVII) Plutarch *Moralia* 212F. In margin 'shrewd'
 1 See *Adagia* I i 10: *Nihil ad Parmenonis suem* 'Nothing like Parmeno's pig.'

**58** He himself was remarkably modest and accordingly did not tolerate arrogance in others.

A certain Doctor Menecrates had met with success in curing some desperately ill patients and was hailed as Jupiter by the admiring populace. The arrogant fellow was delighted with this appellation and conceitedly incorporated it into his name. When he came eventually to write to Agesilaus also, he had no hesitation in beginning the letter with these words: Menecrates Jupiter wishes King Agesilaus well. The king was displeased by this opening and read no further, but wrote back as follows: King Agesilaus wishes Menecrates health.

He did not use the word *chairein* 'be glad,' which is what the Greeks use when they wish someone well, but *hygiainein* 'be well,' a word which can be used in a good or bad sense, but usually carries a bad implication in that we suggest that someone's mental health needs improvement.[1] Someone once used this same word to censure Caesar's foolish behaviour.[2]

**59** He provided a remarkable demonstration of fortitude even in adverse circumstances.

The Persian king's fleet gave Conon and Pharnabazus[1] control of the sea and they were investing the maritime regions of Laconia. At the same

\* \* \* \* \*

58 (LVIII) Plutarch *Moralia* 212F–213A. In margin 'witty, forbearing'
  1 The normal word used in greeting in Greek was χαίρειν [*chairein*] 'be well, be glad,' and Menecrates used this to address Agesilaus. To translate it, Erasmus employs the equivalent Latin phrase *salutem (dicere)* 'wish well.' He translates ὑγιαίνειν [*hygiainein*] in Agesilaus' sarcastic response by *sanitatem (dicere)* 'wish health, soundness.' The English translation has been expanded to spell out Erasmus' comment, which requires a knowledge of the Greek original to be comprehensible.
  2 The Latin text seems to be at fault and should probably mean 'Caesar used ... to censure someone's foolish behaviour.' See Plutarch *Moralia* 508B (*On talkativeness*), where Augustus Caesar answers with *hygiaine* the greeting *chaire* of a man who had foolishly blabbed confidential information to his wife. As *hygiaine* could mean 'Fare well,' the man in this case took it as a command to commit suicide.

59 (LIX) Plutarch *Moralia* 213B. In margin 'brave'
  1 At this point in the long rivalry between Sparta and Athens, the Athenians were allied with the Persians. The Athenian admiral Conon was working in conjunction with the Persian fleet and shared the naval command with Pharnabazus, governor of the north western Persian territories, which included some Greek cities.

time Athens had got walls built round it again. As Pharnabazus was providing the money,[2] the Spartans made peace with the king, and sent one of their citizens, Antalcidas, to Tiribazus, betraying to the king the Asiatic Greeks on whose behalf Agesilaus had waged war. As a result, a certain amount of the disgrace occasioned by this action unfairly fell upon Agesilaus.[3] For Antalcidas was an enemy of Agesilaus, and for that reason made peace on any chance that offered, being jealous of Agesilaus' renown, and thinking that the war gave him importance and made him great and famous. This setback did not however discourage Agesilaus. In fact, when someone commented that the Spartans were now 'siding with the Medes,' he said, 'No, rather it is the Medes who are siding with the Spartans'[4] – meaning that fortune could not change the character of his people for the worse.

60 Agesilaus was once asked which was the superior virtue, bravery or justice. He gravely replied that there was no place for bravery without justice, but if everyone were just there would be no need of bravery.

* * * * *

2  The words 'As Pharnabazus was providing the money' should have been translated by Erasmus with the previous sentence; see Plutarch *Agesilaus* 23.1. The Spartans had destroyed the Long Walls linking Athens with its port Piraeus at the end of the Peloponnesian War in 404 BC. These had now been rebuilt by Conon in 393 BC with Persian money and this signified the potential resurgence of Athens as a power. However, the visit of the Spartan Antalcidas in 392 BC to Tiribazus (Persian governor of Western Asia, including the Greeks living in Ionia) persuaded the Persians to realign themselves with the Spartans. The terms of the agreement in 386 BC included the abandonment of the Greek cities of Ionia to Persian overlordship. For Agesilaus' campaigns on their behalf, see 1.12–16 and 1.39 above. Apophthegms of Antalcidas are recorded at 1.123–30 below.
3  A variant reading (adopted in modern texts of Plutarch) gives the meaning: 'So Agesilaus had absolutely no share in this shameful business.' See also Plutarch *Agesilaus* 23.
4  The words 'in fact ... siding with the Spartans' occur as a separate apophthegm in Plutarch. 'To side with the Medes' *Mēdizein* was to accept Persian policies and influence (and support) and so betray Greek values and Greek freedom and independence. In practice this meant abandoning the Greek cities of Asia Minor to Persian rule. The verb *Mēdizein* was used in fifth to fourth century BC political invective to denote the ultimate treachery, as the various states shifted their alliance according to where they saw the best advantage. Persian money was a powerful factor in all this.

60  (LX) Plutarch *Moralia* 213C. In margin 'just'

An attitude worthy of a great leader, for he was of the opinion that nothing should be done by strength divorced from justice, and was well aware of the difference between daring and bravery.

61 The Asiatic Greeks were accustomed to call the Persian king 'The Great King.' Agesilaus remarked, 'In what way is he greater than I am, unless he is more just and more disciplined?'[1]

This splendid man despised the external goods which are so admired by the common man and measured man's whole felicity by the goods of the mind. Such a sentiment was often on the lips of philosophers, but this military man expressed it with genuine feeling.

62 Observing the perverse licentiousness of the Greeks who lived in Asia (corrupted as they were by the practices of the local peoples), he used to say, 'Over there the wicked are the free men, whereas the virtuous are the slaves.'[1]

This was because vice was there without restraint, virtue was abhorred.

63 On being asked how a man could best win an honourable reputation, he said, 'If his words are the best and his actions the finest.'

How could it be put more briefly or more incisively? Socrates likewise in answer to the same question said, 'If you try really to be the sort of person you want to be thought to be.'[1] Glory won by false pretences is not only not true glory, it does not last either.

64 There is another famous remark by Agesilaus which princes should take to heart – namely that the proper course for a commander is to

\* \* \* \* \*

61 (LXI) Plutarch *Moralia* 213C. In margin 'spirited'
  1 Cf a similar remark made about Pompey, 5.461 below.

62 (LXII) Plutarch *Moralia* 213C. In margin 'weighty'
  1 The Greek probably means 'the inhabitants were poor freemen but good slaves.' See 1.206 below, where similar Greek words are so interpreted by Erasmus.

63 (LXIII) Plutarch *Moralia* 213C. In margin 'wise'
  1 See Xenophon *Memorabilia* 1.7.1; *Adagia* IV i 92: *Cura esse quod audis* 'Take care to be what you are said to be'

64 (LXIV) Plutarch *Moralia* 213C. In margin 'just, restrained'

display boldness in the face of opposition but to treat kindly those who submit.

Virgil[1] said the same thing in that noble line: 'Spare the defeated and beat down the proud in war.' A man is not truly victorious if he cannot bridle his wrath when it clamours for revenge.

65 When someone asked him what children should learn especially, he replied, 'Things that they will still find useful when they are grown up.'[1]

This wise man believed quite rightly that virtue alone should be our very first study, 'right from our baby finger-nails,'[2] and that no portion of life should be devoted to trifling activities which may well seem praiseworthy when children pursue them, but which are not going to be suitable for adults or useful to people with a serious vocation.

66 Agesilaus was sitting as judge in a lawsuit where the prosecutor put up a good case, the defending counsel a poor one – he merely kept on repeating as the case proceeded, 'Agesilaus, a king should back up the law' (implying that he had a good case and the law supported him). Agesilaus put a stop to the man's effrontery by saying, 'If someone broke into your house or stole your clothes, would you be looking for the architect or clothes manufacturer to come to your assistance?'

This suggests that a king is so to speak the architect of the law, and that it would not be right for him to help someone who had done something contrary to the law.

67 After peace had been agreed,[1] a letter from the Persian king was delivered to Agesilaus, brought to Sparta by Perses[2] and Callias. In it the Persian king proposed that he and Agesilaus should enter into a relationship of

* * * * *

1 Virgil *Aeneid* 6.853.

65 (LXV) Plutarch *Moralia* 213D. In margin 'wise'
  1 Cf 1.233 below.
  2 See *Adagia* I vii 52: *A teneris unguiculis* 'Since the time their nails were soft.'

66 (LXVI) Plutarch *Moralia* 213D. In margin 'witty'

67 (LXVII) Plutarch *Moralia* 213D–E. In margin 'uncorrupted'
  1 This is the peace negotiated by the Spartan Antalcidas between the Greeks and Persians in 386 BC. See 1.59 n2 above.
  2 Perses is not a personal name but 'the Persian.' See eg Xenophon *Agesilaus* 7.3.

hospitality and friendship.[3] Agesilaus did not accept this proposal, but told them to take back the message that there was no need to write to him privately; if it were clear that the king was indeed of a friendly mind towards the Spartans and the Greeks, he too would show himself a staunch friend; but if the king were caught acting treacherously, 'then,' he said, 'he need not think he will have me as a friend, even if I receive many, many letters from him.'[4]

Could anything be nobler than such an attitude? In every situation his sole aim was to consider what was good for the state.

68 He was extremely fond of his children, and there is a story that one day he was playing with them at home and riding a hobby-horse. One of his friends happened to see this, and Agesilaus asked him to tell no one what he had seen until he had children of his own.

This request indicated in a light-hearted way that the game was not a sign of silliness on his part but of fatherly affection; and that his behaviour could not appear foolish to anyone who knew from experience how powerful an emotion is parents' love for their children.

69 Agesilaus was constantly fighting against the Thebans, and when he was wounded in one of the battles, Antalcidas,[1] according to the story, remarked, 'Agesilaus, you are getting a fine fee from the Thebans for your instruction, since you taught them to fight when they neither wanted to fight nor knew how to.' They do indeed say that the Thebans became much more warlike than they had been as a result of the Spartans' frequent expeditions against them. For that reason, Lycurgus,[2] the famous early law-giver, in the laws called Rhetrae (that is, god-given pronouncements),[3] forbade making

\* \* \* \* \*

3 Cf 1.53 above.
4 A similar story is told of Epaminondas in book 5.233 below.

68 (LXVIII) Plutarch *Moralia* 213E. Cf a similar story of Socrates playing with his children with a hobby-horse, Valerius Maximus 8.8 ext. 1. In margin 'affectionate, affable'

69 (LXIX) Plutarch *Moralia* 213F. In margin 'sharp'
  1 An opponent of Agesilaus. See 1.59 above.
  2 For Lycurgus see 1.258–87 below.
  3 Literally, 'covenants, agreements, ordinances.' See Plutarch *Lycurgus* 6 where *rhetra* is originally the name given to an oracle obtained by Lycurgus from Delphi, giving divine support to his first reforms. The name was then used for other Spartan ordinances; see Plutarch *Lycurgus* 13.

war frequently on the same people, lest the foe should learn to fight by practice.[4]

This apophthegm however is not one of Agesilaus'.[5]

70 Agesilaus had heard that the allies were grumbling about the number of military expeditions,[1] especially since the allies were numerous, while the Spartans who led them were few in number. Agesilaus accordingly, wishing to demonstrate the size of the Spartan force, ordered all the allies to sit down in one place, all mixed together, and the Spartans by themselves in another place. Then through a herald he ordered all the potters to stand up first; when they had done so, he next ordered the smiths to stand, then the carpenters and builders; and so on with all the other trades. In this way, practically all the allies stood up, but not one of the Spartans, because Spartans, being trained for military service, were forbidden to practise or learn any trade or sedentary occupation. Agesilaus then laughed and said, 'Well, men, you see how many more <soldiers>[2] we take into battle than you do.'

By this device this famous general showed that what matters is not the number of troops you take into battle but their bravery and expertise.

71 At the battle of Leuctra[1] many Spartans ran away and should have paid the penalty prescribed by law.[2] The ephors, bearing in mind that a state short of men is deficient in soldiers, wanted to pardon the soldiers for their

\* \* \* \* \*

4 Cf 1.128 and 1.266 below.
5 For this cf the dedicatory epistle 9 above.

70  (LXX) Plutarch *Moralia* 213F–214A. In margin 'ingenious'
  1 Sparta's allies were obliged to provide contingents of soldiers for Sparta's military expeditions. They were for many years citizen soldiers, not professionals.
  2 The necessary word 'soldiers' is supplied from modern texts of Plutarch.

71  (LXXI) Plutarch *Moralia* 214B. In margin 'ingenious'
  1 Leuctra was a place in Boeotia where, in 371 BC, the Spartans and their allies, under King Cleombrotus I (see 1.211 below) were routed by a Theban force under Epaminondas, for whom see 1.72–3, 1.82, and 5.221–55 (000–000) below. This marked the beginning of the end of Spartan power and influence. Agesilaus had remained in Sparta; see 1.81 below.
  2 This meant total disgrace, entailing exclusion from holding any public position and from marriage, utter rejection by society, and the wearing of a degrading and ludicrous garb. See Plutarch *Agesilaus* 30; Xenophon *Respublica Lacedaemoniorum* 9.4–6. Xenophon remarks that death is preferable to a life so ignominious.

disgraceful behaviour, yet at the same time maintain the laws. So they appointed Agesilaus to promulgate new laws. He advanced onto the platform and said, 'I am certainly not going to put through different laws, for I am not going to add anything to or subtract anything from the laws you have, nor change anything at all. But it seems to me right that the laws you already have should have force and authority – from tomorrow.'

By this clever move our experienced hero was able to deal with the present crisis and also avoid introducing the dangerous precedent of changing laws, simply by suspending the laws for one day.

72 An example of his presence of mind and imperturbability is provided by the following occasion. Epaminondas was attacking[1] with tempestuous force and violence, so that the Thebans and their allies were already congratulating themselves on winning the victory. Nonetheless Agesilaus kept the city of Sparta safe. The defenders were very few, yet he compelled the enemy to retire.

You can call this anything you like, but it certainly can't be called an apophthegm.[2]

73 That incident demonstrated resoluteness. The following wins our admiration for his decisiveness and good sense.

During the battle of Mantinea,[1] he instructed the Spartan contingent to ignore all the rest and concentrate the force of their attack on Epaminondas alone, saying that only men of intelligence were brave and they alone were the architects of victory. 'If we take him,' he said, 'we will easily subdue the rest, as they are men of no sense and no account.' That is exactly what

\* \* \* \* \*

72 (LXXII) Plutarch *Moralia* 214C. In margin 'resolute'
  1 Epaminondas, leader of the Thebans, invaded Spartan territory after Leuctra with 70,000 men. This was in 370 BC, and was the first time that Spartan territory had ever been invaded in 600 years. For more details see Plutarch *Agesilaus* 31.
  2 This remark was added in 1532. For Erasmus' criticism of anecdotes involving stratagems rather than sayings, see the dedicatory epistle 11 and General Index: stratagems.

73 (LXXIII) Plutarch *Moralia* 214C–D. In margin 'sensible'
  1 At this second battle of Mantinea in 362 BC, the Spartans, the Athenians, and their allies met the Thebans and their allies under Epaminondas, and had in fact lost the fight at the point when Epaminondas was killed. As a result of his death, terms were agreed which Sparta refused to recognize.

happened: the victory began to go Epaminondas' way, but, with quite a number of troops in retreat, while he was encouraging his men and calling them back,[2] one of the Spartans dealt him a fatal wound. After he fell, the troops with Agesilaus began to stand their ground and the fight became much more evenly balanced, with the Thebans being much less effective and the Spartans making more impression.

This is how the general's good sense secured the safety of his men, who would otherwise undoubtedly have perished. At the same time, he demonstrated that one really sensible and intelligent man carries more weight in war than a whole crowd of fools.

74 When Sparta was unable to wage war because there was no money to pay mercenary troops,[1] Agesilaus went to Egypt to serve for pay there in answer to a call from Thacos,[2] king of Egypt. But the people of the country treated him with contempt because of his plain appearance and simple dress – they expected a Spartan king to look like the Persian king, with his person splendidly attired, for they had a quite erroneous conception of kings (thinking their worth was to be measured by outward appearance rather than by inner virtues). Agesilaus however made no alteration to his simple garb and manner of life, but made it clear while he was there that majesty and honour should be accorded to kings not because of their magnificent robes but because of their wisdom and valour.

His attitude was also a criticism of the common run of kings, who have nothing kingly left once you take away the crown, the purple, the gold, and the jewels.

This same incident also demonstrated his outstanding love of his country, as he went to Egypt without complaint in order to serve the common weal, and did not try to make his advancing years (he was almost eighty) an

* * * * *

2 There is a misunderstanding here. The Spartans, not the Thebans, were in retreat, and the Greek means 'while he was turning round and encouraging his men ...'

74 (LXXIV) Plutarch *Moralia* 214D–E. In margin 'patriotic'
  1 At first an unpaid citizen and allied army had sufficed for Sparta's wars, but by the fourth century BC it had become necessary to hire mercenary troops because of Sparta's decline, due to adverse economic conditions and the decrease in the number of Spartiates, said to be down to 1500 from the original 9,000.
  2 The name Thacos (properly Tachos) is taken from Plutarch *Agesilaus* 36, from which other material is added at the end of the section.

excuse for not performing military service in a foreign country if by doing so he could help his own country in its need.

Athenaeus tells the story as follows: Agesilaus went to Egypt to provide support for King Tachos, and the king laughed at him because he was such a small man, quoting the lines: 'The mountain laboured, Jupiter was afraid, / and forth there came – a mouse.'[3] Agesilaus replied, 'One day you will think me a lion.' And in fact later on, when Agesilaus did not come to his aid, he was indeed driven from his kingdom and took refuge with the Persians.[4]

75 He observed that the men he was about to lead out into battle were very fearful of the dangers ahead of them because of the size of the enemy – 200,000 of them – and because they were so few in number themselves. He therefore decided to perform a sacrifice before the conflict, as if seeking a good omen from the entrails. Unknown to everybody, he wrote the word 'victory' backwards on the palm of his left hand. Then he took the liver from the diviner, laid the hand with the secret writing on top of it, and held it for some time, pretending to be deep in thought and giving the impression of a man wondering what to do, until the marks of the letters had been transferred to the liver. Then he showed it to the troops whom he was about to lead into battle, saying that the gods by these letters assuredly predicted victory. The men, thinking they had a sure sign of future victory, were powerfully encouraged for the fight.[1]

This ruse was much more effective than a speech, however long and carefully composed. Again, this is a stratagem, not an apophthegm.[2]

76 The enemy were in process of encircling Agesilaus' army with a trench, as they were numerous enough to do this easily, and Nectabius,[1] whom

* * * * *

3 A Greek proverbial expression; see Diogenianus CPG 1 8.75; Horace *Ars Poetica* 139; *Adagia* I ix 14.
4 Athenaeus *Deipnosophistae* 14, 616D–E. See also 1.76 n1 below.

75 (LXXV) Plutarch *Moralia* 214E. In margin 'ingenious'
  1 This incident occurred during Agesilaus' campaigns as a mercenary in Egypt, immediately before the battle described in 1.76 below.
  2 The last sentence was added in 1532 and 1535. A similar ruse is attributed to Alexander in Frontinus *Strategemata* 1.11.14.

76 (LXXVI) Plutarch *Moralia* 214F–215A. In margin 'spirited'
  1 Nectabius (ie Nectanabis) was cousin to King Tachos and succeeded in claim-

Agesilaus was supporting, was of the opinion that they should make a sortie and involve the enemy in fight, to prevent them completing the investment. Agesilaus said that they should not interfere, as the enemy were thus putting themselves on equal terms with their opponents, not making their position superior. (The trench of course prevented *both* sides from fighting.) However, when the trench was all but complete, he drew up what troops remained to him in the narrow intervening space and, equal numbers[2] now being involved on both sides, he put the foe to flight, and with the few troops he had, inflicted great slaughter on them, and out of the spoils sent a huge sum of money to Sparta.

77 He died on his way home from Egypt, falling ill at Port of Menelaus.[1]

On his deathbed, he instructed those present to make no statue or any kind of representation of him.[2] 'If I have performed any noble exploit,' he said, 'that will be my memorial; if not, all the statues in the world, being but the work of common artisans of no significance, will not add lustre to my memory.'

Who would not admire such a philosophical mind in a man of war?

78 When addressing his troops, he constantly urged them not to ill-treat prisoners as if they were criminals, but to look after them as fellow men. When children were captured in war, he made sure that they were all collected in one place, so that they would not be left behind and perish when camp was broken. He showed the same consideration for old men taken prisoner, so that they should not be savaged by dogs and wolves when they could

\* \* \* \* \*

ing the Egyptian throne through the support of Agesilaus and his Spartan mercenaries, who had changed sides.
2 'Equal numbers' translates the reading of *1531* (*inter pares*), which agrees with the Greek text.

77 (LXXVII) Plutarch *Moralia* 215A. In margin 'modest'
1 The name of the place has been supplied by Erasmus either from Plutarch *Agesilaus* 40, or from Nepos *Agesilaus* 8.6.
2 These words do not occur in Plutarch's account of the death of Agesilaus, but are found in an earlier section of his *Life of Agesilaus* 2.2. Cf 1.27 above.

78 (LXXVIII) The remaining sections on Agesilaus are taken from other sources: 1.78 is from Xenophon *Agesilaus* 1.21–2, while 1.79–82 are derived fairly closely from Cornelius Nepos, known as Aemilius Probus in Erasmus' time, with paraphrase and incorporation of whole phrases from the original Latin text. For Nepos/Probus, see the source note to 1.79 below. In margin 'merciful'

not keep up with the army. This humane attitude won him great goodwill among the prisoners and other people as well.

Nowadays men consider themselves members of the human race when they slaughter infants and the old, and carry off captive those of an age fit for lust or labour or both. What depths this brutal savagery has attained!

79 The Athenians, Boeotians, and their allies endeavoured to bar Agesilaus' path at Coronea,[1] but he inflicted a severe defeat upon them. It was a splendid victory in itself, and enhanced by an incident demonstrating Agesilaus' respect for religion. Many who fled from the battle had taken refuge in the temple of Minerva, and when he was asked what he wanted done with them, he said sanctuary should not be violated. He had been wounded several times in the course of that battle, and he was obviously extremely hostile to all those who had taken up arms against him at that time. Nonetheless, religion carried more weight with him than resentment. It was not only in Greece that he held the temples of the gods sacred; among the barbarians too he reverently preserved images and altars as if exempt from the rules of war. A striking remark was often on his lips: he said he was amazed that men were not considered sacrilegious when they ill-treated people who had flung themselves on their mercy, appealing to them in the name of the gods; and amazed that men who diminished religion were not punished more severely than those who robbed temples.

He quite rightly considered that the gods had more care for the safety of human beings than for the lifeless objects adorning temples.

\* \* \* \* \*

79 (LXXIX) Nepos *Agesilaus* 4.5–8. This apophthegm was preceded by the heading 'Taken from Aemilius Probus,' covering 1.79–82. In margin 'reverent'
Nepos, c. 110–24 BC, was a prolific writer, most of whose works have been lost. What has survived apart from fragments is twenty lives of great generals of non-Roman nations and, from his work on Roman historians, a brief account of Cato the Elder and the life of Cicero's friend Pomponius Atticus. The foreign lives were edited by a grammarian Aemilius Probus, who dedicated his edition to the Emperor Theodosius II (AD 408–50). Consequently, for centuries the foreign lives were thought to be his work and only *Cato* and *Atticus* the work of Nepos, as eg in the *editio princeps* of 1471 (Nicolaus Jenson, Venice). This distribution was being questioned already in the fifteenth century (eg by Siccus Polenta, c. 1430), but it was not until Giphanius' edition of 1566 and Lambinus' of 1569 that all the lives were definitively reclaimed for Nepos. Erasmus follows the traditional assignment on the few occasions when he mentions Probus/Nepos (see eg Ep 406; *Ciceronianus* 28.410)
1 See 1.47 above.

**80** Next we have an example of bravery tempered with mercy.

After Agesilaus had broken the strength of Corinth[1] in a great car-
nage and had forced the inhabitants back behind their walls, many urged
him to lay siege to the city, but he refused, saying that to do so would not
be consonant with his high standards of conduct – while he could compel
wrongdoers to do what they ought to do, he was not one to overthrow the
noblest cities of Greece. This showed remarkable self-control, but his next
remark demonstrated his admirable good sense. If we are prepared, he said,
to wipe out those who have stood beside us and faced the barbarian foe,[2]
we will destroy ourselves without the enemy lifting a finger. If our allies
are ruined, the enemy will crush us without difficulty any time they want.

**81** My next example seems to display something superhuman in his make-up.

When the expedition to Leuctra,[1] which turned out to be so calamitous
for the Spartans, was being set in motion, Agesilaus refused to go,[2] though
many urged him to do so. It was as if he had a premonition of the irreparable
disaster.

**82** Now we have an incident demonstrating quickness of mind on his part. By
this he saved the state.

Epaminondas was making a violent onslaught on the city of Sparta[1]
(and Sparta was not protected by walls).[2] A number of youths, terrified at
the enemy's approach, decided to desert to the Thebans and had already occupied a piece of high ground outside the city. Agesilaus realized that there
was no possibility of preserving the city if the general population learned
that some people were trying to desert to the Thebans. So, without disclosing

* * * * *

80 (LXXX) Nepos *Agesilaus* 5.2–4. In margin 'forbearance, wise'
  1 This seems to refer to his campaigns of 390 BC, in which he occupied Lechaeum,
    the port of Corinth.
  2 The Corinthians took part in the naval battle of Salamis, 480 BC, in which the
    Persian invaders under Xerxes were defeated.

81 (LXXXI) Nepos *Agesilaus* 6.1
  1 See 1.71 above.
  2 The Spartan army at Leuctra was commanded by King Cleombrotus I, and a
    relief force was sent out under Archidamus, Agesilaus' son.

82 (LXXXII) Nepos *Agesilaus* 6.1–3. In margin 'resourceful'
  1 See 1.72 above.
  2 See 1.30 n1 above, and cf 5.212 (Pisistratus) below.

anything, he went out with his men to where the group of youths was. As if they had acted in good faith, he praised their initiative in occupying the place, and said he had been intending to do the same thing himself. By thus pretending to praise them, he undermined their resolution. He then made the place secure by leaving some of his companions with them. The lads, who had secretly planned to desert, saw that they were now outnumbered by men who had no share in the plan and so they dared not make any move. They acquiesced the more readily because they thought their intentions had not been discovered.

Undoubtedly Sparta would no longer have been Sparta if Agesilaus had not preserved it by his quick thinking. The same clever ruse remedied the young men's folly rather than punishing it.

### Agesipolis, son of Cleombrotus

83 Someone once, in the presence of Agesipolis, Cleombrotus' son, was extolling King Philip of Macedon's destruction of the city of Olynthus, which he had brought about in just a few days, as if this were some splendid achievement. 'By heaven,' said Agesipolis, 'he won't build such a city in a much longer period of time.'

He meant that it was a more kingly activity to build cities than to demolish existing ones.

84 Another person commented on the fact that Agesipolis, though king, had himself served as a hostage[1] together with other men of the same age as himself, and not their wives and children. (This person seemed to think it was dishonourable for a king to be surrendered into the power and juris-

\* \* \* \* \*

83 (LXXXIII) Plutarch *Moralia* 215B. In margin 'merciful'
The son of Cleombrotus (I) was Agesipolis II, king of Sparta 371–370 BC, and later in time than Agesipolis, son of Pausanias, Agesipolis I (see 1.86 below), whose nephew he was. However, the apophthegms here, 1.83–5, seem more appropriate to Agesipolis III, grandson of Cleombrotus II, king of Sparta 219–215 BC, who was in exile after being driven from Sparta by Lycurgus, his colleague in the kingship, who set himself up as sole ruler.
In any case, this occurred too late for Agesipolis II. Philip II of Macedon destroyed Olynthus in 348 BC, as punishment for its double dealing with respect to himself and Athens.

84 (LXXXIV) Plutarch *Moralia* 215B. In margin 'just'
1 This is unlikely to refer to Agesipolis II, who only reigned for one year.

diction of other people. Other kings usually give their wives and children as hostages in their place.) 'And quite right too,' said Agesipolis. 'It is only fair that we bear the consequences of our own mistakes.'

He meant that if any military or national disaster occurs, it is due to a failing on the part of kings, and accordingly, justice requires that kings, who have brought about the disaster, should be singled out for punishment. The accepted practice of surrendering innocent wives and children as hostages is quite unjust.

85 When this same king ordered some young dogs to be dispatched to him from Sparta,[1] someone commented that the Spartans did not export pups. He replied, 'They did not export men at one time, but they have started doing so now.'[2]

By this humorous remark he was indicating that in a well-organized state everything tends to get better. In the past the Spartans had barely been able to defend their own territory; later they boldly made war on distant kings and nations. The appropriate discipline makes men useful to the state in war; training makes dogs good for hunting.

### Agesipolis, son of Pausanias

86 Agesipolis, son of Pausanias, was in dispute with the city of Athens, and the Athenians chose the city of Megara as arbiter to settle their mutual complaints. 'It's a shameful thing,' said Agesipolis, 'if the people of Megara know better where justice lies than these Athenians who have acted as the guides and leaders of the Greeks.'

The Megarians had a bad reputation among the Greeks. It was commonly said of them that they were neither first nor second nor third nor fourth nor anywhere at all,[1] whereas the Athenians dominated the greater

* * * * *

85   (LXXXV) Plutarch *Moralia* 215B. In margin 'witty'
  1 Spartan hunting dogs were famous. See eg Virgil *Georgics* 3.44, 405.
  2 Agesipolis was presumably referring to the practice of Spartan soldiers enlisting as mercenaries from the fourth century BC onwards, as eg in 1.74 above.

86   (LXXXVI) Plutarch *Moralia* 215C. In margin 'noble'
  Agesipolis, son of Pausanias, ie Agesipolis I, king of Sparta 394–380 BC.
  1 The Megarians were generally despised. See *Adagia* II i 79: *Megarenses neque tertii neque quarti* 'The Megarians are neither the third nor the fourth.' In particular, they were thought to be mean and grasping; see Plutarch *Moralia* 526C (*On love of wealth*).

part of Greece.[2] The king accordingly wanted the dispute settled by the very Athenians with whom he was at variance. He thus demonstrated both his confidence in his own case and his belief in the honesty of his adversaries, preferring to lose by the adjudication of a famous city than to win by Megarian arbitration.

### Agis (1)

87 Agis, son of Archidamus, was told by the ephors, 'Take the troops and go to this man's country, for he will personally guide you into the citadel.' He replied, 'How can it be right, ephors, to entrust so many young men to a man who has betrayed his own country?'

He thus gravely reminded them that those who have been traitors to their native land can be safely trusted in nothing.

88 When he was asked what was the main concern of education in Sparta, he replied, 'Learning how to rule and to be ruled.'[1]

At Athens many branches of learning were cultivated, most of them pandering to intellectual curiosity rather than serving any necessary end in the good government of the state.

\* \* \* \* \*

2 This was true at the time of Athens' greatest power, glory and prestige in the fifth century BC, when she had an empire.

87 (LXXXVII) Plutarch *Moralia* 215C–D. In margin 'shameful treachery'
There are several examples of Spartan kings with the same name: Agesipolis (1.83, 1.86); Agis, as here (1.87, 1.105, 1.107); Archidamus (1.140, 1.148); Cleomenes (1.212, 1.229); Leotychidas (1.231, 1.236); see also Pausanias (not a king 1.312, a king 1.318). These are distinguished in Plutarch by the name of the father. As Erasmus usually incorporates this into his translation, he needs some other means of separating them. He does so (Agis and later) by giving them a number, but this may not correspond with the actual regnal number of the king concerned, which Erasmus probably did not know. Agis, son of Archidamus II, will be Agis II, king of Sparta 427–401 BC. (The first Agis was a shadowy figure belonging to the very early years of Sparta's history, possibly the tenth century BC.) Some apophthegms attributed to Agis II have been wrongly assigned in the tradition. Incidents involving Philip II of Macedon must concern Agis III, son of Archidamus III; see 1.105–6 below. This apophthegm too should probably be assigned to Agis III; see Plutarch *Moralia* 191E (*Sayings of kings and commanders*). For Agis IV see 1.107 below.

88 (LXXXVIII) Plutarch *Moralia* 215D
1 Cf 1.49 and 1.50 above, and 1.195 below.

89 The following spirited words are also attributed to him: 'Spartans should
    not ask how many the enemy are, but where they are.'
        This means that victory depends not on the numerical strength of an
    army but on its courage and speed in action, for a man who asks where the
    enemy are wants to engage at once.

90 At Mantinea[1] some people tried to dissuade Agis from joining battle because
    the enemy were numerically superior. He replied, 'Anyone who wishes to
    rule many must fight many.'

91 When someone asked Agis how many Spartans there were, 'Enough,' he
    replied, 'to repel the wicked.'[1]
        This means that what matters to a state is the bravery of its men, not
    their number.

92 When he was passing the walls of Corinth and observed how high and
    strong and extensive they were, 'What women,' he said, 'live in this place?'
        He meant that brave men don't need walls.[1]

93 A certain sophist[1] declared in his hearing that speech was the finest of all
    things (a remark intended to glorify his own profession). 'So when you are
    speechless,' said Agis, 'you are of no value?'
        He meant that it was much more impressive to do magnificent deeds
    than to have a tongue ever ready to utter magnificent words.

                    * * * * *

89   (LXXXIX) Plutarch *Moralia* 215D. In margin 'spirited'

90   (XC) Plutarch *Moralia* 215D. In margin 'spirited'
    1 A great battle was fought at Mantinea in 418 BC between the Spartans
      (under Agis II), the Athenians, and their allies on both sides. Large num-
      bers of troops seem to have been involved. The Spartans were eventually
      victorious.

91   (XCI) Plutarch *Moralia* 215D. In margin 'shrewd'
    1 The same remark is attributed to Ariston at 1.135 below.

92   (XCII) Plutarch *Moralia* 215D. In margin 'witty'
    1 See 1.30 above.

93   (XCIII) Plutarch *Moralia* 215D. In margin 'witty'
    1 See n3 on Erasmus' preamble 19 above.

**94** Agis had defeated the Argives in battle, but they had reassembled their forces and were now coming at him with even more ferocity. Seeing that many of the allied troops were wavering, he called out, 'Keep your courage up, men. If we who have conquered are trembling, what do you think the ones we have defeated are doing?'

By these words this resourceful general rekindled his men's courage.

**95** The inhabitants of Laconia[1] were noted for being men of few words, so that brevity of speech, taking its name from that region, is known as *Laconismus*.[2]

So when an ambassador from Abdera, after making a lengthy speech before Agis, at long last with great difficulty brought himself to a stop and was asking what answer he should take to his city, Agis replied, 'Tell them that all the time you took for talking I spent listening in silence.'

These words expressed his disapproval of the stupid speaker's empty prating which deserved no reply.

**96** Some people were lauding the inhabitants of Elis for their just administration of the Olympic Games. He said, 'What's great or remarkable in acting justly merely on one day in five years?'

This wise man considered that only someone who practised justice in every action throughout his whole life could properly be praised for justice. The Olympic Games were celebrated only once in a five-year period.[1]

**97** Some people told Agis that certain members of the other family[1] were

\* \* \* \* \*

**94**  (xcɪv) Plutarch *Moralia* 215E. In margin 'resourceful'

**95**  (xcv) Plutarch *Moralia* 215E–F. A very similar incident is reported at 1.101 below. In margin 'loquacity censured'
  1 Ie the area surrounding and dependent on the city of Sparta.
  2 See *Adagia* ɪɪ x 49: *Laconismus* 'Laconic.' There are many illustrations of the famous Spartan 'Laconic' speech throughout *Apophthegmata*. See General Index: Laconismus, Laconic speech.

**96**  (xcvɪ) Plutarch *Moralia* 215F. In margin 'just'
  1 The Olympic Games were celebrated at four-yearly intervals at the great shrine of Zeus in Elis in the Peloponnese. The Greeks, like the Romans used 'inclusive reckoning,' so a four-year period ended for them in the fifth year. The last sentence was added in 1535.

**97**  (xcvɪɪ) Plutarch *Moralia* 215F. In margin 'envy censured'
  1 Ie the other royal family – the Spartans had two royal lines and two kings

envious of him. 'Then they will have double trouble,' he said, 'for their own misfortune will make them miserable, and they will be tormented by the good fortune of myself and my friends as well.'

A fine remark, telling us that those in the grip of envy deserve pity rather than anger, because the envious man pays a heavy penalty even if no one exacts retribution from him.

98 When someone suggested that Agis should let the retreating enemy troops make their escape, 'And how,' said he, 'shall we fight those who are brave enough to stay, if we don't fight those who run away?'

This intrepid man felt that no opportunity should be lost where an enemy was concerned.

99 On the question of Greek liberty, someone brought forward a noble proposal but one extremely difficult to put into practice. 'Friend,' said Agis, 'your words require strength and money.'

He thus neatly indicated that it is pointless discussing things which one hasn't the means to carry out. When taking counsel one must consider not only what would be the most prestigious thing to do but what is actually possible.[1]

100 When someone remarked that Philip[1] was going to make it impossible for the Spartans to set foot in the rest of Greece, 'Friend,' he replied, 'as far as we are concerned, our own country is adequate for us to live in.'

Here we have a heart prepared for either contingency, happy to extend the bounds of empire if things so fall out, or contentedly accepting what fortune grants, however modest it may be. The majority of princes on the other hand neither deal wisely with what they have received nor remain content, whatever accessions are made to their realms.

\* \* \* \* \*

ruling simultaneously. Agis was, in spite of his name, a 'Eurypontid' king; the others were 'Agiads.' See 1.328 nn1 and 2 below.

98 (xcviii) Plutarch *Moralia* 215F. In margin 'shrewd'

99 (xcix) Plutarch *Moralia* 216A
   1 Cf 2.170 below.

100 (c) Plutarch *Moralia* 216A. In margin 'temperate'
   1 Philip II of Macedon. See 1.87n above, 1.148 n1 below.

101 A spokesman who had been sent to Sparta from Perinthus addressed Agis
at great length, and when he had concluded his speech asked him what
answer was to be taken back to the Perinthians. 'Only that you found great
difficulty in coming to an end,' he replied, 'whereas I said nothing.'

This apophthegm is very like the remark recorded above, where he
censured the wordiness of the ambassador from Abdera.[1]

102 He undertook an embassy to Philip[1] and went without any entourage. When
the king said in surprise, 'What's this? Is there just the one of you?' he
replied, 'Why not? I have come to talk to one.'

This was a sharp condemnation of other leaders' ostentation. They exhaust the public purse with extravagant and showy embassies, when one
man of sense could do everything that the national interest requires.

103 When Agis was an old man he heard an elderly fellow lamenting that the
ancient laws and old customs were being done away with while new bad
ones were coming in their place, and that Sparta was being turned upside
down and destroyed, with everything topsy-turvy. Agis jokingly replied, 'If
that's the case, then things are proceeding quite normally, for when I was a
boy, I used to hear my father saying that already in those days things were
being turned upside down.' If they are being turned upside down again,
they must have gone back to their original position. That was a joke;[1] but
he used to say in all seriousness that when he was a boy he also heard his
father saying that it was not at all surprising if things went to the bad, but
it would be amazing if they got better or stayed the same.

While he found fault with the habit old men have of complaining about
things getting worse, he also noted that it is in the nature of things to go
steadily downhill.

\* \* \* \* \*

101   (I) Plutarch *Moralia* 216A. In margin 'loquacity'
    1 See 1.95 above.

102   (II) Plutarch *Moralia* 216B. In margin 'unaffected'
    1 See 1.87n above. Cf Plutarch *Moralia* 511A (*On talkativeness*), where the same
      words are spoken to Demetrius I (king of Macedonia) by an unnamed Spartan
      ambassador. 'One to one' became a saying: see *Adagia* II ii 42: *Unum ad unum*.

103   (III) Plutarch *Moralia* 216B. In margin 'humorous'
    1 There is nothing corresponding to 'If they are being turned ... a joke' in the
      Greek text. It is presumably Erasmus' own humorous comment.

104 When someone asked Agis how a man might preserve his liberty, 'By despising death,' he said.[1]

The fear of death, which, we are told, is one of the things affecting the man who does <not>[2] remain constant, keeps many people from performing great exploits. The man who is free of it can follow what is right in every circumstance, and has no reason to fear the wicked. These, though they plot their worst, can do no more than kill him.

### Agis (2)

105 When Demades[1] remarked to the younger Agis that Laconian swords were so short that fairground performers used them for their sword-swallowing act, 'Ah,' he said, 'but with these swords Spartans get through to enemies armed with longer weapons.'

This remark made it plain that what matters is not the means by which something is achieved but the importance of the achievement. When a man has little to defend himself with apart from his courage, his victory is all the more impressive.[2]

106 Likewise, when some knavish fellow kept asking him who was the best man among the Spartiates, he replied, 'The one least like you.'

Being a noble-spirited man, he was incensed that a person riddled with vices should discuss grades of virtue.

\* \* \* \* \*

104 (IV) Plutarch *Moralia* 216C
  1 Cf 1.36 above.
  2 In spite of the unanimous reading of the editions, the sense requires the insertion of a negative. Accordingly *in constantem* has been emended to *in inconstantem virum* (BIK). For this idea, see eg Seneca *Epistulae morales* 85.16: *non cadit autem in sapientem haec diversitas mentis*, 'such inconstancy is not compatible with the nature of the wise man.' The whole paragraph discusses anger and fear.

105 (V) Plutarch *Moralia* 216C. In margin 'urbane'
  This must be Agis III, king of Sparta 338–331 BC. See 1.157 n1 below.
  1 Demades is presumably the Athenian fourth-century BC orator and politician Demades, who had a cruel wit. See 6.377–82 below for some of his sayings.
  2 Erasmus' comment suggests he did not get the point here, or at 1.130 below, but compare 2.144 below, which he explains correctly.

106 (VI) Plutarch *Moralia* 216C. In margin 'frank'

**The last Agis**

107 Agis, the last of the Spartan kings, was taken through treachery and undeservedly condemned to death by the ephors. When he was being led off to
be strangled and saw one of the execution squad weeping for the shameful-
ness of the deed which he was obliged to carry out, Agis said to him, 'Man,
do not weep on my account. In dying thus unjustly and undeservedly I am
better and happier than those who kill me.' With these words he readily
thrust his head into the noose.

  This outstanding young man demonstrated not in word but in deed a
fortitude surpassing anything taught by any Stoic, measuring happiness by
virtue alone, and judging those who injure others to be more wretched than
those who are injured.[1]

**[Acrotatus]**

108 When his parents asked him to support them in some unjust act, he refused for some time, but when they insisted, he replied in these words:
'When I was in your house,[1] I had no knowledge at all of justice, but now
that you have entrusted me to my country and to my country's laws and
have done your best to have me taught justice and honourable conduct, I

* * * * *

107 (VII) Plutarch *Moralia* 216D. In margin 'brave'
    'Agis, the last of the Spartan kings,' is Agis IV, king of Sparta, 244–241 BC.
    Although the last to bear the name Agis, Agis IV was not the last Spartan
    king, as kings continued to be appointed for some years after his death. He
    could perhaps be called the last 'real' king. Sparta was now in decline, her
    constitution in disarray, and eventually after a period of turmoil and attempts
    at resuscitation, the city succumbed in the second century BC to Rome and
    Roman governance.
  1 A philosophical commonplace; see eg Hesiod *Works and Days* 265–6; Socrates
    in Plato *Gorgias* 469; Aristotle *Nicomachean Ethics* 5.11.7; Plutarch *Moralia* 36B
    (*How to study poetry*); Cicero *Tusculan Disputations* 5.19.56; *Adagia* I ii 14: *Malum
    consilium* 'Bad advice.'

108 (VIII) Plutarch *Moralia* 216D–E. In margin 'just, weighty'
    This anecdote should be told of Acrotatus, son of Cleomenes II. The name
    seems to have been missing in Erasmus' Greek text, consequently he assigns
    the saying to Agis. Erasmus then adds more anecdotes about Agis IV, derived
    from Plutarch's *Life of Agis and Cleomenes* before returning to the *Moralia* with
    Alcamenes (1.111 below). There are several anecdotes about rulers refusing to
    commit an injustice to oblige their friends, eg 5.143, 5.176, 5.379 below.
  1 Spartan boy-children lived with their mothers until the age of seven, when
    they left to embark on the communal life of discipline and training in tradi-
    tional Spartan ways. The heir-apparent was however exempt from this.

shall strive to obey these rather than you. Since your will is that I should
do what is best, and since what is just is best, both for the ordinary citizen and even more so for a ruler, I will do your will. Your request I shall
refuse.'

We are told that Agis was brought up in the greatest luxury as a boy,
but as soon as he was promoted, while still a young man, to the government
of the state, there was an incredible change. He renounced the pleasures of
his early life and bent all his energies to recalling to its original sobriety
the state of Sparta[2] which was by this time thoroughly corrupted by the
morals of both foreigners and Greeks. It was this that brought about his
downfall.

I wish that other princes, whose early years are usually corrupted
with luxury and extravagance, would at least like Agis turn over a new
leaf when they take the reins of government, and follow the pattern set by
him, if anyone asks something of them which is contrary to law and moral-
ity. This splendid young man did not hurt his parents' feelings by refusing in a rough and churlish manner but replied with admirable courtesy
that he obeyed his parents by doing what was their settled will and what
they would applaud in the long run, rather than falling in with a transient
impulse on their part.

**109** When an ephor asked him when he was in the prison whether he regretted
the things he had done, he fearlessly replied that he felt not the slightest
regret for a course of action that embodied both wisdom and honour, even
though he was well aware that he would get no reward but death.

He knew well that virtue was its own reward, whatever the outcome.

**110** The ephor Agesilaus successfully carried a proposal to abolish all debts.[1]
When the promissory notes had been brought into the forum which they

* * * * *

2 From Plutarch *Life of Agis and Cleomenes* 4. Agis became king at an early age
(19) and reigned for four years only. See 1.110 n1 below.

**109** (IX) Plutarch *Life of Agis and Cleomenes* 19.7–8. In margin 'resolute'

**110** (X) Plutarch *Life of Agis and Cleomenes* 13. In margin 'unprincipled'
  1 This incident, which at first sight seems to have nothing to do with Agis, was
    concerned with Agis' reforms and in particular his attempt to break up the big
    estates acquired by the rich and to restore the old Spartan system of citizen
    land allotments. His high-handed overriding of opposition provoked a counter
    coup and led to his execution by the ephors. See 2.157 below.

call Claria[2] and set alight and the flames were leaping up, he began to taunt the other creditors who were gloomily watching, saying that he had never seen a brighter light or a purer fire.

This was because he himself owed large sums of money and also possessed great estates, but he had no intention of paying anybody anything. It's wickedness carried to the limit to add insult to injury.

**Alcamenes**

111 When Alcamenes, son of Telecrus, was asked how a ruler might best preserve his kingdom, he replied, 'By not being over concerned with his own advantage.'

In this he showed a very different attitude from the general run of princes, for these endeavour to make their position secure simply by building up their own resources at the expense of the citizens, whereas justice and equity are the things that really put sovereignty on a secure footing.

112 On another occasion, when he was asked why he had refused the gifts offered by the Messenians,[1] he replied, 'Because if I had accepted them, I could not have kept peace with the laws.'

Here we see a mind fit to rule, a mind that gave the authority of the law precedence over great gain ready for the taking. Where does this leave the people who cry, 'What the prince pleases has the force of law,' people who say that the prince makes laws but is not bound by them?

113 Somebody was censuring Alcamenes for living frugally and abstemiously when he had a considerable fortune. He replied, 'A man who has great possessions must live as reason dictates, not desire.'

By this he meant that wealth brings ruin unless the possessor has a mind superior to wealth, able to regulate the use of it not on the basis of what he possesses but of what he needs.

\* \* \* \* \*

2 This should be 'brought the promissory notes, for which the Spartan word is *claria*, into the forum.'

111 (XI) Plutarch *Moralia* 216E. In margin 'weighty'
Alcamenes was an early king of Sparta, c. 785–754 BC. For Telecrus, see 1.339–42 below.

112 (XII) Plutarch *Moralia* 216E–F. In margin 'upright'
1 See 1.25 n2 above.

113 (XIII) Plutarch *Moralia* 216F. In margin 'temperate'

**Anaxandridas**

114 A certain person was taking it very hard that he was being sent into exile
from the city. Anaxandridas, son of Leon, said to him, 'My good friend,
do not dread being made to depart from the city. The dreadful thing is to
depart from justice.'

He knew that people are not pitiable when misfortune befalls them if
they have done nothing to deserve it and their integrity is unimpaired. The
really pitiful are those who of their own free will have abandoned honour,
whether or not misfortune follows.

115 Someone was once making some relevant points to the ephors, but at too
great length. Anaxandridas said to him, 'Friend, you apply a necessary thing
where there is no necessity.'[1]

He meant that something that is both right and expedient has no need
of a long speech, because the excellence of the cause easily commends itself.
If there ever is a place for verbosity, it should be used on bad causes.

116 When someone asked him why the Spartans, instead of cultivating their
fields themselves, entrusted the farming of them to the Helots[1] (this was
the name given to those whose social class lay between slave and free),
he said, 'Because we acquired the Helots not for their benefit but for
ours.'

In this he censured the folly of those who keep servants in idleness simply for ostentation, and prefer their attendants to be partners and ministers
in their pleasures rather than have them busied with useful activities.

117 Someone put forward the view that glory and reputation were harmful
things and that the happy man was therefore the one who shunned them.
'Well then,' said Anaxandridas, 'if what you say is true, then wrongdoers

\* \* \* \* \*

114  (xiv) Plutarch *Moralia* 216F. In margin 'wise'
Anaxandridas ii was king of Sparta, c. 560–520 BC.

115  (xv) Plutarch *Moralia* 216F. In margin 'loquacity'
1 See 1.241 below, where Erasmus translates identical Greek words differently.
The meaning of the Greek phrase is not immediately obvious. Erasmus takes
it to refer to speech.

116  (xvi) Plutarch *Moralia* 216F–217A. In margin 'neat'
1 See 1.25 n2 above.

117  (xvii) Plutarch *Moralia* 217A. In margin 'witty'

will be happy. For how can the man who commits sacrilege or some other crime possibly have any concern for reputation?'

This remark censured those who reject praise and then do nothing praiseworthy out of idleness. In fact, a great name naturally attaches itself to excellence, and in noble souls a passion for praise is an inborn stimulus to great achievements.

118 When he was asked why the Spartan warriors exposed themselves so fear-lessly to danger, 'Because,' he replied, 'we train ourselves to have respect for our lives but not to fear[1] for them like other men.'

He meant that a controlled concern for one's life is a spur to brave ac-tions, but an excessive terror of death frightens men away from noble deeds.

119 Someone asked Anaxandridas why, among the Spartans, the elders[1] took many days to consider their verdict in capital cases, and why, if the accused were acquitted, he remained liable to retrial. 'They spend many days on their investigation,' he said, 'because if they make a mistake where capital punishment is involved there is no possibility of correcting the decision. If acquitted, the accused should still be answerable to the law, because it is possible that on the basis of that same law a sounder decision in the case may yet be arrived at.'

By thus avoiding extremes they sought to prevent the innocent being executed and the guilty escaping. Even if the guilty is acquitted by a mistake on the part of those passing judgment, he can be prosecuted again under the same law and pay the legally prescribed penalty.

### Anaxander

120 When Anaxander, son of Eurycrates, was asked why the Spartans did not have a state treasury, he replied, 'To prevent the people in charge of it from being corrupted.'

* * * * *

118  (xviii) Plutarch *Moralia* 217A. In margin 'sensible'
  1 Cf 2.189 below.

119  (xix) Plutarch *Moralia* 217A–B. In margin 'sensible, just'
  1 The elders formed a council of twenty-eight men over the age of sixty (plus the two kings), first established by Lycurgus and appointed for life. They were drawn from an inner circle of aristocratic families. They dealt, among other things, with important criminal cases. See 1.242 n1 and 1.299 n4 below.

120  (xx) Plutarch *Moralia* 217B. In margin 'uncorrupted'
  Anaxander was king of Sparta, c. 640–615 BC.

What little concern people show for their own integrity when they store away private wealth in a chest, whereas this man of wisdom feared the effect on the morals of his fellow citizens of public moneys of which they were to be custodians only, not masters!

### Anaxilas

121 When someone expressed his surprise that the ephors[1] did not rise as a mark of respect to the kings, especially as the ephorate had been established by kings, Anaxilas replied, 'They do not rise for the very reason that they are ephors.'

The Spartans have an office, the holders of which are called ephors. The early kings instituted them to be kings' ministers, but their powers subsequently increased to such an extent that they controlled the kings and eventually even executed them. The above remark witnesses to a temperate spirit. What the questioner saw as insolent and arrogant, Anaxilas interpreted as legitimate right.

### Androclidas

122 A certain Spartan named Androclidas who was lame in one leg presented himself in the line of fighting men. Some of them rounded on him, intending to expel him because of his lameness, but he said, 'War needs a man who will stand his ground, not one who will run away.'

He amusingly presented himself as a better soldier by reason of his handicap than the rest who had nothing wrong with their feet.

### Antalcidas

123 When Antalcidas was being initiated in Samothrace, the priest asked him if he had done anything noteworthy[1] in his life. 'If I have,' he said, 'the gods know of it.'

\* \* \* \* \*

121 (XXI) Plutarch *Moralia* 217C. In margin 'temperate'
   Anaxilas was king of Sparta, c. 645–625 BC.
   1 The first ephors were appointed in the seventh century BC. See 1.12 n3 above.

122 (XXII) Plutarch *Moralia* 217C.
   Androclidas was an otherwise unknown Spartan. Cf 1.35 above, 2.139 below.

123 (XXIII) Plutarch *Moralia* 217D. In margin 'modest'
   Antalcidas, a Spartan general in the fourth century BC, opposed to Agesilaus.
   See 1.69 above.
   1 The word *deinon* in the original probably means 'shocking, dreadful' and refers to crimes. Cf the similar story in 1.298 below, and 2.67 below.

Antalcidas thought it foolish to commend himself to the gods by a recital of his achievements, when they knew about them, whether he declared them or not. He could of course have lied to the priest. We can take this as an example both of modesty and of a noble belief about the divine.

124 A certain Athenian called the Spartans ignorant. 'Well then,' he said, 'we are the only people who have learned nothing bad from you.'
   He felt that the arts on which the Athenians prided themselves were more fitted to ostentation, idleness, and pleasure than to government. The Spartans were not lacking in any discipline that contributed to that.

125 Another Athenian was boasting, 'Of course, we've often driven you back from the Cephisus!' 'But,' said Antalcidas, 'we've never made you retreat from the Eurotas!'
   He meant that the real sign of valour was that the Spartans had often dared to advance right up to the river Cephisus in Athenian territory, whereas the Athenians had never managed to reach the Eurotas, Sparta's river.

126 Someone asked him how a man could make himself popular. 'By addressing people as pleasantly as possible,' he said, 'and doing what will help them most.'
   This advice means that one should use a pleasant tone in speaking and perform services with a view to the other person's good. Some people deserve criticism because they are genuinely persons you can rely on, but they spoil the service they do you by their brusque manner. Worse than these are people who address you kindly but do you actual harm. Worst of all are those who are both unpleasant in speech and harmful in action.

127 A sophist[1] was about to give a reading from a book, and Antalcidas asked

* * * * *

124 (xxiv) Plutarch *Moralia* 217D. Cf 1.331 below. In margin 'weighty'

125 (xxv) Plutarch *Moralia* 217D. In margin 'witty'

126 (xxvi) Plutarch *Moralia* 217D. In margin 'wise'

127 (xxvii) Plutarch *Moralia* 217D. In margin 'witty'
   1 See n3 on Erasmus' preamble 19 above.

him what it was about. When told that it was in praise of Hercules, he said, 'But who speaks ill of him?'

He thought it pointless to waste effort on eulogizing someone whom everyone was unanimous in praising. Hercules was revered most devoutly by the Spartans.[2]

128 When Agesilaus was wounded in battle against the Thebans, Antalcidas said to him, 'That's the payment for your lessons – you taught them how to fight when before they neither knew how to fight nor wanted to.' The Thebans had seemingly turned into fighters as a result of Agesilaus' frequent expeditions against them.

Antalcidas meant that it was not a good idea to be constantly fighting the same adversary, for fear they might acquire expertise in warfare through practice.

129 This same Antalcidas used to say that the walls of Sparta were the young men of Sparta, and that the bounds of Spartan jurisdiction were the points of their spears.

In other words, a city had no need of walls[1] when it reared young men fit for war, and the authority of the Spartans extended as far as they could reach with their weapons.[2] The bounds of empire must be extended by valour, not by guile or money.

130 When someone asked why the Spartans used short dagger-like weapons[1] in battle, 'Because,' he replied, 'we engage the enemy at close quarters.'

He wittily turned into a proof of valour the very thing by which the other man intended to make it appear that the Spartans were less effective as a fighting force.

\* \* \* \* \*

2 See 1.302 n2 below.

128 (xxviii) Plutarch *Moralia* 217E. An anecdote repeated from 1.69 above.

129 (xxix) Plutarch *Moralia* 217E
1 See 1.30 above.
2 See 1.29 above, 1.149 below.

130 (xxx) Plutarch *Moralia* 217E. In margin 'witty'
1 See 1.105 above.

**Antiochus**

131  When the ephor Antiochus heard that King Philip had granted the Messenians possession of their territory,[1] he kept asking whether Philip had also
given them the strength to guard the land they had been given against
anyone fighting to get it.

**Argeus**

132  Some men were expressing admiration not of their own wives but of other
people's. 'Good heavens!' said Argeus, 'No one should talk lightly about
good respectable women. In fact no one should have any idea at all what
they are like, except the husbands they live with.'

   Among the ancients, the modesty of girls and married women was
so important that for them to be seen by anyone other than their parents
or their own husbands was considered a step in the direction of shamelessness. Such precautions were taken to guard their reputation that a
woman was considered immoral if it was possible for even unfounded
rumour to spread concerning her. In fact, the highest praise accorded to
a chaste married woman was that she lived her life so confined to her
home that there was no one who could speak of her, either for good or
ill.[1] For a married woman to be gossiped about and become the subject of talk was considered a form of prostitution. Anyone who praises
another man's wife appears to be acquainted with the woman whose
praise he sings, and this in itself damages her reputation as a chaste
woman.

   What would that fine man think of married women who like going,
without their husbands, to parties where young men are present, who are
always running about to festivals and markets in other towns, who join

                    * * * * *

131  (xxxi) Plutarch *Moralia* 217F. In margin 'shrewd'
        Antiochus was a Spartan ephor 338/7 BC.
     1 The Spartans lost control of the subject territory of Messenia (see 1.25 n2
       above) after three hundred years of domination, as a result of the disaster of
       Leuctra in 371 BC. Philip II of Macedon later, after the battle of Chaeronea in
       338 BC, confirmed the independence from Sparta of various states in the Pelo-
       ponnese. Sparta in fact had now no hope of recovering her former power and
       influence.

132  (xxxii) Plutarch *Moralia* 217F. In margin 'modesty in wives'
        Argeus: this should read Areus, ie Areus I, king of Sparta, 309–265 BC.
     1 This ideal is famously enunciated in Pericles' Funeral Oration, Thucydides
       2.45.2. Plutarch criticizes it at *Moralia* 242E–F (*Bravery of women*). Cf 1.177 below.

in dances where men and women dance together, and display their naked bodies in the baths for any man to see?

133 Argeus was once travelling via Selinus,[1] when he saw this elegiac verse inscribed on a tomb:

> These while they were quenching tyranny did savage Mars destroy.
>     They fell close by the walls of Selinus.

'You deserved to perish,' he remarked, 'since you tried to quench tyranny while it was blazing. It would have been better to leave it until it burned itself out.'

It was the word 'quench' that suggested this joke to him. Anything that is suppressed is quenched, but so is a blaze.

## Ariston

134 Someone was extolling a remark made by Cleomenes when he was asked what a good king should do. He had replied, 'Do good to his friends and ill to his enemies.' 'But, my good sir,' said Ariston, 'how much better it is to do good to one's friends and turn enemies into friends.' It was undoubtedly Socrates who first uttered this maxim,[1] and it is ascribed to him as the originator.

135 When someone asked how many Spartiates there were, 'As many as suffice,' said Ariston, 'to repel the wicked.'[1]

*  *  *  *  *

133 (xxxiii) Plutarch *Moralia* 217F
  1 Plutarch's Greek identifies Selinus as a town in Sicily. Areus however campaigned in Crete. The saying is attributed to an unnamed Spartan in Plutarch *Lycurgus* 20.5.

134 (xxxiv) Plutarch *Moralia* 218A. In margin 'civilized'
  Ariston was king of Sparta, c. 550–515 BC. For his co-monarch Cleomenes I (c. 520–490) see 1.212–58 below.
  1 See possibly Plato *Republic* 335B–C. A similar saying is ascribed to Cleobulus at Diogenes Laertius 1.91, but Erasmus omits sayings of Cleobulus when dealing with The Seven Sages in book seven. See 7.38 n2 below. Plutarch describes this saying as a *chreia*. See Introduction xxiv–xxvii.

135 (xxxv) Plutarch *Moralia* 218A
  1 The word *echthros* in the Greek text can mean both 'hateful' and 'hostile.' While the second meaning might seem more appropriate here, cf 1.91 above, where

**136** An Athenian was reading out in Ariston's presence a funeral oration composed in honour of those who had been killed in battle by the Spartans. 'Then what do you think our men are like,' he said, 'who defeated the ones you are praising?'

It was an Athenian custom that those who had fallen in battle should be publicly lauded in a speech called by them an epitaph.[1] In this speech first Athens and the Athenian people were elaborately eulogized, then those in particular who had bravely met their end in battle. This generous man did not resent this rhetorically exaggerated praise of Athens, but turned it to the glory of his own people. Consequently the effect of the speech was to light up the valour of the Spartans rather than that of the Athenians. In the same way, Homer extols Hector's bravery in all kinds of ways in order to make Achilles' victory over him the more impressive.[2]

**[Archelaus]**

**137** Archelaus, who was Charilaus' colleague in the kingship,[1] used to say of him, 'How could Charilaus possibly not be a good man, when he isn't unpleasant even to wrongdoers?'

Charilaus is said to have had a very gentle nature. In my next example this apophthegm occurs in a form which expresses the very opposite idea, and in my opinion this makes it more incisive. Possibly in this passage from the *Life of Lycurgus* the first 'not' should be omitted.[2] Moreover, I suspect that Charilaus and Charillus[3] are the same person.

\* \* \* \* \*

the same apophthegm is quoted in the Greek text with the word *kakos* 'evil' instead of *echthros*. Erasmus translates by *malus*, 'wicked,' in both places.

**136** (xxxvi) Plutarch *Moralia* 218A–B. In margin 'astute'
  1 See Thucydides 2.34–46, which describes the rite and records Pericles' famous Funeral Oration; see 1.132 n1 above.
  2 Immediately Homer *Iliad* 22.90–6, but also in the narrative generally.

**137** (xxxvii) Plutarch *Life of Lycurgus* 5.5.
  Archelaus was king of Sparta in the eighth century BC.
  1 See 1.97 n1 above.
  2 Cf Plutarch *Moralia* 537D (*On envy and hate*) and 55C (*How to tell a flatterer*) where the negative is omitted.
  3 For Charillus, see next apophthegm, also 1.343–7 below.

## Archidamidas

**138** When someone was praising Charillus on the grounds that he had been
equally mild and gentle to all, Archidamidas said, 'How can anyone possibly have the nerve to praise someone who presents a mild front to wrongdoers?'

   This fine man was well aware that gentleness must be combined with
justice. Otherwise a prince's softness towards criminals is nothing but cruelty to the virtuous.

**139** Someone was finding fault with Hecataeus, the teacher of rhetoric,[1] because,
after being admitted to their dining-club, he said nothing. Archidamidas
retorted, 'You don't seem to realize that a man who has learned how to
speak has also learned the right moment to speak.' [2]

   In supreme councils, law-courts, and public meetings, on diplomatic
missions and on other official occasions, there is a place for the orator. At
parties where the wine flows the man of knowledge does better to keep silence than to speak. Likewise the experienced soldier knows when to retreat
as well as how to fight.

## Archidamus

**140** When someone asked him who ruled the Spartan state, Archidamus, son of
Zeuxidamus, replied, 'The laws, and the legally appointed magistrates.'[1]

                              * * * * *

**138** (xxxviii) Plutarch *Moralia* 218B. In margin 'just'
   It is not known who Archidamidas was. Cf Plutarch *Moralia* 55E (*How to tell
   a flatterer*), but that passage gives no clue as to Archidamidas' identity either.
   For Charillus see 1.343–347 below.

**139** (xxxix) Plutarch *Moralia* 218B. In margin 'silence when appropriate'
   1 It is not clear who this Hecataeus was – it could be the fourth-century BC
   Hecataeus of Abdera, but he is not usually described as a sophist/teacher of
   rhetoric.
   2 This is another common anecdote – a similar tale is told of the sage Bias in
   Plutarch *Moralia* 503F (*On talkativeness*). For the sentiment, see 1.170 below, and
   7.176 and 7.252 below.

**140** (xl) Plutarch *Moralia* 218C. In margin 'authority of the laws'
   This Archidamus was Archidamus II, king of Sparta, 469–427 BC. See 1.154n
   below. Archidamus I was king in the seventh century BC.
   1 Better, 'and the magistrates, in accordance with the laws,' which is what Erasmus' comment suggests. See 1.171 and 1.318 below.

Archidamus whole-heartedly believed that in a well-conducted state supreme authority must be vested in the laws, and that no magistrate had the right to attempt anything contrary to the laws of the nation.

**141** He once heard someone talking enthusiastically about a man who sang and played the lyre, and marvelling at his musical talents. 'Really, my good fellow,' he said, 'how ever will you praise and reward good men, when you speak so highly of a singer?'

He was quite rightly finding fault with the inverted values held by the crowd and by princes too. These latter often set more store by an actor or a court fool than a wise and loyal counsellor. A singer, whose skills serve not the public good but mere pleasure, was in his eyes so far from deserving praise that he did not even classify him as a good man.[1]

**142** A certain person wished to commend a musician to him and said, 'This man is a fine performer.' Archidamus replied, 'Well, as far as we're concerned, he's a fine cook,' implying that it was all one whether someone gave pleasure by means of music or by tasty dishes and savouries.[1]

At Athens, musicians were held in high repute, whereas cooks were not so honoured. The Spartans did not approve of any art which made the citizens soft instead of inciting them to valour.

**143** Archidamus was promised on one occasion that the wine would be good. 'What use is that?' he said. 'It means more will be drunk and all that characterizes brave men[1] will be made ineffective.'

Here we have a truly masculine mind, despising all self-indulgence.[2]

\* \* \* \* \*

**141** (XLI) Plutarch *Moralia* 218C. In margin 'useless arts'
 1 See General Index: trivial pursuits.

**142** (XLII) Plutarch *Moralia* 218C. In margin 'useless arts'
 1 See *Adagia* II v 35: *Bonus cantor, bonus cupediarius* 'A good fiddler or a good pastrycook, all's one.' See General Index: trivial pursuits.

**143** (XLIII) Plutarch *Moralia* 218D. In margin 'temperate'
 1 The Greek phrase τὰ ἀνδρεῖα, which Erasmus translates by *quae fortes decent viros*, is one of the names given to the communal meals taken by the Spartiate men (see 1.262 below), and here probably means 'the practice of eating together.'
 2 A similar remark is attributed to a woman, Gorgo, at 2.122 below.

**144** When Archidamus was besieging the city of Corinth, he saw hares leaping up from a spot near the city walls. Turning to his fellow-soldiers, he said, 'We have an easy enemy to defeat.'

He seized on this chance event as an omen, for the Greeks call soft and womanish persons 'hares.' This is shown in that line from comedy: You're a hare, and you go chasing game?'[1]

**145** He was chosen as arbiter by two people who were unable to agree, so he took them to the sacred grove of Minerva of the House of Bronze,[1] and there exacted an oath from them that they would abide by his decision. When they had sworn, he said, 'I declare that you are not to leave this place until you have abandoned your quarrel and are reconciled to one another.'

He very cleverly found a way of avoiding either giving offence to both parties if he refused to act as arbiter, or antagonizing one of them if he decided in favour of the other. The Spartans considered it shocking to break any promise made in the shrine of Minerva.

**146** Dionysius, despotic ruler of Sicily,[1] sent Archidamus' daughters a present of some magnificent and very expensive clothes. He refused to accept them, saying, 'I am afraid that if they wear these, my daughters will look ugly to me.'

This wise man understood that girls are best dressed simply. Silks, jewels, and gold degrade them rather than making them prettier. Extravagant dressing is a sign of a frivolous mind, and it arouses lustful thoughts rather than an attitude of respect in the mind of the beholder. A young maid should be absolutely and in every respect a virgin, and give no suggestion at all of a mind not innocent.

* * * * *

**144** (XLIV) Plutarch *Moralia* 218D. In margin 'clever'
   1 Terence *Eunuch* 426. The words are addressed to a young boy, himself of desirable age, who is making a pass at a woman. See *Adagia* I vi 7: *Tute lepus es et pulpamentum quaeris* 'A hare thyself and goest in quest of game.' For the incident, cf 1.297 below. Hares were a stock example of weakness and timidity.

**145** (XLV) Plutarch *Moralia* 218D. In margin 'ingenious'
   1 The Roman goddess Minerva was equated with the Greek Pallas Athene and Erasmus has here inserted the Latin name to explain Plutarch's elliptical used of the cult title 'She of the House of Bronze' without the name Athena. Cf 1.10 above.

**146** (XLVI) Plutarch *Moralia* 218E. In margin 'strict'
   1 This will be Dionysius I, despot of Syracuse in Sicily, 430–367 BC. The same story is told of Dionysius and Lysander, 1.288 below.

**147** He saw his son fighting Athenians[1] with the bold recklessness of youth, and said to him, 'You need more strength or less high spirits.'

He was saying that boldness is dangerous unless there is the strength to back up the daring.[2]

### Archidamus (2)

**148** After the battle of Chaeronea,[1] Archidamus, son of Agesilaus, received a letter from King Philip of Macedon, written in a rather peremptory tone. He wrote back to this effect: 'If you measure your shadow, you will find it no bigger than it was before your victory.'

This weighty remark reminds us that a man of sense does not swell with pride when fortune grants him some success, while he himself is no greater than he was before. A proper course is to measure oneself by achievements and qualities that really are one's own, not by external success that Fortune gives or takes away as she pleases.

**149** When he was asked how much territory the Spartan warrior class controlled, he replied, 'As much as they can get with the spear.'

There is an allusion here to surveyors, who measure land with ten-foot rods.

**150** Periander was a celebrated and highly regarded physician, but he wrote very poor verse. Archidamus said to him, 'What has got into you, Periander?

\* \* \* \* \*

**147** (XLVII) Plutarch *Moralia* 218E. In margin 'dangerous boldness'
1 Archidamus led invasions into Attica early in the Peloponnesian War.
2 Erasmus added all this in 1526 to *Adagia* IV ii 90: *Aut minus animi aut plus potentiae* 'Less ambition or more strength.'

**148** (XLVIII) Plutarch *Moralia* 218E–F. In margin 'arrogance'
This Archidamus was Archidamus III, son of Agesilaus II, king of Sparta 360–338 BC.
1 At Chaeronea in 338 BC, King Philip II of Macedon had defeated the combined Athenians and Thebans with their allies and asserted his authority over the whole of Greece north of the Peloponnese. The Spartans had not been involved in the battle. This anecdote must either be placed before Chaeronea or not associated with Archidamus, as he was killed fighting in Italy as a mercenary at that time.

**149** (XLIX) Plutarch *Moralia* 218F. See 1.29 and 1.129 above.

**150** (L) Plutarch *Moralia* 218F. In margin 'degeneration'

Why do you want to be known as a bad poet rather than an exclusive physician?'[1]

These words are a criticism of the way people who have taken up a worthwhile activity abandon it for some vulgar pursuit, when the best thing is for each person to practise the skill in which he excels.[2]

151 In the war against Philip,[1] some people put forward the opinion that Archidamus should meet with the enemy somewhere well outside his own country. He replied, 'That's not what one should consider. It's by fighting well[2] that we shall defeat the enemy.'

He meant that what matters is not so much where you meet the enemy, but how lively general and soldiers show themselves to be in the fight.

152 Someone was praising Archidamus for his victory over the Arcadians.[1] 'It would have been more glorious,' he said, 'if we had shown ourselves superior in intelligence rather than physical strength.'

This distinguished general knew that the most brilliant victory is one obtained by ability, since even the brute beasts surpass us in strength.

153 After invading Arcadia, he received information that the people of Elis were

* * * * *

1 All this is repeated in *Adagia* III iv 85: *Pro eleganti medico malus poeta* 'Instead of an exclusive physician, a bad poet'
2 See Aristophanes *Wasps* 1431; Cicero *Tusculan Disputations* 1.18.41; *Adagia* I vi 15: *In dolio figularem artem discere* 'To learn the potter's art on a big jar'

151 (LI) Plutarch *Moralia* 218F. In margin 'resolute'
  1 During the years preceding Chaeronea (see 1.148 above), the Spartans were involved in various alliances and military manoeuvres designed to keep alive Spartan influence and halt the establishment of Philip II's hegemony over Greece.
  2 Erasmus translates the Greek text found in Aldus' edition. An alternative Greek text gives the meaning 'one should consider where a battle is likely to be won,' ie one should not choose a battle-site that will avoid destructions to one's own country, but one that is likely to contribute to victory.

152 (LII) Plutarch *Moralia* 218F. In margin 'specious victory'
  1 This victory was won in 368/7 BC. He is credited with not losing a single Spartan soldier in the engagement. He was not yet king, as his father Agesilaus II was still alive, but left military affairs to his son. See Plutarch *Agesilaus* 33 and 1.81 n2 above.

153 (LIII) Plutarch *Moralia* 219A. In margin 'succinct'

sending help to his opponents. He sent the Eleans this message: 'Archidamus to the Eleans. Quiet is good.'

In the fewest possible words he advised them what was in their best interests and also warned them of the consequences if they tried anything out of line. Such brevity befits a commander, especially a Spartan one.[1]

**154** During the Peloponnesian War,[1] his allies asked him how much money would be needed and requested him to state the exact amount they were to contribute. He replied, 'War does not look for fixed amounts.'

He meant that people who embark on a war must surrender themselves entirely to the requirements of the war, and there is no fixed limit to these, for all kinds of unforeseen situations develop in wartime.

**155** When he saw a missile designed to be hurled by a catapult, an idea newly introduced from Sicily, he cried out. 'Ye gods, man has lost his virility!'[1]

In a battle, whenever machines are used to shoot weapons or rocks and strike at a distance, it makes little difference whether a man is brave or a coward; but when the action is at close quarters, then it is obvious who are men and who are not.

**156** When the Greeks were unwilling to rescind the agreement they had made with Antigonus and Craterus[1] and accept the liberty Archidamus was

* * * * *

1  A reference to the famous Spartan 'Laconic' speech. See 1.95 n2 above. The same saying is attributed to Periander in Diogenes Laertius 1.97, but see 7.38 n2 below.

**154** (LIV) Plutarch *Moralia* 219A. In margin 'uncertainties of war'
1  This conflict occupied Sparta and Athens from 431–404 BC. Consequently this apophthegm must belong to Archidamus II (see 1.140–7 above), or else refer to the fourth-century disagreements between Athens and Sparta.

**155** (LV) Plutarch *Moralia* 219A. In margin 'forceful'
1  For a similar sentiment, see 1.280 and 2.43 below.

**156** (LVI) Plutarch *Moralia* 219A–B. In margin 'devious'
1  Athenian policy throughout the later fourth century BC fluctuated between resistance and submission to Macedonia. Sparta was at the same time trying to stir up Greek resistance to Macedonia and reassert her lost authority. Antipater (who should be read for Antigonus) and Craterus were two of Alexander's generals, who endeavoured to impose Macedonian sovereignty on the warring Greek city states while Alexander was away in Asia from 334 BC onwards. As

offering them – they were in fact afraid they would find the Spartans more oppressive than the Macedonians – he said, 'A sheep can only say *baa*, but a man says all kinds of different things, until he has achieved what he had in mind.'

This saying suggests that one should break one's word if there is sufficient advantage in doing so. Indeed, no animal has such a wide range of expression as man. The remark could seem unworthy of a Spartan, if it were not for the fact that the integrity of the Spartan people had degenerated in the course of time through contact with non-Greek races. An honourable application of the words could be made to express the idea that one should vary the tenor of one's speech to fit the occasion and the circumstances.[2] There are times for speaking bluntly and times for being conciliatory; times for pleasant words, times for harsh ones. If no treachery is involved, this is sensible behaviour. Stupid men who do not know how to adapt to people and circumstances[3] are called 'muttonheads.'[4] So Archidamus attributed to stupidity the persistence of the Greeks, who were unwilling to change their tune when freedom was offered them.

### Astycratidas

157 After Agis[1] had been defeated in battle fighting Antigonus at Megalopolis, someone said, 'What are you going to do now, Spartans? Are you going to be subject to the Macedonians?' Astycratidas replied, 'What a suggestion! Has Antigonus the power to forbid us to die fighting for our country?'

What noble words, expressing the idea that the liberty of one's city is dearer than one's own life, and that a man does not die ignobly if he dies

\* \* \* \* \*

Archidamus died in 338 BC, this saying should perhaps be assigned to his son Agis III (338–331 BC). See 1.157 n1.

2 See 1.231 below.

3 Cf 1.231 and 1.264 below.

4 See *Adagia* III i 95: *Ovium mores* 'The character of a sheep'; Apostolius CPG 2 14.80.

157 (LVII) Plutarch *Moralia* 219B. In margin 'noble'

1 Ie Agis III, king of Sparta 338–331 BC, son of Archidamus III (see 1.148–156 above). Using Persian money, he organized the resistance of some Greeks (Athens refused to collaborate) to the power of Macedonia after Philip II's death, while his successor Alexander was absent in Asia. Megalopolis was one of the cities that refused to join him, and while he was besieging it he was defeated by Antipater (not Antigonus) and died in battle. See Plutarch *Agesilaus* 15.4 and 2.52 below. Astycratidas is unknown apart from this incident.

fighting for his native land. Since no enemy can deprive him of the power to die, anyone who despises death has the means of claiming his liberty whenever he wishes.[2]

The saying does indeed argue a mind of remarkable courage, but no good man should copy the example offered here. There is more fortitude shown in enduring long servitude, however harsh, than in putting an end to one's misery by dying. Socrates gave much holier guidance when he taught that it was sinful for the soul to desert its post in the body except by order of the commander.[3]

## Bias of Sparta

158 Bias the Spartan was trapped in an ambush by the Athenian general Iphicrates.[1] When his soldiers asked him what was to be done in this extremity, he said, 'Only this. You are to save yourselves, but I shall die fighting.'

Cato of Utica was of the same mind: he urged the rest to look to their own safety, but himself escaped base servitude by taking his own life.[2]

## Brasidas

159 Brasidas caught a mouse[1] among some figs, and when it bit him, let it go. He then said to those with him, 'There is no creature so tiny that it can't save itself, provided it has the courage to turn on its attacker.'

With these words this brave and courageous leader filled his men with courage in face of the enemy.

\* \* \* \* \*

2 This is another philosophical commonplace, especially among the Stoics. See eg Cicero *Tusculan Disputations* 5.40.117; Seneca *Epistulae morales* 12.10, 77.15; Seneca *De ira* 3.15.4; and 1.158 n2 below.
3 See Plato *Phaedo* 62b; cf Cicero *Tusculan Disputations* 1.30.74.

158 (LVIII) Plutarch *Moralia* 219C. In margin 'brave'
  1 Iphicrates was a distinguished Athenian general in the earlier part of the fourth century BC. This incident took place in 388 BC near the Hellespont and seems to have involved the Spartan commander Anaxibius, not Bias.
  2 See Plutarch *Cato the Younger* 70–2 (793D–794C); *Moralia* 781D (*To an uneducated ruler*). Cato was a Stoic; see 1.157 n2 above and 4.164 n1 below.

159 (LVIX) Plutarch *Moralia* 219C. In margin 'resourceful'
  Brasidas was a most distinguished and effective Spartan general in the earlier part of the Peloponnesian War between Sparta and Athens (431–404 BC). He was ephor in 429 BC.
  1 Cf a similar story concerning Agesilaus, 1.11 above.

**160** Once in a battle Brasidas was wounded by a weapon which pierced his shield. He plucked the spear from the wound and with it killed the foe who had wounded him.

It is very satisfactory to beat a foe with his own weapons. This is not an apophthegm.

**161** When someone asked him how he got the wound, he laughingly replied, 'My shield let me down.'

We so often meet with misfortune through the very people whose support makes us believe ourselves secure.

**162** When he set off for the war, he wrote to the ephors, 'Whatever misfortune befalls in the war, I shall either rise superior to it or die.'[1]

These words reveal an attitude of mind proper to a brave leader, for the outcome of things does not lie in the hand of man.

When he fell in battle while trying to liberate the Greeks[2] living in Thrace, a delegation bearing the news was sent to Sparta. They went to his mother Archileonis, and the first thing she asked was whether Brasidas had met an honourable end. When the Thracians praised his valour and said there was no one to equal him among the Spartans, she replied, 'Gentlemen, you do not know what the Spartans are like. Brasidas was indeed a good man, but Sparta has many superior to him.'

What should we admire more in this woman? Is it her nobility of spirit? Far from weeping a woman's tears for the death of her son, she judged it something to glory in, because it was an honourable one. Or is it her modesty

\* \* \* \* \*

**160** (LX) Plutarch *Moralia* 219C. This and 1.161 are one item in Plutarch and should be read together.

**161** (LXI) Plutarch *Moralia* 219D. In margin 'humorous'

**162** (LXII) Plutarch *Moralia* 219D (Brasidas to the ephors), 219D–E (his death). In margin 'brave'
   1 The apophthegm is quoted in Plutarch in Laconian dialect and this seems to have caused problems in Erasmus' Greek text. The original words meant, 'As far as the war goes, I will achieve what I want or die in the attempt.'
   2 One of Sparta's moves in the war was to encourage to rebel or to 'liberate' various city-states that, willingly or unwillingly, had been drawn into membership of the Athenian confederacy. Brasidas was campaigning against various cities situated in the Chalcidic Peninsula in Thrace, and at the battle for Amphipolis was killed in the moment of victory in 422 BC.
   For his death see 2.120 below.

and love of her country? She was not prepared for her son to be praised in a way that detracted from the glory of the other Spartan warriors.

## Damonidas

163 Damonidas was assigned a position at the back of the chorus by the chorus-master. 'Splendid!,' he said. 'Sir, you have found a way of making even this undistinguished position a place of honour.'

The noble-souled youth, confident of his own worth, was not afraid of being humiliated by the ignominious position. Rather he was of the opinion that his presence there would make it a place of distinction. There are numerous accounts telling how the noble character of the holder has won respect for an office in itself despised and insignificant.[1]

## Damis

164 When Alexander the Great sent a missive to the Spartans requesting them to pass a decree giving him divine honours and enrolling him among the gods, Damis said, 'Very well, let us grant Alexander that, if he so wish, he be called a god.'

What contemptuous amusement he showed at the foolish aspirations of a prince who imagined that gods could be made by those who were but men themselves, or if he did not actually think so, was foolish enough to find a source of pride in an empty title without substance.

## Damindas

165 When Philip invaded the Peloponnese,[1] someone said, 'Unless the Spartans come to an agreement with Philip, it's very likely that they will suffer badly.'

\* \* \* \* \*

163 (LXIII) Plutarch *Moralia* 219E.
Damonidas is an unknown Spartan. Cf 2.79 below.
1 See eg 1.8 and n2 above.

164 (LXIV) Plutarch *Moralia* 219E. In margin 'self-aggrandizement censured'
Damis is an unknown Spartan. There are numerous anecdotes illustrating Alexander's desire to be recognized publicly as a god, and acquiescing in the adulation, while secretly acknowledging its folly. See Index of Classical Persons: Alexander (1). Cf 1.26 above.

165 (LXV) Plutarch *Moralia* 219F. In margin 'contempt for death'
Damindas is an unknown Spartan. For the saying cf 1.157 above.
1 Philip II of Macedon invaded the Peloponnese and marched through Laconia, Sparta's own territory, in 338 BC, after the battle of Chaeronea. See 1.148 n1 above.

'You pansies!' Damindas replied. 'What suffering can befall us when we have no fear of death?'

### Dercylidas

**166** Pyrrhus had entered Spartan territory with his army and Dercylidas was sent as official representative to find out what his intentions were. Pyrrhus ordered the Spartans to take back their king Cleonymus,[1] or else they would find out that they were no braver than anyone else. Dercylidas replied 'If Cleonymus is a god, we are not afraid of him, as we have done nothing wrong. If he is a man, he is on the same level as us.'

This alternative proposition showed what he thought of the king's arrogant threat. Gods can harm whom they will and suffer no harm in return, but they only hurt the wicked. Men however are on level terms when it comes to fearing and being feared. Accordingly, those who threaten others as if from a position of superiority either think themselves gods or do not recall that the very thing with which they threaten others can be turned upon themselves.

### Demaratus

**167** After Orontes had had a very outspoken exchange with Demaratus, someone remarked that Orontes had been very blunt with him. Demaratus replied, 'He has done me no wrong. The people who do harm are those who speak to curry favour, not those who make offensive remarks out of ill-will.'

This sensible man was well aware that nothing is more pernicious than flattery, for even if it does not deceive, it makes a man arrogant, whereas someone who is hostile and outspoken does no harm to his hearer. In fact,

\* \* \* \* \*

**166** (LXVI) Plutarch *Moralia* 219F. In margin 'noble'
Dercylidas is an unknown Spartan.
1 Although he was the son of Cleomenes II, Cleonymus did not become king. He was exiled from Sparta after a fairly unsuccessful military career, and induced King Pyrrhus of Epirus to invade Spartan territory in 272 BC in an attempt to place him on the throne. For Pyrrhus see 5.119–31 below.

**167** (LXVII) Plutarch *Moralia* 220A. In margin 'flattering talk'
Demaratus was deposed from the Spartan kingship in 491 BC on grounds of illegitimacy and took refuge at the Persian court of Darius I and then of Xerxes, whom he accompanied on his invasion of Greece in 480 BC. The anecdotes 167–74 seem to be nearly all set in the Persian court. Orontes is presumably a Persian of the royal court.

he sometimes does positive good, especially if the other knows how to glean some advantage from an enemy.[1]

**168** When someone asked why at Sparta those who jettisoned their shields were branded with infamy (they were called by the insulting name of 'shield-ditchers'),[1] while those who abandoned helmet and breast plate were not, Demaratus replied, 'Because they wear helmet and breast plate for their own benefit, but they carry the shield for the sake of the army of which they are all fellow members.'

By this he meant that each person should set more store by the common good than his own. A man who has thrown away helmet or breastplate betrays and exposes to danger himself only. If he abandons his shield he betrays the whole troop: the screen of shields protects the entire line from enemy missiles.

**169** He was once listening to a singer demonstrating his expertise. The only praise he gave him was to say, 'He seems to be quite good at playing the fool.'

Such was his contempt for skills which, however much application they involved, merely delighted the ears and brought no real benefit to the state.

**170** Demaratus was once asked at a meeting whether he said nothing because he was a fool or because of inability to speak. He replied, 'A fool wouldn't be able to keep silent.'

Some people think it's brilliant to keep talking all the time, whereas it's the clearest sign of silliness. On the other hand, to say nothing when it is not the moment for speaking is the mark of wisdom.[1]

*  *  *  *  *

1 'How to glean some advantage from an enemy' is the title of a work by Plutarch, *De capienda ex inimicis utilitate,* often quoted by Erasmus: Plutarch *Moralia* 86B–92F (*How to profit by one's enemies*); see especially 89B, 90B.

168 (LXVIII) Plutarch *Moralia* 220A. In margin 'communal benefit'
1 See *Adagia* II ii 97: *Abiecit hastam. Rhipsaspis* 'He threw away his spear'; see 2.110 with n2 below.

169 (LXIX) Plutarch *Moralia* 220A. See General Index: trivial pursuits. In margin 'useless art'

170 (LXX) Plutarch *Moralia* 220A–B. In margin 'timely silence'
1 Cf 1.139 above.

171 When someone asked him why he was exiled from Sparta in spite of being king, he said, 'Because in Sparta the laws have the greater power.'[1]

He meant by this that in Sparta the king was the head of the state, but was not above the laws. The king was just as much subject to these as the citizens were. He found admirable the very feature in the Spartan constitution which obliged him to live in exile. At the same time, he provided a fine example of self-control in that he calmly accepted an exile imposed by the authority of the laws and did not rail against his country or complain that the laws were unfair.

172 A certain Persian had finally succeeded in wheedling away a boy that Demaratus loved by constantly sending him presents. Crowing over this, he said, 'Well, Spartan, I've hunted down your boyfriend.' 'Good heavens!' Demaratus replied, 'you didn't hunt him, you went shopping for him.'

Other people 'raise Hell'[1] when humiliated like this, but he made a joke of it. At the same time, he suggested that it is not very impressive to win through money.

173 One of the Persian king's subjects had defected, but Demaratus persuaded him to change his mind. When he returned home, the king intended to execute him, but Demaratus said, 'Your majesty, while he was your enemy you had no power to punish him for deserting. It would be a base act to desire his death when he has become your friend.'

These wise words of Demaratus moderated the king's displeasure and saved the life of the man he had persuaded to return. To both his advice was beneficial, in that one was persuaded to do nothing unworthy of a merciful monarch, and the other had no cause to regret that he had listened to Demaratus when he urged him to abandon his wrong-headed action.

\* \* \* \* \*

171  (LXXI) Plutarch *Moralia* 220B. In margin 'self-restraint'
   1 See 1.140 above and 1.318 below.

172  (LXXII) Plutarch *Moralia* 220B. The last sentence, 'At the same time ...,' was added in *1532* only. In margin 'self-control'
   1 Literally 'mingle sky and earth together'; *Adagia* I iii 81: *Mare caelo miscere*: 'To mingle sea and sky.'

173  (LXXIII) Plutarch *Moralia* 220B–C. In margin 'merciful'

174 The Persian king's jester kept making jokes about Demaratus' exile. 'My friend,' said Demaratus, 'I am not going to fight you as I've no rank any more.'

This joke depends on the two meanings of the Greek word *taxis* – it can mean either a position or a line or rank of troops drawn up for battle. Someone who has no rank left is not in a position to fight, and a king who has become an exile is finished with his former rank in life.

### Emerepes

175 The ephor Emerepes cut two strings out of the musician Phrynis' nine-stringed lyre,[1] saying 'Don't ruin the music.'

Earlier generations had known only seven strings, and he thought it a corruption of the art to add to these and make music complicated instead of simple. Simplicity and frugality appealed to the Spartans in every sphere.

### Epaenetus

176 Epaenetus was in the habit of saying that 'liars were the source of all wrong-doing and injustice.'

This saying accords with the writings of the Hebrews, where we are told that it was the serpent's falsehood that first opened the doors to every kind of sin.[1] 'Liars' includes flatterers, slanderers, treacherous counsellors, and depraved guardians of the young. These are the source of almost all the evils that cause such turmoil in human life.

### Euboidas

177 When Euboidas heard some men discussing the wives of various people in favourable terms, he reproved them, saying that 'no comment whatsoever

\* \* \* \* \*

174  (LXXIV) Plutarch *Moralia* 220C. In margin 'self-controlled'

175  (LXXV) Plutarch *Moralia* 220C. In margin 'frugal'
     The name is also recorded as Ekprepes or Emprepes. For the apophthegm, cf 2.97 below; *Adagia* IV iii 14: *Ne vities musicam* 'Don't spoil the music.'
   1 Phrynis was a fifth-century BC musician and poet, whose musical innovations were much ridiculed.

176  (LXXVI) Plutarch *Moralia* 220C. In margin 'untruth'
     Epaenetus is not otherwise known.
   1 This is not an exact biblical reference but recalls Genesis 3 in general and verses such as 1 John 3:8 and others.

177  (LXXVII) Plutarch *Moralia* 220D. Euboidas is an unknown Spartan.

should be passed on the character and accomplishments[1] of wives in the presence of people outside the family.'

As he was not prepared to allow praise of other people's wives, what would be his reaction to criticism of them? The chief praise which can be accorded to a chaste married woman is to be known to no one except the husband with whom she shares her bed.

### Eudamidas

178 Eudamidas, son of Archidamus and brother of Agis, heard Xenocrates in his old age conducting a philosophical discussion in the Academy with his friends.[1] He asked who the old man was and was told that he was a wise man, one of those who sought virtue. 'And just when,' said he, 'is he going to put it into practice, if he is still looking for it?'

The Spartan thought it silly to spend one's whole life discussing virtue as if it were something on which different opinions could be held, when one ought to have definite views on what constitutes honourable conduct firmly fixed in one's mind from earliest youth. One should direct one's conduct according to virtuous principles, not ask questions about virtue, as the philosophers do. They cross swords acrimoniously with each other on the question of the supreme good and the supreme evil, and can't even agree to any extent as to what goodness or happiness is.

179 He had listened to a lecture by a philosopher who put forward the view that only the wise man would be a good general.[1] 'The words are marvellous,' he said, 'but the speaker doesn't carry conviction because he has never had the trumpet sounding in his ears.'

* * * * *

1 Erasmus translates by *de moribus ingenioque* 'on the character and accomplishments' the Greek words περὶ φύσεως in Plutarch, which could however refer to physical attributes rather than mental ones. Cf 1.132 above.

178 (LXXVIII) Plutarch *Moralia* 220D. In margin 'shrewd'
   Eudamidas I was king of Sparta, 331–305 BC, succeeding his brother Agis III. See 1.105–6 above.
   1 For Xenocrates as head of the Academy founded by Plato in Athens see 7.171–9 below.

179 (LXXIX) Plutarch *Moralia* 220E. In margin 'experience'
   1 See *Adagia* IV iii 54: *Dives promissis* 'Rich in promises,' (where the name is given as Eudaemonidas). As Erasmus there conjectures, the philosopher was probably a Stoic, as the Stoics taught the supremacy and perfection of the (Stoic) wise man in every sphere.

He approved of the thesis, but pointed out that no one can convince his audience if he is speaking about something of which he has no experience.

180 One day Eudamidas arrived when Xenocrates had completed his exposition of the topic he had chosen for discussion, and had actually stopped speaking. One of Eudamidas' companions remarked, 'Now that we've arrived, he's stopped speaking.' 'Quite right,' replied Eudamidas, 'if he's said what he wanted to say.' Then the other said, 'It would have been good to hear him,' (thinking that to please him Eudamidas would ask Xenocrates to give his entire lecture again from the beginning). Eudamidas said, 'Suppose we had arrived just as he had finished dinner. Surely we wouldn't be asking him to start eating again?'

As a considerate man, he did not wish to force the philosopher to repeat his exposition, as this would have been tiring for him. As a man of Spartan virtue, he had more admiration for displays of noble action than for discussions of virtue.[1]

181 When someone asked him why he had spoken against war with Macedon when the citizens were calling for it, he replied, 'Because I don't want to prove that they are lying.'

This was his way of showing that he knew that the Spartans were demanding war more for appearances' sake than because they really wanted it. If he too had supported war, he would have shown them up, as he believed that the citizens would in that case back down. As it was, he made it appear that he was responsible for the rejection of military action, and so left the citizens with their reputation for bravery intact, as if they really had the spirit and readiness for war.

182 Someone was speaking in favour of war with Macedon and supporting the proposal with reference to the glory and the trophies which the Spartans had brought back from their victorious encounters with the Persians.[1]

* * * * *

180 (LXXX) Plutarch *Moralia* 220E. In margin 'considerate'
   1 See 1.178 above.

181 (LXXXI) Plutarch *Moralia* 220E–F. In margin 'civility'

182 (LXXXII) Plutarch *Moralia* 220F. In margin 'shrewd'
   1 'Victorious encounters with the Persians' presumably refers to the exploits of King Agesilaus in the fifth century BC, for which see 1.13–16 above. The confrontation with Macedon belongs to the fourth century BC.

Eudamidas remarked, 'You don't seem to realize that that's like someone who has defeated a thousand sheep having a fight with fifty wolves.'

He meant that it had not been difficult to defeat the Persians who were rendered impotent by luxury and indulgence and were therefore quite unwarlike, but it was a different thing to have dealings with a bellicose race like the Macedonians. Anyone who proposed that a war with Macedon should be started on the grounds of victories won from the Persians was talking as much sense as someone saying to a person who had defeated a thousand sheep, 'As you've defeated so many sheep, now dare to take on fifty wolves.'

183 He was asked what he thought of a singer[1] who had given a fine performance. 'A considerable charmer,' he said, 'in a trifling activity.'

He had no time for an art that required great application but brought no reward apart from a little empty and transitory gratification of the ears.

184 When someone was extolling the city of Athens, he said, 'How can anyone be justified in praising a city which no one has ever loved because he became a better man there?'

He did not consider worthy of any praise a city so corrupted by pleasure and vice that no one who lived there from choice was improved by it, rather everyone became worse. He implied that Sparta was preferable to Athens, in that living there made people better.

185 A citizen of Argos was remarking that the character of the Spartans degenerated when they went abroad,[1] because while there they fell away from the laws and institutions of their ancestors. 'But you,' retorted Eudamidas, 'when you come to Sparta, finish up not worse but better.'

Eudamidas turned the remark back on the Argive citizen, for in effect the Argive's words criticized his own people rather than the Spartans. At the same time he pointed out the importance of the kind of people you live with.

\* \* \* \* \*

183 (LXXXIII) Plutarch *Moralia* 220F. In margin 'useless art'
  1 See General Index: trivial pursuits.

184 (LXXXIV) Plutarch *Moralia* 220F. In margin 'uncorrupted'

185 (LXXXV) Plutarch *Moralia* 220F–221A. In margin 'clever retort'
  1 The Spartans were in fact notorious for corruption and tyranny once they got away from Spartan discipline and found themselves in a position of power. See 2.99 below; 2.136–7 below.

**186** At the Olympic Games Alexander had an announcement made that all exiles
had the right of returning to their own countries, except for the Thebans.[1]
'An unhappy announcement for you, men of Thebes,' said Eudamidas, 'but
one that does you honour. You are the only people Alexander fears.'

Being a man of resource, he put this interpretation on the situation to
bring the Thebans comfort. Anyone who allows exiles to return home has
no fear that they will plot revenge. Accordingly, Alexander did fear such a
thing from the Thebans, but from no one else.

**187** When someone asked him why the Spartans sacrificed to the Muses before
going into battle[1] (for there seemed to be no connection between the Muses
and Mars the god of war), he replied, 'So that our exploits may receive
honourable commemoration.'

The Spartans assumed that the glory of success would be theirs, but the
celebration of their exploits in splendid words they considered something
they must request of the Muses, the guardians of all splendid utterance,
because they themselves paid no attention to the study of eloquence.

This remark also reminds us that one should not expect tributes of
praise unless one has earned them by virtuous acts.

**Eurycratidas**

**188** When Eurycratidas, son of Anaxandridas, was asked why the ephors pro-
nounced judgment every single day[1] in cases of bargain and contract, he
replied, 'So that we may have mutual confidence in one another even amidst
our enemies.'

\* \* \* \* \*

188 (LXXXVI) Plutarch *Moralia* 221A. In margin 'shrewd'
   1 Alexander (the Great) succeeded his father Philip II of Macedon in 336 BC.
   This decree belongs to the year 323 BC, as does Alexander's demand to be
   recognized as a god by the Greek states. See 1.164 above and Index of Classical
   Persons: Alexander (1).

187 (LXXXVII) Plutarch *Moralia* 221A. In margin 'noble'
   1 See 2.97 below. Cf Plutarch *Lycurgus* 21.7, where the purpose of the sacrifice
   is to inspire the warriors to perform deeds worthy of commemoration.

188 (LXXXVIII) Plutarch *Moralia* 221B.
   Eurycratidas was king of Sparta, c. 615–590 BC. After this apophthegm, modern texts of Plutarch, following the Greek alphabet, have two sayings of Zeuxidamus. These seem to have been misplaced in Erasmus' text and will be found
   at 1.308–9 below.
   1 Two of the five ephors accompanied the army on campaign.

Even more harm is done to a nation when agreements are broken while a war is on, but people who are accustomed to play false at home break their word also when away at the war.

## Herondas

189 Herondas happened to be in Athens and was told of someone who had been found guilty of the crime of not having an occupation and was being escorted home in distress by his grieving friends. Herondas asked to have pointed out to him this person who was prosecuted for behaving like a free man.

The Spartans expected every kind of trade or practical activity to be carried out by their slaves, the Helots, and not by the citizens.[1] Accordingly, Herondas was amazed that anyone could be brought to trial for not practising a servile occupation, and that in Athens a way of life was considered criminal that in Sparta would be thought honourable and appropriate to a free man.

## Thearides

190 When Thearides was sharpening his sword on a whet-stone, someone asked him if it was sharp. 'Sharper than slander,' he said.

This effectively reminds us that slander is the deadliest thing there is.

## Themisteas

191 Themisteas, in his capacity as a prophet, predicted to King Leonidas that there would be total annihilation of the king and his fellow soldiers at Thermopylae.[1] Leonidas tried to send Themisteas back to Sparta on the pretext

* * * * *

189 (LXXXIX) Plutarch *Moralia* 221C. In margin 'noble-spirited'
    Herondas is an unknown Spartan.
  1 See 1.25 and 1.70 above, 2.117 below; Plutarch *Lycurgus* 24.

190 (XC) Plutarch *Moralia* 221C. In margin 'slander'
    Thearides is a Spartan of unknown date.

191 (XCI) Plutarch *Moralia* 221C–D. In margin 'considerate [Leonidas], brave [Themisteas]'
    Nothing is known of Themisteas apart from this incident. He was killed in the battle.
  1 This is the site in southern Thessaly of the famous exploit of Leonidas and his 300 Spartiates, who died trying to delay the invading Persian hordes under Xerxes from getting through the narrow pass and on into the rest of Greece in 480 BC. See 1.242–56 below.

of announcing what was to happen, but in reality to save him from perishing with the rest. He would have none of it, saying, 'I was sent here to fight, not to carry messages.'

Who would not admire this resolute spirit in the prophet? He foresaw destruction, but did not desire to escape it, though he had a fair pretext for doing so. One must also respect Leonidas' self-control. When the prophet gave him bad news, he did not fly into a rage as the general run of princes do,[2] but tried to preserve both the man's life and his reputation.

### Theopompus

192 When Theopompus was asked how a ruler could preserve his kingdom in safety, he replied, 'By allowing his friends due liberty, while at the same time exercising great vigilance to make sure his subjects do not become the victims of injustice.'

Many princes have been destroyed because they allowed their friends total liberty of action and ignored the injustices inflicted on the people. A middle course should be followed here: a ruler should neither alienate his supporters by tyrannical harshness, nor let them abuse their familiarity with him and do what they like to the common people with complete disregard for justice; for the common people, when goaded beyond endurance, have often thrown off their rulers.

193 A visitor was boasting to Theopompus that among his fellow-citizens he was known as 'a man who loves Sparta.' Theopompus replied, 'It would be better if you were called "a man who loves his country" rather than "a man who loves Sparta."'

The other expected to be commended for his pro-Spartan attitude. Theopompus however censured him for preferring to be known as an admirer of another state rather than his own. One's first affection is owed to one's own country. Anyone who is enthusiastic about another country is to some extent showing dissatisfaction with his own.

\* \* \* \* \*

2 See *Adagia* v ii 1: *Nuncio nihil imputandum* 'Don't blame the messenger.'

192 (XCII) Plutarch *Moralia* 221D. Cf 1.18 above. In margin 'moderation'
Theopompus was king of Sparta, c. 720–675 BC.

193 (XCIII) Plutarch *Moralia* 221D–E. In margin 'sharp'

**194** Here is a similar incident. An ambassador from Elis stated that his fellow-
citizens had chosen him as representative because he was the only one who
expressed admiration for the Spartan way of life.[1] Theopompus asked him
which he thought better, the way of life of the other citizens or his own.
When he replied, 'My own,' Theopompus said, 'How ever can that state be
saved where, among so many, there is only one good man?'

This neat retort showed what he thought of the want of sense shown
by a spokesman who praised the Spartans and himself and criticized his
fellow-citizens. The man thought the Spartan way of life a good thing, but
he was the only one of the Eleans who did – which implied that among
the citizens of Elis there was only one single good man who approved of
virtuous conduct.

**195** When it was remarked that the Spartan state stood firm because the kings
knew how to command, Theopompus replied, 'No, it's because the citizens
know how to obey.'[1]

With remarkable modesty he transferred this praise of the kings to
the citizens. The integrity of the ruler is of great moment, but even more
depends on a proper attitude among the citizens.

**196** When the people of Pylos[1] published a decree awarding Theopompus the
highest honours, he wrote back, 'The passage of time increases modest honours, but erases excessive ones.'

What a splendid attitude! He rejected when it was freely offered the
very thing that others either arrogantly assume or foolishly go touting for.
This remark showed how modest he was himself and also reminded his
friends that moderation is best in everything. Moreover, he was well aware
that things that grow fast, like beets and gourds, do not last long, whereas

* * * * *

**194** (XCIV) Plutarch *Moralia* 221E. In margin 'witty'
  1 The Greek implies that the man tried to copy the Spartans in his daily life.

**195** (XCV) Plutarch *Moralia* 221E. In margin 'weighty'
  1 Cf 1.49–50 and 1.88 above.

**196** (XCVI) Plutarch *Moralia* 221F. In margin 'modest'
  1 Theopompus with his colleague Polydorus (1.332 below) won the first Messe-
    nian war, in which Sparta acquired control over Northern Messenia. Pylos
    was an ancient city in Southern Messenia, an area which retained nominal
    independence for a time.

things that develop slowly, like oaks and box-trees, stand the passage of time.

197 When someone was showing Theopompus the walls of his city and asked whether he thought them high and strong, 'Not at all,' he replied, 'if the inhabitants are women.'

He meant that a city has protection enough if it has real men; if not, defence-works are useless, however elaborate.

198 When his wife berated him, complaining that he would hand on to his sons a kingdom smaller and less powerful than the one he had received, he replied, 'No, greater because more likely to last.'[1]

This comes from Plutarch's *Life of Lycurgus*. Things that are kept to modest size stand the test of time, and for this reason they are better.

**Thectamenes**
199 After the ephors had sentenced him to death, Thectamenes smiled as he left the place. The bystanders asked him if he was actually showing contempt for the laws of Sparta. 'Not at all,' he said, 'I am happy because this fine is to be paid by me, and I have never imposed it on anyone else, nor have I borrowed it from anyone.'

He was innocent, but did not rail against his country's laws. He thought himself happy in that, being sentenced to die, he himself had brought death upon no one and owed life to no one but himself. He humorously called the penalty of death a fine, using a milder word[1] for a dreadful thing. A

* * * * *

197 (xcvii) Plutarch *Moralia* 221F. This apophthegm is not found in some mss of Plutarch and was presumably missing in Erasmus' text, as a marginal note in *1531*, *1532*, and *1532* comments: 'This is not in the Greek but is Philelphus' translation.' For Filelfo see the dedicatory epistle 7 n20 above. In *1532* and *1535* there is a marginal note, 'This is found twice elsewhere' (ie 1.92 above and 1.310 below).

198 (xcviii) Plutarch *Life of Lycurgus* chapter 7. In margin 'wise'
  1 Theopompus had agreed to the appointment of the first ephors, who were from the beginning a check on the autocratic power of the kings. See 1.12 n3 above.

199 (xcix) Plutarch *Moralia* 221F. In margin 'death scorned'
  This apophthegm and the next (1.200) are inverted in modern texts of Plutarch. Neither person is otherwise known.
  1 Ie in the figure of speech known as *meiosis*.

man is rightly compelled to pay out money when he has either extorted it or borrowed it from another.

Cicero has the following version of this aphorism in book I of the *Tusculan Disputations*.[2] A certain Spartan, whose name is not even recorded, showed such contempt for death that when he was being led off to execution after the ephors had passed sentence, he was smiling and cheerful. When one of his enemies asked, 'Do you treat the laws of Lycurgus[3] with such disrespect?' he replied, 'No, I feel great gratitude towards him, for he has imposed a fine on me that I can pay without borrowing or raising a loan.' What a man, truly worthy of Sparta! As he showed such a noble spirit, I am sure he was innocent when convicted. Cicero seems to have translated the Greek word *diaitēsanta* 'imposing' by *versura* 'raising a loan.'[4]

Thectamenes so despised death that he made a joke of it, as if death were a lesser penalty than a monetary one, because anyone can pay the fine of death out of his own resources. To pay a monetary fine many have to borrow or raise a second loan.

**Therycion**

200 When Therycion was returning from Delphi, he found the narrow neck of land at the Isthmus of Corinth occupied by Philip's forces. 'Men of Corinth,' he exclaimed, 'the Peloponnese has poor gate-keepers in you!'[1]

He was referring to the fact that citizens who have been entrusted with the city gates are punished severely if they guard them carelessly. The

* * * * *

2 Cicero *Tusculan Disputations* 1.42.100.
3 Lycurgus is the famous lawgiver and architect of the Spartan constitution. See 1.258–87 below.
4 Erasmus' remarks and also his translation of the apophthegm show that his Greek text of Plutarch offered the reading οὖτε διαιτήσαντα [*oute diaitēsanta*], 'neither having imposed (?)' (see lines 4–5). Modern texts read the more straightforward οὖτε τι αἰτήσαντα [*oute ti aitēsanta*], 'neither begging,' and the version of the story available to Cicero must have had something similar. The remark makes more sense in this form, and this is no doubt why Erasmus quotes Cicero's version, even though, faced with a different reading in Plutarch, he is puzzled by Cicero's translation.
Strictly speaking, *versura* is a second loan raised at a higher rate of interest to pay off an earlier creditor. See *Adagia* I x 23: *Versuram solvere* 'To pay by a switching loan.'

200 (c) Plutarch *Moralia* 221F.
Therycion (or Thorycion) is an otherwise unknown Spartan.
1 The saying is the subject of *Adagia* IV ii 52: *Malus ianitor* 'A bad gate-keeper.'

Corinthians were far more guilty, in that they had betrayed to Philip the gates of the whole Peloponnese.

## Hippodamus

**201** When Agis had his forces drawn up ready to do battle against Archidamus, Hippodamus was ordered to go with Agis to Sparta to organize what was needful.[1] 'Surely,' he said, 'it is more honourable to meet my end playing the part of a good and brave man for Sparta's sake?' Thereupon, taking his weapons and stationing himself at the king's right hand, he died fighting.

They were acting out of consideration for his age, for he was well on in years and not really likely to contribute much to the battle, whereas he would be of use back home. He was more than eighty years old,[2] but he granted himself no concessions.

## Hippocratidas

**202** Hippocratidas received from the Persian governor of Caria a letter informing him that a certain Spartan who had known of a plot against the governor had kept quiet instead of reporting the matter. The governor also wanted to know what he should do about him. Hippocratidas replied, 'If he has received any great benefit at your hands, execute him. If not, expel him from your territory, as being too cowardly for any right action.'

He was of the opinion that ingratitude towards a benefactor should be punished by death, whereas for something motivated by fear rather than by some evil impulse exile was an adequate response. The man in question had not been involved in the plot himself, but had failed to betray it out of fear.

\* \* \* \* \*

**201** (1) Plutarch *Moralia* 222A. In margin 'death scorned'
Nothing more is known of this aged Spartan, Hippodamus.
1 The account here is confused because Erasmus has mistranslated Plutarch's *paretasseto* which means 'to do battle *alongside*.' He is following the Latin version offered by Filelfo and Regio. See the dedicatory epistle 7–8 nn20 and 21 above. The incident is however not made clear in the Greek without some explanation. The king is Archidamus III who fought against the state of Megalopolis in 352 BC. Agis is presumably Archidamus' son, the heir to the throne and the future Agis III.
2 This information is part of Plutarch's narrative. Erasmus has included it in his comment.

**202** (II) Plutarch *Moralia* 222A–B. In margin 'temperate'
Hippocratidas was king of Sparta, c. 600–575 BC.

203  He once met a youth who blushed because he had his lover with him. Hippocratidas said, 'You should go walking with persons who won't make you embarrassed if you're seen.'

This pointed out that bad company brings nothing but shame and humiliation.

### Callicratidas

204  The admiral Callicratidas was offered fifty talents by friends of Lysander[1] to allow them to kill one of their enemies. Although he was in desperate need of money to pay the sailors' wages, he would not agree to the proposal. One of his staff-officers, Cleander,[2] said, 'If I'd been you, I would have taken it.' Callicratidas replied, 'So would I, if I'd been you.'

What a marvellous example of integrity! The admiral could not be bribed by any sum of money, however much he needed it, to allow an injustice to be inflicted on a single individual. His remark also reminds us that every action should be in keeping with one's character and status. What might have been in accordance with Cleander's character would not have been suitable for Callicratidas. What a private citizen might do is not always appropriate for a prince.

205  Callicratidas went to Sardis to have an audience with Cyrus the Younger,[1] who was at that time supporting the Spartans in their military operations. He was intending to ask for a subvention for his fleet. The first day after he arrived, he sent a message that he wished to speak with Cyrus. When he was informed that Cyrus was holding a drinking party, 'I will wait,' he said, 'until he has finished drinking.' So this time he went away, as he realized that there was no possibility of getting an audience that day, for he did not wish to give the impression of not knowing the proper way to behave.[2]

* * * * *

203  (III) Plutarch *Moralia* 222B. In margin 'decency'

204  (IV) Plutarch *Moralia* 222B–C. In margin 'honourable'
Callicratidas was a Spartan naval commander in the Peloponnesian War between Sparta and Athens, 431–404 BC.
  1 For the Spartan commander Lysander, see 1.288–303 below.
  2 See 1.209 below.

205  (V) Plutarch *Moralia* 222C–D. In margin 'spirited'
  1 Cyrus had been instructed by his father Darius II, king of Persia, to support the Spartans in the war with Athens and provide subventions of money.
  2 Again Erasmus' Greek text seems to differ from more modern ones which

The next day however, when he was again told that Cyrus was drinking and that there would be no audience, he announced that, while money was important, one should not for the sake of it do anything unworthy of Sparta. He then went straight back to Ephesus, cursing those who had first met with insolence from the barbarians and, by submitting to it, had taught them to think their wealth entitled them to treat others in a high-handed manner. He assured his companions most vehemently that as soon as he got back to Sparta he would do everything in his power to make the Greeks settle their differences. Then the barbarians would consider them something to be reckoned with, and the Greeks would no longer need to apply to the king for help in pursuing their internal quarrels.[3]

What will men not do and suffer when pressed by financial hardship? Yet the noble spirit of this Spartan preferred to ignore financial considerations rather than submit to a third demonstration of arrogance on the part of this voluptuary of a king. Other people are prepared for reasons much less pressing to accept it without complaint if they have to wait a whole six months before being admitted to put their case to the king. Secondly, Callicratidas said nothing against the barbarians or their king, but heaped his indignation on those who by their submissive behaviour had taught them so to flaunt themselves on account of their vast riches. If they had all been like the Spartans, despisers of wealth and pleasure, the barbarians would never have reached such heights of insolence. Thirdly, in his wisdom he saw that the Greeks could become something the barbarians needed to take seriously only by setting aside their internal quarrels and solemnly agreeing to keep the peace.

206 When Callicratidas was asked what sort of persons the Ionians were, he replied, 'Bad freemen, but good slaves.'[1]

He meant that they did not know how to command and exercise freedom, but accepted servitude without discontent, and so were to be assigned to Hesiod's second class of men who have no wisdom of their own but obey one who has understanding.[2]

\* \* \* \* \*

offer: '... an audience that day, thus giving the impression of being somewhat boorish.'
3 See 1.59 nn1, 2, and 4 above.

206 (VI) Plutarch *Moralia* 222E
1 Cf 1.62 above, 5.39 below. They acquiesced in Persian domination.
2 Hesiod *Works and Days* 295; see 1.212 n2 below.

207 When Cyrus had sent the money to pay the soldiers[1] and included a separate gift for Callicratidas as a mark of friendship, Callicratidas accepted the money but sent back the present, saying that it was not for him to have a special private relationship with Cyrus; the public relationship that Cyrus had with all Spartans operated between Cyrus and himself also.

Such an attitude demonstrates the highest integrity, wholly concerned with what is good for the country.

208 Just before the naval battle at Arginusae,[1] Hermon, Callicratidas' captain,[2] said that he would do well to withdraw because the Athenian fleet was numerically far superior. He replied, 'What of it? Fleeing will bring disgrace on Sparta and harm her too. The honourable course is to stand one's ground and either die or conquer.'

He valued glory above life – the public glory of his country, not his own personal glory.

209 When he had performed the pre-battle sacrifice, the seer, looking at the burnt offering, declared that victory was indicated for the Spartan force but death for its commander. No whit perturbed, Callicratidas said, 'Sparta does not depend on one person. If I die, my country will be no worse off, but if I yield to the foe my country will be diminished.' So he appointed Cleander commander in his place, engaged the enemy in the naval battle, and died fighting.

**Clearchus**
210 Clearchus was always drumming into his soldiers that 'a soldier should fear

* * * * *

207  (VII) Plutarch *Moralia* 222E
   1 See 1.205 above

208  (VIII) Plutarch *Moralia* 222E–F. In margin 'contempt for death'
   1 The battle of Arginusae was an important sea battle in 406 BC, in which the Spartans were heavily defeated by the Athenians and Callicratidas was killed.
   2 Hermon was a skilled captain and was honoured by Lysander with a statue at Delphi for his services a year later in 405 BC at the battle of Aegospotami, in which Lysander annihilated the Athenians. See 1.293 below.

209  (IX) Plutarch *Moralia* 222F. In margin 'contempt for death'

210  (X) This is not in Plutarch's *Apophthegmata Laconica*, but is taken from Valerius Maximus 2.7 ext. 2.

his general more than he fears the enemy'[1] – words that promised death to any soldier who displayed less than adequate vigour on the battlefield.

It is more creditable to surrender one's life to one's country with honour than to yield it to execution with disgrace. Not every soldier would submit to such a dictum, but the Spartans did so easily – their mothers at home used to tell them plainly 'either to come back victorious carrying their shields or be carried back dead on them.'[2]

### Cleombrotus

211 A visitor from another country was arguing with Cleombrotus' father, Pausanias,[1] about moral worth. Cleombrotus said, 'My father is a better man than you, until you too become a father.'

He politely stopped the man arguing further by indicating that his father was superior for the very reason that he had provided a son for his country, whereas the other was as yet without offspring.

### Cleomenes (1)

212 Cleomenes, son of Anaxandridas, was accustomed to say that Homer was the poet of the citizens of Sparta, Hesiod the poet of the Helots (that is, of slaves), because Homer told how to wage war,[1] Hesiod how to cultivate the land.[2]

As I said earlier, Spartans were trained purely for military activities, and for that reason assigned all humbler tasks and manual skills to their slaves, whom they called Helots.[3]

213 This same Cleomenes arranged a seven-day truce with the people of Argos,[1] but when he had discovered by observation that, relying on the truce, they

\* \* \* \* \*

1 Also quoted in Frontinus *Strategemata* 4.1.17
2 Cf 2.142 below.

211 (xi) Plutarch *Moralia* 223A. In margin 'courteous'
Cleombrotus later became king of Sparta, 380–371 BC, and was killed at the battle of Leuctra 371 BC.
1 See 1.318–24 below.

212 (xii) Plutarch *Moralia* 223A. This was Cleomenes I, king of Sparta, c. 520–490 BC. In margin 'shrewd'
1 A reference to Homer's *Iliad*, the story of the Trojan War.
2 The author of *Works and Days*, a poem partly about agriculture.
3 See 1.25 n2 and 1.116 above.

213 (xiii) Plutarch *Moralia* 223A–B. In margin 'cunning'
1 Cleomenes attacked Argos in 494 BC.

were all fast asleep on the third night, he attacked them, killing some and capturing others. When he was reviled for this violation of his sworn word, he replied, 'The agreement to which I swore referred to the days only; the nights were not included.[2] In any case, any evil one can inflict on an enemy is judged superior to justice by gods and by men as well.' These arrogant words were not upheld by subsequent events – he failed to capture the city, to achieve which he had violated the agreement,[3] because the women fetched down the weapons dedicated in the temples of the gods and took their revenge on him (as if the very gods whom he had treated with such contempt were exacting the penalty from him).[4] Later he lost his wits and gouged out his flesh with a dagger, cutting himself up from ankles to vitals, and so died, grinning and laughing.

There is nothing worthy of imitation in this apophthegm, but it is a useful example to show that one's given word should not be broken.

214 The seer urged him not to advance on Argos, for, he said, he would return thence covered in shame; but after Cleomenes had brought his troops up to the place and could see the gates barred and women standing on the walls, he said, 'So you think it's shameful to return from a place where the gates have been barred by the women because the men have been killed?'

A bold spirit, if it had been combined with right and just principles.

215 When some of the Argives called him a godless perjurer, he said, 'You have the power to speak ill of me, but I have the power to do ill to you.'

This reminds us that it is not safe to provoke with insults those who have it in their power to do actual harm when they choose; also that the powerful should not let themselves be unduly angered by the words of lesser people – there is sufficient retaliation in the knowledge that they, the powerful, can exact vengeance whenever they will, whereas the others have nothing at their command but words of abuse.

\* \* \* \* \*

2 A tale of similar treachery on the part of the Thracians is found in Zenobius CPG 1 4.37.
3 He was in fact prosecuted in the ephors' court (and acquitted) for failing to take the city.
4 For the women's act, see next apophthegm (1.214). The words 'took their revenge' should be: 'drove him off.'

214 (XIV) Plutarch *Moralia* 223C. In margin 'bold'

215 (XV) Plutarch *Moralia* 223C. In margin 'restrained'

216 The people of Samos sent a delegation to Cleomenes to urge him to declare war on Polycrates,[1] despot of the island. They spoke at far greater length than was necessary[2] and he replied after this fashion: 'What you said first I can't remember, and for that reason I can't grasp the middle either. What you said last I reject.'

This reminds us that verbosity is not only tedious for the listener but contributes nothing towards gaining our end, especially when directed at rulers who have much on their minds and are very choosy as to what they listen to.

217 A pirate was ranging about in Spartan territory, looking for plunder. He was captured and when asked why he had done this bold thing, replied, 'I was short of supplies to give to my men, so I came to take it by force from those who had but would not willingly give.' At this, Cleomenes remarked, 'A succinct crime.'

He was incensed at the robber's wicked deed, but approved of the brisk brevity of his words.[1]

218 When some low person kept reviling him with insults, Cleomenes said, 'Are you slandering everyone so that, if we decide to reply to your charges, we will not have any time left to talk about your own nasty tongue?'

What lofty contempt he showed for this scurrilous fellow! He considered this remark both a sufficient response and a sufficient punishment for a contemptible creature whose only weapon was his slanderous tongue.[1]

\* \* \* \* \*

216 (xvi) Plutarch *Moralia* 223D. In margin 'loquacity'
   1 Polycrates was the sixth-century BC ruler (tyrant) of the island of Samos. He was helped in establishing his sole rule by Lygdamis, sole ruler of the island of Naxos, for whom see 2.66 below. The Greeks were generally antagonistic to rule by any one person and the Spartans did in fact send a force to support the people of Samos in their rebellion against Polycrates. This expedition was a failure. It took place in 525 BC, which is before Cleomenes became king.
   2 See 1.95 n2 above.

217 (xvii) Plutarch *Moralia* 223D. In margin 'assurance'
   1 Ie *Laconismus*, see 1.95 n2 above.

218 (xviii) Plutarch *Moralia* 223D. In margin 'restraint'
   1 Cf 1.215 above and 1.236 below.

**219** Cleomenes heard one of the citizens saying that a good king ought to be absolutely mild and gentle towards everyone.[1] 'Yes,' he said, 'but not enough to make them despise him.'

He meant that to show too much kindness towards the evil-doer is of no use to the state. He was also referring to certain people who learn to despise outstandingly good and merciful rulers when they ought to be devoted to them. To be sure, approachability and gentleness in a ruler is a very fine thing; but because of the wickedness of people it has to be tempered, so that the prince retains his authority.

**220** He was afflicted by a long-term illness[1] and took to consulting soothsayers and performers of purificatory rituals, which he had not been in the habit of doing before. When someone expressed surprise at this, he said, 'Why are you surprised? I am not the man I was. As I am a different man, I choose different things.'

He thus deflected the charge of inconsistency, but it is true that an old man does not find pleasure in the things that pleased him in his youth.

**221** A sophist was giving a long disquisition on courage. Cleomenes laughed, and when the other asked, 'What do you find so funny, Cleomenes, in hearing someone talking about courage, especially when you are a king?' 'My friend,' said the king, 'if a swallow were talking about courage, I should laugh as I do now; but if an eagle were talking, I should listen in total silence.'

He thought it ridiculous for anyone to talk impressively about courage when he had himself never done anything courageous[1] and could do nothing better than twitter like a swallow.

**222** The people of Argos declared that they would repair the defeat inflicted on them earlier by having another fight. 'I'm surprised,' Cleomenes said, 'if the addition of two syllables makes you better than you were before.'

* * * * *

219  (XIX) Plutarch *Moralia* 223E. In margin 'courteous'
  1 Cf 1.138 above.

220  (XX) Plutarch *Moralia* 223E. In margin 'witty'
  1 Cf possibly 1.213 above.

221  (XXI) Plutarch *Moralia* 223F. In margin 'suitability'
  1 Cf 1.179 above.

222  (XXII) Plutarch *Moralia* 223F. In margin 'humorous'

The point of this witty remark cannot be reproduced in a Latin translation. In Greek, the verb *machesthai* means 'to fight'; *anamachesthai* means 'to
fight again.' The only difference between the two words is that the second
is longer by two syllables, ie *ana*.[1]

223 Someone taunted him with being a voluptuary. 'That, at any rate,' he said,
'is better than being unjust – and you're ruled by love of money, though
you have plenty for your needs.'
   This quick retort implied that no one dominated by a passion for amass-
ing more than he needs can possibly live without deviating from just principles. Moreover, it is foolish to censure someone else for a lesser fault when
he can immediately retaliate with a more serious charge against you.

224 Someone was telling Cleomenes how good a certain singer was. As well as
praising him on various specific counts, he asserted that he was the finest
singer in all Greece. Cleomenes pointed to one of the people in the room.
'Believe you me,' he said, 'I have this man who's an artist in creating soups.'
   He had no time for a skill which served no end but pleasure.

225 In consequence of the Persian invasion Maeander, despot of Samos,[1] fled to
Sparta. He showed Cleomenes what monies[2] he had brought with him and
offered to give him as much as he wanted. Cleomenes accepted none of it
himself, but he was afraid that Maeander would give something to other
citizens. So he went to the ephors and told them it would be best if they
were to ban his Samian guest from the Peloponnese, to prevent him from
persuading any of the Spartan citizens to become a bad man. The ephors

* * * * *

1 The Argives used the Greek verb *anamachesthai*, which means 'to fight again'
   and carries the implication of success at the second attempt. Erasmus feels that
   there is no two-syllable Latin word or prefix which will neatly express this,
   and translates the word by *iterato praelio sarcire*, 'repair by a repeat battle.'

223 (XXIII) Plutarch *Moralia* 223F. In margin 'nice retort'

224 (XXIV) Plutarch *Moralia* 224A. See 1.56 n4 and 1.142 above. In margin 'useless
   art'

225 (XXV) Plutarch *Moralia* 224A–B. In margin 'integrity'
   1 Maeander (Maeandrios) succeeded Polycrates as sole ruler of Samos in 522 BC;
      see 1.216 above. He sought help in Sparta in 516 BC. Cf 2.121 below.
   2 The Greek text has 'gold and silver cups.'

took his advice and on that same day issued an edict expelling Maeander from the Peloponnese.

How this man despised wealth! He considered it no less lethal to his fellow-citizens than a virulent poison, yet most people think their country happy only if it has vast resources of wealth.

Herodotus, in book 3, calls this Maeander Maeandrius.[3]

226 Someone asked him why the Spartans hadn't destroyed the Argives who were always fighting against them, when they had so often defeated them in battle. 'We wouldn't even want them to be destroyed,' he said. 'We need someone to give our young men some practice.'[1]

This splendid leader knew only too well that young men go to the bad if left to idleness, which teaches them indiscipline and every kind of evil.

227 Someone asked Cleomenes why the Spartan warriors did not dedicate to the gods the spoils they had stripped from their defeated foes. 'Because,' he said, 'they have come from cowards.'

It is not right for young men to have before their eyes things acquired from men captured because of their cowardice, nor for such things to be offered to the gods in dedication. He held the view that in war one should either defeat the foe or courageously meet one's end. He considered fear of death to be such a disgraceful thing that reminders even of other people's cowardice should be kept from the eyes of young men.

228 One of Cleomenes' friends took a guest to the common dining-hall and offered him nothing but black wine[1] and hard biscuit. Cleomenes was angry and said to him, 'You shouldn't behave too much like a Spartan towards visitors.'

It is discipline to make oneself submit to a harsh régime, but uncouth to force it upon a guest.

\* \* \* \* \*

3 Herodotus 3.148

226 (xxvi) Plutarch *Moralia* 224B. In margin 'purposeful'
   1 See 2.23–4 below; 6.336 below.

227 (xxvii) Plutarch *Moralia* 224B. In margin 'bold'

228 (xxviii) Added from Xenophon *Cleomenes* 34(13)D–E
   1 'Black wine' should be 'black broth,' the notorious Spartan dish. See 2.84 below.

### Cleomenes (2)

**229** Somebody presented Cleomenes, son of Cleombrotus, with some fighting-cocks, and (seeking to enhance his gift by praising it) said that they would die fighting for victory. Cleomenes replied, 'Then give me some of the cocks that kill these, for they are superior.'

Being a military man, he made everything apply to war. If you praise the defeated, you enhance the conqueror's glory.[1]

### Labotus

**230** When someone addressed him at excessive length, Labotus said, 'Why spin out this great introduction to a tiny subject? Your speech should match your subject in size.'[1]

All Spartans had this characteristic of finding fault with speech that was longer than the occasion demanded.[2] They admired economy in everything. To apply a superfluous spate of words to a modest topic is a form of self-indulgence.

Herodotus calls this Labotus Leobotas, which means 'shepherd of the people.'[3]

### Leontychidas (1)

**231** Someone reproached Leontychidas, the first of that name, with being too ready to change. 'I do change,' he replied, 'but only as circumstances demand, not out of inbuilt weakness like you.'

A wise man alters his plans to fit the circumstances, but to be constantly changing for no reason is inconsistency, which is a fault.[1]

\* \* \* \* \*

**229** (xxix) Plutarch *Moralia* 224c. In margin 'humorous'
This is Cleomenes II, king of Sparta, 370–309 BC, son of Cleombrotus I, for whom see 1.211 above. This Cleomenes was much later than Cleomenes I, c. 520–490 BC.
1 Cf 1.136 above.

**230** (xxx) Plutarch *Moralia* 224c. In margin 'loquacity'
Labotus (Labotas) was an early king of Sparta, c. ninth century BC.
1 Cf 1.5 above; 2.115 below.
2 Cf 1.95 n2 above.
3 Herodotus 1.65

**231** (xxxi) Plutarch *Moralia* 224c–D.
Leotychidas (*sic*) I was king of Sparta, c. 625–600 BC.
1 See *Adagia* I i 93: *Polypi mentem obtine* 'adopt the outlook of a polyp.'

232 When someone asked Leontychidas how a man could preserve the possessions he had, 'By not entrusting all to fortune,' he replied.

Fortune has no power over the riches of the mind. As for material possessions, we will put these on a surer basis if we lay some aside and do
not entrust them to fickle fortune. There are rulers who, out of desire to extend their dominion, put themselves in danger of losing the realm they have.
There are also men of wealth who, out of desire to increase their possessions,
entrust all they have to some maritime adventure.

233 When he was asked what in particular free-born boys should learn, he said,
'Things that will be useful to them when they reach man's estate.'

234 When someone asked him why the Spartiates were so abstemious in their
drinking habits, 'So that we may make decisions for others,' he replied, 'and
not others for us.'

A smart answer, indicating that wine-bibbers are not fit to take part in
deliberations. Sobriety is the mother of healthy decisions.

235 Leontychidas, a Spartan elder – there were twenty-eight of them, we are
told[1] – was having dinner at Corinth. He asked his host whether logs grew
square in Corinth. When he said they did not, Leontychidas then said, 'Well
then, if they grew square, would you make them round?'

So Plutarch relates the incident in his *Life of Lycurgus*,[2] though the story
is recorded elsewhere, with a different speaker, ie Agesilaus.

* * * * *

232 (xxxii) Plutarch *Moralia* 224D. In margin 'sagacious'

233 (xxxiii) Plutarch *Moralia* 224D. Cf 1.65 above and 3.153 below.

234 (xxxiv) Plutarch *Moralia* 224D. In margin 'sobriety'

235 (xxxv) Added from Plutarch *Life of Lycurgus* 13.7 where the speaker is called
Leotychidas. This Leotychidas could be the son of Timaea, wife of Agis II (for
whom see 1.87–104 above). He was excluded from the kingship on grounds
of illegitimacy. But the Greek probably means 'Leotychidas the Elder,' ie Leotychidas I, to whom the saying is attributed at 1.265 below. In any case, his
seventh-century date fits the anecdote better.
   1 For elders, see 1.119 above; 'there were twenty-eight ... told' is Erasmus'
   addition.
   2 See 1.28 above. The name Agesilaus was added in 1535.

**Leontychidas (2)**

236 Someone told Leontychidas, son of Ariston, that Demaratus'[1] supporters were speaking ill of him. 'Upon my word,' he said, 'I'm not surprised. None of them could speak well of anyone.'

This shows us that we should pay no attention to malicious talk, which has its origin not in considered opinion but in a sickness of the mind. It is obvious that those who go about slandering everyone do it because of some fault in their own make-up, not because of anything in their victims that justifies it.

237 A snake had wrapped itself round the key of a door near-by, and the interpreters of signs declared that this was a portent. 'I don't think so at all,' he said. 'If the key had wrapped itself round the snake, now that would be a portent.'[1]

He wittily made fun of the superstition of human beings, who are terrified by perfectly normal chance occurrences. This mental weakness is nourished by diviners, soothsayers, fortune-tellers, and clairvoyants. But when someone instigates some wicked scheme that disregards all justice and honour, then we should recoil in horror at the portent and expect some great evil to follow.

238 A certain Philippus was a leader in the Orphic sect and used to initiate others into its mysteries. He was extremely poor, and one day he remarked in Leontychidas' hearing that those who were initiated into the Orphic rites at his hands would be happy after death. 'Well then, you silly man,' said Leontychidas, 'why don't you bring your life to an end as soon as possible, so you can stop complaining about your misfortunes and your poverty?'

* * * * *

236 (xxxvi) Plutarch *Moralia* 224E. In margin 'malicious talk'
   Leotychidas (*sic*) II was king of Sparta, c. 491–469 BC.
 1 Demaratus was king of Sparta from c. 515 until 491 BC when he was deposed on a false claim of illegitimacy manufactured by his colleague and enemy Cleomenes I (see 1.212–28 above) and his successor Leontychidas. His supporters therefore had good reason to speak against Leontychidas.

237 (xxxvii) Plutarch *Moralia* 224E. In margin 'humorous'
 1 For a similar story about Cato, see 5.383 below.

238 (xxxviii) Plutarch *Moralia* 224E–F. In margin 'freedom from superstition'

There we have a mind free of all superstition! It is those who have lived their lives here dutifully and justly who will be happy in the next life, not someone initiated into illusory rites. The Spartans were convinced that those who had lived dutifully in this life would become divine after death.

**Leon**

239 Leon, son of Eurycratidas, was asked if there was any city in which a man could live in safety. 'Yes,' he replied, 'one where the inhabitants possess neither too much nor too little, a place where justice flourishes, injustice is powerless.'

This was a solemn reminder that equality nourishes peace and tranquillity, whereas inequality is a seed-bed of sedition; and that there is no place for justice where greater power implies greater licence to oppress the weak.

240 This same Leon observed at the Olympic Games that the runners were trying to get a starting position that would give them an advantage and help them to win.[1] 'How much more concerned they are with speed,' he said, 'than with fairness!'

This man of integrity wanted fairness to be a consideration even in games and was of the opinion that the aim should be not to cross the line first but to win fairly.

241 Someone was discussing matters of some importance in an inappropriate manner. 'Friend,' said Leon, 'you are using a convenient thing in an inconvenient way.'[1]

Speech is the noblest of gifts, provided you are not too prodigal in bringing out the treasures of your tongue.[2]

\* \* \* \* \*

239 (XXXIX) Plutarch *Moralia* 224F. In margin 'equality'
Leon was king of Sparta, c. 590–560 BC.

240 (XL) Plutarch *Moralia* 224F. In margin 'fair'
1 It seems that the runners in the centre of the starting line had a slight advantage. See Harris 71–2.

241 (XLI) Plutarch *Moralia* 224F
1 See 1.115 above, for a different translation of the identical Greek words.
2 See 1.95 n2 above.

**Leonidas**

242 Someone once said to Leonidas, son of Anaxandridas and brother of Cleomenes, 'Apart from being king, you are no different from us.' 'But,' said
he, 'if I were not better than you, I would not be king.'

With these restrained words he both parried the taunt and asserted his
own status. Where men are made kings not by birth but by the choice of the
citizens,[1] the very fact that the prince has by popular election been called to
rule shows that the people have judged him to be better than the rest.

243 When he was setting off for Thermopylae to fight the Persians,[1] his wife
Gorgo asked him if he had any instructions for her.[2] 'Marry good men,' he
said, 'and bear good children.'

These words showed that he had a premonition of his death, but this
foreboding did not frighten him into cancelling the expedition – he believed
that it was a glorious thing to die fighting for one's country.

244 When the ephors commented that he was taking only a small force with him
to Thermopylae, 'Of course I am,' he said, 'in view of the business we're
engaged on.'[1]

\* \* \* \* \*

242 (XLII) Plutarch *Moralia* 225A. In margin 'restrained'
     Leonidas I was king of Sparta, 490–480 BC, and hero of Thermopylae; see 1.191
     above and 1.243–56 below.
   1 The transmission of the kingship of Sparta was, as far as we know, based on
     birth without any element of election in normal circumstances. It was confined
     to two noble families (see 1.97 n1 above) and the succession passed to a son
     or brother of the deceased king. The apparent heir could however be rejected
     or a king deposed in favour of the next heir on grounds of illegitimacy, phys-
     ical deformity, or other indication of unsuitability. See 1.27 n2, 1.167n, and
     1.235n above. Such decisions were probably taken by the Council of Elders,
     but there is some evidence for a disputed succession being settled by appeal
     to the people. See eg Xenophon *Hellenica* 3.3.1–3. Leonidas was half-brother to
     Cleomenes who died without male issue.
     For the Council of Elders (Gerousia) see 1.119 n1 above.

243 (XLIII) Plutarch *Moralia* 225A. In margin 'serious'
   1 This was after Xerxes I invaded Greece in 480 BC. See 5.9n below.
   2 For sayings of Gorgo see 1.268 and 2.121–4 below.

244 (XLIV) Plutarch *Moralia* 225A
   1 This refers to the famous 300 Spartiates who perished at Thermopylae. See
     1.191 n1 above. They were a suicide squad, resolved to die; see the next

He meant that he was taking plenty of men with him if they went with the aim of dying in battle. It was better for few to perish rather than many.[2]

245 Again when the ephors asked him if he intended to do anything else, 'Just this,' he replied, 'in theory to block the barbarian invasion, but in reality to die for Greece.'[1]

A splendid demonstration of a fearless spirit, not to shrink even from an inevitable death in an honourable and patriotic cause.

246 When Leonidas reached Thermopylae, he addressed his fellow-soldiers in these words: 'They say the barbarian foe is close by, but we are wasting time. For now we have come upon the foe, and them we must either defeat or else be conquered and die ourselves.'

247 One of the men said, 'We won't even be able to see the sun for the barbarian arrows.' 'Won't it be nice then,' Leonidas replied, 'if we're going to fight them in the shade?'

Could anything be braver than the spirit shown by this man? He was marching to his death, yet he could even make a joke, and this had the effect of freeing his men's minds from fear. Cicero records this aphorism in book one of the *Tusculan Disputations*,[1] attributing it to some unnamed person: When they were parleying, the Persian foe boastfully declared, 'You will not see the sun for the number of our spears and the shade cast by our arrows.' 'Well then,' replied one of the Greeks, 'we shall fight in the shade.'

* * * * *

apophthegm 1.245. Erasmus' Latin text reads *nimirum*, 'of course,' which is probably a mistake for *nimium*, 'too many, more than enough,' translating Plutarch's *pleonas*.
2 The last sentence was added in 1535.

245 (XLV) Plutarch *Moralia* 225A. In margin 'contempt for death'
1 The Greek text suggests that this paragraph should be punctuated differently, ie: 'asked him if he intended to do anything else but block the barbarian invasion. 'That in theory,' he replied, 'but in reality to die for Greece.'

246 (XLVI) Plutarch *Moralia* 225B. In margin 'bravely'

247 (XLVII) Plutarch *Moralia* 225B. In margin 'joking'
1 Cicero *Tusculan Disputations* 1.42.101.

**248** Another of the soldiers said, 'They're very close to us.' Leonidas replied, 'And so are we to them.'

He meant that the situation entailed just as much danger to the enemy as to themselves.

**249** When someone said, 'Have you come here like this to try the fortunes of war with just a few men pitted against a great army?' Leonidas replied, 'If you think I have come here relying on numbers, not even the whole of Greece would be enough, for she is just a small fraction compared to the barbarian horde. But if relying on courage, even this number will suffice.'

He was of the opinion that the quality of one's troops is more significant than their number.

**250** When someone else commented that he was leading only a few troops out to face a large force, 'No,' he replied, I am leading out a large number, since they are going to die.'

This agrees with what he said to the ephors earlier.[1]

**251** Xerxes had written to Leonidas, saying, 'If you cease to fight against the will of heaven[1] and come and serve with my army, you can become king of Greece.' He replied, 'If you had any idea what was honourable in life, you would have refrained from coveting what belongs to others. As for myself, I would rather die for Greece than submit my fellow Greeks to the rule of an autocrat.'

Is there any wicked deed that people in general will not do in order to extend their sphere of influence? But the man we have here preferred to meet an honourable end endeavouring to set his friends free rather than become king and oppress with servitude the very people from whom he had set out with the intention of warding off the threat of servitude to barbarians.

\* \* \* \* \*

**248** (XLVIII) Plutarch *Moralia* 225B. In margin 'spirited'

**249** (XLIX) Plutarch *Moralia* 225C. In margin 'courageous'

**250** (L) Plutarch *Moralia* 225B–C
1 See 1.244 above.

**251** (LI) Plutarch *Moralia* 225C. In margin 'honourable'
1 Erasmus gives 'fight against the will of heaven' in Greek: θεομαχεῖν [*theomachein*]. See *Adagia* II v 44: *Cum diis pugnare* 'To fight against the gods.'

252 On another occasion, when Xerxes sent a message saying, 'Hand over your arms,' he wrote back, 'Come and take them.'

    He preferred to die with his weapons rather than surrender them and ignominiously treat with the enemy for his life.

253 Leonidas was getting impatient to join battle with the enemy, but the military commanders[1] urged him to wait for the remaining allied forces to arrive.[2] 'The people who are going to fight are here, aren't they?' he said. 'Don't you realize that the only people who fight the enemy are those who respect and fear their own rulers?'[3]

    He did not think they ought to wait for people who had not presented themselves by the time specified by the commander-in-chief. Even if the others were present, they would not be fighters.

254 He addressed his troops, saying, 'Eat your breakfast, my fellow-soldiers, like men who expect to have dinner in the place of the dead.'

    These words would have terrified the cowardly, but they inspired those courageous men, urging them not to enter the fight heavy with food and wine, or at any rate bidding them for their country's sake bravely to meet their inevitable end.

255 When he was asked why brave men prefer a glorious death to an inglorious life, Leonidas replied, 'Because they hold that one is natural, the other is characteristically their own.'

    Even the most cowardly of men have life as a gift from nature, but only those endowed with courage can die nobly.

         \* \* \* \* \*

252 (LII) Plutarch *Moralia* 225D. In margin 'spirited'

253 (LIII) Plutarch *Moralia* 225D. In margin 'weighty'
  1 'The military commanders' were polemarchs, high military officials in the Spartan army. Erasmus does not reproduce the technical term.
  2 In fact only the Thespians fought beside Leonidas and his 300 Spartiates at Thermopylae, as the contingents from other states had been dismissed by Leonidas because they had no heart for the fight; see Herodotus 7.222. For troops not arriving, cf the battle of Plataea the following year (479 BC), when contingents from Mantinea and Elis were suspiciously late in turning up for the battle.
  3 Cf 1.210 above; 1.335 below.

254 (LIV) Plutarch *Moralia* 225D

255 (LV) Plutarch *Moralia* 225D. In margin 'wise'

**256** Leonidas wanted to keep the unmarried lads out of the battle to save their lives, but he knew they would not by any means acquiesce in this. So he gave each of them a *scytala* (a form of secret dispatch used by the Spartans) and sent them off to the ephors. He also wanted to save three of the older lads who had already taken wives, and tried to send them away home on a similar pretext. They however saw through this subterfuge and would not accept the dispatches. One of them excused himself by saying, 'I joined your force as a combatant, not a courier.' The second said, 'I will be a better man if I stay here'; and the third, 'I will not be the last of these to enter the fight, but the first.'

What commands our admiration the more here? Is it the commander's attitude? He had no concern for his own safety but wanted to preserve those whose continued existence would be of advantage to their country. Or is it such unconcern for life displayed by young men in the flower of their youth?

### Lochadas

**257** Lochadas, son of Polyaenides and father of Siron,[1] was told that one of his two sons had died. 'I knew long ago,' he said, 'that he would have to die.'

He could see nothing remarkable in a mortal man dying, nor did he think it made much difference whether he departed this life a little sooner or later, as he would have to go before long anyway.[2]

### Lycurgus

**258** Lycurgus, the architect of the Spartan constitution, wished to convert his fellow citizens away from their existing habits to a more disciplined way of life and to create in them a desire for bravery and rectitude, since they were soft with self-indulgence. So he took two pups from the same

*     *     *     *     *

**256** (LVI) Plutarch *Moralia* 225E. In margin 'considerate, spirited'

**257** (LVII) Plutarch *Moralia* 225E. In margin 'resolute'
   Little is known of Lochadas (Lochagus), a Spartan of the fourth century BC.
   1 The text should read: 'father of Polyaenides and Siron.'
   2 A very similar remark is famously attributed to the philosopher Anaxagoras in many places; see 7.126 n1 below

**258** (LVIII) Plutarch *Moralia* 225F–6B. In margin 'upbringing'
   Lycurgus was the famous law-giver and reputed founder of the peculiar Spartan constitution, traditionally eighth century BC. Much of the material in the succeeding apophthegms is to be found also in Plutarch's *Life of Lycurgus*.

litter.[1] One of them he kept in the house and fed on dainty foods, the other
was taken outside and trained to hunt. He then assembled the population
in the town centre and brought in the two dogs. He laid out on one side
some bones and tasty morsels. Then he released a hare. Each dog dashed towards the thing it was familiar with, one seizing the food, the other the hare.
'Now, citizens,' he said, 'surely you can see that those two pups have turned
out quite differently though they are of the same breed, because they have
been trained differently. Upbringing carries more weight than heredity in
the forming of good character.'

Another version of the story says that the two pups were not from the
same litter. One was of an inferior breed of the sort used as guard dogs, the
other of a breed kept for hunting. The pup of inferior stock was trained to
hunt, while the one with the better pedigree was kept just as a pet. After
each dog had made for what it was used to, and Lycurgus had thus demonstrated to all of them the importance of upbringing for both good and ill,
he said, 'In just the same way, citizens, noble lineage, which men so admire,
and our descent from Hercules[2] will do us no good, unless we do the deeds
which made Hercules the most famous and noble of mortal men, and unless
we, all our lives, study and work at what is honourable.'

Being an ingenious man, he found a way of setting a visual representation of Virtue before the general populace who were little suited to ab-
stract argument. What we see stirs us and makes more of an impression on
us than what we hear. Now every head of a family in his own home, every
instructor with his own group, can do what Lycurgus did at the national
level. Heredity is a powerful force, but upbringing has an even greater effect, correcting a bad nature and changing it to good. No one has any control over the kind of children born to him, but it lies within our power to
ensure that they develop into good persons through proper upbringing.

259 Lycurgus was well aware of the supreme importance of equality in fostering
thrift and concord.

So he made a fresh distribution of land and allocated an equal share
to each citizen.[1] We are told that some time later he was returning from a
visit abroad and was travelling through territory where the fields had just

* * * * *

1 This story is used again in Plutarch *Moralia* 3A (*The education of children*).
2 See 1.302 n2 below.

259 (LIX) Plutarch *Moralia* 226B. In margin 'equality'
1 According to tradition 9,000 'true Spartans' each received a share.

been harvested. When he saw the stooks of sheaves all of the same size and standing in line, he was delighted at the spectacle and said to his companions with a smile, 'The whole territory of Sparta looks like land belonging to many brothers who have just divided the inheritance between them.'

A good ruler finds nothing more delightful than civic concord. A tyrant finds nothing more disquieting.

260 After Lycurgus had delivered from debt all those who owed money by wiping the slate clean, he then tried to get everyone's private possessions redistributed in equal shares, in order to eliminate differentiation and inequality of wealth from Spartan society. When he saw that they would not tolerate this open confiscation of their property, he set about achieving the same end by indirect means. He abolished gold and silver coinage and established iron as the sole medium of exchange. Also, in so far as the practicalities of the situation demanded, he limited the amount of a person's wealth that could be converted to the new currency.[1] As a result of this, all wrong disappeared from Sparta. As the iron currency could not be hidden and possessing it gave one no status and using it involved risk and importing or exporting it was not safe, no one was able any more to steal it or use it to bribe others or be bribed with it or rob its owners of it by malpractice or violence.

By this ingenious scheme he prevented the people whom he could not induce to despise wealth from making use of wealth, took away from them any desire to hoard it, and deprived them of the possibility of using it for trade.

261 Furthermore, Lycurgus had everything unnecessary removed from the country, with the result that no merchant or itinerant lecturer or soothsayer or huckster or maker of fancy goods visited Sparta. For he did not allow the existence of any money there that would be of use to such persons. The only

* * * * *

260 (LX) Plutarch *Moralia* 226C–D. In margin 'disregard for wealth'
  1 Erasmus seems to have had difficulty with the interpretation of the Greek text here. His first version did not render it adequately and second thoughts led him to add 'in so far as ... demanded' (*quatenus postulabat usus*) in 1535. Probably the passage means 'He also limited the time one could keep one's property before changing it.'

261 (LXI) Plutarch *Moralia* 226D. In margin 'unnecessary skills'

units of currency issued were of iron, each weighing about half a kilo on the Aeginetan scale[1] and worth four copper coins.

These measures drove out avarice.

262 Having decided to wage war on refinements and luxuries and eliminate the attraction of wealth in that sphere too, Lycurgus established *syssitia*, that is, communal eating arrangements.[1] When someone asked him why these were organized in such a way that each mess consisted of a small group of men who kept their weapons by them at table, he replied, 'So that they remain at the ready to obey any order; if any disaffection arises, the evil is confined to a small group; and everyone has an equal share of food and drink. In fact, it applies not only to eatables and drinkables – in coverlets and tableware and every single thing the rich man is treated no better than the poor man.' By these tactics he removed the desire for riches, as there was eventually no one left who could either use wealth or make a show of it. Then he often said to his friends, 'What a splendid thing it is, my friends, to have demonstrated in practical terms the nature of wealth. It is indeed blind itself – and there is besides no one to see it or wonder at it.'[2]

He also made sure that no one came to the public dinners stuffed with non-prescribed food after eating at home. If anyone did not eat and drink with the group, the others taunted him with growing soft on illegitimate foodstuffs and being unfitted for the communal life. Anyone who was found out was fined. That was why a fine was imposed on Agis, (who was king long after the time of Lycurgus).[3] He had returned home after a victory over the Athenians, and wanted for one day to have dinner with his

\* \* \* \* \*

1 'Half a kilo,' literally 'a mina,' which probably weighed 460 grammes. The coinage of Aegina provided a standard weight, as the first silver coins minted west of the Aegean were produced in Aegina. Sparta's earliest monetary units may have been in the form of iron skewers: Plutarch *Lysander* 17.4–5.

262 (LXII) Plutarch *Moralia* 226D–E. In margin 'living together'
   1 Each *syssition* or 'mess' probably had about twenty members drawn from men of all age classes, excluding young boys still undergoing training. Members had to contribute to the common table produce from their land-holdings, worked for them by their Helots, and from spoils of the hunt.
   2 'and there is besides ... wonder at it' is an addition by Erasmus to the Greek text. He seems to be making a play on the two meanings of the Latin word *caecus*, 'blind,' ie 'unable to see,' 'unable to be seen.'
   3 This Agis is probably Agis II, who, during the Peloponnesian War in 413 BC, built a permanent fort in Athenian territory ten miles north of Athens, and

wife. So he asked for his allocation of food from the common table, but the military commanders [4] would not send it. The next day the ephors learned what had happened and imposed a fine on him.

This incident offers us an example of two things; the first of frugal living; the second of strictness, since the laws did not spare even the king in this minor offence.

263 The fate that befalls most people who launch a campaign against corruption in society then befel Lycurgus.

The rich did not take kindly to these arrangements and rose against him, not merely shouting at him but pelting him with stones in an attempt to kill him. When they closed in on him, he managed to make his escape across the market-place, and gave most of them the slip. But a man called Alcander kept up the pursuit and when Lycurgus turned his head to look behind him, hit him with his club and blinded him in one eye. This Alcander was sentenced to be punished by decree of the people and handed over to Lycurgus to be dealt with. Lycurgus neither exacted any form of retribution from him, nor even reproached him, but made him a sharer in his daily life, with the result that Alcander in the end had nothing but praise for Lycurgus himself and for the way of life he had shared with him, and became an advocate not only of the practical arrangements for the citizens' lives but of the whole system which Lycurgus had introduced. Lycurgus dedicated a memorial of this unfortunate incident in the temple of Minerva Chalkioikos (so called from her shrine of bronze),[1] and gave her the additional title of 'Optiletis.' *Optiloi* (derived from the Greek verb *opto*, meaning 'see') was the word for 'eyes' among the Dorians who lived in the territory round Sparta.[2]

Again we have an incident demonstrating two things. First it tells us that it is a dangerous thing to try to reform the corrupt morals of society and make it wholesome. Secondly it shows us an example of remarkable

* * * * *

inflicted great hardship on the city. See 1.87–104 above. Lycurgus traditionally belongs to the eighth century BC.
4 See 1.253 n1 above.

263 (LXIII) Plutarch *Moralia* 227A–B. In margin 'forbearance'
  1 For Minerva Chalkioikos, see 1.10 above.
  2 The Dorians were one of the chief tribal divisions of the ancient Greek people, the others being the Ionians and Achaeans. There were various Dorian states, mainly in the Peloponnese, of which Sparta with its dependent territory was the most important. The Spartans spoke a distinctive dialect of Doric Greek.

forbearance which turned an enemy to the death into a friend and supporter. Even if he had executed Alcander, as he had every right to do, Lycurgus would not have got his eye back and he would have had one person less to lend support to his reforms.

264 When someone asked him why he did not have written laws,[1] he replied, 'Because properly trained and instructed citizens will know what is the appropriate response to the circumstances.'

He meant that what is written is fixed, whereas a sound and sensible man often has to modify his plans in the light of changed circumstances.[2] It is not possible to legislate specifically for every event. It is enough if the citizens have acquired sound principles, for then they will of themselves see what action is required in any situation.

265 On another occasion Lycurgus was asked why he had decreed that workmen were not to use any tool other than an axe when putting the roof on a house, and only a saw for making doors. He replied, 'So that the citizens will avoid any extravagance in their household goods and own none of the things which are so admired elsewhere.'

It would indeed have looked silly to carry in through a crude rough entrance furnishings that were out of the ordinary, expensive and elaborately decorated. The door itself practically spoke out against any such thing.

This accounts for the story told about Leontychidas, the first king of the Spartans.[1] He was a guest at dinner somewhere and observed that the roof was constructed with sumptuous ornamentation and fitted with decorative panels, so he asked his host whether trees grew square in their country.[2]

He was of the opinion that spoiling what was natural with artifice was extravagant and self-indulgent.

* * * * *

264 (LXIV) Plutarch *Moralia* 227B. In margin 'sagacious'
   1 There was in fact a *rhetra* forbidding the writing down of the laws. Cf 1.69 n3 above, and see Plutarch *Lycurgus* 13.6.
   2 See 1.231 n1 above.

265 (LXV) Plutarch *Moralia* 227C (both anecdotes). In margin 'frugal'
   1 Erasmus' Latin appears to mean this. It should read 'Leontychidas the first, king of the Spartans.' See 1.235 above (where the subject of the story is made a Spartan elder).
   2 Cf a similar remark attributed to Agesilaus at 1.28 above.

**266** When Lycurgus was asked why he had forbidden the Spartans to keep on launching military expeditions against the same enemy, he replied, 'To prevent them from constantly defending themselves and so learning how to fight a war by experience.' This is why Agesilaus was criticized so sharply – his frequent expeditions and campaigns against Sparta's enemy, Thebes, had provoked them into fighting back. When Antalcidas saw that Agesilaus himself had been wounded, he taunted him with instructing the Thebans in the art of fighting, when hitherto they had neither known how to conduct a war nor wanted to. 'You have a fine reward,' he said, 'for your instruction. The Thebans had no mind for war nor any expertise in it, yet you have accustomed them to waging war even against their will and taught them how to do it.'[1]

This same tactic can be applied to other situations, for example one should avoid constantly going to law or engaging in a dispute with the same people, otherwise they will get used to us and either treat us with contempt or get the better of us.

**267** Someone asked Lycurgus why he subjected girls to vigorous exercise, making them participate in running, wrestling, and throwing the discus and javelin. He replied, 'To ensure that any children they conceive may from the very moment of implantation get a strong start in strong bodies; next, that the girls themselves, when the time of delivery comes, may easily and with spirit cope with the effort and pains of childbirth; and finally, that they may be able, should the need arise, to fight for themselves, their children, and their country.'

The wise man was well aware that idleness and having nothing to do are a bane to a society, whereas moderate physical activity makes bodies stronger and healthier as well. For this reason he did not let the young girls – any more than the boys – spend their time on idle pursuits but, by submitting them to masculine exercises, in a way he made them masculine too. In most societies self-indulgence and pleasures turn the men into women.

\* \* \* \* \*

266  (LXVI) Plutarch *Moralia* 227C–D
  1  This same story involving Agesilaus and Antalcidas is told earlier in 1.69 and 1.128 above.

267  (LXVII) Plutarch *Moralia* 227D. In margin 'manly women'

**268** Lycurgus made the young girls participating in processions and ceremonial games go naked for all to see.[1] Some people took exception to this and asked why he had instituted this practice. 'To give them the same training as the boys,' he replied, 'so that their bodies are absolutely equal to theirs in health and strength and their minds in courage and spirit and ambition to earn true praise, while despising vulgar glory.' This accounts for the following story, or something like it, told of Gorgo, wife of Leonidas. Some woman or other, probably a foreigner, said to her, 'You Spartans are the only women who rule the men.' 'Naturally,' she replied, 'we are the only women who give birth to men.'[2]

 You must not think that this practice is to be imitated either in the case of boys or of girls. We can however learn this from it at least: children must at a tender age be freed from that silly self-consciousness which often acts as an obstacle to honourable action,[3] and must learn, right at the beginning, that the only thing to be ashamed of is base conduct. You will find countless girls who would blush with confusion if they were seen not dressed, but never change colour in the slightest degree if they do or say something discreditable. There are countless others whose cheeks would redden with shame if they had to wear poor clothes or a rather plain outfit, while they think it something to be proud of if they appear in public gorgeously dressed – but they are indifferent to the things which bring true honour and real praise.

**269** Citizens who shunned marriage, preferring a bachelor life, were prohibited from attendance at those events where the young people participated naked,[1] and were also subjected to other forms of humiliation.[2] By such measures Lycurgus made sure that the citizens took seriously the matter of

\* \* \* \* \*

268  (LXVIII) Plutarch *Moralia* 227E
  1 This probably does not mean stark naked, but wearing some kind of athletic strip, possibly a short tunic with one shoulder bare. Cf 1.344 below. The Athenians professed to be shocked by this practice. See Plato *Republic* 452B.
  2 *Adagia* IV iii 17: *Solae Lacaenae viros pariunt* 'Only Spartan women produce men'; Plutarch *Lycurgus* 14.4. For Gorgo see 1.243 n1 above.
  3 See Plutarch *Moralia* 529A (*On compliancy*); Younger Pliny *Epistulae* 4.7.3: *recta ingenia debilitat verecundia* 'diffidence undermines right-thinking minds.'

269  (LXIX) Plutarch *Moralia* 227F. In margin 'condemnation of the unmarried state'
  1 This refers chiefly to the *Gymnopaidiai*, athletic contests in high summer for naked boys.
  2 See Plutarch *Lycurgus* 15.1–2; Xenophon *Respublica Lacedaemoniorum* 9.5.

begetting children. It was a Spartan custom that younger men should show
great honour and respect to their elders. Lycurgus took this honour away
from those who refused to take wives and add to the number of citizens.[3]
For this reason no one took exception to the remark that was made to Dercylidas, experienced military leader though he was.[4] When a certain young
man did not rise as he approached,[5] Dercylidas complained, 'You did not
rise and give place to me.' The other replied, 'And you have not fathered
anyone who will give place to me.'

The Spartan people would never have stood for such an impertinent
remark from a young man to an older one, and one famous for his military
successes at that, if they had not considered as the worst type of citizen those
who were childless from choice and refused to honour their obligations to
their country. If you think about it, there is not much difference between
a man who kills a citizen and one who refuses to provide the state with a
citizen when he can.

270 When someone asked Lycurgus why he had introduced a law decreeing that girls should be given in marriage without a dowry, Lycurgus
replied, 'To prevent any of them being left unmarried through poverty,
or sought after because of wealth, and to ensure that each young man
considers the character of the girl and makes his choice on the basis
of virtue.' For the same reason he banished from the city all cosmetics
and adornments which other girls use to fake good looks or to enhance
them.

This splendid man promoted equality in every sphere!

271 He fixed the age at which both girls and youths should marry. When he
was asked why he thought such a regulation necessary, he replied, 'To ensure that the offspring are healthy and vigorous, being born of parents of
sufficient maturity and in the prime of life.'

* * * * *

3 Erasmus inserts the words 'who shunned ... bachelor life' and 'from those
  who refused ... citizens' thus emphasizing the importance of marriage and
  making it clear that children were to be born in wedlock. Plutarch simply calls
  them 'the unmarried.'
4 For Dercylidas, see 1.166 above.
5 Cf 1.341, 2.10, 2.53, 2.54, and 2.92 below.

270 (LXX) Plutarch *Moralia* 227F. In margin 'choosing a wife'

271 (LXXI) Plutarch *Moralia* 228A

If women conceive children when they are too young, not only are their own bodies damaged, but the children are born sickly. Also, those who father children before they are ready cannot exercise that authority over them which maturity commands. On the other hand, those who beget children much later on in life neither get pleasure out of their offspring nor see their upbringing through to the end, being overtaken by old age and death.

272 Someone expressed curiosity as to why Lycurgus had forbidden husband and wife to sleep together, but decreed that each of them should spend most of the day with the members of his or her own age group[1] and sleep the whole night in their company, the husband only meeting by stealth and privately to have intercourse with his spouse. He replied, 'First, to ensure that they are strong in body, since they do not engage in intercourse long enough to be utterly satisfied; secondly, to ensure that their mutual affection for each other lasts and remains fresh and strong; and finally, to ensure that they bring stronger children into the world.'

Now that really is fulfilling the role of Father of the Country – to be watching everywhere for ways to promote the interests of the state and to provide for the physical and mental well-being of the citizens even in points of detail. Many persons in positions of authority however, consider themselves to be properly fulfilling their office if they exact as much as possible from the citizens by way of taxes and assessments and punish a few heinous crimes, while at the same time putting incentives to crime in the way of their own supporters.

273 He even went so far as to ban perfumes, calling them 'a contamination and a waste of oil.'

Oil mixed with perfume[1] is of no use either for cooking or for rubbing into the body, and when people waste a necessity of life on frivolities, supplies of it run short.

\* \* \* \* \*

272 (LXXII) Plutarch *Moralia* 228A. In margin 'intercourse restricted'
  1 Spartan boys started their training at the age of seven and moved with their contemporaries through the successive stages until reaching the status of full citizens at the age of thirty. Even then they could not live entirely as they chose, though husbands were then allowed to sleep at home. See Plutarch *Lycurgus* 15.3.

273 (LXXIII) Plutarch *Moralia* 228B. In margin 'perfumes'
  1 Ancient perfumes used an oil base.

**274** He also forbade the practice of dyeing, calling it 'a flattery of the senses.'

Indeed, when colour offers its blandishments to the eyes, the true nature of the object is spoiled.

In short, he debarred from entering the city of Sparta anyone who made anything designed to enhance the body with spurious adornment, saying that such persons 'corrupted good arts by their evil arts.'

Lycurgus did this because delights of this sort distracted the citizenry from healthy and serious interests.

**275** In those days wives were so chaste and so free from the lax morals which later infected them, that it was unbelievable at that time that any true Spartan woman would commit adultery. People still recount the story of what was said by Geradas, a man who lived in Sparta in very early times.[1] Some stranger asked him what was the penalty for adultery in Sparta, as he had not discovered any enactment of Lycurgus relating to it. 'My friend,' said Geradas, 'we don't have any adulterers.' The other persisted, 'Suppose you did, what then?' 'He will make payment of an ox,' said Geradas, 'so huge that it can stretch out its neck over Mount Taygetus and drink out of the Eurotas.' The other laughed and said, 'There couldn't be such a huge ox.'[2] To which Geradas replied, 'And how could there be an adulterer in Sparta, when wealth, frivolous luxuries, and extraneous bodily adornment are all considered disgraceful there, whereas decency, modesty, and the habit of proper obedience to the magistrates are approved and admired?'[3]

Geradas was wise enough to see that vices cannot take root where nothing is allowed that could act as a seed-bed. No interest is ever shown in anything that earns contempt rather than admiration. This is the kindest way of healing depraved morals and stimulating the desire for moral rectitude.

**276** Someone demanded of Lycurgus that he turn the state into a democracy (that

* * * * *

**274** (LXXIV) Plutarch *Moralia* 228B (both quotations). In margin 'frivolities'

**275** (LXXV) Plutarch *Moralia* 228B–C. In margin 'adultery'
   1 The Greek words could equally mean 'a very old-fashioned type.'
   2 'He will make ... a huge ox' was added to the story from Plutarch *Lycurgus* 15.17–18. Taygetus was the mountain range close to the city of Sparta to the west and the river Eurotas flowed past the city to the east.
   3 The anecdote is used in *Adagia* IV ii 59: *Bos porrecto ultra Taygeton capite* 'An ox putting its head over Taygetus,' added to *Adagia* in 1526.

**276** (LXXVI) Plutarch *Moralia* 228C–D. In margin 'trenchant'

is, one where the people rule) instead of an aristocracy (that is, one where the best classes rule). He replied, 'You go and establish democracy first in your own home.'

This was a quick way of showing that no form of government is good for a state if no one is prepared to have it in his own household. The state is nothing but the household writ large.[1]

277 When he was asked why he had made a regulation that all sacrifices were to consist of small and inexpensive things, Lycurgus replied, 'So that we may never find ourselves without the means of honouring the divinity.'

Now everyone would say that splendour and magnificence should characterize the solemn worship of the gods. But this wise man realized that the divine power is more pleased with modest offerings than with expensive sacrificial victims, as this prevents religion acting as a pretext for extravagance or, more likely, impoverishment. God does not need great outlay on our part – rather he cares for men, and that expenditure could have been used to supply their needs.

278 Lycurgus only allowed contests in which the hands were not raised. Someone asked him the reason for this. He replied, 'To prevent them getting into the habit of wearing themselves out with hard physical effort.'[1]

The purpose of exercise is to strengthen the body, not to exhaust it. People who constantly tire themselves out with exercise soon collapse when they embark on necessary hard work, because they come to it in a weakened state.[2]

\* \* \* \* \*

1 This definition was added in 1532.

277 (LXXVII) Plutarch *Moralia* 228D. In margin 'inexpensive sacrifices'

278 (LXXVIII) Plutarch *Moralia* 228D. In margin 'exercise'
  1 Erasmus doesn't seem to have recognized 'raising the hands' here as a gesture of surrender and has taken the Greek verb *apaudan* as 'faint, grow weary' (ie 'wear themselves out,' line 3), rather than 'cry off, cry quits,' in a hard struggle. The point is that the contestants should not get used even in play to the gesture of raising the hands in surrender. Lycurgus for this reason forbade boxing and the *pancration* which combined boxing and wrestling (Herodotus 9.105), in which sports the contestants conceded defeat rather than relying on an umpire (Plutarch *Moralia* 189E). See however *Adagia* I ix 79: *Dare manus* 'To put one's hands up,' ie surrender.
  2 See Plutarch *Moralia* 8C (*The education of children*).

279 Someone asked Lycurgus why he made the Spartan army keep moving camp. He replied, 'In order to inflict more damage on the enemy.'

The Spartans took only a small amount of equipment with them and so could move the army from place to place with very little trouble. But it was not so easy for their enemies, as they took huge amounts of baggage and equipment with them and furthermore usually fortified their camps with ditches, ramparts, and palisades.

280 When someone asked why he had forbidden assaults on walled cities, he replied, 'To prevent the finest soldiers from being killed by a woman or a boy, or by some man or other not very different from a boy or a woman.'

He did not approve of a form of fighting in which there was no place for valour. A boy or a woman can throw stones down from a tower and kill a man, however brave he is. So what place is there for valour in our wars, in which the chief part is played by cannon?[1]

281 The people of Thebes sought Lycurgus' advice about the sacrifice and ritual mourning which they were accustomed to offer to Leucothea.[1] 'If you believe her to be divine,' he said, 'you should not mourn her. If you think her human, you should not offer sacrifice to her as to a goddess.'

He thus tellingly censured the contradictory practices of the Thebans. Mourning and sacrifice are not compatible – you cannot ask help from one who is herself in dire distress and a cause of grief and mourning.

282 Some citizens asked him how they could avoid enemy raids. 'By being poor,' he said, 'and none of you wanting more than another.'

When men have possessions and are loaded with potential loot, the

* * * * *

279 (LXXIX) Plutarch *Moralia* 228D. In margin 'stratagem'

280 (LXXX) Plutarch *Moralia* 228D. In margin 'stratagem'
   1 Cf 1.155 above.

281 (LXXXI) Plutarch *Moralia* 228E. In margin 'astute'
   1 A minor deity worshipped at several sites in Greece. As a woman, Ino, she threw herself and her child into the sea in a fit of madness and was transformed into a sea-nymph by Neptune (Ovid *Metamorphoses* 4.512–42). Her ritual involved mourning for her death, but sea-farers prayed to her in her divine form.

282 (LXXXII) Plutarch *Moralia* 228E. In margin 'poverty travels light'

prospect of winning it attracts the enemy, and it is not easy to escape when hampered by baggage and equipment. Furthermore, equality and the concord that results from equality are a defence against enemy attack.[1]

283 The same people asked why Lycurgus would not let the city have defensive walls built round it. 'A city is not without walls,' he replied, 'if it is encircled not by bricks but by men.'

He meant that physical defence works suggested that the citizens were cowards rather than brave men.[1]

284 The Spartan warriors made a point of letting their hair grow long, and Lycurgus gave a reason for this too. 'Hair enhances good looks,' he said, 'and makes the ugly look more terrifying to the enemy.'

Hair looks good on the handsome and lends an alarming and somewhat bestial air to those endowed with a less fortunate outward form. A good head of hair is a natural adornment and costs practically nothing. Lycurgus did not object to adornment of this kind as it neither depended on elaborate workmanship nor replaced plainness with extravagance. He did not approve of artificial beautifying and false adornments procured at great expense. So we ought to find even more abhorrent the topsy-turvy ideas of people who take the trouble to pluck and shave those parts of the body which nature endowed with hair in the interests of comeliness or modesty or even health, and contrariwise, artificially produce a forest of hair[1] where nature decreed hairlessness.

285 Lycurgus was always telling them that, in a war, after they had put the enemy to flight and had gained the upper hand, they should pursue them as they fled only long enough to make the victory secure and should then quickly return to base. It was, he said, not the Greek way to slaughter those who yielded, and to spare them was not only honourable but

*　*　*　*　*

1 Cf 1.279 above.

283 (LXXXIII) Plutarch *Moralia* 228E. In margin 'resolute'
   1 See 1.30 above.

284 (LXXXIV) Plutarch *Moralia* 228F. In margin 'hair'
   1 See *Adagia* III iii 94: *Penicissare* 'To wear a wig,' which Erasmus considers a form of deception.

285 (LXXXV) Plutarch *Moralia* 228F. In margin 'moderation in victory'

advantageous. If the enemy they were engaged with knew that the Spartans spared those who yielded but slew those who stood their ground, they would think it in their own interest to run away rather than make a stand.

Desperation often lends great courage, just as much as expectation of victory. As men imbued with concepts of law and discipline, it was expected of Greeks to observe clemency even in war; only barbarian savages behave with ferocious cruelty when people are at their mercy. On the other hand, clemency needs to be exercised with caution or it may do us harm – the enemy often feigns retreat in order to recombine and launch a fiercer attack on the victor.

286 When someone asked why he would not let the Spartan army pillage enemy corpses, Lycurgus replied, 'To prevent them being so keen on looting that they forget about fighting, and to make them keep their simple way of life as well as their position in line.'

This wise man was always concerned about the effect on his citizens of wealth, which he saw as the source of most evils. The average man desires wealth above all else, believing it to be the chief safeguard of human happiness.

287 A constant saying of his was that 'the state is maintained by two things, reward and punishment.'[1]

This is recorded in Cicero's *Letters to Brutus*.

**Lysander**

288 Lysander would not accept the expensive clothes which Dionysius had sent for his daughters.[1]

'I am afraid,' he said, 'that if they wear these they will look ugly.'

\* \* \* \* \*

286 (LXXXVI) Plutarch *Moralia* 228F–9A. In margin 'stratagem'

287 (LXXXVII) Cicero *Letters to Brutus* 1.15.3, where the saying is attributed to Solon. This apophthegm was added in *1535*.
  1 Cf 1.299 below.

288 (LXXXVIII) Plutarch *Moralia* 229A. For Lysander, see 1.51n above.
  1 As Plutarch's Greek text explains, Lysander had on this occasion (and the one reported in 1.289) been sent to Dionysius I, ruler of Syracuse, as ambassador from Sparta, to ask for naval support in the war with Athens. The two apophthegms should be read together.

289 When a little later the same Dionysius sent him two dresses, telling him to choose one to send to his daughter, he said, 'She will choose better herself,' and departed with both.

This anecdote contains nothing fit to be emulated, nothing worthy of a Spartan. One would not expect of this leader anything except villainous duplicity.

290 Lysander became marvellously adept at giving a false impression and putting a cunning gloss on his cruel and greedy acts. Justice for him was expediency and right simply what was advantageous. He went so far as to agree that 'truth had the advantage over falsehood' but 'the standing and value of either depended on the use one could put it to.'

This wicked man inverted the philosophical doctrine that what is right is also to our advantage[1] – he said that whatever offered some advantage was also the right thing to choose.

291 He was attacked for using guile and deceit in pursuit of his aims and achieving them by underhand and dishonourable methods, in this showing himself an unworthy descendant of Hercules, (the founder of the Spartan race).[1] He laughed and said that 'where the lion-skin[2] wouldn't stretch to what he wanted, it would have to be extended with a fox-skin.'

He meant that one should use deceit and guile where one couldn't achieve one's purpose by honourable means.[3]

\* \* \* \* \*

See earlier, 1.146 above, where the story is told of Archidamus II. A marginal note in 1531 and 1532 records that 'this occurs earlier [ie 1.146 above] and is not in Aldus' text.' It was however translated by Filelfo and Regio, for whom see the dedicatory epistle 7–8 nn20 and 21. Cf 1.197n above.

289 (LXXXIX) Plutarch *Moralia* 229A. In margin 'cunning'

290 (XC) Plutarch *Moralia* 229A–B. In margin 'expediency preferable to right action'
   1 This is a Stoic doctrine. See Cicero, *De officiis* 3.5.20.

291 (XCI) Plutarch *Moralia* 229B. In margin 'guile'
   1 For Spartiate descent from Hercules, see 1.302 n2 below.
   2 One of Hercules' 'Labours' was the destruction of the lion of Nemea. After killing the beast he thereafter wore its skin, which, together with his club, became his characteristic garb.
   3 This is expanded in *Adagia* III v 81: *Si leonina pellis non satis est, vulpina addenda* 'If the lion's skin is not enough, a fox's must be added.'

292 Others censured him for violating the agreement he had made in Miletus,[1] confirming it with solemn oaths. He commented, 'Boys have to be tricked with knuckle-bones, grown men with oaths'[2] – as if tricking people with broken promises were fit behaviour for a man.

293 After overcoming the Athenians at the River Aegis,[1] not by valour but by trickery, and then starving them into surrendering the city to him, he wrote to the ephors, 'Athens is taken' – as if he had taken it by force, giving a false impression so as to enhance his own glory.

294 The people of Argos were in dispute with the Spartans over the boundaries of their territory and declared that they had the juster cause. Lysander drew his sword and said, 'When it comes to boundaries, the strongest argument belongs to the one who has the upper hand through this.'

This arrogant fellow disregarded what was right and just and appealed to force.

295 He was marching through the territory of the Boeotians,[1] who were undecided and had not committed themselves to either side. He sent messengers to ask them 'whether he was to pass through their lands with lances upright or sloped.'

\* \* \* \* \*

292 (xcii) Plutarch *Moralia* 229B. In margin 'perfidy'
1 By this agreement made with the Persian Tissaphernes in 412 BC, Sparta abandoned the Greek cities of Asia Minor to Persian domination in return for money to finance the war against Athens. Later the Spartans set out to recover the same cities.
2 The same remark is attributed to Dionysius II, ruler of Syracuse, at Plutarch *Moralia* 330E (*The Fortune of Alexander* I).

293 (xciii) Plutarch *Moralia* 229B. In margin 'boastful'
1 This refers to the naval battle at Aegospotami in Asia Minor in 405 BC, at which Lysander killed 3–4000 Athenian troops and annihilated Athenian sea-power. The Athenian fleet was caught unprepared, but treachery may have been involved. Lysander then sailed unopposed to Athens and blockaded its port of Piraeus. The city was eventually starved into surrender. Cf 1.51n above.

294 (xciv) Plutarch *Moralia* 229C. In margin 'aggressive'

295 (xcv) Plutarch *Moralia* 229C. In margin 'bold'
1 This incident could be dated to 395 BC. Lysander was killed in that year at Haliartus in Boeotia. Cf the attitude of Agesilaus 1.41–2 above.

He meant by this that whether the Boeotians were friendly or hostile, he was going to continue on his way regardless, except that if he was to proceed through enemy territory the lances would be in the 'ready' position, prepared to repel any who stood in their way; if through friendly territory, they would be in the resting position, as a sign that he intended to harm no one. This remark sounds typically Spartan – he would neither ask favours of enemies nor act threateningly towards a friendly state.

296 An inhabitant of Megara spoke very freely against him in a public meeting. 'My friend,' he said, 'your words require a city.'[1]
    He meant that anyone was free to say what he thought in a meeting of civilians, but the same freedom of speech was not allowable in time of war.

297 The inhabitants of Corinth had rebelled, and when Lysander brought his troops up to the walls of the city he observed that his men were not eager to make an assault. By chance a hare that had been disturbed was seen leaping the ditch.[1] 'Are you not ashamed, you men of Sparta,' he said, 'to feel afraid of an enemy who are so spineless that they let hares sleep in their walls?'
    Lysander was an astute general who could turn this chance occurrence into something that would fire his men's courage.

298 When Lysander consulted the oracle in Samothrace,[1] the priest ordered him to declare the most wicked thing he had ever done in his life. He asked the priest, 'Is it by your order or by order of the gods that I have to do this?' When the priest answered, 'By order of the gods,' he said, 'Well then, you take yourself off, and I will tell the gods if they ask me.'

* * * * *

296 (xcvi) Plutarch *Moralia* 229C. In margin 'outspokenness'
    1 For similar apophthegms see eg 1.55 and 1.99 above. In view of these, the remark here probably meant that bold words require the strength of a city to back them. It also suggested that Megara did not count as a city. See 1.86 above, 4.100 below. Erasmus' comment implies a different interpretation, seemingly based on the version of the story in Plutarch *Moralia* 71E (*How to tell a flatterer*) which sets the incident in a military context.

297 (xcvii) Plutarch *Moralia* 229D. In margin 'astute'
    1 Cf the same story told at 1.144 above, of Archidamus II.

298 (xcviii) Plutarch *Moralia* 229D
    1 Cf the similar story, told of Antalcidas, 1.123 above and 2.67 below.

It is up to the reader to decide whether to applaud here a mind free of all superstition or the alertness of a man who saw through the subterfuge of the priest, who wanted to get a hold over him through knowledge of his wickedness. The Spartans never undertook any fresh course of action without consulting an oracle.[2] Lysander had no religious belief of any kind, yet he used religion, like everything else, to cloak his vices with an appearance of virtue, though without great success.

299 A Persian asked him what kind of state he most approved of. 'One,' he said, 'in which appropriate rewards are given to the brave and to the cowardly.'[1]

He knew that valour is drawn out by recognition and cowardice stirred into action by disgrace. It was seeing brave men receive no more recognition than cowards that made Achilles so resentful in Homer.[2] This remark of Lysander's is of relevance not merely in public life but in the private household. These two things, honour and disgrace, are of prime importance in maintaining discipline in any group of people. Honours nourish not only arts, as the proverb says,[3] but also virtue. What is important is not whether we have monarchy, aristocracy, democracy, or some form of government combining elements of all three,[4] but whether under any constitution a distinction is made at public level between those who contribute to the state and those who serve only their own base pleasures.

300 Someone was boasting to Lysander that he was always singing Lysander's praises and defending him against criticism. Lysander replied, 'I have two

* * * * *

2 See 1.12 above.

299 (XCIX) Plutarch *Moralia* 229E. In margin 'reward for bravery'
   1 Cf 1.287 above, and 7.56 below.
   2 'The Wrath of Achilles,' the main theme of the *Iliad*, was occasioned when the girl Briseis, who had been allocated to him as the spoils of battle after his great exploits, was taken away from Achilles and given to King Agamemnon, who had done nothing. See *Iliad*, book 1 in general.
   3 *Adagia* I viii 92: *Honos alit artes* 'Honours nourish arts'
   4 Among Greek political theorists of the fourth century BC and later, Sparta was admired for its constitution which, in theory at least, owed its stability to a combination of monarchy (with its two royal houses), aristocracy (its council of elders, the Gerousia), and democracy (the assembly of full Spartiate citizens). See 1.119 n1 above and 1.328 n1 below; Polybios 6.10; also Cicero *De republica* 1.30, 35; 2.28.

300 (C) Plutarch *Moralia* 229E. In margin 'praise from men'

oxen in the country. Neither says a word, but I know well which one is lazy and which works hard.'

He knew that true virtue does not need men's praises, as praise and honour follow it naturally.[1] It is those who do nothing admirable who need someone to cry them up.

301 Someone kept shouting insults at him. 'Keep talking, my little friend,' said Lysander, 'keep on and on and don't leave anything out. Maybe you'll be able to empty your mind of all the nasty things you seem to be full of.'

This was truly a sign of a great mind – not to respond to the insults even with anger, when he could well have punished the man.

302 A little later, after Lysander's death, a disagreement arose about a military alliance, so Agesilaus went to Lysander's house to look for some papers relating to it which Lysander had kept. He also found there a document written by Lysander containing proposals for a change in the constitution. Lysander had said there that the kingship ought to be taken away from the Eurytiontids and Agis (as it was, kings could be created only from these families) and made subject to election, the choice of king to be made from the best persons.[1] This would mean that this high office would be bestowed not on those who were directly descended from Hercules[2] but on those who were like Hercules in moral worth, since it was moral worth and not noble lineage that had exalted him to a place among the gods.[3] Agesilaus was eager to publish this document, hoping to show

* * * * *

1 *Adagia* IV viii 71: *Virtus gloriam parit* 'Virtue begets glory'

301 (I) Plutarch *Moralia* 229E. In margin 'forbearance'

302 (II) Plutarch *Moralia* 229F. This whole incident is given at 1.51 above.
  1 The Spartan kings were not derived from all the noble families of Sparta but only from two branches, the Eurypontidae and Agiadae (both given wrongly in Erasmus' text); see 1.328 n2 below. Lysander, who, according to this story, fancied himself as king, was not even noble, but a commoner like Brasidas. His family had actually lost its Spartiate status through poverty and he had had to win back full citizenship.
  2 The Dorian Greeks, of whom the Spartans became the most important, believed that they had occupied the Peloponnese c. 1000 BC under the leadership of princes who were descended from Hercules and were the direct ancestors of the two Spartan royal houses.
  3 As a reward for his benefits to mankind in performing the Twelve Labours and other exploits, Hercules was exalted to heaven and given a place among

the people what sort of citizen Lysander had really been and also to discredit Lysander's supporters. We are told however that Cratidas, who was
then chief among the ephors, was afraid that if people read the speech they
would agree with it, so he persuaded Agesilaus not to carry out his intention, saying that 'they should not resurrect Lysander, but rather bury
the speech with him,' as it seemed to him cunningly and persuasively
written.

The story demonstrates Lysander's depraved ambition – he left nothing untried in his attempts to gain the kingship. It also demonstrates Agesilaus' self-control, in that he put the good of the state before personal
animosity.

303 The men who had sought the hand of Lysander's daughters in marriage
withdrew their offer soon after his death, when it became known that he
was poor.[1] The ephors imposed a fine on them for cultivating a man they
believed to be rich and then throwing him off when he was shown to be
fair and honest by his modest means.

While this is not a 'saying,' it is a good example of firm principle,
and tells us that in arranging marriages one should look for good character
rather than wealth; also that friends who measure friendship by what they
can get out of it are false and unreliable – when there is nothing more to be
gained they immediately cease the acquaintance. It also reminds us that it
is better to be rich in reputation than in money.

### Namertas

304 When Namertas was acting as ambassador for his country, a citizen of the
place he was visiting called him a lucky man to have so many friends. So
Namertas asked him what kind of test a man with many friends could use
to see if he had a genuine, honest friend. The other said he did not know
but would be glad to be told. Namertas replied, 'Misfortune.'[1]

\* \* \* \* \*

the gods. He had to overcome the disadvantage of illegitimacy, being the son
of Zeus and the mortal Alcmene.

303 (III) Plutarch *Moralia* 230A. In margin 'uncompromising'
   1 For all his lack of scruple, Lysander was believed to be above taking bribes.
   See Plutarch *Lycurgus* 30. For his poverty, see 1.302 n1 above.

304 (IV) Plutarch *Moralia* 230A–B. In margin 'a test for friendship'
   Namertas is a Spartiate of whom nothing more is known.
   1 Cf *Adagia* IV v 5: *Amicus certus in re incerta cernitur* 'Uncertainty sees a certain
   friend'; cf 2.174 below)

## Nicander

305 Someone told Nicander that the citizens of Argos were speaking ill of him.
'And the people who speak ill of the good,' he said, 'are not paying the
penalty, are they?'[1]

He meant that a country had low moral standards if its people were
allowed to slander with impunity those who had deserved no ill.

306 The same person asked why the Spartans let their hair and beards grow.[1]
'This adornment is the most beautiful a man can have,' he replied, 'it is
special to him and it costs nothing.'

307 An Athenian remarked to Nicander, 'You Spartans are too keen on not working.' 'True enough,' he replied, 'but we don't try, like you, to achieve leisure
by any and every means.'

He meant that leisure created by honest means had no blame attached
to it, but that it was reprehensible to go to any lengths to achieve a life of
indolence. But what the Athenian meant by 'not working' was 'not engaging
in a trade.'[1]

## Zeuxidamus

308 When someone asked him why the Spartans kept their laws about bravery
in oral form instead of writing them down and giving them to the young

* * * * *

305 (v) Plutarch *Moralia* 230B.
    Nicander was king of Sparta in the eighth century BC, the son of Charillus, for
    whom see 1.343 below.
  1 Erasmus' translation and comment suggest that he read οὔκουν 'certainly not'
    in his Greek text and took the words as a question, in this agreeing with Filelfo
    (see the dedicatory epistle 7 n20 above). More recent texts of Plutarch offer,
    with a different accentuation, οὐκοῦν 'certainly' and make the words a state-
    ment: '... are indeed paying the penalty ...' Nicander was at the time invading
    the territory of Argos and laying it waste. See Pausanias *Periegesis* 3.7.4.

306 (vi) Plutarch *Moralia* 230B
  1 See 1.284 above.

307 (vii) Plutarch *Moralia* 230B
  1 See 1.70 above.

308 (viii) Plutarch *Moralia* 221B–C.
    Zeuxidamus has been misplaced. In Plutarch's text he comes after Eurycratidas
    (1.188 above). Zeuxidamus was the son of Leotychidas II (1.236–8 above), but
    he died before his father and so never became king.

men to read,[1] Zeuxidamus replied, 'Because they must learn to put their minds to great deeds, not to reading.'

It is a form of laziness to talk about fortitude like the philosophers. Bravery needs to be given immediate practical expression, and a few precepts are enough to instil it.

**309** A citizen of Aetolia remarked that those who were keen to combine virtue and valour would prefer war to peace. 'Heavens, no!' said Zeuxidamus, 'but they should put death before life.'

The man from Sparta corrected the Aetolian – war is not to be desired, but neither in war nor in peace can one defend liberty unless one has ceased to fear death.

**Panthoidas**

**310** Panthoidas went on an embassy to Asia and was shown a strongly built fortification. 'Good heavens, sir!' he said, 'a fine set of women's quarters.'[1]

**311** When he had listened to a long philosophical debate in the Academy on the subject of virtue, Panthoidas was asked what he thought of discussions of that sort. 'They are good, of course,' he replied, 'but absolutely useless in your case, as you don't make use of them.'

He wittily put his finger on an Athenian characteristic: they always had virtue on their lips but did not demonstrate it in practice.

**Pausanias (1)**

**312** The inhabitants of Delos were in dispute with the Athenians about the

\* \* \* \* \*

1 Cf 1.264 above.

**309** (IX) Plutarch *Moralia* 221C

**310** (X) Plutarch *Moralia* 230C.
This could be the Panthoidas who was sent from Sparta in 403/2 BC to capture Byzantium. He was killed at Tanagra in 377 BC fighting Pelopidas (for whom see 5.255–62 below).
1 Cf 1.197 above.

**311** (XI) Plutarch *Moralia* 230C. In margin 'sharp'

**312** (XII) Plutarch *Moralia* 230C–D. In margin 'pointed'
This Pausanias was regent of Sparta for his under-age cousin Plistarchus (see 1.328–30 below) from 479 BC onwards, and was commander at the

sovereignty of the island. While putting their case, they remarked that according to local custom no woman was allowed to give birth on the island and no one could be buried there. Pausanias, son of Cleombrotus, commented, 'How can this island be a homeland for you, when none of you has ever been <born> there or ever will be?'[1]

This was a witty criticism of the foolish custom of the Delians who would not let their own citizens either be born alive or buried dead in their native land. A country, like a woman, cannot be a mother unless it gives birth; and it would be unthinkable for a loving mother to refuse burial to her children.[2]

313 The Athenian[1] exiles were trying to persuade him to take his army and attack Athens, saying that when the herald announced his victory at the Olympic Games, only the Athenians had booed. He replied, 'If they did that when I had done well by them, what do you think they will do if I treat them ill?'

We have here a remarkable example of emotions under control, in that he was quite unmoved by this gross insult. The incident also demonstrates his quick wit in turning into an argument for the opposite course of action the thing they put forward as an incentive for starting hostilities.

\* \* \* \* \*

battle of Plataea in 479 BC. The apophthegm itself raises various historical problems which are not relevant to Erasmus' translation. The situation is too late for Pausanias for one thing. For the actual events, see Thucydides 3.104.
1 There is a problem in the text of Plutarch here, which reads οὔτε γέγονε τις ὑμῶν οὔτ' ἔσται. Literally, this means 'none of you has been or will be.' One solution offered by editors has been to take γέγονε as 'has been born' and to emend ἔσται 'will be' to κείσεται 'will lie' (buried). Erasmus seems to have translated the problem text literally, as his Latin version appears to mean 'none of you has been or will be,' but as the previous text and his comment indicates, some reference at least to birth is required. Accordingly, the word 'born' has been inserted in the English translation.
2 Delos was supposed to be the birth-place of the gods Apollo and Artemis, and the purpose of the regulation was to keep the sacred island free from pollution.

313 (XIII) Plutarch *Moralia* 230D. Cf a similar saying attributed to Philip of Macedon at 4.25 below. In margin 'forbearance'
1 Erasmus has added the word 'Athenian.' Possibly the exiles were Delians, as the Athenians had expelled them from the island.

**314** When someone asked him why they had given the poet Tyrtaeus Spartan citizenship,[1] he replied, 'So that we should not be seen to have had a foreigner as general.'

Poets were not esteemed by the Spartans,[2] and Tyrtaeus did not merit the honour of citizenship on that score. He had shown himself a vigorous leader in war, and so they thought they should claim the glory of that for their own country.

**315** A weakling was urging Pausanias to risk a battle with the enemy by land and sea. 'Are you prepared to strip and show us what you are like,' he said, 'you who are so keen that we should fight?'

So he wittily made fun of the man who encouraged others to take a course of action to which he himself could contribute nothing.

**316** People were admiring the expensive clothes that had been taken as spoils from the barbarians.[1] 'It would have been better,' Pausanias remarked, 'if they had been worth a lot themselves, rather than owning things worth a lot.'

He thus checked their admiration and put them in the way of admiring truly good things.

**317** After defeating the Medes at Platea, Pausanias ordered his men to serve up the Persian banquet which the barbarian enemy had prepared before the battle. It was rich and sumptuous. 'Persian,' he said, 'you were a greedy fellow to come for our barley-cakes when you had all these delicacies.' Barley-cakes were a cheap type of bread, generally looked down on.

\* \* \* \* \*

**314** (XIV) Plutarch *Moralia* 230D. In margin 'clever'
  1 Tyrtaeus was a poet active in Sparta in the seventh century BC. His works, now fragmentary, seem to have included marching songs and other material appropriate to a militaristic society. The story was that an oracle had ordered the Spartans in their second war with the Messenians (c. 650 BC) to take a leader from among the Athenians and Tyrtaeus had been chosen. See the geographer Pausanias *Periegesis* 4.15.6.
  2 See 2.39 n2 below.

**315** (XV) Plutarch *Moralia* 230E. In margin 'witty'

**316** (XVI) Plutarch *Moralia* 230E. In margin 'wise'
  1 This booty was taken from the Persians (also called Medes; cf 1.59 and n4 above) after the battle of Plataea in 479 BC, at which the Persian king Xerxes, who had invaded Greece with a vast army, was finally repulsed. See 1.317 below.

**317** (XVII) Plutarch *Moralia* 230E–F. In margin 'humorous'

He here reminds us that it is folly for those with possessions to fight people who have very little that can be taken from them. If the lottery of war favours them, their gain is minimal. If it goes against them, the loss is great. But the real point of the remark is that it is an arrogant kind of faddiness to ask for cheap food, such as humble people eat, in the midst of all kinds of delicacies. Rich people sometimes do this,[1] when they are sickened by a constant supply of luxuries.

## Pausanias (2)

318 Someone asked Pausanias, son of Plistonax, why the Spartans were not allowed to change any of their ancient laws. 'Because,' he said, 'the laws should have authority over men and not men over laws.'[1]

319 He was in exile in Tegea[1] and when he praised Sparta, someone said to him, 'Why ever didn't you stay in Sparta instead of going into exile?' He replied, 'Because doctors too spend their time among the sick and not among the healthy.'[2]

He wittily turned the taunt of exile back on the citizen of Tegea, for the corrupt morals of that people were in need of Spartan discipline.[3]

320 Someone asked Pausanias how they could defeat the Thracians. He replied, 'By choosing the best man to conduct the war.'

He reminded them to what extent victory is dependent on the commanader-in-chief. Indeed, in every undertaking, the character of those who are put in charge is of the utmost importance.

\* \* \* \* \*

1 See Seneca *Epistulae morales* 18.5ff; *Ad Helviam* 12.3.

318 (xviii) Plutarch *Moralia* 230F. In margin 'authority of the laws'
This Pausanias was king of Sparta, 409–395 BC.
1 Cf 1.140 and 1.171 above.

319 (xix) Plutarch *Moralia* 230F. In margin 'witty'
1 Pausanias was condemned to death for a military reverse in 394 BC, in which Lysander (for whom see 1.288–303 above) was killed, and he spent the rest of his life in exile.
2 The saying, a common sentiment, is ascribed also to Antisthenes (see 7.60 below), to Aristippus in Diogenes Laertius 2.70 (3.117 below), and to Diogenes in Stobaeus 13.25 (Meineke I 261).
3 Cf 3.327 below.

320 (xx) Plutarch *Moralia* 230F. In margin 'a good leader'

321 A doctor who was paying Pausanias a visit told him he had nothing wrong
with him. 'That's because I don't make use of your professional services,'
he replied.

So far from attributing his freedom from illness to doctors, Pausanias
was of the opinion that the only people who enjoyed good health were those
who made no use of doctors. While this is not always true, it is nonetheless beyond dispute that the majority of illnesses are caused by doctors, because of their inexperience, carelessness, ambition, or concern for making
money.[1]

322 A friend took him to task for speaking ill of a certain doctor who had done
him no harm, of whom in fact he had no experience. 'And if I had,' he
replied, 'I wouldn't be alive.'

323 A certain doctor remarked to Pausanias that he had reached a good age.
'That's because I never employed you as my doctor,' he replied.

The doctor thought that it was due to his profession if anyone reached
old age. Pausanias was of the opinion that those who employ doctors hardly
ever achieve ripe years.

324 Pausanias considered that the best doctor was one who didn't let his patients
rot but got them buried as soon as possible.

This seems rather a brutal idea, but it is not all that different from Socrates' view. He suggested that people in a very poor state of health, who could
no longer serve the state in any useful capacity, ought contentedly to depart
this life, not meaning that any should lay violent hands on themselves,[1] but
that they should pass away while still able to do what was right.[2] Certainly it

* * * * *

321 (xxi) Plutarch *Moralia* 231A. In margin 'scorn for medicine'
  1 Erasmus is often uncomplimentary about doctors. See General Index: doctors.

322 (xxii) Plutarch *Moralia* 231A. In margin 'hater of doctors'

323 (xxiii) Plutarch *Moralia* 231A. In margin 'hater of doctors'

324 (xxiv) Plutarch *Moralia* 231A. In margin 'the best doctor'
  1 For Socrates' rejection of suicide, see Plato *Phaedo* 61B–62C.
  2 Cf Cicero *De senectute* 20.72, which spells out what seems to be meant here:
    ideally one should live doing one's duty as long as this is possible, leaving the
    crumbling edifice of the body to fall apart naturally, without doing anything
    either to hasten, or (the point being made here) to delay the end.

is by no means clear what good is being achieved when a dozen or so doctors strive for a long time at huge expense to extend for a month or two the life of an old woman who is already half dead. They are just using their skills to spin death out, as if any sane person would wish to be a long time a-dying. Wise men have declared that the best death is a sudden and a quick one.[3]

### Paedaretus

**325** When someone pointed out how large the enemy force was, 'All the more glory for us,' replied Paedaretus, 'as we shall kill more.'

What the other saw as a reason for cowardice, he turned into a spur to bolder action. One can use the same weapon against anyone who pleads the difficulties of the right course of action as a reason for not embarking on it.

**326** A man who was soft by nature was nonetheless praised by the citizenry for his kindness. Paedaretus remarked that 'no praise should be given to men who are like women, nor to women who are like men, unless some extreme situation forces such behaviour on a woman.'

He saw that one kind of behaviour was appropriate for a good man, another for a good woman. He accepts that extreme circumstances may force a woman to act the man, but there is no excuse for a man who degenerates into a woman. Likewise, a prince should not be praised for the same things as a subject, nor a person in public life for the same things as a private citizen.

**327** When he was not chosen to be one of the three hundred,[1] an honour which confers the highest status in Spartan society, in spite of his rejection

\* \* \* \* \*

The Stoics however taught that one should voluntarily end one's life when no longer able to live virtuously. See Seneca *Epistulae morales* 58.32–6. Erasmus as a Christian can, of course, not agree with this. Cf 1.157 above.
3  Eg Julius Caesar; see Suetonius *Divus Iulius* 87.

325  (xxv) Plutarch *Moralia* 231B. In margin 'resolute'
Paedaretus was a Spartiate general in the Peloponnesian War (431–404 BC).

326  (xxvi) Plutarch *Moralia* 231B. In margin 'appropriateness'

327  (xxvii) Plutarch *Moralia* 231B. In margin 'unaffected'
1  When Spartiate youths became young adults, the ephors appointed the three most outstanding of the age group as commanders. Each of these in turn picked a group of a hundred to form an élite corps. See Xenophon *Respublica Lacedaemoniorum* 4.3. .

Paedaretus left the place cheerful and smiling. The ephors called him back and asked what he was smiling about. 'I am glad for my country,' he said, 'because it has three hundred citizens much better than me.'

What a philosophical attitude! He did not feel aggrieved at being passed over, nor complain at the ephors' decision, but found more satisfaction in the general good of his country than he would have felt if he had received the honour.

### Plistarchus

**328** Someone asked Plistarchus, son of Leonidas, why the kings of Sparta did not bear a name derived from the earliest kings. 'Because,' he said, 'the early kings preferred to lead rather than rule, but their successors took a very different view.'

The first of all the Spartan kings was called Agis, and this name did pass down to some of the later ones.[1] 'Agis' is derived from the word for 'leading,'[2] because the early kings commanded, even if in a kindly manner. It is the function of kings to command, not persuade. 'Plistarchus' in fact means 'commanding many.'

**329** A defence counsel in a lawsuit kept making jokes. Plistarchus interrupted

\* \* \* \* \*

**328** (xxviii) Plutarch *Moralia* 231c. In margin 'temperate'
Plistarchus was king of Sparta, 480–459 BC.
  1 The first Spartan kings were in actuality the shadowy Eurysthenes and Procles, but the two Spartan royal houses, the Agiads and Eurypontids, were named after Agis I, possibly tenth century BC, son of Eurysthenes, and Eurypon, grandson of Procles. The early kings became increasingly autocratic, and Theopompus, king in the eighth to seventh century BC, appointed the first ephors as a check on royal power, see 1.12 n3 above.
    For Agis II, III and IV see 1.87–110 above. Erasmus seems to be commenting on the fact that not many were called Agis.
  2 Ie Greek *agein*. Erasmus' translation of the apophthegm and forced comment on 'lead' suggest that he was endeavouring to make sense of and explain a reading in his Greek text *agein ē basileuein echrēizon*, which he renders as 'preferred to lead rather than rule.' A modern emendation of the text offers *agan basileuein echrēizon* 'needed to rule excessively' ie autocratically. The Greek verb *chrēizō* can mean either 'desire' or 'need.'

**329** (xxix) Plutarch *Moralia* 231c. In margin 'foolish talking'
After this some MSS of Plutarch have an apophthegm which repeats the substance of one attributed to Agesilaus (1.57 above). It may not have been in Erasmus' text of Plutarch, but see the dedicatory epistle 10 n31 above.

him and said, 'You had better take care, my friend, not to be constantly raising a laugh. People who constantly practise wrestling turn into wrestlers,
and you are in danger of becoming a joke yourself.'

This excellent man was well aware that people should be forgiven the
occasional lapse, but when a fault has turned into a habit and regular behaviour the evil is past healing. If our friends constantly commit the same
fault, we should challenge them,[1] as Plistarchus did here, and check them,
so that they do not get used to doing whatever it is and the fault becomes
second nature.

330 Someone told Plistarchus that he was being praised by a man who was
always speaking ill of people. 'I wonder,' he said, 'if someone has told him
I was dead. He couldn't speak well of anyone living.'[1]

This fine man took no pleasure in praise coming from a man of evil
reputation.

**Plistonax**

331 When a certain Athenian orator accused the Spartans of being ignorant,
Plistonax, son of Pausanias, replied, 'Yes, we are the only Greeks who have
learnt nothing bad from you.'

\* \* \* \* \*

1 Cf 2.173 below.

330 (xxx) Plutarch *Moralia* 231D
   1 Cf 7.57 and 7.69 below.

331 (xxxi) Plutarch *Moralia* 231D
   Plistonax was king of Sparta, 459–409 BC. Here Froben in *1538* included
   the following: 'A note by Erasmus: Plistonax is called the son of Pausanias, though shortly before two Pausaniases are mentioned, one the son
   of Cleombrotus [1.312 above], the other the son of Plistonax [1.318 above].
   Plutarch writes here "Plistonax of Pausanias." The Greeks use the father's
   name like this to distinguish the son. I am not sure whether the father can
   likewise be distinguished by the name of the son. I included this apophthegm from the Greek of Plutarch's collection, but it is not in Filelfo's version, nor in Raffaele's [see the dedicatory epistle 7–8 nn20 and 21 above],
   and I suspect it was added to Plutarch's text without good reason, especially since the same saying is earlier attributed to Antalcidas [1.124
   above]. Aldus used as the basis of his edition [of Plutarch's *Moralia*] a
   not very sound text, and for that reason Lascaris advised him to post-
   pone the edition until he had acquired an improved text, but he was not
   listened to.'

The Spartans classed as bad anything that did not contribute to the improvement of the state.

### Polydorus

332 A certain man kept on making threats against his enemies. Polydorus, son of Alcamenes, said to him, 'Don't you realize you are squandering the greatest part of your vengeance?'

Anyone who has decided to take revenge on an enemy achieves nothing by issuing threats except to forewarn him and reduce his own scope for injuring him. Brave men hurt those who deserve to be hurt by what they do, not by what they say.

333 When he had marched out into Messenian territory,[1] someone asked him if they were going to fight against their brothers.[2] 'No,' he replied, 'we are just moving into that part of the land which has not yet been allocated.'[3]

He misled the questioner by giving this false impression of what he planned to do. This can provide another example of concealing your intention when you want to harm someone.

334 After the famous Battle of the Three Hundred,[1] the people of Argos sus-

\* \* \* \* \*

332 (XXXII) Plutarch *Moralia* 231D. In margin 'noble-spirited'
Polydorus was king of Sparta, c. 700–665 BC. This odd saying is also attributed to the sage Chilon. See 2.173 below.

333 (XXXIII) Plutarch *Moralia* 231E. In margin 'misleading'
1 Sparta gradually extended her territory beyond the bounds of Laconia in a series of aggressive wars against Messenia to the north and west, taking over the land and reducing the Messenian inhabitants to the status of Helots. Polydorus was believed to have contributed to bringing the first Messenian War to a successful conclusion in the seventh century BC with his colleague Theopompus (see 1.196 n1 above).
2 The Messenians were probably Dorians, like the Spartans. See 1.263 n2 above.
3 Occupied Messenian territory was divided into additional lots which were allocated to individual Spartans and worked by Helot serfs for the upkeep of their masters. The original allocations were in Sparta's own territory of Laconia (see 1.259 above). Polydorus left behind a reputation as a popular fair-minded king and a distributor of land.

334 (XXXIV) Plutarch *Moralia* 231E. In margin 'self-control'
1 For this battle in 546 BC between Sparta and Argos, see Herodotus 1.82. It was fought by 300 picked warriors from each side to avoid a general engagement. Two Argives survived and one Spartan. As both sides claimed the victory for different reasons a conventional battle was then fought, which the Spartans

tained another military defeat. Polydorus' associates urged him not to let the opportunity slip but to attack the walls and take the enemy city. This, they said, would be easy, because the men had been killed and only women were left. He replied to this effect: 'I consider it right and proper to defeat rebels on the battle-field where both sides have an equal chance. But I do not think it fair, when I have fought to win land, then to want to capture the city. I came here to recover territory, not to capture a city.'

This high-minded man was of the opinion that even in dealing with an enemy one's conduct should be governed by equity, whereas most people think that anything is permissible where an enemy is concerned. Even if the dispute is over some pathetic little town, the victor thinks he has the right to occupy the whole territory of the vanquished. Polydorus further considered that it would stain his reputation to make war on people who did not have the means of fighting back. From such a victory comes not the renown accorded to bravery but the infamy due to cruelty.

335 When someone asked him the reason why the Spartan warriors exposed themselves so courageously to danger in war, he replied, 'Because they have learned to respect their commander rather than fear him.'[1]

Respect is linked with love, but we fear above all those whom we hate. A man who wholeheartedly does what he is required to do does it better than one who does it from fear of evil consequences.

### Polycratidas

336 Polycratidas was sent with others on an embassy to the King's[1] generals. When he was asked whether they had come privately or officially, he replied, 'Officially, if our request is granted; if not, privately.'

This remark reveals his loving concern for his country. If the embassy went the way they wanted, he wished the glory of it to go to the state; if not, he did not want the humiliation of being refused to be linked with his country.

\* \* \* \* \*

won. Polydorus did attack Argos and was defeated in 669 BC, but the famous battle occurred long after his reign.

335 (xxxv) Plutarch *Moralia* 231F. In margin 'wise'
  1 Cf 1.210 and 1.253 above.

336 (xxxvi) Plutarch *Moralia* 231F. In margin 'concern for country'
  Polycratidas is an otherwise unknown Spartan.
  1 Ie the king of Persia, known as The Great King. See 1.61 above.

### Soebidas

337 When the Spartans were about to expose themselves to the chances of war in the battle of Leuctra,[1] someone remarked, 'Today will show the good man.' Soebidas replied, 'A splendid day – if it can show the good man unharmed.'[2]

He foresaw that many fine men would bravely meet their end in that battle, men that he would prefer to stay alive for the country's sake.

338 When [Soos] found himself penned in by the enemy forces on rugged terrain with no water supply, he made the following pact with the enemy, as the story goes: he would cede to them the territory he had won in the war if his men and he himself could drink from the nearby spring – the enemy had control of this. When the agreement was ratified, he called all his men together and promised to grant dominion over that region[1] to any man who did not drink. Not one of them mastered his thirst, but all of them drank. After everyone else, he himself went down into the spring and splashed himself with water. Then, with the enemy force still there, he went off and seized the area on the grounds that he alone had not drunk.

By this ruse he delivered the army from the perils of thirst and tricked the enemy and by his physical endurance kept the kingdom for himself. He was not bound to the enemy by the terms of the agreement because it was not the case that everyone had drunk including himself. Nor had he tricked his men because no one apart from himself had refrained from drinking. If the enemy had resorted to arms at this point, he could now meet them on equal terms as he had a strategically better position and control of the spring.

### Telecrus

339 Telecrus was told that his father was saying unpleasant things about him.

\* \* \* \* \*

337 (xxxvii) Plutarch *Moralia* 231F. In margin 'pointed'
   'Soebidas' should be Phoebidas, Spartiate general and brother of Eudamidas I.
   1 The Spartans were heavily defeated at the battle of Leuctra (371 BC; see 1.71 n1 above). Phoebidas however had already met his end fighting the Thebans at Thespiae (see Plutarch *Pelopidas* 15).
   2 'Unharmed' translates Aldus' text of *Apophthegmata* which reads *sōon*, a mistake for *Sōos*, which should be the first word of the next item.

338 (xxxviii) Plutarch *Moralia* 232A. This story should be told of Sous, a very early king of Sparta (see Plutarch *Life of Lycurgus* 2). In margin 'wily'
   1 'Dominion over that region' should read 'the kingship,' as in Plutarch's text; cf line 12 below.

339 (xxxix) Plutarch *Moralia* 232B. In margin 'filial piety'
   Telecrus (Teleclus) was the son of Archelaus, king of Sparta in the eighth cen-

He replied, 'He wouldn't be saying them if it weren't necessary.'

He preferred to take the blame on himself rather than make it appear that his father had spoken without thinking. Here you have an example of filial piety and an absence of self-conceit.

340 Telecrus' brother complained that the citizens did not show towards himself the same consideration as they did towards him, but treated him rather callously in failing so far to elect him ephor.[1] 'You don't know,' Telecrus replied, 'how to submit to injustice. I do.'

He meant that anyone who desires to enjoy public favour must learn not to react to a great deal of unfair comment.[2]

341 When he was asked why it was customary in Spartan society for the young to show respect for their elders by rising from their seats,[1] he replied, 'To ensure that, being accustomed to show respect to persons not related to them, they may honour their parents the more.'

It is a splendid way of accustoming people to doing what they ought to do, if we teach them to do more than is actually required. For example, if a man is accustomed to living with his own wife in a controlled and continent manner, he will not be so likely to make improper advances to other people's wives.[2]

342 When he was asked how much he possessed, 'No more,' he replied, 'than enough.'

He measured wealth by need, not greed.

\* \* \* \* \*

tury BC. He himself became king later, and was active in expanding Spartan territory southwards c. 750–740 BC, and in sending colonists to annex part of Messenia.

340 (XL) Plutarch *Moralia* 232B. In margin 'good-humoured'
  1 The words 'in failing so far to elect him ephor' have nothing to correspond in the text of Plutarch, which reads 'though he belonged to the same (royal) family.' They seem to have been imported from a comparable story about Chilon and his brother, recorded at 2.161 below.
  2 *Adagia* III viii 89: *Magistratum gerens audi iuste et iniuste* 'When in office expect both just and unjust criticism'

341 (XLI) Plutarch *Moralia* 232B. In margin 'weighty'
  1 See 1.269 n5 above.
  2 See Plutarch *Moralia* 522B (*On being a busybody*).

342 (XLII) Plutarch *Moralia* 232B

**Charillus/Charilaus**

343 When Charillus was asked why Lycurgus had established so few laws for the Spartans, he replied, 'Because people who don't say much don't need many laws.'

   He knew well that nearly all evils arise from excessive talking. The Spartans were characterized by their laconic speech.[1]

344 Someone else asked him why the Spartans let their unmarried girls appear in public lightly clad,[1] but kept their married women covered up. He replied, 'Because girls have to find husbands, wives have to be kept by those who have got them.'

   This custom was intended to ensure that girls were not left without husbands and that wives were not seduced. This is different from other nations, where young girls are religiously kept from men's eyes but wives are available for all to look at.

345 When a Helot slave spoke to him rather insolently, he said, 'If I weren't so angry, I would kill you.'

   He believed so strongly that an angry man cannot say or do anything right that he would not even punish his slave while his emotions were at all roused.[1]

346 When he was asked what he considered the best type of political constitution, 'The one,' he replied, 'under which the majority of citizens compete with each other in the attainment of excellence, without however generating sedition.'


\* \* \* \* \*


343 (XLIII) Plutarch *Moralia* 232B–C. In margin 'loquacity'
   Charillus was an early king of Sparta, c. 775–750 BC, supposedly nephew of Lycurgus. See 1.137 n3 above.
   1 For 'Laconic' speech see 1.95 n2 above.

344 (XLIV) Plutarch *Moralia* 232C
   1 Cf 1.268 above.

345 (XLV) Plutarch *Moralia* 232C. In margin 'controlled'
   1 This saying was ascribed to several people. See eg 7.155 below. Cf Plutarch *Moralia* 10D (*The education of children*), where it is ascribed to Archytas and Plato. See also Seneca *De ira* 3.12.3–5.

346 (XLVI) Plutarch *Moralia* 232C. In margin 'wise'

In most states, people strive for wealth and office; for excellence, hardly anyone. Yet even the pursuit of excellence should not be prosecuted so passionately that it results in strife – if it reaches that stage, it is not what is honourable that is the point at issue, but self-seeking. A man truly endowed with excellence has no end in view but service to his country. Civil strife however is a virulent poison in the national body.

347 Someone asked Charillus why all the statues of gods in Sparta were represented bearing arms.[1] He replied, 'So that the reproaches which are heaped on men for cowardice cannot be ultimately turned against the gods; and so that the young may pray to the gods only when carrying their arms.'

This explanation was meant to instil the idea in the citizens' minds that the gods loved bravery and hated cowardice; also that the young should get used to being armed, as this would make them less inclined to idle pursuits and better prepared for military service, if it was not allowed to lay aside one's weapons even for religious reasons. Idleness and self-indulgence often creep into a society under cover of religion.

* * * * *

347 (XLVII) Plutarch *Moralia* 232D. After this apophthegm, Plutarch's text has (not in all MSS) one that repeats the one attributed to Nicander in 1.306 above. In margin 'idleness'
1 Cf 2.105 below.

# BOOK II

**Sayings of unnamed Spartans**

1 Ambassadors from Samos had presented their case at inordinate length.[1] The citizens of Sparta replied, 'We have forgotten what you said first, and because we don't remember the beginning, we haven't understood the end.'

2 The Thebans were making their point with some vehemence. 'You should have less spirit,' the Spartans commented, 'or more strength.'[1]

3 An aged Spartan was asked why he wore his beard long and bushy. 'So that I may look at my grey hairs,' he said, 'and do nothing that shames them.'
    A good man tries to find incentives to virtue everywhere.

* * * * *

1 (I) Plutarch *Moralia* 232D.
    This group of apophthegms, 2.1–71, is translated from Plutarch *Moralia* 232D–236E. After this apophthegm, modern texts of Plutarch have an incident similar to 1.95, but using different words. It is not in Erasmus' Latin text, and he may simply have omitted it. See the dedicatory epistle 10 n31 above.
    1 Cf 1.216 above, another version of the incident.

2 (II) Plutarch *Moralia* 232E. Cf 1.55 and 1.99 above. The city of Thebes had a varied political history and this incident no doubt occurred during one of its less influential periods. Contrast 2.21 and 2.159 below. See General Index: Thebes.
    1 *Adagia* IV ii 90: *Aut minus animi aut plus potentiae* 'Less ambition or more strength.'

3 (III) Plutarch *Moralia* 232E. In margin 'grey hairs'
    After this apophthegm, Plutarch's text has a saying that repeats in substance one found above at 1.105. Again this is not in Erasmus' Latin text. See 2.1n above.

**4** Someone was bestowing exaggerated praise on some splendid warriors.[1] 'Yes,' said the Spartan, 'at Troy.'

He meant that there were such warriors in those days, but men like that hadn't existed for a long time.

**5** Another Spartan, on hearing that some people were being compelled to drink after dinner, remarked, 'They aren't being forced to eat as well, are they?'

He censured the Greek custom of making everyone down a certain number of cups.[1] That was just as stupid as making a man who wasn't hungry eat a certain number of dishes, except that people didn't find the former silly because it was the custom.

**6** When someone quoted Pindar's line about 'Athens, the mainstay of Greece,'[1] a Spartan remarked that 'Greece would collapse if it depended on a prop like that.'

This remark censured the Athenians' moral flabbiness which he felt in no way merited the poet's praise, or, if not that, censured the poet's insincerity in bestowing such praise on undeserving subjects.

\* \* \* \* \*

**4** (IV) Plutarch *Moralia* 232E. In margin 'witty'
 1 A better reading in Plutarch's text gives 'some Argive warriors,' which makes more sense. Sparta was often at odds with Argos, a powerful city to the north. The Trojan War took place, according to Greek tradition, in the early twelfth century BC, and Agamemnon, king of Mycenae, the leader of the Greek forces, is described at Homer *Iliad* 2.108 as 'ruling all Argos.' Mycenae was in the area known as the Argolid.

**5** (V) Plutarch *Moralia* 232E. In margin 'excessive drinking'
 1 Lycurgus had abolished this practice in Sparta; see Xenophon *Respublica Lacedaemoniorum* 5.4.

**6** (VI) Plutarch *Moralia* 232E. In margin 'frank'
 1 This is a famous line surviving from one of Pindar's dithyrambs (elaborate choral odes). See Plutarch *Moralia* 349A–350B (*On the fame of the Athenians*), where Plutarch lists glorious Athenian achievements, including the battle of Marathon when, in 491 BC, a modest Athenian force withstood the Persian invaders under Darius. Plutarch tells us that Pindar was inspired by all this to award this accolade to the Athenians, to their great delight.
 Sparta and Athens were continually jostling (and fighting) for acknowledged supremacy in the whole of Greece, and indulging in mutual denigration.

**7** Someone was looking at a picture representing Spartans being slaughtered by Athenians. 'Oh, brave Athenians!' he exclaimed. A Spartan who heard him retorted, 'Yes – in the picture.'

He meant that it was ridiculous to congratulate oneself on the strength of a picture, since a picture can lie just as much as a poet.

**8** There was a person who was very ready to lend an ear to slander directed at others. To him a Spartan said, 'Stop listening against me.'

He felt that people who slander others deserve censure, but so do those who listen to their insinuations. It is a form of injury to give ear to malicious attacks on those who have done nothing to deserve it, for there would be no slanderers if they had no one to heed them. That was why the Spartan took the man to task for listening to the fellow who was slandering him.

**9** A slave who was being punished kept saying, 'I didn't intend to do it.' The other replied, 'Then take your punishment without intending to.'

It's a common enough excuse but a feeble one to say 'I didn't intend to.' The person should have been taking care not to do wrong by mistake.

**10** A man who was away from Sparta saw men sitting on stools.[1] 'I hope I never sit on a seat,' he exclaimed, 'where I cannot rise and give place to an older person.'[2]

These refined persons sat on such seats with their legs stretched out, and the low roof prevented them from getting up. But the Spartan considered it reprehensible for a young man not to rise and show respect for an older one.

**11** Some people from Chios who were visiting Sparta, after dining, first of all

* * * * *

7   (VII) Plutarch *Moralia* 232F. In margin 'witty'

8   (VIII) Plutarch *Moralia* 232F. In margin 'being slandered'

9   (IX) Plutarch *Moralia* 232F. In margin 'neat'

10   (X) Plutarch *Moralia* 232F. In margin 'censorious'
  1 The Greek reveals that this occurs in a privy, as Erasmus obliquely indicates in his comment.
  2 See 1.269 n5 above.

11   (XI) Plutarch *Moralia* 232F–233A. In margin 'toleration'

vomited in the ephors' hall and then fouled the seats on which the ephors sat. Immediately a rigorous inquiry was instituted to find out who had perpetrated this crime, in case they were citizens, but when it was discovered that they were from Chios, an announcement was made to the effect that 'they had no objection to Chians acting like louts.'

Fine men pay no attention to insults coming from the openly disreputable. Even praise from such people is unacceptable.

12 A Spartan saw two 'hard' almonds[1] being sold for twice the normal price. 'Are stones so scarce here?' he asked.

He saw no difference between 'hard' almonds and stones. As a Spartan he was so unacquainted with luxuries that he didn't know that the kernel is hidden inside two outer layers. It seems that this species of tree was not known in any and every region, since Pliny is not sure whether it had reached Italy in Cato's time.[2]

13 A Spartan plucked a nightingale and found very little flesh. 'You are just a voice,' he said, 'nothing else.'

The same can be said of people who have nothing but a fluent tongue and high-sounding words.[1]

14 Another man saw Diogenes 'the Dog' with his arms round a bronze statue on an extremely cold day. He asked him if he was cold. When the other said no, he said, 'Well then, what great thing are you doing?'

The philosopher, who was obsessed with winning glory, thought it was a marvellous thing that he had so inured his body to all hardships that

* * * * *

12  (XII) Plutarch *Moralia* 233A. In margin 'witty'
  1 As there is nothing suggesting 'two' (*duas*) in the Greek, the word should probably be deleted as a mistake based on a repetition of *duras* 'hard.'
  2 Ie the Elder Cato, second century BC; see Pliny *Naturalis historia* 15.90, and also 15.114, where we are told that the almond, like the chestnut and walnut, has two layers over the kernel. As Erasmus mentions the two layers, he presumably understands that the almonds were being sold in their shells, rather than being a harder species of nut, which is what the Greek suggests.

13  (XIII) Plutarch *Moralia* 233A. In margin 'loquacity'
  1 For Erasmus' comment, cf the same moral drawn in Aesop 201 (Chambry), where a tiny frog makes a great croaking and is contemptuously squashed by a wolf.

14  (XIV) Plutarch *Moralia* 233A. For Diogenes the Cynic ('the Dog') see 3.164–388 below. In margin 'telling'

he could endure contact with a cold statue on a frosty day and not feel discomfort. The Spartan thought this was no more admirable than someone doing much the same thing in summer without any ill effects.

15 When a Spartan accused the people of Metapontum[1] of cowardice, a citizen of the place a retorted, 'All the same, we do possess a lot of land belonging to other states!' 'Well,' said the Spartan, 'in that case you are not only cowardly but unscrupulous as well.'

He meant that anyone who was craven and unwarlike could possess much that rightfully came under another's jurisdiction only if it had been acquired by sharp practice.

16 A man who was visiting Sparta was standing on one leg and putting his sandal on the other foot. He said to one of them, 'I don't think you can stand on one leg as long as I can.' The Spartan retorted, 'I agree. But any goose can do what you're doing.'

He was right to pour scorn on a man who had by long practice acquired a skill which contributed nothing of any use to his country. The same is true of the skills of jugglers, tight-rope walkers, and suchlike.

17 A man was boasting of his art as an orator. 'By the Twin Gods,'[1] a Spartan commented, 'without a grasp of the truth there is no art, nor ever will be.'

This was a criticism directed at professional orators who openly claim to say what is convincing even if it is not true.[2]

18 A citizen of Argos declared, 'There are many tombs of your Spartan warriors in our country.' A Spartan took him up on this. 'There isn't a single Argive

* * * * *

15 (xv) Plutarch *Moralia* 233A–B. In margin 'telling'
   1 A city founded by Greek colonists on the Gulf of Taranto in Italy. The remark may have been made by Cleonymus, son of Cleomenes II (see 1.166 above) who took the city in 304 BC during an expedition sent out in support of neighbouring Tarentum, a Spartan settlement.

16 (xvi) Plutarch *Moralia* 233B. In margin 'ridiculous'

17 (xvii) Plutarch *Moralia* 233B. In margin 'weighty'
   1 The Twin Gods were Castor and Pollux, the Heavenly Twins. This oath was characteristic of the Spartans. See 1.9 above.
   2 Probably another dig at the ancient sophists, Cf 1.1 n2 above.

18 (xviii) Plutarch *Moralia* 233C. In margin 'neat'

tomb in ours,' he said, meaning that the Spartans had always invaded Argive territory, but the Argives had never invaded Sparta.[1]

The Spartan neatly turned what the other had said, intending to praise his country, into something to be ashamed of.

19 A Spartan was taken prisoner of war. He was being sold by auction and the auctioneer announced, 'Next lot, a Spartan.' The Spartan stopped the auctioneer's mouth and said, 'Say you are auctioning a prisoner.'[1]

He accepted his own fate but could not bear the disgrace of having his country held up to shame at the auction.

20 One of the soldiers serving for pay under Lysimachus[1]. was asked by him whether he was not one of the Helots[2] (that is, the serfs of the Spartans). He replied, 'Do you imagine a Spartan would come for the few cents you pay?'

He would rather pass as a serf than have the shame of the situation attach to the name of Sparta.

21 After defeating the Spartans at the battle of Leuctra,[1] the Thebans penetrated right to the Eurotas.[2] One of them triumphantly exclaimed, 'Where are the Spartans now?' A Spartan warrior whom they had captured retorted, 'Not here, or you would not have got this far.'

Not even in defeat and capture could he forget his Spartan character and endure the enemy's boasting.

22 After surrendering their city,[1] the Athenians asked to be allowed to keep

* * * * *

1 Cf 1.125 and 2.4 n1 above.

19 (xix) Plutarch *Moralia* 233C
   1 Cf 2.37 below.

20 (xx) Plutarch *Moralia* 233C
   1 From the fourth century BC onwards, Spartans often enlisted as mercenary soldiers under foreign commanders. Lysimachus was one of the successors of Alexander the Great, and became king of Thrace c. 323 BC
   2 See 1.25 n2 above.

21 (xxi) Plutarch *Moralia* 233C. In margin 'noble'
   1 See 1.71 above.
   2 The Eurotas was the river flowing past the city of Sparta.

22 (xxii) Plutarch *Moralia* 233D. In margin 'pointed'
   1 Ie to the Spartans at the end of the Peloponnesian War in 404 BC. The island

just Samos. The Spartans replied, 'You don't own yourselves, and you ask to own others?' This gave rise to the proverb, 'He who owns not himself asks for Samos.'[2]

23 After the Spartans had taken a certain city by force of arms, the ephors remarked, 'Our young men have lost their training ground; they will not have anyone to fight against now.'

They were pleased with the victory, but sorry that the young men no longer had anyone on whom to practise their warrior's craft.

24 One of the Spartan kings swore that he would raze to the ground a certain city that had often been a trouble to the Spartans. The ephors forbade him to do so, saying, 'You shall not wipe out and destroy the whet-stone of our young men.'

They called the hostile city the 'whet-stone of the young men' because the young men sharpened their military skills on it.

25 The Spartans did not have instructors to teach the boys wrestling, as they wanted it to be a contest of courage rather than skill. So when Lysander[1] was asked how Charon had come to defeat him, he replied, 'By knowing lots of moves.'[2]

The Spartan people did not consider any kind of victory impressive if it were won by cunning counsels rather than strength of mind and body.[3]

* * * * *

of Samos had been a member of the Athenian Confederacy and the Athenian naval base.

2 Quoted in Diogenianus CPG 1 7.34; Apostolius CPG 2 13.5. See *Adagia* I vii 83, where Erasmus comments 'this will suit people who demand something outrageous.'

23 (XXIII) Plutarch *Moralia* 233D. With this and the following apophthegm, cf 1.226 above and 6.336 below.

24 (XXIV) Plutarch *Moralia* 233E. See 2.23n above. In margin 'noble'

25 (XXV) Plutarch *Moralia* 233E
  1 For Lysander, see 1.288–303 above, but the text should probably read Lysanoridas. He was one of the Spartan garrison commanders in Thebes, who had to surrender to Charon and his fellow liberators in 397 BC. The occupying Spartan forces had actually engaged in wrestling matches with the Theban population. See Plutarch *Pelopidas* 7.
  2 Cf 2.71 below.
  3 But contrast 2.102 below.

The further any skill departs from the simplicity of nature the closer it approaches to deceit.

26 Philip entered Spartan country[1] and sent them a message enquiring whether they wished him to come as friend or foe. They sent back the reply: 'Neither.'

In one word they said what they had to say, which was typical of Spartans,[2] and boldly denied the king passage, which was typical of brave men.

27 The Spartans sent an ambassador to Antigonus, son of Demetrius.[1] Although he returned bringing from Antigonus a measure of wheat for each person at a time when there was a great food shortage, they fined him because they heard that he had addressed Antigonus as 'king.'

Such was the rigour of Spartan law that not even the relief of the famine by such a generous subvention could earn leniency and allow them to condone their successful ambassador's use of the one little word.

28 A man of evil morals made an excellent proposal. They approved the proposal, but setting aside the proposer, attributed it to a man of blameless character.

They were absolutely convinced that no standing in the community should be granted to evil-livers. They changed the proposer so that the appearance of his name should not bring discredit on the state. They did not change the proposal, as they did not want it to appear that they had allowed the public good to suffer because of private infamy.

Aulus Gellius records this incident.[1]

\* \* \* \* \*

26 (xxvi) Plutarch *Moralia* 233E. In margin 'frank'
  1 See 1.165 above.
  2 See 1.95 n2 above.

27 (xxvii) Plutarch *Moralia* 233E–F. In margin 'deed of note'
  1 Ie Antigonus II, king of Macedonia, 276 BC onwards. In 272 BC, Sparta appealed to Antigonus for help in resisting an invasion of their territory by Pyrrhus, king of Epirus.

28 (xxviii) Plutarch *Moralia* 233F. In margin 'deed of note'
  1 Aulus Gellius *Noctes Atticae* 18.3.2–8. The story is also to be found in Plutarch *Moralia* 41B (*On listening to lectures*).

**29** Two brothers were quarrelling. The Spartans fined the father for failing to deal with the disagreement between his sons.

They were of the opinion that the young men could be forgiven, but any fault they had committed in the hot-headedness of youth the Spartans laid at the father's door, as his authority should have ensured that no contention arose between his sons.

**30** A musician who was visiting Sparta was fined for playing his lyre with his fingers, and not with a plectrum.[1]

They were totally opposed to any change in accepted custom. The same attitude caused the famous incident when a Spartan cut two strings out of a nine-stringed lyre.[2]

**31** Two boys were fighting and one dealt the other a fatal blow.[1] As he lay dying, the other boys promised revenge, saying they would kill the boy who had injured him. But he said, 'Do not do it, for heaven's sake! It would not be right, for I would have done the same to him, if I had got in first and had been strong enough.'

What a truly Spartan character! Though conquered and dying he spoke up for the one who had beaten him in fair fight, winning by fighting ability and not by trickery. How happy such characters would have been if they had been brought up from their earliest years to seek true virtue rather than the toughness demanded of soldiers!

**32** At the time when it was the Spartan custom to let the free-born boys steal anything they could, though only if they did not get caught, which was a disgrace, some boys stole a live vixen-cub and gave it to one of their number

\* \* \* \* \*

**29** (xxix) Plutarch *Moralia* 233F. In margin 'deed of note'

**30** (xxx) Plutarch *Moralia* 233F. In margin 'an uncompromising act'
   1 Presumably because playing with the fingers would give more scope for ornamentation. Erasmus has added the explanatory words 'and not with a plectrum.'
   2 See 1.175 above.

**31** (xxxi) Plutarch *Moralia* 233F. In margin 'noble'
   1 Erasmus neglects to say that the fatal blow was struck with a sickle. Perhaps he thought this unfair. Cf his comments on unfair practices at 2.41 below.

**32** (xxxii) Plutarch *Moralia* 234A–B. In margin 'courageous'

to keep. When the owners came looking for it, he kept it hidden under his cloak. The creature, maddened, gnawed right through the boy's side to his vitals, but, to prevent the theft being discovered, he made not a sound and didn't give the secret away. After the others had gone and the boys saw what had happened, they reproached him, saying 'It would have been better to let the vixen be discovered than conceal it to the death.' 'Never,' he replied. 'It is better to die in agony than be branded with the infamy of saving through weakness a life ever after tainted with shame.'[1]

There could be nothing more perfect than this, if the true wisdom had been added to spirits so richly endowed by birth.

33 Some people met some Spartans on the road, and said, 'You're lucky, Spartans. Some robbers have only just left here.' 'By Enyalius,' they retorted (that's the Spartan name for Mars).[1] 'We're not lucky. They're the lucky ones, because they didn't meet us.'

The Spartans were quite unafraid of all the things that normal people fear.

34 A Spartan was asked what skills he had. 'I am a free man,' he replied.

The Spartan race was not trained either in philosophical disciplines or in crafts.[1] They simply guarded their liberty with independent spirit, not submitting readily either to men or to vice.

35 A Spartiate boy was captured by King Antigonus[1] and sold as a slave. He obeyed the man who had bought him in everything that he felt a free-born person could properly do. However, when he was asked to bring a chamber-

* * * * *

1 For the ignominies suffered at Sparta by those branded as cowards see 1.71 n2 above; Xenophon *Respublica Lacedaemoniorum* 9.4–6. Xenophon remarks that death is preferable to a life so ignominious.

33 (XXXIII) Plutarch *Moralia* 234B. In margin 'spirited'
   1 Mars is the Roman name for the god of war. Enyalius was a title of Ares, the corresponding Greek god of war.

34 (XXXIV) Plutarch *Moralia* 234B. In margin 'noble'
   1 See 1.189 above.

35 (XXXV) Plutarch *Moralia* 234B–C. In margin 'noble, resolute'
   1 Sparta and Athens resisted King Antigonus II of Macedonia in the period 267–263 BC.

pot, he would not brook that, but said, 'I will not be a slave.' When his master insisted, the boy went up onto the roof, and declaring, 'You will find out what kind of a purchase you have made,' threw himself down from the height and was killed.[2]

He could live as a captive, but he could not perform slave tasks, and he won his freedom by death.

36 Another boy, when he was being sold, was asked by the prospective purchaser, 'Will you be a good reliable boy if I buy you?' He replied, 'Yes, and if you don't buy me too.'

Not even a slave's fate could teach him slave's words. A naturally honest person will be honest everywhere and with everybody.

37 Another boy was captured and when he was being sold, the auctioneer announced the sale of a slave. 'You villain,' he cried. 'Announce the sale of a captive, will you?'[1]

He was not ashamed of his hard lot, but he was ashamed of being called 'slave.' Such was his passion for liberty.

38 A certain Spartan had as a device on his shield a fly, painted life-size. When some people made fun of it and said he had done it so as not to be noticed, he retorted, 'On the contrary, it's to make me stand out. I go so close to the enemy that they can see for themselves what my device is like.'

He smartly turned the reproach of cowardice into a proof of valour.

39 On another occasion, after dinner, a lyre was brought in. A Spartan present commented, 'Spartans don't indulge in silly activities.'

In this they differed markedly from other Greeks, who considered no dinner party really satisfactory without music. The Spartan thought this

* * * * *

2 Seneca records the story at *Epistulae Morales* 77.14, an essay on suicide. See also 2.156 below)

36    (xxxvi) Plutarch *Moralia* 234C

37    (xxxvii) Plutarch *Moralia* 234C
    1 Cf 2.19 above

38    (xxxviii) Plutarch *Moralia* 234C–D. In margin 'smart'

39    (xxxix) Plutarch *Moralia* 234D. In margin 'stern'

silly, being of the opinion that it was more civilized to spice up the after-dinner drinking with decent and humorous conversation[1] than by listening to the empty twanging of the lyre.[2]

40 A citizen of Sparta was asked whether the road to Sparta was safe. 'It depends,' he replied, 'what sort of person you are when you make the journey. Lions going in that direction weep, but hares lurking in the shadows we hunt.'[1]

He meant that it wasn't safe for wild and violent men to go in the direction of Sparta, nor for soft, unmanly ones, because those who approached with hostile intent would get a dusty reception from those who were stronger than they were, and they wouldn't allow fops to indulge their perverted appetites in the shadows.

41 During a wrestling bout (for which the Spartan word is *cheirapsia*, 'clinch'), one of the contestants was gripping the other by the neck and was to no effect and against the rules hitting him and dragging him down. The other, who was being forced into submission as his opponent hung onto him, felt

* * * * *

1 Cf the dedicatory epistle 15 above, for Lycurgus' encouragement of humour at Sparta (Plutarch *Lycurgus* 25.1–2).
2 Erasmus' comment is no doubt based on various Spartan sayings already translated which disparaged musical expertise: eg 1.141–2, 1.169, 1.183, 1.224. He has yet to translate various sayings which on the other hand illustrate the Spartans' appreciation of music of a rousing and inspiring nature and its importance in their educational curriculum, provided it was in a traditional and non-innovative style: eg 2.60 n1, 2.95, 2.97. His comment here is rather superficial and the wording perhaps reveals his own attitude towards musical expertise. His remarks in various places indicate that he thought that the time spent on becoming an expert player or athlete would be better spent on cultivating the mind and on activities conducive to moral worth. The philosophers also frequently condemn such trivial pursuits. See General Index: trivial pursuits.

40 (XL) Plutarch *Moralia* 234D. In margin 'incisive'
  1 Textual problems have arisen in the transmission of the Greek text, occasioned by the use of Laconian dialect in Plutarch. Erasmus translates the reading as found in Aldus' text and follows Regio's interpretation in the words 'hares in the shadows we hunt.' See the dedicatory epistle 8 n21 above. One suggested modern emendation of the text gives a meaning, 'Lions wander where they will, but hares we chase over those lands.'

41 (XLI) Plutarch *Moralia* 234E. In margin 'neat'

his strength going, so he bit the arm that gripped him. The other cried, 'Spartan, you bite like a woman!' He retorted, 'No, like a lion.'[1]

How quickly he turned the taunt of cowardice into a proof of courage! The worst disgrace known among the Spartans was the reproach of womanish weakness. He was right to save himself by biting, when the loser was attacking him contrary to the rules of the contest.

42 A lame man who was going off to fight was laughed at by the others. 'It's not people who run away who are needed,' he said 'but those who stand fast and keep their place in the line.'[1]

43 One of them was wounded by an arrow[1] and as he lay dying said, 'I am not distressed at dying, but at being killed by a skulking archer, no better than a woman, and I am sorry to die without having achieved anything impressive.'

It is a solace to the conquered to fall to the courage and skill of a warrior. The Spartans fought with the sword at close quarters and did not

* * * * *

1 In translating this anecdote Erasmus seems to be thinking of a passage in Galen which he had added in 1528 to *Adagia* I ix 79 *Dare manus* 'To put one's hands up': '. . . like one of those unskilled wrestlers who, when they have been thrown by the wrestling-master and are lying on their backs on the ground, are still so far from admitting the fall that they continue to hold those who have thrown them by their necks, refusing to let them go, and think that this is evidence that they have not been beaten.' As the last sentence of his comment makes clear, Erasmus assumes that the contestant on top did the biting as a last resort because the loser was refusing to follow the rules and acknowledge defeat as soon as he had been floored. Consequently he has added the words *praeter legem* 'against the rules' (line 3) for which there is nothing in the Greek text (and see again at the end, *praeter ius certaminis* 'contrary to the rules of the contest.') At Plutarch *Moralia* 186D (*Sayings of kings and commanders*) 5.184 below, it is Alcibiades, the loser, who bites his opponent. Erasmus there comments that it is the opposite of this story. See Cicero *Tusculan Disputations* 5.27–77 for the determination of Spartan youths to win at all costs.

42 (XLII) Plutarch *Moralia* 234E
    1 Cf 1.35 and 1.122 above, 2.139 below.

43 (XLIII) Plutarch *Moralia* 234E. In margin 'noble'
    1 According to Plutarch *Aristides* 17.7, this was one Callicrates, killed at the battle of Plataea (see 1.316 n1 above). The invading Persians and their allies employed bow and arrow, a weapon not used by the Greeks. It was on the same occasion that the incident concerning Pausanias took place; see 2.116 n5 below.

think it brave to kill someone by shooting an arrow from a distance, as even women can do that.[2] Men can depart this life more contentedly if they leave behind them the memory of things well done.

44 A Spartan went into an inn and gave the innkeeper some fish to prepare. The innkeeper asked him for cheese and oil. 'What!' said he. 'If I had cheese, I wouldn't need fish!'[1]

The innkeeper asked him for cheese and oil to make the fish tasty. The Spartan, who was satisfied with very plain fare, thought it unnecessary to combine one food with another when either was enough on its own. How different is the attitude of those who combine a hundred different items in one dish!

45 A man was speaking admiringly of Lampis of Aegina[1] and saying how lucky he was, because he owned a large merchant fleet and must be very rich. A Spartan commented, 'I am not impressed by good fortune that hangs on ropes.'

All wealth is in the hand of fortune, but especially wealth which merchants entrust to ships. If the ropes break, shipwreck follows, with the loss of all the goods. This is why a philosopher[2] who was asked whether he thought the living were more numerous than the dead, asked in his turn how he should classify those who take to ships – they were hardly to be counted as really living when their whole existence was spent in peril of their lives.

* * * * *

2 For the cowardice of shooting from a distance instead of engaging hand to hand, see 1.155 above.

44 (XLIV) Plutarch *Moralia* 234E–F. In margin 'abstemious'
  1 See *Adagia* III iv 89 *Si caseum haberem, non desiderarem opsonium* 'If I had cheese, I wouldn't want meat.' Though *opsonium* can mean any kind of prepared dish, including meat, in this apophthegm Erasmus interprets it as 'fish,' possibly basing this on Plutarch *Moralia* 667F–668A (*Table-talk*), where it is said that at Athens it had come to mean primarily 'fish,' which was there considered a great delicacy. The same information is found at Athenaeus *Deipnosophistae* 276E–F, another source much used by Erasmus. As Erasmus did not like fish, he no doubt thinks 'fish' more appropriate for an ascetic Spartan.

45 (XLV) Plutarch *Moralia* 234F. In margin 'astute'
  1 Lampis of Aegina was a shipowner famed for his wealth. Aegina is an island lying between Athens and the Peloponnese.
  2 Ie Anacharsis, one of the Seven Sages; see 2.161 below.

46 Someone accused a Spartan of lying. 'Of course,' he said, 'we are free men. Others get beaten if they don't tell the truth.'[1]

　　The Spartan was quite unabashed by the shocking accusation and turned it with a joke, incidentally taunting the one who made it with not being a Spartan and so not being free, because a whipping is what slaves get to teach them a lesson if they tell any sort of lie.

47 A man was trying to get a corpse to stand upright without success. After trying everything, 'By Jove,' he said, 'there must be something inside.'

　　This Spartan had the idea that a spirit or an evil genius was lurking within the corpse. Corpses are stood upright on the funeral pyre.[1]

48 Tynnichus bore the death of his son Thrasybulus with great fortitude. The following epigram was composed in the son's memory:

> To Pitane[1] you came, Thrasybulus,
> 　Dead upon your shield.
> With seven dread wounds returned to us
> 　From Argive battle field,
> And all upon your breast displayed.
> 　I, Tynnichus, your sire,
> With these words your corpse have laid,
> 　All bloodied, on the pyre:
> 'Tears are for cowards shed. You I shall not weep.
> True son of father and of fatherland you sleep.'

49 The bath attendant was supplying Alcibiades the Athenian[1] with a great

*　*　*　*　*

46　(XLVI) Plutarch *Moralia* 234F. In margin 'clever'
　1 Spartan boys were trained to be cunning and live by their wits. The crime for which they would be beaten was being found out. See 2.32 above and 2.94 below.

47　(XLVII) Plutarch *Moralia* 234F
　1 Cf 3.187 below

48　(XLVIII) Plutarch *Moralia* 235A. In margin 'brave'
　1 Pitane was one of the districts of the city of Sparta. See 2.116 n7 below.

49　(XLIX) Plutarch *Moralia* 235A. In margin 'witty'
　1 During one phase of his brilliant but erratic career, Alcibiades defected to

deal of water. A Spartan who observed this said, 'What have we here? He's pouring extra water as if he's not clean but very dirty.'

This jibe pointed the finger at Alcibiades' notorious life-style.

50 King Philip of Macedon wrote to the Spartans, giving them some orders. They answered, 'In reply to yours, no.'[1]

They answered the king's long missive with the monosyllable, NO, which they wrote in huge letters filling up the space usually taken up by the text of the letter.[2] In this they displayed both the economy of words for which the Spartans were famous and also their usual boldness.[3]

51 On another occasion Philip had entered Spartan territory with his army and things had reached such a pass that the Spartans would, it seemed, all perish to a man. The king remarked to one of the Spartan warriors, 'What will you do now, you Spartans?' To which he replied, 'What else than die bravely, since we alone of all the Greeks have learned to be free and not obey others.'[1]

No one who is prepared to die is compelled to be a slave.[2] What a good sweet thing is liberty bought at the price of death; what a wretched thing is a servitude worse than death! What mental attitude shall we then ascribe to people who deliberately surrender themselves to a bondage from which there is no escape, either by ransom or by free release?[3]

\* \* \* \* \*

Sparta during the Peloponnesian War and lived like a Spartan, taking cold drenches. See Plutarch *Moralia* 52E (*How to tell a flatterer*). The bath attendant poured water over the bathers. If this incident occurred at Sparta, Alcibiades wanted more than the usual modest amount with which Spartans were satisfied. See 5.191 below.

50 (L) Plutarch *Moralia* 235A
  1 All three editions of *Apophthegmata* have a marginal note, 'This is not in our Greek text but in Philelphus.' For Filelfo, see the dedicatory epistle 7 n20 above.
  2 This detail comes from Plutarch *Moralia* 513A (*On talkativeness*).
  3 See 1.95 n2 above.

51 (LI) Plutarch *Moralia* 235B. In margin 'brave'
  1 Cf 1.157 and 1.165 above.
  2 See 1.157 n2 above.
  3 This last sentence possibly refers to the binding vows of the monastic profession. See Ep 447:34–7, 169–74.

52 After defeating Agis in battle, Antipater[1] demanded fifty boys as hostages. Eteocles, who was an ephor at the time, replied that he would not hand over boys for fear that they would get used to living without correction and become incapable of accepting the discipline of their native land, and so would not even be citizens.[2] He would however hand over twice as many women and old men. Antipater threatened them with dire retribution if they did not accede to his demands. The people replied with one voice, 'If the thing you demand is worse than death, we shall find death the easier thing.'

It would not be so wonderful maybe to find this kind of courage in one or two people in the citizen body, but to see such unanimity in the whole people is really extraordinary. This story also reminds us how carefully we should approach the task of bringing up those of tender years and imbuing them with sound principles, since the Spartans did not consider that young persons left to grow up undisciplined should be treated as citizens. This is like a mother rejecting the son she has borne if his moral standards do not measure up to those of his ancestors.

53 At the Olympic Games an old man wanted to watch a contest that had already started but there were no seats left. He went from place to place being laughed at and made the butt of jokes, because no one would let him in. When he came to the Spartans, not only did all the boys rise from their seats but many of the men too offered him their place.[1] All the other Greeks assembled there applauded and spoke admiringly of this traditional Spartan behaviour, but the old man 'shaking his grey beard and grizzled locks,'[2] said with tears in his eyes, 'How sad it is that all the Greeks know what is the right thing to do, but only the Spartans do it.'

* * * * *

52 (LII) Plutarch *Moralia* 235B–C. In margin 'outspoken'
1 Antipater 397–319 BC was a trusted Macedonian general serving first under Philip II. Under his successor Alexander he held important administrative posts and was regent of Macedonia during Alexander's absence. He defeated Agis III of Sparta at Megalopolis in 311–310 BC, after Sparta had organized rebellion against Macedonia. After Alexander's death he was one of the successors contending for domination.
2 Only those who submitted to the traditional Spartan discipline could be full Spartiate citizens. See 2.99 n1 below.

53 (LIII) Plutarch *Moralia* 235C–D. In margin 'telling'
1 See 1.269 n5 above; 2.54 and 2.59 below.
2 Homer *Iliad* 22.74, 24.516.

**54** The same thing is said to have occurred in Athens during the Panathenaea.[1] The Athenians were making fun of an old man, pretending to offer him a seat and then closing up when he approached. After he had walked round nearly all of them, he came to where the Spartan spectators were sitting. They all rose from the benches and offered him a place.[2] The people were delighted with this and showed their appreciation with clapping and signs of approval. Meantime one of the 'true Spartans' remarked, 'In the name of the Twin Gods, the Athenians know what's the right thing, but they don't do it.'

    Philosophy was much in vogue at Athens, teaching what was base and what was honourable. The 'true Spartans' would not countenance such studies, but, following their ancestral code of conduct, demonstrated virtue both in character and in action. So it came about that Athens had the words of philosophy while the Spartans had the real thing. The Spartan's comment reminds us that it is disgraceful to know the proper thing to do and yet do the opposite.

**55** A beggar asked a Spartan to give him something. He replied, 'If I give you something, it will confirm you as a beggar. The person who first gave you something started you on your shameful way of life and made you idle.'

    The Spartans condemned begging because they hated being idle and were content with very little. Generosity to beggars looks like a virtue, but this goodness on the part of pious persons often feeds the selfish laziness of the reprobate.

**56** A Spartan saw someone making a collection for the gods. 'I've no time,' said he, 'for gods who are poorer than myself.'

    This anecdote shows that the practice of going out with a begging-bowl under the pretext of religion is nothing new. Very often what is donated

\* \* \* \* \*

54  (LIV) Plutarch *Moralia* 235D–E
  1 The Panathenaea was the great annual festival held at Athens in honour of Pallas Athene, the patron goddess of Athens. At the Greater Panathenaea, held every four years, there were athletic and musical contests open to people from all over Greece.
  2 Cf 2.53 just above. The story is also related by Cicero *De senectute* 63 but that is not Erasmus' source here.

55  (LV) Plutarch *Moralia* 235E. In margin 'sharp'

56  (LVI) Plutarch *Moralia* 235E

because people think it is for some religious cause is not spent on the gods, who have no need of anything, but used to supply the extravagance and lusts of villainous men.

**57** A Spartan caught an adulterer in bed with his wife,[1] who was an ugly woman. 'Poor fellow,' he said, 'whatever drove you to this?'

First of all we have here an example of self-control. Who would keep his temper when faced with an adulterer caught in the act? This man seems rather to have felt sorry for the other, who, it appears, had been driven by some dire compulsion to have sex with an ugly woman. It seemed unlikely that the adulterer would get himself into that particular tricky situation just for pleasure's sake.

**58** Another Spartan heard an orator weaving together his swathes of circumlocutory speech. 'By the Twin Gods,' he commented. 'What a powerful fellow! He has nothing to say, yet he can roll his tongue round it splendidly!'

The Spartans appreciated a speech only if it were brief, truthful, and dealt with a serious subject. So this man thought it ludicrous that the speaker could generate such a wealth of words on an imaginary topic.[1]

**59** A man who was visiting Sparta observed the respect shown there by the younger men to the older ones. 'Sparta is the only place,' he commented, 'where there are advantages in growing old.'

Poverty is a wretched, heavy burden as the comic writer says.[1] But the greatest misery is that it makes men laughing-stocks as well, as says the Satirist.[2] So among the disadvantages brought by advancing years, one of the greatest is that old men are usually treated with mockery and contempt.

\* \* \* \* \*

57  (LVII) Plutarch *Moralia* 235E. In margin 'forbearing'
 1 Erasmus has got the idea that it is the man's own wife who was involved from a similar story in Plutarch *Moralia* 525D (*On avarice*), used in 6.270 below. Adultery was supposed to be unthinkable in Sparta: see 1.275 above. The original remark is in Spartan dialect.

58  (LVIII) Plutarch *Moralia* 235E. In margin 'loquacity'
 1 For numerous aphorisms on this subject, see 1.95 n2 above.

59  (LIX) Plutarch *Moralia* 235F. In margin 'honoured old-age'
 1 Ie the Roman dramatist Terence, in *Phormio* 94.
 2 Ie the Roman satirist Juvenal, in *Satires* 3.153.

Accordingly, many people saw Sparta as the most honourable home for old age.[3]

60  A Spartan was asked what he thought of the poet Tyrtaeus. 'Good,' he said, 'for corrupting[1] the minds of the young.'

Plato considered that the poetry of Homer had nothing to contribute to the kind of republic he wanted to see established.[2] Likewise, the Spartans had no time for poets who wrote verse that pleased rather than improved.

61  A man with very bad eyes went off to the war. Several people said to him, 'Where are you off to with that complaint of yours? What do you expect to do?' 'If nothing else,' he replied, 'you will find I have certainly blunted the enemy's sword.'

I haven't made up my mind whether this was a witty remark or a brave one.

62  Two Spartans, Buris and Spartis, volunteered to go to Xerxes, the Persian king, and pay the penalty which the Spartans had incurred, as declared by the oracle, for killing the envoys the king had sent.[1] When they came before

* * * * *

3  This translates the reading of 1531. The later editions have 'the honourable home of virtue.' See *Adagia* IV ii 68: *In sola Sparta expedit senescere* 'Only in Sparta does it pay to grow old.'

60  (LX) Plutarch *Moralia* 235F. In margin 'a useless skill'
  1  The meaning of the Greek word (possibly a Laconian dialectal word) translated by Erasmus as 'corrupting' is dubious, but more likely means 'sharpening.' This meaning is spelt out at Plutarch *Moralia* 959B (where the saying is attributed to Leonidas). Erasmus follows Filelfo here rather than Regio, who opts for the second meaning. See the dedicatory epistle 7–8 nn20 and 21 above. The fragments of Tyrtaeus' poetry suggest battle songs and a military context. See 1.314 above.
  2  Plato *Republic* 10.607A

61  (LXI) Plutarch *Moralia* 235F. In margin 'brave'

62  (LXII) Plutarch *Moralia* 235F–236B. In margin 'love of country'
  1  The Persian envoys came to various cities in Greece after the collapse of the Ionian revolt in 494 BC, demanding submission. Athens and Sparta executed them. The oracle emanated from the shrine of Talthybius (Agamemnon's herald), situated at Sparta.

him, they asked him to execute them as representatives of the Spartans, choosing whatever manner of death he thought appropriate. The king, impressed both by their patriotism and by their bravery, released them from all punishment and asked them to stay in his court. 'How can we live here,' they replied, 'leaving our country, its laws and its men, when it is for their sake that we have made this long journey for the purpose of dying?' Indarnus, the king's general, also tried to persuade them, saying that they would have the same status as those held in highest honour among the king's associates. They replied to this, 'You do not seem to be aware what an enormous blessing liberty is and that no sane man would exchange it even for the whole realm of Persia.'

This incident sets before us an example of patriotism, of unshakable love of liberty and of a mind free from the terror of death.

Herodotus in book 7 calls the pair Sperthies and Boulis.[2]

63 A man had avoided asking a Spartan friend to stay with him the day before, but the next day, having borrowed bed-covers, he gave him a lavish welcome. But the Spartan threw the covers down and stamped on them, saying, 'Because of these, I wasn't allowed to sleep even on a rush mat last night.'

This was a witty dig at people of modest means who try to appear rich by borrowing or hiring furniture, especially to entertain visitors or for weddings or any other sort of special occasion. While it is foolish to make a parade of one's wealth, it is even more ridiculous to show off furnishings belonging to other people, sometimes even hired for the occasion. The Spartans however invited not just king's ambassadors but kings[1] themselves to their common dining-hall, being of the opinion that the simplicity observed there would actually earn them great respect.

64 Another Spartan, when visiting Athens, observed people hawking pickles and delicatessen, and pursuing various dishonourable occupations, such as tax-collecting[1] and pimping, seeing no activity as shameful. When he

* * * * *

2 Herodotus 7.133–6, who also calls the Persian general Hydarnes, the form of the name used in LB. The last sentence was added in 1535.

63 (LXIII) Plutarch Moralia 236B. In margin 'witty'
1 For example, Dionysius I, tyrant of Sicily. See 2.84 below.

64 (LXIV) Plutarch Moralia 236B–C. In margin 'lack of restraint'
1 Tax-collecting was a speculative profit-making business in ancient times, which usually enriched the operators. As Spartiates were forbidden to engage in any

returned home, his fellows asked him how things were in Athens. 'Everything is OK,' he replied, sarcastically indicating that at Athens everything was acceptable, nothing considered disreputable.

The wit of the remark lies in the fact that it can be taken in more than one way.

65 Another Spartan, when asked some question or other, answered, 'No.' The questioner then said that he was lying. To which he replied, 'Don't you see how stupid it is to ask a question to which you already know the answer.'

This was his smart criticism of the other's fault of talkativeness, since he was trying to manufacture something to talk about out of nothing.[1]

66 Some Spartans came on an embassy to the despot Lygdamis.[1] Their audience with him was constantly being postponed on various pretexts. At last, after all the other excuses, they were told that he was not in very good health and was feeling rather weak. The ambassadors replied, 'Good God, we haven't come to wrestle with him but to have a talk with him!'

This was a neat criticism of the barbarian king's arrogance and foppishness since he neglected serious business for any reason, however frivolous.

67 A Spartan was about to be initiated into the holy mysteries and the officiant asked him what was the worst thing in his whole life that his conscience accused him of. He replied, 'The gods already know that.' The other pressed him, saying, 'You have to declare it.' The Spartan

* * * * *

money-making activity or craft or sedentary occupation (see Xenophon *Respublica Lacedaemoniorum* 7.2), they no doubt considered tax-collecting, like the other activities mentioned, a degrading occupation for a free citizen. 'Craft or sedentary occupation' is Erasmus' version of τέχνη βάναυσος 'artisan skill,' which covers smithing, building, carpentry, etc, and strictly sedentary occupations such as potting, weaving, tailoring. See 1.70 above, 2.117 and 3.12 below.

65 (LXV) Plutarch *Moralia* 236C
  1 See Plutarch *Moralia* 512B (*On talkativeness*).

66 (LXVI) Plutarch *Moralia* 236C
  1 'The despot Lygdamis' was sole ruler of the island of Naxos 560–524 BC. See 1.216 n1 above.

67 (LXVII) Plutarch *Moralia* 236D. Cf 1.123 above.

then asked him, 'Do I have to tell you or the god?' When the other answered, 'The god,' he replied, 'You remove yourself then, so that I can tell him.'

**68** A Spartan was once passing a tomb at night and thought he saw a ghost. He ran at it with his lance levelled and as he struck at it, cried out, 'Spirit, where can you run to escape from me? You will now die a second time.'

What a mind utterly free of all terrors, quite undaunted by spectres and hobgoblins!

**69** A certain Spartan took a vow to jump off the Leucadian cliff,[1] but when he climbed up and saw how high it was, he turned back. When people jeered at him for this, he replied, 'I didn't think my vow needed an even greater vow.'

He thus jokingly deflected the charge of cowardice and not sticking to his resolution. Anyone who sees himself performing some challenging deed should first pray the gods for a spirit equal to the deed.

**70** In the thick of battle a Spartan had his sword drawn and was about to plunge it into an enemy soldier when the signal was given to withdraw, so he did not make the fatal thrust. Someone asked him why he had not killed the man when he had him at his mercy. He replied, 'Because it is better to obey one's commander than kill the foe.'

We have here an example of military discipline. How far removed from such obedience are those who use war as a pretext for mere brigandage! In earlier days one was not allowed to strike the foe unless the trumpet had given the signal, and once the withdrawal was sounded killing a foe was treated as murder.

\* \* \* \* \*

**68** (LXVIII) Plutarch *Moralia* 236D. In margin 'absence of superstition'

**69** (LXIX) Plutarch *Moralia* 236D. In margin 'humorous'
  1 The Leucadian cliff was a high cliff on the island of Leucas off the northwest coast of Greece, from which unhappy lovers used to leap into the sea. Some, it is said, survived and were cured of their passion, others drowned. The poetess Sappho was supposed to have been the first to take the plunge. The leap became proverbial.

**70** (LXX) Plutarch *Moralia* 236E. In margin 'military discipline'

71 Someone said to a Spartan who had been defeated in a contest at the Olympic Games, 'Spartan, your opponent was better than you.' 'No,' he replied, 'just better at throws.'[1]

The contest was one of skill, not courage, so the Spartan did not consider himself inferior for being defeated. The wit of the remark depends on the ambiguity of the word 'better.' It means both 'more good' and 'more powerful,' 'stronger' or 'superior.'

72 The Aetolians once raided Spartan territory and took away 50,000 slaves. An elderly Spartan wittily commented, 'The enemy have done Sparta a great service, as they have relieved us of such a crowd.'

73 It was a Spartan custom that the king should go into battle preceded by a man wearing a garland on his head who had at some time won a victor's crown in an athletic contest. A certain Spartan at the Olympic Games was offered a large bribe, which he rejected with scorn. In the contest he eventually threw his opponent after a long hard struggle and took the victor's crown. Someone said to him, 'Well then, Spartan, what will you get out of your victory?' He smiled and promptly replied, 'I will march to meet the enemy in front of the king, wearing my crown.'

It is a noble spirit that loves glory more than money.

74 A certain Spartan soldier had been brought to the ground and the enemy was kneeling on his back ready to kill him. He asked his assailant to turn him over and plunge his sword into his breast rather than his back. When asked

* * * * *

71  (LXXI) Plutarch *Moralia* 236E. In margin 'witty'
    This is the last of Plutarch's *Sayings of Spartans*. The remaining Spartan apoph-thegms are taken from various sources, mainly other works of Plutarch.
    1 Cf 2.25 above.

72  (LXXII) Plutarch *Life of Agis and Cleomenes* 39 [18].3.

73  (LXXIII) Plutarch *Life of Lycurgus* 22.4. The prizes for victory offered at the major Greek athletic contests were in themselves of no value, consisting of wreaths of greenery (eg laurel, olive), though the victors expected other more tangible rewards from their home cities. Plutarch does not actually say that they wore the garland into battle. In margin 'noble'

74  (LXXIV) Plutarch *Life of Pelopidas* 18.4

why, he replied, 'So that my lover[1] may not see my body with sword-cuts dealt from behind and be shamed.'

75 Diagoras of Rhodes[1] saw his own sons and also the sons of both a son and a daughter crowned as victors at the Olympic Games. A Spartan said to him, 'Time to die, Diagoras. You won't ascend to Olympus.'

He meant that it was best to depart this life at the highest point of happiness and success. The story is found in Plutarch's *Lives*. Cicero also records it in the *Tusculans*, book 1.

What gives the remark its point is the ambiguity of the word Olympus. Olympus is a hill where the Olympian contests were held at the end of every five year period,[2] and it also signifies Heaven.[3]

76 A Spartan tutor took on the charge of a boy and when he was asked what he was going to teach him, 'I will make sure,' he said, 'that he takes pleasure in what is honourable and detests what is evil.'

Nothing contributes more to true happiness than loving virtue for itself and hating vice for itself.

\* \* \* \* \*

1 It was customary in Sparta for men and boys to enter into close relationships and share each other's fame and disgrace. See Plutarch *Lycurgus* 18; also 2.89 below.

75 (LXXV) Plutarch *Life of Pelopidas* 34 and Cicero *Tusculan Disputations* 1.46.111
   1 Diagoras of Rhodes was the first Olympic victor in a distinguished family of athletes, winning the boxing in 464 BC, a victory celebrated by Pindar in his seventh Olympian Ode. His son Damagetus won the pankration in 452 and 448, at which meeting a younger brother Acusilas won the boxing. A third son, Dorieus, won the pankration in 432, 428, and 424. In 404 Eucles, his daughter's son, won the boxing, and another grandson, Pisorrhodus, won the boys' boxing contest. See Harris 123.
   2 See 1.96 n1 above.
   3 The famous Mount Olympus (height 2911 metres) was the home of the gods, far above the concerns of men and 'to ascend to Olympus' signified becoming divine and joining the company of the gods, as eg Hercules did. Diagoras has achieved all an ordinary man can hope for. The mountain was in the far north of Greece, on the extreme border of Thessaly, and nowhere near Olympia in Elis in southern Greece where the Olympic Games were celebrated. However, several other hills bore the name Olympus, and one of these overlooked the plain where the Olympic sanctuary and the site of the games lay.

76 (LXXVI) Plutarch *Moralia* 452D (*On moral virtue*)

77 A traditional-type Spartan was asked what good it did to assign tutors to boys. 'They see to it,' he replied, 'that what is honourable becomes pleasurable to them as well.'

78 [a] In the Peloponnesian War, Callicratidas, the Spartan general, was urged to withdraw the fleet from Arginusae[1] and not engage with the Athenians. He refused to comply, saying that if the Spartans lost that fleet they could replace it, but they could not flee without incurring dishonour.

[b] Agesilaus said that it gave him pleasure to be praised by people who were not afraid to take him to task if they found fault with anything.

If such people praise anything, they do so out of conviction, not from fear or in order to flatter.

79 When Demonides[1] had his sandals stolen, he prayed that they would fit the thief's feet.

This looked like a blessing prayer, but actually it was a cursing prayer, as he was asking that the thief might have deformed feet like his own.

80 The Spartans sent relief supplies to the people of Smyrna when they were in need. They began to thank them profusely, but the Spartans interrupted. 'It's nothing,' they said. 'We and our horses went without dinner for one day and this is the proceeds.'

A favour is more acceptable if the one who bestows it makes light of it. Those who exaggerate their generosity (which is what most people do), lose much of the recipient's gratitude.

* * * * *

77   (LXXVII) Plutarch *Moralia* 439F (*Can virtue be taught?*)

78   (LXXVIII) [a] was used in *1531* and was replaced by [b] in *1532*, *1535*. [a] Cicero *De officiis* 1.84; [b] Plutarch *Moralia* 55C (*How to tell a flatterer*). See also Xenophon *Agesilaus* 11.5
   1 See 1.208 above, from a different source.

79   (LXXIX) Plutarch *Moralia* 18D (*How to study poetry*)
   1 This (the Latin form of the name) could be the same person as in 1.163. A similar story is told of Dorion in Athenaeus 338A. It is ascribed to one Damon and identified as a *chreia* 'in the form of a prayer' in Theon *Progymnasmata* 5.199 (Spengel II 100); see Introduction xxiv–xxvii.

80   (LXXX) Plutarch *Moralia* 64B (*How to tell a flatterer*). See also 2.190 below.

**81** When Cephisicrates was standing trial for treason, Lacydes, an intimate of Arcesilaus,[1] came with his other friends to support him. When the accuser demanded the production of a ring which could have proved his guilt, Cephisicrates stealthily dropped it on the ground. Lacydes observed this and put his foot over it. So Cephisicrates denied the charge and was acquitted. Then when the defendant was thanking the jury in the customary way, one of them, who had seen what happened, told him to thank Lacydes as well.

**82** Arcesilaus was suffering from a very painful attack of gout. Carneades[1] came to call on him and was sadly going away, but the other, pointing to his feet and his breast, said, 'Stay, Carneades. Nothing from there has reached here.'

He meant that his feet were in pain but his mind was free from pain.

### Early Spartan Customs

**83** As each person entered the common dining hall,[1] the oldest person present pointed to the door and said, 'No word goes out through here.'

This was to remind them not to blab if anyone said anything unguarded over the meal. This custom was instituted by Lycurgus.

**84** The Spartans set great store by a 'black broth' as they called it. In fact the

\* \* \* \* \*

**81** (LXXXI) Plutarch *Moralia* 63E (*How to tell a flatterer*). 2.81 and 2.82 do not seem to have any very obvious Spartan connection.
  1 Arcesilaus was an Ionian, born at Pitane in Asia Minor. (An area of Sparta was also called Pitane – this might have occasioned an association with Sparta in Erasmus' mind.) He was the founder of the sceptical Middle Academy at Athens and died c. 240 BC. Lacydes was his pupil and succeeded him as head of the Middle Academy. See 7.181–6, 7.336 below.

**82** (LXXXII) For the incident see Cicero *De finibus* 5.94 (where, however, the visitor is Charmides, an Epicurean).
  1 Carneades was a native of Cyrene in North Africa, a Doric settlement. He was the founder of the New Academy at Athens in the second century BC. See 1.1 n1 above, 7.217–8 below.

**83** (I) Plutarch *Moralia* 236F. The section on Early Spartan Customs (2.83–2.119) is translated from Plutarch *Moralia* 236F–240B (*The ancient customs of the Spartans*). In margin 'silence'
  1 For 'the common dining hall' see 1.262 above.

**84** (II) Plutarch *Moralia* 236F. In margin 'exercise as seasoning'

older men took it instead of meat, which they left to the younger men. For this reason, Dionysius, the despot of Sicily, we are told, bought a Spartan cook and ordered him to prepare this broth for him, no expense spared; but when he tasted it, he found it revolting and spat it out. The cook then remarked, 'You have to eat this broth, your majesty, after exercising in Spartan fashion and swimming in the Eurotas.'

Cicero in book 5 of the *Tusculans* has a more amusing version of the same story which is somewhat different from Plutarch's.[1] He tells us that Dionysius had dinner in the common mess-hall at Sparta and after the meal said that he had not liked the black broth which had been the main dish. The man who had prepared the broth said that it wasn't surprising that he hadn't liked it, as it didn't have the proper seasonings. When Dionysius wanted to know what these might be, he replied, 'The hard work of the hunt, sweating, running after a swim in the Eurotas, hunger, and thirst. These are the seasonings used in Spartan meals.'[2]

85 The Spartans drink in moderation at their communal meals and afterwards leave the hall without using any torches, as they are not allowed to light their way on this route or any other. This is to get them used to travelling boldly and fearlessly at night in the dark.

In wartime this practice sometimes become a necessity.

86 These same Spartans did indeed learn to read and write but would have nothing to do with other, foreign, intellectual disciplines, refusing to admit either the people who taught such things or even books on the subjects. Their scholarship was summed up in this: obey the magistrates wholeheartedly, bear toil patiently, and in battle conquer or die.

At one time some of the Romans were of the same mind, the ones, that is, who expelled the Greek philosophers from Rome because their novel teachings were enticing the young away to idleness and neglect of duty, teaching them to talk, to be sure, but making them unfit to fulfil their obligations to the state.[1] What would these Romans have said if they had come

\* \* \* \* \*

1 Cicero *Tusculan Disputations* 5.34.98
2 For hunger and thirst as the best seasoning see 4.44 and 5.93 below.

85  (III) Plutarch *Moralia* 237A. In margin 'getting used to the dark'

86  (IV) Plutarch *Moralia* 237A. In margin 'simple philosophy'
1 See n1 on Erasmus' preamble 19 above.

across those sophistical conundrums, the stultifying complications of the nominal and the real?[2]

87 They always wore a single garment without a tunic and had grubby bodies, as they abstained almost entirely from baths and the use of body lotions.[1]

People like this, who are both poor and tough, are not readily attacked. Nor were they driven to seek wealth by evil means, being content with so little. This was how the Spartans lived, knowing nothing of either philosophy or Christ. Are we not ashamed of our self-indulgence? We call people religious when they are content with four layers of clothing.

88 The young men slept by troop and company in communal dormitories, on beds of vegetation which they collected for themselves, pulling by hand without any implement the tops of the rushes which grew along the Eurotas. In winter they added a layer of a kind of moss which they mixed with the rushes, as it was believed to have heat-giving properties.

Now what about those people who sleep stretched out on goose feather mattresses and complain that the hard bed gives them a pain in the side?

89 It was acceptable among the Spartans to become emotionally attached to boys of good character for their qualities of mind, but it was considered disgraceful to have physical relations with them, as this suggested love for

* * * * *

2 Nominalism and Realism were schools of thought dealing with such topics as language, meaning, reality, existence, knowledge, and universals – logical problems bequeathed to the Middle Ages in part by Aristotle's *Categories* – and were the stuff of mediaeval logic, metaphysics, and theology. Erasmus of course had had direct experience of all this in his own education and often expresses impatience with its hair-splitting complexity and irrelevance. He often calls mediaeval scholasticism 'sophistry.'

87 (v) Plutarch *Moralia* 237B. In margin 'thrifty'
 1 This paragraph refers to the training of boys; see Plutarch *Lycurgus* 16.12. The wearing of a single garment was enforced from the age of twelve. Adult Spartans did not take hot baths, which were considered effeminate and enervating, but they did take cold drenches; see 2.49 above. Plutarch considered the taking of cold baths ostentatious and bad for the health; see Plutarch *Moralia* 131B (*Advice about keeping well*).

88 (vi) Plutarch *Moralia* 237B. In margin 'thrifty'

89 (vii) Plutarch *Moralia* 237C. In margin 'love of the mind'

the body rather than the mind. If anyone was accused of improper conduct towards boys, he was a social outcast for the rest of his life and ineligible for any public position.

Thus the law, protecting those of tender years, allowed older persons to love them, but without any sordid implications.[1] This holds good not only with children, but with spouses too. A man does not truly love his wife if he loves her for her body rather than herself.

90 It was customary for youths, when they were going somewhere, to be asked by the older men where they were going and for what purpose. Anyone who didn't reply or offered a frivolous reason was given a dressing-down. An older man who failed to take to task a youth who did something wrong before his very eyes had to pay the same penalty as if he had done the deed himself. Anyone who resented being corrected brought shame on himself.

It is only right to blame the faults of children on those whose task it is to control or correct them. Furthermore, the older men had a compelling reason not to let the boys see them doing anything unseemly themselves, for how could they have the face to censure the younger generation if they were deserving of censure themselves?[1]

91 Anyone caught doing wrong was compelled to walk round a certain altar in the city, reciting a chant about his own shortcomings. This had the effect of making him blame himself in his own words.

Boys of a noble disposition are directed more effectively towards good by shame and the desire for commendation. To be whipped or beaten is only for slaves.[1]

92 Furthermore, it was expected that the young should not only respect and obey their own parents, but also honour all older persons,[1] standing aside

* * * * *

1 Cf Plato *Republic* 3.403; Plutarch *Moralia* 11F (*The education of children*).

90 (VIII) Plutarch *Moralia* 237C. In margin 'wise'
1 For this whole paragraph see Plutarch *Moralia* 14A (*The education of children*).

91 (IX) Plutarch *Moralia* 237C. In margin 'reprimand'
1 For this paragraph, see Plutarch *Moralia* 9A (*The education of children*). Cf 2.46 above.

92 (X) Plutarch *Moralia* 237D. In margin 'communal living'
1 Cf 1.341 above.

for them in the street, rising to offer them their seats,[2] and not talking or making a noise when they went by. As a result of this, each person had authority not only over his own children, slaves, and possessions as in other states, but had as much right over his friends' and neighbours' children and possessions as over his own. So everything was to be held totally in common and everybody was to look after what belonged to other people in the same way as he looked after what was his own.

They realized the advantages to be gained from common ownership not imposed from outside but arising naturally from mutual goodwill. Pythagoras was ultimately responsible for the idea that 'everything is shared among friends,'[3] and this concept they wished to have the widest possible application in their society. For all fellow-citizens are friends. How much more those who share the same faith! Indeed, all human beings should be motivated by mutual benevolence simply because they are members of the same human race.

93 If a boy was punished by someone and complained to his father, the father would be censured if he did not thereupon give his son another beating. Their ancestral constitution had given them such mutual confidence in each other that they believed no one would order anyone else's son to do anything improper, as they treated other people's children as if they were their own.

Children do not yet understand right and wrong and so need correction. But when boys are beaten by their teachers they usually complain to their parents of the cruelty of those who have corrected them. Because this undermines the authority of other older persons, the Spartans did not leave their children this opening, with the result that all older persons had the same authority over the boys as their parents.

94 In Sparta boys steal anything they can,[1] including food, learning to take

* * * * *

2 See 1.269 n5 above.
3 See *Adagia* I i 1: *Amicorum communia omnia* 'Between friends all is common'; Diogenes Laertius 8.10.

93 (XI) Plutarch *Moralia* 237D–E. In margin 'the discipline of children'

94 (XII) Plutarch *Moralia* 237E–F. In margin 'the art of stealing'
1 Cf 2.32 above. See also Xenophon *Respublica Lacedaemoniorum* 2.5–6 for this whole paragraph. A marginal note reads: 'This is not Plutarch's style. It comes from Xenophon.'

people unawares when they are asleep or not being sufficiently careful. The punishment if they are caught is a beating and going without food. They are kept on short rations anyway in order to make them bold and cunning, since they have to use their wits if they don't want to go hungry. This was one reason why they were made to suffer hunger. But another reason for giving them so little to eat was to get them used to never having enough to satisfy them and to being able to endure the pangs of hunger. They thought that this practice would make them more effective soldiers, if they could go without food and still continue to function efficiently. Furthermore, they would have more disciplined bodies able to subsist on poor fare, if they lived for long periods at small expense. Not only that, they believed that, if they were used to not having anything fancy and to eating gladly anything put in front of them, their bodies would grow healthier and taller, because less food means more height, since the body is not weighed down and so can grow upwards rather than sideways, and it also looks more attractive. A thin spare physique also contributes to mobility; fatness due to overeating hinders movement because of the weight.[2]

That race made no concessions to pleasure and indulgence but in everything put the good of the state first! In this they totally disagreed with the majority, who have this idea that there is nothing better than stuffing children with far too much food and drink, when in reality this not only makes them slow and useless for any work but makes their bodies ugly and their brains thick.

95 They paid as much attention to the style of music, melody and song as they did to food, dress, and the other things mentioned earlier. Their music was such that it stirred the mind and spirit and inspired an ardour for doing great things, in effect not unlike the divine afflatus.[1]

The other Greek states preferred soothing music that debilitated the spirit, inclining it to pleasure and softness. Plato thinks it very important what kind of music a nation listens to.[2]

\* \* \* \* \*

2 Similar ideas are expressed in Aulus Gellius 4.19.

95 (XIII) Plutarch *Moralia* 238A. In margin 'virile music'
   1 Erasmus here uses the phrase *adflatus divinus* 'divine afflatus' which Cicero uses quite often (eg at *Divinatio* 2.167) to translate the Greek word ἐνθουσιώδης [*enthousiōdēs*] which is in Plutarch's text here.
   2 See Plato *Republic* 398C–399E.

96 Their oratory was simple and unaffected, without refinement or frippery, and it was employed only in praise of those who had lived bravely and nobly, had given their lives for Sparta, and were extolled by all as blessed beings; or else it was employed in denouncing those who, for fear of danger, had never done anything out of the ordinary and because of their cowardice in the face of death were living lives of anguish and misery.[1] Finally it was employed in making declarations appropriate to each person's stage in life, that would inspire deeds of valour by implanting in their souls a passion for glory. To this end, there were three choirs put together at the festivals, drawn from each of the three age groups. The choir of older men began by singing, '*Valiant young warriors in days gone by were we*'; the second choir, made up of men in the prime of life, sang, '*Such are we now; try us if you will and see*'; and a third choir of boys sang, '*We in days to come the best by far shall be.*'

97 Moreover they marched in time to certain rhythms[1] which had the effect of stirring their spirits to courage, audacity, and contempt for death. They employed these rhythms in their choral dancing too, as well as when they advanced to engage with the enemy to the accompaniment of pipes.[2] Lycurgus indeed combined army drill with the practice of music to ensure that their impetuous eagerness for battle should be disciplined by musical rhythms and display harmony and unison. Hence it was the custom for the king to sacrifice to the Muses before joining battle, so that the fighting men should perform deeds worthy of honoured remembrance in the spoken and the written word.[3]

They allowed no one to introduce innovations[4] into the traditional music. Even Terpander,[5] the most senior and the finest lyre player of the age,

* * * * *

96   (xiv) Plutarch *Moralia* 238A–B. In margin 'three choirs'
  1 See 2.32 n1 above.

97   (xv) Plutarch *Moralia* 238C–D (music in battle) and 238B (innovations). In margin 'type of music'
  1 Cf 1.37 and 2.95 above. See Athenaeus 14.630F for Spartan warriors chanting the songs of Tyrtaeus (see 1.314 above) as they marched into battle.
  2 For 'pipes,' see 1.37 above.
  3 Cf 1.187 above.
  4 Cf 1.175 and 2.30 above.
  5 Terpander was a seventh-century BC poet and musician, who came originally from Lesbos but worked in Sparta. He was believed to be the first to win the music competition at the Carneian Games (see below n7).

and a great celebrant of heroic deeds, was fined by the ephors, who snatched away his lyre and nailed it to the wall because he had added just one unnecessary string in order to give a greater variety of pitch. They approved of only the simplest of melodies. When Timotheus[6] was competing in the Carneian Games (this was a festival in honour of some prophet or other called Carnes, though Pausanias[7] tells us that the Spartans gave Apollo the title Carneius), one of the ephors took his sword and asked him from which side of the lyre he would prefer to have the strings that exceeded the number seven cut out.

How the Spartan people practised frugality and abhorred excess in every sphere, fearing to depart from ancestral custom, because everything that brings destruction on a nation takes its origin from that!

98 Lycurgus went so far as to abolish all superstitious practices connected with tombs. He not only allowed burials within the city but allowed the burial places to be close to religious buildings. He did away with the rites for expiating the pollution occasioned by a death and allowed nothing to be buried with the corpse. (Other nations used to put in the grave anything which had been particularly dear to the departed during his life, a wasteful and silly superstition, suggesting that the dead still have some sort of sensation.) Lycurgus ordered everyone to be buried in exactly the same way, wrapped in a red cloth and with olive leaves. He forbade the addition of any name or inscription to the tomb, except in the case of those who had fallen in battle. He also abolished ritual mourning and dirges.

People in general used to mark a death with incredible expense and elaboration, even hiring mourners for the occasion, all of which was a very foolish procedure, suggesting that the departed retained consciousness, and

* * * * *

6 Timotheus was a musician and poet of the fifth to fourth century BC, famed for his bold musical innovations, which were not at first well received anywhere. In his hands, the seven-stringed lyre, which had gradually had more strings added, seems to have acquired an eleventh string, to facilitate his use of chromatic figuration.

7 Pausanias *Periegesis* (*Description of Greece*) 3.13.4 ff, where we read of a prophet Carnus, another figure Carneus who had an old-established worship in the Peloponnese, and of Apollo Carneus, who likewise was worshipped at various places in the Peloponnese. The Carneian Games in honour of Apollo (the god of music) at Sparta lasted for nine days and included music competitions as well as more directly military activities.

98 (XVI) Plutarch *Moralia* 238D. In margin 'superstitions connected with funerals'

that if they did, they still took pleasure in the things they had loved in life, and loved indeed not by rational choice but through some folly of the mind.

99 They were not allowed to visit foreign countries. This was to prevent them catching the contagion of foreign ways and undisciplined living. They even kept foreigners from coming into their city, so that they should not gradually infiltrate and become tutors to the citizens in some evil practice or other. Any citizen who objected to his children being educated in the traditional way[1] was deprived of citizen rights. We are also told that any foreigner who was capable of submitting himself to the traditional institutions of the Spartan state was, according to the decision of Lycurgus, admitted to that share in the citizen body that had been determined in the earliest days.[2] But no one was allowed to sell the rights of citizenship.

The wise Lycurgus was well aware that even well constituted states are corrupted by trade and foreign contacts, since all men are more receptive of vice than of virtue. But no admixture is more pernicious than the one that results from the carrying abroad and extension of imperial power. Rome lost her manliness through the influx of Greeks. Even Sparta eventually, through her dealings with barbarian nations, became utterly corrupt after being totally undefiled.[3] Likewise, France lost its masculinity by the admixture of foreign races, and so did Germany to some extent.

100 It was accepted that anyone could make use of his neighbour's servants just as if they were his own, likewise his dogs and horses, unless maybe the master needed them himself. Even out in the country, if a man was short of anything, he would open someone's storehouse, take enough to supply his immediate needs, then reseal the doors and depart.

\* \* \* \* \*

99 (xvii) Plutarch *Moralia* 238E–F. In margin 'foreign customs'
  1 Plutarch's Greek probably means 'would not submit to the traditional boy's education.'
  2 This may mean that he received a *kleros*, an allocation of land, like Spartan citizens, but there is some doubt about the Greek text of Plutarch here. See 1.259 above.
  3 The extension of Spartan influence beyond the Peloponnese involved contact with many other states and peoples, especially the Persians in the fifth century BC onwards. For the resultant corruption, see 1.185 above and 2.136 below.

100 (xviii) Plutarch *Moralia* 238F. In margin 'communal living'

In a society like this, what place was there for insatiable greed? For the rapacity that claims others' possessions for its own? For the arrogance derived from wealth? For the violence of thugs who murder some unknown innocent traveller for a paltry sum? You could call the Spartans true Christians if they had had Christ as their lawgiver instead of Lycurgus.

101 In war they wore red tunics, either because they thought this a manly colour, or because the blood-red hue would inspire more terror in inexperienced enemy troops, or to keep the enemy from noticing immediately if anyone had been wounded, as the tunic, being the same colour as blood, would conveniently conceal the fact.

102 If ever they defeated the enemy by a clever stratagem, they sacrificed a bull to Mars, but if in straight fight, a cock. This got the military leaders used to the idea that they should not only engage battle boldly but devise cunning tactics against the enemy.

They thought it more impressive to defeat the enemy bloodlessly by tactics than by fighting a battle involving bloodshed on both sides.[1]

103 When they pray to the gods they always include a petition that they may be able to submit to injustice.

This was because they considered no one fit to wield authority or undertake important functions in general if he were upset by unjust treatment of any sort.[1]

104 The sum total of their prayers was that the gods should grant honour to good men – apart from that, nothing.

They sought no reward for virtue other than fair fame. Other nations employ very different prayers, with vain repetitions, ineffective, and even asking the gods very often for shameful things.

\* \* \* \* \*

101 (xix) Plutarch *Moralia* 238F. In margin 'wily'

102 (xx) Plutarch *Moralia* 238F. In margin 'counsel in war'
    1 Cf 1.152 above.

103 (xxi) Plutarch *Moralia* 239A. In margin 'acceptance'
    1 Cf 1.340 above, 2.161 below.

104 (xxii) Plutarch *Moralia* 239A. In margin 'prayers'

**105** They worship a Venus in armour (whom they call Morpho).[1] In fact, all their divinities, both gods and goddesses, are represented lance in hand,[2] as this signifies that all of them are possessed of warlike valour.

They considered nothing worse than cowardice, nothing finer than martial valour, and so they made their gods represent what they saw as their citizen ideal. The beliefs about the gods in other Greek states made them out to be inactive and peaceable and so they represented them in a recumbent posture. Since the model for all that is good is to be sought in the divine, it is dangerous for a state to make gods of such a nature that, if anyone were to imitate them, he would become useless or even harmful to the state.

**106** They had a well-known saying that 'your own hand you must first apply when on Fortune you would call.'[1] They meant that when we call on the gods for aid, we must put out our own hand and make some effort ourselves, otherwise our prayer will be in vain.

It is true that we must see it as the gift of God if anything turns out well in human affairs, but the Divinity does not show favour to the idle and lazy. He wants his blessings to come to us as a result of our own endeavours, as it would look foolish if he showed favour to those who despise what he has given them.

**107** They used to display to the boys slaves made tipsy with wine, so that they would decide that drunkenness was disgusting.

The boys would see what a revolting spectacle was a man reeling with excessive drink and behaving like a madman. The Spartans even used to force Helots to drink to excess and then perform a silly dance and sing vulgar songs.[1] Others waste many words on trying to persuade the young that sobriety is a fine thing and that drunkenness is totally unworthy of a human being, whereas the Spartans gave them a quick practical demonstration,

* * * * *

**105** (xxiii) Plutarch *Moralia* 239A. In margin 'gods in armour'
  1 The information about Morpho is derived from Pausanias *Periegesis* 3.15.8.
  2 Cf 1.347 above.

**106** (xxiv) Plutarch *Moralia* 238A. In margin 'effort'
  1 *Adagia* II ii 81: *Manum admoventi fortuna est imploranda* 'Set your hand to the work before you appeal to Fortune.'

**107** (xxv) Plutarch *Moralia* 239A. In margin 'drunkenness'
  1 See Plutarch *Lycurgus* 28.9.

using slaves, however, as it is particularly shameful for free-born men to sink to their level.

108 It was the custom among the Spartans not to knock on the outside door but to call the person out if they wanted anything.

They wanted nothing done in secret but everything to be open for all to see.

109 They took off the sweat with scrapers made of cane, not metal.

They used such scrapers in the baths because they could be acquired easily and cheaply. They tried to be economical and to save in every situation.

110 They did not watch either comedies or tragedies, as they did not want to hear spoken, either seriously or in jest, anything that contravened the laws.[1]

The laws forbid fornication, incest, and adultery; they forbid trickery, injustice, theft, and other crimes; but poets represent the gods as doing all these things in the tales they tell. The Spartans were not impressed by the justification put forward by some, that stories were invented to give pleasure, not to be taken as the literal truth. Pleasure of that sort corrupts simple minds.

For this reason the Spartans expelled the poet Archilochus[2] from Sparta as soon as he arrived, because they learned that he had expressed the view in his poems that it was better to throw away one's weapons than die. The poem in question runs as follows:

\* \* \* \* \*

108 (xxvi) Plutarch *Moralia* 239B

109 (xxvii) Plutarch *Moralia* 239B. In margin 'economical'

110 (xxviii) Plutarch *Moralia* 239B (the second paragraph is Erasmus' commentary).
   1 Cf Diogenes Laertius 1.59 (Solon, the Athenian lawgiver, prohibited Thespis from performing tragedies on the ground that fiction was pernicious); Plato *Laws* 7.817C–D.
   2 Archilochus was a lyric poet of the eighth to seventh century BC, originally from Ionia, who spent many years in the island of Thasos in the north Aegean. He lost his shield in a battle with Thracians inhabiting the nearby mainland. Erasmus translated into Latin verse the faulty three-and-a-half line Greek original as given in his text of Plutarch. He does not comment on the faulty verse, as he usually does. Modern texts have an additional half-line supplied from Sextus Empiricus (Bergk PLG 2.384 / Archilochus 6). Cf 1.168 above.

> Some Thracian chap enjoys my shield –
> nice one it was, I didn't want to lose it! But
> I dropped it in the darksome wood.
>    I'll have to say goodbye to that.
> But never mind! One day no doubt
> I'll get another just as good.

**111** Girls and boys attended the same religious rites.

This like everything else was to ensure that the girls developed masculine strengths.

**112** The ephors fined Sciraphidas[1] because many people treated him unjustly.

They assumed that his timidity was the cause of so many people doing him wrong. If you tamely submit to one injury, you invite another.[2] If the first man who wronged him had been brought to book and had paid the legal penalty, the rest would have refrained from harming him.

**113** They executed a shield-bearing soldier, because he added a bit of purple trimming to his shield.[1]

They were so wary of foreign extravagance and the example it might give, knowing well that from the tiniest beginnings an unstoppable flood of filthy vice could come pouring in, so that it was safest to make a stand at the very outset. For that reason they inflicted the severest of penalties on those who were the first to do something. Anyone who opens a window of opportunity to evil does great harm to the state.

\* \* \* \* \*

**111** (xxix) Plutarch *Moralia* 239C

**112** (xxx) Plutarch *Moralia* 239C. In margin 'the wrong sort of mildness'
   1 Sciraphidas was an ephor contemporary of Lysander; see 1.288–303 above. It has been suggested that he was the victim of a hate campaign organized by political opponents.
   2 A common-place. See Publilius Syrus 587, *Qui culpae ignoscit uni suadet pluribus*.

**113** (xxxi) Plutarch *Moralia* 239C. In margin 'severity'
   1 Erasmus has been misled by Filelfo's version here. See dedicatory epistle 7 n20 above. At some point σάκκος [*sakkos*] 'coarse garment' in Plutarch's Greek has been confused with σάκος [*sakos*] 'shield.' The meaning should be, 'They executed a man wearing a coarse garment because he inserted a border in it.' There is no word for 'soldier' in the original.

**114** They censured one of the youths who exercised in the gymnasium for knowing the road to Pylea.[1]

They were very anxious to keep their citizens from travelling outside
the city and gaining knowledge of foreign things, for fear this might occasion a falling away from ancestral custom, especially since Arcadia, the
country where Pylea was situated, was corrupt with self-indulgence and
exotic creature-comforts.

**115** They expelled one Ctesiphon,[1] who claimed to be able to talk all day on
any topic whatsoever, saying that a good speaker should keep his words
commensurate with his subject.[2]

They were of the opinion that the most appropriate place for the application of economy was in speech, which Hesiod says should be brought
out of store sparingly, like a precious treasure, for use and not for display.[3]

**116** It is the custom among the Spartans for boys to be flogged all day[1] at the
altar of Diana Orthia[2] (so called by them for her irrepressible valour). This
they often endure to the point of death, cheerful and exultant, vying with
each other to see which of them can triumph by holding out for the longest

\* \* \* \* \*

**114** (XXXII) Plutarch *Moralia* 239C. In margin 'foreign customs'
  1 It is not certain what 'the road to Pylea' means. It has been suggested that
    Pylea indicates a market (full of temptations for a Spartan) just outside
    the city. See S.A. Naber 'Observationes miscellaneae ad Plutarchi Moralia I'
    *Mnemosyne* 28 (1900) 134–8. But see also CPG 1 Zenobius 5.36 and *Adagia* II vii
    57: *Novit haec Pylaea et Tyttygias*, where it is identified as a place in Arcadia
    where stolen goods were sold on. For the corrupt morals see General Index:
    Arcadia.

**115** (XXXIII) Plutarch *Moralia* 239C. In margin 'loquacity'
  1 Ctesiphon, or Cephisophon as in Plutarch, is in either case unknown.
  2 See 1.95 n2.
  3 Hesiod *Works and Days* 719.

**116** (XXXIV) Plutarch *Moralia* 239C–D. In margin 'hard childhood'
  1 The custom was still observed in Plutarch's day in the second century AD.
    See Plutarch *Lycurgus* 18.1. It had by that time become something of a tourist
    attraction.
  2 The name Orthia means 'Upright.' The image of the goddess was ancient and
    made of wood, and was supposedly found standing upright in a thicket (see
    the geographer Pausanias, as in n6 below).

time with the greatest courage. The winner makes a great name for himself. This type of contest is called 'The Scourging'[3] and is held every year.

Plutarch gives the origin of this custom in his life of Aristides:[4] When Pausanias[5] was performing the sacrifice at a little distance from where his troops were positioned, some Lydians made a sortie and destroyed the sacrifice and everything connected with it. He rounded on them with his companions but because they had not got their weapons with them, attacked them with whips. The contest above mentioned was founded in memory of this incident.

Pausanias[6] gives a different explanation in his book dealing with Laconia: The inhabitants of Limnae, Cynosura, Mesoa, and Pitane[7] were offering sacrifice to Diana, when a disagreement arose between them. The disagreement turned into a fight so bitter that bodies were strewn all over the altar. The survivors were carried off by plague. Consequently a pronouncement from an oracle declared that the desecration of Diana's altar must be expiated with human blood. When they set about performing the sacrifice with victims chosen by lot, Lycurgus substituted the flogging of the young men for the actual slaughter. As a result the altar was purged with human blood but without human sacrifice.

While it would be foolish to follow this example, it does tell us how wrong it is to treat children with excessive lenience. We bring them up so indulgently that they are unfit even for the demands of study and become resentful of any correction, however mild.

117  Whatever we think of that, Lycurgus does seem to have secured for his citizens one particular thing that contributed to an honourable and happy way of life. And what was that? It was plenty of free time, as they were absolutely forbidden to touch any sedentary craft.[1] Indeed, they had no need to exercise any laborious and demanding craft in order to make money,

\* \* \* \* \*

3  Erasmus quotes the name in Greek, διαμαστίγωσις.
4  Plutarch *Aristides* 17.8
5  This is Pausanias, regent of Sparta, and the incident occurred at the battle of Plataea against the Persian host, which included contingents of Lydians. See 2.43 above.
6  This is a different Pausanias, the author of *Periegesis*, book three of which deals with Laconia. For this incident see *Periegesis* 3.16.9ff.
7  Limnae, Cynosura, Mesoa, and Pitane were all districts of the town of Sparta. The second is properly Conooura.

117  (xxxv) Plutarch *Moralia* 239D–E. In margin 'civilized leisure'
  1  See 2.64 n1 above.

since Lycurgus had done away with any admiration or respect for riches. The Helots (that is, the slaves) cultivated the fields for them and paid a rent in kind, the amount of which had been fixed by the ancestors.

There are people nowadays who copy them, using slaves or hired servants, or children they turn into slaves, for nearly everything, but they do this not to give themselves time for meditation on lofty subjects, but to be free for drinking and playing dice.

118 There was a curse on anyone who asked more than the prescribed rent for the land. This made the slaves work more cheerfully for their masters, since they could expect some profit for themselves, and it stopped the citizens from trying to get more than the customary amount.

What wisdom that nation showed in thus directing everything that could be a source of evil onto their slaves and diverting it away from those of free birth! How differently other nations behave – they claim for their children all that is productive of self-indulgence, lust, avarice, and drunkenness, but force their servants to practice poverty and economy.

119 They were forbidden to sail ships or engage in naval battles, though later on they did win control of the sea through naval engagements; but when they realized that the character of their citizens was degenerating, they gave up their sea power. But they changed their minds again in this as in everything else. When money was first introduced into Spartan territory, they executed those responsible for bringing it in, as an oracle had been given to the two kings Alcamenes and Theopompus[1] that 'love of money would destroy Sparta.'[2] All the same, after defeating the Athenians, Lysander brought in a huge amount of gold and silver, and they not only accepted the money but honoured the man.[3] As long as Sparta observed the laws of Lycurgus and did not break her word, she held first place among the Greeks, for six hundred years, through the fairness and fame of her laws. However, as they gradually fell away from these, and love of money and the evil of avarice came flooding

* * * * *

118 (XXXVI) Plutarch *Moralia* 239E

119 (XXXVII) Plutarch *Moralia* 239E–240B. In margin 'money a pernicious thing, degeneration'
  1 Alcamenes and Theopompus were kings of Sparta in the eighth century BC.
  2 See *Adagia* II vii 94, 'Love of money will be Sparta's undoing and nothing else.'
  3 For apophthegms attributed to Lysander, see 1.288–303 above. For his bringing home huge spoils to Sparta at the end of the Peloponnesian War in 404 BC, including quantities of silver coinage, see Plutarch *Lycurgus* 30.1; *Lysander* 16.

in as a result, not only did their power decline, but they now found hostile
to them those who had formerly been their friends and allies in war. Yet, in
spite of their changed ways, after the victory of King Philip of Macedon at
Chaeronea,[4] when all the other Greeks acknowledged him as supreme ruler
by land and sea, and his son Alexander after him, the Spartans were the only
people, once Thebes had been overthrown, who would not ally themselves
in war either with other Greeks or, later, with the Macedonian kings, or make
common cause with them,[5] and this in spite of the fact that their city was not
defended by walls,[6] their numbers had been seriously reduced by constant
warfare, and their weakness, compared with their past strength, made them
vulnerable. They were able to act like this because they still cherished a few
faint sparks of the Lycurgan constitution. Nor were the Spartans reduced to
paying tribute until the time when they lost all respect for Lycurgus' laws
and were oppressed by a tyranny exercised by their own citizens.[7] Nothing
then remained of their ancestral constitution and they became like the rest,
stripped of the glory and the liberty they once enjoyed and reduced to servitude. Now, just like the rest of the Greeks, they are subject to the Romans.[8]

This is a serious warning to us all that dominion is won by bravery,
but through greed, indiscipline, and indulgence it is either lost or turned
into tyranny.

### Sayings of Spartan women

120   After the death of Brasidas,[1] men from Amphipolis came to Sparta to visit his

* * * * *

4 In the decisive battle at Chaeronea in 338 BC Philip II of Macedon defeated the
   allied Greeks led by Athens and Thebes. The Spartans were not involved in
   the actual battle.
5 This is more likely to mean 'either with them (ie Philip and Alexander) or the
   Macedonian kings who came after them.' What happened during this period
   is however very confused with constantly shifting alliances.
6 See 1.30 n1 above.
7 The reforming Spartan kings Agis IV and Cleomenes III of the third century
   BC were regarded as autocratic and tyrannous by their political opponents, see
   1.12 n2, 1.107–10 above and 2.157 below. Nabis, a violent reforming ruler at
   the end of the century, succumbed to Roman authority.
8 Plutarch (if he is the author) was writing in the period first to second century
   AD, when Greece had been subject to Rome for about 250–300 years.

120 (1) Plutarch *Moralia* 240C. This section (2.120–56) is translated from Plutarch
      *Moralia* 240C to 242D.
   1 For Brasidas see 1.159–62 and 1.162 n2 above. The saying also occurs at *Moralia*
      190C (*Sayings of kings and commanders*), which provides *Adagia* III iv 17: *Brasidas
      quidem vir bonus* 'Brasidas indeed is a good man.'

mother Archileonis. She asked them whether her son had died honourably, as befitted a citizen of Sparta. They began to extol the young man's bravery and say that he was the finest military man in all Sparta. She replied, 'Friends, my son was indeed a fine spirited man, but Sparta has many men better than he.'

121 Aristagoras of Miletus was trying to persuade King Cleomenes to start a war against the King of the Persians in support of the Greeks of Ionia. He offered him a considerable sum of money and when Cleomenes persisted in refusing, he made the promised sum ever larger. Gorgo, Cleomenes' daughter said, 'Father, this little foreigner will corrupt you if you don't throw him out instantly.'[1]

Where does this leave the people who call women money-lovers, since Gorgo urged her father to refuse money, not accept it?

122 This same Gorgo was instructed by her father to give some corn to a certain individual by way of thanks. The father added as a commendation, 'He taught me to enjoy my wine.' She replied, 'So, father, more wine will be drunk and those who drink will become more self-indulgent and lesser men.'[1]

How can one adequately praise this girl who had stricter standards than either her elderly father or the other man? Though the female sex in general is much taken by attractive things.

123 When Gorgo saw Aristagoras having his shoes put on by one of his slaves,[1] she exclaimed, 'Whatever next, father! Hasn't this foreigner got any hands?'

She had no time for the foppery of a man who wasted his servants' energies on doing what he could do for himself with his own two hands. How ashamed those people should be who find ten servants hardly enough

\* \* \* \* \*

121 (II) Plutarch *Moralia* 240D. In margin 'contempt for money'
   1 Aristagoras, the ex-ruler of Miletus, was fostering rebellion among the Greek states subject to the Persians, and sought assistance from Cleomenes I in 499 BC; cf 1.225 above for a similar story about Cleomenes' incorruptibility. Gorgo was only eight years old at the time; see Herodotus 5.51.

122 (III) Plutarch *Moralia* 240D–E
   1 Cf 1.143 above.

123 (IV) Plutarch *Moralia* 240E. In margin 'censorious'
   1 See 2.121 above. Aristagoras had adopted the luxurious customs of Eastern rulers.

to get them dressed and their hair arranged! When they go to the toilet, they
need one servant to untie their hose and another to pass them grass or wool
to wipe themselves, and all but do the wiping for them.[2]

124 A foreigner was somewhat effetely and with difficulty trailing his rather
long garment. Gorgo gave him a push and said, 'Off with you! You can't
even do what women do!'

It is for women to wear fringed garments reaching down to the ground.
Sometimes they have long trains behind as well. However, they don't find
them heavy, or else they loop them up.

125 Gyrtias' grandson Acrotatus[1] – his mother was Gyrtias' daughter – was
carried home for dead after a fight with other boys in which he had
been severely injured. Everyone else in the household started weeping, but
Gyrtias observing them, said, 'Cease your noise! He has shown of what
blood he comes.' She added that 'the brave need to be cared for, not wept
over.'[2]

\* \* \* \* \*

2 Cf 3.239 below.

124 (v) Plutarch *Moralia* 240E. In margin 'censorious'
Both the text and the meaning of the Greek are debatable here. Modern editors, following all the manuscripts which read μαλακῶς σχολῇ 'languidly, without making an effort,' with no word στολήν [*stolēn*] 'garment,' have suggested
either that the man was making mild and ineffectual advances, or that he was
walking in a mincing and effeminate manner (interpreting the verb as intran-
sitive, 'advancing'). Raffaele Regio, either finding a reading σχολῇ στολήν 'in
a leisurely way ... a garment' or emending the text himself, translated *cum
peregrinus quidam vestem molliter traheret* 'when some foreigner was trailing his
garment in a languid way.' Erasmus took account of this text and translation
(see the dedicatory epistle 7 n21 above), and made a marginal note στολήν 'garment' in his copy of the Aldine *Moralia*. He spelt out the meaning more clearly
in 1535 by adding 'with difficulty' and changing the verb from 'pulling on'
to 'trailing.' Letting one's clothes trail sloppily was a sign of effeminacy. Cf
4.303 below.

125 (vi) Plutarch *Moralia* 240E–F. In margin 'brave'
1 Gyrtias' grandson Acrotatus was the son of King Areus I, and later on briefly
king of Sparta, 265–c. 262 BC.
2 Erasmus follows the interpretation of Filelfo and Regio. See dedicatory epistle
7–8 nn20 and 21 above. The text may mean: 'the brave should do something
helpful, not weep.' See *Adagia* III ix 41: *Non luctu, sed remedio opus in malis*
'Misfortunes need healing, not mourning.'

126 When Gyrtias received news from Crete of Acrotatus' death,[1] she said,
'When he went off to war, was it not inevitable that he would be killed
himself or else kill the enemy? It is more satisfying to hear that he met his
end in a manner worthy of himself, his country, and his family than have
him tamely live out the life of a coward.'

Grandmothers tend to have a more indulgent and emotional attitude
to their grandchildren than the children's mothers have. What justification
have women for ending their own lives if their children die, when Gyrtias
would have no lamenting over her grandson when he was at death's door,[2]
and did not consider mourning appropriate when he had perished fighting
bravely?

127 Damatria heard that her son's conduct on the battle-field showed him to be
unworthy of her, so when he came home, she killed him. The following
epigram was written concerning the incident:[1]

> The city and its laws he failed
> And by his mother's hand was slain.
> Damatria as true Spartan stood revealed.
> He was no Spartan but in name.

This terrible deed is more akin to barbarian savagery than to true bravery. All the same, we can use it to point up the folly of the excessive indulgence mothers show their children – in fact they often love them all the
more intensely just because they are bad characters.

128 Another Spartan woman also killed her son for being unworthy of his country, when he had deserted his station in the battle-line and fled. She com-

* * * * *

126 (VII) Plutarch *Moralia* 240F. In margin 'brave, wise'
   1 Acrotatus died in battle c. 262 BC, but at Megalopolis in the Peloponnese,
     not in Crete. See Plutarch *Agis* 3.6. His father Areus had campaigned in
     Crete (Plutarch *Pyrrhus* 27), and this may have caused confusion. See 1.133n
     above.
   2 See 2.125 just above.

127 (VIII) Plutarch *Moralia* 240F. In margin 'resolute'
   1 The English version translates Erasmus' Latin verse translation of the Greek
     verse quoted in Plutarch, which Erasmus does not quote in Greek.

128 (IX) Plutarch *Moralia* 241A. In margin 'resolute'

mented, 'This is no sprig of mine.' There is an epigram about her too:[1]

Useless sprig, through the shadows away!
Even to timorous deer
Eurotas his waters would deny,
So strong his hate for you.
Worthless whelp, rotten remnant,
To the depths of hell now go.
Go, unworthy son of Sparta, go,
A son I never bore.

Another woman, hearing of her son's brave death in battle, said:

Tears are for cowards shed. You I shall not weep.
True son of mine and of your native land, you sleep.

This verse was earlier attributed to Tynnichus,[2] but Filelfo[3] records it without any specific reference.

129 Another woman heard that her son was alive but had fled in the face of the enemy. She wrote to him, 'There is a nasty rumour going about concerning you. Either disprove it, or cease to exist.'
She thought it better to die than to live in disgrace.[1]

130 The sons of another woman came to her after fleeing from battle. 'Where are you going, you cowardly runaway varlets?' she said. Then showing them her belly, she asked them, 'Do you think you can creep back in here from where you came forth?'[1]
This remark would do credit to a follower of the Cynic sect.[2]

*  *  *  *  *

1 This translates Erasmus' Latin verse translation of the Greek verse quoted in Plutarch as also at line 11. These again Erasmus does not quote in Greek.
2 For Tynnichus, see 2.48 above.
3 For Francesco Filelfo (1398–1481) see the dedicatory epistle 7 n20 above.

129 (x) Plutarch *Moralia* 241A. In margin 'spirited'
1 Cf 2.136 below

130 (xi) Plutarch *Moralia* 241B. The last sentence was added in 1532. In margin 'crude'
1 Cf 6.586 below.
2 The Cynics were quite without inhibition where body parts and bodily func-

131 A woman saw her son approaching and asked him, 'How goes the country?'
When he replied, 'Everyone is dead,' she threw a tile at him and killed him,
saying, 'So they sent you to tell us the bad news, did they?'

She considered him unfit to live since he had not had the courage to
die with his fellow-soldiers.

132 A man was telling his mother how nobly his brother had died. 'And isn't it
disgraceful' she said, 'that you didn't manage to keep company with him?'[1]

133 A woman whose five sons had gone off to the war was standing just outside
the city waiting to hear how the fighting had gone. Someone came up to her
and told her that all her sons were dead. 'That's not what I was asking, you
cowardly menial,' she replied, 'but how the country fares.' When he told
her that the country had the victory, 'Well then,' she said, 'I am quite happy
about the death of my sons.'

This splendid woman put her love for her country above her private
affection for her sons.

134 A woman was burying her son. Some contemptible old hag came up to her
and said, 'Oh what a sad thing, you poor woman!' But she retorted, 'No,
by the Twin Gods, a good thing! For my son has died for Sparta and I have
seen fulfilled the purpose for which I brought him into the world.'

This brave woman turned the old woman's commiseration into con-
gratulation. Cicero refers to this woman in the first book of the *Tusculan
Disputations*.[1]

135 A woman from Ionia was boasting about a tapestry she had woven as a

\* \* \* \* \*

tions were concerned. See 7.290 below; *De copia* 1.11 *Indecent words* (CWE 24
315 / LB 1.11D).

131 (XII) Plutarch *Moralia* 241B. In margin 'resolute'

132 (XIII) Plutarch *Moralia* 241B. In margin 'spirited'
    1 Cf 2.148 below.

133 (XIV) Plutarch *Moralia* 241C. In margin 'resolute'

134 (XV) Plutarch *Moralia* 241C. In margin 'resolute'
    1 Cicero *Tusculan Disputations* 1.43.102

135 (XVI) Plutarch *Moralia* 241D. In margin 'worthy'

thing of great value. A Spartan woman pointed to her four well-mannered sons and said, 'This is the kind of work for a good and honourable woman. These are the achievements she should take pride in and boast about.'

The inhabitants of Ionia find time to create elaborate tapestries depicting various scenes. But the Spartan woman declared that her finest work was bringing up sons of good character. These are more of an adornment to a country than Ionian hangings or garments.

**136** Another Spartan woman heard that her son was behaving disgracefully while he was abroad.[1] She wrote to him, 'There is a nasty rumour going about concerning you. Either scotch it or stop living.'

**137** Some exiles from Chios came to Sparta, complaining of the way Paedaretus was acting.[1] His mother Teleutia sent for them, and when she had learnt what their grounds of complaint were and had realized that her son was in the wrong, she wrote to him to this effect: 'His mother to Paedaretus. He is to improve his conduct or stay where he is, giving up all expectation of living safe in Sparta.'

That forceful woman threatened her son with death unless he improved his conduct.

**138** Another woman said to her son, who was on trial for some crime or other, 'Free yourself from this charge, my son, or else free yourself from life.'

The mother was harder on her son than the judge, as she preferred him dead rather than living with a bad name.

**139** Another woman was walking beside her lame son as he left for the war. 'Son,' she said, 'with every step mind you think of valour.'

Lameness might well make other mothers anxious, but this woman urged her son to find inspiration for brave action in his very handicap, on

* * * * *

**136** (xvii) Plutarch *Moralia* 241D
  1 Cf 1.185 above, 2.138 below.

**137** (xviii) Plutarch *Moralia* 241D–E. In margin 'stern'
  1 Paedaretus was a commander stationed by the Spartans on the island of Chios in 412–411 BC, during the Peloponnesian War against Athens, where he acted with great harshness and injustice. See 1.325–7 above.

**138** (xix) Plutarch *Moralia* 241E. In margin 'stern'

**139** (xx) Plutarch *Moralia* 241E. In margin 'lame'

the grounds that running away is no help to a lame man;[1] he must either win or die.

140 Another woman's son came home from the war with a wound in the foot which gave him great pain. She said to him, 'If you remember your bravery, my son, you will not only not feel the pain, but will be of good heart.'

Mothers usually make their sons' suffering worse by fussing and weeping. She gave her son strength to bear the pain.

141 A Spartan was so badly wounded in the war that he could not walk normally but had to crawl on all fours. He felt humiliated when people laughed at him, but his mother took him to task: 'It would be better, my son, to take pride in your courage rather than blush at the laughter of fools.'

Cicero has a similar story about the mother of Spurius Claudius,[1] but he ascribes to her the words found in the example quoted earlier.

142 Another Spartan woman, as she hung her son's shield upon him, gave him these words of encouragement: 'Son, either with this or on this.'

With Spartan economy of words she gave him to understand that he must so conduct himself on the battle-field as to bring home his shield in triumph or else be carried home upon it dead.[1]

143 Another woman as she hung the shield upon her son as he set off for the war said to him, 'Your father always kept this shield safe for you; mind you always keep it safe, or else stop living.'[1]

\* \* \* \* \*

1 Cf 2.42 above.

140 (xxi) Plutarch *Moralia* 241E–F. In margin 'resolute'

141 (xxii) Plutarch *Moralia* 241F. In margin 'resolute'
  1 Cicero *De oratore* 2.249. The story is used at 6.207 below. The subject there is Spurius Carvilius, whose mother says 'With every step you take, remember your valorous exploits.' For similar stories, see 2.139, 2.140 above, 4.94 (Alexander to Philip) below.

142 (xxiii) Plutarch *Moralia* 241F. In margin 'resolute'
  1 Cf 1.210 above. See *Adagia* iii v 10: *Aut manenti vincendum aut moriendum* 'He must stay and conquer or die.'

143 (xxiv) Plutarch *Moralia* 241F. In margin 'resolute'
  1 Cf 1.168 above and 2.142 just above.

144 When her son remarked that his sword was short, a Spartan woman said, 'Well, add a pace to it.'[1]

She meant that the short sword would be no disadvantage if he went up close to the enemy.

145 Another woman heard that her son had perished fighting bravely on the battle field. 'Of course,' she said, 'he was mine.'

She did not feel aggrieved at the death of her son, but congratulated herself on his courage.

When however she heard that her other son had survived because he had refused to fight out of cowardice, she said, 'Of course, he was not mine.'[1]

She believed that those who fell short of their parents' standards should not be considered as their children.

146 Another woman heard that her son had been slain in battle. 'Lay him aside,' she said, 'just where he was stationed,[1] and let his brother take his place.'

You would be hard put to find such strength of mind in a man! She had no fear of being left childless, provided her sons gave their lives for their country.

147 Another woman was taking part in a procession in a religious ceremony when she received the news that her son had been victorious in battle but was dying from his many wounds. She did not remove the garland from her head[1] but said exultantly to her companions, 'How much more splendid it is, my friends, to die victorious in battle than to win a victory at the Olympic Games and live!'

\* \* \* \* \*

144  (xxv) Plutarch *Moralia* 241F. In margin 'trenchant'
  1 Cf 1.105 and 1.130 above.

145  (xxvi) Plutarch *Moralia* 242A. In margin 'resolute'
  1 Cf 2.128 above.

146  (xxvii) Plutarch *Moralia* 242A. In margin 'resolute'
  1 Modern editors punctuate differently and take the Greek phrase translated by the words 'just where he was stationed' together with 'slain in battle.' Erasmus here follows Filelfo. See dedicatory epistle 7 n20 above.

147  (xxviii) Plutarch *Moralia* 242A–B. In margin 'resolute'
  1 Taking the garland from her head would have been a sign of mourning. Cf the aftermath of the battle of Leuctra (Plutarch *Agesilaus* 29), when the religious ceremonies were not interrupted in spite of the bad news of the shattering defeat. See 1.337 n1 above.

This forceful woman had quite different ideas from other people. They believe that to take first place at the Olympics puts one almost up with the gods, yet the contest there is about expertise and the spending of large sums of money, not about bravery.[2] They also believe that nothing is more terrible than death and that there is nothing so precious that it is worth losing one's life to gain it. She believed that the most impressive victory was one gained for one's country and that no death was more desirable than one linked with the glory of that achievement.

148 A man was telling his sister how bravely her son had perished in the battle. 'I am glad about my son's death,' she said, 'but sorry for you, because you didn't stay in such good company.'[1]

149 A man sent a message to a Spartan woman asking whether she would agree to an assignation with him. She sent back the answer, 'When I was a girl, I was taught to obey my father and that is what I did. When I became a married woman, I obeyed my husband. If this man wants to meet me for some honest purpose, he may discuss it with my husband first.'

150 A poor girl was asked what dowry she would bring her husband. 'The modesty traditional in our family,' she replied.
    A noble declaration – a girl who brings purity to her marriage bed is well endowed.

151 A Spartan woman was asked whether she had made advances to her husband. 'No,' she replied, 'but he has to me.'
    She implied that she had relations with her husband not to satisfy desire but in obedience to her parents and what the law required of her. It was disgraceful for a woman to take the initiative.

*  *  *  *  *

2 Cf 1.48 above.

148 (xxix) Plutarch *Moralia* 242B
    1 Cf 2.132 above.

149 (xxx) Plutarch *Moralia* 242B. In margin 'chaste'

150 (xxxi) Plutarch *Moralia* 242B. In margin 'chaste'

151 (xxxii) Plutarch *Moralia* 242C. In margin 'chaste'

**152** A girl who was pregnant as a result of a secret encounter brought on an abortion, and bore up so bravely under the pain that she uttered not a sound. In fact the abortion took place without her father and others who were close by realizing what was happening. The shame combined with her self-respect overcame the excruciating pain.

Because she was a proud girl, she could not face disgrace. To escape the shame consequent on what she had done, she suffered in silence the pangs of labour which make other women cry out in distress.

**153** Another Spartan girl was being sold as a slave, and when she was asked what she knew, replied, 'To be faithful.'

She was of the opinion that faithfulness in a slave was better than any practical skill.

**154** Another captive likewise, when asked what she could do, replied, 'Manage a house well.'

This is no common ability in a woman.

**155** Another girl was asked by a prospective purchaser if she would be good if he bought her. 'Yes,' she replied, 'and if you don't buy me.'

**156** Another girl was asked by the auctioneer what she knew. 'How to be a free person,' she replied.

She meant that she might well be a captive, but that she would not obey if ordered to do things not appropriate to a free-born person.

So when the person who had bought her ordered her to perform some tasks not fitting for a free-born woman, she said, 'You will regret not letting yourself keep such a valuable possession,' and proceeded to kill herself.

\* \* \* \* \*

**152** (xxxiii) Plutarch *Moralia* 242c. In margin 'brave'

**153** (xxxiv) Plutarch *Moralia* 242c. In margin 'noble'

**154** (xxxv) Plutarch *Moralia* 242c

**155** (xxxvi) Plutarch *Moralia* 242c. Cf the same story told of a boy, 2.36 above.

**156** (xxxvii) Plutarch *Moralia* 242D. Cf the similar story told at 2.34 above. This anecdote was the basis of a *chreia*.
'End of *Sayings of Spartan Women*' is marked in the text after this apophthegm. The remaining four sayings are taken from other works by Plutarch.

**157** When Agesistrata saw her son Agis lying dead,[1] she kissed his face and said, 'My dear son, you were too good and gentle and compassionate, and so destroyed yourself and us too.'

Agis had been trying to reform the degenerate character of the Spartans and bring back the old-fashioned discipline, a noble scheme but one that generated much hostility. While he tried to offend no one and please everyone he brought about his own destruction.

**158** The same woman, putting her head in the noose, said, 'In this at least I was useful to Sparta.'[1]

This noble-spirited woman was grieved that her son was not permitted to do the good he would for his country.

**159** The Thebans invaded Spartan territory and took away captives of both sexes, including large numbers of Helots. These they ordered to sing the songs of the Spartan poets Terpander, Alcman, and Spendon, but they refused, saying that 'their masters' daughters would not allow it.'

The authority of these girls who were their fellow captives carried more weight with them than the commands of those who had conquered them.

Some people took this incident as proof of the saying that in Sparta the free man was more free than anywhere, but a slave was more a slave than anywhere.[1]

This is taken from Plutarch's *Life of Lycurgus*.

**160** When Theano[1] was putting on her cloak, she accidentally uncovered her

\* \* \* \* \*

**157** (xxxviii) This and the following incident are taken from Plutarch *Life of Agis* 20.
   1 This is Agis iv, king of Sparta 244–241 BC. See 1.107–110 and 2.119 n7 above.

**158** (xxxix) Plutarch *Life of Agis* 20. In margin 'patriotism'
   1 Agis' mother and grandmother were strangled because they supported his reforms and protested at his unjust execution.

**159** (xl) Plutarch *Life of Lycurgus* 28. Plutarch says that the Helots had been allowed to sing only low songs and not the literary, inspiring ones of Spartan poets such as Terpander and Alcman. Spendon is otherwise unknown. Cf 2.97 and 2.107 above. In margin 'an entourage of slaves'
   1 *Adagia* iv ix 35: *Spartae servi maxime servi* 'Nowhere more a slave than at Sparta.'

**160** (xli) Plutarch *Moralia* 142C (*Advice to bride and groom*)
   1 Theano was the wife of the philosopher Pythagoras.

arm. When some man remarked, 'What a pretty arm!' she retorted, 'But not one for general approbation!'

She indicated that only one person was entitled to find it attractive, not anybody, and she also reprimanded the man who had thus expressed admiration for his failure to control himself, looking with curiosity at a body that was not his to look at.

### Sayings of Chilon the Spartan

161  I am quite sure that the Spartan Chilon, who was said to be one of the Seven Sages of Greece,[1] displayed true Spartan character in his sayings, though this does not come through in the sayings that are attributed to him, no doubt through the fault of the writers. The following sayings are taken from Diogenes Laertius.

When his brother complained that he was not made ephor when Chilon was,[2] Chilon replied, 'I know how to submit to injustice, you don't.'[3]

\* \* \* \* \*

161  (i) Diogenes Laertius 1.68. In margin 'controlled'
This section is mainly derived from Diogenes Laertius 1.68–73. Erasmus, however, did not have the text of Diogenes Laertius in Greek at this stage, but used Traversari's Latin translation. See Introduction xvi above.

1  The list of the Seven Sages was not fixed – various selections were made from a list that in its fullest form included seventeen names, though Thales, Bias, Pittacus, and Solon were nearly always in, Chilon often. See book 7 (preliminary note) 765 below. Their utterances were variously reported and attributed now to one, now to the other. They are recorded in many places in Greek and Latin literature – Erasmus tells us (line 5) that he is here using Diogenes Laertius as his main source for Chilon (ie 2.161–87). He has supplemented this in 2.187–91 below with material from a poem attributed to Ausonius (a fourth-century AD Christian poet from Gaul), ie *Appendix Ausoniana* I *Septem sapientum sententiae* (VI *Chilon Lacedaemonius*). This whole poem first appears in an edition of Ausonius by Thaddaeus Ugoletus (Parma 1499) and is nowadays considered to be spurious. Thaddaeus made numerous additions to the accepted text of Ausonius. The list of Sages given here in Ausonius is: Bias, Pittacus, Cleobulus, Periander, Solon, Chilon, and Anacharsis the Scythian (or Thales). Erasmus' comments on Chilon's sayings in several places echo the utterances attributed in Ausonius and Diogenes Laertius to other sages, but the sayings are all commonplaces in Greek and Latin literature. See also 7.38 n1 below.

2  Chilon, like the other Sages, was a real figure, and held the office of ephor in Sparta in 556 BC. He was also made a member of the Gerousia, the council of elders (Aristotle *Rhetoric* 2.23 1398b4). He came to be worshipped in Sparta as a hero. Ephors were elected annually by the assembly of Spartiate citizens. There were no formal restrictions as to who could be chosen. See 1.12 n2.

3  Cf 1.340 above.

He meant that no one was fitted for bearing office if he couldn't pretend on many occasions not to notice unfair and hurtful comments, as in the famous line,[4] 'Ruler, accept impartially both fair and unfair words.'

162 When Aesop[1] asked him what Jupiter was doing, he replied, 'Putting down the exalted and raising the humble.'[2]

He meant that the affairs of men swing up and down in accordance with the divine will.

163 When Chilon was asked what distinguished the informed from the ignorant, he replied, 'Good expectations.'

By 'informed,' he meant people of good character, brought up under good laws, living disciplined lives. They are superior to the bad, though equal in other respects, in that they hope for a reward after this life for their good deeds. The Spartans believed that outstanding characters after their deaths were translated to a blessed life and became divine.[1]

164 Chilon used to say, 'As the touchstone tries gold, so gold tries men.'[1] The stone when rubbed against the gold reveals its quality, but the gold itself reveals what sort a man is.'

This is like the proverb: 'Tis the place that shows the man.'[2]

* * * * *

4 See CPG 2 Apostolius 4.3; CPG 1 Diogenianus 2.99. It is there ascribed to Solon. See also *Adagia* II vii 89: *Magistratum gerens audi et iuste et iniuste* 'When in office expect both just and unjust criticism.'

162 (II) Diogenes Laertius 1.69. In margin 'life's vicissitudes'
    1 Aesop is the famous writer of fables. A meeting is not chronologically impossible. They are both among the guests at the *Dinner party of the seven sages* described in Plutarch *Moralia* 146B–164D.
    2 See Hesiod *Works and Days* 4–7.

163 (III) Diogenes Laertius 1.69. In margin 'rewards of virtue'
    1 As Chilon himself was. See 2.161 n2 above.

164 (IV) Diogenes Laertius 1.71. In margin 'gold the touch-stone'
    1 See *Adagia* I v 87: *Lydius lapis sive Heraclius lapis*; II iv 51: *Quod index auro, id aurum homini.*
    2 'Place' in the sense of power and official position. See *Adagia* I x 76: *Magistratus virum indicat* (ἀρχὴ τὸν ἄνδρα δείκνυσιν).

**165** When Chilon had become a very old man, he used to say he could not recall any act which he regretted save one. He had been called in as arbiter to settle a dispute between two friends. He did not want to do anything contrary to the law, so he persuaded one of them to take the matter to others for a decision. In this way he both kept the law and kept his friend.[1]

What was worrying the old man's conscience was that a person of perfect integrity would not have been deflected from strict legality by any sort of consideration, nor would he have set much store by the friendship of a man who would cease to be his friend if judgment was given to suit the law rather than himself. What could be more saintly than this soul that had committed only this one sin throughout his whole long life?

**166** A number of writers, including Aulus Gellius, attribute to Chilon the following saying: 'Love allowing for a change to hate, hate allowing for a change to love.'[1]

This warns us not to be so bitterly at odds with anyone that all hope of reconciliation is precluded, nor to be so trusting of friends that you give them the means of destroying you if they become your enemies.

**167** He used to say we should 'never indulge in invective, for if we say what we enjoy saying we may have to listen in turn to what we don't enjoy hearing.'[1]

The sick urge to hurl abuse at people does provide its own kind of pleasure, but this is very often counterbalanced by the unpleasant experience of being on the receiving end ourselves. This is what Cicero meant

\* \* \* \* \*

**165** (v) Diogenes Laertius 1.71. In margin 'clear conscience'
   1 The version of the story actually given in Diogenes Laertius 1.71 and also in Aulus Gellius *Noctes Atticae* 1.3.4–7 is less creditable: Chilon secretly voted for conviction in a trial but persuaded his fellow-judges to vote for acquittal. Erasmus is using Traversari's version (see Introduction xvi–xvii above).

**166** (vi) Diogenes Laertius 1.71. In margin 'controlled'
   1 Aulus Gellius *Noctes Atticae* 1.3.30. See *Adagia* II i 72: *Ama tamquam osurus, oderis tamquam amaturus*. It is there attributed to Bias, another of the Seven Sages.

**167** (vii) Diogenes Laertius 1.70. In margin 'abuse'
   1 See Hesiod *Works and Days* 721; Plutarch *Moralia* 88c (*How to profit by one's enemies*); *Adagia* I i 27: *Qui quae vult dicit, quae non vult audit* 'He who says what he would will hear what he would not.'

when he warned Sallust that any satisfaction he had derived from making his abusive attack would be wiped out when he had to listen to himself being trounced.[2]

**168** He used to say that 'one should never let one's tongue outrun one's thoughts.'

He meant that one should think what one is going to say before the tongue embarks on speech. For 'a word once spoken never recalled can be.'[1] A first thought can often be corrected by a second thought that is better, as the proverb says,[2] but this is not true of a word.

**169** 'Loss,' said Chilon, 'is better than dishonest gain. One regrets the former at the time, the other for ever.'

Material loss can easily be made up, but a stained reputation can hardly ever be restored. Loss grieves one temporarily, but a guilty conscience is a continuous torment. So gains made by dishonest means are not gains but loss.[1]

**170** 'One should not attempt the impossible.'[1]

There are enterprises which are splendid and laudable, but they only damage a country if they cannot be carried through. The chief function of a

* * * * *

2 Included in the corpus of the historian Sallust's works were two spurious speeches of invective, one supposedly by Sallust, attacking the famous orator and statesman Cicero, and the other Cicero's reply. Erasmus seems to have misremembered here: this warning occurs in the opening of Sallust's attack on Cicero (*In M. Tullium Ciceronem invectiva* 1.1). But cf in Cicero's reply (*In C. Sallustium Crispum invectiva* 8.21): 'Anyone who intends to make a speech of attack ought to be free of all taint himself. It is the man who has no truths to fear who can safely fulminate against others.'

**168** (VIII) Diogenes Laertius 1.70. In margin 'headlong speech'
1 Horace *Ars poetica* 390.
2 *Adagia* I iii 38: *Posterioribus melioribus* 'Better luck next time'

**169** (IX) Diogenes Laertius 1.70. In margin 'dishonest gain'
1 See *Adagia* III iii 52: *Lucrum malum aequale dispendio* 'Gain ill-gotten is as bad as loss,' for other occurrences of this sentiment.

**170** (x) Diogenes Laertius 1.70. In margin 'impossibles'
1 See *Adagia* v ii 2: *Quod fieri non potest nec incipiendum quidem est* 'Do not even begin what cannot be achieved.'

good adviser is to identify not only what is the best thing in absolute terms, but what is feasible in the circumstances.

171 When Chilon was asked to name something difficult, he replied, 'To keep a secret.'

The tongue is the most slippery and uncontrolled thing there is, though you might well think nothing was easier than to say nothing.

172 He used to tell people also that 'they should guard their tongues always, but especially at a party.'

At a party the food and drink encourage recklessness.[1] Where there is more danger, there is need of more caution.

173 'One should not make threats,' not only 'because it is characteristic of women to do so' rather than men, but because threatening a person you intend to harm warns your enemy to be on his guard and reduces your chances of damaging him.[1] As for friends, it is uncivilized to use threatening language to them. All the same, it is right to do so when we intend the threat to be the means of correcting a person[2] and are minded to punish him no further.

174 'One should rally round one's friends in ill fortune rather than good fortune.'

Some people come running when things are going well, even people who are hardly friends. True friends are the ones who stand by you when fortune goes against you.[1]

* * * * *

171 (XI) Diogenes Laertius 1.69. In margin 'silence'

172 (XII) Diogenes Laertius 1.69. In margin 'careless talk at a party'
   1 Cf Plutarch *Moralia* 503E–F (*On talkativeness*) and General Index: mouth, keeping shut

173 (XIII) Diogenes Laertius 1.70. In margin 'pointless threats'
   1 Cf 1.332 above.
   2 See *Adagia* III viii 52: *Amicorum est admonere mutuum* 'It is the duty of friends to admonish each other'; also Ausonius (2.161 n1 above) *Anacharsis* 5: *Cum vere obiurges, sic inimice iuvas* 'Just reproof is help in unfriendly guise'; Plutarch *Moralia* 50B, 55C, 59B (*How to tell a flatterer*).

174 (XIV) Diogenes Laertius 1.70. In margin 'a true friend'
   1 *Adagia* IV v 5: *Amicus certus in re incerta cernitur* 'Uncertainty sees a certain friend'

**175** 'Marry a poor wife with few possessions.'

Otherwise you will take home not a wife but a ruler.[1] A girl has a good enough dowry if she brings with her modesty and good character.[2] That is why it was a Spartan custom for girls to be married without a dowry.[3]

**176** Chilon forbade speaking ill of the dead. Because it was cowardly to attack those who could not answer back, and despicable to wrestle with ghosts and spirits,[1] for that is exhuming the dead in a way.

**177** Chilon taught that the young should reverence the old.

Then, when they became old themselves, they too would be esteemed by others. This was useful in two ways: the authority and standing of the old deterred the disorderly young from doing wrong, and the old took care not to do anything that would either make them a laughing-stock to the young because of folly, or a danger to them because of moral turpitude. There was the same respectful relationship between the whole older and younger age groups as between parents and their own children.[1]

**178** Chilon warned against 'applauding or smiling on a man made arrogant by good fortune.'

Good fortune becomes bad fortune if it makes a man conceited and then it merits not cheers but tears. Those who encourage self-conceit are worse than those who display it. The people often cry out against the prince's avarice and tyranny, but it is from the people that princes learn these things.[1]

\* \* \* \* \*

**175** (xv) Diogenes Laertius 1.70. In margin 'a humble wife'
  1 See Plutarch *Moralia* 13F (*The education of children*); *Adagia* I viii 1: *Aequalem uxorem quaere* 'Seek a wife of your own sort.'
  2 Cf 2.150 above.
  3 See 1.270 above.

**176** (xvi) Diogenes Laertius 1.70. In margin 'spare the dead'
  1 See *Adagia* I ii 53: *Cum larvis luctari* 'To wrestle with ghosts.'

**177** (xvii) Diogenes Laertius 1.70. In margin 'respect for old age'
  1 See 2.92 above.

**178** (xviii) Diogenes Laertius 1.70. In margin 'arrogance'
  1 For this idea see Plutarch *Agis* 1.3–4.

One copy of the Greek text had 'Do not mock (or insult) the unfortunate.' To do so marks the depths of inhumanity.[2]

179 Chilon taught that 'power must be combined with clemency, so that the ruler does not so much screw fear out of his subjects as invite and receive respect.'

Love accompanies respect, hatred accompanies fear. To be loved is not only more honourable, it is also safer.

180 He urged 'every man to look after his own house well.'

We owe our first responsibility to our immediate household, and no one is fit to administer public affairs if he cannot give proper direction to his personal ones. A household is but the state writ small.[1]

181 'Anger must be conquered.'

Anger is the most powerful of all emotions and to defeat it demands more valour than laying low an armed foe. Anger is as destructive to mortal men as a human enemy.

182 'Prophecy,' said Chilon, 'is not to be despised.'

* * * * *

2 This section from 'One copy of the Greek text' was added in 1532. The first version, translating a reading εὐτυχοῦντι μὴ ἐπιγελᾶν, literally, 'Do not laugh at the successful' is based on Traversari (see Introduction xvi–xvii above). Erasmus found this puzzling. His explanation is perhaps based on Diogenes Laertius 1.88, where the maxim 'Do not praise an unworthy man because of his wealth' is accredited to Bias. The easier variant reading ἀτυχοῦντι μὴ ἐπιγελᾶν 'Do not laugh at the unfortunate' found in Froben's edition of Diogenes Laertius 1533 is supported by Ausonius (2.161 n1 above) II Pittacus 4: 'The fool laughs at the grief of the unfortunate'; also Quintilian Institutio oratoria 6.3.33, 'It is uncivilized to make jokes about the unfortunate.'

179 (xix) Diogenes Laertius 1.70. In margin 'control'

180 (xx) Diogenes Laertius 1.70
  1 Cf 1.276 above.

181 (xxi) Diogenes Laertius 1.70. In margin 'anger'

182 (xxii) Diogenes Laertius 1.70 (prophecy), 1.68 (foreseeing events), and 1.71–2 (Cythera). In margin 'prophecy'

He believed that the ability to foresee events was a gift from the gods and could be exercised rationally by a man endowed with outstanding ability.[1]

He himself predicted that much harm would come to the Spartans from the island of Cythera.[2] When he observed its nature and situation, he said, 'I wish this island had never existed or that it had sunk the moment it was born.' For when Demaratus fled from Sparta,[3] he went to Xerxes and urged him to station a fleet at that island. If Xerxes had followed Demaratus' advice, he would undoubtedly have conquered Greece. Later on, Nicias[4] gained control of it, put a garrison of Athenians there, and inflicted a number of defeats on the Spartans.

183 Chilon is also credited with the saying, 'Do not rush along the street.'

The way a man walks reveals his temperament. A headlong rush indicates a hasty man, an excessively slow pace a dullard. In public it is proper to display a calm manner. Perhaps Chilon meant that one should avoid hasty decisions.[1]

184 Very like this is the saying, 'Do not wave your hands about when speaking, for that looks crazy.'

That is why we read in the book of Proverbs that the fool speaks with his fingers.[1]

* * * * *

1 A comparison with the actual Greek text shows that Erasmus is adapting Traversari. See Introduction xvi–xvii above.
2 Cythera was a large island lying off the southern coast of Laconia and commanding the Laconian Gulf.
3 Demaratus was exiled from Sparta and took refuge first with Darius I and then with Xerxes, the Persian king who invaded Greece via the Hellespont and was finally repulsed at Plataea in 479 BC. See 1.167–74 above for anecdotes from Demaratus' time in exile.
4 Nicias was an Athenian commander who occupied Cythera during the Peloponnesian War against Sparta and from there made incursions onto the mainland.

183 (XXIII) Diogenes Laertius 1.70. In margin 'conduct in public'
1 The last sentence is found in 1532.

184 (XXIV) Diogenes Laertius 1.70
1 Prov 6.12–13: 'A naughty person ... speaketh with his feet, he teaches with his fingers.'

**185** Chilon insisted that 'the laws must be obeyed.'

This applies particularly to rulers who think they are above the law. A lively respect for law contributes more than anything else to national well-being, and tyranny cannot arise where everything is done in obedience to long-established laws.

**186** He used to say, 'Quiet is highly desirable,' that is, if honourable leisure comes our way, which agrees with that well-known Greek saying, 'Quiet is a good thing.'[1] There is nothing safer or pleasanter than being still. And no business is more dangerous than war.

**187** He is also credited with the saying, 'Watch out for yourself.' Perhaps it should be taken to mean 'Watch yourself,' or 'Beware of yourself,' or 'Keep an eye on yourself,' since the Greek means 'Guard yourself.'[1] So he is telling us that we should be an object of suspicion to ourselves. We all try to protect ourselves from others, but a man's worst enemy is often himself, when he allows himself to be guided by lust, rage, or ambition.

I wonder what authority Ausonius was following when he attributed the following sentiments to him.[2]

**188** 'One should so direct one's life that subordinates are not terrified nor superiors contemptuous.'

To be feared by those under us is the mark of a tyrant; but to earn the contempt of those above us shows supineness. This saying can be related

* * * * *

185    (xxv) Diogenes Laertius 1.70. In margin 'the authority of the law'

186    (xxvi) Diogenes Laertius 1.70. In margin 'leisure'
  1 Cf 1.153 above.

187    (xxvii) Diogenes Laertius 1.70. In margin 'watch yourself'
  1 'Or "Keep an eye ... Guard yourself"' is not in the first edition 1531.
  2 See 2.161 n1 above for Erasmus' use of Ausonius here. Each of Ausonius' seven sections, in different metres and each dealing with one of the Seven Sages, is made up of seven lines. See eg the editions in PL 19 col 878; BT 1886 (ed Rudolphus Peiper) 408; Loeb 1921 (ed H.G. Evelyn White) 2.276; Green 676. Chilon is treated in section 6, and Erasmus quotes only six lines of this section as it stands today: 2.188 quotes line 1, 2.189 lines 2–3, 2.190 line 4, 2.191 lines 6–7. For line 5 see 2.190 n2 below. Erasmus' headings are paraphrases of Ausonius' words, not quotations. He gives the actual quotations later.

188    (xxviii) Ausonius *Septem sapientum sententiae* 6.1 (see 2.187 n2 just above). In margin 'to be loved without being despised'

to your stage in life: you should so conduct yourself that younger persons love rather than fear you, and older persons do not find you contemptible. Excessive severity generates fear. To be torpid, wine-sodden, senseless and so on stirs contempt. This saying can also be applied to one's fortune: if it is extremely large, it is more likely to occasion fear than affection or respect; if it is humble, it lays one open to contempt. In this case as in others, the avoidance of either extreme is best.

Ausonius' poem puts it this way:

No fear of me from humbler men,
Nor scorn, I hope, from greater!

**189** Moreover, 'We should despise death, but still take care to preserve ourselves.'[1]

It is folly, not courage, recklessly to put one's life in danger. But whenever inescapable necessity leaves us no choice or a serious and honourable cause gives us reason, then it is the mark of a brave spirit to treat death as unimportant. When one is ill, one does not have to fear death, but one should still apply reasonable medication. In war one must prepare oneself to face death, but in the meantime fight bravely for victory.[2] I think the line in Ausonius' poem should read:

Live ever mindful of your end,
Yet take thought for living too.[3]

We could take this to mean: 'Remember that you must die, and so refrain from sin and useless concerns, but meanwhile assume that many

* * * * *

**189** (XXIX) See Ausonius *Septem sapientum sententiae* 6.2–3 (see 2.187 n2 above). In margin 'how far death to be disregarded, friend as supporter'
1 See 1.118 above.
2 The omission of the negative in line 4 ('When one is ill, one does not ...') might create a more satisfactory *comparatio in maius*, ie a parallel progressing to something greater: When one is ill, one should be aware of the possibility of death, but still take the prescribed medicine. In war, one *must* prepare oneself to face death, but still fight bravely for victory. See *De copia* book 2, method 9, CWE 24 592.
3 Ausonius *Septem sapientum sententiae* 6.2: *Vive memor mortis, item vive memor salutis.* Erasmus does not say what reading he is emending. Ugoletus' text had: *immemor ut sis vive salutis.* Erasmus' emendation *uti sis memor et salutis* is adopted in PL 19 column 878; *item vive* for Erasmus' *uti sis* is read in MGH, BT (1886), and the Loeb text (II 274). See 2.187 n2.

years lie ahead of you and so give thought to all that contributes to an honourable and happy life.' Brooding on death inhibits many people from pursuing worthwhile activities; while ignoring it encourages them to sin more recklessly.

One could also interpret the saying to mean: 'Fear death, but don't for that reason live in apprehension and misery,[4] but let hope of life temper the horror of death.' This last sense is suggested by the line that follows:[5]

> Triumphing over all that hurts
> Through courage or support of friends.

Life is subject to many miseries, but the most depressing thing is that death is the most certain thing in it, the day of death the most uncertain.[6] But we must rise above everything, either through a courageous spirit or through the support of friends. There is nothing more helpful in a time of trouble than to confide our worries and inner torment to friends, whose encouragement and sympathy lift the greater part of the burden.[7]

**190** 'One should forget that one has conferred a favour, remember that one has received one.'[1]

People usually do just the opposite. If they have done someone a favour, they boast about it endlessly and blow it up out of all proportion.

\* \* \* \* \*

4 Cf Seneca *Epistulae morales* 54.7: 'follow the man who is prepared to die but is still glad to live'; see also ibidem 78.25.
5 Ausonius *Septem sapientum sententiae* 6.3
6 For the whole section, cf Cicero *De senectute* 20.74.
7 Erasmus has many adages on the value of true friendship, eg 1 i 1 *Amicorum communia omnia* 'Between friends all is common'; 1 i 2: *Amicitia aequalitas* 'Friendship is equality' (containing *Amicus alter ipse* 'A friend is another self'); II ii 75: *Amicus magis necessarius quam ignis et aqua* 'A friend is more necessary than fire and water'; IV v 5: *Amicus certus in re incerta cernitur* 'Uncertainty sees a certain friend'; IV v 26: *Amicitias immortales esse oportet* 'Friendships should last forever.'

190 (xxx) Ausonius *Septem sapientum sententiae* 6.4 (see 2.187 n2 above). In margin 'gratitude'
1 See *Adagia* III x 68: *Benefactorum memoria* 'The memory of good deeds'; III i 83: *Simul et misertum est et interiit gratia* 'No sooner is he pitied than his gratitude is dead.' A similar saying to Chilon's is there attributed to Seneca. See Seneca *De beneficiis* 2.10.4: the whole chapter is relevant to Erasmus' remarks here.

If someone has done something for them, they either forget it very soon, or pretend it was never done or belittle it. Ausonius' poem puts it like this:

> If some kindness you bestow,
> Forget you ever did it.[2]

191  Ausonius also attributes to Chilon the opinion that 'a youthful old age is desirable, a senile youth burdensome.'

Most of the ills that give old age a bad name are the result of men's vices. Old age in fact brings a number of advantages: remembering and enjoying many things in retrospect, being able to give advice, receiving respect, exercising authority. If these advantages are present and the disadvantages absent, this kind of old age is preferable to the youth that is experienced by many, trickling away in vice and indolence. You see in many young people the feebleness associated with age, the lethargy associated with age, the fearfulness, the bad temper associated with age. The youth of such persons is worse than old age. They are not old but they are aged.

Ausonius put it like this:

> Age will no burden prove to man
> When youthful thoughts remain.
> But youth if prematurely old
> Becomes a sad affliction.

192  Pliny also attributes to Chilon that famous saying, which was considered to have the force of an oracle: 'Stand surety and ruin is at hand.'[1]

* * * * *

2  Modern editions of Ausonius have an additional line here: *Quae bene facta accipias perpetuo memento* 'But of some benefit received / Keep the memory ever.' Erasmus was possibly using the edition of Ausonius by Thaddaeus Ugoletus (Parma 1499) which omits the line (see 2.161 n1); Aldus had a copy of this edition which he annotated by hand. Erasmus' heading may be based on Seneca, see n1 above.

191  (xxxi) Ausonius *Septem sapientum sententiae* 6.6–7 (see 2.187 n2 above). In margin 'youthful old age'

192  (xxxii) Pliny *Naturalis historia* 7.32.119 but he does not quote these actual words; see also Diogenes Laertius 1.73.
   1  The saying is the subject of *Adagia* I vi 97: *Sponde, noxa praesto est.*

**193** Aulus Gellius in book I, chapter 3, of the *Attic Nights* attributes to Chilon
the following saying, and does so on the authority of Plutarch in the *De
anima*. Someone was boasting that he had no enemy, so Chilon asked him
whether he had any friend either, as he was of the opinion that friendships
and enmities follow in each other's train. Anyone who has many friends
must inevitably have many enemies.

So, if you please, let this serve as the second course[1] of our banquet. We will
follow it with some philosophers, not all of them or there will be no end,
but a few of the most distinguished. The change will prevent boredom in
the reader. If anyone wants more of this dish, Diogenes Laertius will easily
satisfy his appetite,[2] provided he is not too hard to please.

\* \* \* \* \*

**193** (xxxiii) Aulus Gellius *Noctes Atticae* 1.3.31, quoting Plutarch's *De anima*, a work
that survives in fragmentary form. The story is also found in Plutarch *Moralia*
86c (*How to profit by one's enemies*) and 96A (*On having many friends*). In margin
'friendship linked with enmity'

1 This metaphor of a banquet with various courses and dishes is set up in the
dedicatory epistle (11 above) and reappears not only here but with more or
less elaboration in the Prefaces to books 5–8 and in passing in 4.256. The
first five books are seen as the five main courses of the meal (*cena*), the sixth
is the desert (*mensae secundae*), and books 7–8 (added in 1532) represent the
sweetmeats served afterwards. For the frequent metaphor of a book as a meal,
see eg Pliny *Letters* 2.5.7–8. Often a whole work is presented as a record of
a discussion over dinner, eg Plato *Symposium*, Macrobius *Saturnalia* (see 1.1
there), Aulus Gellius *Noctes Atticae* (7.13), Plutarch's nine books of *Table-talk*,
and Athenaeus *Deipnosophistae* (*Doctors at Dinner*) – a banquet of food and talk,
a feast of many dishes and many topics, which provides an important source
for Erasmus, in book 6 below.
2 Diogenes Laertius' *Lives of Eminent Philosophers* treats of the *Seven Sages of
Greece* as well as early philosophers. Erasmus will draw on it for Socrates,
Aristippus, and Diogenes in book three, using Traversari's Latin version. See
Introduction xvi–xvii above. He will himself provide more, returning to this
source in book seven, for stories of many other philosophers.

# BOOK III

## SOCRATES AND HIS SCHOOL

It seems to me that Socrates comes very close to the Spartan temperament, not just in his incorruptible behaviour, his precepts, and his witty sayings, but in his capacity for endurance: so you might say he was Athenian by birth but Spartan by intellect – except that he did not practise Spartan brevity, since he preferred to put virtue across by persuasion rather than precept. He was particularly fond of using similes and inductive argument, which the Greeks call *eisagogai*, for this purpose, and the famous laconic brevity of the Spartan was ill suited to this type of speech. But though he may have been outdone by the Spartans in this respect, he far surpassed them in the holiness of his pronouncements. So it will be in order to review a number of these sayings.

**[Socrates]**

1 Socrates used to say that the gods were the best and most blessed of all, and the nearer anyone came to resembling them, the better and more blessed he would be.

\* \* \* \* \*

Erasmus provides a title *Socratica* for book 3, suggesting 'material relating' to Socrates and his followers. *Socratici* is a common term for Socrates, his followers, and the various schools they founded. His many followers included, besides Plato and Xenophon, the proto-Cynic Antisthenes (see 7.39–46 below and some isolated sayings in other books), as well as Aristippus and Diogenes to whom much of book 3 is devoted.
There was a mass of anecdotal literature, much of it no doubt tendentious, since Socrates' followers tended to father different schools of thought. For Erasmus' sources in book 3, especially his use of Diogenes Laertius, see Introduction xv, xvi–xvii above. References given to Xenophon's *Memorabilia* (passim 3.1–3.25), like those to the dialogues of Plato, often do not necessarily point to an exact source, as Erasmus tends to summarize, paraphrase, and combine memories of more than one passage.

1  (1) Xenophon *Memorabilia* 1.3.2. In margin 'be like God'

If you correct the number of that one word to the singular, there could no more Christian sentiment.

2 He said one should not ask anything from the gods except things intrinsically good, although men usually pray for a wife with a good dowry, for riches, office, power, and long life, as if they were advising the deity what he should do. But God knows best what is good for us and what is not.

3 Socrates wanted sacrifices to cost as little as possible, since he said the gods did not need men's property, and were more concerned with the feelings of those who made sacrifices than with their wealth. Otherwise, since the worst men are always the most wealthy, human affairs would be beyond hope, if the gods took more pleasure in the offerings of bad men than good. So he greatly approved of the following line of verse: 'Man must offer the immortals gifts that he can afford.'[1]

This precept concerns us Christians too, when we decorate our sacred buildings and conduct our services and our rites for dead relations at outrageous expense, although we would be more pleasing to God, if we assigned to our brothers in need whatever is left after decent thrift.[2] He declared that one should show the same thrift in entertaining guests, and applied the same rule: 'offer what you can afford.'

4 When a friend reproached Socrates for providing too modest a spread to entertain his guests, he said, 'If they are good men it will be enough: it will be more than enough if they aren't.'

* * * * *

2    (II) Xenophon *Memorabilia* 1.3.3 with material from Valerius Maximus 7.2 ext. 1. In margin 'what sort of prayers'

3    (III) Xenophon *Memorabilia* 1.3.3–4. In margin 'sacrifices to cost little'
  1 Hesiod *Works and Days* 336: Καδδύναμιν δ' ἔρδειν ἱέρ' ἀθανάτοισι θεοῖσι
  2 Erasmus backs up Socrates' precept of making offerings according to one's resources by moralizing about the expenditure of contemporary Christians on erecting chapels, or on church furnishings and services. He adds *parentalia*, the Roman festival of offerings to the family dead, whose Christian equivalent would be masses for the souls of departed relatives, which a priest would be paid to say.

4    (IV) Diogenes Laertius 2.34. In margin 'pointed'

5 He declared that one should avoid foods that provoked a man to eat when he was not hungry, and drink which enticed a man who was not thirsty to drink. For it is wrong to indulge in such things beyond the needs of the body.

6 He said hunger was the best seasoning,[1] because it sweetened everything so well, and cost nothing. This was why he always ate and drank with pleasure, because he did neither unless he was hungry and thirsty.

7 Socrates even practised enduring hunger and thirst; for when he had built up a sweat from the exercise ground, at a time when other men desperately wanted a drink, he never drank from the first pitcher; asked why he refused he said it was, 'In case I get used to obeying my desires.'

For sometimes even when you are thirsty, it is dangerous to drink; in this case when reason advises self-control, and desire is urging you to drink, you should listen to reason.

8 He said that men who had practised self-control and thrift had far more pleasure and less pain than men who wasted effort on procuring delicacies from all over the world.

This was because the pleasures of the profligate not only caused the torment of bad conscience, disgrace, and poverty, but often brought the body more discomfort than enjoyment into the bargain. On the other hand the things that are best also become the most pleasurable, if one has become accustomed to them.

\* \* \* \* \*

5 (v) Plutarch *Moralia* 124D (*Advice about keeping well*); cf 513D (*On talkativeness*) and 661F (*Table-talk* book 4); Xenophon *Memorabilia* 1.3.6. In margin 'abstemious'

6 (vi) Xenophon *Memorabilia* 1.3.5; Diogenes Laertius 2.27. In margin 'abstemious'
  1 Cf 2.84 above and 3.30 below.

7 (vii) Cf Plutarch *Moralia* 512F (*On talkativeness*). In margin 'physical urges controlled'

8 (viii) Xenophon *Memorabilia* 1.3.15. In this and the next citation Erasmus passes over material in Xenophon that he must have felt unsuitable, avoiding Xenophon's views on the desire for beautiful boys. He resumes with Socrates' comments on food and drink (3.8) and condemnation of enslavement to money (3.9). In margin 'pleasure from doing right'

9 Socrates declared it was shameful for anyone to choose to be a slave of pleasures, and make himself into the kind of fellow that no one would want to
have in his home as a slave. There was no hope of salvation for such men unless others prayed to God for them to find good masters, since they were committed to being slaves. Indeed he thought no one experienced more vile and
wretched slavery than those who were slaves of pleasure in mind and body.

10 Once, asked why he did not take part in public life, since he understood
government so well, Socrates replied that a man was more use to the state
if he trained many to be fit to govern, than if he alone governed well.

In fact Niccolò Leoniceno of Ferrara[1] gave me the same reply, when I
expressed amazement that he did not himself practise the art of medicine,
which he taught. 'I do more good' he said, 'by teaching all the doctors.' And
I had a similar reply from that great patron of my studies William Warham,
Archbishop of Canterbury,[2] when I wrongly declined preferment to a parish
and said to him, 'How could I have the effrontery to enjoy the money of
men whom I cannot preach to, since I do not know their language? Nor can I
support them by warning or consolation, or provide any of the services of a
good shepherd.' He answered, 'As if you were not doing more by teaching
all the shepherds with your books, than if you devoted yourself to one little
country parish!' I admitted that he spoke like a good friend, but he did not
convince me.

11 When someone asked Socrates how he could achieve a good reputation, his

\* \* \* \* \*

9    (IX) Xenophon *Memorabilia* 1.5.5. In margin 'slavery to pleasures'

10    (X) Xenophon *Memorabilia* 1.6.15. Socrates did fulfil the obligations of an ordinary Athenian citizen. In margin 'being useful to many'
  1 This is Niccolò Leoniceno, originally of Vicenza. Erasmus met him in Ferrara,
    where he taught medicine and other subjects for sixty years. Erasmus had a
    high opinion of him. See CEBR 2 323.
  2 On Erasmus' relationship to his generous patron Archbishop Warham see CEBR
    3 427–31 (William Warham), and cf 8.152 below. In March 1512 Erasmus was
    appointed rector to the parish of Aldington in Kent, but resigned four months
    later. Warham presumably expected him to appoint a curate to perform the
    parish duties (as was often done) and use the revenues of the parish to support
    himself in his studies and writing. After his resignation Erasmus was allowed
    to draw a pension from the living.

11    (XI) A paraphrase and summary of Xenophon *Memorabilia* 1.7.1–5. In margin
'how to win a reputation'

reply was, 'By striving to be what you want men to think you are.'[1] It is just like wanting to be thought a good piper: a man must demonstrate the skills he sees displayed in respected pipers. A person without training in medicine doesn't become a doctor because he has a doctor's position and is commonly called Doctor.[2] In the same way a man elected by popular vote does not immediately become prince or a magistrate, unless he knows the art of governing.

12 Socrates used to say it was utterly absurd that no one would, without suffering disgrace, practise sedentary skills[1] which he had not learned, nor would anyone commission a bookchest from a man ignorant of the craft, yet men were admitted to public office who had never studied the disciplines without which no man could hold office properly. Anyone would damn a man who took the helm with no knowledge of piloting. Surely then men deserved far greater curses for entering politics without knowledge of political science. In fact he did not really think a man should be called a trickster for taking money or plate he could not return from someone who trusted him; but men should certainly be called tricksters when they deceitfully persuaded others that they were fit to govern, although they were good for nothing.

This comment is even more appropriate to Christian princes, magistrates, and bishops, than to pagans.

13 He often said that no treasure was more precious than a real and good friend, and nothing could give so much benefit and pleasure. So it is quite perverse of people to be more distressed at waste of money than the loss of a friend, or to protest that they have wasted a favour freely given, when this has won them a friend more precious than any profit.[1]

14 We commission statues from men whom we already know as the creators of a number of tasteful statues. Accordingly, we should not invite men into

* * * * *

1 *Adagia* IV i 92: *Cura esse quad audis* 'Take care to be what you are said to be'
2 Erasmus adds the example of the doctor.

12 (XII) Xenophon *Memorabilia* 1.2.9 and 1.7.5. In margin 'the art of governing'
  1 For 'sedentary skills' see 2.64 n1 above.

13 (XIII) Xenophon *Memorabilia* 2.4.1–4. In margin 'a true friend'
  1 Cf 3.31 below.

14 (XIV) Xenophon *Memorabilia* 2.6.6–7. In margin 'judge according to behaviour'

our friendship unless we have already found them to be faithful and useful friends to others.

15 When someone was punishing a slave rather savagely, Socrates asked him why he was raging so. The other replied, 'Because he is the greatest glutton and the laziest worker, the greediest, and the most idle.' To which Socrates said, 'Have you never thought which of you needs more beatings, you or your slave?'

Whenever anyone finds himself punishing in others a fault he forgives in his own case – or if not the same fault then an even worse one – if only he said to himself what Socrates said to this fellow.

16 When someone wanted to go to Olympia but was put off by the effort of the journey, Socrates said, 'At home you often walk around all day, before lunch and again before dinner. If you kept on with your local walks for five or six days you would easily get to Olympia.'

He cleverly showed the fellow that what deters us in undertaking some effort is more one's imagining than the effort itself. If any risk, expense, or effort is to be made for the sake of something honourable, we make excuses and cry off, and shudder, though we often voluntarily go to more trouble in trivial and even shameful matters. So some people when invited to take part in intellectual activities, make excuses of their health, the sleeplessness, the cost of books, yet they stay up all night dicing, and get a fever or gout or dropsy or weakened eyesight from drinking, and paralysis or the new disease they call the French pox from whoring.[1]

17 Once a man complained that he was tired by the long journey, so Socrates asked if his slave could keep up with him. 'Of course,' he said. 'Was the slave unburdened or carrying a load?' 'He was carrying quite a lot of bag-gage,' said the other. 'Well then,' said Socrates, 'does he complain that he

*****

15  (xv) Xenophon *Memorabilia* 3.13.4. In margin 'punishing others for what one does oneself'

16  (xvi) Xenophon *Memorabilia* 3.13.5. In margin 'effort undertaken voluntarily'
 1  A virulent form of syphilis appeared in Europe about 1500, perhaps brought back from the New World by sailors. It was variously known as 'the Neapoli-tan scab' or 'the French disease'.

17  (xvii) Xenophon *Memorabilia* 3.13.6. In margin 'slave better than his master'

is tired?' When the other said no, Socrates went on 'Aren't you ashamed of your softness, when you are tired walking without a load, although he carries his load without complaining that he is tired?'

Thus Socrates showed that the slave was superior to the master in that, being better exercised for hardship, he felt less discomfort.

18 Socrates used to remind men that what was called in other lands simply 'dining' or 'feasting,' was called *euocheisthai* 'to be well fed / to fare well' by the Athenians, and this was meant to remind us that food should be taken in such moderation that neither mind nor body was burdened.

He explained it this way, I think, because *ocheisthai* means 'to be carried' (hence *oxeion*, 'vehicle, carriage' though *oxē* 'support' can also mean 'food, sustenance') and *eu* 'well' was added to the verb so that an unreasonably heavy burden was not put upon the body.

19 He said good training should be especially applied to well-born and free-born young people. The same thing tended to happen with them as with horses: among horses the proud ones with a noble nature, if they are well trained from their early years, grow up superb and adapted to every use, but if they are not trained, they are wild and ungovernable and good for nothing.

So the most talented natures are ruined through the ignorance of their teachers, who quickly turn horses into donkeys because they don't know how to command lofty and free-born spirits.

20 Another thing Socrates used to say was that a cowherd who reduced the size of his herd would be acting shamelessly if he expected still to be thought a good cowherd, but it was much more absurd if someone expected to be thought a good statesman when he reduced the number of citizens.[1] He aimed this comment at Critias and Charicles who had killed

\* \* \* \* \*

18   (XVIII) Xenophon *Memorabilia* 3.14.7. In margin 'moderation in food'

19   (XIX) Xenophon *Memorabilia* 4.1.3–4. In margin 'a lofty spirit'

20   (XX) Xenophon *Memorabilia* 1.2.32–3 (cowherd/statesman); Xenophon *Memorabilia* 1.2.37–8 (Charicles and Critias).
   1 Cf Xenophon *Cyropaedia* 'education of Cyrus' 8.2.14, where a good king is likened to a good shepherd.

many citizens.[2] This came to their ears, and Critias threatened Socrates that if he did not keep quiet, he too would reduce his herd; and what he threatened he carried out, for it was through him that Socrates met his death.

21 Socrates had chosen some lines from the old authors which he often used like proverbs, one of which is that line of Hesiod: 'It is no dishonour to work, but idling is dishonour.'[1]

He used this to discourage young men not just from idleness but also from unprofitable activities; certainly he called men idle who wasted their life in dicing, drinking, and whoring.

22 Another favourite was this line of Homer, as Gellius and Diogenes Laertius report: 'The good or ill that's wrought in our own halls.'[1]

Socrates quoted this to deter his hearer not just from inquisitiveness into other men's affairs, but from unnecessary skills, such as a precise knowledge of astrology, or geometry, or natural science, or the study of things beyond this world, towards learning ethics, the knowledge of which enables us to know ourselves and administer our private and public business profitably.[2]

23 This is the drift of another saying ascribed to him, which is particularly famous: 'What is above us is none of our business.'[1]

* * * * *

2 Critias was leader of the so-called thirty tyrants who imposed an oligarchic revolution on Athens in 404. Charicles, who had once been a rabble-rousing demagogue, also became one of the tyrants. They had both been followers of Socrates.

21 (xxi) Xenophon *Memorabilia* 1.2.56–7. In margin 'dishonourable idleness'
  1 Hesiod *Works and Days* 311: ἔργον γ' οὐδὲν ὄνειδος, ἀεργείη δέ τ' ὄνειδος.

22 (xxii) Aulus Gellius 14.6.5; Diogenes Laertius 2.21. In margin 'curiosity'
  1 *Odyssey* 4.392: ὅττι τοι ἐν μεγάροισι κακῶν τ' ἀγαθῶν τε τέτυκται, a line also cited by Plutarch *Moralia* 122D (*Advice about keeping well*), and 1063D (*Against the Stoics*). The saying and quotation are also attributed to Aristippus.
  2 Erasmus' comment is based on the context of the remark in Diogenes Laertius. See *Adagia* I vi 85.

23 (xxiii) Diogenes Laertius 2.21. In margin 'curiosity'
  1 *Adagia* I vi 69: *Quae supra nos nihil ad nos* 'The things that are above us are nothing to us'

This was his customary reply to those who expressed amazement that he always talked about ethics and never about stars or celestial phenomena.

24 When someone deliberately kicked him in the street, and others were surprised that he put up with it, he asked what he was supposed to do. When they urged him to sue the man, he said, 'That's absurd. If a donkey had struck me with his hoof, would you have told me to sue him?'[1]

He thought there was no difference between a donkey and a stupid man without virtue, and it seemed to him utterly absurd not to accept from such a man what you would accept from a brute creature.

25 Once a man he had greeted did not return his greeting. Socrates did not resent this, but his friends were amazed and indignant at the man's discourtesy. Then he said to them, 'If someone passed us by who was in a worse state of bodily health than we are, we would not be angry with him, so why should I be angry with someone who is in a worse state of mental health than I am?'

26 Euripides once brought Socrates a book written by Heraclitus,[1] and after he had read it to him asked him what he thought of it? 'By god,' he said, 'what I understood seems to me splendid, and I suppose the same could be said of what I didn't understand, but it needs some kind of Delian swimmer.'[2]

This was a very witty way of commenting on the artificial obscurity of that writer, from which he was nicknamed 'The Dark One.' As for the Delian swimmer we have explained that in the *Adages*.[3]

\* \* \* \* \*

24 (xxiv) Diogenes Laertius 2.21. In margin 'acceptance'
  1 Cf Plutarch *Moralia* 10c (*The education of children*).

25 (xxv) Xenophon *Memorabilia* 3.13.1. In margin 'forbearing'

26 (xxvi) Diogenes Laertius 2.22. In margin 'witty'
  1 The Ionic natural philosopher Heraclitus wrote natural philosophy in gnomic prose so oracular and allusive that he was called 'the Obscure.' Only fragments survive. His doctrines of *logos* 'thought', constant flux, and fire as a basic element of the universe were developed by the Stoics.
  2 Cf Diogenes Laertius 9.12 where Crates makes the same comment. Delian divers did not just dive and surface; they could swim under water.
  3 *Adagia* I iv 29: *Delius natator* 'A Delian diver.'

27 When Alcibiades[1] presented him with an extensive piece of ground on which to build a house, he said, 'What! If I needed shoes, would you give me a whole hide to make them from? And if you gave it to me, wouldn't I seem a fool to accept it?'

He used this comparison to refuse a useless gift.

28 When Socrates was walking through the marketplace looking at the quantity of goods for sale there, he used to say to himself: 'What a lot of things I don't need!'

Yet others torture themselves thinking 'how many things I lack.' Socrates was congratulating himself that because he lived according to nature and was used to very little, he neither wanted nor needed gold, purple, jewels, ivory, tapestries, and all the other things rich men delight in. Indeed he used to say they were needed more to stage tragedies than for real life.

To support this he often quoted these iambic lines from some poet or other:

> those vessels wrought of silver, purple cloths,
> are suited to those acting tragedies
> but make no contribution to good life.[1]

29 Another of his sayings was that the most godlike man was the one who needed least, since the gods need absolutely nothing.

But people usually think the wealthy are like the gods, although nothing is enough for their enjoyment. Hence the remark about rich men in the comedy of Terence 'How easily you live your lives!'[1] Now this was what

\* \* \* \* \*

27  (xxvii) Diogenes Laertius 2.24. In margin 'a useless gift'
   1 Alcibiades, nephew of Pericles and Athenian statesman, was Socrates' most extravagant and unstable pupil. See 5.184n below.

28  (xxviii) Diogenes Laertius 2.25. In margin 'abstemious'
   1 Erasmus quotes the Greek: Τἀδ' ἀργυρώματ' ἐστιν, ἤ τε πορφύρα / Εἰς τοὺς τραγῳδοὺς χρήσιμ', οὐκ εἰς τὸν βίον.
   The last section ('To support this . . .') was added in 1532. By this date Erasmus has a copy of Diogenes Laertius with the Greek verse inserted; see Introduction xvi above. Stobaeus 56.15 (Meineke II 336) attributes the iambic quotation to the comic dramatist Philemon (*incerta* fr 105 PCG), who could not have been quoted by Socrates, since Philemon lived and wrote after Socrates' death.

29  (xxix) Diogenes Laertius 2.27. In margin 'abstemious'
   1 Terence *Adelphi* 501

Homer ascribed to the gods, whom he called ῥᾷον ἄγοντας [rhaon agontas], that is, 'easy livers.'[2] But the man lives most easily who is happy with least possessions.

30 Socrates used to say that a man who could eat bread with enjoyment did not need a cooked dish, and someone who would enjoy drinking anything did not hanker for a drink other than what was available.

For hunger and thirst season everything best.[1]

31 He also said that it was easy for anyone to list his prize possessions, and yet it was most difficult for him to list his friends, although no possession was more precious than these.[1]

By this comment he criticized the popular values, which treated most carelessly the things which everyone should value most. A man who has acquired money thinks himself richer, and curses his misfortune if he loses it, but the man who has won a good friend does not see himself as better off, nor does he weep for the loss if he loses him.

32 To Euclides, who was very keen on rather tricky arguments,[1] Socrates said 'Euclides, you know how to associate with sophists but not with men.'

In this way he made it clear that sophistic skills were useless for public purposes. Anyone who aspired to take part in public life should not play with riddles and empty quibbles, but adapt himself to the ways of men.

33 He said that knowledge was the only good, and conversely ignorance the only evil.

*  *  *  *  *

2 Cf eg Homer *Iliad* 6.138, *Odyssey* 4.805, 5.122 (actually *rheia zōontes*).

30 (xxx) Diogenes Laertius 2.27. In margin 'abstemious'
   1 Cf 2.84 above.

31 (xxxi) Diogenes Laertius 2.30. In margin 'a true friend'
   1 Cf 3.13 above, 4.71 below.

32 (xxxii) Diogenes Laertius 2.30. Euclides of Megara (c. 450–380 BC) was the founder of the Megarian school of philosophy. He was particularly interested in logical disputation. In margin 'common sense'
   1 Erasmus has corrected his translation of the 1531 edition, where he referred to Euclides' passion for court cases, instead of intellectual disputes.

33 (xxxiii) Diogenes Laertius 2.31

Men who commit an injustice blunder because they do not know what each man is entitled to; on the other hand brave men are brave only in knowing that they must seek what the common people think should be dreaded; again intemperate men go wrong because they think things are sweet or admirable which are nothing of the sort. So he declared that the highest good was the knowledge of what one ought to seek and what one ought to shun.

34 When someone said Antisthenes the philosopher had a Thracian mother, as if it were an insult to the man to call him of mixed race, having an Athenian father but a barbarian mother,[1] Socrates protested, 'Do you think such a fine fellow could have come from Athenian parents on both sides?'

He was censuring the depraved morals of the Athenians, which made it more likely that a good man would have a Thracian or Scythian mother than an Athenian, and he thought Antisthenes' virtue should be credited to his mother.

35 Socrates used to say leisure was the best of all possessions.

But he understood leisure not as being idle but as being untroubled by upsetting business and desires that interfere with peace of mind.

36 The most famous of his sayings is that he knew nothing except that he knew nothing, for he went around asking questions as though he was uncertain, not because he did not really know anything; but by this irony he made apparent his modesty and reproached the arrogance of others, who declared there was nothing they didn't know, though in fact they did not know anything.[1]

* * * * *

34    (xxxiv) Diogenes Laertius 2.31. In margin 'humorous'
   1 For Antisthenes see 7.39–100 below. This jibe is repeated at 7.47 and 7.76. If Antisthenes had a foreign mother he would not be entitled to Athenian citizenship. Low birth was considered a legitimate target for wit; see 3.329 and 7.116 below.

35    (xxxv) Diogenes Laertius 2.31. In margin 'honourable leisure'

36    (xxxvi) Diogenes Laertius 2.32. In margin 'modest'
   1 Socrates explains in Plato's *Apology* 21 and the following narrative, that his loyal disciple Chaerephon asked the Delphic oracle of Apollo whether there was anyone wiser than Socrates. The oracle said there was no one and Socrates, puzzled, came to realize from questioning experts that he alone knew that he knew nothing, and was superior to them in this respect.

Indeed sophists publicly claimed that they would reply on the spot
to any theme set before them, and Socrates often exposed their arrogant
ignorance.[2] And as he saw it, this was the reason he was judged to be wise
by Apollo, that although he shared general ignorance with everyone else, he
was superior to them because he recognized his own ignorance while they
were unaware of theirs.

37 Diogenes Laertius also credits Socrates with the saying that 'the beginning is half the job.'[1] For he used to say half a task was completed once
a man had started it. For some people waste all their lives in delaying and
planning. Indeed there is a half line of Hesiod, 'The beginning is half the
whole.'[2]

38 He would say that men who bought fruits ripened early at high prices must
have given up hope of living until the normal season for ripening.
      Otherwise it would be stupid to pay a higher price for an inferior prod-
uct, when one could soon buy better fruit for less. In this way he constantly
recalled men's irrational greed to sound judgment.

39 Once Euripides was speaking about virtue and said: 'Such random things
should best be left alone,' as if virtue could hardly be found anywhere.[1]
Then Socrates got up and said this was absurd. If a slave could not be found

* * * * *

2 For this sophistic practice compare Gorgias' claim at Plato *Gorgias* 447C and
   Cicero *De Oratore* 1.103; see 8.27 below.

37 (XXXVII) Diogenes Laertius 2.32. In margin 'delay an evil'
   1 Cf 3.93 below.
   2 Hesiod *Works and Days* 40: Ἀρχὴ ἥμισυ παντός. See *Adagia* I ii 39: *Principium
     dimidium totius* 'Well begun is half done.'

38 (XXXVIII) Diogenes Laertius 2.32. In margin 'haste'

39 (XXXIX) Diogenes Laertius 2.33. In margin 'virtue to be sought'
   1 Κράτιστον εἰκῇ ταῦτα ἐᾶν ἀφειμένα. Erasmus introduced the Greek words and
     changed Traversari's translation (see Introduction xvi–xvii above) in 1532, after
     he had access to the Greek text. The 1531 edition simply says 'Euripides, when
     speaking about virtue, said it was best to let virtue go, since it could scarcely
     be found.' The line occurs at Euripides *Electra* 379, but is attributed by Laertius
     to the lost play *Auge*. Erasmus has omitted 'and went out' after 'Socrates got
     up,' obscuring the fact that the incident occurred in the theatre, as Diogenes
     Laertius makes clear.

at once we would think it worth while to search for him. It was absurd to think virtue not worth a search if it didn't come to a man at once.

40  When a young man asked him whether it was better to marry a wife or not,[1] Socrates said, 'You will be sorry whatever you do.' He judged that both bachelor life and marriage had their inconveniences, for which one must prepare the spirit. The bachelor's lot means loneliness, childlessness, the end of the family line, an outsider as heir; but marriage means endless harassment, constant complaints, reproaches about dowry, the raised eyebrow of in-laws, the chatter of a mother-in-law, a betrayer in wait to ruin other men's marriages, no guarantee of how children will turn out, and countless other disadvantages.

Accordingly this was not a choice between good and bad, but between more or less tiresome nuisances.

41  One of his friends was complaining that everything cost too much at Athens – Chian wine cost a mina, purple three minae, half a pot of honey five drachmae. So Socrates took him by the hand into a grain merchant's store. 'Look', he said, 'a half measure costs an obol, so wheat is cheap.' Then he took him to the oil store and said, 'A whole measure is just two brass bits. So not everything in the city costs a lot.'

The man who is content with a few essentials makes food cheap for himself.

42  King Archelaus had invited Socrates with lavish promises.[1] But Socrates answered that he did not want to come in order to take favours from him, since

*  *  *  *  *

40  (XL) Diogenes Laertius 2.33 for the general sentiment; the details are added from Valerius Maximus 7.2 ext. 1. In margin 'marriage'
1  A question frequently put to philosophers. See General Index: marriage. It was used as a *chreia*, ie the subject for elementary exercises in composition (*progymnasmata*). See Introduction xxiv–xxvii above. Aphthonius *Progymnasmata* 13.109–114 (Spengel II 49–53) takes it as a *thesis* and gives sample arguments pro and con.

41  (XLI) Plutarch *Moralia* 470F (*On tranquillity of mind*). In margin 'abstemious'

42  (XLII) Seneca *De beneficiis* 5.6.2. In margin 'gifts scorned'
1  Archelaus, son of Perdiccas, was king of Macedonia from 413–399, and invited to his court both Socrates (who declined) and Euripides (who accepted). Erasmus quotes some of his sayings at 5.87–91 below.

he could not return them. Seneca criticizes this saying, on the grounds that a philosopher who teaches contempt for gold and silver gives more than if he were to give gold and silver.

43 Once when he came back from market he said to his friends 'I would have bought a cloak, if I had any money.' He didn't ask for anything but modestly reminded them of his need. Soon there was a contest among his friends as to whom Socrates would take it from. 'Yet anyone who was eager after that remark,' Seneca commented, 'was already late in giving.'

44 A certain man complained that his travels had done him no good. 'That is what you deserve,' Socrates said, 'for you travelled in your own company.' Many people think that wisdom is gathered from long journeys, although Horace declares 'Men change the sky, not their mood, when they cross the sea.'[1] It is the association of wise men that brings good judgment, not mountains or oceans.

45 When a fellow struck him in the street he made no answer, except to say that men never knew when they should go out wearing a helmet. Laertius gives the same witticism to Diogenes.[1]

46 Socrates used to say he wondered why sculptors who tried so hard to make stone look like the man, didn't take as much trouble not to look like stone and actually be like stone themselves. Now there is a belief that Socrates had been a statue maker before he took to philosophical leisure.

47 He always urged young men to gaze in a mirror, so that if they were good looking, they would take care not to act in a manner unworthy of their

* * * * *

43   (XLIII) Seneca *De beneficiis* 7.24.1–2. In margin 'unsolicited kindness'

44   (XLIV) Seneca *Epistulae morales* 104.7. In margin 'travel useless'
  1 Horace *Epistles* 1.11.27

45   (XLV) Diogenes Laertius 6.41. In margin 'forbearing'
  1 See 3.228 below.

46   (XLVI) Diogenes Laertius 2.33 (the saying) and 2.19 (Socrates as sculptor). Cf 3.122, 7.234, and 7.249 below. In margin 'witty'

47   (XLVII) Diogenes Laertius 2.33. In margin 'development of mind'

looks; but if not, they would compensate for their physical deficiencies by
the development of their intellect and character.[1]

This great man was always so eager to seize any opportunity for urging
men towards virtue.

48 Socrates had asked some rich men to dinner. Xanthippe was worried about
this, because they had very few provisions. 'Keep calm,' he said 'for if they
are modest and self controlled they will make the best of it, but if not, we
shouldn't worry about them.'

These alternatives should eliminate our laborious and costly pretensions in entertaining guests.

49 He used to say that many lived to eat and drink, but he ate and drank
in order to live, indulging in these things not for pleasure but to satisfy
nature.

This is how the satirist adapted the saying: 'Don't live to eat but eat so
you can live.'[1]

50 Socrates declared that those who trusted the ignorant mob behaved like a
man who questioned and rejected a single tetradrachm, but approved and
accepted a whole pile of similar coins.

If you wouldn't trust a man by himself, you should trust him even
less in a crowd of others like him. It doesn't make any difference how many

* * * * *

1 See also Plutarch *Moralia* 141D (*Advice to bride and groom*).

48 (XLVIII) Diogenes Laertius 2.34. Cf 3.4 above. In margin 'frugality'

49 (XLIX) Diogenes Laertius 2.34; also quoted in Aulus Gellius 19.2 and Macrobius 2.8.16. In margin 'indulgence'
   1 'The satirist' usually means Juvenal, but this is from Alexander de Villa Dei
   *Doctrinale* 2611; see ASD IV-4 589 p208.
   This was an elementary instruction manual in verse on various points of Latin
   usage and forms of nouns and verbs. This line comes from chapter 12 on
   figures of speech. It was a basic school text and there were many MSS and
   printings. It was used in Hegius' school in Deventer; it was published there
   c. 1484 and frequently thereafter (see the preface to Dietrich Reichling *Das
   doctrinale des Alexander de Villa-Dei: kritisch-exegetische Ausgabe* [Berlin 1893] li).
   So this may be a distant memory from Erasmus' school-days (see CEBR 2 173
   [Hegius]), hence the wrong attribution.

50 (L) Diogenes Laertius 2.34. In margin 'what sort of coin'

they are, only how reliable, for a counterfeit coin remains a counterfeit coin however big the pile.[1] This was his argument against a crowd of witnesses and the verdicts of the ignorant rabble.

51 Aeschines wanted to be one of Socrates' pupils, and modestly excused his poverty, being embarrassed because Socrates' other wealthy friends poured money on him, while he had nothing to offer but himself. So Socrates said, 'Don't you realize what a great gift you are giving me, unless perhaps you don't think much of yourself? In that case I will take care to return you to yourself better than I found you.'[1]

Although other sophists taught sheer nonsense, they took no pupil without a large fee, but Socrates took in the penniless as gladly as the well off.

52 When someone said to him 'the Athenians have condemned you to death' Socrates answered, 'and Nature has condemned them!'

He felt it was not a great evil if someone was put to death since he would die soon anyway, even if no one executed him. But some people attribute this remark to Anaxagoras.[1]

53 His wife wept, the way women will, and said, 'Dear husband you are going to die although you are innocent,' but he said 'Well, wife, would you rather I died guilty?'

* * * * *

1 This entry was heavily remodelled from the first edition (1531) which offered: 'He used to say that those who trusted the common crowd which hates poverty but admires wealth, behaved ... a pile of similar coins, as if numbers increased value. If a coin is good in itself, why is that one rejected? If it is not, what does having more of them contribute?'

51 (LI) Diogenes Laertius 2.34. In margin 'gracious'
1 This is Aeschines of Sphettus, 'the Socratic,' whom Laertius 2.64 distinguishes from the famous orator and others of the same name.

52 (LII) Diogenes Laertius 2.35. In margin 'death inevitable'
1 See 7.127 below, where Diogenes Laertius attributes the remark to Anaxagoras.

53 (LIII) Diogenes Laertius 2.35. This anecdote is given as a *chreia* (with Apollodorus, see 3.54 below, in place of Xanthipppe) in Theon *Progymnasmata* 5.208 (Spengel II 99). Erasmus' comment seems to be suggested by Theon's conclusion. In margin 'death not to be lamented'

We should shed fewer tears over the death of good men, because they are dying undeservedly; but men deserve twice as many tears when they are paying the penalty for their wicked deeds. It is far more pitiable to deserve punishment than receive it.

54 The day Socrates was due to drink the poison Apollodorus brought him a very valuable cloak to comfort him, so that he could die in it.[1] But he refused the gift, saying 'Do you think my cloak, which suits me well alive, will not suit me dead?'

Thus he condemned the pretentiousness of people who take strange pains to have a funeral procession and be buried as grandly as possible.

55 A friend reported that someone was speaking ill of him: 'I suppose,' Socrates said, 'he has not learnt to speak well,'[1] attributing the man's sick tongue not to malice but ignorance. He didn't think it mattered to him what men said who spoke out of a mental affliction, not from judgment.

56 When the Cynic Antisthenes had a torn cloak and turned round to let everyone see the tear, Socrates said, 'Through that hole in your cloak I can see your – vanity.'[1]

This was a neat way of pointing out how it was more shameful to be pretentious about the cheapness of one's dress than about a splendid garment. If only there were not many like Antisthenes among the Christians, who conceal more self-satisfaction under a dark cheap dirty robe than other – wealthy – men have in their robes of pure silk or muslin.

57 When someone was amazed that Socrates was not upset with a fellow who assailed him with insults, Socrates said, 'It's not me he is abusing, since what he is saying isn't true of me and doesn't apply to me.'

* * * * *

54 (LIV) Diogenes Laertius 2.35. In margin 'concern for one's funeral'
1 Apollodorus, a devoted pupil of Socrates, was present at Socrates' death and is the spokesman who reports Plato's *Symposium* (174a).

55 (LV) Diogenes Laertius 2.35. In margin 'forbearance'
1 Cf 1.236 above.

56 (LVI) Diogenes Laertius 2.36; 6.8. In margin 'pretentious squalor'
1 The story is repeated in 8.204 below. There are several anecdotes on this topic.

57 (LVII) Diogenes Laertius 2.36. In margin 'forbearance'

Yet most men are more upset if accusations are undeserved. When good men are spoken ill of, they congratulate themselves on being innocent of the evils that are cast in their teeth, and do not believe that these are anything to do with them. It's like someone with poor eyesight addressing Plato as Socrates and then abusing Socrates. He would not be abusing Plato, but the man he thought Plato was.

58 The Old Comedy regularly insults men under their own names.[1] Although most people were afraid of this licence, Socrates said it was in a person's interest to offer himself knowingly and willingly as a target. 'For if they attack us for something that deserves reproach,' he said, 'we will take warning and correct it, and they will have done us good: but if they sling false insults at us, that's nothing to do with us.'

59 When Socrates had put up with Xanthippe scolding him indoors for a long time, and had finally gone to sit wearily outside the doorway, she was even more enraged by her husband's calm, and poured a chamber pot onto him out of the window. The passers-by laughed and Socrates laughed with them, saying, 'It was easy to guess that after such thunder rain would follow.'

60 Alcibiades was amazed that Socrates endured the unbearably quarrelsome Xanthippe at home. Socrates said, 'I have been accustomed to this for so long now, that I am no more irritated than if I were listening to the screech of the wheel that hauls water from the well.'
    For this noise is very disturbing to those who are not used to it, but the man who hears it every day is so little troubled that he doesn't know he is hearing it.

61 When Alcibiades made another similar remark, Socrates said, 'But don't you endure the squawking of hens at home?' 'Yes, I do,' said Alcibiades, 'but

* * * * *

58  (LVIII) Diogenes Laertius 2.36. In margin 'profit from insults'
 1  For Aristophanes' comedy about Socrates see 3.83 below.

59  (LIX) Diogenes Laertius 2.36. In margin 'witty, mild'

60  (LX) Diogenes Laertius 2.36. In margin 'familiarity makes things tolerable'

61  (LXI) Diogenes Laertius 2.36. In margin 'reason for enduring a wife'

they lay eggs and hatch chickens.' 'Well,' said Socrates, 'Xanthippe has given me children.'

62 Some people believe Socrates kept two wives at home at the same time, Myrto and Xanthippe.[1] So when someone wondered aloud what need he had to keep two wives, especially quarrelsome ones, and why he did not drive them out, Socrates said, 'They teach me endurance at home, which I need to use in public. Now I have been trained by their behaviour I will be better adjusted to the company of others.'[2]

Aulus Gellius gives this question to Alcibiades.[3]

63 When Xanthippe tore his cloak off Socrates in public and his friends urged him to avenge this wrong with his fists, he said 'Fine! So that you can cheer us on as we fight, one saying 'Go it Socrates,' another 'Go it, Xanthippe' (for these are the kind of cries with which supporters encourage two people having a fight).

He wisely preferred to offer an example of tolerance, than provide the absurd spectacle of a husband fighting his wife.

64 He told a man who asked why he kept Xanthippe, since her temper was so disagreeable, 'We should practise living with bad-tempered wives the way men learn horsemanship: they get horses of a fierce temperament and if they control them and can bear with them, they can handle others more easily. So the man who has learnt to bear the ways of a bad-tempered wife, will associate much more easily with any kind of person.'

* * * * *

62 (LXII) Diogenes Laertius 2.26 and 2.27; Aulus Gellius 1.17.2–3. In margin 'mildness'
   1 Laertius (2.26) attributes this report to Aristotle. Towards the end of the Peloponnesian war when many young Athenian men had been killed, a law was passed to make it legal for one citizen to have two wives; Laertius notes that Socrates married Myrto, daughter of Aristides, as a second wife.
   2 Cf 3.64 below.
   3 Aulus Gellius 1.17.1–3, but Erasmus has misremembered – the question there is only about Xanthippe.

63 (LXIII) Diogenes Laertius 2.37. In margin 'mildness'

64 (LXIV) Diogenes Laertius 2.37 and Xenophon *Symposium* 2.10. In margin 'mildness'

65 When Lysias read to Socrates the speech he had composed as his defence, Socrates said, 'It is a fine and elegant speech, but it doesn't fit Socrates.' For it was more suited to law court practice than to a philosopher, and such a philosopher. So when Lysias asked why he thought the speech wouldn't suit him if it was a good one, he said, 'Can't a garment or a shoe be smart and elegant and still not fit a man?'[1]

   Valerius Maximus tells the same story in a more offensive form and one less worthy of Socrates. For he reports that Socrates answered Lysias, 'Take it away, for if I could be persuaded to utter it in the remotest Scythian desert, I would really think I deserved the death penalty.'

66 When the jury disagreed on the penalty that Socrates deserved, he said, 'Personally I think that for what I did I deserve to be fed in the city hall.'[1]

   This was the honour paid to men who had served the State exceptionally well. Cicero reports this in the first book of *The Making of an Orator*. This is what he says: 'At Athens when the accused had been found guilty, and assuming it was not a capital offence, the determination of the sentence was assigned to the jury. They then used to ask the defendant what sentence he thought he most deserved. Now when Socrates was asked this he said that he deserved to be heaped with the greatest honours and rewards, and be offered his daily meals at state expense in the city hall – for this was considered the highest honour by the Greeks. But the jury was so enraged by this reply that they condemned this totally innocent man to death.'[2]

67 Socrates came upon Xenophon in some side street and when he recognized that the young man had an exceptional nature he stretched out his stick and barred his path. Once he had stopped, Socrates asked him where various

* * * * *

65  (LXV) Diogenes Laertius 2.40 and Valerius Maximus 4.4 ext. 2. Defendants had to plead their own case and often commissioned a speech from a speech writer, such as the famous and prolific Lysias. See 3.120, 3.125 below. In margin 'appropriate to the individual'
   1 The story is also found in Cicero *De oratore* 1.232, cited in the next anecdote.

66  (LXVI) Diogenes Laertius 2.42 and Cicero *De oratore* 1.232–3. In margin 'confidence based on good acts'
   1 This comes from the second part of Socrates' defence, in which he proposed his own penalty (or reward) after hearing the verdict: Plato *Apology* 36–7.
   2 The supplementary material from Cicero was added only in 1535.

67  (LXVII) Diogenes Laertius 2.48. In margin 'training of the mind'

products that men generally used were made and sold; so after Xenophon had given ready answers, Socrates asked, 'Where were good men made?' When the young man said he didn't know, Socrates said, 'Follow me, so that you will find out.' From this time Xenophon was a pupil of Socrates.[1]

Now it is absurd to know where you can get a decent garment or cup and not know where you can obtain training for your mind.

68 Once when Socrates was energetically walking about in front of his house into late evening, one of the passers-by said, 'What are you doing, Socrates?' He replied 'I am getting the appetizers for my supper.'

He meant the hunger he was working up by this physical exercise. Cicero's version says 'to enjoy my dinner better I am giving my hunger a first course by walking about.'[1]

69 Socrates said perfumes should be left to women, and no perfume smelt better on young men than the oil they used while exercising. For if you think of herbal oils like marjoram and nard, they make a slave and a freeman smell just the same. They asked him what old men should smell of and he said, 'Honesty.' So they asked where it was sold and he recited the line of Theognis: 'Whoever is good, learn what is good from him.'[1]

Xenophon gathers a number of such sayings in his *Symposium*.

70 When a wealthy man sent his young son to Socrates for him to assess his character, and the boy's attendant said, 'His father has sent his son for you to look him over, Socrates,' Socrates said to the boy, 'Speak then, so I can see you,'[1] meaning that a man's character did not shine forth so clearly from

* * * * *

1 This is Xenophon, the philosopher and historian. See 1.49 and Introduction xv above.

68 (LXVIII) Athenaeus 4.46, 157E. In margin 'abstemious'
1 Cicero *Tusculan Disputations* 5.97

69 (LXIX) Xenophon *Symposium* 2.3–4.
1 Theognis 1.69: Ἐσθλῶν μὲν γὰρ ἀπ' ἐσθλὰ διδάξεαι; *Adagia* IV viii 37: *A bonis bona disce* 'Learn goodness from the good.' For Socrates' dislike of perfume cf Plutarch *Moralia* 401C (*The oracles at Delphi*) and 713D (*Table-talk* book VII).

70 (LXX) Apuleius *Florida* 2.1 with Plato *Charmides* 154E. Cf 3.101, 3.184–5 below. In margin 'speech the mirror of the mind'
1 Erasmus is fond of quoting the words of Socrates. See eg *Lingua* CWE 29 326; *Adagia* I vi 50: *Qualis vir, talis oratio* 'As the man is, so is his talk'; *Adagia* II vi

his face as from his speech, since this is the surest and least deceitful mirror of the mind.

71 Socrates used to claim that the female sex was just as fit to learn the disciplines and all the virtues including courage (which the Greeks called manliness as if it were peculiar to men), provided they were properly taught. He inferred this from the little dancing girl who was brought to the dinner party and threw twelve hoops into the air and then caught them with amazing skill, controlling both the height of each and the rhythm of her steps so well that she never missed; she also danced fearlessly among the sharpest swords, to the great horror of the spectators.

72 When Agathon had invited Socrates to dinner and he had bathed and was wearing party slippers, contrary to his practice, a friend met him and asked why he was smarter than usual, and Socrates said playfully, 'To look handsome as I go to visit a handsome fellow,' though no one was more remote from this kind of passion.[1]

73 The day he was due to drink the poison, when his shackles were removed he rubbed his legs and felt pleasure at the sensation. He said to his friends, 'How marvellously nature has ensured that these two things, pleasure and pain, go together; for if there had not been the discomfort before, I would not be feeling this pleasure now.'

* * * * *

54: *Pluris est oculatus testis quam auriti decem* 'One eye-witness is worth more than ten ear-witnesses.' Here Erasmus has enlivened the anecdote with the addition of the wealthy father and the attendant. No single direct source is suggested.

71 (LXXI) Xenophon *Symposium* 2.7–12 summarized. In margin 'the female sex fit to learn everything'

72 (XXII) Plato *Symposium* 174A. In margin 'like to like' (1531)
   1 This is the opening scene of Plato's *Symposium*. Erasmus adds the remark in order to dispel any idea that Socrates could have had homosexual relationships. For his relationship with eg Alcibiades see Plato *Symposium* 218E–219D and see 7.198 n1 below. This is in line with the mildly deprecatory moral stance he usually takes on this subject throughout the *Apophthegmata*. Agathon was a celebrated tragic poet, ridiculed by Aristophanes for passive homosexual leanings.

73 (LXXIII) Plato *Phaedo* 60B. In margin 'pleasure linked with pain'

74 When the prison attendant offered him the hemlock in a cup, Socrates asked how this medicine should be taken, since the attendant was an expert (this was a reference to the way sick people find out from doctors when and how they should take the doctors' mixture). The slave said he should drink it in one gulp if he could and walk around a little until he felt heaviness in his legs, and then lie down in bed on his back, and then the drug would take its usual effect. Socrates asked whether he might use some of it for a libation (as it is the practice at dinner parties to pour out a small part of the wine and offer it by name to some god or other), but the attendant said he had only mixed as much as was needed, implying there was nothing left over to pour out. Then Socrates said, 'Still, it is right and proper to pray to the gods that my journey hence be blessed and fortunate.'

75 When the slave uncovered his face because he was already growing chill around the heart, he said 'Crito, we owe a cock to Aesculapius;[1] please don't forget to offer it' – as if he had regained his health by taking the draught. For Crito had worked with all his might to make Socrates preserve his life.[2] But there was such a natural spring of wit in the man that he even joked when dying. For they say this was his last utterance.

76 Socrates taught that one should love the beauty of the soul rather than of the body, and that we should transfer the pleasure which the sight of a lovely face produces in us to the far more beautiful but hidden appearance of the mind. But really we need philosophical eyes to see this.

He was aware that the Greek verb *phileisthai* was an ambiguous word, describing both kissing and loving, of which the first is an act of those loving the body, the second of those loving the mind.

* * * * *

74 (LXXIV) Plato *Phaedo* 117A–C. In margin 'cheerfulness in unhappy circumstances'

75 (LXXV) Plato *Phaedo* 118A. In margin 'cheerfulness when dying'
 1 Aesculapius as the son of Apollo was a god of healing. Those who were healed by him customarily offered the sacrifice of a cock. Possibly Socrates meant that he was now cured of the disease of life.
 2 See 3.77 below

76 (LXXVI) Possibly Plato *Symposium* 218E–219A (beauty) and Xenophon *Symposium* 4.26 (loving); also Xenophon *Symposium* 8.36 – the whole speech from 8.6–42 is on this theme. In margin 'pure love'

77 When Crito passionately urged him, if he was personally indifferent to his
life, at least to save himself for his children who were still young and for
his friends who depended on him, he said, 'God who gave them to me will
care for them; when I leave, I will either find friends like you or better than
you. What is more, I will not even feel the lack of your company, for before
long you will soon join me in the same place.'

78 Socrates said men who only loved the body were like beggars who were
always in need, and always pressuring others with demands; but those who
were friends rather than lovers were like men who owned an estate which
they were always trying to improve. A lover seeks to satisfy his own pleasure, whereas a friend does not aim at his own advantage but thinks he is
all the richer for making his friend a better man.

79 At Xenophon's dinner party, when individuals were told to say what skill or
asset they were particularly proud of, and the turn came round to Socrates,
he said jokingly that he was most proud of his pimping.

He meant that he was procuring real virtue, which made its possessor most attractive, and which both in private and in public life wins the
goodwill and love of men.

80 A physiognomist who claimed to be an expert in determining the natures of
men from looking at the build of their body and at their facial features examined Socrates and said he was dumb and stupid, a womanizer, lecherous
in the love of boys, a wine-bibber and a profligate. Socrates' friends were
furious and threatened the fellow, but Socrates controlled them, saying, 'He
didn't lie; I would have been all of these things if I had not surrendered
myself to the guidance of philosophy.'[1]

* * * * *

77 (LXXVII) Plato *Crito* 45C–D (children), *Phaedo* 69E and 115A (afterlife). Crito had
offered Socrates the chance of escape into exile in Thessaly (Plato *Crito* 45A–B).
In margin 'a holy death'

78 (LXXVIII) Xenophon *Symposium* 8.23 and 25. In margin 'pure love'

79 (LXXIX) Xenophon *Symposium* 3.10, 4.56–64. In margin 'pimping'

80 (LXXX) Cicero *De fato* 5.10; *Tusculan Disputations* 4.80, which names the physiognomist as Zopyrus. In margin 'philosophy changes a man's nature'
1 For the benefits of philosophy see General Index: philosophy, benefits of.

81 When Socrates' pupil Aristippus sent him twenty minae from his fees, which he was the first of the Socratics to charge for teaching, Socrates immediately sent the money back to him, saying his own daimon would not let him take it. For Socrates said he had a personal daimon which stopped him by a secret signal if he was attempting something dishonourable.

In my opinion this daimon was Reason. But at any rate, this was a polite way of telling Aristippus that he did not approve of Aristippus teaching philosophy for pay, and he rejected the gift as if it had been won by sacrilege.

82 Socrates was going home from the exercise ground when he chanced to meet Euthydemus and asked him to dinner. While they were discussing all sorts of things together Xanthippe got up angrily from the table and hurled a lot of abuse at her husband; but he was not at all affected, until in the end she turned the table over. Euthydemus was very upset and got up to leave, but Socrates said, 'What is the matter? Didn't the same thing happen at your home, when a hen flew up and knocked over what was on the table? But we didn't get indignant about that.'

83 In Aristophanes' comedy *The Clouds*, Socrates was attacked with many bitter insults, and one of the bystanders said, 'Don't you resent all this, Socrates?' 'No, by Jove,' he said, 'I don't mind being stung by witty abuse in the theatre any more than I would mind if it happened at a huge dinner party.'

Indeed the custom still persists among some Germans of inviting some jester to crowded dinner parties make jokes about the diners, and it is thought very uncivilized to be upset by them.

84 He used to say that anybody who exercised using dance movements needed

* * * * *

81 (LXXXI) Diogenes Laertius 2.65 (Aristippus); Plato *Apology* 40A (daimon). For Aristippus see 3.102–163 below. In margin 'disregard for money'

82 (LXXXII) Plutarch *Moralia* 461D (*On the control of anger*). In margin 'forbearance' This is Euthydemus of Chios, a sophist.

83 (LXXXIII) Plutarch *Moralia* 10C–D (*The education of children*). In margin 'comic licence'

84 (LXXXIV) Plutarch *Moralia* 130E (*Advice about keeping well*). In margin 'moderate exercise'

a large house for it,[1] but any space would be enough for a person using singing or declaiming, whether he stood or reclined.

By this saying he gave his approval to moderate exercise, especially after taking food, and expressed disapproval of the more violent movements.

85 When Socrates scolded a friend rather seriously at a dinner party Plato said, 'Wouldn't it have been better to take him aside and say this?' To which Socrates said, 'And wouldn't you have done better to take me aside too and say what you are saying?'

This was a very witty way of censuring Plato for committing the same offence by his reproaches as the one he was himself reproaching.

86 Once at a dinner, Socrates saw a young man greedily devouring the cooked dish and often dipping his bread in the sauce. 'Fellow guests,' he said 'which of you is treating the bread as the cooked dish and the cooked dish as the bread?' This caused a discussion among the guests, and when the young man realized, he blushed and began to eat the cooked dish with more restraint.

87 When someone asked Socrates what was a particular merit in young men, he said, 'Not to overdo anything.'

For the heat of youth scarcely allows them to keep within limits. This was what Terence had in mind in his report on young Pamphilus.[1]

88 Socrates said that writing, which the common crowd thinks was invented

* * * * *

1 Socrates used dancing as a healthy exercise (Diogenes Laertius 2.32).

85 (LXXXV) Plutarch *Moralia* 70E–F (*How to tell a flatterer*). In margin 'witty'

86 (LXXXVI) Athenaeus 186D and Xenophon *Memorabilia* 3.14.2–4. Cf *Adagia* II iv 64: *Edax currus* 'Greedy as a racing car.' In margin 'delicacies'

87 (LXXXVII) Diogenes Laertius 2.32. In margin 'moderation'
  1 Pamphilus is the devoted young lover in Terence's *Andria*. His father is deluded in thinking his son has done 'nothing to excess.' See *Andria* 55–60; also *Adagia* I vi 96: *Ne quid nimis* 'Nothing to excess.'

88 (LXXXVIII) This is the gist of the reproach voiced by Thamus to Thoth on his invention of writing in the myth at Plato *Phaedrus* 274E–5B. See also Quintilian 11.2.9 and 7.53 below. In margin 'memory'

to assist memory, was a serious obstacle to memory. For formerly if men
heard anything worth knowing they wrote it not in books but in their minds.
Their memory was strengthened by this exercise, they easily retained whatever they wanted, and everyone had whatever he knew ready to hand. Then
when writing was discovered, coming to rely on books, they did not take
equal pains to fix in their minds what they had discovered. So with the neglect of memory training, their knowledge of things was less lasting and
each man knew less; for we only know as much as we can keep in our
memory.

89 When the time to die was already at hand, Socrates was asked by Crito how
he wanted to buried: 'My friends,' he said, 'I have wasted a lot of effort,
if I haven't persuaded Crito here that I will fly away from here and leave
nothing of myself behind. But really Crito, if you can catch up with me, or
if you find me anywhere, bury me as you choose. But believe me, once I
have got out of here, none of you will catch up with me.'[1]

Socrates felt that the mind was the real man, whereas the body was
simply the tool or residence of the mind. Thus those who worry about how
they will be buried are being foolish.

90 He used to say, too, that death was like a deep sleep or a very long journey
to someone else.[1]

A really deep sleep takes away all consciousness, and the mind, sepa-
rated from the body, will some day return to its home.

91 He also used to say that if all the misfortunes of all men were heaped together and then equal shares of that pile were distributed to individuals,
what would happen would be that each man would prefer to take back his
own misfortunes rather than receive his fair share of the common lot.

This he said as a criticism of men's common behaviour, envying others,
and deploring their own lot.

* * * * *

89 (LXXXIX) Cicero *Tusculan Disputations* 1.103. In margin 'the soul immortal'
  1 Cf Plato *Phaedo* 115C–116A.

90 (XC) Plutarch *Moralia* 107C (*Consolation to Apollonius*). In margin 'death and
  sleep'
  1 Cf 3.372 below.

91 (XCI) Plutarch *Moralia* 106B (*Consolation to Apollonius*). In margin 'everyone dis-
  satisfied with his lot'

92 Socrates was quite old when he learnt to play the lyre, and learnt among
children: and when men were surprised at this as if it were absurd, he said
it was not at all absurd for a man to learn what he didn't know.

No one is blamed for acquiring things he needs if he has not got
them. It's not the person's age that matters, it's the fact that he's without
something.

93 He said beginning well was not trivial but almost trivial.[1] The Greek puts it
this way: εὖ ἄρχεσθαι, μικρὸν μὲν μὴ εἶναι παραμικρόν δε [eu archesthai mikron
men mē einai, paramikron de], which the translator of Laertius[2] has rendered:
'to begin well is not small but very great.' Yet Socrates' words have a different meaning: he means, if I am not mistaken 'to begin well is not small but
is considered unimportant,' or 'making a good start is not trivial but next
to trivial.' For one must begin gradually, because those who are hasty at the
beginning reach the end late, referring to Hesiod's command that we add
little to little.[3] The wit of the saying is in the Greek words, and cannot be
turned into Latin.

94 Socrates advised that geometry should be studied up to the point when a
man could both take over and pass on land knowing its size.

The Greek puts it thus: ἔφασκε δεῖν γεωμετρεῖν, μέχρι ἄν τις μέτρῳ δύνηται
γῆν παραλαβεῖν τε καὶ παραδοῦναι [ephaske dein geometrein, mechri an tis metrōi
dunētai gēn paralabein te kai paradounai] 'He said one should "geometrize"
until a man could ...' I think he meant that you should get modest estates such as it is comfortable to receive from ancestors and pass on to your
heirs. For large possessions cannot be obtained without trouble, nor do they
pass down to heirs without lawsuits. The wit of the saying lies in the word

* * * * *

92  (CII) Diogenes Laertius 2.32. Erasmus added apophthegms 3.92–100 in the second edition (1532), and 3.101 in the third (1535).

93  (XCIII) Diogenes Laertius 2.32. See 3.92n above.
    1 This is an alternative version of 3.37 above, inserted when Erasmus had access
      to the Greek text (see Introduction xvi–xvii). Erasmus was clearly puzzled by
      this saying. Cf 7.328 below, where he gives a different interpretation of similar
      words.
    2 This is Traversari; see Introduction xvi above.
    3 A paraphrase of Hesiod Works and Days 361–2, quoted in Plutarch Moralia 9F
      (The education of children).

94  (XCIV) Diogenes Laertius 2.32. See 3.92n above.

'geometrize,' which has a double sense, referring to both geometry and land surveyors.

95 When someone complained that he had been passed over when the thirty tyrants took over the government,[1] he said, 'Is that anything to regret?'

Socrates felt one should not resent being despised by wicked men, and no one should be discontented on this account, only if he did anything which rightly displeased himself and other good men. For it does one credit to displease wicked men.

96 When a figure in a dream said to him 'You should come to Phthia as soon as the third dawn rises,'[1] he told Aeschines 'I shall die on the third day.'

He interpreted the Homeric verse as an oracular saying, and this indeed happened. Phthia in Thessaly was Achilles' homeland, and Socrates' friends tried to persuade him to flee to Thessaly, because he had good friends there.[2]

97 Socrates said that men should obey the laws of the state, and wives should obey the practices of the husband with whom they lived.

A husband is the rule for his wife, and she lives rightly if he obeys the public laws.

98 He used to remind people that pleasures should be avoided like sirens by anyone who is as eager to set eyes on Virtue as if he had his sights set on his native land.

He was referring to Ulysses, who sailed past the Sirens with his ears stopped with wax, so that he might see the smoke of Ithaca arise.[1]

* * * * *

95 (xcv) Diogenes Laertius 2.34. See 3.92n above.
　1 On the 'thirty tyrants' at Athens see 3.20 n2 above.

96 (xcvi) Diogenes Laertius 2.35. See 3.92n above.
　1 Ἥματι μὲν τριτάτῳ Φθίην ἐρίβωλον ἵκοιο, *Iliad* 9.363, in which Achilles considers the future life open to him if he abandons the Trojan expedition to return home to Phthia.
　2 See 3.77 above.

97 (xcvii) Stobaeus 74.58 (Meineke III 62). See 3.92n above.

98 (xcviii) Stobaeus 5.81 (Meineke I 132). See 3.92n above.
　1 Erasmus has misremembered Homer (*Odyssey* 12.47–52 and 192–200). Ulysses

99 When Socrates heard the *Lysis* of Plato read aloud he said 'Great god, how many lies the young fellow tells about me!'[1]

Either his modesty prevented him from recognizing the praises that Plato gave to him, or else Plato invented a great deal about Socrates in the dialogue.

100 Aeschines was oppressed by poverty,[1] and Socrates used to advise him to 'borrow from himself' with or without interest and he added the explanation of the method, which was to reduce his own food supplies. This agrees with that well known saying: Thrift is a great source of revenue.[2] The quickest way of increasing your income, is to reduce your expenditure.

101 When someone asked him about Archelaus son of Perdiccas who was thought to be very powerful at that time,[1] wanting to know whether Socrates thought him happy, he said, 'I don't know: I've never talked to him'; and when the man added that you might just as well question whether the king of Persia was happy, Socrates said, 'Of course, since I don't know how wise or good he is.'[2]

Socrates measured a man's happiness by the real blessings of the mind. The story is quoted by Cicero in the fifth book of *Tusculans*, from Plato's *Gorgias*.

\* \* \* \* \*

sailed past the Sirens with his own ears unblocked, but tied himself to the mast so that he would not be bewitched by hearing the Sirens' song, while his men rowed past with their ears stopped with wax.

99 (XCIX) Diogenes Laertius 3.35. See 3.92n above.
1 Laertius adds that Plato included in the dialogue much that Socrates never said. See Athenaeus 505D and 507D for other denials of the truth of Plato's dialogues.

100 (C) Diogenes Laertius 2.62
1 Cf 3.51 above.
2 Cicero *Paradoxa Stoicorum* 6.3.49

101 (CI) Cicero *Tusculan Disputations* 5.35; Plato *Gorgias* 470D–E. The second part of this is given as a *chreia* of the type that gives a reason for what is said; Theon *Progymnasmata* 5.204 (Spengel II 98). See Introduction xxiv–xxvii. This entry was added only in *1535*; see 3.92n above.
1 On King Archelaus of Macedon see 3.42 above.
2 Cf 3.70 above with n1.

**Aristippus**

I think it is appropriate to follow the teacher with the pupil next to him in age and authority. No philosopher had a more nimble mind or one more adaptable to every circumstance of life, nor was anyone wittier or more amusing in his sayings, even if he does not seem to have shown the same probity of life which everyone admires in Socrates.

102 There was considerable competition between Aristippus and Diogenes the Cynic, because of their different way of life. Diogenes called Aristippus the king's dog because he paid court to Dionysius, tyrant of Sicily.[1] Aristippus in return said, 'If Diogenes knew how to handle kings he would not live on raw greens.' To which Diogenes retorted, 'If Aristippus had learnt to be content with raw greens, he would not be the king's dog.'

103 Once when he had had his slaves buy a partridge for fifty drachmae, someone denounced luxury in a philosopher, so he said, 'and wouldn't you buy one too, if it were sold for an obol?' When the other agreed that he would buy it in that case, Aristippus said, 'Well, that is all fifty drachmae are worth to me.'

What the other condemned under the name of luxury, Aristippus turned into a creditable contempt for money. For if anyone is put off buying by the high price, it is not that he despises the food, but that he puts more value on money. But to the philosopher fifty drachmae meant no more than an obol to the other man. So Aristippus matched him in desire for delicacies, but was superior to him in contempt for money.

* * * * *

102 (1) Diogenes Laertius 2.66, 2.68. In margin 'frank speech'
Aristippus (fourth century BC) was an associate of Socrates and possibly the founder of the Cyrenaic school of philosophy, which posited the sensory pleasure of the moment as the supreme good. He was famous for his self-indulgent and self-seeking life-style, but also for his inconsistency, alternating wildly between ostentatious extravagance and harsh self-denial. Many of the following anecdotes relate to the period when Aristippus, as a dependent of the Sicilian despot Dionysius I (403–377 BC), was living comfortably at the tyrant's expense. Plato too is recorded as associating with Dionysius (cf 3.110), but he offended him (Diogenes Laertius 3.18 and 3.147 below) and was sold by him into slavery according to some sources (7.151 below). In contrast to Aristippus, Diogenes the third philosopher (treated below 3.164–388) was a follower of the proto-Cynic Antisthenes and lived in deliberate poverty at Athens. For testimonia and fragments of Aristippus and Diogenes see Introduction xv n8.
1 For Diogenes' nickname as 'dog' see 3.192 n1 below.

103 (11) Diogenes Laertius 2.66. Cf 3.133, 3.137, 3.141 below. In margin 'pointed'

104 When Dionysius offered him three lovely courtesans, urging him to choose
the one he liked, he claimed them all, saying 'It wasn't safe even for Paris
to prefer one to the others': but he escorted the girls to the antechamber of
the court and dismissed them, finding it as easy to cast them away as to
embrace them.[1]

105 Straton, or Plato as others say, said to Aristippus, 'You alone are able to wear
either a chlamys or a rag.'
    The chlamys is the dress of satraps, a rag belongs to beggars. Horace
commented on this when he said every colour suited Aristippus.[1]
    He danced in front of Dionysius in purple, but sometimes wore a cheap
ordinary garment, always keeping an eye on what was appropriate.[2]

106 When Dionysius spat upon him, he took it in good part, saying to those
who were indignant at this insult, 'When fishermen catch a gudgeon they
let themselves be drenched in seawater. When I catch a whale, shouldn't I
put up with being spattered with saliva?'
    By the reference to a whale he meant the king whom he was patiently
striving to win over to the pursuit of philosophy. For a great deal of good
arises from wisdom on the part of sovereigns.

107 Asked what benefit he got from his devotion to philosophy, he said, 'Thanks
to philosophy I can speak freely to anyone I choose.'[1]
    He was not afraid of the powerful, nor contemptuous of the humble.
Since his mind was equally free of hope and fear he was a slave to no man,
and flattered no one contrary to his true opinion.

      * * * * *

104 (III) Diogenes Laertius 2.67. In margin 'humorous'
    1 Aristippus compares himself with the Trojan shepherd prince Paris who being
      called to judge the beauty contest between three goddesses, chose Aphrodite,
      and provoked the hatred of Hera and Athene.

105 (IV) Diogenes Laertius 2.67, but Straton (of Lampsacus) is too late.
    1 Horace *Epistles* 1.17.23. The chlamys was a short military cloak, not an elaborate
      robe as worn by Persian governors.
    2 See 3.149 and 7.170 below.

106 (V) Diogenes Laertius 2.67. Cf 3.351 below. In margin 'shrewd'

107 (VI) Diogenes Laertius 2.68. In margin 'freedom'
    1 Philosophers were often questioned about the benefits of philosophy. For var-
      ious replies see General Index: philosophy, benefits of.

**108** When certain men reproached him for being a philosopher, but living in luxury and refinement, he said, 'If this were a vice, it would not be the practice in honouring the gods.'

For on such occasions of worship men usually dress magnificently and enjoy the richest preparation of foods. So, since gods are angered by vices, they would not be appeased but enraged by this kind of magnificence if it was associated with vice. So he did indeed escape the reproach, but failed to indicate the best course of behaviour.

**109** When Dionysius asked what extraordinary quality philosophers had beyond other men, Aristippus said, 'Even if all the laws were abolished, we would go on living as we do now.'[1]

For the crowd is prevented from sinning by the terms of the laws, but the philosopher has reason as his guide instead of the laws and he does not do right because the law has commanded it, nor does he shun crime because the law has forbidden it, but he acts so from knowledge that one thing is intrinsically right, and the other wrong.

**110** Both Aristippus and Plato courted Dionysius, but Aristippus did not forgo the luxuries of the court when they were available, whereas Plato strove to observe frugality even amid royal luxury. So when Plato reprimanded Aristippus because he indulged so freely in delicacies, Aristippus asked what his opinion was of Dionysius – did he seem a good man? When Plato replied that he seemed good, Aristippus retorted, 'But he lives a lot more extravagantly than I! So there is nothing to forbid the same man to live in comfort and live well.'

**111** When Dionysius asked how it was that philosophers crowded the doors of the wealthy, and not the other way round, he said, 'because philosophers know what they need, and the rich do not.'

Philosophers know that one cannot live without money; so they seek

* * * * *

108  (VII) Diogenes Laertius 2.68. In margin 'witty'

109  (VIII) Diogenes Laertius 2.68. In margin 'the fruits of philosophy'
  1 Cf the comparable remark of Aristotle at 7.240 below. See 3.107 n1 above.

110  (IX) Diogenes Laertius 2.69. In margin 'humorous'

111  (x) Diogenes Laertius 2.69. Cf 3.117 below. In margin 'philosophy necessary'

out those who can give what they need. If rich men had an equal realization
of their lack of wisdom, they even more would crowd the thresholds of
philosophers. For poverty of mind is more wretched than poverty of body.
So the rich are more wretched in their need because they do not realize what
a precious and necessary thing they lack.

112 Asked the difference between educated and uneducated men, Aristippus
said, 'The same as between broken-in horses and unbroken ones.'

Just as an unbroken horse is useless for anything because of its ignorance and wildness, so the man carried away by the emotions which only
philosophy can tame is useless for every association in life.[1]

113 Once when he visited a prostitute, he noticed one of the very young men
who were with him blushing as if it was disgraceful for a philosopher to
enter a brothel. He turned to the young man and said, 'Young man, it is no
disgrace to come in here, only to be unable to leave.'

He felt it was pardonable if a man indulged moderately in permitted
sex, but not if he was enslaved to pleasure. This sentiment could be approved in that age when no law forbade associating with a prostitute, but
now it has nothing to recommend it except the witticism.

114 Someone once proposed a logical problem and eagerly urged Aristippus to
solve it. 'You fool!' he said, 'why do you want me to let it loose when it is
giving us such trouble tied up?'

He was making a pun. For one can solve a problem and one can untie
a man, or a beast, that is tied up, but it is stupid to untie a madman or a
dangerous beast, so that it will do even more harm.[1]

\* \* \* \* \*

112 (XI) Diogenes Laertius 2.69. In margin 'the fruits of philosophy'
  1 Defining the difference between the educated and uneducated man was
    a test case for philosophers. Chilon (Diogenes Laertius 1.69) said the dif-
    ference lay in good expectations (2.163 above); Aristotle (Diogenes Laer-
    tius 5.19) said they differed as much as the living differed from the dead
    or live men from statues (7.234 and 7.249 below). Cf 3.115 and 3.122
    below.

113 (XII) Diogenes Laertius 2.69. In margin 'moderation in sexual activity'

114 (XIII) Diogenes Laertius 2.70. In margin 'witty'
  1 The pun depends on the fact that in both Greek and Latin the same verb can
    mean 'solve' or literally 'untie.'

**115** Aristippus said it was better to be a beggar than an ignorant man, since the beggar only lacks money, but the other lacks what makes a human being.

The man without money is no less a man, but the man without wisdom is no man. A man without money asks passers-by for it; while a fellow without wisdom does not pester anyone in order to get it.

**116** When he was being harassed with insults by some fellow, he went away without a word; but when the abuser followed him as he left, saying, 'Why are you running away?' he said, 'Because you have the power to abuse me, but I have the power not to listen.'

This was a very witty condemnation of the fellow's shamelessness, in assuming the right to abuse, but not allowing the other even the right to withdraw, and stop listening to abuse. For the question 'Why are you running away?' was as if he were complaining about an injury.[1]

**117** Someone pouring out complaints against philosophers added that he always saw them hanging around the doors of the rich. Aristippus answered, 'Doctors visit the houses of sick patients, but no one would rather be a sick man than a doctor.'[1]

This was a smart way to turn around the abuse. Philosophers preach happiness which they claim for the wise man alone and yet they constantly associate with the rich, hunting for something from them, from which the other inferred that rich men were better off than philosophers. But Aristippus interpreted it that philosophers particularly cultivated the rich because their luxury and wealth made them more stupid and corrupt than other mortals, and so in greater need of philosophical instruction. For the

\* \* \* \* \*

**115** (XIV) Diogenes Laertius 2.70. In margin 'education profitable'

**116** (XV) Diogenes Laertius 2.70. In margin 'yield to the abuser'
1 The first edition (*1531*) has a very different text: 'You have the ability to abuse me, but I don't have the same ability to put up with it. The philosopher yielded to the stronger, for the other man was more expert in abuse than he in enduring insults, and it is much easier to abuse than endure insults. But here the one who wins is inferior, and the man defeated is superior' (cf 4.372 below). Erasmus changed the translation of the saying on the basis of the Greek text which he acquired (see Introduction xvi-xvii above) and this involved changing his comment.

**117** (XVI) Diogenes Laertius 2.70. In margin 'philosophy the medicine of the soul'
1 Cf the similar remark of Pausanias (2), 1.319 above.

philosopher is the doctor of minds in bad condition. And it is a better thing to be the doctor than the sick man.

118 Once when he was sailing to Corinth and a storm arose and threatened to wreck the ship, Aristippus went pale. Noticing this, one of the passengers, a fat soldier who hated philosophers,[1] began to insult him once the storm was calmed: 'Why do you philosophers who preach that death is not to be feared, grow pale in times of danger, while we ignorant fellows are not afraid?' 'Because you and I do not have lives of equal value to fear for,' said Aristippus.

Aulus Gellius adds 'I am afraid for the life of Aristippus, you aren't afraid for the life of a worthless fellow,' a remark rather too sharp to suit Aristippus, whose wit does not have so much black salt.

We feel least fear for the cheapest things, hence the proverb 'keep the water pot by the door.'[2] So Aristippus joked that the other was not frightened, not because he was braver but because he was worthless, with a mind lacking any virtue at all, so it was small loss if he died. An educated and wise man does not die without a grave loss to the state.

119 When a certain fellow boasted that he was a polymath, that is, a man of many kinds of learning, as if there was nothing he did not know, Aristippus said, 'It is not true that those who eat and excrete[1] the most are healthier than those of us who take just what we need; in the same way it's not the people who read most who should be thought learned and scholarly but the ones who read what is truly useful.'[2]

He criticized strongly those who stuff themselves with random and excessive reading without taking to heart what they read, but just store it in their memory. This makes them neither more learned nor better men.

* * * * *

118 (xvii) Diogenes Laertius 2.71; Aulus Gellius 19.1.10. In margin 'fear of death'
  1 Erasmus seems to have invented this character who does not appear in any other version of the story.
  2 *Adagia* ii i 65: *In foribus urceum* 'The water-jar on the doorstep'

119 (xviii) Diogenes Laertius 2.71. In margin 'variant reading'
  1 The text of Laertius says 'take exercise,' which is how Traversari (see Introduction xvi–xvii above) translates it, *exercentur*. Modern texts omit it. Erasmus obviously felt it was inappropriate and emended it to *excernunt*.
  2 Compare Seneca *Epistulae morales* 2.2–4, 45.1–2, on the need to read much, that is, a few books deeply, rather than many books.

120 An orator defended Aristippus in court, and won the lawsuit. When he, seemingly exalting his art above philosophy, said 'What help was Socrates to you, Aristippus?' Aristippus replied, 'Socrates helped me by ensuring that what you said in my defence was true.'[1]

For he had defended Aristippus as a good and innocent man. But it was Socrates who had ensured that he was the man the advocate said he was, by teaching him philosophy. For an advocate does not make someone good, but makes him seem good to the jury, even if he is not.

So what the philosopher provides is more valuable than what the advocate provides.

121 He brought up his daughter Arete with morally improving precepts, accustoming her to despise whatever was excessive, because the mean is best in all things, and it is an achievement of the greatest virtue in a woman to control her desires.

122 When someone asked Aristippus why his son would become better if he had him trained in literature, he said, 'If nothing else, at least he won't sit in the theatre like one block on top of another.'

For amphitheatres had steps made of blocks of marble on which the people sat to watch, but men also commonly called an uneducated and inarticulate man a block.

123 A father was negotiating with Aristippus to take on educating his son; but when the philosopher asked five hundred drachmas as his fee, the man was put off by the size of the fee and said 'I could buy a slave for less than that.' 'But, said Aristippus, 'here you will have two slaves!'

He realized that with the same money the man would get himself both a useful philosopher and an obedient son.[1] This was a splendid criticism of

* * * * *

120 (XIX) Diogenes Laertius 2.71. Cf 3.125 below. In margin 'oratory better than philosophy'
   1 The words 'seemingly ... philosophy' are Erasmus' insertion.

121 (XX) Diogenes Laertius 2.72. In margin 'moderation'

122 (XXI) Diogenes Laertius 2.72. In margin 'education profitable'

123 (XXII) Diogenes Laertius 2.72. In margin 'proper education'
   1 Erasmus seems to have missed the point, which is that the man will buy a slave to educate his son and so will have two slaves because his son will be

popular judgment, for men are never meaner than in educating their sons properly, and spend more money on their horses than their children.

124 When Aristippus was criticized for taking money from his friends, he said he was not taking it to use it himself, but to teach them the things money should be used for.

For rich men generally waste money on horses or building or on luxury, when it should be spent on good men if they need it.

But you can understand it another way. Aristippus did not use money except for necessities, and so he took from rich men to show them the right way to use it. He could not do this unless they supplied the raw material. In the same way a man who wants to learn the art of writing offers paper and pen to the one who is going to teach him.

125 When he was reproached for having used a hired orator in his own case, he said, 'It is not surprising, for when I am going to serve dinner, I hire a cook.'

The other man wanted to make out that the the orator was superior to the philosopher because the philosopher had hired his services, but Aristippus turned the charge round by implying that the inferior is the one who is hired.

For the task of the orator is too low to be fitting for a philosopher.

126 Dionysius once told Aristippus to give some examples of his philosophy and when he was reluctant, Dionysius insisted, so he said, 'It is ridiculous for you to ask me to talk about philosophy, and then instruct me when I should talk.'

Aristippus realized that it was precisely the philosopher's job to know when to talk and when to be silent. Now the man who asks to hear something

* * * * *

as 'ignorant as a slave.' See Plutarch *Moralia* 4F–5D (*The education of children*), which supports that view. The odd idea that the man is buying himself a tame philosopher who will be as good as a slave to him is repeated at 8.155 below. See also *De pueris educandis* CWE 26 314 / LB I 498A.

124 (XXIII) Diogenes Laertius 2.72. In margin 'the use of money'

125 (XXIV) Diogenes Laertius 2.72. Cf 3.65, 3.120 above. In margin 'philosopher superior to orator'

126 (XXV) Diogenes Laertius 2.73 (first paragraph); Diogenes Laertius 2.73 (third paragraph). In margin 'frank speech, the man honours the place'

philosophical is saying he wants to learn philosophy from a philosopher, but if he compels him to talk he seems more learned than the philosopher, inasmuch as he knows better the time to talk than the philosopher himself.

The king was angry with this reply of Aristippus and ordered him to be seated in the lowest position at dinner. At this Aristippus was not at all offended. He said 'O king, you want to distinguish this position and make it a source of honour,' indicating that the position did not make the man worth less but the man's dignity added honour to the place.[1]

**127** Aristippus could not stand it when someone was very pleased with himself for his skill in swimming: 'Aren't you ashamed,' he said, 'to boast so shamelessly about skills that belong to dolphins?'

It would have been wittier if he had said 'to frogs.' For it befits a man to boast about the skills proper to a man, and nothing is becoming to a man more than skill in reasoning. After all no one swims so well he cannot be outdone by dolphins.

**128** When he was asked how a wise man differed from an ignorant one, he said, 'Send them both naked among strangers and you will see.'

He meant that the wise man carried in his breast the means to win approval from anyone. Hence if you send an educated man and an ignorant one in the same way to a foreign country where they are both equally unknown, the wise man will immediately find money and friends by bringing out his own riches, but the other naked man will be laughed at as a madman and risk dying of hunger.

**129** A fellow boasted to him that he drank a lot but didn't get drunk. 'Why boast,' said Aristippus, 'when a mule can do the same?'

**130** Someone reproached Aristippus with having a relationship with a courtesan. Aristippus silenced him with a Socratic induction: 'Tell me,' he said

\* \* \* \* \*

1 Cf Athenaeus 12.544C–D. See also 1.8 and 1.163 above.

127 (xxvi) Diogenes Laertius 2.73

128 (xxvii) Diogenes Laertius 2.73. Cf 3.162 below. In margin 'education profitable'

129 (xxviii) Diogenes Laertius 2.73. In margin 'bibulousness'

130 (xxix) Diogenes Laertius 2.74

'does it matter whether you take a house that many men have lived in or no one?' When the man said it didn't matter, he said, 'Well, does it matter whether you are carried in a ship that has carried many passengers or none?' When he said no to this too, Aristippus said, 'So what difference does it make whether I have a relationship with a woman who has made herself available to many or to no one?'[1]

This remark too can be approved of for its wit by people who do not regard plain fornication as an offence.

131 When a man criticized him because he was a pupil of Socrates but took money contrary to Socrates' practice, he said, 'I am right to do this, for many rich friends sent Socrates wheat and wine; he would keep a little for his needs and return the rest. It seems he had the leading Athenians as his stewards, but I only have my slave Eutychides whom I bought.'

He meant that he despised money no less than Socrates, but Socrates enjoyed more generous friends. This argument could be used by men even today to excuse themselves for professing the greatest contempt for money, when their money is deposited with their friends. At one time they had generous custodians of their stores, but now they would starve well enough if they didn't have some cash laid up somewhere.

132 Aristippus is said to have had an affair with the famous courtesan Lais. When he got a bad reputation on this account, and someone objected that he, a philosopher, was in thrall to Lais, he said, 'On the contrary, I have Lais, she does not have me!'[1]

He meant it was no disgrace to enjoy lawful pleasure, but to be a slave to it should be thought shameful.

\* \* \* \* \*

1 The Socratic *eisagoge*, also called *epagoge*, was inductive reasoning based on an accumulation of examples; see 221 above (Erasmus' introductory paragraph to book 3).

131 (xxx) Diogenes Laertius 2.74. Aristippus was the first of the sophists to charge fees for his teaching, see 3.81 above. In margin 'provision of necessaries'

132 (xxxi) Diogenes Laertius 2.75
1 A much quoted story, cf Athenaeus 12.544C, 13.588E, 599B. For anecdotes about Lais see 6.572–3 below.

**133** Again this is how Aristippus silenced a man who complained that he enjoyed fancy foods: 'Wouldn't you buy these foods for three obols?' When the would-be despiser of luxury nodded, he said, 'Then I am not as devoted to pleasure as you are to avarice.'

For the other man would have indulged in the delicacies if they had been free or very cheap. In the same way, some countries accuse the Germans of drunkenness and the English of greed, although no nation is more greedy than these same people if they are offered a chance to indulge their gluttony for nothing. So they are more avaricious, not more self-controlled. The anecdote about the partridge which I reported above is very like this.[1]

**134** Dionysius' steward, called Simus, a Phrygian by birth, showed Aristippus his house, which was magnificent in every way, even with an exquisite mosaic pavement. After he had seen it all, Aristippus spat on Simus' beard and when Simus was angry, he said that he had seen nothing in the whole house more convenient for spitting into, implying that in the whole house nothing was uglier or more unclean than the barbarian's face, although it should have been the cleanest part of a man.[1] Admittedly this remark fits better some Cynic than Aristippus, for all that it is ascribed to him.[2]

**135** Once when he was delighted by a splendid perfume he said, 'A curse on those horrible perverts who have discredited such a fine thing,' thinking that many things were rejected through the fault of those who misused them.[1]

**136** When asked how Socrates had died, Aristippus said, 'As I would wish to die,' meaning that such a death was preferable to any life.

Indeed he couldn't have described a happy death more succinctly.

\* \* \* \* \*

**133** (xxxii) Diogenes Laertius 2.76. In margin 'fancy foods'
   1 For the story of the partridge see 3.103 above. Cf 3.137 and 3.141 below.

**134** (xxxiii) Diogenes Laertius 2.75. In margin 'uninhibited'
   1 Erasmus gives no reason for this behaviour. Phrygians had a reputation as idle worthless slaves: CPG 2 Apostolius 18.1 'If you beat a Phrygian he'll be better and more useful.'
   2 It is attributed to the Cynic philosopher Diogenes in Diogenes Laertius 6.32.

**135** (xxxvi) Seneca *De beneficiis* 7.25.1
   1 Cf 3.163 below.

**136** (xxxv) Diogenes Laertius 2.76

But the wit of the remark lies in this, that the philosopher answered differently from what the questioner expected.[1] For he was asking about the type of death, had he died of illness, by the sword, by poison, or by falling from a precipice, whereas Aristippus thinking it immaterial, answered that he had died happily.

137 The sophist Polyaenus went into Aristippus' house, and saw beautifully dressed women and a dinner splendidly laid out; then he began to criticize such luxury in a philosopher. Aristippus pretended not to notice the rebuke and said a little later, 'Can you be our guest tonight?' When the other did not decline, he said 'So why do you accuse me? For you seem not to be reproaching a lavish table so much as the expense.'

If the dinner had offended just by being lavish, he would have declined to be a guest. But to approve the display but take offence at the expense seems more characteristic of an avaricious than a thrifty man.

138 I can hardly believe what Bion reports of Aristippus, that when the slave carrying his money on a journey was wearied by the burden he said, 'Throw away what is too much for you and carry what you can.'[1]

139 Once he was on a voyage and realized it was a pirate ship, so he took out his gold and began to count it and soon threw it in the sea groaning loudly, pretending he had dropped it accidentally. With this clever ruse he took care of his life, by taking from the pirates the reason to kill him or tie him up. Some people say he also added, 'It is better for this to be lost through Aristippus than for Aristippus to be lost on account of this.'

140 When Dionysius asked why Aristippus had left Socrates and come to Sicily,

* * * * *

1 This is an example of humour depending on an unexpected reply; see General Index: replies, unexpected. It was a recognized form of *chreia*: Theon *Progymnasmata* 5.209 (Spengel II 100). See Introduction xxiv–xxvii.

137 (xxxvi) Diogenes Laertius 2.76–7. In margin 'witty'

138 (xxxvii) Diogenes Laertius 2.77. In margin 'passion for philosophy'
1 Erasmus rather disingenuously gives the impression he got the anecdote from Bion's (lost) diatribes, rather than from Laertius' reference to them.

139 (xxxviii) Diogenes Laertius 2.77. In margin 'clever'

140 (xxxix) Diogenes Laertius 2.78. In margin 'frank'

he said, 'To share what I have and receive what I haven't.' Some say he gave this answer: 'When I was short of wisdom I went to Socrates; now I am short of money I have come to you.'

141 Aristippus said to Plato, who criticized him for buying a lot of fish, that he had bought them for an obol. So when Plato said, 'I would have bought them too at that price,' he commented 'You see, Plato I am not greedy for delicacies, but you are for money.' We have already reported other similar remarks.[1]

142 He kept company with Phryne in Aegina at the feast of Poseidon, and when someone reproached him with spending so much money on a woman who had served Diogenes for nothing, he said, 'I supply her with money so that I can enjoy her, not so that no other man can.'

It is said of Phryne that although she was incredibly beautiful she would let anyone use her body without discrimination, whether they were rich or poor, disdaining nobody. So she had a crowd of lovers. Horace is thinking of this when he writes, 'The freedwoman Phryne torments me, not content with one man.'[1]

143 When Aristippus kept company with Phryne this is how Diogenes reproached him: 'Aristippus' he said, 'you are having an affair with a public whore. You should either play the dog like me or give up.' Aristippus refuted him by the following inductive argument: 'Does it seem absurd to you, Diogenes, to live in a house which others lived in before you?' When he said no, Aristippus said, 'What about travelling in a ship which has already carried many passengers?' When he said this wasn't absurd either, Aristippus said, 'So why do you think it absurd to make love to a woman whom many have used before you?' This has been reported already except that Athenaeus is the source of this version.[1]

\* \* \* \* \*

141 (XL) Athenaeus 8.343B. In margin 'sharp'
  1 See 3.103, 3.133, and 3.137 above.

142 (XLI) The story should be told of Lais, not Phryne; Athenaeus 13.588E. Erasmus has misread the text. In margin 'unaffected'
  1 Horace *Epodes* 14.16

143 (XLII) Athenaeus 13 588F
  1 This is another version of the anecdote told above at 3.130. Again the courtesan is Phryne.

144 When he lost a very pleasant estate and someone lamented his sad misfortune, he said, 'Don't you know that you have only one little piece of land whereas I have three fields left?' The other nodded, and Aristippus said, 'Then why don't we lament your misfortune instead?' He felt it was foolish to grieve for what was lost rather than rejoice for what was left.

145 When someone asked him, 'You aren't everywhere, are you?' He laughed and said, 'I'm not wasting my fare if I am everywhere.'
  Aristippus was making fun of the sophistic problem of whether the same body could be in different places, by answering that there was no risk he would waste his fare. For a man wastes his fare who pays the price and doesn't reach his destination.
  It can also be understood this way, 'Well then, I have wasted my fare.'[1]

146 He was once defeated in an argument by a confident man who was also crazy and stupid, and when he saw the man was triumphant and puffed up with his victory he said, 'I am leaving defeated, but I shall sleep more sweetly than you who refuted me.'

147 One of Plato's contemporaries, Helicon of Cyzicus, had foretold an eclipse of the sun; so after it happened as he had predicted, he received a talent of silver from Dionysius. Then Aristippus told the other philosophers, 'I too have got something miraculous to foretell!' When they begged him to tell them he said, 'I foretell that there will soon be a quarrel between Plato and Dionysius.'
  For he felt the king had long been concealing his real feelings.[1]

148 The thing Aristippus particularly condemned in men's behaviour was that

        * * * * *

144 (XLIII) Plutarch *Moralia* 469D–E (*On tranquillity of mind*). In margin 'enjoy what's left'

145 (XLIV) Plutarch *Moralia* 439E (*Can virtue be taught?*). In margin 'humorous'
  1 The doctrine in question is that body (matter) is continuous and interchangeable. The last sentence, added in *1535*, is a better interpretation of the Greek.

146 (XLV) Plutarch *Moralia* 80C (*Progress in virtue*). In margin 'forbearance'

147 (XLVI) Plutarch *Life of Dion* 19.6–7
  1 This last remark is based on the previous section in Plutarch (ie *Dion* 19.4–5).

148 (XLVII) Diogenes Laertius 2.78. In margin 'choosing friends'

at auctions they looked carefully at objects before buying them, but they did not examine the lives of those they made their friends.

Yet you have more advantage from loyal friends than from objects and more harm if you do not exercise choice.

149 Once at a dinner Dionysius ordered his guests to dance one at a time in a purple robe.[1] (Now wearing purple used to be the privilege of kings, but now it is common even for a tailor.) Plato refused to do so, quoting these dramatic trimeters:

> I scarce can put me on a woman's dress,
> myself a man and born from race of men.

But Aristippus did not refuse, but dressing in the purple all ready to dance he recited these verses with a clever change:

> for at the rites of Father Liber
> a mind that's pure cannot be made corrupt.[2]

150 Once he was appealing to Dionysius on behalf of a friend, and when the king would not grant his prayers, Aristippus threw himself down and embraced the king's feet and so got his request. When someone criticized this behaviour as beneath a philosopher, he said, 'I am not to blame but Dionysius, for keeping his ears in his feet.'

His was a nature ready both to do and to excuse anything at all.

\* \* \* \* \*

149 (XLVIII) Diogenes Laertius 2.78. In margin 'good-humoured'
  1 Another illustration of Plato's pride and Aristippus' indifference to what he was wearing. Cf 3.105 above.
  2 Plato quotes Euripides *Bacchae* 836: Οὐκ ἂν δυναίμην θῆλυν ἐνδῦναι στολὴν / Ἄρρην πεφυκὼς, καὶ γένους ἐξ ἄρρενος (the protest of Pentheus about to capitulate and wear women's clothes), Aristippus wittily misquotes *Bacchae* 317–18: Καὶ γὰρ ἐν βακχεύμασιν / ὁ νοῦς ὁ σώφρων οὐ διαφθαρήσεται, spoken by the prophet Teiresias earlier in the same play, 'for at the rites of Bacchus a woman that's pure cannot be made corrupt' changing 'a woman that's pure' to 'a mind that's pure.' The second line of Plato's quotation, which appears thus in many early texts, has been excised from modern editions. For misquoting verse see 3.283 n1 below.

150 (XLIX) Diogenes Laertius 2.78. In margin 'abject entreaty'

151 When he was in Asia he was arrested by the satrap Artaphernes. When someone asked him then whether he still had his usual confidence he said, 'Silly man, as if I was ever more confident than now, since I am going to talk to Artaphernes.'

For philosophy gave him this advantage that he feared no man, but spoke freely to them all.

152 Aristippus said that if men were educated in the liberal arts but neglected philosophy they were like Penelope's suitors, since they had affairs with Melantho and Polydora the maids, expecting to get anything but marriage with their mistress.[1] He felt that the liberal arts were like attendants on moral philosophy, which was the most important thing to be acquired, and for whose sake men should learn everything else. They say Ariston made a similar remark about Ulysses, who went down to the underworld and talked to nearly all the shades although he could not even see the queen herself.

153 Asked what it was most important for young men to learn, he said, 'What will be profitable to them as men.' His remark is also attributed to others.[1] For we should learn the best things first, and youth should not be busy with superfluous things when it is most teachable.

154 After Aristippus had acquired a great sum of money and Socrates said in amazement, 'Where did you get so much from?' Aristippus said, 'Where did you get so little?'[1]

\* \* \* \* \*

151 (L) Diogenes Laertius 2.79. In margin 'a mind free from fear'

152 (LI) Diogenes Laertius 2.79–80. In margin 'philosophy the queen'
  1 The point is that Aristippus treats the liberal arts (poetry) as mere hand-maids of philosophy, which men settled for just as Penelope's suitors con-tented themselves with seducing her maids when she refused to choose any of them. Plutarch *Moralia* 7D (*The education of children*) attributes this remark to Bion (7.214 below). Ariston is probably Ariston of Chios, whom Laertius treats briefly at 7.160–3. Erasmus has a few anecdotes: see 6.560, 7.300, 7.335, 7.352, and 8.101–2 below.

153 (LII) Diogenes Laertius 2.80. In margin 'the best things first'
  1 See 1.65 and 1.233 above.

154 (LIII) Diogenes Laertius 2.80. In margin 'a rich philosopher'
  1 Erasmus followed Traversari (see Introduction xvi–xvii above) in taking

For he thought it no less amazing that so great a philosopher as Socrates, with such important friends, should be poor.

155 When a prostitute said to him, 'I'm pregnant by you, Aristippus,' he said, 'You can no more be sure of this than if you walked through dense thorns and said, 'This is the one that pricked me!'

156 When he was reproached with neglecting and abandoning his son, as if he had not fathered him, he said, 'Don't we get rid of both the mucus and the lice which we produce because they are good for nothing?'

He felt one should not treat as sons children who had nothing to commend them to a parent's affection except being born from them. This is what the old man says in the comedy: 'I want you to be mine only while you act worthily of yourself.'[1]

157 When Aristippus accepted money from Dionysius, but Plato was given books, he was rebuked by someone for this as if he were more interested in money than Plato. But he said, 'What difference does it make? I needed money, Plato needed books,' meaning that neither should be blamed.

158 Asked why Dionysius contradicted him he said, 'For the same reason that everyone else does,' meaning that a philosopher's freedom of speech is inconvenient to everyone, so it was not surprising that it was unwelcome to the king.

But he also implied that the king's judgment was no different from that of the crowd, because fortune does not add wisdom.

\* \* \* \* \*

Aristippus' remark as a question, but it is more witty if taken as a statement: 'From the place where you got so little.'

155 (LIV) Diogenes Laertius 2.81. In margin 'witty'

156 (LV) Diogenes Laertius 2.81. In margin 'degenerate children'
   1 Cf Terence *Hautontimoroumenos* 106, but Erasmus has quoted from memory, reordering the words and disturbing Terence's metre.

157 (LVI) Diogenes Laertius 2.81. In margin 'avarice in things other than money'

158 (LVII) Diogenes Laertius 2.81. In margin 'truth unwelcome'

159 Aristippus once asked Dionysius for a talent and the king seized the opportunity of refuting him, saying, 'Didn't you declare that a philosopher needed
nothing?' He said, 'Give it me and then we'll discuss the point.' Once he
had received the money he said, 'Wasn't I right to say that a philosopher
needed nothing?'

  For a man is not in need if he has a source of money when he needs it.

160 When Dionysius recited a verse of a Sophoclean tragedy

  whoever betakes himself to a tyrant's hall
  becomes his slave although he freely came,[1]

Aristippus replied by correcting the second verse to 'He's scarcely slave if
he came there free.'[2]

  He meant that no one was truly free unless philosophy had set his
mind free from hope and fear. For a man is not really free by being free-
born. Some people attribute this saying to Plato.

161 When a quarrel broke out between Aristippus and Aeschines, someone said,
'So where is your friendship now?' He said, 'It is sleeping, but I will wake
it up.' So Aristippus healed the quarrel by a gracious and open appeal. To

* * * * *

159 (LVIII) Diogenes Laertius 2.82. In margin 'the philosopher needs nothing'

160 (LIX) Diogenes Laertius 2.82. In margin 'true liberty'
  1 In the same kind of literary exchange as at 3.149 above, Dionysius quotes
    this passage of Sophocles (Nauck Sophocles fr. 789): Πρὸς τὸν τύραννον ὅς τις
    ἐμπορεύεται / Κείνῳ 'στι δοῦλος, κἂν ἐλεύθερος μόλῃ to assert that Aristippus
    has enslaved himself. Aristippus retorts by changing Sophocles' second line
    to οὐκ ἔστι δοῦλος, ἂν ἐλεύθερος μόλῃ. The first lines are also quoted by Plutarch
    Moralia 33D (How to study poetry) and taken up by Pompey going to his death,
    Plutarch Pompey 78 (4.251 below). As the Greek was not quoted in Traversari
    or Curio (see Introduction xvi–xvii above) Erasmus has supplied the first two
    lines direct from the Greek sources and apparently reconstructed Aristippus'
    retort from Traversari's Latin version.
  2 In 1531, Erasmus has Aristippus interrupting with his line before the couplet
    is completed.

161 (LX) Diogenes Laertius 2.82–3, amplified from Plutarch Moralia 462D (On the
    control of anger), which contributes the opening remark about sleeping friend-
    ship; but the last two exchanges are the same. In margin 'reconciliation'

prevent the evil growing worse, as usually happens, through silence, he voluntarily went to Aeschines and said, 'Can't we become friends again as soon as possible and stop being silly? Or shall we wait and provide scope for jesters to talk about us at drinking parties?' When Aeschines answered that he would be glad to be reconciled, Aristippus said, 'Remember, then, that although I was older I came to you first.' Then Aeschines said, 'Indeed you are a much better man than I, since the quarrel began with me, but mending the goodwill began with you.' This is how their friendship was restored.

162 Once Aristippus was sailing with some fellow citizens and was shipwrecked. When he saw mathematical figures drawn in the sand, he said, 'Friends, it is all right. I see the traces of men,' and he went into the nearby city and enquired what students of philosophy there were there. When he met them they treated not only him but his companions too with the greatest humanity and even provided travel money for their return. Finally when those who had come with Aristippus were preparing their return to their country and asked him if he wanted any message taken to his fellow citizens, he said, 'Tell them to strive to obtain the resources that do not perish in a shipwreck but float ashore with their owner.'[1]

Vitruvius tells the same tale in *On Architecture* book 6, adding that it was Rhodes Aristippus came to on that occasion.[2]

163 When Socrates was inveighing against men who drenched themselves with perfumes[1] Charondas, or as others say Phaedo, asked who was this man soaked in perfume. Aristippus said, 'I, wretched fellow, and the king of Persia who is even more wretched than I am. But see,' he said, 'he's not superior to any other animal by reason of this, and he's not of more consequence than any other man either.'[2]

\* \* \* \* \*

162 (LXI) Galen *Protrepticus* 5 and Vitruvius 6 preface (first paragraph). In margin 'the true possessions of the mind'
  1 Erasmus' version of Galen translated at CWE 29 225–39, this anecdote 227
  2 Syracuse in Galen. Cf 3.128 above and 7.59 below.

163 (LXII) Diogenes Laertius 2.76. In margin 'frank speech'
  1 See 3.69 above, from where Erasmus has introduced Socrates into this anecdote.
  2 The Greek probably means, 'No other creature is diminished by wearing perfume, nor is a man.' In Diogenes Laertius the anecdote concludes with the

He felt that a man was not made a better man in any way by external goods, and that a horse smeared with marjoram smelt the same as a king; and a beggar smeared with the same perfume does not smell any less pleasing than the highest priest.

## The Cynic Diogenes

I do not think it will seem out of order if we follow Socrates' witty purity and Aristippus' cheerful frankness by recalling Diogenes of Sinope, who far excelled all others in the varied charm of his sayings; although I personally think all three should be respected for different virtues, but on equal terms. However different they were, you would say they were equal in merit.

**164** When Diogenes first set out for Athens he approached Antisthenes. Though he was repeatedly sent away[1] (for Antisthenes did not take any pupils) he did not give up attaching himself to him; indeed when Antisthenes finally shook his stick at him, Diogenes deliberately submitted his head to the stick, saying, 'Beat me if you want, but you won't find any stick hard enough to drive me away from you while you have something to say.'

This is an extraordinary example of devotion to wisdom.

**165** Once when he saw a mouse running around in Megara[1] without looking for its hole, or taking fright at the crowds,[2] or seeking food, he said, 'A splendid example of liberty,' and soon after he rejected everything and began to live in a storage jar.

\* \* \* \* \*

remark recorded at 3.135 above. Aristippus is actually defending the wearing of perfume.

**164** (I) Diogenes Laertius 6.21. In margin 'devotion to wisdom'
For Diogenes of Sinope (and testimonia and fragments), see Introduction xv (and n8) above.
1 On Antisthenes' initial rejection of Diogenes cf also Aelian *Varia historia* 10.16. For Antisthenes see 7.39–100 below.

**165** (II) Diogenes Laertius 6.22. In margin 'freedom'
1 Diogenes Laertius says: 'As Theophrastus says in *The Megarian* (sc. *Dialogue*) ...'; Erasmus was misled by the punctuation in Traversari (see Introduction xvi–xvii above), understanding 'in [the town of] Megara.'
2 'Crowds' instead of 'dark' translates a reading proposed in BAS and LB.

**166** People were amazed that Diogenes had no house in which to eat, but he pointed to the portico of Zeus and said the Athenians had constructed a magnificent residence for him to feed in.

He treated what was public as available for his use, and he certainly could not have wanted a more splendid dining hall.

**167** He called Euclides' school *cholē*, that is 'bile and trouble,' because it taught ideas that were clever but useless for good living. (The Greek word *scholē* means 'leisure'). He also called Plato's *diatribē*, that is 'way of life,' *katatribē*, that is 'waste of life,' altering the word for the worse, because Plato kept apart from public life and grew old with discussions, whereas Diogenes lived in public and preferred to live in a philosophical fashion rather than just discuss.[1]

**168** As for the contests of the Dionysia[1] (which were celebrated at Athens in honour of Bacchus at enormous expense), he called them a great marvel for fools, because everything that happened on this occasion was ridiculous.

**169** Orators were highly esteemed in Athens but he called them 'lackeys of the crowd,' because they were forced to speak to please and to flatter the stupid crowd in servile fashion.[1]

He also said that crowns were pustules of glory, in Greek *exanthēmata*, such as burst into bloom on some men's nose or face from biliousness.[2]

\* \* \* \* \*

**166** (III) Diogenes Laertius 6.22. In margin 'humorous'

**167** (IV) Diogenes Laertius 6.24. In margin 'useless skills'
   1 The hostile puns are evidence of Diogenes' disapproval of formal teaching on any subject; for him philosophy was a practice, or way of life. For Euclides see 3.32 n1 above.

**168** (V) Diogenes Laertius 6.24. In margin 'foolish parade'
   1 These were the festivals at which the surviving tragedies and comedies of the great dramatists were performed.

**169** (VI) Diogenes Laertius 6.24 and Diogenes Laertius 6.41 (second paragraph). In margin 'orators'
   1 Socrates argued that political orators were slaves of the people in Plato's *Gorgias* 502, and Diogenes makes the same point to Demosthenes 3.196 and 8.174 n1 below.
   2 This was added in 1532.

170 Whenever he considered in human affairs the governors of states, the doctors and philosophers, he said, 'No animal was wiser than man.' But then looking at dream-interpreters, diviners, holy men, and others of this kind, or those enslaved to glory and wealth, he said nothing seemed to him more stupid than man.

He meant that the human mind was fit for the best achievements if it was exercised, but if it degenerated into vice it was far below dumb animals.

171 Diogenes used to say that one should in life more often provide a speech than a noose.

Men in despair resort to the noose, when they should resort to a speech of consolation. For speech is a doctor to a sick mind.[1] Indeed the sentiment is not absurd if you understand 'speech, word' as 'reason.'[2]

172 When he saw Plato at a lavish dinner eating none of the delicacies, but feeding simply on olives, he said, 'Wisest of men, what has happened? You went to Sicily to get this kind of dinner and now you're here you are abstaining from it when it's laid before you.' Plato replied, 'By Hercules, Diogenes, I was quite content with this kind of food in Sicily too.' 'So why did you need to sail to Syracuse?' said Diogenes. 'Didn't Attica produce olives then?' Some people ascribe this saying to Aristippus.[1]

173 Once when Diogenes was eating figs he met Plato and offered them to him saying, 'You may share them.' When Plato accepted them and ate them, he said, 'What I said was share them, not eat them all up.' This joke can be

* * * * *

170 (VII) Diogenes Laertius 6.24. In margin 'man the stupidest of creatures'

171 (VIII) Diogenes Laertius 6.24
  1 *Adagia* III i 100: *Animo aegrotanti medicus est oratio* 'To a sick spirit speech is a physician'
  2 Greek *logos* has many meanings, including speech, reason, wisdom (see John 1). Traversari (see Introduction xvi–xvii above) had translated with *sermo* 'speech,' but a marginal note gave Erasmus the Greek original, *logos*.

172 (IX) Diogenes Laertius 6.25. In margin 'the philosopher at court'
  1 According to Diogenes Laertius it was the second-century sophist Favorinus (see 7.44 n1 and 8.8–9 below) who made the ascription to Aristippus. See *Adagia* II ii 91: *Concupivit assam farinam* 'He lost his heart to wheaten loaves.' See 3.110 above.

173 (x) Diogenes Laertius 6.25. In margin 'abusing permission'

adapted to serious matters, especially against men who abuse the permission of a prince or instructor or parents to do things that are not granted – for instance, if someone is advised that it is not useless to sample dialectic but then devotes his entire life to that pursuit.

The saying is reported by Laertius in such a way that you are not sure which of them offered the other the figs.

174 Plato was certainly thrifty, but inclined to elegance whereas Diogenes was dirty. So he trampled on Plato's cushions and said to some friends of Dionysius whom Plato had invited to dinner, 'I am trampling on Plato's pretences.' To which Plato said, 'But how swollen your pride is, Diogenes, to think you are trampling another man's pride underfoot.' This story is better told by other sources. When Diogenes said, 'I am trampling on Plato's pretences,' Plato said, 'Yes, you are, but with a different kind of pretentiousness.'

For this too was a kind of arrogance, to boast of contempt for elegance. Men who glory in shabbiness are no less pretentious than those who dress splendidly, just in a different way. Yet it is a more shameful form of pretentiousness to seek honour from a false show of virtue. But Sotion does not attribute this to Diogenes, but to Plato the Cynic.[1]

175 Diogenes had asked Plato for a little wine, and then for some figs. Plato sent him a flagon, and the Cynic thanked him like this: 'When you are asked how much is two and two, do you answer twenty? So you don't give the amount you are asked for, nor do you answer the question you are asked.'

He criticized Plato as excessively talkative, a feature Aristotle also criticized in his writings.

176 Someone asked where he had seen good men in Greece: 'I saw no good men anywhere,' he said, 'but good boys at Sparta.'[1]

* * * * *

174 (xi) Diogenes Laertius 6.26. In margin 'concealed vanity'
  1 Sotion of Alexandria, was a Peripatetic philosopher of second century BC. Erasmus has followed Traversari's version (see Introduction xvi–xvii above). As there does not seem to be a 'Plato the Cynic,' it has been suggested either that the text of Laertius is corrupt or that it can be interpreted as meaning, 'It is Sotion in his fourth book who reports that the Cynic said this to Plato.' Sotion was one of Diogenes Laertius' sources.

175 (xii) Diogenes Laertius 6.26. In margin 'excessive generosity'

176 (xiii) Diogenes Laertius 6.27. In margin 'few good men'
  1 The first of several anecdotes in which Diogenes withholds the name of men,

This was a criticism of the corrupt behaviour of all Greece, so much so that even among the Spartans, that least corrupt of nations, old-fashioned innocence only existed in the boys. Diogenes also implied that in the rest of Greece not even the boys were good, and that the men were worse than the boys, although they should be training the boys to honest ways.

177 Once when he was talking about a serious topic he found no one was listening, so he began to sing a silly song as if there was going to be some dancing. When a large crowd had assembled he scolded them for coming in large enthusiastic numbers to a stupid and silly entertainment, but not gathering around for serious instruction useful for good living, or listening to it attentively.

This is very like the story attributed to Demosthenes about the ass's shadow.[1]

178 Diogenes reproached men for training to become skilled in wrestling, kicking, and suchlike, whereas no one made an effort to become good and honest.

179 He did not restrain his wit against any kind of man. He said he was surprised by grammarians who investigated the misfortunes of Ulysses with such enthusiasm without being aware of their own misfortunes. (For in those days grammarians were especially concerned with the poems of Homer, and in the *Odyssey* Homer records the various wanderings of Ulysses.) He also accused musicians in the same way, saying that they carefully tuned the strings of the lyre to obtain harmony, but their morals were out of tune.[1] He also reproached astronomers because they gazed at the sun, moon, and stars, and did not see what was at their feet. He used to criticize orators, because they took care to speak justly but not to behave justly.

* * * * *

ie good men, from those he met. See 3.188, 3.193, 3.221, 3.226, 3.234, 3.317, 3.318 below.

177 (xiv) Diogenes Laertius 6.27. In margin 'silly things preferred to worthwhile'
   1 CPG 1 Zenobius 6.28; pseudo-Plutarch *Moralia* 848A–B (*Lives of the Ten Orators*); *Adagia* I iii 52: *De asini umbra* 'About an ass's shadow.' See 8.142 below.

178 (xv) Diogenes Laertius 6.27. In margin 'misplaced application'

179 (xvi) Diogenes Laertius 6.27–8. In margin 'misplaced studies'
   1 Cf 3.345 below.

And he scolded misers because they abused money when they spoke, but valued it highly in their minds.

For this is a peculiar quality of misers, that nobody curses avarice more than they.

180 Diogenes condemned the common crowd for calling people good because they despise money, although they did not imitate the men they praised so passionately, but rather followed the wealthy whom they abused. He also let off his spleen against those who sacrificed to obtain good health, and gorged themselves on excessive feasting at the actual rite, acting against the interest of their health. He said he was amazed at slaves who saw their masters indecently greedy and did not snatch their food away. For this would show concern for their masters' health, and greed is more appropriate to slaves.

181 So far I have reported those whom he reproached and on what score. Now hear whom he praised: he praised those who were going to marry and did not do so, those who were going to sail and then did not, who were going to rear children and did not, who were going to take part in public life and then did not, who prepared themselves to associate with influential men, and then did not.

He meant that one should avoid all these activities and so he thought men wise who were invited to such things but changed their mind in good time, since once they had started they would no longer have the option of declining, even if they regretted their undertaking. A man who has married is no longer his own master; a man who has trusted himself to the sea must be carried away by the winds, the man who has entered public life must be a slave to this theatre,[1] and, even if he longs to, it is not safe for him to return to private life.

182 This puzzling saying is credited to Diogenes: 'You should not hold out your hands to your friends with your fingers curled up.'

He meant that it was not enough for us to be courteous to friends,

* * * * *

180  (XVII) Diogenes Laertius 6.28

181  (XVIII) Diogenes Laertius 6.29. In margin 'what to be avoided in life'
  1  *Adagia* I i 91: *Servire scaenae* 'To be a slave to your theatre'

182  (XIX) Diogenes Laertius 6.29. In margin 'generosity'

but that generosity must accompany courtesy. Men who treat their friends courteously are said in Greek to 'right hand' them.[1]

183 When Diogenes was captured and sold in Crete, and the auctioneer asked what skills he had, and under what title he should recommend him to a purchaser he said, 'Say you are selling a man who knows how to command free men.' A certain Xeniades of Corinth, impressed by the novelty of the auction entry, approached Diogenes to find out whether he really knew what he claimed to know. And when he discovered from conversation that Diogenes was educated and wise, he bought him and took him home, and put him in charge of educating his children. Diogenes took charge of them and gave them a gentlemanly education. First he taught them the liberal arts, then he taught them to ride horses, shoot a bow, twist a sling, hurl a weapon. However, at the wrestling ground he would not let the trainer exercise them like athletes with strenuous exercise, but only allowed as much exercise as would foster their complexion and good bodily health.

He made sure they learnt by heart the best excerpts from the poets and other writers, because we really know only what we have in our memory. In short he reduced to a compact form for them the total of all knowledge, so that they would understand it faster and hold it more faithfully in their memory. He also trained them to wait on their parents at home and to be content with a cheap and light diet and water to drink. While the others grew their hair long to enhance their beauty, he ordered them to cut it very short. If ever they had to go out in public he sent them out uncombed and without tunics, unshod and silent. He also trained them in hunting, in imitation of the Spartans. As a result he was respected by the children and through them won the goodwill of their parents.

Others say the auctioneer was instructed by Diogenes to say this: 'Does anyone want to buy a master?'[1]

* * * * *

1 Erasmus gave the word in Greek *dexiousthai* and added the translation in 1532.

183 (xx) For apophthegms 3.183–7, Laertius quotes two (lost) sources for the stories associated with Diogenes' supposed enslavement, both called 'the Sale of Diogenes,' one by the satirist Menippus (or possibly the Peripatetic biographer Hermippus), the other by the comic playwright Eubulus. Erasmus has recast and re-ordered Diogenes Laertius 6.29–31 and added details from Diogenes Laertius 6.74, Aulus Gellius 2.18.9, and elsewhere. In margin 'a sober education'
1 Diogenes Laertius 6.30

**184** When he sat at the auction he was forbidden to sit and told to stand, I suppose so that the buyer could more easily inspect what he was buying. But Diogenes said, 'What difference does it make? Fish are bought no matter how they lie.'

This was a criticism of the stupidity of the crowd, who take care when they buy a slave that no physical fault escapes them, but are more careless about his mental condition. That can be discovered from speech.[1]

**185** Diogenes said he was amazed that men did not buy a pot or lid without testing it by the sound when it was struck, but when they bought a man they were content with seeing what he looked like.

He meant that a man could be known by nothing so well as his speech. People planning to buy an earthenware dish for a few pennies strike it with their fingers, and can tell from the ringing it produces whether it is intact, of good clay, and well baked. Similarly before they buy a man for several minae, they should provoke him into talking, and discover from his speech what kind of man he is.[1] This is the point of the earlier saying: a fish is silent and it doesn't matter how it lies, since it is just a fish. Just so a man's physique is irrelevant if you buy him without making him speak.[2]

**186** He said to Xeniades who had bought him, 'Although I am a slave you will have to obey me, because anyone who has a slave as ship's helmsman or doctor has to obey him if he wants to get any value out of him.'

**187** He is supposed to have grown old with this man Xeniades, and been buried by his pupils. When Xeniades asked him how he wanted to be buried, he

* * * * *

**184** (xxi) Diogenes Laertius 6.29 and see 3.183n just above. In margin 'speech reveals the mind'
  1 In 1532, Erasmus added his own comments to the bare anecdote: 'Naturally men usually purchased slaves to perform physical tasks, and so examined their physical condition but not their intellectual qualities.' See 3.70 above.

**185** (xxii) Diogenes Laertius 6.30 and see 3.183n above.
  1 Cf 3.148 above.
  2 See 3.184 just above.

**186** (xxiii) Diogenes Laertius 6.30 and see 3.183n above. In margin 'obey a wise slave'

**187** (xxiv) Diogenes Laertius 6.31–2 and see 3.183n above. In margin 'burial'

said, 'On my face.' Xeniades asked why, and he said, 'Because very soon it will come to pass that the things below will be above,' referring to the fact that the Macedonians had come to power, and from being humble had become lofty.

So if everything was going to be turned upside down, a corpse would soon change from being prone to being supine. Perhaps he meant that it made no difference in what condition a dead body was buried, although the crowd had a great superstitious preoccupation with this: the dead were carried out for burial with their feet stretched towards the door, and cremated standing. And today as I hear the Jews are buried standing; certainly all Christians are buried lying supine.[1]

188 Diogenes once shouted out as he stood in the forum, 'Come here men, one and all' as if he was going to make a speech to the people. And when they had gathered in large numbers, and he didn't stop shouting, 'Come here men, one and all' someone said indignantly, 'Well, here we are, say something.' Then Diogenes drove him away with his stick, saying, 'I said "Come here, men, not trash from a dungheap."'

He did not think the title of man fitted those who did not live according to reason, but were moved by their emotions like brute beasts.[1]

189 When Alexander the Great was at Corinth he approached Diogenes sitting in front of his jar and talked to him at length. When he left, the king's friends were indignant that he had shown so much honour to this 'dog,'[1] who had not even thought fit to get up for the king. 'No,' said Alexander, 'if I were not Alexander I should want to be Diogenes.'[2]

Such was his admiration for this free spirit who rose above all human affairs, that he thought nothing was closer to being a king. Kings are particularly blessed because they serve nobody, but can easily do whatever they want, and they lack nothing: but philosophy provides a man

* * * * *

1 For Diogenes' indifference to the manner of his burial, see 3.284 and 3.372–3 below.

188 (xxv) Diogenes Laertius 6.32. In margin 'men like cattle'
1 See 3.176 above.

189 (xxvi) Diogenes Laertius 6.32
1 See 3.192 n1 below.
2 Only the last sentence is an actual translation. The rest seems to be a conflation of the many versions of this story. See 3.209–10 below.

with this very state much more truly than monarchy provides it for kings. Although Alexander thought being Alexander was something greater than being king.[3]

190 Diogenes said it was not the deaf or blind who should be called weak and crippled, 'but those without a bundle.'

He was playing on the resemblance between the words: for *anapēros* in Greek means 'crippled or amputated' and *apēros* means 'without a bundle.' He meant, I think, that a man was useless for every function of life if he was ignorant of philosophy, for a bundle was the Cynic's travelling equipment.[1]

191 Once he went to a dinner party of young men with his head half shaved, and far from being received politely was sent away with many blows. He took his revenge in this way: he wrote on a tablet the names of the young men who had beaten him up, and wearing it on his forehead he strolled about in Leucon, the most crowded part of the city where lawsuits are conducted.[1] As he walked around with his cloak thrown open the marks of the blows showed what he had suffered and the tablet declared those responsible.

Thus he exposed those coarse young men to universal censure and condemnation.

192 Since he was a Cynic he was called a dog.[1] Many praised this way of life but nobody imitated it. So he used to say that he was the dog of those who

* * * * *

3 Cf Plutarch *Alexander* 14.2–5 and Plutarch *Moralia* 331F *On the fortune of Alexander.*

190 (XXVII) Diogenes Laertius 6.33. In margin 'philosophy'
   1 See 3.204 below.

191 (XXVIII) Diogenes Laertius 6.33. In margin 'civilized revenge'
   1 'Wearing it ... conducted' translates the reading of *1531* (cf 7.273 below). 'In Leucon' seems to be derived from Traversari's translation (see Introduction xvi–xvii). It is a doublet of *in albo* 'on a (white) tablet' (*leukos* means 'white'). It is unknown on what Erasmus based his explanation (*1531*) of this fictitious place. In *1532* onwards this was changed to: 'he strolled about with his cloak thrown open.'

192 (XXIX) Diogenes Laertius 6.33. In margin 'virtue merely praised'
   1 This is one of many allusions to the name 'dog,' applied first to Diogenes and then to his 'Cynic' followers. Cf 3.220 below, in which Plato calls him dog; also in book 3: 242, 248, 326 below, and finally 3.298 below,

praised him, but none of the praisers dared to go hunting with the dog they praised.

193 When someone was boasting, saying that 'I can beat men in the Pythian games,' he said 'I can beat men, but you only beat slaves.' Again he was playing on the similarity between the Greek words 'men' *andras* and 'slaves' *andrapoda*. For he called all those who were enslaved to their passions 'slaves.'[1]

It is nobler to defeat passions through philosophy than defeat men at the Pythian games.

194 When someone advised Diogenes that now he was an old man he should rest from his labours, he said, 'If I were running in the footrace, should I slacken my pace near the winning post, or quicken it?'

He rightly felt that devotion to virtue should be all the more intensified as less of life remained, because it would be despicable to cool off and abandon one's honourable and established way of life at that stage.

195 Once when he was invited to dinner he said he would not go. When he was asked why, he said, 'Because yesterday they did not thank me.'

The mass of men expect to be thanked as if for a great favour if they invite anyone to dinner: but Diogenes, though poor, thought he was entitled to thanks because he was prepared to attend the dinner, since he never went without a contribution but nourished the souls of the host and fellow guests more generously with philosophical conversations than the host fed their bodies with feasting.

\* \* \* \* \*

where Erasmus cites Diogenes' own interpretation of the name. 'Cynic' κυνικός [*kunikos*] is derived from κύων [*kuōn*] 'dog.' The insulting name was applied to Diogenes for what people saw as his sordid and shameless way of life, flouting all conventions of accepted behaviour, but essentially for his biting criticism of the attitudes and beliefs of his contemporaries. 'Cynic' and 'Cynicism' did not originally imply being cynical in the modern sense.

193 (xxx) Diogenes Laertius 6.33. In margin 'truly slaves'
  1 See 3.176 n1 above.

194 (xxxi) Diogenes Laertius 6.34. In margin 'the passion for rectitude to be intensified'

195 (xxxii) Diogenes Laertius 6.34

196 Diogenes once caught young Demosthenes taking supper at a public inn and when he retreated inside at the sight of Diogenes he said, 'You will be even further inside the inn that way.'

He meant that Demosthenes would become even more the talking point of dinner guests if he not only frequented an inn, but even hid himself as if he was involved in a crime. This was more worth remarking on than the fact that he was drinking there. Others report this as said to a certain young man who might well be Demosthenes. A simple interpretation is to take it that the young man was advised to flee not inside but outside the inn. For the further he withdrew into the inn the more he was in the inn.[1]

197 When some visitors were eager to see the celebrated Demosthenes, he stuck out his middle finger and said, 'Here is the famous Demosthenes, the advocate of Athens.'

Now the finger next to the thumb is called the index, because we extend it when we want to point to something. But the middle finger was shameful among the ancients for a reason that ought to not be mentioned here,[1] and Demosthenes had a bad reputation with the general public, for being unmanly. Diogenes had this in mind when he preferred to point to Demosthenes with the middle finger rather than the index.

198 Someone dropped a loaf of bread and left it lying there because he was ashamed to pick it up. Diogenes wanted to censure this man, so he put a rope round the neck of a pitcher and dragged it through the Ceramicus, doing to the vessel what the other was ashamed to do to the bread.

199 When he was judged by many to carry philosophy to excess, he replied that

*  *  *  *  *

196 (XXXIII) Diogenes Laertius 6.34
  1 This is only one version of the story in which Diogenes finds the orator in a tavern: cf Plutarch *Moralia* 82C–D (*How to profit by one's enemies*) and 847F (*Lives of the ten orators*). In a different version (8.174 below from Aelian *Varia historia* 9.19) Diogenes ironically tells Demosthenes to enter the tavern freely since his master (ie the common folk) goes there often.

197 (XXXIV) Diogenes Laertius 6.34. In margin 'here he is'
  1 The middle finger was associated with soliciting homosexual intercourse; see also 3.200 below. Cf *Adagia* II iv 68 *Medium ostendere digitum* 'To show the middle finger.'

198 (XXXV) Diogenes Laertius 6.35. In margin 'pointless shame'

199 (XXXVI) Diogenes Laertius 6.35. In margin 'outstanding examples'

he was imitating the choral trainers who used to aim above the right pitch so that the others would reach the correct one.

For whatever goes beyond the limit, even to a fault, is useful for rousing other men's slackness. Thus the cloak and jar of Diogenes reproached rich men for their luxury.

200 He said most men were crazy in more than a finger. If someone constantly extended his middle finger instead of his index finger, he was generally thought mad; but if he extended his index finger he was thought sane.[1]

But there are very many men who, in matters of importance, do far more seriously crazy things than pointing one finger instead of another, yet they are not usually considered mad. Just so parents even today punish it as a serious offence in children if they use the left hand instead of the right; but they don't punish them in the same way when they choose shameful instead of honourable behaviour.

201 Diogenes also criticized men's folly for buying and selling precious things for very little and cheap things for a great deal. For a statue could be bought for 3000 sesterces whereas a measure of flour sold for two pennies.

But a statue was no use for living, whereas one could not live without flour. So it would have been right for flour to cost a lot more than statues. The philosopher assessed the worth of things by their natural use, whereas the crowd assesses them from a foolish persuasion.

202 The story about Xeniades that we told above[1] is told by some sources in this way: When Diogenes had been purchased, as if he had himself bought Xeniades, he said to him, 'Be sure to obey my orders.' When the other said, 'rivers run backwards,'[2] meaning that things really were back to front, if the

\* \* \* \* \*

200 (xxxvii) Diogenes Laertius 6.35. In margin 'forms of madness'
  1 See 3.197 above.

201 (xxxviii) Diogenes Laertius 6.35. In margin 'topsy-turvy values'

202 (xxxix) Diogenes Laertius 6.36 and Diogenes Laertius 6.29 (second paragraph). In margin 'slave wiser than his master'
  1 See 3.183 above.
  2 The opening line of the chorus in Euripides *Medea* 401, comparing the reversal of justice in society with the impossible phenomenon of rivers running uphill. Cf *Adagia* I iii 15: *Sursum versus sacrorum fluminum ferunter fontes* 'The springs of the sacred rivers flow backwards.'

slave ordered his master, Diogenes said, 'If you had bought a doctor when you were sick, would you obey his prescriptions, or would you say "rivers run backwards?"'

If a crippled master listens to a slave with expertise in medicine, then a sick mind has all the more reason to listen to a slave expert in philosophy. What the medical art offers the body, philosophy provides for the mind: the one cures a fever, the other corrupt desires. And as the mind is more important than the body, so its illnesses are more serious. Laertius added that when Diogenes was asked by the auctioneer under what title he wanted to be advertised, he said, 'As one who knew how to give orders to free men.' Then when he saw a smartly dressed man passing, he said, 'Sell me to this one, because he needs a master.'

203 When someone applied to be taken as a pupil in philosophy by Diogenes and he took him on probation, he gave him a ham to carry in the street and ordered the man to follow him, but the other was ashamed and discarded what he was carrying and stealthily sneaked away. A little later he happened to meet him and laughing said, 'That ham destroyed your and my friendship.'[1]

Diogenes meant that the other was not suited to study philosophy, because he could not rise above a foolish embarrassment. For it is not disgraceful to carry a ham, but it is to retreat from honest enterprise.

Diocles tells this story too in a slightly different way.[2] When someone eager to become Diogenes' pupil said to him: 'Diogenes, order me to do something,' Diogenes made him one of his household and gave him a piece of cheese to carry. When the other refused out of shame, Diogenes said, 'A little bit of cheese destroyed our friendship.'

204 Once when he saw a boy drinking from the hollow of his hand, he said, 'This boy has outdone me in thrift, for I have been carrying around useless equipment,' and he pulled his wooden cup out of his bundle and threw it away. 'I did not know,' he said, 'that nature had taken thought for us even in this.' When he saw another boy whose dish had broken holding his lentil

* * * * *

203 (XL) Diogenes Laertius 6.36. In margin 'pointless shame'
  1 Following Traversari (see Introduction xvi–xvii above), Erasmus has a ham where Laertius has a tuna-fish.
  2 Diocles of Magnesia, mid to late first century BC, wrote on the history of philosophy and was a major source for Diogenes Laertius.

204 (XLI) Diogenes Laertius 6.37. Cf 3.199 above. In margin 'thrift'

porridge in a hollow crust of bread, he threw away his wooden dish as a superfluous object.

I will allow these acts to seem absurd, provided we admit that an example of simplicity taken to extremes can serve to make us ashamed of our luxury.

205 Diogenes used this syllogism to deduce that the wise man lacked nothing: All things belong to the gods, but wise men are friends of the gods, and friends have everything in common, so wise men have everything.[1]

But the same syllogism could have been used to refuse him when he asked for anything: 'Why do you ask when you have everything?'

206 When he saw a woman who was reverencing the gods bowing her body so deeply that from behind parts of her body were seen that should not be bared to the eyes of men, he went up to her saying, 'Aren't you afraid, woman, that when god stands behind you (for everything is full of him) you are not acting very decently?' He is said to have dedicated to Aesculapius a thug who would come running and beat up people who prostrated themselves, by this fancy idea deterring people from superstition, when they think that the gods will not listen to them unless they supplicate them with an unseemly physical gesture.[1]

207 He used to say as a joke that tragic curses had befallen him, since he was 'without home, city, and country, a pauper, and a wanderer and living from day to day.' He was alluding to some passage in tragedy.[1] We have spoken about the curses of Oedipus in the adage collection.[2]

* * * * *

205 (XLII) Diogenes Laertius 6.37. In margin 'the wise man rich'
  1 See *Adagia* I i 1: *Amicorum communia omnia* 'Between friends all is common,' where the whole saying is mistakenly attributed to Socrates. Cf 3.159 above.

206 (XLIII) Diogenes Laertius 6.37. In margin 'decency at all times'
  1 As Aesculapius was the god of healing, perhaps Diogenes meant that he hoped the thug would be preserved to continue the good work.

207 (XLIV) Diogenes Laertius 6.38. In margin 'tragic destitution'
  1 The play is unknown, but Erasmus seems to deduce that its subject was Oedipus (Nauck *adespota* fr 284). Erasmus quotes the words in Greek, but as he was using Traversari's Greekless version of Diogenes Laertius (see Introduction xvi–xvii), he may well have made his own Greek version of the quotation, as it appears in a very different form in Laertius' Greek text.
  2 *Adagia* I ii 84: *Devotionis templum* 'Temple of cursing'; I vii 61: *Oedipi imprecatio* 'The curse of Oedipus'

208 Diogenes is also supposed to have said this: He set self-confidence against
fortune, nature against prescription, and reason against the emotions, since
by these three principles men's peace of mind is won and kept.

A fearless heart preserves the wise man against the storms of fortune;
he follows Nature as a substitute for prescription, and if prescription con-
flicts with Nature, he despises it; moreover he crushes the turmoil of desires
with the aid of reason.

209 When Alexander the Great went to see Diogenes he found him sitting in
the Craneion[1] in front of a storage jar, and joining together torn pages with
glue. When the king had talked with him at length and was about to go he
said, 'Diogenes, think what you would like to ask of me, for you will get
whatever you choose.' Diogenes replied, 'We'll talk about other things later.
Meantime, just move away a bit.' After the king had moved away, suppos-
ing Diogenes wanted to think it over, Diogenes was silent for some time.
Alexander approached him again: 'Ask what you want, Diogenes.' 'That was
what I wanted,' Diogenes said, 'for before you were cutting out the sun-
light which I need for my task.'[2] Others report that he said, 'Don't put me
in the shade,' because he wanted to enjoy the sun.[3]

210 Another version of the tale is that Alexander had said, 'Here I am, Diogenes,
I have come to help you, since I see you are in need of many things.' Then
Diogenes replied, 'Which of us needs more? I, who want nothing except my
bundle and cloak, or you, who have not been content with your ancestral

\* \* \* \* \*

208 (XLV) Diogenes Laertius 6.38. In margin 'the life of the philosopher'

209 (XLVI) Diogenes Laertius 6.38
    1 The Craneion was the gymnasium of Corinth.
    2 Erasmus seems to be recalling various sources other than Laertius (6.38) as
      the story was often told. See eg Plutarch *Alexander* 14.2–4; Valerius Maximus
      4.3 ext. 4; 3.210 below. The strange detail of Diogenes gluing pages together
      comes from pseudo-Diogenes epistola 33 in R. Hercher ed *Epistolographi Graeci*
      (Paris 1873) 247; see ter Meer, edition of *Apophthegmata* ASD IV-4 749 p248. Cf
      Aristophanes *Thesmophoriazusae* 54–7, where the playwright Agathon is gluing
      scraps together.
    3 Cicero *Tusculan Disputations* 5.92

210 (XLVII) Erasmus' version does not seem to reflect any source exactly. For
    Alexander not being content with the whole world, see Juvenal 10.168: 'One
    world does not suffice the youth from Pella.' Cf 4.33 below. In margin 'the
    philosopher has few needs'

kingdom but expose yourself to so many dangers to increase your rule, so that it seems the whole world will scarcely be enough for your desire?'

211 Once, when he had been reading a very long time and finally reached the point where the paper was blank, he said, 'Be of good cheer, friends, I have sighted land.'[1]

He was playing on the idea of men weary after a long voyage, who recover their spirits when they see the harbour in the distance.

212 Someone deduced by sophistical arguments[1] that Diogenes had horns; so he rubbed his brow and temples with his hands and said, 'But I don't see them.'

He preferred to make fun of a silly argument rather than refute it.

213 When Zeno was lecturing in his classes and proved by the sharpest arguments that no motion existed or could exist, Diogenes got up and began to walk about. Zeno was amazed and said, 'What are you doing, Diogenes?' 'I am refuting your arguments' he said.[1]

This is how he criticized an empty display of cleverness.

214 A certain sophist wanted to display the keenness of his wits to Diogenes, and argued in this fashion: 'What I am, you are not.' When Diogenes agreed, he said, 'I am a man, therefore you are not a man.' Then Diogenes said, 'Start with me and your deduction will be right.'

He did not think it worthwhile explaining the fallacy in the argument, but preferred to make fun of a man who was proud of such silly trifles. If

\* \* \* \* \*

211 (XLVIII) Diogenes Laertius 6.38. In margin 'humorous'
  1 In Diogenes Laertius, the reader is an unknown person, and Diogenes utters a cry of relief, which makes the story more amusing. *Adagia* IV viii 18: *Terram video* 'I see land'

212 (XLIX) Diogenes Laertius 6.38. In margin 'silly subtleties'
  1 Ie 'What you have not lost you still have. You have not lost horns. Therefore you still have horns.'

213 (L) Diogenes Laertius 6.39
  1 Erasmus identifies the lecturer as Zeno of Elea. The doctrine certainly suggests Zeno of Elea, famous for paradoxes about motion, but he is chronologically too early for Diogenes. For Zeno see 7.379–82 below and Diogenes Laertius 9.72.

214 (LI) Aulus Gellius 18.13.7–8. In margin 'silly subtleties'

the sophist had made his premise, 'You are a man' it would have followed that the sophist was not a man.

215 When someone was lecturing at length on the heavenly bodies, Diogenes asked, 'How recently have you come from heaven?' In this he was echoing Socrates, who made the well-known judgment, 'What is above us has nothing to do with us.'[1]

216 A eunuch of foul reputation had inscribed on his house 'Let nothing bad enter here.' When Diogenes saw this, he said, 'So where is the master's entrance?'

  The eunuch had set up this inscription for a good omen, so that no evils would affect the house, but Diogenes reinterpreted it to mean evil of mind, which are the only real evils.

217 He got some ointment and anointed his feet with it, contrary to popular practice. When people expressed surprise, he said 'I did it because ointment poured over the head rises and perfumes the air, but scent coming from the feet rises to the nostrils.'

  Just so another man criticizes the public practice of putting garlands on the head when it would be more fitting to put them under the nostrils, since the odour of perfume does not sink but rise.

218 The Athenians used to urge Diogenes to be initiated into the mysteries, adding that the initiated held sway over the underworld. Diogenes gave them this answer: 'It is quite absurd if Agesilaus and Epaminondas[1] are kept lingering in the mud while that thief Patetion and other completely

* * * * *

215 (LII) Diogenes Laertius 6.39. In margin 'talking about the unknown'
  1 *Adagia* II i 69: *Quae supra nos nihil ad nos* 'The things that are above us are nothing to us.' Cf 3.23 above.

216 (LIII) Diogenes Laertius 6.39. Cf 3.266 below. In margin 'real evils'

217 (LIV) Diogenes Laertius 6.39 and Lucian *Nigrinus* 32 (last paragraph). In margin 'ridiculous'

218 (LV) Diogenes Laertius 6.39. In margin 'initiation not enough'
  1 Agesilaus king of Sparta and Epaminondas the Theban commander were both fourth-century heroes: Erasmus has quoted many sayings of the Spartan Agesilaus from Plutarch's *Sayings of the Spartans* in 1.3–82 above, and will

worthless men will be in the Isles of the Blest because they have got themselves initiated.'[2]

He severely criticized the behaviour of priests who for the sake of
profit appealed to the superstition of inexperienced men, persuading them
that initiation bestowed blessedness after this life, when this is the reward
of those who have earned it by pious and glorious achievements, whether
they are initiated or not.

219 When Diogenes first began to be a philosopher, living in his jar and feeding
only on dry and mouldy bread, he heard the whole city humming with
celebration (for it was a feast day) and felt some discouragement, and for a
long time seriously considered abandoning his way of life. But finally when
he saw the mice creeping up and eating the crumbs of his bread, he said to
himself, 'Why be discontented? You are quite grand enough; look, you even
support your own hangers-on.'

220 When Plato called him a dog because of the shabbiness of his life he said,
'Quite right, since I ran back to those who sold me.'[1]

For when dogs are sold they often return to their old masters. He was
not offended by the insult, but turned it neatly. When he was sailing to
Aegina he was caught by pirates and taken to Crete, and sold there. I think
the pirates were Corinthians, or Athenians, or if not, Aeginetans.[2]

221 When Diogenes was returning from the baths and someone asked him

* * * * *

assemble more than thirty sayings of Epaminondas from various sources in
5.221–55 below.
2 Diogenes challenges the claim of salvation through initiation into the mysteries; cf Plutarch *Moralia* 21F (*How to study poetry*). See the remarks at 1.238
above and 7.46 below.

219 (LVI) A combination of Plutarch *Moralia* 77E–78A (*How to profit by one's enemies*)
and Diogenes Laertius 6.40. In margin 'humorous'

220 (LVII) Diogenes Laertius 6.40. In margin 'a dog's mockery'
1 Another retort to the abusive name of dog; see 3.192 n1 above.
2 A journey from Athens to Aegina was very short, but capture by pirates (also
alleged to have happened to Plato) served to explain his enslaved status when
he was put up for sale, although born free (see 3.183, 3.202 above). Diogenes
lived in both Athens and Corinth.

221 (LVIII) Diogenes Laertius 6.40. In margin 'men no men'

whether there were a lot of men there, he said there weren't. But when he was asked if there was a great crowd, he agreed that there was, meaning that the name of man fits very few.[1]

222 Here is another, almost incredible story. Plato had defined man as a two-legged creature without feathers. When Plato's pupils applauded this definition, Diogenes brought to the school a cockerel plucked of its feathers and wingless and said, 'Here you are: here is Plato's man!' So Plato added to the definition 'with broad nails' because birds do not have nails of that sort.

223 When someone asked what time a man should eat dinner, Diogenes said: 'If he is rich, when he wants; if he is poor, when he can.'

224 Once in Megara Diogenes saw the sheep wearing jackets of skin to protect them against the cold, while the Megarians' own children went bare. Then he said, 'It is better to be a Megarian's sheep than his child.'[1]

It is generally reported of the Megarians that they are careless about the way they treat their children.[2]

225 Someone carrying a long beam through the street accidentally hit Diogenes and quickly said, 'Watch out!' out of habit. But Diogenes said, 'Why? You don't want to strike me again do you?'

Others tell the story like this: When the man said, 'Watch out,' Diogenes struck the man on the head with his stick and followed the blow with 'Watch out!' giving tit for tat. For he should have said 'watch out' before the blow.

*  *  *  *  *

1 See 3.176 n1 above.

222 (LIX) Diogenes Laertius 6.40. In margin 'ridiculous'

223 (LX) Diogenes Laertius 6.40. In margin 'witty'

224 (LXI) Diogenes Laertius 6.41; Aelian *Varia historia* 12.56 (last paragraph). In margin 'education'
 1 The jackets were to protect the fleece from damage; see Varro *De re rustica* 2.2.18.
 2 Plutarch *Moralia* 526c (*On love of wealth*) says that the Megarians taught their children only how to make money and did not educate them properly, hence Erasmus' marginal comment.

225 (LXII) Diogenes Laertius 6.41. In margin 'a warning too late'

226 Diogenes once walked around the market-place in full daylight carrying a lighted lamp like someone searching. When men asked what he was doing, he said, 'I am looking for a man,'[1] thus criticizing the behaviour of the community as hardly worthy of men.

227 On another occasion he got a drenching and stood there dripping all over. Some bystanders as you might expect, sympathized with him for suffering undeservedly. But Plato, who happened to be there said to them, 'If you want to show sympathy for Diogenes, go away,' thus commenting on the philosopher's love of glory.

For as Diogenes took pleasure in being a spectacle, he was happy rather than pitiable; but if he had been soaked without a witness he would have been really pitiable.

228 When someone boxed his ears he said, 'I didn't know I was walking about with a helmet on my head.'

In jest he called the flat of the man's hand a helmet. This was his only retaliation against the man who struck him. Unless we should read 'I didn't realize I ought to go around wearing a helmet.'[1]

229 But he didn't put up with Midias so submissively. Midias hit him on the head and said, 'I have deposited three thousand for you at the banker's table,' mockingly congratulating him because so much money in compensation for the blow would come to him from the fine if he sued. But Diogenes the next day took a boxer's leather thong, struck Midias with it, and said aping his words, 'And there's three thousand deposited at the banker's table for you.'[1]

* * * * *

226 (LXIII) Diogenes Laertius 6.41. In margin 'a man hard to find'
   1 This is identified as a *chreia* in the rhetoricians. See the dedicatory epistle xxiii-xxiv above; see also 3.176 above.

227 (LXIV) Diogenes Laertius 6.41. In margin 'concealed vainglory'

228 (LXV) Diogenes Laertius 6.41. In margin 'forbearing'
   1 The first translation was suggested to Erasmus by Traversari's version. See Introduction xvi above. The Greek probably means 'How come I forgot about taking a walk with a helmet on my head?' Cf 3.45 above.

229 (LXVI) Diogenes Laertius 6.42; Aulus Gellius 20.1.13 (last paragraph). In margin 'tit for tat'
   1 Midias is presumably the same thug as the one against whom Demosthenes delivered a powerful prosecuting speech (oration 21). The thong was wrapped around the hand and by this time was loaded with metal studs.

Aulus Gellius tells a story about a man who like to hit others and then order the fine to be counted out from the purse he carried round for the purpose. But Diogenes made it known that not everyone was so long-suffering as to be content with a fine.

230 Philosophers are generally abused either for not believing in the gods or for despising them. With this in mind Lysias kept asking Diogenes whether he believed in the gods? Diogenes replied, 'How could I not believe in the gods, when I am sure you are hateful to them?'[1] Some attribute this saying to Theodorus.[2]

Diogenes did not answer the question but turned the exchange against his questioner's insulting manner.

231 When he saw someone sprinkling himself with river water on religious grounds – for this is how men of old used to purify themselves, if they thought they had committed some sin – he said, 'Wretched man, when you make a mistake in grammar you are not excused because you sprinkle yourself, so it is far less likely that a sprinkling will free you from sins in life.'

He was right to comment on men's superstition, for believing that stains of the soul could be cured by a physical element, without cutting away wicked desires.

232 Diogenes vigorously reproached people who blamed fortune if something bad happened, as most men do. He said, 'It was rather men themselves who should be blamed for asking fortune not for what is really good, but for things that they think good.'

For if they trusted the gods to give what they thought best, they would do so, but as it is they feel no shame in blaming the gods when they get what they asked for.

233 He used to make fun of the superstition of men terrified by dreams by

*　*　*　*　*

230 (LXVII) Diogenes Laertius 6.42. In margin 'witty'
1 Diogenes Laertius says Lysias was a *pharmakopolēs* or hawker of quack remedies and drugs, a despised trade.
2 Possibly Theodorus the Atheist; see 7.133 and 7.291 below.

231 (LXVIII) Diogenes Laertius 6.42. In margin 'superstition'

232 (LXIX) Diogenes Laertius 6.42. Cf 3.238 below. In margin 'stupid prayers'

233 (LXX) Diogenes Laertius 6.43

saying, 'You don't worry about what you do when you are awake, but you anxiously investigate what you dream when asleep.'

For what a man experiences in his dreams is not as relevant to his happiness or unhappiness as what he does when awake. He ought to fear the anger of the gods and a bad consequence whenever he actually does something shameful, not if he sees something in a dream.

234 When the herald at Olympia announced, 'Dexippus has defeated the men,' Diogenes corrected him: 'He has defeated slaves,' he said, 'but I have defeated men.'

He meant that the competitors at Olympia were not real men, but slaves to glory. Only the philosopher defeats men. This is like the story we told above.[1]

235 When Philip's army was at Chaeronea, Diogenes went there and was seized by the soldiers and brought to the king. He looked at Diogenes, whom he did not know, and said, 'A spy!' Diogenes replied, 'Quite right, I am a spy. I came here to examine your folly in not resting content with ruling the Macedonians, but seeking other men's territory at the risk of losing both your kingdom and your life.' Amazed at the man's frankness, the king bade him go free.[1]

236 Alexander king of Macedon sent a letter to Antipater through a messenger called Athlios. Diogenes was there at the time and said, like a true Cynic, 'Wretch from a wretch by reason of a wretch to yet another wretch.'[1]

Now *athlius* in Greek means 'wretched, enduring many sufferings,' hence the word 'athlete.' The philosopher realized that princes whose ambition drove them to make troubles in constant warfare were really wretched. Those who abetted the desires of princes were equally wretched.

\* \* \* \* \*

234 (LXXI) Diogenes Laertius 6.43. In margin 'admirable victory'
  1 See 3.176 above.

235 (LXXII) Plutarch *Moralia* 606c (*On exile*). In margin 'ambition'
  1 Erasmus has enriched the version in Plutarch *Moralia* 606 with elements from 70E (*How to profit by one's enemies*) and Diogenes Laertius 6.43.

236 (LXXIII) Diogenes Laertius 6.44
  1 Diogenes' comment is in trochaic verse. To spell it out, Alexander the Great, a king and the son of a king (Philip II of Macedon) writes via Athlios to Antipater, a general and governor of Macedonia.

237 When he was invited to go to Alexander he refused, and when the commander Perdiccas threatened to kill him if he didn't come[1] he said, 'That won't be a great achievement, since the cantharis and phalangium can do the same.' (A cantharis is a little insect rather like a scarab,[2] but its poison is instantaneous: a phalangium is a deadly kind of spider.) He didn't hesitate to threaten Perdiccas in return, saying that he would be happy if he lived without Perdiccas, meaning that those who lived with Perdiccas were unhappy.

238 Diogenes said the gods were generous in giving men life, but men did not realize this when they craved sweetmeats and perfume and other kinds of self-indulgence.

    For men who enjoy these luxuries think they are living, when only wisdom provides real life that is calm and sweet. So it is not the gods who deserve reproach, but men who in their stupidity do not ask the gods for life but for pleasures.

239 When he saw a pampered man having his shoes put on by a slave he said, 'You haven't yet attained felicity, unless he also wipes you clean; that will happen when you've lost the use of your hands.'

    It seemed to Diogenes not much less absurd to use a slave's help to put on his shoes, if a man can do it for himself, than if after evacuating he employs a slave to wipe his arse.[1] Though this could be understood of wiping his nose.[2] To the pagan philosopher it seemed outrageous luxury for a pagan to be shod by a slave, but I know a Christian, a priest and theologian, not crippled in any limb, who used to summon servants when he went to the latrine to undo his laces and tie them up again when he returned. When I saw this I thought to myself: 'If only Diogenes were here to see him!'

    \* \* \* \* \*

237 (LXXIV) Diogenes Laertius 6.44. In margin 'free speech'
   1 Perdiccas was a distinguished military commander close to Alexander.
   2 Erasmus has replaced *cantharos* 'dung-beetle' in the original with *cantharis* 'blister-fly.' This had medicinal uses but could prove fatal. See *De copia* CWE 24 564:3n and Pliny *Naturalis historia* 29.4.93–4, no doubt Erasmus' source. See 8.136 below where the same story is told of Lysimachus.

238 (LXXV) Diogenes Laertius 6.44. Cf 3.232 above. In margin 'pleasure'

239 (LXXVI) Diogenes Laertius 6.44. In margin 'affectation'
   1 Cf 2.123 above.
   2 This alternative translation of wiping the nose was added in 1532.

240 Diogenes once saw a man being led off to execution who had stolen a bowl from a treasure house – he was escorted by the magistrates the Greeks called *hieromnemones*.[1] Diogenes said, 'The big thieves are arresting a little one!'

If only this could not be said truthfully of some Christian magistrates who sometimes hang a man who has stolen ten pence, but themselves get rich without punishment from great thefts, or rather embezzlement.

241 On another occasion he saw a youth throwing stones at a cross, and said, 'Fine, you will reach your target.'

He meant that one day the youth would be put on the cross.

242 A group of young men stood around Diogenes and jeered at him, calling him, 'Dog, dog!' but then began to run away as if scared. Then he asked them why they were running away and they said, 'In case you bite us, you dog.' He said, 'Don't worry, my boys; a dog doesn't eat beets,' an indirect way of accusing them of effeminacy.[1]

243 One fellow was very pleased with himself for walking around clad in a lionskin. Diogenes said, 'Stop putting the dress of courage to shame.'

He thought it unbecoming for an effeminate fellow to wear the costume of Hercules. The same thing can be said to those who by their extraordinary clothing make a show of holiness to which their lives do not correspond.

244 When people said the philosopher Callisthenes[1] was lucky to be welcomed

\* \* \* \* \*

240 (LXXVII) Diogenes Laertius 6.45
  1 These were magistrates in charge of temples and religious matters.

241 (LXXVIII) Diogenes Laertius 6.45. In margin 'witty'

242 (LXXIX) Diogenes Laertius 6.45. In margin 'witty'
  1 See *Adagia* II iv 72: *Betizare, Lachanizare* 'To wilt like beet or salad,' where this incident is quoted. See also 3.192 n1 above.

243 (LXXX) Diogenes Laertius 6.45. In margin 'acting a part'

244 (LXXXI) Diogenes Laertius 6.45
  1 Callisthenes was Aristotle's nephew, and served as historian to Alexander's expedition, but provoked the king and was executed on a charge of conspiracy in 317 BC.

by Alexander with lavish hospitality, Diogenes said, 'No, he is unlucky, because he will have to lunch and dine when it suits Alexander.'

He meant that nothing was fortunate without freedom. This Callisthenes is the pupil of Aristotle who was finally thrown into prison by Alexander and died there. Some sources substitute Aristotle[2] himself for Callisthenes, and add that when men praised his good luck for living with the king's son, Diogenes said, 'Aristotle will lunch when Alexander chooses, but Diogenes when Diogenes chooses.'

245 If ever he was short of money he used to take it from friends, but when men criticized him for asking, a beggar's practice and contrary to the dignity of a philosopher, he said, 'No, I am not asking, but asking back.'[1]

For we ask back a loan or a deposit. Now a friend who gives to a friend in need does not make a present, but returns what he owes. Whoever holds on to money in such a situation is holding back another man's due.[2]

246 When a rather fancily dressed young man put a question to Diogenes. Diogenes said, 'I won't answer you until you lift up your clothes[1] and show me whether you are a man or a woman.'

He identified the fellow's effeminacy from his unmanly costume.

247 Another young man was showing some skill in a lover's game in the baths which the Greeks call *kottabizein*.[1] Diogenes said, 'The better you play the worse you are.'

\* \* \* \* \*

2 For Erasmus' alternative version 'Aristotle dines at Alexander's pleasure, etc' cf Plutarch *Moralia* 604D (*On exile*).

245 (LXXXII) Diogenes Laertius 6.46, expanded. In margin 'generosity'
1 Erasmus added the Greek in 1535, οὐκ αἰτῶ, ἀλλ' ἀπαιτῶ.
2 Erasmus here omits two coarse anecdotes, but then gives the first at 3.367 below

246 (LXXXIII) Diogenes Laertius 6.46. In margin 'effeminacy'
1 'lift up your clothes': omitted in 1531

247 (LXXXIV) Diogenes Laertius 6.46. In margin 'a shameful ability'
1 Athenaeus has a long section (15.665B–668E) on the *kottabus* game. It consisted of throwing the last drop of wine remaining in a cup to hit a metal target, and sounds innocent enough, though obviously involving noisy drinking. Erasmus' identification of it as 'a lover's game' is perhaps based on Athenaeus' statement that one could invoke the lover's name when making the throw. Diogenes was probably condemning it as a waste of time.

He was condemning a skill he disapproved of – dicing is another – for the better a man is as player, the worse he is as a man.

248  When Diogenes was at a dinner-party, the diners called him, 'You dog,' and threw bones to him, as this is what people do to dogs. He in turn, as he left, pissed on the diners from behind, to show that this too went with being a dog.[1]

249  He called public speakers and others who did everything for glory 'thrice-men,' an ambiguous phrase.
     For while the generality of people won't call anyone a man if he is neither educated nor humane, the philosopher called a man 'wretched' if he had nothing apart from being a man. Now, according to Homer no creature is more wretched than man.[1] So when he called them 'thrice-men' he meant 'thrice wretched,' for devoting all their efforts to a worthless thing and enslaving themselves to the common crowd, a many-headed beast.[2]

250  He called a certain uneducated rich man who was splendidly dressed 'a sheep with a golden fleece.'[1]
     For the poets say there were such sheep.[2] Those who were weak of mind were proverbially said to be just like sheep.[3]

251  When he passed the house of a spendthrift which had a notice up 'for sale,'

*  *  *  *  *

248  (LXXXV) Diogenes Laertius 6.46. In margin 'what dogs do'
     1 Another 'dog' story (see 192 n1 above); this time Diogenes answers by action not words.

249  (LXXXVI) Diogenes Laertius 6.47. In margin 'thrice-men'
     1 Homer *Iliad* 17.466–7
     2 See Horace *Epistles* 1.1.76.

250  (LXXXVII) Diogenes Laertius 6.47
     1 In one among several versions of this *chreia* Diogenes calls a rich but ignorant boy 'filth in a silver covering' (Theon *Progymnasmata* 5.203 [Spengel II 97]).
     2 See the story of the Argonauts and the quest for the Golden Fleece, related most notably by Apollonius Rhodius (third century BC) in his four book epic poem *Argonautica*. See also Virgil *Eclogues* 4.42–4, where the sheep will have gold-coloured fleeces at the return of the Golden Age.
     3 *Adagia* III i 9: *Ovium mores* 'The character of a sheep.' Erasmus there quotes Aristophanes and Plautus.

251  (LXXXVIII) Diogenes Laertius 6.47. In margin 'extravagance'

he said, 'I could easily guess that your excessive drinking bouts would make you vomit up your house.'[1]

The man had already swallowed his house before he put it up for sale. So this was really more a sicking up than a selling up.

252 When a young man complained that many people were upsetting him, Diogenes said, 'Stop letting it show that you are upset by it then,' meaning that the tiresomeness of men who aim to hurt is best brought to an end if the victim conceals his distress. For men who attack someone in order to torment him will stop if they see he is unmoved by it.

I suspect the Greek words have another meaning: when the young man said lots of people were bothering him, Diogenes' reply really meant, 'You too stop giving out signals of your inclinations,' ie of being a passive effeminate.[1]

253 There was an incompetent lyre player of huge bulk whom everyone found fault with and Diogenes was the only one to praise. When they wondered why he did this, he said, 'I praise him because, being like that, he prefers to play the lyre rather than practise robbery.'

He meant that being strong in body but weak in talent the man was better suited to robbery than music.

This is a joke based on the unexpected.[1]

254 Another lyre player was deserted by the audience whenever he sang. Diogenes used to greet him when they met with 'Hail, rooster!' When the other

* * * * *

1 Diogenes Laertius actually says the opposite: 'make you (the house) vomit up your owner,' which has more point. Erasmus seems to have misread *dominum* in Traversari's version as *domum* (see Introduction xvi–xvii). He may have been influenced by 3.275 below. See also Job 20:15: He hath swallowed down riches and he shall vomit them up again.

252 (LXXXIX) Diogenes Laertius 6.47. In margin 'distress concealed'
  1 The first version misinterprets Traversari's Latin translation of Diogenes Laertius' Greek. The corrected interpretation was added in 1532 after Erasmus had been able to consult the Greek original (see Introduction xvii above).

253 (XC) Diogenes Laertius 6.47. Erasmus has again passed over one of Laertius' anecdotes, but will insert it as 281 below. In margin 'witty'
  1 The last sentence was added in 1532. For 'a joke based on the unexpected' see 3.136 n1 above.

254 (XCI) Diogenes Laertius 6.48. In margin 'witty'

was offended by the strange salutation and said, 'Why do you say that?' he said, 'because when you sing you make everyone get up.'

He made a joke depending on the ambiguity of the Greek verb: for a man is said *anegeirein* when he rouses someone from sleep, as roosters do when they crow in the morning, but also when he provokes a man to rise from his seat, which is what that man did.

255 Once a great many people were staring at a beautiful youth, so Diogenes bent over and filled the fold of his cloak with lupin beans. When everyone turned to stare at this sight, he said he was amazed that they forgot the youth and stared at him,[1] thus commenting on their lack of self-control.

256 A very superstitious fellow prone to terror of ghosts and ghouls once threatened to kill Diogenes, saying, 'I will smash your skull at a blow.' 'But if you do that' said Diogenes, 'I will stand on your left and make you shudder.'[1]

He meant that once dead he could terrify even the man who despised him alive. This state of mind possesses a lot of people even nowadays: they are aggressive against the living but terrified of ghosts.

257 When Hegesias asked him to lend him some books he said, 'Hegesias, you are not wise: you pick real figs, not painted ones, but you neglect real training and betake yourself to a written version.'

This remark was an adverse comment on all those who spend their life doing nothing more than reading the books of philosophers which contain' rules for good living, when virtue is better learned from practice than reading. Now in Greek *graphein* means both 'to write' and 'to paint.' So virtue expressed in books is like a painting of virtue. It does seem absurd to be selective about figs but not about virtue.

\* \* \* \* \*

255 (XCII) Diogenes Laertius 6.48
  1 Misled by Traversari, Erasmus has omitted that the young man was giving a demonstration speech and Diogenes gobbled the beans to attract attention.

256 (XCIII) Diogenes Laertius 6.48. In margin 'superstition'
  1 Erasmus is following Traversari whose text seems to have read *parōn* 'standing by' instead of *ptarōn* 'sneezing.' See Introduction xvi–xvii above. A sneeze on the left was an ill omen for a Greek.

257 (XCIV) Diogenes Laertius 6.48. In margin 'reading dead'
  Hegesias was possibly a pupil of Diogenes and, like him, from Sinope in Pontus (see 3.259 below).

**258** When a man taunted Diogenes with being exiled from his country Diogenes said, 'Wretched fellow, that is why I took to philosophy.'

Either exile had compelled Diogenes to take up philosophy, or he had learnt philosophy in order to bear exile and similar misfortunes calmly.[1]

**259** Another fellow said to him as an insult; 'The people of Sinope have condemned you to exile.' But I,' said Diogenes, 'condemn them to staying put.'

He meant that, having been ordered to change country he was no worse off than those who stayed in their native land and would not be able to bear exile calmly. For it is as wretched to be forced to stay as to be forced to leave. To a philosopher any land is his country; if he is ordered to go into exile, he is exiled only from one community. But the man who cannot live anywhere except in his own country is an exile from many lands. Now Diogenes, it is thought, was ordered to change country for debasing coinage. For he was a native of Sinope.[1] This is how Plutarch reports the tale in his book *On exile*: 'The people of Sinope have ordered you to become an exile from Pontus.' 'But,' said Diogenes, 'I condemn them to the penalty of forever remaining confined to the region of Pontus and the far shores of the Black Sea.'

Diogenes had changed his native land, but for the better: it was the people allotted to that barren region who were really in exile.[2]

**260** When Diogenes came upon an Olympionices (which means 'a competitor at the Olympic games') pasturing sheep, he said, 'My famous friend, how quickly you have taken yourself from Olympia to Nemea!' playing on words. For the Nemea are games called after the place, like the Olympia.[1] But in Greek *nemo* means 'I pasture,' and *nemos* means 'pastures.'

\* \* \* \* \*

**258** (xcv) Diogenes Laertius 6.49. In margin 'exile profitable'
  1 For the benefits bestowed by philosophy, see 3.107 n1 above.

**259** (xcvi) Diogenes Laertius 6.49; Plutarch *Moralia* 602A (*On exile*) (second paragraph).
  1 The claim that Diogenes was exiled from his city Sinope for debasing its coinage when he was a mint-master is found at Diogenes Laertius 6.20.
  2 The last sentence was added in 1532. See 3.334 below.

**260** (xcvii) Diogenes Laertius 6.49. In margin 'humorous'
  1 As well as the famous Olympian Games, there were the Pythian, Nemean and Isthmian, as well as various minor athletic festivals.

261 Asked once why athletes had no feeling, he replied, 'Because they have been
reared on pork and beef.'

For athletes are fed on heavier foods, which give strength to the body
but blunt the edge of the mind. The double meaning made the joke possible. For both the Greek word 'to feel' and the corresponding Latin *sentire*
concern the mind as much as the body. But the questioner was asking why
athletes were not upset by blows, as if they felt nothing, whereas Diogenes
preferred to criticize their dull minds.

262 He used to go up to statues from time to time and ask them for something.
When men wondered why he did this, he said, 'to get into the habit of not
minding if ever I don't get what I ask for from men.'

263 After Diogenes had been driven by poverty to start begging, he used to
accost men with these words: 'If you have given to anyone else then give to
me, but if you have not given to anyone, then start with me.'

He meant that he was no worse than other beggars, so it was fair that
a man who had given to anybody else should give to Diogenes; but if a man
was too stingy to give to anyone, then it was time for him to start giving.

264 Once when asked by a tyrant what sort of bronze should be used to make
statuary, he said, 'The bronze from which they moulded Harmodius and
Aristogeiton.'[1]

This implied that the man should be removed, since they were tyrant-
killers.

265 Someone asked him how Dionysius treated his friends: 'Like wineskins' said

* * * * *

261 (XCVIII) Diogenes Laertius 6.49. In margin 'dullness of mind'

262 (XCIX) Diogenes Laertius 6.49. In margin 'long experience reduces distress'

263 (C) Diogenes Laertius 6.49. In margin 'beggary'

264 (I) Diogenes Laertius 6.50. In margin 'outspoken'
    1 Harmodius and Aristogeiton were the famous killers of Hipparchus, tyrant
      of Athens at the end of the sixth century, who were revered as heroes of
      democracy. 'The tyrant' is Dionysius I, tyrant of Syracuse, but the story really
      belongs to Antiphon, see 7.372 below.

265 (II) Diogenes Laertius 6.50. In margin 'witty'

Diogenes; 'when they are full he hangs them up, when they are empty he throws them away.'

He meant that the tyrant killed the rich and neglected the poor.

266 A man once wrote a boastful inscription over his house: 'Callinicus Hercules, son of Jove, lives here; let no evil enter in.' Diogenes detected the man's stupidity from the inscription and added the words 'help after the war.'[1]

He meant that it was too late to pray to avert all evils after such a horror had moved in. Hercules was worshipped as 'averter of evil' and he should have moved into the house before the master, since the master himself was a great evil.[2]

267 Once seeing a debauchee eating olives in a tavern he said, 'If you had lunched like that, you would not be dining like that.'

He meant that the fellow was not eating olives as an economy, but because his stomach was weighed down with too rich a luncheon, so he wanted nothing for dinner. For a light luncheon is the best seasoning for dinner.

268 Diogenes used to say that love of money was 'the stronghold' 'the metropolis' of all evils, a turn of phrase not far from the saying of Solomon who said, 'love of money was the root of all evils.'[1]

* * * * *

266 (III) Diogenes Laertius 6.50. In margin 'too late'
  1 Callinicus, 'glorious in victory,' is a cult title of Hercules. *Adagia* III vi 17: *Post bellum auxilium* 'Help when the war is over.'
  2 Erasmus has missed the all-important fact that the man was newly married: the evil that has entered is the wife. Diogenes was a notorious misogynist: see 3.278, 3.282, 3.288, 3.344 below. Erasmus is perhaps recalling 3.216 above.

267 (IV) Diogenes Laertius 6.50. In margin 'indulgence'

268 (V) Diogenes Laertius 6.50. In margin 'avarice'
  1 The Greek word *philargyria* 'love of money' is translated by Erasmus with the Biblical word *cupiditas*. See 1 Tim 6:10, *Radix omnium malorum est cupiditas* 'Love of money is the root of all evils' (AV). Possibly Erasmus is thinking of the Wisdom of Solomon 14:2, *cupiditas acquirendi* 'desire of gain.' This book (in the Apocrypha) was known as The Proverbs of Solomon at one time.
    Diogenes' words are identified as a *chreia* and attributed to Bion (see 7.187–215 below) in Theon *Progymnasmata* 5.207 (Spengel II 99). It was a well-known aphorism, attributed also to Bias and Democritus among others.

**269** Diogenes said good men were visual representations of the gods.

The gods are by nature completely good, and it is their characteristic to do all men good, and harm nobody. This concept is illustrated with greater clarity in wise and good men than it is in statues, since the gods are incorporeal.

**270** Love, he said, was the business of people with time on their hands.

Certainly this emotion chiefly seizes those with nothing to do. So while they have time for idleness, they fall into something that requires a great deal of busy involvement and yet at the same time they do nothing worthwhile.

**271** To someone who inquired what was most wretched in life, he said, 'A needy old man.'

Yes indeed: when the protection of nature deserts a man, the weakness of age has to be buttressed by external advantages. But a man should not be counted needy who has provided himself with noble arts and good friends, the surest travelling fund for old age. That man is most wretchedly in need who is endowed with no virtue.

**272** He was asked what creature had the most deadly bite: 'If you are asking about wild animals,' he said, 'a slanderer, but if you mean tame ones, a flatterer.'[1]

For a slanderer displays his hatred openly, while in the guise of a friend a flatterer hurts much more severely.

**273** Diogenes once saw a very badly painted picture of two centaurs fighting, and asked, 'Which of them is worse?'

This was his criticism of the painter's incompetence, pretending not

*  *  *  *  *

269  (VI) Diogenes Laertius 6.51. In margin 'good men like the gods'

270  (VII) Diogenes Laertius 6.51. See 8.76 below. In margin 'base love'

271  (VIII) Diogenes Laertius 6.51. In margin 'old age'

272  (IX) Diogenes Laertius 6.51
    1 Cf 7.38 below.

273  (X) Diogenes Laertius 6.51. In margin 'witty'

to know which of them was worse painted. But he was making a pun, for *cheiron* means both worse, and one worsted in a fight.[1]

274 He used to call a flattering but insincere speech that was composed to please 'a honeyed noose,'[1] because it throttled a man while giving him a pleasant embrace.

275 He called a pampered belly a Charybdis of life, because it devoured everything and was never sated.[1]

Charybdis only swallows what sails on the sea, and finally regurgitates what she has swallowed; but neither air nor land nor rivers suffice the stomachs of gluttons, but they swallow up whole estates and houses and do not regurgitate them.

276 When some men reported to Diogenes that Didymon had been caught in adultery he said, 'He deserves to be hanged by his name.'[1]

Now testicles are called *didymi* in Greek, so he wanted the man to be hanged by the source of his name and the instrument of his offence.

277 A certain scientist asked Diogenes why gold was pale yellow: he replied, 'Because it is pursued by so many assassins.'

For men that are afraid turn pale and yellow.

* * * * *

1 There is a pun here, but not the one Erasmus explains: *Cheiron / cheiron* is also the name of the most famous centaur, teacher of Achilles, Jason, and others. Diogenes actually asks, 'Which centaur is worse / Cheiron?' Erasmus inserts 'fighting,' to support his interpretation of *cheiron* as 'the loser.' See 3.315 below.

274 (XI) Diogenes Laertius 6.51. In margin 'sweet talk'
  1 See *Adagia* I viii 58: *Letale mulsum* 'A deadly honey-brew.'

275 (XII) Diogenes Laertius 6.51. In margin 'the belly devouring all'
  1 The use of Charybdis, the engulfing sea-monster in the *Odyssey*, for bottomless extravagance became classic in ancient rhetoric.

276 (XIII) Diogenes Laertius 6.51. In margin 'adultery'
  1 This was a *chreia*: Theon *Progymnasmata* 5.211 (Spengel II 102), where the man, there called Didymos, is identified as a pipe-player. See 3.363 below.

277 (XIV) Diogenes Laertius 6.51. In margin 'love of gold'

278 When Diogenes saw a woman in a litter he said, 'The cage doesn't suit the creature.'

He implied that such a wild and dangerous animal needed to be in an iron cage. Now a litter is a kind of seat enclosed with a grille, so that it gives something of the appearance of a cage; rich and spoilt women are accustomed to sit and even be carried in these.

279 Seeing a runaway slave sitting by a well he said, 'Be careful that you don't get dislodged, young man,' making a pun.

For the man who falls into a well gets dislodged, and he also 'gets dislodged' if he is driven from a place. I think wells were once sacred and it was not right to drag anyone away from them, as in the case of temples and statues of the emperor.[1]

280 When he saw a clothes thief in the baths, he said to him, 'Have you come *ep' aleimmation* "to get a bit of a rubdown" (or *ep' all' imation* "to get another garment?"')

Again he was playing on a resemblance between the Greek words, which cannot be represented in Latin. The Greek phrases differ only by a slight change of sound: *aleimma*, from *aleiphō* 'anoint,' is 'a rub-down' (hence *aliptai* 'masseurs') and this diminutive *aleimmation* is 'a lit-tle rubdown.' *All' imation* is two words, but the elision makes them seem almost one; if you remove the elision you get *allo imation* that is, 'another garment.' For men used to rub themselves with oil in the baths, and that is also where thieves carried on their trade, since it is usual for bathers to take off their clothes. So he reprimanded the thief who had stolen one garment somewhere else and had come to steal another.

\* \* \* \* \*

278 (xv) Diogenes Laertius 6.51. In margin 'luxurious'
   For Diogenes the Cynic's misogyny see 3.266 n2 above. See also General Index: women, attitudes to.

279 (xvi) Diogenes Laertius 6.52. In margin 'ambiguous'
   1 Temples regularly offered sanctuary in the Greek world, as did the statues of deified emperors (or their temples) in the Roman Empire. See Seneca *De clementia* 1.18.2.

280 (xvii) Diogenes Laertius 6.52

281 Diogenes once entered a dirty bath and said, 'Where do the men who bathe
here go to bathe?'

He meant that even clean men would get dirty there, and if they had
bathed there would need another bath to get clean in.

282 On one occasion when he saw women who had been hanged dangling from
an olive tree he said, 'If only other trees bore similar fruit!'

For Diogenes was a *misogynēs*, that is, a woman-hater, and so he wanted
to see them all hanged.

283 Noticing someone with a bad reputation for robbing tombs, Diogenes
greeted him with a Homeric verse:

> Why has thou come hither, fine fellow?
> Perhaps to strip one of those whom black death has seized?[1]

284 Once when asked whether he had a slave or slave girl, he said no. But when
the questioner added: 'Then who would bury you if you died?' He said,
'Whoever needs a home.'

Many are superstitiously anxious about how they will be buried and
by whom. Diogenes was completely indifferent to this, having no doubt that
someone would throw out his body, if only to clear the house for himself.
And yet he did have an honourable burial.

\* \* \* \* \*

281 (XVIII) Diogenes Laertius 6.47. In margin 'filth'

282 (XIX) Diogenes Laertius 6.52. See 3.266 n2 above. In margin 'misogynist'

283 (XX) Diogenes Laertius 6.52. In margin 'sacrilege'
  1 Cf *Iliad* 10.343, 387. The introductory words are Homeric-sounding but not
    part of the quotation. Quoting an apt line of verse on the spur of the moment
    or deliberately making a small change in the original to make it fit the situation
    seems to have been a traditional form of wit. The main source was Homer, who
    would be instantly recognizable as the Homeric poems were the foundation of
    Greek education. The equally well-known dramatists were also drawn upon.
    Diogenes seems to have been particularly good at this. See 3.285–6, 3.297,
    3.306, 3.335, 3.350, 3.356–7, 3.384 below. For Aristippus, see 3.149 and 3.160
    above.

284 (XXI) Diogenes Laertius 6.52 and 6.78 (burial). For Diogenes' indifference to
    his own death, see 3.187 n1 above. In margin 'burial'

285 When he noticed a youth sleeping carelessly, Diogenes prodded him with
his stick and uttered a verse of Homer: 'Get up: "lest someone spears you
in the back as you sleep." '[1]

286 To a man who was indulging excessively in fancy food and luxury, Diogenes
applied the Homeric tag: 'O my son, you will be short of living.'[1]
    He meant that he would bring on his death with luxury.

287 Even Aristotle laughed at the Platonic ideas, that is the forms. Once when
Plato was talking at length about the ideas and trying to explain this imaginary thing in invented language – bringing to his lips table-hoods and cup-
hoods, by which he meant the 'ideas' of a table and a cup – Diogenes, mocking these subtle triflings, said, 'I see a table and a cup, but I cannot see a
table-hood and a cup-hood.' (Just so there are men today who think themselves clever talking of happen-hoods and this-hoods.)[1] But Plato retaliated:
'I'm not surprised,' he said, 'for you have eyes to see cups and tables, but
no mind to see table-hoods and cup-hoods.'

288 When someone asked when he should take a wife, he said, 'A young man
should not take one yet and an old man never.'
    This is neater in Greek with the similar sounding *mēdepō* 'never' and
*mēdepōpote* 'not at any time yet.' He was implying that one should completely
avoid marriage. But the questioner wanted to know what year of his life,
or what time of the year, it was advantageous to take a wife, as Aristotle
recommended for the girl the eighteenth year and for the man the thirty-

* * * * *

285 (XXII) Diogenes Laertius 6.53
    1 This is another witty adaptation of a line in Homer *Iliad* 8.95: μή τίς τοι εὕδοντι
    μεταφρένῳ ἐν δόρυ πήξῃ 'lest someone spears you in the back as you flee.' 'Get
    up' is not part of the quotation.

286 (XXIII) Diogenes Laertius 6.53. In margin 'luxury'
    1 Homer *Iliad* 18.95: ὠκύμορος δή μοι, τέκος, ἔσσεαι. The final two words were
    omitted in Traversari's translation (see Introduction xvi–xvii) and these con-
    tained the essence of the joke. The original line said '... short of living by
    reason of your speaking.' Diogenes made it '... by reason of your shopping.'

287 (XXIV) Diogenes Laertius 6.53, expanded. In margin 'silly subtleties'
    1 *Sorteitates ... ecceitates*: terms, used by mediaeval logicians to express individ-
    uation. 'But Plato retaliated ...' The rest was added in 1532.

288 (XXV) Diogenes Laertius 6.54. In margin 'matrimony to be avoided'

fifth,[1] and the Romans thought April and June favourable for weddings, but May inauspicious.[2]

289 When someone asked Diogenes what he would want for a box on the ears, he said, 'a helmet.'

This is another joke depending on the unexpected;[1] for the other expected to find out what compensation Diogenes would take for a box on the ears.

290 When he saw a young man dressing himself up, he said, 'If that is for men, it is in vain, if it is for women, it is unfair.'

This is a wittier joke in Greek because of the similar words, *atucheis* 'you are unlucky' and *adikeis* 'you are unjust.' For a man dresses up for another man in vain, since there can be no marriage between them, and a young man is acting unfairly if he deceives the weaker sex by making himself look good, since a wife is to be won not by specious attractiveness but by sound character.

291 Once, when a young man was embarrassed by his own blushing, Diogenes said, 'Don't worry; that is the colour of virtue.'[1]

292 When he heard two legal experts disputing, he cursed them both, on the grounds that one had committed a theft but the other had not lost anything.

He meant that both deserved death. The wit of the saying is this: the man who robs makes a profit, and the one robbed is afflicted with a loss. But

* * * * *

1 Aristotle *Politics* 7.1335a
2 On Roman taboos against marrying in May see Ovid *Fasti* 6.219–34; *Adagia* I iv 9: *Mense Maio nubunt malae* 'Bad women marry in May.' For Diogenes' misogyny see 3.266 n2 above.

289 (xxvi) Diogenes Laertius 6.54. In margin 'joke from the unexpected'
1 See 3.136 and 3.229 above

290 (xxvii) Diogenes Laertius 6.54. This is given as a *chreia* in Theon *Progymnasmata* 5.208 (Spengel II 99). In margin 'effeminacy'

291 (xxviii) Diogenes Laertius 6.54. In margin 'modesty'
1 Cf 5.332 below.

292 (xxix) Diogenes Laertius 6.54. In margin 'thievishness'

here something absurd had happened: one had stolen the other's property, and yet the man robbed had not lost anything, because he had himself stolen the thing the other took from him.

293 Someone asked which wine he preferred; he answered, 'Someone else's.'
   Here too the *aprosdokēton* – the unexpected point[1] – adds wit to the saying. For the questioner expected something different, that is, he was thinking of the type of wine.

294 A man told him, 'Most people laugh at you.' 'Ah,' he said, 'but I am not laughed at.'
   Now this seems an impossibility, that someone strikes you and you are not struck; but Diogenes said he was not laughed at either because he was not laughable, or because he thought men's mockery did not concern him.

295 When someone said life was wretched, he said, 'It is not living that is wretched, but living badly.'
   The common crowd calls a life wretched if it is exposed to toils, pains, sicknesses, losses, periods of exile, and many misfortunes of this kind. But the philosopher thought nothing bad or wretched unless it was combined with what was shameful.

296 Diogenes had a servant called Manes. When he ran away from his master his friends advised him to search for the fugitive. 'But it's absurd' said Diogenes, 'if Manes can live without Diogenes, but Diogenes cannot live without Manes.'
   Yet many pursue their slaves to be revenged on them, whereas Diogenes looked to the advantage to himself. For a philosopher is better if he needs fewer things. So our man did not want to seem inferior to a slave.

* * * * *

293 (xxx) Diogenes Laertius 6.54. In margin 'nicer if it's other people's'
   1 See 3.136 above.

294 (xxxi) Diogenes Laertius 6.54. Cf Socrates at 3.57 above, and 3.312 below. In margin 'disregard for hurt'

295 (xxxii) Diogenes Laertius 6.55. In margin 'life wretched'

296 (xxxiii) Diogenes Laertius 6.55. In margin 'thrifty'

297 Once he was lunching on olives, and when a cake was brought in as well
he threw it away, quoting that famous tag from tragedy: 'O stranger, from
tyrants far betake yourself,' followed by a Homeric verse: 'sometimes he
drove them on with whips.'[1]

Diogenes called himself a tyrant as the despiser of sweetmeats, which
he wanted driven far from him.

298 Diogenes was commonly called a dog. Now there are many kinds of
dogs: hunting dogs, retrievers, sheepdogs, guard dogs, and lap dogs. So
when someone asked what kind of dog he was, he gave a splendid answer: 'When starving I am a Maltese spaniel, but when full a Molossian
hound.'[1]

His point was that he would fawn when he wanted food but once sated
he would bite.

299 When someone asked him whether philosophers ate cakes, he said: 'Yes,
everything, just like the rest of mankind.'

Again he answered a different question than the one that was asked.
For his questioner wanted to know whether it was proper for philosophers who professed moderation to eat cakes, the food of the pampered.
But Diogenes replied, feigning misunderstanding, as if philosophers were
not men,[1] and yet fed on human foods. For brute beasts do not eat everything available: the ox eats hay, the lion doesn't touch it; sheep love
willow leaves, but horses love oats. Some birds feed on juniper berries,
some feed on flesh, and some on fish. This was the point of Diogenes'
joke.[2]

* * * * *

297 (xxxiv) Diogenes Laertius 6.55
    1 The quotations come from Euripides *Phoenissae* 40: Ὦ ξένε τυράννοις ἐκποδὼν
      καθίστασο, and from *Iliad* 5.366 and 8.45: ἄλλοτε μάστιξεν δ᾽ ἐλάαν. Cf a similar
      story about Philoxenus (6.511 below where the joke will be explained). This
      second story suggests that Diogenes threw away the olives not the cake. See
      3.299–300 below.

298 (xxxv) Diogenes Laertius 6.55. In margin 'Diogenes the Dog'
    1 Another 'dog' story (see 3.192 n1 above). The famous fierce hunting dogs
      from Molossis in Epirus were also used as guard dogs. See eg Horace *Satires*
      2.6.112–5.

299 (xxxvi) Diogenes Laertius 6.56. In margin 'the philosopher human'
    1 For philosophers not counting as human, see 7.151 below.
    2 Erasmus added the parallel about animal and bird diet in 1535. See also 8.279
      below.

300 Once when Diogenes was eating cake at a dinner party, one of the guests
said, 'What are you eating, Diogenes?' thinking that a Cynic philosopher did
not know what cake was. 'Some nicely baked bread,' he said, pretending not
to know what he was eating.

   To others it was cake, to Diogenes, who did not eat for pleasure, it was
bread.[2]

301 When someone inquired why men gave generously to other beggars but not
to philosophers, he said, 'Because they hope they'll become blind or lame
sooner than they'll become philosophers.'

   Those who pitied the afflicted, and most beggars are afflicted, do it
in contemplation of men's common lot: thus they help a blind man, thinking, 'This could happen to me,' but they don't have the same idea about a
philosopher. The saying is rather witty because of its misinterpretation of
the word *sperare* which can mean 'expect' as well as 'hope': one may well
hope to become a philosopher, but nobody hopes for blindness or lameness.[1]

302 Diogenes was asking a miser for some help, but when he saw him hesitating
and about to refuse, he said, 'Good man, I am asking you for food, not a
funeral,' to render the similarity of the Greek words as best I can. For in
Greek *trophē* is 'food,' and *taphē* is 'burial.'

303 Someone reproached him for having once falsely coined money; for as men
say, he was ordered into exile for this.[1] 'I admit,' he said, 'there was a time
when I was just as you are now; but you will never be what I am now.'

   He was criticizing those who condemn the errors of youth in others,
although they do not correct their own even in old age.

        * * * * *

   300 (XXXVII) Athenaeus 3.80, 113F. In margin 'pretence'
     2 Erasmus has transformed the very brief original with several interpolations
       and has omitted the fact that Diogenes was gobbling the cake. In Athenaeus,
       the story comes in a section on greedy eating. The joke is presumably similar
       to the one in 3.299, but this time Diogenes plays along with the questioner.

   301 (XXXVIII) Diogenes Laertius 6.56. In margin 'witty'
     1 The joke seems to be that the words can be misinterpreted to mean 'anything
       rather than become a philosopher.'

   302 (XXXIX) Diogenes Laertius 6.56. In margin 'giving reluctantly'

   303 (XL) Diogenes Laertius 6.56. In margin 'error corrected'
     1 On Diogenes' debasement of the coinage see 3.259 above.

304 When someone else reproached him with this same crime, he defended the offence on the grounds of his youth, saying, 'I pissed more quickly then, but now it is different.'

He censured his juvenile years with a Cynic's circumlocution; for youth more easily pours liquid from the bladder, but old men suffer from *dysouria*.

305 Diogenes once travelled to Myndus, and found that the gates were huge and magnificently built, whereas the town itself was tiny. 'Men of Myndus,' he said, 'shut your gates in case your city gets away.'

He meant that the town was so small it could leave through the gates.

306 When he saw a thief arrested who stole purple clothes, he adapted a Homeric verse to fit him: 'Now you,' he said, 'purple death has grasped and violent destiny.'[1]

307 Craterus, a commander under Alexander the Great, and a very wealthy man, had invited Diogenes to move into his house.[1] He replied, 'I would rather lick salt[2] at Athens than enjoy a delicate table at Craterus' home.'

He believed liberty however poor was to be preferred to all the luxury of the wealthy, where liberty is impaired.

308 The rhetoric teacher Anaximenes[1] was weighed down by a big belly. Dio-

* * * * *

304  (XLI) Diogenes Laertius 6.56. In margin 'youthful error'

305  (XLII) Diogenes Laertius 6.57. In margin 'amusing'
Myndus was the capital of Caria in south-west Asia Minor.

306  (XLIII) Diogenes Laertius 6.57. In margin 'witty'
1 *Iliad* 5.83. The original line said: 'Him purple death . . .' See 3.283 n1 above.

307  (XLIV) Diogenes Laertius 6.57. In margin 'liberty'
1 It was a matter of prestige for public figures to attach philosophers to their households, and it was the main source of support (often in relative luxury) for such men. Although Craterus was one of Alexander's chief generals, Diogenes asserted his independence.
2 'To lick salt' meant to have an impoverished life-style. See *Adagia* III vii 33: *Salem lingere* 'to lick salt.'

308  (XLV) Diogenes Laertius 6.57. In margin 'obesity'
1 The historian and rhetorician Anaximenes of Lampsacus (c. 380–320 BC) was a prosperous glutton.

genes went up to him and said: 'Share your stomach with us poor fellows; for you will be relieved of a burden and do us a favour.'

309 Once, when Anaximenes was orating, Diogenes held out a ham[1] and turned the audience's attention to himself. Anaximenes was angry at this and fell silent, abandoned by his audience. Then Diogenes said, 'An obol of expense has paid off Anaximenes' discourse.'

He meant that the other was talking about silly matters, which did not keep the audience attentive enough.

310 When certain men reproached him with eating in the market-place, he said, 'What is surprising about that? The market-place is where I get hungry.'

He was arguing from corresponding opposites: if a man did *not* feel hungry in the market-place, it might well be inappropriate for him to eat there. But on the same principle he could have defended himself for evacuating or urinating in the market-place.[1]

311 Some writers also credit Diogenes with this retort: They say Plato came upon him rinsing greens and said in his ear, 'If you had humoured Dionysius you wouldn't be rinsing greens now.' Diogenes in turn said in Plato's ear, 'And if you rinsed greens, you wouldn't have been a slave to Dionysius.'

But really this seems modelled on a story we told before (about Aristippus),[1] as the next one is.[2]

312 Someone once said to Diogenes, 'There are many who laugh at you, Diogenes!' and he replied, 'And most likely donkeys laugh at them.' And when

\* \* \* \* \*

309 (XLVI) Diogenes Laertius 6.57. In margin 'humorous'
  1 Once again Erasmus has changed Diogenes' gesture by substituting a ham (which would cost more than an obol) for the fish mentioned by Laertius, no doubt because of his own distaste for fish.

310 (XLVII) Diogenes Laertius 6.57. In margin 'eating in public'
  1 As the Cynics did as a gesture; it was natural and therefore nothing to be ashamed of. See 3.367 below.

311 (XLVIII) Diogenes Laertius 6.57. In margin 'liberty'
  1 See 3.102 above (Aristippus); also 3.110 above.
  2 See 3.312, similar to 3.294 above.

312 (XLIX) Diogenes Laertius 6.58. See 3.294 above. In margin 'mockery ignored'

another butted in, 'But these folk take no notice of donkeys,' Diogenes answered, 'Nor do I take any notice of them.'

He credited donkeys with laughing because when they bare their teeth they give the appearance of laughter. Again men making fun of someone put their hands to their ears to imitate donkeys' ears. So too a donkey that twitches its ears seems to make fun of people but nobody takes offence.

313 Diogenes noticed a very young man studying philosophy and said, 'Bravo! You are diverting lovers of physical beauty towards the beauties of the mind.'[1]

He meant that by concentrating on enriching his mind with virtue and honourable studies the young man would come to have far superior friends. For nothing is more beautiful than wisdom, or more lovable than virtue.

314 Once men who had been rescued from danger used to hang up votive gifts in temples as if attributing their safety to the gods. So when he was shown votive offerings in Samothrace dedicated by men saved from war, sickness, a voyage, or some other hazard, he said, 'But there would be a lot more offerings if those who had not survived had dedicated them.'

I think he felt that those who were saved were saved by chance, not as a favour from the gods. For if we must credit the gods when someone is rescued, we must also lay it to their charge that more perish than are saved. Some writers attribute this to Diagoras of Melos, the atheist.[1] Certainly the Samothracians were afflicted with great superstition in these matters.

315 When a handsome young man was going to a dinner-party Diogenes said, 'You will come back worse for it!' So when the young man returned and

* * * * *

313 (L) Diogenes Laertius 6.58. In margin 'cultivation of the mind'
  1 The editor of the Loeb text suggests that Diogenes addresses philosophy.

314 (LI) Diogenes Laertius 6.59. In margin 'offerings'
  1 This information also from Laertius 6.59. See also Cicero De natura deorum 3.89. Diagoras of Melos was a philosopher and a lyric poet of the fifth century BC, whether justly or not, particularly regarded as an atheist for his nonconformity with traditional religious views. Samothrace was a centre of worship of the Cabiri, deities especially invoked by sailors.

315 (LII) Diogenes Laertius 6.59. In margin 'bad associates'

said, 'I went and I haven't come back worse,' Diogenes said 'Indeed you have come back worse.'[1]

He meant that it was impossible for a young man to escape being the worse for a drunken and wanton party.

316 Diogenes asked a big favour of Eurytion,[1] and when Eurytion characteristically refused it with these words, 'I'll do it, if you can persuade me,' Diogenes said, 'If I could, I would have persuaded you to hang yourself long since.'

But there is nothing to admire here except Cynic licence.

317 He had paid a visit to Sparta and when he returned to Athens someone asked him, as men do, where he was going and where had come from. 'From a land of men to one of women,' he said, as a criticism of the Athenian way of life that had become effeminate from luxury, whereas the Spartans were given a tough training.[1]

318 Once on his return from Olympia he was asked whether he had seen a great crowd. 'A huge crowd,' he said, 'but hardly any men.'

This story seems to be an imitation of the earlier one about the baths.[1]

* * * * *

1 This story depends on a pun on the names of the wise centaur Cheiron (whose name also meant 'worse') and another, violent, centaur Eurytion (whose name meant 'broad- or slack-arsed'). Cf 3.273 above. Diogenes' final retort to the young man was 'Indeed you haven't come back Cheiron/worse, you've come back Erytion/slack-arsed!' In Erasmus' version the negative is omitted ('Indeed you have come back worse') and Erytion's name has somehow been incorporated into the next saying. This does not seem to be an example of Erasmus censuring a risky anecdote; rather he seems to have been misled by Traversari's version (see Introduction xvi–xvii above).

316 (LIII) Diogenes Laertius 6.59. In margin 'uninhibited'
   1 See n1 on 3.315 just above. In Laertius, the other person is 'a bad-tempered man.'

317 (LIV) Diogenes Laertius 6.59. In margin 'fancy living'
   1 For the benefit of this criticism of Athenians, Diogenes honours the Spartans as real men; but usually he denies anybody the name of 'real man'; see 3.176 n1 above.

318 (LV) Diogenes Laertius 6.60. In margin 'men are few'
   1 Ie 3.221 above.

319 He said that men who squandered their estate in self-indulgence on cooks, whores, play-boys, and flatterers, were like trees growing on a precipice, because no man could taste their fruit, but they were eaten by vultures and crows.

His point was that those who were slaves of their throats and bellies were not men.[1]

320 If the Greeks want to curse anyone they tell them to 'go to the crows.'[1] But Diogenes used to say that it was much more dangerous to fall among flatterers than among crows.

We have lost the joke here which depends on the resemblance of the Greek words. For they call crows *korakas* and with a change of one letter they call flatterers *kolakas*. This saying is also credited to Antisthenes.[2]

321 The courtesan Phryne dedicated a golden Venus at Delphi, and when Diogenes saw it he added an inscription: 'The spoils of Greek wantonness.'[1]

He implied that the Greeks were excessively addicted to lust since a whore had accumulated so much gold from her disgraceful trade.

322 Some people also credit this saying to him. When Alexander the Great came to see Diogenes and greeted him, Diogenes asked who he was; and when he replied, 'I am the famous King Alexander' Diogenes replied, 'And I am the famous dog Diogenes.' He was as proud of his freedom of speech as Alexander was of his kingdom. And when he was asked how he had earned

\* \* \* \* \*

319 (LVI) Diogenes Laertius 6.60. In margin 'squandering'
  1 Erasmus' last sentence shows he has missed Diogenes' point, that debauchees were preyed upon by con-men as the fruit from fig trees on a cliff edge was only consumed by vultures. Cf 7.283, where the saying is ascribed to Crates.

320 (LVII) Athenaeus 6.254C. In margin 'flattery'
  1 *Adagia* II i 96: *Ad corvos* 'Off with you to the crows'
  2 Diogenes Laertius 6.4 (see 7.51 below)

321 (LVIII) Diogenes Laertius 6.60
  1 This story is also told at Plutarch *Moralia* 336D (*On the fortune of Alexander*). Erasmus quotes sayings of Phryne in 6.575–81 below. There were at Delphi many dedications set up by states from the spoils of enemies defeated in war. This is the joke. See 6.472 below.

322 (LIX) Diogenes Laertius 6.60. In margin 'freedom of speech'

the nickname dog, he said, 'Because I fawn on those who make me gifts, I bark at those who don't, but bad men I even bite.'[1]

323 When Diogenes was plucking some fruit from a fig tree and the orchard keeper said to him, 'A man hanged himself from this tree a few days ago,' Diogenes said, 'But I will clean it up.'[1]

  The other man thought Diogenes would take the warning and stay away from the deadly tree that had carried a corpse. But he was free of all superstition and thought the fruit no more unclean for that.

324 When he saw an Olympic victor staring so fixedly at a whore that he turned his head to gaze at her after she passed, he said, 'See how that champion ram is led away bound with his neck in a noose by a mere street woman.'[1]

  He thought it absurd for a man to compete with champions and be dragged around like a prisoner by a cheap girl without even being bound.

325 He said that beautiful whores were like sweet wine mixed with deadly poison, because they brought pleasure at first, but one followed by unending pain.

326 Once when Diogenes was lunching in the open street and many crowded round him because of the strangeness of the sight and kept shouting, 'Dog, dog!' he said, 'No, you are the dogs, to stand around someone when he is eating his lunch.'

  For this is a particularly common habit of dogs.[1]

\* \* \* \* \*

  1 Another interpretation of the nickname 'dog'; see 3.192 n1 above.

  323 (LX) Diogenes Laertius 6.61. In margin 'no superstition'
    1 Possibly Diogenes is making a pun and means he will strip the tree of its fruit.

  324 (LXI) Diogenes Laertius 6.61. In margin 'sensual pleasure'
    1 Cf Plutarch *Moralia* 521B (*On being a busybody*), who names the Olympic champion as Dioxippus. See *Adagia* IV ix 50: *Obtorto collo* 'With one's neck in a noose.'

  325 (LXII) Diogenes Laertius 6.61. *Adagia* I viii 58: *Letale mulsum* 'A deadly honeybrew.' In margin 'whore'

  326 (LXIII) Diogenes Laertius 6.61. In margin 'uninhibited speech'
    1 Another Diogenes dog story; see 3.192 above.

327 When someone mentioned a boy who was a rent-boy, Diogenes was asked
where he was from and made a pun saying, 'He's a Tegeate.'
        Now Tegea is a community in Arcadia: but *tegos* is sometimes used to
mean 'brothel': hence the philosopher called the common whore a Tegeate.[1]

328 He saw someone who had previously been a wrestler, but a poor one, claiming to be a doctor and said to him, 'So are you going to lay low the men
who used to lay you low?'
        A wrestler lays a man low when he defeats him, and a doctor lays low
those he sends to their beds or even their deaths. Diogenes guessed he was
as bad as a doctor as he had been as a wrestler. There is a joke like this in
Martial about the man who changed from a doctor into an armed gladiator,
and did the same thing as a gladiator that he had done as a doctor.[1]

329 When a bastard son of a courtesan was throwing stones at the crowd, Diogenes said, 'Mind you don't hit your father!'[1]
        Since he was a whore's son his father was unknown.

330 When some people were hymning the generosity of a man who had made
Diogenes a present, he said, 'Why don't you praise me too, for deserving to
receive it?'
        It is greater to deserve a kindness than to give it, according to the
saying of Publius the Mime-writer:
        Who gives a kindness well-deserved receives one.[1]


                    * * * * *


327  (LXIV) Diogenes Laertius 6.61. In margin 'punning'
    1 See General Index: Arcadia.

328  (LXV) Diogenes Laertius 6.62. In margin 'bad doctor'
    1 Cf Martial 8.74.

329  (LXVI) Diogenes Laertius 6.62
    1 In the first edition the boy is simply illegitimate; his mother's profession was
      added in 1532. For wit exercised on disreputable birth cf 3.34 n1 above.
      This is given as a *chreia* in Theon *Progymnasmata* 5.209–10 (Spengel II 100–1)
      classified as 'mixed,' both 'figurative' and 'jesting.'

330  (LXVII) Diogenes Laertius 6.62. In margin 'a benefit deserved'
    1 This is from the collection of apophthegms of the first-century BC Roman
      mime-writer Publilius Syrus (*Sententiae* B55 Meyer.)

331 Diogenes made a very witty retort to someone who asked him to give back
a cloak: 'If you gave it me, I am keeping it; if you lent it, I am still using it.'
   He meant that he didn't intend to return it, whether he had received it
as a gift or a loan. It is shameful to demand back something you have given
away,[1] and unkind to snatch away something the user needs.

332 When a supposititious man[1] said about Diogenes that he 'had gold wrapped
in his cloak,' Diogenes countered the insult: 'That's right, so I sleep on something pushed in underneath.[2]
   Now supposititious birth is the name they give when men pretend
to be born from a womb they didn't come from. We 'sleep on' a treasure
to keep it safe, and we 'shut our eyes to' something we disregard. And
Diogenes used his cloak as a pillow at night.[3]

333 When he was asked what profit he got from philosophy, he said, 'If nothing
else, at least I am ready for every kind of luck.'
   This saying hardly sounds like Diogenes, even if it is credited to him.

334 Somebody asked Diogenes where he came from and he said 'kosmopolites,'

* * * * *

331 (LXVIII) Diogenes Laertius 6.62
   1 Adagia IV viii 98: Quod recte datum est 'What's once given'

332 (LXIX) Diogenes Laertius 6.62
   1 Supposititious: 'put in under,' said of a child fraudulently set up to displace
     the real heir.
   2 This not very accurate rendering of Diogenes Laertius' Greek has coloured Eras-
     mus' comment. The meaning of the passage is not immediately clear in any case,
     but it seems to mean: When a supposititious man said to Diogenes that he had
     gold in his cloak, 'Yes,' he said, 'and for that reason you sleep with it pushed in
     underneath'; or: 'for that very reason you sleep as one pushed in.' This alterna-
     tive interpretation depends on dividing the words differently and the remark
     could be deliberately ambiguous as many of Diogenes' quips are.
   3 Traditionally it was said that fraudulent babies were smuggled into the birth
     room in a cloak. Diogenes both sleeps on his folded cloak (see Diogenes Laer-
     tius 6.22) and ignores the remarks of a 'smuggled in' or 'pushed in underneath'
     man.

333 (LXX) Diogenes Laertius 6.63. In margin 'the philosopher'

334 (LXXI) Diogenes Laertius 6.63. In margin 'every land a homeland to the brave'

'I'm a world citizen,' meaning that wherever a philosopher spent his time, he was living in his own country.[1]

335 Once when he asked for alms, he addressed the *eranarches*, that is the charity commissioner, in a Homeric verse: 'Despoil the rest, from Hector hold your grasp.'[1]

   The wit lies in the wordplay. He substituted *enarize* 'strip of arms' for *eranize* 'give a contribution' and by Hector's name he meant himself. For a man who denies to the needy is taking spoils. Indeed this kind of man is prone to thieving.

336 Diogenes said that whores were 'queens of kings' because they asked and got whatever they fancied from kings. That is, he called them queens of kings, not because they were like wives, but because they held sway over kings. Kings do not always get what they want from the people, but nothing is denied to a whore. I think barbarian kings must have been like this.

337 To flatter Alexander the Athenians decreed that he should be treated and

* * * * *

1 On Diogenes as a citizen of the world see J.L. Moles 'Cynic cosmopolitanism' 105–111 in Bracht Branham and Marie Odile Goulet-Cazé eds *The Cynics: the Cynic movement in antiquity and its legacy* (University of California Press 1996). Moles rejects the authenticity of similar stories about Socrates, eg Plutarch *Moralia* 600F (*On exile*) and Cicero *Tusculan Disputations* 5.108. Arrian *Epictetus* 1.9.1 attributes the claim to Epictetus. The quotation in the margin is from Ovid *Fasti* 1.493. Cf 3.259 above.

335 (LXXII) Diogenes Laertius 6.63. In margin 'humorous'
   1 This verse is not in our text of Homer, but some editors added it in the past after *Iliad* 16.82 or 90. This anecdote had already been garbled in Traversari's Latin version (see Introduction xvi–xvii) hence Erasmus' muddled paragraph. Diogenes was being asked for a contribution, not requesting alms for himself. As on many occasions, he made a joke by deliberately changing a Homeric line (see eg 3.285 above), substituting *eranize* 'ask a contribution' for Homer's *enarize* 'strip (a fallen foe) of arms.' The similar sounding Greek words have been muddled in the text, spoiling the joke. Diogenes actually said 'ask the others for a contribution' instead of 'despoil the others.'

336 (LXXIII) Diogenes Laertius 6.63. In margin 'imperious whore'

337 (LXXIV) Diogenes Laertius 6.63

worshipped as Father Liber. Diogenes made fun of this honour saying, 'And make me Serapis!'[1]

For as Bacchus is among the satyrs, so Serapis is worshipped by the Egyptians in the form of a bull.[2]

338 When he was censured for going into dirty and dishonourable places, he said, 'But the sun enters latrines without being fouled.'

He felt that an honest man was not damaged by the ill fame of a place.

339 When he was eating dinner in a shrine and they put down dirty rolls beside him, he threw them out of the shrine saying, 'Nothing dirty should come into a temple.'

340 One man asked him saucily why he called himself a philosopher when he knew nothing. Diogenes said, 'If I pretend to be a philosopher, this too is practising philosophy.'

\* \* \* \* \*

1 There are other stories of protests by eg Pytheas (5.212 below) and Damis (1.164 above) against the deification of the still living king, but the status of god was generally bestowed upon him after death, in keeping with Greek cult of ancestor heroes. Alexander was quite prepared to accept the adulation and liked to equate himself with Dionysus Bacchus (Father Liber in Latin; Erasmus prefers to use Latin rather than Greek names for divinities.)
2 The point of Diogenes' quip may simply be that the Egyptian Serapis was associated with a three-headed animal (dog, lion, wolf), also with the dog-headed divinity Anubis. (For Diogenes as 'dog' see 3.192 n1 above.) Serapis however became a syncretistic Greco-Egyptian deity about this date, identified with Osiris and the bull-headed Apis. In Egypt the Greek Dionysus was identified with Osiris: Herodotus 2.42, 2.144, Plutarch *Moralia* 362B (*On Isis and Osiris*). See J. Servais 'Alexandre-Dionysus et Diogène-Serapis. A propos de Diogène Laerce VI 63' *L'Antiquité classique* 28 (1959) 98–106 (reference supplied by Dr ter Meer). Among his many representations, Bacchus was depicted on coins with horns, either of a ram or a bull. The Satyrs were Dionysus / Bacchus' drunken, half-animal companions. Erasmus' cryptic comment only adds confusion to an unclear anecdote.

338 (LXXV) Diogenes Laertius 6.63. In margin 'a place does not defile'

339 (LXXVI) Diogenes Laertius 6.64. In margin 'keep sacred things clean'

340 (LXXVII) Diogenes Laertius 6.64. In margin 'pretence of philosophy'

He implied that philosophy was such a difficult matter that even to affect it was a great part of the art. In the same way a man has much of the nature of a king who can play the role of king skilfully. And to pretend is to imitate and to imitate philosophers is to practise philosophy, that is, to be devoted to philosophy.

341 Someone brought a boy to Diogenes for him to share in Diogenes' learning, and to recommend him to the philosopher he said that the boy was of excellent intellect and fine character. Then Diogenes said, 'So what does he need from me?'[1]

He was reproaching the man's excessive praise, for crediting the boy with the qualities which boys are sent to philosophers to acquire. It would have been enough to mention the boy's decent character and promise.

342 Diogenes said that men who talked about virtue and did not live rightly were like a lyre which was useful to others for its sound, but neither understood nor heard anything itself.

This comment is not very different from St Paul's saying about the tinkling cymbal.[1]

343 One day when the crowd was leaving the theatre, Diogenes was making his way in, pushing against the flow of people. When he was asked why he was doing it, he said, 'This is what I aim to do in all my life.'

His point was that philosophy consisted of acting as far as possible in opposition to the crowd, because the mass of men are driven by desires not by reason.

344 When he caught sight of a very young man whose clothing and gestures were unmanly he said, 'Aren't you ashamed to choose something worse for

* * * * *

341 (LXXVIII) Diogenes Laertius 6.64. In margin 'excessive praise'
  1 This story treats Diogenes as if he were a regular teacher, like most of his philosophical peers.

342 (LXXIX) Diogenes Laertius 6.64. In margin 'teaching without moral application'
  1 1 Cor 13:1. Cf 7.341 below.

343 (LX) Diogenes Laertius 6.64. In margin 'nothing pleases the crowd for right reasons'

344 (LXXXI) Diogenes Laertius 6.65. This is another example of Diogenes' notorious misogyny; see 3.266 n2 above. In margin 'degeneracy'

yourself than nature intended for you? For Nature made you a man and you have remodelled yourself as a woman.'

This can be said against most men whom nature has made human but who of their own accord sink into being cattle.

345 When Diogenes saw a foolish singer of undisciplined lifestyle tuning his zither he said, 'Aren't you ashamed that you know how to make sounds harmonize with wood but don't know how to tune your life to the right way of living?'

This apophthegm too seems to have been put together from earlier ones.[1]

346 He was urging someone to the pursuit of wisdom and the man said, 'I am not suited to philosophy.' 'So why do you keep on living,' he said, 'if you're not interest in living rightly?'

For a man does not live just to stay alive but to learn how to live. Nature gives us life, philosophy the right way of life.[1] Nature begets men so they can learn virtue; she does not beget them already learned.

347 He said to a son who was expressing contempt for his father, 'Aren't you ashamed to despise the man to whom you owe your own self-satisfaction?'[1]

The elegance of the saying lies in the play of opposites; for being despised and pleased with oneself are contraries.

348 When he heard a young man of respectable appearance using disreputable language, he said, 'Aren't you ashamed to draw a leaden sword out of an ivory scabbard?'

* * * * *

345 (LXXXII) Diogenes Laertius 6.65. In margin 'we neglect what is best'
    1 Cf 3.179 above.

346 (LXXXIII) Diogenes Laertius 6.65. In margin 'life without learning is death'
    1 The usual form of the saying is 'Parents give us life, teachers living aright.' See 7.235 n1 below. For the marginal heading see Seneca *Epistulae morales* 82.3 'leisure without learning is death.'

347 (LXXXIV) Diogenes Laertius 6.65. In margin 'lack of respect for father'
    1 This seems to be another 'unexpected reply' (see 3.136 above): he should be ashamed for despising the father to whom he owed – the very fact that he could feel superior. Cf Seneca *De beneficiis* 3.29.

348 (LXXXV) Diogenes Laertius 6.65. In margin 'disreputable language'

For ivory was once very expensive. The mind is concealed by the body, but shines through the speech.

**349** When someone made it a reproach to him that he drank in an inn, Diogenes said, 'Yes, and I get shaved at a barber's!'

His point was that it was no more dishonourable to drink than to have a haircut or shave. Just as nobody blames a man for being shaved at a barber's, since that is the purpose of his shop, so it should not seem shameful to drink in an inn, if a man does it moderately. For to drink immoderately is shameful anywhere.

**350** To a fellow who reproached him with accepting a cloak from King Philip, he answered with the Homeric verse: 'The glorious gifts of gods should not be spurned.'[1]

What Homer said of physical beauty, which is a gift of the gods, Diogenes applied to the cloak given by the king. And I myself could chant the same line to those reproaching me because I sometimes accept gifts from princes or bishops that are presented to do me honour. There is no one from whom I have ever asked for a gift, either openly or indirectly; but what men freely bestow I gladly accept, less as gifts than as commendations, especially when their wealth is too great for them to feel the gift as a loss.

**351** When Diogenes was speaking earnestly about avoiding anger, a certain rude young man, as if to test whether Diogenes could practise what he preached, spat in his face. He took it mildly and wisely: 'I am not angry,' he said, 'but I am wondering whether I should be angry!'[1]

\* \* \* \* \*

349 (LXXXVI) Diogenes Laertius 6.66. In margin 'eating anywhere'

350 (LXXXVII) Diogenes Laertius 6.66 (where the gift is from Antipater). In margin 'gifts of kings'
   1 Iliad 3.65: Οὔτοι ἀπόβλητ᾽ ἐστι θεῖων ἐρικυδέα δῶρα

351 (LXXXVIII) Seneca De ira 3.38.1. In margin 'mildness'
   1 Both the motif of submitting to being spat at (see 3.106 above and 4.274 below) and resistance to anger (see 1.345 above and 7.155–6 below) are recurrent themes. Erasmus replaced Diogenes Laertius 6.66 with this anecdote, because Diogenes Laertius was here reporting on earlier story (see 3.225 above).

352 Seeing someone entreating a courtesan to get what he desired he said, 'What is it you want, you poor fool? It is better not to get what you are asking for.'

For it is happier to be sent away by a whore than to be invited in. Yet most men urgently solicit their own harm and pay a great price for it.

353 Diogenes said to a fellow with heavily perfumed hair oil: 'Take care that the sweet odour of your head does not put your life in ill odour!'

We are trying to catch the neat resemblance of the Greek words *euōdia* 'nice smell' and *dysōdia* 'bad smell' as best we can. Of course perfume in a man suggests effeminacy of behaviour, and a man's repute is his perfume as it were. Martial said something similar: 'Naevolus, a man doesn't smell good, if he always smells good.'[1]

354 He said there was no difference between slaves and bad masters except their name; the slaves served their masters, the masters their lusts.

He meant that both groups were slaves, but that the masters are more wretchedly enslaved than the slaves, if they are bad men. For a man led by the whim of his emotions has many masters, and they are both shameful and ruthless.

355 Greek calls slaves, especially runaways, *andrapoda*, a word apparently compounded of *andra* and *pod-* 'man' and 'foot,' though grammarians give a different etymology.[1] So when a corrupt man asked Diogenes why runaway slaves were called *andrapoda*, he said, 'Because they have the feet of men but a soul like yours who ask me this question.'

He meant that the other man too had the mind of a farm animal, not of a man.

\* \* \* \* \*

352  (LXXXIX) Diogenes Laertius 6.66. In margin 'consorting with whores'

353  (XC) Diogenes Laertius 6.66. In margin 'perfumes'
  1 Martial 2.12.4, but 'Naevolus' is in error for 'Postumus.'

354  (XCI) Diogenes Laertius 6.66. In margin 'slavery to vice'

355  (XCII) Diogenes Laertius 6.67. In margin 'witty'
  1 See eg *Etymologicum magnum* which, suggests derivations from words of similar sound meaning 'exhibit' or 'man' and 'shackles,' and says 'they put shackles on because they run away.' Also *Suda* A 2155, which suggests 'man' and 'foot': 'because the foot is below the whole body as the slave is subject to his master.' For slaves equated with farm animals see Aristotle *Politics* 1254b.

356 Diogenes once tried to beg a whole mina from a spendthrift.[1] The other was amazed at the outrageous demand and asked, 'Why do you ask me for a whole mina when you usually ask others for an obol?' Diogenes replied, 'Because with other men I can hope that I will receive some money on another occasion, but "it lies in the lap of the gods" whether I will ever again get anything from you.'

He worked in this Homeric half-line,[2] implying by it that a spendthrift was at risk of being soon reduced to penury, without even an obol left.

357 When some fellows reproached Diogenes with begging, since Plato did not do it, he said, 'On the contrary, he begs too, but "with head up close so that no one else may hear."'

He mis-applied the Homeric verse, from the first book of the Odyssey,[1] to indicate that Plato was no less prone to begging, except that he begged discreetly, whereas Diogenes did it openly.

358 When he saw someone hurling the javelin incompetently, he sat next to the target and when he was asked why, replied, 'So that he won't accidentally hit me.'

He was implying that the man would hit anything rather than the target, but the other spectators put themselves as far as possible from the target so as not to be struck.

359 Men who miss the target are commonly said in Greek *atuxein*, that is, 'to fail.' But Diogenes said men did not fail by missing the target, but by making pleasures the target of their endeavours.

They hope for happiness from pleasures, whereas they are brought by them to utmost wretchedness.

\* \* \* \* \*

356 (XCIII) Diogenes Laertius 6.67. In margin 'extravagance'
    1 This was an extravagant demand, since one mina was six hundred obols, more than a craftsman's annual wage.
    2 Eg Homer *Iliad* 17.514, *Odyssey* 1.267: θεῶν ἐν γούνασι κεῖται. See *Adagia* II viii 58: *In quinque iudicum genibus situm est* 'It lies on the knees of five judges.'

357 (XCIV) Diogenes Laertius 6.67. In margin 'concealed begging'
    1 *Odyssey* 1.157, also 4.70. 'Odyssey 1' was added in 1535. In the original context, the goddess Athena whispers to Telemachos. See 3.283 n1 above.

358 (XCV) Diogenes Laertius 6.68. *Adagia* II vi 78: *nec propius ferire* 'Nowhere near the mark.' In margin 'humorous'

359 (XCVI) Diogenes Laertius 6.68. In margin 'pleasure'

**360** Asked once whether death was a misfortune, he said, 'How can it be a misfortune when we do not notice its presence?'

For what is not present is a misfortune to nobody. While a man is conscious, he is alive, so death is not present; for if it were, there would be no consciousness. And what cannot be perceived is no misfortune. Some attribute this argument to Epicurus. Indeed death is not a bad thing, but the approach to death is wretched.[1] If we fear that, what else is a man's whole life except the approach to death?[2]

**361** They say Alexander the Great stood by Diogenes and asked him if he was afraid of him. But Diogenes said, 'What are you? A good thing or a bad one?' Alexander answered that he was good. 'Well then,' said Diogenes, 'who is afraid of a good thing?'

He demonstrated that a king was not to be feared unless he declared himself to be a bad thing. By the same syllogism he could deduce that God was not to be feared either.

**362** He recommended learning to everyone with the claim that it brought young men sobriety, old men comfort, poor men wealth, and rich men adornment: for it controlled youth, which was naturally at risk and kept it from excesses, it softened the discomforts of old age with an honourable consolation, it was as good as resources for the poor, since men who have been instructed do not feel need, and it adorned the wealth of the rich.

**363** Didymon, who was commonly thought of as an adulterer, was treating a maiden's eye. Diogenes said to him, 'See you don't harm the pupil.'[1]

This witticism loses its charm in Latin. For in Greek the word *korē* means both a maiden and the pupil of the eye. So Diogenes was exploiting the double meaning.

\* \* \* \* \*

360 (xcvii) Diogenes Laertius 6.68. In margin 'is death an evil?'
  1 Diogenes Laertius 10.125. See also Plutarch *Moralia* 110A (*Consolation to Apollonius*), said by Arcesilaus
  2 Seneca *Dialogues* 11.11.2 (*Ad Polybium de consolatione*)

361 (xcviii) Diogenes Laertius 6.68. In margin 'neat'

362 (xcix) Diogenes Laertius 6.68. In margin 'learning'

363 (c) Diogenes Laertius 6.68. In margin 'joke depending on ambiguity'
  1 The seducer Didymos (sic) is identified as a flute-player at 3.276 n1 above, though this anecdote suggests he was a doctor.

**364** After someone warned him that he should be careful because his friends were laying a trap for him, Diogenes said, 'What are you to do if we have to associate with friends and enemies on the same terms?'

   For we protect ourselves from enemies but trust our friends. But if we must protect ourselves equally from both, life is just not pleasant.

**365** When asked what was best in life, he said, 'Freedom.'

   But a man is not truly free who is a slave to vices, nor can a man be free who feels the need of many things: the miser, the ambitious man, and one given to indulgence feel the need of a great many things.[1]

**366** Once the Muses used to be painted in schools as presiding over studies. So when he entered a school and saw many Muses but few pupils, he said to the teacher, 'If the gods are with you, you have a lot of pupils.'[1]

   He was playing on the ambiguity of the phrase, for the Greeks say 'with the gods' when we would say 'with the gods' good favour.' Greek *syn*, 'with,' also means 'together with'; for instance 'I with many others defended you' means 'many defended you together with me.'

**367** Diogenes used to say that whatever was not inherently shameful was not shameful even in public. This is how he argued the point: 'If it is not bad to dine, then it is not bad to dine in the market-place; but there is nothing bad about dining, so it cannot be bad to dine in the market-place either.'[1]

   One could endure the Cynic syllogism this far, but who would put up with his inferring in the same way that to evacuate or urinate or copulate with one's wife or undress is not bad, therefore it is not bad in public either. For decent men like modesty everywhere.

* * * * *

364  (I) Diogenes Laertius 6.68. In margin 'friends to be trusted'

365  (II) Diogenes Laertius 6.69. In margin 'freedom'
   1 Misled by Traversari (see Introduction xvi–xvii), Erasmus has taken 'freedom' wrongly. In Laertius it is 'freedom of speech.'

366  (III) Diogenes Laertius 6.69. In margin 'joke depending on ambiguity'
   1 Cf the anecdote about Stratonicus at 6.482 below.

367  (IV) Diogenes Laertius 6.69. In margin 'what is shameful is shameful everywhere'
   1 See 3.310 and 3.363 n1 above.

When he had 'plied his hand' in public in full sight of everyone, he said, 'If only one could satisfy one's hunger by rubbing one's belly like this.' He knew that agitation of the body brought on a desire to evacuate and he wanted to be free from that necessity. Scholars likewise find it very annoying to be called away from their books by the demands of nature.[2]

368 Diogenes used to say that practice and exercise produced both speed and ease in mental and moral, just as in physical, performance.

369 He said there was no law without a community and no community without the law.

370 He said that nobility and other similar kinds of ornaments of fortune were nothing but cloaks of vice.
    For rich men are no better than others, but they sin with less restraint, as Horace says about the wealthy man: 'and whatever he wants, this he hopes will bring him great repute, as if it were achieved by virtue.'[1] In fact nobles generally allow themselves every kind of indulgence even nowadays.

371 When he was a slave of Xeniades, his friends discussed ransoming him, but he said, 'Not at all. Don't you know that lions do not serve the men who feed them, but rather their trainers serve the lions.' For a lion is a lion wherever he is.

372 After he was woken from a deathly sleep and the doctor asked 'How are things?' he said, 'Fine; one brother is embracing another,' alluding to Homer

* * * * *

2 This paragraph occurs only in *1531* and *1532*. Erasmus omitted it in *1535*, no doubt realizing its indecency. His comment suggests that he had missed the point earlier, but see 3.245 n2 above.

368 (v) Diogenes Laertius 6.70; Erasmus gives the gist of the whole paragraph.

369 (vi) Diogenes Laertius 6.72

370 (vii) Diogenes Laertius 6.72. In margin 'gifts of fortune'
    1 Cf Horace *Satires* 2.3.98–9.

371 (viii) Diogenes Laertius 6.75. In margin 'freedom'

372 (ix) Plutarch *Moralia* 107E–F (*Consolation to Apollonius*). Erasmus now has a run of extracts mainly from Plutarch. In margin 'humour in face of death'

who made 'death' and 'sleep' brothers, because sleep is the semblance of death.[1]

373 Asked how he wanted to be buried, he told them to throw away his body without burial. Then his friends said, 'What, for the birds and beasts to eat?' 'Not at all,' he said, 'put a stick beside me for me to drive them away.' They answered, 'How can you, since you won't be conscious?' 'Well then,' he said, 'what harm will the mauling of wild beasts do to me, if I'm not aware of anything?'

374 When Plato was praising someone because he was very kind to everyone, Diogenes said, 'What kind of tribute should we pay to the man who has spent so many years in philosophy and caused no man any grief?'[1]

He meant that the proper role of philosophy was to heal men's vices, but this could not be done without fear and grief, that is, fear of shame and grief at present humiliation.

375 Once seeing a stranger in Sparta who was earnestly preparing for a holy day he said, 'What are you doing? Isn't any day a holy day for a good man?'

He felt that this world was a shrine worthy of god, and once man was set in it he should always behave honourably as if in the sight of all-seeing God. He adapted to this situation the proverb 'For lazy men it is always a feast day.'[1]

376 Diogenes used to say to young men, 'Go into courtesans' houses to see what worthless creatures are bought at so great a price.'

\* \* \* \* \*

1 *Iliad* 14.231 (focused on sleep) or 16.682 (focused on death).

373 (x) Cicero *Tusculan Disputations* 1.104. There are various versions of this; see eg Diogenes Laertius 6.79. See 3.187n above, for Diogenes' indifference regarding his burial. In margin 'burial'

374 (xi) Plutarch *Moralia* 452D (*On moral virtue*). In margin 'leniency bad'
   1 Cf 1.137 and 1.138 above.

375 (xii) Plutarch *Moralia* 477C (*On tranquillity of mind*). In margin 'every day a holy day for the wise man'
   1 *Adagia* II vi 12: *Ignavis semper feriae sunt* 'For sluggards it is always holiday'

376 (xiii) Plutarch *Moralia* 5C (*The education of children*). In margin 'whores'

Terence refers to this: 'To know all this is salvation to young men.'[1]

377 Diogenes said that for our salvation we need either loyal friends or fierce enemies, because the ones advise and the others speak bluntly to us.

So both groups benefit us in different ways but to the same degree, since we learn our faults through them. Laertius credits this to Antisthenes, but Plutarch to Diogenes.[1]

378 Asked by someone how he could best be revenged on an enemy, Diogenes said, 'If you show yourself to be a good and honourable man.'

For the man who does this does himself most good and gives his enemy most torment. If an enemy is tormented by seeing a farm well cultivated, what will he feel if he sees you yourself adorned with real good qualities?

379 When Diogenes went to see Antisthenes lying sick, he said, 'Do you have any need of a friend?'

He meant that in suffering one should make use of loyal friends who can either help materially or by consoling soften the discomfort.

380 On another occasion when he heard that Antisthenes was enduring his illness badly from love of life, he went in with a dagger, and when Antisthenes said, 'Who will free me from these agonies?' Diogenes held out the dagger and said, 'This will do it.' Antisthenes retorted, 'I said from agonies, not from life.'

* * * * *

1 See Parmeno's speech in Terence *Eunuchus* 50–70.

377 (XIV) Plutarch *Moralia* 74C (*How to tell a flatterer*), 82A (*Progress in virtue*). In margin 'reprimand'
    1 Diogenes Laertius 6.12 (Antisthenes on enemies, see 7.93 below); see also Plutarch *Moralia* 89B (*How to profit by one's enemies*, Antisthenes on friends and enemies).

378 (xv) Plutarch *Moralia* 87B (*How to profit by one's enemies*). In margin 'the best revenge'

379 (XVI) Diogenes Laertius 6.18. In margin 'a friend a consoler'

380 (XVII) Diogenes Laertius 6.18. In margin 'death releases from torment'

**381** He went to Corinth and entered the school which Dionysius had opened when he was driven into exile, and heard the boys singing badly. Meanwhile Dionysius came in and thinking Diogenes had come to comfort him, said, 'You are very kind, Diogenes. This is the way human lives are turned upside down.' 'No I'm not,' said Diogenes, 'in fact I am amazed you are still alive, after committing so many evils in your monarchy, and I see you are no better as a schoolmaster than you were as a king.'[1]

**382** Diogenes also used to say, 'For other mortals, life is pleasant and death odious if all is well with them; but if they are unfortunate, life is a burden and death desirable.[1] But tyrants experience the misery of both situations: on the one hand their lives are more unpleasant than those of the people who long for death, while at the same time they fear death as much as if they lived a delightful life.

**383** When someone showed him a clock, he said, 'By Jove, a fine instrument to make sure we don't miss dinner.'

He felt that the mathematical disciplines were useless like all the others.[1]

**384** Another fellow boasted of his expertise in music, so Diogenes replied:

\* \* \* \* \*

**381** (xviii) Cf Plutarch *Moralia* 783D (*Old men in public affairs*) and *Timoleon* 15 8–9, but these are not the precise source here. In margin 'the evil man is evil wherever he is'
  1 It was a notorious reverse of fortune that the Sicilian despot Dionysius II (the younger Dionysius) supposedly went to Corinth in exile and supported himself by school teaching. See 7.152 below; *Adagia* I i 83: *Dionysius Corinthi* 'Dionysius in Corinth.'

**382** (xix) Dio Chrysostom 6.46–7 (*On kingship*). This and the six following sayings were added in 1535.
  1 A common sentiment; cf Publilius Syrus (Meyer 438): *o vita misero longa, felici brevis*; Seneca *Controversiae* 7.3; Stobaeus 121.34 (Meineke IV 119).

**383** (xx) Diogenes Laertius 6.104
  1 The Cynics cancelled geometry, astronomy, music, and such like disciplines (Diogenes Laertius 6.73, 104)

**384** (xxi) Diogenes Laertius 6.104

'By wisdom are cities governed well,
And a house also – not by tunes and twanging strings.'[1]

385 When Speusippus was paralysed and was brought into the Academy in a
carriage, he met Diogenes by chance and said, 'I wish you well.' Diogenes
replied, 'But I don't wish you well, when you are so badly afflicted and can
bear to live.'

He felt it was the act of a real philosopher to bring on his own death
once he ceased to be useful to human life. And Speusippus actually did this
later.

386 When he saw a boy behaving badly he struck his attendant with a stick,
saying, 'Why do you train him like this?' He wanted to show that it depends
on those who shape children's first years whether they grow up into young
men with bad morals or otherwise. Aphthonius and Priscian report this.[1]

387 When someone reproached him with poverty to insult him, though the man
himself was criminal, Diogenes said, 'I have not seen anyone tortured for
poverty, but many for vice.'[1]

\* \* \* \* \*

1 See 3.383 above. Diogenes as usual adapts well-known verse to fit his purpose.
For the original see Nauck TGF 419, Euripides *Antiope* 200.1–2 where the second
line ends 'and it is mighty too in war.'

385 (XXII) Diogenes Laertius 4.3. Speusippus succeeded Plato as head of the
Academy 347–339 BC.

386 (XXIII) Aphthonius and Hermogenes 3.63 and 3.19, Priscian 2.8 (see n1).
1 Cf Plutarch *Moralia* 439E (*Can virtue be taught*) where Diogenes catches the
boy eating candy and beats his escort. This is a *chreia* demonstrating speech
combined with action, given as an example by Aphthonius and Hermogenes
*Progymnasmata* 3.63 and 3.19 (Spengel II 23 and 6). See also Quintilian 1.9.5.
For Priscian, see his *Praeexercitamina* 2.8 (K. Halm ed *Rhetores Latini minores*
[Leipzig 1863] 552). This was a Latin version of Hermogenes *Progymnasmata*,
written about AD 500. Aphthonius (fourth century AD) made an abridgment (in
Greek) of Hermogenes and this was adapted into Latin by Rodolphus Agricola
and others.

387 (XXIV) Stobaeus 95.12 (Meineke III 199). In margin 'poverty'
1 For the general sentiment 'poverty is no crime,' originating with Pericles in
Thucydides 2.40, see Plutarch *Moralia* 533A (*On false shame*) and 822E (*Precepts
of statecraft*).

**388** Diogenes called poverty 'self-taught' virtue.

For rich men need many rules to make them live decently, exercise their bodies by hard work, not delight in showy adornment of the person, and countless other things, all of which poverty teaches of itself.[1]

To the Spartans who rightly win first prize in the matter of Apophthegms, I have appended three philosophers, each exceptional of their kind, to whom I will now add just three kings who are most famous for their civilized sayings, so as not to crush the reader with a mass of material.

* * * * *

388  (xxv) Stobaeus 95.19 (Meineke III 200)
  1 This again is a commonly expressed sentiment. A similar saying is attributed to Xenocles: Stobaeus *Florilegium Monacense* 220 (Meineke IV 285).

# BOOK IV

In my opinion there has never been a king of the Greeks to match Philip, king of Macedon, the father of Alexander, in either the adroitness of his mind or the wit of his sayings.

## [Philip of Macedon]

1 Philip used to say he thought the Athenians very fortunate to find ten men to appoint as generals every year,[1] because he had only found one real general in many years, and that was Parmenion.[2]

He meant that it was pointless for the state to keep changing leaders, and far better not to change the man you had found to be capable and loyal. Moreover in warfare it did not matter how many leaders there were, only how fit they were to conduct the war.

\* \* \* \* \*

In this book Erasmus returns to Plutarch, this time selecting the most prominent figures from *Sayings of kings and commanders* (*Moralia* 172B and following). Omitting Plutarch's reported sayings of Persian kings and Sicilian tyrants (to which he will return in book v) he begins book IV with Philip II of Macedon.

1 (1) Plutarch *Moralia* 177C *Sayings of kings and commanders*. In margin 'don't change a good man when you've got one'
  In his long rule (382–336 BC) Philip took control of mainland Greece by a mixture of diplomacy and conquest, defeating Thebes and Athens at the battle of Chaeronea in 338 BC. See General Index: battles.
  1 The Athenian democracy had its ten tribes elect ten generals each year, though not all of them would serve on campaign rather than acting as presiding magistrates in the city.
  2 Parmenion was Philip's most powerful and effective military commander and continued in that role under Alexander after him.

2 When the news was brought to him of many successes obtained on one
day (for he had won the four horse chariot race at Olympia, and Parmenion
had defeated the Dardanians in battle, and Olympias had born him a male
child)[1] Philip stretched out his arms to the heavens and said 'Fortune, in
return for these great blessings, inflict some trivial misfortune upon me!'

Shrewd as he was, he did not become over-excited by his material success, but was wary of Fortune's indulgence. He knew her tendency to be-
guile with new success the men she was planning to destroy. The story told
by Pliny about Polycrates of Samos is a case in point.[2]

3 When Philip had conquered the Greeks, and some counsellors advised him
to control the cities with garrisons so that they would not rebel, he replied,
'I would rather be called good and tolerant for many years than master for
a brief moment.'

He felt that rule maintained by kindnesses and goodwill was long
lasting, but one depending on force and intimidation was short-lived.

4 There was an insolent fellow who used to hurl abuse at Philip, so that the
king's companions urged him to send the man into exile. But he surprised
them by refusing. When they asked him why, he said, 'I don't want him to
wander around abusing me to a lot more people.'

Not having the slanderer crucified could be seen as clemency if he
forgave him, or nobility of spirit if he thought him beneath notice, but not
sending him into exile was an act of prudence. For he would have done
Philip a lot more harm.

* * * * *

2   (II) Plutarch *Moralia* 177C. In margin 'fortune's spite'
  1  '(for he had won ... child)' was added 1535 from Plutarch *Moralia* 105A–B
     (*Consolation to Apollonius*). For Parmenion see 4.1 n1 above.
  2  The tale of the tyrant Polycrates of Samos in Pliny *Naturalis historia* 37.3–4
     is based on Herodotus 3.41–2. Polycrates was so disturbed by his own good
     fortune that he tried to counter it by throwing his favourite ring into the sea,
     but it was returned by a fisherman who found it in a fish he had caught.
     Polycrates took this as a sign that the gods would bring about his downfall.
     After surviving an unsuccessful popular revolt (see 1.216 and n1 above) he
     was lured into a trap by the Persian satrap Oroetes, who had him crucified.
     Cf Aemilius Paulus' remark, 5.322 below.

3   (III) Plutarch *Moralia* 177C–D. In margin 'fear a poor guarantee of permanence'

4   (IV) Plutarch *Moralia* 177D. In margin 'the abuser scorned'

5 Smicythus kept reporting to the king that Nicanor incessantly spoke ill of
him, and when Philip's friends urged him to have Nicanor arrested and
punished, Philip replied, 'Nicanor is not the worst of the Macedonians, so
we must be careful in case we are neglecting our duty in some respect.' So
when the king discovered that Nicanor was suffering dreadful poverty but
he had overlooked giving him any relief, he ordered the man to be given
a gift of some kind. After this when Smicythus reported that Nicanor was
incessantly uttering Philip's praises to everyone, Philip said, 'You see, it
depends on us whether we are well or ill spoken of.'

How appallingly far from the behaviour of this ruler are those men
who never think they have been praised enough although they are doing
nothing that deserves praise, men who make no effort to win men's goodwill by kindnesses, but prefer to be feared rather than loved. Indeed they
often behave abominably, and quite blatantly, and yet anyone who dares to
utter a word is done for.

6 Philip used to say he felt very grateful to Athenian politicians because their
abuse had made him improve in both eloquence and character, 'as I tried to
prove them liars both by my words and by my deeds.'

This king truly had a philosophical nature, in knowing how to derive benefit even from his enemies. Instead of behaving like most people,
who aim only to harm those who abuse them, he aimed to improve himself,
taking warning from their abuse.

7 Philip had released all the Athenians captured at Chaeronea without asking
a ransom, yet they asked for the return of their clothes and bedding and
wanted to sue the Macedonians for them. Philip laughed, saying, 'What
next? It looks as if the Athenians imagine they've lost to us at a game of
dice, doesn't it?'

* * * * *

5   (v) Plutarch *Moralia* 177D. Neither Smicythus or this Nicanor are otherwise
known. In margin 'it depends on us whether we are well spoken of'

6   (vi) Plutarch *Moralia* 177E. In margin 'the abuser useful'
Demosthenes made his reputation as an orator by denouncing Philip's aggressive intentions towards Athens, and was followed by other Athenian politicians such as Demochares (4.35 below). Philip saw this as an opportunity
to profit from his enemies (the subject of a Plutarch essay much used by
Erasmus.)

7   (vii) Plutarch *Moralia* 177E. See 4.1 n1 above. In margin 'ingratitude tolerated'

Such was the restraint with which he, as victor, bore the ingratitude of the defeated, although they did not thank him for letting them go free and unharmed, but even charged him with not returning their clothes and bedding as well, as though they did not know the code of war, and as if competing in battle was no different from competing in a children's game like dice.

8 When Philip broke his collar-bone in battle and the doctor who was treating him asked for something new each day, he said, 'Take as much as you want, for you are in charge of my key.'

He was playing on words, for Greek *kleis* means both a key to open a desk or door, and the link between the shoulder and the chest.[1] What could be more modest than this attitude, in a man ready to joke while in pain and facing a greedy doctor. The pain did not spoil his good humour nor did the shamelessness of the demands make him lose his temper.

9 There were two brothers, one called Amphoteros, which is the Greek for 'both,' the other called Hekateros, which in their language is 'either.' Philip noticed that Either was clever and adaptable whereas Both was clumsy and incompetent, so he altered their names, saying, 'Either is Both, and Both is Neither.'[1]

He meant that one brother, Hekateros (Either), possessed the virtues of both, so that nothing was left to the other. So he changed the name of the one called Amphoteros (Both) to its opposite, that is, he was called Oudeteros (Neither) meaning that he was worthless.

10 When his advisers encouraged him to treat the Athenians more harshly, he answered that it was unreasonable to urge a man who did and suffered everything for glory to throw away an opportunity of parading his glory for all to see.

He meant that his purpose was not to destroy Athens, but to win approval for his virtues from a famous city rich with an abundance of most learned men.

\* \* \* \* \*

8   (VIII) Plutarch *Moralia* 177F. In margin 'joking in illness'
  1 The collar-bone is similarly *clavicula* 'small key' in Latin, clavicle in English.

9   (IX) Plutarch *Moralia* 177F. In margin 'joke based on wordplay'
  1 Phrase from the translation by W. Hinton 'The Apophthegms or Remarkable Sayings of Kings and Great Commanders' in William W. Goodwin (corr and rev) *Plutarch's Morals* 5 vols (Boston 1878) 1 195.

10  (x) Plutarch *Moralia* 178A. In margin 'clemency'

11 Two equally vicious men were bandying mutual accusations when Philip
was acting as judge. After hearing the case he gave the verdict that 'one
should be exiled from Macedonia and the other should pursue him.'
  This sounds more amusing in Greek because the verb *phugein* means
both to run away and to be exiled, and when someone runs away we pursue
him. So Philip acquitted neither man but condemned both to exile.[1]

12 When he was preparing to pitch camp in a fine situation and someone
warned him that there was no fodder for the pack animals, he said, 'What
sort of life is this, if we have to live to suit even the convenience of donkeys?'

13 Once he was determined to capture a heavily fortified citadel and its garrison, but his scouts reported that it was utterly difficult, indeed impossible.
Then Philip asked whether it was so steep that not even a donkey loaded
with gold could enter.
  He was hinting that no place was so well fortified that it could not
be stormed with gold. This is what the poets meant by the myth of Danaë
seduced by Jupiter, when the god turned himself into gold. Hence Horace's
'gold delights to pass through the midst of bodyguards and break through
camps more powerfully than steel.'[1]

14 When the supporters of Lasthenes[1] complained indignantly that some of
Philip's escort called them traitors, Philip retorted, 'Macedonians are obviously unsophisticated peasants, who don't know any name for a spade but
a spade.'
  He was alluding to the famous proverb 'calling figs figs and tubs tubs.'[2]

* * * * *

11  (XI) Plutarch *Moralia* 178A. In margin 'witty judgment'
 1 The joke is that the Greek verbs also mean 'stand trial' and 'accuse.'

12  (XII) Plutarch *Moralia* 178A. In margin 'a wretched sort of campaign'

13  (XIII) Plutarch *Moralia* 178B. In margin 'nothing that cannot be stormed with
    gold'
 1 For Danaë enclosed in a tower but impregnated by Zeus in the form of a
    shower of gold and the moral, see Horace *Odes* 3.16, 1–11 (misquoted, *saxa
    potentius / ictu fulmineo*)

14  (XIV) Plutarch *Moralia* 178B. In margin 'truth'
 1 The Olynthian Lasthenes betrayed his city to Philip: cf Plutarch *Moralia* 97D
    (*On chance*).
 2 CPG 2 Apostolius 15.95B, 16.10; quoted in *Adagia* II iii 5: *Ficus ficus, ligonem
    ligonem vocat* 'He calls figs figs and a spade a spade.' See also Apostolius 1.24a

He implied of course that the men really were traitors, for peasant truthfulness calls everything by its own name.

**15** Philip used to advise his son Alexander to keep on friendly terms with the Macedonians, so as to win strength and power by acquiring general goodwill while someone else was ruling and he could still afford to be humane.

He realized that nothing so sustained authority as the goodwill of citizens: but it was very difficult for anyone exercising a monarchy to be humane with all and sundry, not only because royal power is exposed to jealousy, but because a state cannot remain unharmed unless crimes are disciplined by punishment. So kings must dilute their humanity towards their citizens enough to preserve their royal authority. For too much kindness often breeds contempt.[1]

**16** He also advised his son to make friends of men influential in the state, whether good or bad, and to employ the good, but exploit the bad.

It is a special art of kingship not to reject anyone but to adapt all men's services to the public good. Just as God, the sole monarch of the world, makes use of evil spirits and impious men for the benefit of the church, so clever rulers know how to employ both good and evil men, not to do harm by means of the wicked, but to make use of them as instruments to punish other wicked men. But there are many rulers who perversely exploit the good and employ the bad. They use men renowned for holiness to implement tyrannical decisions so that the crowd may believe that what they do is good and pious.

**17** When Philip was a hostage in Thebes, he enjoyed the hospitality of Philon

* * * * *

'I'm a peasant calling a tub a tub.' Erasmus is responsible for the well-known 'spade' version. See CWE 33 384.

**15** (xv) Plutarch *Moralia* 178B. In margin 'benevolence on the part of kings'
  1 See 1.219 above

**16** (xvi) Plutarch *Moralia* 178c. A further illustration of how to make use of one's enemies; cf 4.6 above. Erasmus presents his own Christian version in which God, being almighty, makes use of the devil and wicked men for the benefit of the Church. In margin 'use the good, exploit the bad'

**17** (xvii) Plutarch *Moralia* 178c. In margin 'beneficence'

of Thebes and received many kindnesses at his hands.[1] When Philon would
not take any gifts from Philip in return, Philip said, 'Don't outdo me in
generosity and deprive me of my glory that, until now, I have never been
outdone by any man in kindnesses.'

This was a spirit worthy to rule! He thought it nobler to win by kindness than by power.

18 When many prisoners of war were up for sale Philip was sitting at the auction with his cloak embarrassingly hitched up. Then one of the prisoners
being sold cried out, 'Pardon me, Philip, for I am a friend of your father.'
When Philip asked him, 'How is that? What was the origin of this friendship?' he said, 'I would like to come closer and tell you.' So he was allowed
to approach and as if telling a secret, he said, 'Pull down your cloak a little,
because the way you are sitting now is not decent.' Then Philip said, 'Let
this man go free, for I did not realize he was truly a friend and well-wisher.'

Such a great king was not offended by either the deception or the advice of a stranger, but covered up his deception by a reciprocal deception,
and rewarded this small service with the great prize of liberty.

19 Once he was invited to dinner by a guest-friend, and brought with him as
uninvited guests several men he happened to meet on the way.[1] When he
realized the host was upset because the food prepared was not enough for
so many, he sent a slave round the guests individually in advance to urge
them to save space for the cake;[2] they obediently ate very little while they
waited for the cake and so the dinner was sufficient to go round them all.

* * * * *

1 This was probably in 369–367 BC when Macedonia was in danger of dissolution
through civil war and foreign invasion, some years before his accession to the
throne.

18 (XVIII) Plutarch *Moralia* 178C–D. Erasmus' comment does not condemn the mild
deception, but praises Philip for using his own pretence to endorse the tact-
ful subterfuge of the prisoner of war. There is a similar praise of deception in
4.19 below. In margin 'welcome admonition'

19 (XIX) Plutarch *Moralia* 178D–E. In margin 'civilized deception'
1 Erasmus has mistranslated: Philip was invited while on the road and the men
were part of his retinue, not random travellers he met on the way.
2 *Plakous* in Greek, *placenta* in Latin. It was served at the dessert stage of the
meal. The recipe given in Cato *De agricultura* 76 suggests that the Roman version was substantial (and filling), consisting of alternate layers of pastry and
sheep's cheese mixed with honey.

By this witty jest he both deceived his friends and relieved his host's embarrassment.

20  When Hipparchus of Euboea died, Philip showed how bitterly he grieved over his death. So when someone wanted to console his grief and said, 'But his death was timely, when he was already old,' Philip replied, 'Yes, timely for him, but premature for me: for death took him too soon, before he had received a kindness from me worthy of our friendship.'[1]

It is very rare that a prince feels the emotion of gratitude; instead they mostly treat their friends like horses, caring for them while they are useful, but discarding them when they grow useless. Indeed they strip them rather than help them by favours.

21  When Philip heard that his son Alexander was complaining that his father had children by many women, he encouraged him in these terms: 'Since you have many rivals to the throne, take care to grow up honourable and virtuous, so that it will be clear that you won the throne not through me but through your own qualities.'[1]

With truly royal prudence Philip did not comfort his son but increased his anxiety so as to stimulate him to virtue. He showed him that he could not hope for his father's kingdom unless he proved himself worthy of the succession, and that it was less glorious to obtain the throne than to deserve it.

22  He also urged Alexander to pay attention to Aristotle, who had been entrusted with teaching him, and devote himself to philosophy, 'so that you will not make the many mistakes which I now regret making.'

This excellent prince realized that no man ignorant of philosophy was fit for ruling, and was not ashamed to admit that he had made many mis-

* * * * *

20  (xx) Plutarch *Moralia* 178E. In margin 'gratitude'
  1  Hipparchus was made tyrant of Eretria in Euboea in 343 BC, no doubt in return for bringing his city under Macedonian control, and died soon after 342 BC.

21  (xxi) Plutarch *Moralia* 178E–F. This and the next item form one unit in Plutarch, who tells the same story in his *Life of Alexander* 9. In margin 'kingship to be sought by virtue'
  1  Philip divorced Olympias, the mother of Alexander, in 337 and married Cleopatra, daughter of one of his generals. In the disruption that followed, Alexander went into temporary exile in Illyria. Of Philip's many other wives, one was named Phila, possibly the sister of Machaetes in 4.24 below.

22  (xxii) See 4.21 above. In margin 'philosophy necessary for a king'

takes because he had not been steeped from earliest childhood[1] in the precepts of philosophy. For men who learn to run a kingdom by trial and error, however talented their nature, still become good kings only late and at great cost to the state. But the man who comes to the throne prepared by philosophy, if he has a sound mind, can hardly stray from what is honourable. So where are those who insist that the study of literature and philosophy is quite useless for governing the state?

23 Philip had enrolled one of Antipater's friends in the panel of judges. But later when he found out that he dyed his beard and hair he disqualified him, saying that a man not trustworthy about his hair did not seem fit to be trusted in public life.

The man used deception in dying his hair where little profit was involved, so he was much more likely to use deception in public business, where fraud sometimes brings a huge profit. This should be the special concern of kings, to set men of integrity to judge cases. How can this happen when the position of judge is for sale and a judge is appointed not because he is a better man but because he is quicker or more lavish in bribery? But with Philip not even Antipater's authority was strong enough to prevent him demoting a dubious figure from the rank of judge.

24 Philip was on the bench to hear the case of Machaetes, but he was sleepy and did not pay enough attention to the rights of the case and so found against him. But when Machaetes cried out that he would appeal against the verdict the king said angrily, 'To whom?' For kings hate the word 'appeal.' Then Machaetes said, 'To you yourself, King, if you will rouse yourself and listen with more attention to my case.' At the time the king simply adjourned the court, but after he had weighed up the case more carefully in his mind, and realized Machaetes had been wronged, he did not rescind his decision, but he personally paid the fine imposed on Machaetes.

* * * * *

1 *Adagia* I vii 52: *A teneris unguiculis* 'Since the time their nails were soft.'

23 (XXIII) Plutarch *Moralia* 178F. The story is also told by Aelian *Varia historia* 7.20 about Archidamus of Sparta instead of Antipater. For Antipater see 2.52 n1 above. In margin 'a sham not to be trusted'

24 (XXIV) Plutarch *Moralia* 178F–9A. A similar tale is told at 4.31 below of the old woman's retort when Philip did not want to be bothered with hearing her case. In margin 'an attentive judge'

How many demonstrations of royal excellence there are in this one action! He did not persist in his anger against a man who had challenged him and publicly accused him of sleeping, but considered the matter more carefully when he was at leisure and his anger had subsided. Let that be credited to him as royal restraint and moderation; it was a mark of shrewdness to relieve the man of his penalty by a clever contrivance so as not to undermine his own royal authority as a judge, paying the fine privately as if he himself had been found liable.

25 Philip's friends were angry at the Peloponnesians for jeering and hissing at him at the Olympic games, especially since they had received particular favours from the king, saying this to make Philip retaliate. But he said, 'So how will they behave if we actually do them any harm?'

Philip wittily turned around his friends' argument: If they are so depraved that they jeer at those who have treated them well, they will do even worse harm if anyone provokes them with mistreatment. It was proof not merely of restraint and clemency but of exceptional nobility of spirit that the king ignored the hisses of these ungrateful men.

26 When Crates, a friend and kinsman of Harpalus, was accused of wrongdoing, Harpalus asked Philip to let the defendant pay the fine but acquit him, since if he was condemned he would be exposed to insult and abuse. Then Philip said, 'It is better for him to be spoken ill of than for us to be maligned on his account.'

He was indulgent to his friends but only as far as was compatible with his reputation as an honest judge.

27 When he woke up after sleeping for a long time on campaign, he said, 'It was safe for me to sleep because Antipater was awake.'

*  *  *  *  *

25 (xxv) Plutarch *Moralia* 179A–B. In margin 'affable'

26 (xxvi) Plutarch *Moralia* 179A.  In margin 'a strict judge'
Harpalus, a Macedonian noble, was later a friend of Alexander the Great, and put in charge of the central treasuries of Alexander's empire, which he used to fund a lavish lifestyle. Alexander's return from the east forced him to flee. He eventually reached Athens, where he engaged in political bribery. (See 4.358 below.) He then fled to Crete with a mercenary army, where he was murdered. This Crates seems to be otherwise unknown.

27 (xxvii) Plutarch *Moralia* 179B. For Antipater see 2.52 n1 above. In margin 'a wakeful officer'

He was hinting that a king should not indulge in sleep, especially during a war, but that this sometimes incurred no danger if the king had a trusty and wakeful officer in command. Thus he combined excusing his own sleepiness and praising his friend.

28 On another occasion when Philip was sleeping in the daytime, the many Greeks who had come to his door resented it and reproached the king because they were not instantly admitted to confer with him because of his need to sleep. Parmenion defended the king by saying, 'Don't be surprised if Philip is sleeping now, for when you were sleeping he stayed awake.'[1]

What he meant was that when the Greeks were not giving sufficient thought to the conduct of their affairs, Philip had served as a protection to them.

29 Witty as he was, he was also delighted by other men's witty sayings. So when he wanted to criticize a singer at dinner and was talking about plucking the strings, the singer said, 'May the gods forbid, Sire, that you know more about this than I do.'[1]

This was a courteous way of asserting his professional judgment without offending the king, by declaring him too good to dispute about lyre-playing with a player.

30 He also took calmly quite sharp remarks, provided that they were timely. For when he was quarrelling with his wife Olympias and his son Alexander, Demaratus the Corinthian came to see him and he asked him how relations

* * * * *

28 (xxvIII) Plutarch *Moralia* 179B. In margin 'sleep excused'
  1 A similar anecdote is told about Alexander in Plutarch's *Life of Alexander* 31. Both Philip and Alexander were heavy drinkers and often had to sleep it off. This is often glossed over in the anecdotes, (see 4.99) but see 6.380 and 8.62 below. For Parmenion see 5.113 n1 below.

29 (xxIX) Plutarch *Moralia* 179B. Cf Plutarch *Moralia* 67F (*How to tell a flatterer*) and 334C–D (*On the fortune of Alexander*). Plutarch cites many of the same type of sayings in this essay and the *Apophthegmata*. In margin 'the craftsman to judge the craft'
  1 Greek *citharoedes* accompanied their own song on the lyre. Erasmus has missed the nuance of the Greek: 'Sire, may you never fare so badly that you know this sort of thing better than I.' Cf 4.32 and 6.454 below.

30 (xxx) Plutarch *Moralia* 179C. In margin 'frank reprimand'

between the various Greek states were going.[1] Demaratus answered, 'Of
course harmony among the Greeks must be very important to you, since
your nearest and dearest treat you like this.' What would you expect here
except that the king would take offence at Demaratus' frankness and have
him taken away out of his sight? No; since Demaratus' comment diverted
him from anger to wiser counsels the king heeded his reproach, and setting
aside his anger was reconciled with his family.

31 A poor old woman once appealed to Philip to hear her case, and when she
interrupted repeatedly with her demands, he answered that he did not have
time. Then she cried out, 'Then you should not want to be king.' He was
amazed at her frank criticism, and heard not only her case, but other cases
as well.

Latin writers also attribute this story to the emperor Hadrian.[1]

32 When Philip heard that his son had sung expertly at some social occasion,
he rebuked him courteously, saying, 'Aren't you ashamed to know how to
sing so well?'

He meant that other arts were more worthy of a king.

33 Again when Philip fell while wrestling, and saw the traces of his body in
the dust as he got up, he said, 'By Jove, what a small a portion of earth we
are allotted by nature, and still we seek the whole world!'

* * * * *

1 Philip had long been intervening militarily and diplomatically in turbulent inter-state Greek politics, supporting various warring factions in order
to achieve the ultimate subjugation of all Greece. Demaratus is one of his
friends.

31 (xxxi) Plutarch *Moralia* 179C–D; cf *Life of Demetrius* 42 where the story is told
of Antigonus, and Stobaeus 13.28 (Meineke I 262) where it is told of Antipater.
For the similar story concerning Hadrian, see 6.110 below. In margin 'kings
should hear all'
1 Erasmus is probably thinking of the *Historia Augusta*, but he has misremembered as this story is not found there, but in Dio Cassius; see however Introduction xix–xx above.

32 (xxxii) Plutarch *Life of Pericles* 1.6. This and 4.33–5 have been added by Erasmus from sources other than Plutarch's *Sayings of kings and commanders*. Cf the
story at 4.29 above. In margin 'skills unworthy of a king'

33 (xxxiii) Plutarch *Moralia* 602D (*On exile*). In margin 'ambition'

If only this saying had stayed in his son's heart, for the world itself was too cramped for Alexander's ambition.

34 Scolding his son because he was trying to win the affection of the Macedonians by bribery, he said, 'Dammit, what reason led you to expect that men would be faithful to you whom you have corrupted with money? Are you aiming to have the Macedonians think you not their king but their provisioner?'

35 The Athenians had sent an embassy to Philip. He heard it kindly and as a polite form of dismissal asked them to tell him how he could oblige the Athenians. Then Demochares took him up: 'By hanging yourself' he said. This Demochares was one of the envoys, nicknamed 'Loudmouth' because of his uncontrolled tongue. The king's friends were angry at such a rude a reply, but Philip silenced them, and ordered them to let this Thersites[1] go unharmed. Then he turned to the rest of the envoys and said 'Tell the Athenians that men who say that sort of thing are much more arrogant than those who listen without punishing them.'

Only spirit like this is worthy of monarchy.

**Alexander the Great**

36 Among Philip's sayings none were without wit. They also encouraged good behaviour; and I cannot see anyone more fitting to set next to Philip than his son Alexander.

Even when he was still a boy, when his father enjoyed many successes, Alexander did not exult in them but said to his foster-brothers and peers:

\* \* \* \* \*

34 (xxxiv) Cicero De officiis 2.15.53. In margin 'goodwill to be won by virtue'

35 (xxxv) Seneca De ira 3.23.1–2. For Philip's response to criticism and abuse, cf 4.4–6 above. In margin 'leniency'
   1 Thersites is the ugly common soldier who dares to criticize Agamemnon in Iliad 2, and is punished for voicing an otherwise justifiable opinion out of turn.

36 (1) Plutarch Moralia 179D. In margin 'restless nature'
   This is the formal transition to the group of sayings of Alexander III of Macedon, 'the Great' (356–323 BC). Erasmus follows Plutarch in combining tales of his military prowess with tributes to his education by Aristotle and his love of Homer. Many of the sayings are also quoted in Plutarch's Life of Alexander and the essay On the fortune of Alexander.

'My father will leave nothing for me!' When they disagreed, saying, 'No, he is preparing all this for you,' Alexander said, 'What will it benefit me, if I have so much and achieve nothing?'[1]

Even then you would recognize the spark of his ambitious and restless spirit.

37 Alexander excelled in lightness of body and swiftness of foot, and when his father urged him to compete in the foot-race at Olympia, he said, 'I would do, if I had kings as competitors.'

Here you can recognize his lofty pride, unwilling to yield to any man in the contest for glory and empire. He was not yet king, yet he thought it beneath him to be matched against anyone except kings.

38 When a girl was brought to Alexander to sleep with him very late at night the king asked where she had been for so long, and she replied, 'waiting for her husband to go to bed.' The King summoned his chamberlains and reprimanded them fiercely. 'Take her back' he said, 'through your fault I was almost turned into an adulterer.'

This is a splendid example of chastity, whether in a young man or a monarch. For with Greeks ordinary irregular sexual connection was thought no crime. It is clear too that they observed the custom which still obtains in Italy, that wives slept apart from their husbands unless they were summoned.[1]

39 When Alexander as a boy was making a rather lavish offering to the gods, and constantly running to get more incense,[1] Leonidas, his paedagogus, happened to be present and said, 'Hey, boy, you can make lavish offerings of incense when you have conquered the land that produces incense.' So when

* * * * *

1 Cf Plutarch *Alexander* 5.

37 (II) Plutarch *Moralia* 179C; cf *Alexander* 4, and *Moralia* 331B (*On the fortune of Alexander*). In margin 'what is kingly befits a king'

38 (III) Plutarch *Moralia* 179E. In margin 'adultery'
   1 Compare 4.54 in which Alexander, feeling desire for the woman brought by Antipater to dine with them, is angry when he discovers she is Antipater's mistress and not a casual partner. His code forbade him to take a woman if she belonged to another man.

39 (IV) Plutarch *Moralia* 179E–F; cf also *Alexander* 25 and Pliny *Naturalis historia* 12.62. In margin 'extravagance'
   1 Erasmus talks of Alexander running to get the incense where Plutarch merely has him repeatedly picking up handfuls of it.

Alexander had conquered that region, remembering the saying, he wrote a letter to Leonidas as follows, 'I am sending you some hundredweights of incense and cassia, so that you need not be stingy towards the gods from now on, since you know we have taken possession of the region that produces the perfumes.'

40 When he was about to enter battle at the Granicus river, Alexander urged the Macedonians to eat their fill, since the next day they would be eating the enemy's rations.[1]

This shows a resolute spirit, confident and carefree about the outcome of the war.

41 One of Alexander's friends, Perillus, asked Alexander for a dowry for his daughters. The king ordered him to be given fifty talents, and when he answered that ten would be enough, replied, 'Certainly enough for you to receive, but not enough for me to give.'

A splendid saying, if only the desire to outdo had not spoilt his virtuous nature.

42 Alexander had ordered his treasurer to give Anaxarchus, the philosopher, as much as he asked for, and when the treasurer heard his demand, he was troubled and told Alexander the philosopher was asking for a hundred talents. The king said, 'He is right, because he knows he has a friend who can give so much and is willing to do so.'

Here you might wonder whether to be more amazed by the generosity of the king's gift or the greed of the philosopher's demand, unless we choose to call it confidence instead.

43 When he was at Miletus and saw many statues of victors at the Olympian and Pythian games, all of them huge, he asked, 'Where were those mighty bodies when the barbarians were besieging your city?'

* * * * *

40  (v) Plutarch *Moralia* 179F. In margin 'confidence'
  1 The Granicus river was the scene of Alexander's first victory over the Persians in 334 BC.

41  (VI) Plutarch *Moralia* 179F. This is the first of several illustrations of his generosity. In margin 'generosity'

42  (VII) Plutarch *Moralia* 179F. Anaxarchus of Abdera, a philosopher who accompanied Alexander on his campaigns. In margin 'generosity'

43  (VIII) Plutarch *Moralia* 180A. In margin 'ill-timed display of strength'

This was a witty censure of their foolish pretensions, for boasting of men who had won contests in the games because of their size and strength of body, although none of them displayed the same qualities against the barbarians in their times of danger.[1]

44 When Queen Adas of the Carians was eager to send Alexander constant supplies of dainty foods and pastries skilfully prepared by cooks and confectioners, Alexander said he had better culinary artists: a night march before breakfast, and a skimpy breakfast to give appetite for dinner.

45 Once when all the preparations had been made for battle and he was asked whether he wanted anything else done, he said, 'Nothing, except that the Macedonians should shave their beards.' When Parmenion wondered what he had in mind, he explained, 'Don't you know that in battle the beard is the best handle?'

He meant that they would have to fight at close quarters, a kind of combat in which beards are a nuisance because soldiers can easily be seized by them.[1]

46 Darius offered Alexander these terms: that Alexander should receive ten thousand talents and take an equal share of Asia with him. When Alexander refused, Parmenion said, 'I would have accepted, if I were Alexander,' and Alexander replied, 'So would I, if I were Parmenion.' But this was his reply to Darius: 'As the earth cannot support two suns, so Asia cannot support two kings.'

You might approve his lofty spirit in this case too, if the saying did not suggest an uncontrolled lust for mastery.

* * * * *

1 The defeat and sack of Miletus by the Persians in the early fifth century was notorious and even recorded in a tragedy by Phrynichus. Compare the proverb cited at Athenaeus 523F: 'The Milesians were valiant in days of yore' (*Adagia* I ix 49: *Fuere quondam strenui Milesii*).

44 (IX) Plutarch *Moralia* 180A; cf *Alexander* 22 and *Moralia* 127B (*Advice about keeping well*), 1099C (*On the impossibility of living pleasantly*). In margin 'abstinence'

45 (X) Plutarch *Moralia* 180B; cf *Theseus* 3. In margin 'beards useless in war'
   1 According to Chrysippus, cited at Athenaeus 565a, the practice of being clean-shaven began under Alexander. For Parmenion see 5.113 n1 below.

46 (XI) Plutarch *Moralia* 180B; cf *Alexander* 29 and 4.73 below. This is Darius III. In margin 'rule by one'

**47** When he was about to risk his whole empire at Arbela in an engagement with an array of a million armed men, some will-disposed soldiers came to him and informed on the others for conspiring in camp and plotting not to bring any booty to the king's tent[1] but keep it all for their own profit. When he heard this Alexander smiled: 'That is good news,' he said, 'the talk I am hearing is of men set on winning, not running away.' And his intuition did not deceive him, for many soldiers approached him and said, 'Sire, be confident and have no fear of the enemy's numbers, for they won't even be able to endure the smell of us!'

**48** And when the battle line was drawn up and he saw a soldier just starting to attach the thrower to his javelin, he dismissed him from the force as useless, because he was only getting his weapons ready when he should have been using them.

But this should have been listed among the military tactics, rather than the apophthegms, like the next item which I add here.[1]

**49** Alexander was reading a letter from his mother which contained some secrets and slander against Antipater, and Hephaestion was reading it with the king as usual. In fact the king did not forbid him to read it, but after scanning the letter he pulled his signet ring off his finger and pressed it to Hephaestion's mouth to indicate that he should keep the material secret.

This is a model of trust in his friend and exceptional consideration: he did not want the slander to spread, although he disliked Antipater.

\* \* \* \* \*

**47**  (xii) Plutarch *Moralia* 180c. In margin 'opportune interpretation'
  1 Erasmus followed Filelfo or Regio here, instead of translating 'to the royal treasury' (see dedicatory epistle 7–8 nn20 and 21 above). After defeating the vast army of Darius iii at Gaugamela in Mesopotamia in 331 BC, Alexander pursued the fleeing king to Arbela but failed to capture him, though he captured his family. Darius was later assassinated. Alexander acquired a huge amount of Persian treasure as booty from the captured camp and later from the royal palaces of Babylon, Susa and Persepolis. Persian luxury and wealth were legendary.

**48**  (xiii) Plutarch *Moralia* 180c–d. In margin 'preparing too late'
  1 See the dedicatory epistle 9 and 11 above.

**49**  (xiv) Plutarch *Moralia* 180d. For Antipater see 2.52 n1 above and see also 4.91 below. Hephaestion was Alexander's most intimate friend. See 4.64 and 4.97 below. In margin 'silence'

50 When he was hailed as son of Jupiter by the prophet in the temple of Ammon, he said, 'That is not surprising, since Jupiter is by nature father of all,
but he singles out all the best men to be his own.'

He interpreted the oracle with great modesty: for the prophet called
him son of Jupiter as a piece of flattery, as if he were begotten by Jupiter in
the way that Hercules is believed to be Jupiter's son. Now Alexander admitted that Jupiter was by nature source and parent of all, but claimed that he
acknowledged as his sons those who came closest to divinity by their bravery
and great deeds. It is the divine nature to bestow kindness on all men.

51 When he was wounded in the leg by an arrow and many ran to help who had
often called him a god, he alluded to Homer's epic, saying with a cheerful
and relaxed expression, 'Isn't this blood that you see, and not "the liquid
that flows from the blessed gods?"'

He was making fun of the foolishness of his flatterers, since what had
happened showed he was nothing but a man. He was referring to Iliad 5
and the tale of the wounding of Venus by Diomedes.[1]

52 When several men praised Antipater's thrift, because he lived a plain life
far from all self-indulgence, Alexander said, 'Antipater wears a white cloak
in public, but in private he is all purple.'

He was criticizing Antipater's pretence of economy, since he went to
excess in all other respects.[1]

53 When he was entertained by a friend in winter and chilly weather and he
saw a small hearth and scanty fire, he said, 'Bring in either logs or incense!'
He was hinting that his host was as sparing with the logs as if they

* * * * *

50  (xv) Plutarch *Moralia* 180D. Alexander made an excursion to the desert shrine
of the god Ammon (equated with Jupiter) while he was in Egypt in 331 BC.
See 4.98 below. In margin 'those who are the sons of the gods'

51  (xvi) Plutarch *Moralia* 180D. The story is told again at *Alexander* 28 and *Moralia*
341B (*The fortune of Alexander* 28.3); also by Diogenes Laertius 9.60 (see 7.375
below) and Seneca *Letters* 59.12.
  1 Homer *Iliad* 5.330–51. The reference was added in 1535. Erasmus accidentally
  omitted the negative 'not.'

52  (xvii) Plutarch *Moralia* 180E. Cf *Phocion* 29. In margin 'hypocrisy'
  1 For Antipater see 2.52 n1.

53  (xviii) Plutarch *Moralia* 180E. In margin 'parsimony'

were pure incense, though in such icy weather they should not have spared even the incense; at the same time he meant that there was enough fire to offer a sacrifice of perfume to the gods, but too little to drive away the cold.

54 When he was dining with Antipatrides, and his host brought a beautiful lyre player into dinner, Alexander was seized with passion for her at sight, so he asked Antipatrides whether he was in love with the woman, and when he admitted it Alexander said, 'You wretch, take the woman away from the party immediately.'

How utterly remote was his disposition from seducing another man's wife, if he was so afraid of lusting after his host's girl friend.[1]

55 Again when Cassander wanted to force his embrace on Python, the boy-friend of Evius the pipe-player, and Alexander realized that Evius was upset, he jumped up, angry with Cassander, and shouted, 'So because of us, can no man feel love for anything?'[1]

It was not enough for the king to behave chastely himself; he had to make his officers share his standards. When would he ever have allowed the daughter or wife of a respectable citizen to be raped by his followers, since he wanted even a pipe-player to keep his beloved unviolated, even by a kiss? In short he thought the offences of his generals were his responsibility.

56 Alexander was discharging the sick, crippled and feeble from the Macedonian force to go back to the coast, when he was informed that someone had had himself listed among the sick although he was not sick. When this man was brought before the king and interrogated, he confessed he had pretended to be ill for love of Telesippa, who had left for the coast. Alexander asked him whom he should commission to fetch Telesippa back to the army. But when he discovered she was a free woman he said, 'So we will have to

* * * * *

54  (xix) Plutarch *Moralia* 180F. In margin 'self-control'
  1 See 4.38 n1 above. Antipatrides is otherwise unknown.

55  (xx) Plutarch *Moralia* 180F. In margin 'self-control'
  1 Another instance (see 4.38 n1 above) of Alexander's rule that one should not touch another man's partner, in this case a boy beloved. Cf Plutarch *Eumenes* 2. Cassander was Antipater's son, a general involved in the struggles for succession after Alexander's death. Alexander disliked him intensely. It makes more sense to read *per vos* for *per nos* ie 'because of you.'

56  (xxi) Plutarch *Moralia* 181A. See 4.38 n1 above. In margin 'decent'

persuade Telesippa to stay with us, Antigenes. For it is not our way to use force on a free woman.'

He was indulgent to the love of a good soldier whom he wanted to keep in his force, but not willing to bring back a free woman except by persuading her.

57 When the Greek mercenaries serving with the enemy came into Alexander's power he ordered the Athenians to be shackled, because they were receiving pay from the state, but had served the enemy for wages; he also shackled the Thessalians because they possessed splendid land but were not farming it; but he released the Thebans, saying, 'It is our fault they have nothing left, neither city nor countryside.'[1]

Thus he reduced the penalty, decreeing not death but chains for those who deserved death, and taking the blame for those who could make an excuse of need.

58 When he had taken prisoner a famous Indian archer so skilled he could shoot an arrow through a ring, Alexander ordered him to give a demonstration of his skill, but when the man refused he angrily ordered him to be killed. But as the Indian was being led to execution, he said to his guards that he had not practised his art for many days and so was afraid of missing his mark. When Alexander was told that he had refused not from arrogance but fearing the humiliation of failure, the king was impressed by his passion for glory and released him with a present, because he had preferred to die rather than seem inferior to his reputation.

This shows that the proverbial 'like is friend to like'[1] is not entirely foolish. Alexander in his excessive desire for glory loved the same passion in others.

59 When Taxilas, one of the Indian kings, met Alexander he addressed him like

* * * * *

57  (xxii) Plutarch *Moralia* 181A–B. In margin 'reduction of penalty'
  1 After the battle of Chaeronea in 338 BC, Philip had occupied Thebes with a garrison and freed its dependencies, leaving it weak and helpless. After Philip's assassination in 336 BC, Thebes hopefully rebelled, but Alexander took the city, destroyed it utterly and sold the population into slavery.

58  (xxiii) Plutarch *Moralia* 181C. 4.58–60 record incidents from Alexander's campaigns in India 327–6 BC. In margin 'reputation dearer than life'
  1 *Adagia* I ii 21: *Simile gaudet simili* 'Like rejoices in like.'
59  (xxiv) Plutarch *Moralia* 181C; cf *Alexander* 59. In margin 'a truly royal contest'

this: 'I challenge you, not to battle or war but to another kind of contest. If you are weaker, receive a favour from us; but if you are superior, bestow the favour upon us.' In reply Alexander said, 'Indeed this is the contest we must enter, to see which can surpass the other in bestowing favours.' And he embraced him very courteously, and not only did not deprive him of his wealth but increased it.[1]

60 There was a rock in Indian territory, which was so high that it was called 'birdless' as if inaccessible to birds. When Alexander heard that the place was indeed difficult to storm but its commander was cowardly, he said, 'Now the place is easy to take,' meaning that fortifications were useless unless a brave man was defending them.

For a citadel is not secure with ditches and walls but with men.

61 And when another man was holding a rock that was thought impossible to storm, he surrendered to Alexander; but Alexander not only appointed him as ruler over the area but added to it, saying, 'This man seems to me to have good sense, preferring to trust a good man rather than a fortified position.'

62 When he had captured the rock and his companions declared he had surpassed Hercules in noble deeds, he said, 'But I do not think my achievements while in command can be compared even as a fancy phrase with Hercules' achievements.'[1]

\* \* \* \* \*

1 In the spirit of Homeric heroes, the competition in generosity between Alexander and the Indian king ends in exchanging a pact of friendship. Taxilas surrendered to Alexander rather than face defeat in battle, and established friendly relations with him, entertaining him for three days. He gave Alexander lavish gifts on his departure, which Alexander returned, giving Taxilas some of the rich Persian booty he had with him, as well as other things. See Curtius *Historia Alexandri* 8.12.42–3.

60 (xxv) Plutarch *Moralia* 181C. In margin 'the confidence of a brave man

61 (xxvi) Plutarch *Moralia* 181C–D. In margin 'confidence in one who surrendered'

62 (xxvii) Plutarch *Moralia* 181D
1 This is the same rock as in 4.60 above. In Curtius' account (*Historia Alexandri* 8.11.39–41) the precipitous pinnacle surrounded by a ravine was captured only after a difficult two-day assault in which Alexander lost many men. The

They were flattering him, but no form of flattery pleased his spirit.

63  Alexander fined some of his companions because he realized they were not playing the game of dice as an amusement.

And yet many play dice as if it were a very serious business. For those who risk their fortunes, and even their children, on the whim of the dice are no longer playing a game.

64  Amongst his special and most influential friends he seemed to honour Craterus most, but to love Hephaestion most of all. He said, 'This is because Craterus loves his king, but Hephaestion loves Alexander.'

This is neater in Greek with the words *philobasileus* 'king-lover,' *philalexandros* 'Alexander-lover.' He felt that Craterus was a faithful friend in all that pertained to his royal status, but Hephaestion loved Alexander with a personal affection. So he rewarded differently those who loved him equally but in a different way: he loaded Craterus with honour, but admitted Hephaestion into his intimate friendship.

65  Alexander sent the philosopher Xenocrates fifty talents, and when he declined, saying he did not need it, he asked whether Xenocrates had no friend who needed it, and commented 'I didn't find even the wealth of Darius enough for my friends.'[1]

In this I have not yet decided whose spirit I should admire most; the king so inclined to generosity or the philosopher who returned so great a gift spontaneously offered by such a great king.

* * * * *

defenders fled on the third night. Nonetheless, Alexander treated it as a great victory and (Arrian *Anabasis* 5.26.5) boasted of capturing the rock fortress that, according to local legend, had defeated Hercules.

63  (xxviii) Plutarch *Moralia* 181D

64  (xxix) Plutarch *Moralia* 181D. In margin 'a friend'
Craterus was one of Alexander's chief generals. Hephaestion, also a Macedonian noble, was his dearest friend, but no great military man, in spite of being given commands.

65  (xxx) Plutarch *Moralia* 181E. In margin 'generosity'
1  Alexander had defeated King Darius III of Persia at Gaugamela and had received his possessions on his death. See 47 n1 above. For Xenocrates see 1.178 above.

**66** When King Porus was defeated by Alexander and was asked after the battle, 'How shall I treat you?' he said, 'Royally.' Then Alexander added, 'Is there anything more?' and Porus said, 'Everything is included in this single word "royally."' Marvelling at the man's wisdom and courage Alexander gave him an even wider authority than he had previously held.[1]

He would have given less to a suppliant prostrate before his feet, so greatly did this proud young man love fearless spirits.

Quintus Curtius tells the story a little differently. When Porus was asked what he thought the victor should decree he said, 'What you are persuaded by this day in which you learned how insecure is prosperity.' He was warning the king to use his good fortune with moderation, remembering that what had happened to Porus could happen to himself.[2]

**67** When Alexander found out that someone was assailing him with abuse he said, 'It is a king's lot to act kindly and be spoken of unkindly.'

Nothing is more noble than this saying, though it is also ascribed to others.[1]

**68** When he was near death he looked up at his companions and said, 'I see I will have a mighty funeral oration,' guessing that his achievements would be celebrated by the eloquence of many writers. And his intuition was correct.

**69** When he took Darius' daughters prisoner he greeted them with lowered

* * * * *

66  (xxxi) Plutarch *Moralia* 181E. In margin 'royally'
. 1 Porus, the most powerful of Indian kings, confronted Alexander at the Hydaspes river, barring his progress with a huge army including war-elephants. After a hard-fought battle in which the issue long hung in the balance, Porus, defiant to the last, was badly wounded and captured. This, in 326 BC, was the climax of Alexander's Indian campaign. He was much impressed by Porus' dignity and proud courage.
  2 See Curtius *Historia Alexandri* 8.14.51. This reference was added in 1532.

67  (xxxii) Plutarch *Moralia* 181F; cf *Alexander* 41. In margin 'a truly royal attitude'
  1 See Diogenes Laertius 6.3 (7.45 below), Epictetus *Discourses* 4.6, Marcus Aurelius *Meditations* 7.36.

68  (xxxiii) Plutarch *Moralia* 181F. Alexander died at Babylon in 323 BC, probably from fever, though poison was rumoured.

69  (xxxiv) Plutarch *Life of Alexander* 21.10
From here on Erasmus' anecdotes do not come from Plutarch's *Apophthegms*

eyes, and rarely, for fear of being attracted by their beauty. For he used to say to his intimates 'Persian girls are distressing to the eyes.'

70 He issued a decree forbidding anyone to paint his portrait except Apelles, or to sculpt his likeness except Lysippus, since these were the most distinguished artists of that time. For he thought this too was a matter of royal dignity. He also made an agreement with Choerilus the poet that he would receive a gold Philippic coin for every good verse, and a box on the ears for every bad one.

71 Asked where he hid his treasures, he said, 'With my friends,' meaning that there was nowhere more safe to store one's wealth. For when there is need, it returns to you with interest.

72 When a messenger ran up exultant with joy stretching out his hand, all ready to report a success, he asked, 'What great thing will you tell me, my good man, unless it is that Homer has been restored to life?'
        He meant that all the glory of great deeds must fade away unless they meet a herald such as Homer.

73 There was a city that offered Alexander a part of its territory and half its possessions in order to enjoy peace from his warfare. His reply was 'I came

* * * * *

but from passages in his *Life of Alexander* and *Moralia* 326D–345B (*On the fortune of Alexander*), or from the Greek historians of Alexander. Alexander captured Darius III's family after the battle of Gaugamela; see 4.47 above.

70    (xxxv) On the painter Apelles and Lysippus the sculptor in bronze see Plutarch *Moralia* 335A–B (*On the fortune of Alexander*) and *Life of Alexander* 4.1–3, for Apelles' reported sayings and deeds see 6.523–31 below). The monopolies given to Apelles and Lysippus are quoted by Horace in *Letter to Augustus* (*Epistles* 2.1.232–41), Valerius Maximus 8.11 ext. 2, and Pliny *Naturalis historia* 7.125. For Choerilus and the box on the ears, see 8.202 n3 below. In margin 'arts'

71    (xxxvi) Ammianus Marcellinus 25.4.15. Cf the similar saying given as a *chreia* in Theon *Progymnasmata* 5.208 (Spengel II 2.100). See Introduction xxiv–xxvii above. In margin 'generosity'

72    (xxxvii) Plutarch *Moralia* 85c (*Progress in virtue*). For Alexander's veneration of Homer see 4.85, 4.89, 4.95, 8.202. In margin 'report of achievements'

73    (xxxviii) Seneca *Letters* 53.10. In margin 'imperious'

to Asia not to receive what you offer, but to let you have what I leave over.'

74 Alexander kept Eudaemonicus, a philosopher, but one more ready to flatter than any parasite. When it thundered one day very violently, so that everyone was frightened, he said to Alexander, 'Why don't you do something like that, Alexander, son of Jupiter?' But the king could not stand the remark of so base a philosopher, and said with a laugh, 'Because I don't want to be fearsome, as you would have me be, urging me to serve the heads of satraps and kings at dinner.' This is Athenaeus' version.[1]

But Plutarch tells it a little differently in the *Life*: 'Why are you angry with me for serving fish at dinner and not the heads of satraps?'[2]

75 When Alexander was leading a campaign in winter he sat by the fire and began to review the forces as they passed, but when he saw an old man shivering with cold and stopping by the fire, he bade him sit down in his place, saying, 'If you had been born in Persia it would have been a capital offence to sit in the king's chair, but it is yielded up to a man born in Macedonia.'

76 When Alexander was very young and saw his father Philip was going to discard as if good for nothing a horse that was very fierce and could endure no rider, he said, 'What a horse your men are wasting, because in their ignorance and softness they don't know how to handle him.' And when he had fondled the horse quite marvellously without any blows, and then mounted it and cantered, and then used his spurs, and brought the horse back with a gentle pull on the rein, his father kissed his head as he dismounted and said, 'My son, find yourself another kingdom equal to this since Macedonia cannot contain you.'

* * * * *

74 (xxxix) Athenaeus 6.57, 250F and Plutarch *Life of Alexander* 28.4. In margin 'flattery'
    1 Erasmus has misread Athenaeus. *Eudaemonicus* 'the Happy Man' is a nickname of Anaxarchus the philosopher. Anaxarchus accompanied Alexander on his Eastern campaign. See 7.375–6 below. He was a follower of Democritus, for whom see 7.367 below. Erasmus has interpolated 'but one ... parasite' and 'But the king ... so base a philosopher.'
    2 Plutarch *Alexander* 28.4, where Anaxarchus is named.

75 (xl) Frontinus *Strategemata* 4.6.3. In margin 'unassuming'

76 (xli) A paraphrase of Plutarch *Life of Alexander* 6. This tale introduces Bucephalus, Alexander's favourite warhorse. In margin 'lofty spirit'

That wise man divined that so lofty a spirit would not be content with his father's dominion. But this horse reminds us that many naturally fine intellects are ruined by the fault of their instructors, who mostly do not know how to exercise authority without turning thoroughbreds into donkeys.

77 Alexander also used to regard Aristotle, who had been entrusted with his upbringing from boyhood, with the greatest reverence, saying that he owed him as much as he owed to his father, because he had received the beginning of life from his father but of good life from his teacher.[1]

78 When a pirate was taken prisoner and brought to him, and Alexander asked him how he dared to raid the seas, the pirate retorted neatly, 'Because I raid with one small ship, I am called a pirate, but when you raid with a great fleet, you are called king.'
Impressed by his fearless spirit Alexander spared his life.

79 He went on a journey to Delphi and when the priestess refused to consult the god, because these were ill-omened days on which not even oracles were allowed to speak, he dragged the priestess with him by force and went up into the temple: and when she was overwhelmed by his ruthlessness and said, 'Thou art invincible, my son' Alexander said, 'That is a sufficient oracle for me,' treating the woman's words as an oracular response.

80 After he set out on his expedition he distributed almost all his royal wealth to his soldiers and generals. When Perdiccas asked, 'What is left for yourself now, Sire?' he answered, 'Hope.' Then Perdiccas said, 'That will be shared

\* \* \* \* \*

77  (XLII) Plutarch *Life of Alexander* 8.4. In margin 'reverence for teacher'
   1 It was a much repeated saying that we owe more to teachers than to parents. See 7.235 below.

78  (XLIII) Augustine *City of God* 4.4. In margin 'spirited'

79  (XLIV) Plutarch *Life of Alexander* 14.6–7. This occurred before he left Greece on his campaigns. He wanted a favourable oracle to start with. In margin 'oracle'

80  (XLV) Plutarch *Life of Alexander* 15.4–5. Perdiccas was one of Alexander's senior generals and a contender for power after his death. In margin 'confidence in the outcome'

with us, your fellow soldiers,' and refused the estate that Alexander had marked out for him.

Such was his confidence that the expedition would be successful.

81 When he first sat as a judge in capital cases, he used to block up one ear against the accuser, and when he was asked why, said 'I am keeping one ear unbiased for the defendant.'[1]

82 When his admiral Philoxenus wrote to Alexander that a Tarentine dealer called Theodorus was visiting him with handsome slave boys for sale, if Alexander wanted to buy them, he was very indignant, and exclaimed to his friends, 'What impurity has Philoxenus seen in me to inflict such an insult upon me?'

83 This was the verse he uttered against Callisthenes who could not adjust to the ways of the court, but made clear in word and gesture that it all offended him: 'I loathe a wiseacre who is not wise on his own behalf.'[1]

84 When he was about to storm Nisa, and saw the soldiers were intimidated by the depth of the river that surrounded the city, he leapt up and said, 'Oh! I am the worst of men, for not learning to swim' and then leaning on his shield as if it were a cork raft he was the first to cross.

85 Alexander went to Ilium and set a garland around the statue of Achilles,

* * * * *

81 (XLVI) Plutarch *Life of Alexander* 42.2. In margin 'unbiased judge'
  1 Cf *Education of a Christian Prince* CWE 27 280, which reports the anecdote more clearly.

82 (XLVII) Plutarch *Life of Alexander* 22. The story is also told at *Moralia* 333A (*On the fortune of Alexander*). In margin 'integrity'

83 (XLVIII) Plutarch *Life of Alexander* 53.2. In margin 'serve the times'
  1 Aristotle's nephew Callisthenes accompanied Alexander's expedition as a historian but provoked his own execution by his intransigence. Alexander quotes an apposite fragment of Euripides (Nauck fr 905): Μισῶ σοφιστὴν, ὅστις οὐχ αὑτῷ σοφός.

84 (XLIX) Plutarch *Life of Alexander* 58.6. This is the Indus river (Curtius *Historia Alexandri* 8.9.34). In margin 'the leader's example'

85 (L) Plutarch *Life of Alexander* 15.7–8. In margin 'outstanding blessings'

saying, 'O happy Achilles to have such a friend while you lived and such a herald when you were dead.'

He was talking about Patroclus and Homer: the former was Achilles' most loyal friend, the latter celebrated him throughout the epic *Iliad*.[1]

86 He was hailed as god by many but used to say he knew he was mortal from two things, from sleep and intercourse, because these states betrayed the weakness of the body, but he was unconquerable in all other respects. For sleep is the likeness of death, and intercourse is a kind of seizure.

87 When he entered the palace of Darius and saw a lofty bedchamber with coverlets and tables and everything set out in marvellous array, he said, 'Is this what it was to be ruler?'

He felt that it was not kingly to indulge in such luxury.

88 Again when he got into bed he used to shake out the bedclothes very carefully saying, 'I hope my mother has not slipped in anything luxurious or unnecessary.'

Such was his detestation of womanly luxury.[1]

89 When a little box was brought to him more precious and beautiful than anything else found among Darius' treasures, those present asked what it was intended for. Various suggestions were offered, but he said, 'This is the best place to keep Homer,' meaning that no treasure was more precious to

* * * * *

1 Cf Cicero *pro Archia* 24, *Ad familiares* 5.12.7, Arrian *Anabasis* 1.12. After his death in the Trojan War, Achilles became a divine hero. One of his shrines was on Cape Sigaeum in north-west Turkey near Troy (Ilium).

86 (LI) Plutarch *Life of Alexander* 22.6; cf Plutarch *Moralia* 65F (*How to tell a flatterer*), which Erasmus has also used here. In margin 'intimations of mortality'

87 (LII) Plutarch *Life of Alexander* 20.13. This is after the defeat of Darius III, see 4.47 above. In margin 'luxury unworthy of a ruler'

88 (LIII) Plutarch *Life of Alexander* 22.10
  1 Actually Alexander says his tutor Leonidas (for whom see 4.39 above) did this.

89 (LIV) Plutarch *Life of Alexander* 26.1. For Darius see 4.47 above. In margin 'love of literature'

him than Homer.[1] This is what the young man felt who modelled himself entirely on Achilles.

90 Parmenion urged Alexander to attack the enemy by night, saying that otherwise there would be great danger in risking open combat with so great a multitude. For they estimated from the distant clamour, roaring like the sea, that the number was immense. But Alexander answered, 'I do not win victory by stealth,' refusing to conquer by virtue of darkness.

91 When he read a verbose letter from Antipater, containing many slanders against Olympias, he said, 'Antipater does not seem to know that one tear from a mother will erase many letters.'[1]

92 When he found out that his sister was having an affair with an elegant young man he was not shocked,[1] but said, 'We must allow her too to benefit from our kingship in some small way.'

In this he differed greatly from Caesar Augustus, who was bitterly angry at the wantonness of his daughter and grand-daughter.[2]

\* \* \* \* \*

1 Cf 8.202 below.

90 (LV) Plutarch *Life of Alexander* 31.10–12. For Parmenion see 5.113 n1 below. In margin 'open'

91 (LVI) Plutarch *Life of Alexander* 39.13. In margin 'a mother's tears'
1 Antipater was acting as regent in Macedonia during Alexander's absence, but Alexander's mother the dowager Olympias constantly intrigued at court. Cf 4.49 above. For Antipater see 2.52 n1 above.

92 (LVII) Plutarch *Moralia* 818B (*Precepts of statecraft*). In margin 'good-natured'
1 Alexander's tolerance of his sister's affair was exceptional in a society where fathers and brothers felt their honour damaged by any sexual activity (outside marriage) of a daughter or sister.
2 On Augustus' repudiation of his daughter and granddaughter, see also 4.139 and 4.196 below. Augustus had passed stringent laws to punish adultery, and was driven to exile both his daughter Julia and later her daughter for open adulterous relationships. Having no son, he had used the marriages of his only child to mark her husbands as his successors; and adopted her sons by her second husband Agrippa to be his own 'sons.' But her third marriage to Tiberius ended in estrangement, and her adulteries, if such they were, were political relationships when she was forbidden to obtain a divorce.

93 When Alexander heard Anaxagoras putting forward the theory that there were worlds beyond number, he is said to have wept. And when men asked if something had happened to cause his tears, he said, 'Don't I have good cause to weep if there are countless worlds and I have not yet become master of even one?'[1]

94 Philip was wounded in battle by the Triballi, when his thigh was pierced by a lance. Once he had escaped the risk of death, thanks to a surgeon, he began to grieve that he would continue to suffer the deformity of limping. Then Alexander said, 'Don't be afraid to appear in public, but when you step out remember your own valour.'[1]

95 If ever there was a dispute in conversation or at parties about the epics of Homer, when different men preferred one line or the other, Alexander gave his approbation to this one in particular: 'a good leader and likewise a mighty fighter at arms.'[1]

He used to add that Homer was celebrating the valour of Agamemnon in this verse, but foreseeing that of Alexander.

96 When he had crossed the Hellespont and went to visit Troy, he meditated on the achievements of the ancient heroes, and someone said that if he wished he would give him the lyre of Paris. Then Alexander said, 'I don't need that at all, for I have Achilles' lyre. That courageous warrior used to "sing

* * * * *

93 (LVIII) Plutarch *Moralia* 466D (*On tranquillity of mind*). In margin 'insatiable ambition'
  1 See also Valerius Maximus 8.14 ext. 2. Both sources give Anaxarchus, not Anaxagoras. Anaxarchus accompanied Alexander on his expeditions. See 7.373–8 below. As a follower of the Democritean/Epicurean school, he would believe in a multiplicity of worlds. See 4.76 n1 above.

94 (LIX) Plutarch *Moralia* 331B (*On the fortune of Alexander*). This occurred during Philip's campaigns in Thrace in 340–339 BC.
  1 For similar remarks attributed to others, see 2.20–2 above and 6.207 below.

95 (LX) Homer *Iliad* 3.179 and Plutarch *Moralia* 331C–D (*On the fortune of Alexander*). In margin 'comparison of the Homeric poems'
  1 See *Adagia* III x 75: *Imperator bonus et idem robustus miles* 'A good commander and a hard soldier too.'

96 (LXI) Plutarch *Moralia* 331D (*On the fortune of Alexander*). In margin 'music worthy of a leader'

the praises of gallant heroes"'[1] on this lyre, whereas Paris intoned soft and
wanton tunes on his.'

97 Once he went to visit the womenfolk of Darius with Hephaestion.[1] Now
Hephaestion wore the same costume as the king and was slightly taller, so
Syngambris, Darius' mother, bowed before him as if he were the king. And
when she realized her mistake from the reactions of the bystanders, she was
distressed and changed to greeting Alexander. Then Alexander said, 'Good
mother, there is no need to be distressed, for he is Alexander too.' What he
meant was that his friend was a second Alexander.

98 When he came to the temple of Ammon, an ancient priest greeted him
and said, 'Hail, my son! May you be so named by the god also.' Then
Alexander said, 'I accept it, father, and henceforth I shall allow myself to be
called your son if you grant me dominion over the whole world.' The priest
withdrew inside, and as if he had consulted the god replied that Jupiter
certainly promised what he sought. Then Alexander said, 'I would like to
know whether anyone of my father's assassins has survived unpunished.'
The priest replied, 'All Philip's assassins have paid the penalty, but no mortal man can assassinate your father.' He meant that Alexander was the son
of Jupiter, not Philip.[1]

99 When Darius had drawn up his multitudinous army for battle, Alexander
was seized by a sleep so profound that he could not even be woken up with
the daylight, but finally as the danger drew close his companions went in
and aroused the king, and when they said they were amazed at his great

* * * * *

1 Homer *Iliad* 9.189. Achilles was famed for his skill on the lyre.

97 (LXII) Diodorus Siculus 17.37.5–6. In this and the next two anecdotes, Erasmus
    seems to be abbreviating and paraphrasing the Latin translation of Angelus
    Cospus. See the dedicatory epistle 6 n17 above. See also Quintus Curtius 3.31.
    In margin 'merciful'
  1 See 4.49 and 4.64 above.

98 (LXIII) Diodorus Siculus 17.51.1–3. See also Quintus Curtius 4.32. In margin
    'adulation'
  1 Cf 4.50 above.

99 (LXIV) Diodorus Siculus 17.56.1–4. See 4.28 above. See also Quintus Curtius
    4.49. In margin 'spirited'

calm at this time of crisis, Alexander said, 'King Darius has released me from great anxiety by concentrating all his forces against me at once so that one day can decide the final outcome.'

100 The Corinthians sent an embassy to offer Alexander the Great their citizenship. And when the king laughed at this form of homage, one of the envoys said, 'We have never offered citizenship to any other man except to you and Hercules.' Then the king gladly accepted the honour they offered, pleased partly by its rarity and partly by sharing it with Hercules.

101 He was besieging a city and seeking out the weakest part of the walls when he was struck by an arrow, but still did not abandon his task; only when the blood had been staunched and the pain of the dry wound increased and his leg slung over his horse had gradually become numb, was he forced to give up his undertaking and call for a surgeon. 'Everyone declares I am the son of Jupiter,' he said, 'but this wound proclaims me a man.'

102 Zenophantus used to summon Alexander to arms with a specific melody. But when everybody expressed amazement at the power of his music, someone said, 'If he is such an artist, let him play tunes that will call Alexander back from warring.'

His meaning was that it did not require great artistry to drive a man to what he is naturally inclined to do.

### Antigonus, King of Macedon

103 Antigonus was fierce and strict in demanding tribute. When someone

* * * * *

100 (LXV) Seneca *De beneficiis* 1.13.1–2; a similar story is told about Alexander and the inhabitants of Megara, an insignificant place, in Plutarch *Moralia* 826c (*On government*).

101 (LXVI) Seneca *Letters* 59.12. Cf 4.51 above.

102 (LXVII) The first part of the anecdote appears in more than one source, and different musicians are named: Antigenidas, a Theban lyre-player, in Plutarch *Moralia* 335A (*On the fortune of Alexander*; Timotheus, the most famous of lyre-players in *Dio Chrysostom* 1.1 (*On kingship*) quoted in *Adagia* I ii 46: *Currentem incitare* 'To cheer on the runner'; *Adagia* II v 93: *A Dorio ad Phrygium* 'From Dorian to Phrygian,' where the rousing music is said to be in the Dorian mode; and Xenophantes (sic), the most famous pipe-player, in Seneca *Dialogues* 4.2.6.

103 (I) Plutarch *Moralia* 182A. Erasmus returns (4.103–20) to Plutarch's *Sayings of kings and commanders*, last used at 4.68. In margin 'humorous'

protested, 'But Alexander was not like this,' he answered, 'Quite right, for he harvested Asia, whereas I am gleaning the straw.'

His meaning was that the wealthy land of Asia had already been stripped by Alexander, so that he had to scrape up what he could.

104 Seeing some soldiers playing ball in breastplates and helmets, he was delighted by the sight, and ordered their officers be fetched so that he could commend the soldiers to them: but when he was told that the officers were drinking, he gave their position to the soldiers who played ball in their armour.

In this way he punished the leaders' slackness and honoured the energy of the common soldiers.

105 Everybody expressed amazement that Antigonus had been somewhat harsh at the beginning of his rule, but as he grew old governed his kingdom mercifully and mildly. He replied, 'At first I needed to rule, but now only to enjoy glory and goodwill.'

He felt that rule was often won by force of arms and severity but could only be maintained by good reputation and the citizens' goodwill.

106 When his son Philip asked in front of a crowd, 'When will we break camp?'

* * * * *

Antigonus I (called Monophthalmos 'the One-eyed') was one of Alexander's generals who survived to compete for power after his death. Plutarch (*Life of Demetrius* 3) calls Antigonus 'the oldest and greatest of the successors of Alexander.' He had been governor of Asia (Minor) and was left in control of it after Alexander's death but had to fight Cassander and Ptolemy, two other successors, from 323–310 BC, who eventually ousted him. He then championed the cause of the mainland Greeks with his son Demetrius Poliorketes ('the Besieger'), promising to liberate them from Cassander's occupation, starting with Athens. (See 4.118 below.) The Athenians welcomed him with extravagant honours in 307 BC, and he made it his base. He was killed in battle fighting the other successors in 301 BC. The sayings in Plutarch's collection are often duplicated in his lives of Demetrius and Pyrrhus, and Erasmus will use these as sources later (4.121 onwards). Plutarch did not write an independent life of Antigonus.

104 (II) Plutarch *Moralia* 182A. In margin 'strict'

105 (III) Plutarch *Moralia* 182 A–B. See 4.112 and 4.128–9 below for his mildness. In margin 'stable rule'

106 (IV) Plutarch *Moralia* 182B. Philip was Antigonus' second son. Plutarch in his *Life of Demetrius* 28.10 makes the son in question Demetrius, and Frontinus *Strategemata* 1.1.13 tells this story of Crassus. In margin 'secrecy in war'

he answered, 'What, are you afraid you will be the only one not to hear the bugle?'

He rebuked the young man's indiscretion in asking his father such a question in front of a large audience. The plans of the commanders should be kept secret in war; but whenever camp is to be broken, the bugle sounds the signal to everyone.

107 When young Philip insisted on being lodged with a widow with three beautiful daughters, Antigonus summoned the billeting officer and said, 'Won't you remove my son from this tight spot?'

He did not betray his son's desire, although he knew he was seeking a love affair, but made a pretext of the smallness of a house in which a widow and her three daughters were living.

108 After he had recovered from a serious illness, he said, 'It is none the worse if this illness has reminded me not to be over-confident, since I am mortal.'

Who taught this pagan king this philosophy worthy of a Christian soul? His friends were lamenting as if it was a great misfortune that he had been so gravely ill, but he understood that more good than evil had come from the sickness. It had slimmed down his body but made his mind more moderate; it had reduced some of his bodily strength, but reduced the arrogance of his mind, by far the most dangerous of sicknesses. In short it is not a bad state of affairs when a milder sickness drives away a greater one.[1]

109 Hermodotus described Antigonus in a poem as 'son of Jupiter.'[1] Reading this he said, 'My *lasanus*-bearer never realized this,' wittily mocking the poet's flattery and admitting with equal modesty the humbleness of his birth. (A *lasanus* is an earthenware chamber pot.) So if he was the son of Jupiter this

*****

107 (v) Plutarch *Moralia* 182B. In margin 'sexual purity'

108 (vi) Plutarch *Moralia* 182B. In margin 'utility of sickness'
   1 Erasmus' extended comment recalls his own adaptation of Plutarch's essay *Whether the affections of the soul are worse than those of the body* (*Moralia* 500B–2A) in the preface of his *Lingua* 'On the tongue' CWE 29 257–9.

109 (vii) Plutarch *Moralia* 182C. In margin 'modesty'
   1 Here in Plutarch Antigonus is hailed as 'child of the Sun' (Helios), as also in *Moralia* 360E (*On Isis and Osiris*). Perhaps Erasmus was distracted by his earlier tales of Alexander as son of Jupiter. Nothing is known of this Hermodotus.

had escaped the notice of both the slave who usually carried the pot to his chamber and also of Antigonus, Jupiter's son.

**110** When someone said that everything was just and honourable for kings, he said, 'So they are, by Jupiter, at least for kings who rule barbarians, but for us, only those things are honourable which are honourable, and only those things are just which are just.'

He sternly rejected the flattering remark that claimed kings could do what they chose. For a king is not the measure of what is honourable and just, but its agent. If only Christian ears did not hear such remarks, or if they heard them would reject them with equal severity. What else are men saying who keep chanting, 'Whatever the prince decides has the force of law?' Such men deny that a prince is bound by law and credit him with dual powers, established and unchallenged, one which empowers him to do what is required by laws, contracts, and treaties, the other to do as he chooses.[1]

**111** Marsyas, Antigonus' brother, had a lawsuit but petitioned the king to hear the case privately. Antigonus replied, 'If we are doing nothing against the law, it will be better done in the public court with everyone listening.'[1]

His love for his brother did not persuade the king to deviate even the least bit from justice. Indeed he tied up his brother with this dilemma: 'If you know you have an unjust case, why are you suing? But if it is just, why are you avoiding men's knowledge and withdrawing a public matter into the secrecy of our house, where you will not escape your fellow citizens' suspicion, even if you win in a just cause?'

**112** Once when Antigonus had forced his men to move camp in winter to a place without sufficient essential supplies, and some of the soldiers were

\* \* \* \* \*

110  (VIII) Plutarch *Moralia* 182C. In margin 'kings may only do what is honourable'
  1  Erasmus seizes on this scrupulous principle of Antigonus to trigger an attack on Christian rulers who regard themselves as sole arbiters of the law.

111  (IX) Plutarch *Moralia* 182C. In margin 'strict'
  1  A slight mistranslation: Plutarch says, 'It will take place in public, with everyone hearing whether we are committing injustice.' Erasmus was possibly misled here by Regio's version (see the dedicatory epistle 8 n21 above).

112  (X) Plutarch *Moralia* 182C. Cf *Moralia* 457E (*On the control of anger*), and Seneca *De ira* 3.22.2. In margin 'mild'

damning the king for it, not knowing he was nearby, he opened the flap of his tent with his baton and said, 'You'll be sorry if you don't go further away before you abuse me!'

What could be more mild than this witticism, or more witty than this mildness? He pretended not to mind them abusing him, only that they were so near that they could be heard by the object of their abuse.

113 Aristodemus, one of the king's friends who was thought to be the son of a cook, urged him to reduce his spending and his largess, and the king replied, 'Your words taste of gravy.'[1]

He was hinting that such economy was proper to cooks, not kings, and in giving such advice Aristodemus was forgetting whose friend he was while remembering whose son he was.

114 When the Athenians enrolled a slave of Antigonus in their citizen register to honour him as if he were free-born man, he said, 'I would not want a single Athenian to have a flogging at my hands,' meaning that they had put him in the position of being able to flog one Athenian citizen, that is, his own slave; but that there were more persons than one at Athens who deserved a flogging from the king, for effectively setting free another man's slave.

115 A young pupil of the rhetorician Anaximenes[1] was delivering a speech composed by his teacher which he had been prompted to recite before Antigonus. When Antigonus wanted to know something and interrupted with a question, the young man fell silent. Antigonus said, 'What's the matter?' 'Wasn't that "written on your tablets"?'[2]

* * * * *

113 (xi) Plutarch *Moralia* 182D. In margin 'royal liberality'
 1 Plutarch's Greek text has 'smells of a cook's apron.' Erasmus has followed the versions of Filefo and Regio (see the dedicatory epistle nn20 and 21 above).

114 (xii) Plutarch *Moralia* 182D. See 103 headnote above. In margin 'harsh'

115 (xiii) Plutarch *Moralia* 182E. In margin 'speech written by another'
 1 For Anaximenes, see 3.308–9 above.
 2 The young man only knew what he had learnt by heart. Antigonus quotes a line of Euripides *Iphigenia in Tauris* 787, where the speaker is reading someone else's letter and only partly understands it. Erasmus takes the opportunity to criticize contemporary speakers who deliver speeches by others that have taken six months to prepare. Cf *Ciceronianus* cwe 28 350–4, where Erasmus satirizes contemporary Ciceronians as taking a week to write six sentences.

He thought this absurd in the young man, but people think it a fine thing nowadays for grown men to memorize a speech that has been worked up by a hired speech-maker for six months and deliver it like a parrot even in front of princes. And quite often they dry up even when nobody interrupts them, and are a laughing-stock to everybody.

116  When he heard another rhetorician speaking like this, 'The season that hurls the spears of snows came and rendered the land ungrassed,' he asked him, 'Won't you stop addressing me like a crowd?'

The king was offended by this over-wrought speech, such as orators use to advertise themselves to the ignorant rabble with a fine flourish of words. To act like this before the king was to abuse his patience. I will write down the Greek, because the pretentious figure of speech cannot be appropriately expressed in Latin: χιονοβόλος ἡ ὥρα γενομένη, λειποβοτανεῖν ἐποίησεν τὴν χώραν. He could have said 'winter' for χιονοβόλος ἡ ὥρα 'the snow-hurling season' and λειποβοτανεῖν 'to make poor in grass' is an artificial verb which would be scarcely excusable in a poet.

117  When the Cynic Thrasyllus asked for a drachma, Antigonus said, 'It is not royal to make such a gift.' So the Cynic followed up, 'Then give me a talent.' He retorted, 'But it is not a Cynic's act to take such a gift.'

He rejected the shamelessness of the demand using both alternatives of the dilemma, because he did not think the man deserved a kindness.

118  When he sent his son Demetrius with a huge fleet and large infantry force to liberate the Greeks, he said that glory spread like fire throughout all the world from a beacon lit in Greece.

* * * * *

116  (XIV) Plutarch *Moralia* 182E. The story is repeated in Plutarch *Life of Demetrius* 12. The speaker's words are rhythmical, almost verse, as well as being far-fetched. In margin 'affected language'

117  (XV) Plutarch *Moralia* 182E. So also *Moralia* 531E (*On compliancy*), Seneca *De beneficiis* 2.17. Cynics flaunted their self-imposed impoverished way of life. In margin 'witty'

118  (XVI) Plutarch *Moralia* 182E–F. In margin 'encouragement to win glory' Antigonus sent Demetrius with a large fleet from Asia (Minor) to liberate Athens from Cassander, one of the other successors, promising the city its freedom. He said that Athens was the beacon of Greece because of its glorious reputation. Plutarch *Life of Demetrius* 8.

In this way he used the young man's passion for glory to spur him on to campaign energetically, because fame of such achievement would not be restricted to the boundaries of Greece, but spread throughout the world because of the celebrated name of Greece.

119 Antigonus caught the poet Antagoras in his tent cooking an eel and wielding the pan himself, and standing behind him said, 'Antagoras, do you think Homer was cooking an eel when he composed the deeds of Agamemnon?' Antagoras replied, 'And you, Sire, do you think king Agamemnon had time when he did those deeds, to wonder whether anyone in his army was cooking an eel?'[1]

The king took the retaliation in good part, as if it were an exchange between equals.

120 Antigonus once saw in his dreams Mithridates harvesting a crop of gold, which led him to plot to eliminate him. So when he had informed his son Demetrius, he made him swear silence. But when Demetrius was walking by the sea shore with Mithridates, he wrote in the sand with the butt of his spear, 'Get away from here, Mithridates.' Mithridates understood and went to Pontus and enjoyed uninterrupted rule there.[1]

This is not an apophthegm, but seems to have been added by some interpolator.[2]

121 Antigonus' friends urged him to control Athens, if he captured it, with powerful garrisons in case it might ever revolt, and to guard it with the greatest care as the foundation-stone of Greece; to which he replied that he had

* * * * *

119  (XVII) Plutarch *Moralia* 182F. In margin 'affable'
  1 Antagoras was court poet to Antigonus II Gonatas, who has probably been confused in the tradition with Antigonus I, as in 4.123 below. Antagoras wrote, among other things, epigrams and an epic poem *Thebais*.

120  (XVIII) Plutarch *Moralia* 183A. In margin 'a friend's loyalty'
  1 This is Mithridates I who founded the dynasty of Pontus (in northern Turkey) which ended with the defeat and suicide of Mithridates VI in 63 BC.
  2 See Introduction xix n11 and dedicatory epistle 9 above.

121  (XIX) Plutarch *Life of Demetrius* 8.3. In margin 'merciful'
  Erasmus has now reached the end of the sayings recorded in Plutarch's collection of sayings and uses other sources, from Plutarch and other authors. These further illustrate the confusion in the tradition between Antigonus I and his grandson Antigonus II Gonatas, and also Antigonus III Doson.

always been minded to believe that there was no firmer garrison for a ruler than the goodwill of his citizens.[1]

122 Again when he heard that the kings had conspired to eliminate him, he replied with arrogance that he would put them all to flight with a single stone and a single shout like birds pecking at seeds.

123 When Antigonus kept his army on steep inaccessible ground overlooking the plain and Pyrrhus had pitched camp near Nauplia, Pyrrhus challenged him the next day via a herald to come down to the plain and risk battle. But Antigonus replied that his own campaign depended as much on timing as on forces; as for Pyrrhus, if he had become weary of life, there were quite enough ways open to meet his death.

124 Asked whom of his own generation he thought the most distinguished commander, he said, 'Pyrrhus would be, if he reached old age.'[1] He did not call him best, but said that he would excel if age added experience.

125 Once he saw a soldier who was otherwise energetic and ready to take risks but in poor bodily condition, and asked him why he was pale. When the

* * * * *

1 Cf 1.2 above (Agesilaus) for the same sentiment.

122 (xx) Plutarch *Life of Demetrius* 28.5. In margin 'arrogant'

123 (xxi) Plutarch *Life of Pyrrhus* 31.3–4. In margin 'fighting not always appropriate'
This is Antigonus ii Gonatas who was contemporary with Pyrrhus, not Antigonus i. Pyrrhus was king of Epirus in north-west Greece 319–272 BC. Seeking to extend his territories, he clashed with Antigonus ii in southern Greece, and was ignominiously killed at the battle for the city of Argos, by a tile thrown by a woman, in 272 BC. See 4.131 below. There are sayings of Pyrrhus which Plutarch includes at *Moralia* 184C, almost last among the foreign kings, but which Erasmus postpones until he returns to the collection in 5.119–30 below.

124 (xxii) Plutarch *Life of Pyrrhus* 8.4. This again is Antigonus ii Gonatas.
  1 Hannibal likewise gave high place to Pyrrhus both at Plutarch *Pyrrhus* 8.4 and at *Flamininus* 21.4–5. Pyrrhus had notable successes against the Romans in southern Italy.

125 (xxiii) Plutarch *Life of Pelopidas* 1.2–4. It is not clear which Antigonus this is. In margin 'prosperity makes people fearful'

man admitted he had a secret disease, the king told the doctors to apply remedies if it was at all possible. But after he was cured the soldier began to shirk battle and expose himself less readily to danger. In surprise the king asked him what had changed his attitude. The soldier answered, 'It is your fault: when I lived in poor health I was not very fearful for my wretched existence, but now that you have made my life more precious I am more careful not to lose it.'[1]

126 The old Antigonus[1] said to a sophist who was offering him a book on justice, 'You are crazy to talk about justice to me when you can see I am busy attacking foreign cities.'

He realized that those who wage war on foreign cities to expand their empire and win glory cannot keep the laws of justice.

127 When the old Antigonus had suffered Bias repeatedly making importunate demands he was finally overcome by weariness and said, 'Give Bias a talent, even under compulsion.'[1]

He felt the kindness had not been won but extorted by shameless persistence.

\* \* \* \* \*

1 Compare Horace's story (Epistle 1.7) of the auctioneer enriched by Philippus, with disastrous result.

126 (xxiv) Plutarch *Moralia* 330E (*On the fortune of Alexander*). In margin 'unjust war'
  1 This could be Antigonus I or II. This passage and the next refer to Antigonus as *senior*, either in the sense 'the elder Antigonus' (to distinguish him from his grandson, Antigonus II Gonatas, the contemporary of Pyrrhus of Epirus) or meaning 'Antigonus, when he was an old man.'

127 (xxv) Plutarch *Moralia* 531E (*On compliancy*)
  1 See 4.126 n1 above.
    Modern texts have (since Casaubon) emended the name to *Bion*, ie Bion the Borysthenite, a Cynic philosopher at the court of Antigonus II Gonatas. The MSS however all give Bias, as in Erasmus' version. There is often confusion in the tradition between Bion and the famous Bias of Priene, one of the Seven Sages. Bias (seventh century BC) is too early for either Antigonus. The Greek text here shows that Antigonus was making a pun on the name: 'Give Force a talent,' in Greek *biai*, and this may have occasioned the substitution of the more famous name Bias for Bion. (See the discussion in Plutarque *Oeuvres morales* VII 2, ed and trans Robert Klaert and Yvonne Vernière, Paris 1974, 181 n3). The pun cannot be reproduced in Latin or English.

**128** One night Antigonus heard some of his soldiers uttering every kind of curse on the king for leading them on that route into an inescapable bog. So he went up to those in the worst difficulties, and when he had helped them out, although they did not know who was helping them, he said, 'Now curse Antigonus, through whose fault you fell into this desperate mess: but wish him well too for leading you out of this pit.'

The king's genuine magnanimity was content with this retaliation.

**129** Again when the Greeks were being besieged in a small fortress and, relying on their position, treated the enemy with contempt and made many jokes against Antigonus' ugliness, jeering now at his short stature now at his broken nose, he said, 'I am delighted and expect some good out of this since I have a Silenus in my camp.'[1] And when he had reduced these jesters to starvation he said he would not even have followed the customary treatment of the surrendered, that is enrolling the good fighters in his cohorts and putting the others up for sale, if it had not been good for men with such a nasty tongue to be subjected to a master.

I think this is the same story as told by Plutarch, except that Seneca tells it in a different way.[2]

**130** When he was given a document written in huge letters, he said, 'These are clear even to a blind man,'[1] making fun of his own eye problem, for he was one-eyed. Any other man would have risked his life if he had said this,

\* \* \* \* \*

128 (xxvi) Seneca *De ira* 3.22.2. Seneca ascribes this and the remark in 4.129 to an Alexander, allegedly grandfather of Alexander the Great, but this is a mistake: Alexander's grandfather was Amyntas III, king of Macedon. The subject of both is probably Antigonus I the One-eyed. Cf 4.112 above.

129 (xxvii) Seneca *De ira* 3.22.4–5 and Plutarch *Moralia* 458F (*On the control of anger*); see 4.128n just above.
  1 Antigonus' short stature and snub nose made him resemble Silenus, an enigmatic figure, ugly and debauched on the outside, but wise and inspired within. Socrates was often likened to him. See *Adagia* III i 1: *Sileni Alcibiadis* 'The Sileni of Alcibiades.'
  2 In Plutarch's shorter version (*Moralia* 458F) Antigonus mildly remarks, 'And I thought I was good-looking.'

130 (xxviii) Plutarch *Moralia* 633C (*Table-talk* 2). This saying was added in 1535. This must be Antigonus I, the One-eyed. In margin 'a joke against oneself'
  1 Cf *Adagia* I viii 93: *Vel caeco appareat* 'A blind man might see that'

which is what happened to Theocritus of Chios, who will be mentioned later.[2]

**131** When King Antigonus was informed that his son Alcyoneus had fallen in battle,[1] he bowed his head and thought privately for a little while. Then he burst out with this cry, 'O Alcyoneus, you exchanged life for death later than might have been expected, for you leapt so boldly onto the enemy, paying no attention to your own survival nor to my warnings.'

He did not think he should weep over a man who died by his own fault and brought disaster on himself. This has been taken from Plutarch.

**132** Again, seeing his son treating his subjects too boastfully and arrogantly, he said, 'My son, don't you know our rule is a glorious servitude?'[1]

Nothing could be more shrewd. For a prince is as much compelled to be a servant to the people as the people to him, except that the prince does it with dignity; otherwise it is really reciprocal enslavement.

Now to match the Greeks we will set Julius Caesar against Alexander, Augustus against Philip, and Cicero against Antigonus.

\* \* \* \* \*

2 See 6.492 below. The sophist Theocritus of Chios is reported by Athenaeus as insulting various hosts and rivals.

**131** (XXIX) Plutarch *Moralia* 119C–D (*Consolation to Apollonius*). This and the next apophthegm were not included in *1531* and in *1532* were used in book 8. They were moved to this position in *1535*.
1 Alcyoneus is the son of Antigonus II Gonatas. Little else is known of Alcyoneus. His father had been angered with him for treating with disrespect the severed head of King Pyrrhus of Epirus, instead of honouring a noble opponent. See Plutarch *Life of Pyrrhus* 34, Valerius Maximus 5.1 ext. 4. See 4.132 below, 4.124 above.

**132** (XXX) Aelian *Varia historia* 2.20. See Introduction xx n14. In margin 'to rule is to serve'
1 This too refers to Antigonus II Gonatas. This son is Demetrius II. This anecdote was later repeated; see 8.173A below.

After this saying, Erasmus passes over the rest of Plutarch's *Sayings of kings and commanders* and many of the early figures in his *Sayings of the Romans*. He singles out for inclusion Augustus, Julius Caesar, and Pompey as parallels to his three Macedonian kings. His mention of Cicero here is a mistake; he will appear in the section on orators, 4.257ff, as a counterpart to Demosthenes. Erasmus abandons the order followed in Plutarch's *Sayings of the*

**Octavius Caesar Augustus**

133 When King Rhimirales of Thrace, who deserted Mark Antony for Augustus, was boasting excessively at a party of his services to Augustus, and became a nuisance by endlessly bringing up his alliance in the war, Augustus ignored his rudeness and, offering the toast to another king, said 'I love treachery but cannot praise traitors.'[1]

He meant that men who have been useful by treachery deserve no thanks, for although their service is welcome at the time, they themselves are thought evil treaty-breakers.

134 After Alexandria was taken by storm the Alexandrians expected the worst, but Augustus mounted the tribunal with Arius of Alexandria and said he would spare the city, firstly because of its greatness and beauty, then for the sake of Alexander the Great who founded it, and finally as a favour to his friend Arius.[1]

This was an act of rare clemency, not to sack a city that had been obstinate in rebellion, but he deserves no less praise for his modesty in that he did not claim the credit for this favour for himself but attributed it for the most part to the city, secondly to Alexander, whose memory he knew

* * * * *

Romans, which moves from Pompey (*Moralia* 208B–204E), to Cicero (*Moralia* 204E–205F), to Caesar (205F–206F), to Augustus (206F–208A). Plutarch in his *Lives* likewise pairs Alexander and Caesar, and Demosthenes and Cicero.

133 (I) Plutarch *Moralia* 207A. Erasmus first draws on Plutarch's *Sayings of the Romans* for his sayings of Augustus (4.133–45), omitting the first one, probably because it mentions large sums of money impossible to represent in Latin terms.
'Caesar Augustus' was the final name of Julius Caesar's great-nephew Octavius, who first became Octavianus Caesar by adoption in Caesar's will; he ruled Italy as the main triumvir from 43–33 BC, defeated Antony and Cleopatra at Actium in 31, and conquered Egypt in 30. In 27 BC he was awarded the honorific title Augustus in return for handing over to the senate and people of Rome control of the demilitarized provinces. King Rhimirales had defected after Antony's defeat at Actium. In margin 'treachery welcome'
1 Cf Plutarch *Romulus* 17 where the remark is also attributed to Antigonus I. Stobaeus 54.63 (Meineke II 330) attributes a similar comment to Philip II of Macedon.

134 (II) Plutarch *Moralia* 207A. In margin 'merciful'
1 These events took place in 30 BC. See Suetonius *Augustus* 89.1 for Arius Didymus of Alexandria, the Stoic philosopher, Augustus' former teacher and later adviser.

was particularly cherished by the Alexandrians, and thirdly to Arius, a citizen of that city, commending his friend to his fellow-citizens by giving him this prestigious title.

**135** When Augustus was informed that Eros, his administrator in Egypt, had bought a quail that defeated all others in battle and was absolutely invincible, but had then roasted and eaten it, he had the man brought to him and when he admitted it on interrogation he ordered Eros to be nailed to a ship's mast.

He must have thought Eros did not deserve to live, for sacrificing to such a brief gastronomic pleasure a bird that could have brought pleasure to many by fighting for a long time; and indeed by its good omen promised Caesar continuing success in war.[1]

**136** Augustus made Arius chief magistrate in Sicily instead of Theodorus, but when someone passed a note to him which said, 'Theodorus of Tarsus was a bald-headed thief: what do you think?' he read it and wrote underneath simply, 'That's obvious.'[1]

**137** When the philosopher Athenodorus begged to be allowed to go home, on

* * * * *

**135** (III) Plutarch *Moralia* 207B. In margin 'harsh'
   1 Erasmus' explanation of Augustus' act in executing his procurator (a high fiscal administrator) hardly justifies the savage punishment, but other stories such as that of Vedius Pollio (4.192 below) reflect his dislike of both gluttony and wanton cruelty. Quails were bred for the popular sport of quail-fighting (see 8.44 below), and the bird probably had a considerable following.

**136** (IV) Plutarch *Moralia* 207C. In margin 'witty'
   1 There are problems with this anecdote. It may be about the Athenodorus of 4.137 below, whom Augustus appointed governor of his native city of Tarsus in the Roman province of Cilicia (in south-west Turkey) in 33 BC. In this case Erasmus' *Sicily* (from Plutarch) is a mistake for *Cicilia*, to which it was corrected in BAS and LB (for these editions see Introduction xxviii above). Cicero (*Letters to Atticus* 16.11) calls this man *Athenodorus Calvus*, 'Athenodorus Baldhead,' presumably a nickname. Erasmus' translation suggests that his Greek text of Plutarch read ἦν 'was a thief,' or that he silently emended the reading ἤ 'or,' ie 'a baldhead or a thief.' With ἦν the word order produces a nice ambiguity: either Theodorus Baldhead was a thief, or Theodorus was a bald-headed thief. Augustus chooses the second interpretation.

**137** (V) Plutarch *Moralia* 207C. Erasmus has omitted Plutarch's sixth entry in *Sayings of Romans* for Caesar Augustus, which does not involve a saying or even a wise action. In margin 'a remedy for anger'

the grounds of his increasing age, Augustus granted the request. But as he said goodbye, wanting to present Augustus with something to remember worthy of a philosopher, he said, 'Caesar, do not say or do anything when you are angry until you have recited the twenty four letters of the Greek alphabet.'

The emperor clutched the philosopher's right hand and said, 'I still need you,' and kept him for a whole year, uttering the Greek proverb, 'There are safe rewards for faithful silence.'[1]

Either he approved the philosopher's saying, because it was safe to control one's anger and not let it escape in words, or because he thought it would have benefited the philosopher not to make this pronouncement when he was leaving.[2] Yet such a beneficial precept deserved some magnificent reward.

138 When he heard that at the age of thirty-two after crossing most regions of the world Alexander had wondered what to do in the rest of his life, he expressed amazement that Alexander had not thought it more important to govern well the empire he had won, than merely to acquire a vast territory.[1]

In any case he was right to censure Alexander's insatiable ambition, for thinking that a king had no other purpose than to extend the boundaries of his territory: for it is much nobler and more difficult to enrich the kingdom one has received with correct laws and virtuous morals than to add one kingdom to another by conquest.

139 Augustus passed a law against adulterers, establishing procedures to judge those accused of this charge and how they were to be punished if found guilty. Then in uncontrollable anger he assaulted a young man accused of

\* \* \* \* \*

1 Augustus attached great importance to two philosophers, Arius of Alexandria (cf 4.136 just above and 4.157 below) and Athenodorus of Tarsus.
  The 'Greek proverb' is in fact a line from Simonides (Bergk PLG Simonides 66) also recalled by Horace (*Odes* 3.2.25f); cf *Adagia* III v 3: *Silentii tutum praemium* 'Safety is silence's reward' and CPG 2 Apostius 8.97.
2 There are various sayings on the value of holding one's tongue. General Index: mouth, keeping shut frequently recommended.

138 (VI) Plutarch *Moralia* 207D. In margin 'most important to preserve what has been won'
  1 In contrast with Augustus' adoptive father Julius Caesar, who despaired at not matching Alexander's world conquest (see 4.203 below), Augustus pragmatically stressed the need to organize and administer his new empire; Augustus may never have made this comment, but it reflects his own actual policies.

139 (VII) Plutarch *Moralia* 207D. In margin 'the ruler observant of the law'

having relations with Julia, Augustus' daughter, and beat him up. But when the young man cried out, 'You passed a law on this, Caesar,' he was so remorseful that he refused to dine that day.[1]

It was a serious charge, and one committed against Caesar's daughter. What prince would have controlled his indignation at this? Or who would have waited for the delays entailed by law and the courts? But this great prince was so ashamed that he punished himself for failing to obey in all respects the law he promulgated for others.

140 When he was sending his grandson (his daughter's son), Gaius,[1] to Armenia, he asked the gods that the popularity of Pompey, the boldness of Alexander, and Augustus' own good fortune should accompany him.

He wished for one man to have the exceptional blessings of each of these individuals. But what marked his unique modesty was that this man, distinguished in intellect, learning, and judgment, should attribute his own great achievements to fortune.

141 Augustus used to say he would leave the Romans a successor who never had to deliberate twice on the same problem, meaning Tiberius.[1]

142 Some upper-class young men of good standing in society were staging a

* * * * *

1 Augustus tried to strengthen Roman family life and reproductivity by legislating in 18 BC both to regulate marriage and to punish adultery (ie extramarital affairs by or with wives; a husband could freely sleep with unprotected slave and foreign partners). After her second husband's death, and abandoned by her third husband Tiberius, Augustus' daughter Julia supposedly had adulterous affairs; however, this anecdote does not concern an adulterer, but, as Plutarch reports, a man slandered as having an affair with her. The man reminded Augustus that by his own law, a father could only punish an adulterer if he caught him in the act or if the man was prosecuted and convicted.

140 (VIII) Plutarch *Moralia* 207E. In margin 'prayer'
  1 For Augustus' adoption of his grandsons Gaius and Lucius as 'sons,' see 4.92 above with n2.

141 (IX) Plutarch *Moralia* 207E. In margin 'ready counsel'
  1 After the first two men Augustus had considered as successors died, he marked out his stepson Tiberius for the succession in AD 4. For Tiberius see 6.1–13 below

142 (X) Plutarch *Moralia* 207E. In margin 'authority'

noisy demonstration. Augustus wanted to calm them but when they would not listen to him, but went on creating a disturbance, he said, 'Young men, listen to an old one, whom old men listened to when he was young.'[1]

The fact is that Augustus entered public life as a very young man and held high authority. He disciplined them by this single comment and did not impose any other penalty for the riot they had stirred up.

143 When the Athenian people had, as it seemed, committed some offence he wrote from the city of Aegina,[1] 'I don't think you have missed the fact that I am angry, for I have not come to Aegina to spend the winter.'

He neither said nor did anything else to them, thinking it enough to threaten them if they did not stop it.

144 When one of Euclides'[1] accusers, exploiting his freedom of speech to the full and most tediously, was so carried away that he said something like, 'If these don't seem to you great offences, have him recite Thucydides' seventh book to me,' the emperor was offended, and ordered him to be taken away. But then he heard that he was the last of Brasidas' descendants, so he sent for him and scolded him mildly before letting him go.[2]

145 When Piso built his house from the foundation to the roof-top with the greatest care, Augustus said, 'You make me confident, Piso, building as though Rome would be eternal.'[1]

\* \* \* \* \*

1 This seems to refer to the occasion (Suetonius *Augustus* 34.2) when Augustus had to deal with a protest of unmarried élite men against being penalized for remaining bachelors. See 4.170 n1 below.

143 (XI) Plutarch *Moralia* 207F. In margin 'clemency'
   1 Aegina is an island not far from the coast of Attica.

144 (XII) Plutarch *Moralia* 207F. In margin 'clemency'
   1 Modern texts of Plutarch correctly name the man as Eurycles (possibly the Spartan who fought on Augustus' side at the battle of Actium).
   2 This is the fourth book of Thucydides as they are now numbered, which relates the achievements of the Spartan hero Brasidas. For Brasidas see 1.159–62 above.

145 (XIII) Plutarch *Moralia* 208A. In margin 'opportune interpretation'
   1 There were several Pisos who held consulships under Augustus. It is possible this was Gnaeus Calpurnius Piso, Augustus' colleague in the consulship 23 BC, or his son Gnaeus Calpurnius Piso (consul 7 BC), the friend of Tiberius

He was not offended by the extravagant display of the building, but what another might have thought suggested tyrannical ambition he turned into a happy omen for the empire of Rome.

This is as far as Plutarch goes.

146 Augustus wrote a tragedy called *Ajax* and later, since it did not satisfy him, obliterated it with a sponge. So when Lucius the tragic poet asked him, 'How was Ajax getting on?' the emperor quite wittily said, 'He has fallen on his sponge.'

He was referring to the plot of the play in which Ajax committed suicide by falling on his sword when he learns what he had said and done during his madness.[1]

147 When someone offered him a petition very timidly, now stretching out and now withdrawing his hand, Augustus said, 'What, do you think you are giving a penny to an elephant?'

Children often give a very small coin to an elephant which it picks up with its trunk without hurting the boy's hand, to the great admiration of the spectators. Likewise we see children putting their hands even into the gaping mouth of a bear, though they are frightened to do it. This excellent emperor didn't like people to be afraid of him.

148 When Pacinnius Taurus[1] asked him for a gift and reported that there was

\* \* \* \* \*

who subsequently seems to have undermined if not also poisoned Germanicus on behalf of Tiberius. Certainly we know from the Senate's decree of condemnation that this Piso had a magnificent house.

146 (xiv) Macrobius *Saturnalia* 2.4.2; Macrobius no doubt found this story in Suetonius *Augustus* 85.2. In margin 'humorous'
  Except for 4.157–8 Erasmus now follows Macrobius' collection of Augustus' witticisms in *Saturnalia* 2.4 for 4.146–80.
  1 Erasmus recalls Sophocles' *Ajax*, which may have been the model of Augustus' aborted Latin tragedy. The tragic poet is probably Lucius Varius Rufus, friend of Horace and Virgil.

147 (xv) Macrobius *Saturnalia* 2.4.3. Macrobius' anecdote is also found in Suetonius *Augustus* 53.2. In margin 'a ruler easy of approach'

148 (xvi) Macrobius *Saturnalia* 2.4.4. In margin 'humorous'
  1 The man's name is given in Macrobius as Pacuvius Taurus. He was tribune in 27 BC.

a common rumour that Augustus had given him a great deal of money,
Augustus said, 'Don't you believe it!'

By this smart joke he implied he wouldn't give anything. The man
had thought that the emperor would help out his embarrassment, so that
he would not be made fun of if the rumour was found to be false. But the
emperor offered another solution, to let men say what they chose, provided
that they didn't persuade Pacinnius to believe a falsehood!

149 Another man, who was removed from his command of a cavalry squadron,
actually dared to ask Augustus for a salary, with the argument that he was
not seeking it for the sake of the money but 'So that it may seem,' he said,
'that I have been granted a post on your recommendation, and so may be
thought not to have been dismissed from my previous position but to have
resigned from it.' Augustus answered, 'Tell everyone you have received it
and I won't put out a denial.'

If this petitioner was only prompted by the fear of disgrace, Augustus
showed him a way of protecting his honour just as good as if he had received
the money.

150 Caesar Augustus had ordered the vicious young man Herennius to leave his
camp, and when he was dismissed he with weeping and supplication begged
him with this appeal, 'How can I face returning home, what shall I say to
my father?' The emperor said, 'Tell him I did not meet your satisfaction.'

Since the young man was ashamed to admit that he had not satisfied
Augustus, the emperor allowed him to reverse the saying and put the blame
on him.

151 A soldier was struck by a rock on campaign and his forehead was disfig-
ured by a conspicuous scar. Since he was marked by an honourable wound
he boasted excessively of his deeds, so Augustus gently reproached his arrogance: 'Take care,' he said, 'that you don't look back any time you are
running away.'

He hinted that it was possible that the man had suffered the wound
which he kept bragging about in flight, and not in battle.

* * * * *

149 (XVII) Macrobius *Saturnalia* 2.4.5. In margin 'an amusing way of refusing'

150 (XVIII) Macrobius *Saturnalia* 2.4.6. In margin 'jocose'

151 (XIX) Macrobius *Saturnalia* 2.4.7. In margin 'witty'

**152** Galba's body was deformed by a hump, and the common gossip was that Galba's mind was ill-housed.[1] So when he was pleading before the emperor and kept saying, 'Set me straight, Caesar, if you see anything in me to find fault with,' Augustus replied, 'I can bring it to your notice, but not set you straight.'

For what is criticized is set straight, and so is whatever is changed from being out of shape into the right shape.

**153** When most of the defendants accused by Cassius Severus were discharged,[1] and the man to whom Augustus had given the contract to construct his forum was keeping him waiting for a long time for the work, he said, 'I only wish Cassius had accused my forum!'

He was playing on words, for a thing completed and man acquitted are both called discharged (*absolutus*): the architect discharges a contract and the judge discharges the defendant.

**154** Once men felt great reverence for tombs and memorials, and the part of a field dedicated to a funeral monument was never tilled. So when Vectius, undeterred by any religious scruple, had ploughed up his father's memorial, Augustus made a witty remark: 'This is real cultivation of your father's memorial.'

Again he was playing on words. For we cultivate (*colimus*) both what we worship and a field or suchlike. If would be a double pun if he had substituted *memory* for *memorial*, which I think is what he must have said. In fact we talk about the sacred remembrance of the deceased persons we reverence, and we call funeral monuments remembrances in imitation of the Greeks.[1]

\* \* \* \* \*

**152** (xx) Macrobius *Saturnalia* 2.4.8. In margin 'witty'
   1 Gaius Sulpicius Galba was an orator of moderate abilities. He was the father of Servius Sulpicius Galba who became emperor briefly in AD 68–9. Romans felt no inhibitions about jokes at the expense of deformed or crippled people; see many of Cicero's witticisms reported below. 'Galba ... ill-housed': added by Erasmus from Macrobius 2.6.3.; 6.242 below.

**153** (xxi) Macrobius *Saturnalia* 2.4.9. In margin 'humorous'
   1 Cassius Severus was an eloquent, if dissident, speaker, historian and wit; his oratory is praised by Seneca the elder (*Controversiae* 3 pref. 2–7) and, with qualifications, Tacitus in the *Dialogue on Orators* 19.2, 26.14.

**154** (xxii) Macrobius *Saturnalia* 2.4.10. In margin 'joke depending on ambiguity'
   1 Erasmus has expanded on Macrobius' two-liner with his explanation: Greek *mnema* can be used both of memory and of a physical memorial of the dead.

155  When the report came to Augustus of Herod's cruelty in having all boy
children in Syria under two years old killed, including a child of his own,
he said, 'It is better to be Herod's pig than his son.'

For Herod was a Jew and the Jews by a strange scruple refrain from
eating pig's flesh.[1]

156  Maecenas was esteemed for other qualities but was wanton in his style, often indulging in pretentious language and eccentric sentence structure. Augustus on the other hand used to say one must shun a strange word as
if it were a reef.[1] So when he wrote to others he used a plain style, but
writing to Maecenas,[2] whom he fondly loved, he used to imitate Maecenas,
so extravagantly that in a letter in which he made many frank and wanton jests he ended with: 'Farewell, my honey of the nations, my little gem,
my ivory from Etruria, my spice from Arezzo, my diamond of the north-
west, my pearl of the Tiber,[3] my emerald of the Cilnei,[4] my jasper of potters,[5] my beryl of Porsenna,[6] my precious jewel,[7] in short, my mattress of
adulteresses.'[8]

This is how Augustus mocked his friend's affectations in writing. He
used to jeer at his myrrh-soaked curls and call his far-fetched phrases and
ideas 'stinks.'[9] He loved a correct and elegant diction which would express

* * * * *

155  (xxiii) Macrobius *Saturnalia* 2.4.11. In margin 'cruelty'
  1 This refers to the 'massacre of the innocents' ordered by Herod as ruler of
     Judaea. See Matt 2:16–18. The form of the joke resembles Diogenes' jibe (3.224
     above) that he would rather be a Megarian's sheep than his child.

156  (xxiv) Macrobius *Saturnalia* 2.4.12
  1 Erasmus has added this from Macrobius *Saturnalia* 1.5.2, but he has misre-
     membered; it was said by Julius Caesar.
  2 Augustus' minister, the Etruscan nobleman Maecenas, was notorious for his
     effeminate lifestyle, and a famous letter of the younger Seneca (114) attributes
     his degenerate literary style, parodied in this intimate letter from Augustus
     (which Erasmus knew from Macrobius), to his way of life.
  3 The joke here is that these places in Etruria did not produce these precious
     substances.
  4 The Cilnei were Maecenas' Etruscan clan.
  5 Arezzo (Arretium, in Etruria) was famous for its red-glazed pottery.
  6 Porsenna: the king of Clusium in Etruria who attacked Rome to restore the
     exiled Tarquinic Superbus
  7 Macrobius' text is corrupt here: *carbuculum habeas Italiae*, possibly 'my jewel of
     Italy' or 'my jewel of the Adriatic.'
  8 *Malagma*, or with a variant reading *allagma*, 'my reward of adulteresses.'
  9 Suetonius *Augustus* 86.1

his meaning as clearly as possible. Nor did he spare Tiberius, who sometimes hunted out obscure and obsolete words. He used to abuse Antony for writing for admiration rather than comprehension. Indeed when he praised the intellect of his granddaughter Agrippina, he added, 'But you must take care not to speak tiresomely.'[10]

**157** After occupying Alexandria he spared many for the sake of the philosopher Arius, but he cast off Sostratus, a man of very ready tongue who offended the emperor by wanting to be thought an Academic philosopher without good cause. Then the man began to follow Arius around in mourning and with untrimmed white beard wherever he went uttering this verse: 'Wise men save the wise if they are truly wise,'[1] and by this subterfuge compelled Caesar to pardon him.

**158** When Augustus was already over forty and was in Gaul, he was informed that L. Cinna, a young noble and Pompey's grandson, was plotting against him; the information included when, how, and where they would make the attempt, for they planned to assassinate him while sacrificing. Augustus was already composing the decree of outlawry, but as he expressed out loud now this emotion, now that, Livia came in and said, 'Do what the doctors do: when the usual medicines don't work, they try the opposite. You have gained nothing by severity so far – pardon him instead. Now he has been caught Cinna cannot harm your life, only enhance your reputation.' So he had Cinna brought in alone for interview and when he came in had a chair set for him. 'My first request from you, Cinna,' he said, 'is that you don't interrupt me as I speak; you will have a time to talk yourself.' Then after mentioning his many kindnesses to Cinna – he had saved him when he was found in the enemy camp, he had granted him all his paternal inheritance, he had awarded him a priesthood – Augustus asked why Cinna thought he

* * * * *

10 Augustus was a fastidious but plain stylist. Suetonius (*Augustus* 86.2) reports his criticisms of Tiberius and his enemy Mark Antony, and quotes (86.3) this private letter advising his granddaughter Agrippina to write without affectation. She was the daughter of Augustus' daughter Julia.

157 (xxv) Plutarch *Life of Antony* 80. For Arius see 6.134 above. In margin 'pardon extorted'
  1 Erasmus added a translation of the (unidentified) Greek tragic verse (Nauck *adespota* fr 422: Σόφοι σοφοὺς σώζουσιν, ἂν ὦσιν σόφοι) only in 1532.

158 (xxvi) Seneca *De clementia* 1.9.1–9, abbreviated

should be killed. Cinna was distressed, but Augustus finished his rebuke:
'I am giving you your life for a second time, Cinna, first when you were
my enemy and now when you are an assassin and parricide. Let friendship
between us start today, and let us compete to see whether I show better faith
in giving you your life, or you in owing it to me.' Then he offered him the
consulship.

Do you want to hear the end of the story? He found Cinna a devoted
friend all his life, and was made his sole heir, nor was he ever again the
object of any murderous attempt by anybody.

159 It was Augustus' practice never to refuse an invitation to dinner. So when
he had been entertained by somebody with a very meagre dinner, almost
everyday food, and was saying goodbye, he whispered in his ear just this:
'I didn't think I was such a close friend.'

Another man would have treated such scanty hospitality as an insult,
but he avoided embarrassing his host as well, taking it as intimacy, and that
in his ear, so that the others would not think Augustus had found fault with
his miserliness. What could be more worthy of love than such courtesy in
a monarch, whom scarcely thirty of our present kings put together could
match?

160 He was going to buy some Tyrian purple cloth, but was critical of its dullness; however, when the seller said, 'Hold it higher and look up at it,' he
retorted, 'So do I have to walk in the gallery so that the Roman people will
call me well dressed?'

161 Augustus had an aide (*nomenclator*) who was very forgetful, although men
in this position ought to have an exceptional memory. When he was going
to the Forum he asked Augustus whether he had any instructions. Augustus said, 'Take a letter of recommendation with you, since you don't know
anyone there!'[1]

* * * * *

159 (xxvii) Macrobius *Saturnalia* 2.4.13. In margin 'courteous'

160 (xxviii) Macrobius *Saturnalia* 2.4.14. In margin 'witty'

161 (xxix) Macrobius *Saturnalia* 2.4.15. In margin 'a forgetful name-prompter'
   1 This story plays on two Roman customs; that public men employed a 'name-
      sayer' who stood at their shoulder and whispered the names of those ap-
      proaching, and that the same kind of powerful man would issue letters of
      recommendation to inferiors travelling abroad where they were not known.

Now the special function of name-prompters is to know the names and family names and rank and office of everybody, so as to prompt their masters when needed. This is the source of their title, compounded of Greek and Latin.[2]

162 Even as a young man Augustus scored brilliantly off Vatinius; for Vatinius was liable to gout but wanted to seem cured of the ailment, and was boasting that he could now walk a mile. 'I am not surprised,' said Augustus, 'for the days are getting quite a bit longer,' meaning that Vatinius was no more free from gout than before but the days were getting longer.[1]

163 When a Roman knight died it was discovered that he was so deeply in debt that he owed more than twenty million sesterces, a fact which he had concealed in his lifetime. So when his property was auctioned to pay off his creditors, Augustus ordered men to buy his bed-pillow, and when everyone expressed surprise he added, 'I need that pillow to help me sleep, if he could enjoy sleep on it despite his enormous debt.'

In fact Augustus, because of his immense responsibilities, often spent part of the night unable to sleep.[1]

164 Once he came to the house where Cato of Utica had lived, and when Strabo in order to flatter Augustus condemned Cato's obstinacy, blaming him for preferring suicide to acknowledging Julius Caesar's victory, Augustus said, 'Whoever does not want the current constitution of the state to change is a good man and a good citizen.'[1]

\* \* \* \* \*

2 Erasmus derives the word *nomenclator* from Latin *nomen* 'name' and Greek *kalein* 'to call.' It is actually derived from the archaic Latin verb *calare* 'to proclaim.'

162 (xxx) Macrobius *Saturnalia* 2.4.16. In margin 'witty'
    1 The story of the ailing Vatinius' boast is told again at 4.323 below) where he claims to have walked two miles, not one, and the jibe is attributed to Cicero.

163 (xxxi) Macrobius *Saturnalia* 2.4.17. In margin 'pillow of the man in debt'
    1 See Suetonius *Augustus* 78.1–2.

164 (xxxii) Macrobius *Saturnalia* 2.4.18. In margin 'weighty'
    1 Cato 'of Utica' was a doctrinaire Stoic and fierce republican. He acted as the moral leader of the republican resistance to Julius Caesar, both during the decade from 59 BC and in the African campaigns after the defeat and death of Pompey in 48 BC. When the remnants of the republican army were defeated at

With this one comment he protected Cato's memory and his own position, discouraging any future attempt at revolution. For the current constitution does not just mean the one in force when Augustus spoke but also the constitution at the time of Julius Caesar's assassination.[2] That is, *praesens* in Latin relates to all three tenses, past, present, and future, as in, 'He was not content with the current circumstances,' or 'current life' meaning that being lived now, or 'Let him drop it till the current time' meaning 'the appropriate time in the future.'[3]

**165** Just as Augustus liked to make gentlemanly jokes against others, so he took in good part the jokes and retorts made against himself, sometimes rather too freely. A young man from the provinces once came to Rome so closely resembling Augustus that he attracted everyone's attention. Caesar Augustus heard this and had him brought for interview, gazed at him, and then asked, 'Tell me, young man, was your mother ever in Rome?' He answered 'No,' and getting the point of the joke, retorted 'but my father was often here.'

Augustus had jestingly cast suspicion on the young man's mother, as if she had been seduced by him, but the young man immediately cast it back on the emperor's mother or sister. For the facial resemblance could equally well make him out to be Augustus' brother or nephew as his son.[1]

\* \* \* \* \*

Thapsus (in modern Tunisia) in 46 BC, Cato, who commanded the garrison at Utica, secured the safe conduct of those under his charge but famously took his own life rather than surrender to Caesar. Under the principate of Augustus and after, he was remembered as a martyr of the resistance to autocracy. This is one of a number of ancient stories designed to show Augustus' respect for the republic and its supporters (cf 5.383–99 for sayings of the younger Cato).
2 For the current constitution ... assassination: added in 1532.
3 That is, ... in the future: added in 1535. The last example is from Horace *Ars Poetica* 44.

165 (XXXIII) Macrobius *Saturnalia* 2.4.19–20. In margin 'joking retort to the princeps'
1 Augustus' parents were Gaius Octavius and Atia, Julius Caesar's niece, daughter of Caesar's sister. (Augustus was Caesar's 'son' only by adoption, and in his early career was afraid of any rival like Cleopatra's son Caesarion, claiming to be the actual child of Caesar.) The story is better left without Erasmus' obfuscating 'explanation.' The anecdote implies that Augustus and the young man are step-brothers because they have the same father, either Augustus' father or the young man's. Either way one of the mothers is insulted. The young man coolly throws Augustus' implied insult to his mother back at Augustus'

**166** In the triumviral period[1] when Octavius, Lepidus, and Antony shared power, Augustus wrote Fescennine abusive verse[2] against Pollio as a joke. Then Pollio commented, 'I am keeping quiet, for it is not easy to write (*scribere*) against a man who can write you off (*proscribere*).'

This was how he commented on Augustus' tyrannical power. But Augustus was not offended by his frankness.

**167** A Roman knight called Curtius, who wallowed in luxury, was dining with Augustus and lifted a skinny thrush from his plate asking the emperor whether he might send it out, and when Augustus said, 'Of course,' immediately threw the thrush through the window.

He was making a joke of the word's ambiguity. For food from a dinner was sent out as a gift for friends, a Roman custom, but is also sent out when it is thrown away. And Augustus was not offended by this joke either.

**168** He also paid off unasked the debts of a senator of whom he was fond, disbursing 4,000,000 sesterces on his behalf. When the senator found out, instead of thanking the emperor, he merely wrote 'Nothing for me.'

He was jokingly protesting because Augustus had given money to all his creditors but none to him. A more ill-tempered person would have

\* \* \* \* \*

mother. Macrobius calls the retort 'a cruel jibe.' Cf 6.275 below.

Erasmus seems to reject any suggestion that Augustus himself might be the young man's father although Augustus was well-known to be a serial adulterer and rapist; see Suetonius *Life of Augustus* 68–9.

**166** (xxxiv) Macrobius *Saturnalia* 2.4.21. In margin 'outspoken'
   1 During the triumviral period of 43–33 BC (the so-called Second Triumvirate) Asinius Pollio had been an ally of Mark Antony, but withdrew from politics when Octavian broke with Antony. (Octavius, Octavian, and [Caesar] Augustus are successive names of the emperor Augustus.) He was older than Octavian and his seniority enabled him to remain politically neutral throughout the rest of his life. Compare 4.191 below on his hospitality to the dissident historian Timagenes.
   2 Fescennine verses were an ancient Italian form improvised at triumphs or weddings. Our only examples are in eight-foot trochees (from Caesar's triumph): they often led to an exchange of versified abuse similar to the hexameters of Virgil *Eclogues* 3.

**167** (xxxv) Macrobius *Saturnalia* 2.4.22. In margin 'uninhibited'

**168** (xxxvi) Macrobius *Saturnalia* 2.4.23. In margin 'ingratitude'

treated this joke as ingratitude, but the emperor was delighted by his confidence in their friendship.

**169** Augustus' freedman Licinus[1] used to contribute generous sums to his patron when he started on a new building scheme. So when Augustus was
about to begin a new building Licinus promised him 10,000,000 in writing. There was a gap left after the amount, which was indicated with a superscript symbol.[2] The emperor exploited this opportunity to add another
10,000,000 to the sum which the freedman had written, carefully filling in
the empty space himself and making sure the letters looked the same. So he
received double the amount, and the freedman kept it quiet. But the next
time Augustus began a new public work, the freedman gently drew his attention to this, with the following message, 'Master, I am contributing for
your new work whatever amount you wish.'

He did not name the amount, so that Augustus was free to write what
he wished, since he had doubled the previous offer.

**170** When Augustus was exercising the task of censor, a Roman knight was
reported to him as having reduced his property. But when he was inter-
viewed he proved he had increased it. Then he was accused of not marrying, although the law bade him do so. He then stated that he had a wife
and was father of three children.[1] But the knight was not content merely to

\* \* \* \* \*

**169** (xxxvii) Macrobius *Saturnalia* 2.4.24. In margin 'witty protest'
  1 This was the freedman Licinus, a Gaul whom Julius Caesar had made his stew-
    ard. Augustus made him governor of Gaul, in which office he acquired a vast
    fortune by plundering his fellow-countrymen. He escaped punishment by con-
    tributing to Augustus' building projects. Like Crassus, his name was synony-
    mous with wealth. After Caesar's death, he seems to have viewed Augustus
    as his patron (a title given by a freedman to a former master).
  2 Macrobius says the superscript line, which indicated hundred thousands, had
    already been extended over the space, presumably accidentally. Augustus put
    figures in the space.

**170** (xxxviii) Macrobius *Saturnalia* 2.4.25. The next two anecdotes (4.171–2) also
    demonstrate Augustus' tolerance of opposition in small matters, but in both
    cases from soldiers, who were to some extent privileged. In margin 'frank
    speech based on innocence'
  1 Augustus introduced legislation in 18 BC and AD 9 which, among other things,
    required all men between 25 and 60 to take wives and beget children, and
    penalizing those who did not conform. This was mainly aimed at the wealthy
    knights and upper classes. The begetting of three children brought certain

be let off; he added as a reproach to the emperor's credulity, 'From now on, Caesar, trust respectable sources when you are investigating respectable men.'[2]

He made it quite clear that men who had told Augustus blatant lies were not decent men, and incidentally charged Augustus with entrusting his own responsibility to false informers. And Caesar forgave this frankness too in view of his innocence.

171 Augustus' nights in a certain country house were disturbed because the cries of an owl spoilt his sleep. A soldier skilled in fowling undertook to catch the owl and brought it to Augustus hoping for a huge reward. Augustus thanked him and ordered him to be given only a thousand sesterces. The soldier had the nerve to say, 'Then let it live' and released the owl. Who would not be amazed that the soldier got away with such insolence?

172 When a veteran was threatened by a lawsuit, he openly went to Augustus and asked him to support him. The emperor immediately assigned a member of his staff and recommended the litigator to him. Then the soldier shouted out, 'But when you were threatened in the Actium campaign I did not look for a deputy, but fought for you in person,' and laid bare the scars of his wounds. Augustus blushed and came in person to support him in the suit, fearing to seem not only proud but ungrateful.[1]

173 At dinner he had enjoyed the chorus of the slave-dealer Turonius Flaccus, and gave them a gift of grain, although he usually gave others he listened to

\* \* \* \* \*

rewards. (There was comparable legislation for women.) The legislation was not popular. See 4.142 n1 above.
2 It was the censor's task to examine the finances and moral record of each member of the senatorial or equestrian élite. Knights were required to own a specific amount of property. Augustus declined the title of censor, but exercised the censor's function of scrutiny more than once.

171 (XXXIX) Macrobius *Saturnalia* 2.4.26. In margin 'emperor's clemency'

172 (XL) Macrobius *Saturnalia* 2.4.27. In margin 'emperor's gratitude'
1 The battle of Actium, 31 BC, brought the final defeat of Antony and the end of the Second Civil War.

173 (XLI) Macrobius *Saturnalia* 2.4.28

large sums of money. When Augustus asked for them to perform again at dinner, Turonius excused them by saying, 'They are busy grinding away.'[1]

This is how the man reproached him with the gift of grain. And he got away with this too, though it was a slave-dealer, not a soldier who said it.

174 When Augustus was returning exalted by the victory at Actium, a man appeared among those congratulating him with a crow which had been taught to say, 'Hail victorious Caesar!' Augustus was delighted by the greeting and bought the bird for 6000 sesterces. But the partner of the trainer, who had received no share in the gift, told the emperor that the man had another crow, and asked that he be forced to bring it. When it was brought in it said the words it had learnt, 'Hail Antony, victorious general!' Augustus was not at all angry, but ordered the gift to be shared with the informer.[1]

175 When he had the same greeting from a parrot he ordered its purchase: and impressed by the same trick in a jackdaw, he bought that too. This encouraged a poor tailor to train a crow to make this kind of greeting. But after he ran out of money, he often used to say to the bird when it didn't reply: 'I've wasted my effort and my money.' Finally by persistence he succeeded in making the crow repeat the greeting as rehearsed. But when it greeted Augustus as he passed, he said, 'I have enough greetings like that at home.' Then the crow, remembering the other words it had heard so often said, 'I've wasted my effort and my money.' Augustus laughed and ordered the bird to be bought at a higher price than any of the previous birds.[1]

176 Some poor Greek or other adopted this method of trying to win over Augustus: whenever Augustus left the Palatine he would offer him an epigram in his honour. But when he had often done this in vain and Augustus saw he

* * * * *

1 The point of the joke is that the musicians would have to grind their gift of grain before they could use it, but that grinding grain was itself a punishment for offending slaves.

174 (XLII) Macrobius *Saturnalia* 2.4.29. In margin 'leniency'
1 The word 'informer' in 1532 and 1535 replaces 'partner' in the first edition.

175 (XLIII) Macrobius *Saturnalia* 2.4.30. In margin 'ingenious'
1 Erasmus has already told this story in *Adagia* I iv 62 *Oleum et operam perdidi* 'I have wasted both oil and toil.'

176 (XLIV) Macrobius *Saturnalia* 2.4.31. In margin 'forced generosity'

would not give up, he copied out a neat Greek epigram in his own hand and sent it to the Greek as he came to meet him, as if paying for poems with poems. The Greek took it and read it and not only praised the poem in words but expressed admiration and wonder by his voice and expression and gestures. Then he approached the litter in which the emperor was riding, put his hand in his poor wallet and fetched out a few coins which he gave to Augustus with these words: 'This is not appropriate to your fortune, Caesar, but if I had more I would give it.' When everyone laughed, Augustus called his steward and ordered him to pay out 100,000 sesterces to the Greek.[1]

The Greek did well by openly criticizing the emperor's miserliness.

**177** Julia Augusta once greeted her father and noticed he was offended by her provocative dress, although he kept quiet about it. So the next day she changed her costume before embracing her father. Then Augustus, who had concealed his discontent the previous day, could not suppress his delight. 'How much more that costume suits the emperor's daughter!' he said. Then Julia replied, 'Of course: today I dressed for my father's eyes, yesterday for my husband's.'

**178** Livia[1] and Julia attracted everyone's attention at a gladiatorial show because of the difference in their entourage. Livia was surrounded by dignified older men, Julia accompanied by rakish young men. When her father Augustus warned Julia in a letter to take notice of the difference between the two imperial ladies, she wrote back, 'But these will grow old along with me.'

If you take this favourably it is witty, but if you take it ill, it could seem a wanton remark.

**179** Julia also began to get grey hairs early, and Augustus coming unannounced caught the hairdressers plucking out his daughter's grey hair, for one could

* * * * *

1 Being Greek he spoke in Greek, which Erasmus both quotes and translates.

**177** (XLV) Macrobius *Saturnalia* 2.5.5. The first of Macrobius' set of stories about Augustus' father-daughter relationship. Julia was Augustus' only daughter by his first wife, Scribonia. See 4.92 n1 above. In margin 'clever'

**178** (XLVI) Macrobius *Saturnalia* 2.5.6. In margin 'chosen companions reveal the mistress's character'
   1 Livia, Augustus' last wife (from 39 or early 38 BC until his death in AD 14) was Julia's stepmother.

**179** (XLVII) Macrobius *Saturnalia* 2.5.7. In margin 'deliberate baldness'

see the hairs they had pulled out on their clothing. Augustus made no comment, but after and passing the time with other topics finally brought up the question of age. He took the chance to say, 'In a few years would you rather be grey-haired or bald?' And when she replied, 'I'd rather be grey, father,' he asked, 'Then why are they working to make you prematurely bald?'

He proved her a liar by his witty retort.

180 When a serious friend urged Julia to model herself on her father's thrift, Julia said saucily, 'He forgets that he is emperor, but I remember I am the emperor's daughter.'

181 Two mime-artists[1] were competing turn and turn about with their miming representations. Augustus said one was leaping about, the other was leaping in.[2]

He meant that one mimed too energetically, while the other did not seem to be miming, but to be obstructing the dancer.

182 When the people of Tarraco[1] announced as a joyous omen that a palm tree had sprung up on his altar, he said, 'It's obvious how often you light a fire on it!'

They wanted to credit this to the gods, but he credited it to their negligence, because they never burned incense on Caesar's altar.

183 When the Gauls presented Augustus with a gold torque[1] of a hundred pounds weight, Dolabella,[2] teasing him, finally carried his jest so far as to

* * * * *

180 (XLVIII) Macrobius *Saturnalia* 2.5.8

181 (XLIX) Quintilian 6.3.65; a run of extracts from Quintilian 6.3 follows.
 1 The mime was a simple dramatic piece performed in mime to the accompaniment of words and music. See 8.192 below.
 2 The joke is contained in the two rhyming words in Latin: *saltator* 'dancer, leaper,' *interpellator* 'interrupter'; ie neither of them was truly miming. See 4.199 n1 below. Augustus seem to have been a connoisseur of the mime.

182 (L) Quintilian 6.3.77. In margin 'flattery rejected'
 1 The people of Tarraco (Tarragona) in Spain were among the first to request the right to have a temple of Augustus.

183 (LI) Quintilian 6.3.79
 1 The *torque*, a neck ornament of twisted metal, was a reward for valour.
 2 This may be the Publius Cornelius Dolabella mentioned as Augustus' companion in Plutarch *Antony* 84.1.

say, 'Commander, present me with a torque' and Augustus said, 'I'd rather give you the civic crown.'[3]

This was a witty way of repelling his shameless demand, for Dolabella had never served in a war, and so the civic crown was all the more fitting. This was usually made of oak and ilex leaves, as the triumphal crown is made of gold. Though the other crowns, for being first to enter the enemy camp, or being first to storm a wall, or for being first to board an enemy ship, are also made of gold. See on this Aulus Gellius book 5 chapter 6.[4] But Augustus offered him the civic crown, which was more prestigious, as a joke. For Suetonius[5] notes that Augustus was more inclined to give medals and torques and anything of gold or silver among military honours, than the crowns for mounting a rampart or a wall, which were superior in honour. If you do not know this, you miss the point of Augustus' joke. (Though Suetonius disagrees with Gellius about the material of these crowns.)

184 When he had beautified and reinforced the city of Rome in many ways, and made it secure for the future as far as he was able, he used to say, in justifiable pride, 'I found Rome a city of brick and leave it a city of marble.'

Nothing is more glorious for a prince than to improve the territory he has received.

185 A soldier was shamelessly asking a favour from Augustus. He saw Martianus approaching, whom he suspected of also being about to make an importunate request, so Augustus said, 'My fellow soldier, I am no more going to grant your request than what Martianus is about to ask me.'

186 There was a law that a man who killed his father should be sewn in a sack, but this penalty was only imposed on one who admitted it. To free a man

* * * * *

3 The 'civic crown' or 'crown of gallantry' was awarded by a citizen to another citizen for saving his life in battle, and being made of twigs, cost nothing. Augustus had been awarded it by the Senate as the saviour of Rome.
4 Aulus Gellius 5.6
5 Suetonius *Augustus* 25.3

184 (LII) Suetonius *Augustus* 28.3. Erasmus now draws on Suetonius for 4.184–99 (except for 4.185, 4.191, 4.192). In margin 'a prince's duty to beautify his realm'

185 (LIII) Quintilian 6.3.95

186 (LIV) Suetonius *Augustus* 33.1. In margin 'leniency'

guilty of obvious parricide from this cruel penalty, Augustus asked 'Of
course you didn't kill your father?'[1]

He thus offered the man a way of denying it. Such was the emperor's
leniency when trying cases.

**187** He used to say that nothing was less suited to a perfect commander than
haste and rashness, and often uttered the famous, 'Make haste slowly, for a
safe general is better than a bold one.'[1]

But we have said enough on this in our *Adages*. [2]

**188** When his wife Livia was asking the citizenship for a certain Gaul, he refused but offered him exemption from tax, saying that he would more easily
allow a loss to his treasury[1] than the cheapening of the honour of citizenship.

Of course he preferred the good of the state to his private advantage.

**189** When he was making a public speech and saw many in working clothes or
'Greek clothes' (which I think is the proper reading),[1] he was indignant and
cried out 'Lo, here the Roman people, lords of the world, the togaed race!'[2]

He was so keen to restore old ways of life that he even regretted the
change in dress and costume.

\* \* \* \* \*

1 For more on this penalty see *Adagia* IV ix 18: *Culleo dignus, aut, Non uno culleo
dignus* 'Fit for the sack, or One sack is not enough.' Cf also 6.44 below.

**187** (LV) Suetonius *Augustus* 25.4. In margin 'make haste slowly'
1 Augustus' famous words were in Greek, which Erasmus quotes without translating: Σπεῦδε βραδέως / Ἀσφαλὴς γάρ ἐστ' ἀμείνων ἢ θρασὺς στρατηλάτης.
2 See *Adagia* II i 1: *Festina lente* 'Make haste slowly.' There Erasmus recognized
the quotation as a line of verse, but did not recall its source: Euripides *Phoenissae* 599. The first two words are not part of the quotation but were one of
Augustus' favourite sayings.

**188** (LVI) Suetonius *Augustus* 40.3. In margin 'status cheapened if shared with
many'
1 Roman citizens were exempt from certain forms of taxation levied on inhabitants of provinces.

**189** (LVII) Suetonius *Augustus* 40.5. In margin 'dress'
1 Erasmus is proposing to change *pullati* 'in dark work clothes,' which he read
in his text, into *palliati* 'clad in the Greek *pallium*,' though he does not propose
this in his edition of Suetonius. Both forms of dress would be seen as incor-
rect as opposed to the formal toga, which was heavy and inconvenient and
increasingly neglected. It was supposed to be worn at formal gatherings.
2 Jupiter's proud title for the Romans, Virgil *Aeneid* 1.282

190 When the people were complaining of the shortage and high price of wine, he said sufficient measures had been taken to spare men from thirst when his son in law Agrippa had extended several aqueducts.[1]

For Agrippa had a scrupulous concern to keep the city supplied with water. So Augustus austerely bade the people turn from wine to water.

191 Timagenes the historian had made many wanton accusations against Augustus, his wife, and his whole family, so the emperor advised him to use his tongue with more restraint. When he persisted in his abuse, Augustus simply refused the man access to his home. But Timagenes gave recitations of the books in which he reported Augustus' achievements and then burnt them out of hatred for him, as if wanting to destroy the memory of his achievements. But although he was openly and persistently conducting a feud with the emperor no Roman citizen closed his doors to him, and he grew old in Pollio's household. Yet Augustus never protested to Pollio, his enemy's host, except that he once said in Greek *Thēriotrofeis*, that is, 'You are feeding a wild animal (or a viper).' Then when Pollio began to make excuses, Augustus cut in saying, 'Enjoy him, Pollio, enjoy him.' But when Pollio, still anxious, said, 'If you bid me, Caesar, I will forbid him my house.' Augustus said, 'Do you think I would do that, when I was responsible for reconciling you two?' For Pollio had been angry with Timagenes, and had no other reason for stopping being angry with Timagenes except that Augustus had started.

The prince's leniency took in good part the ill will of both men.

192 Augustus was dining with Atedius or Vedius Pollio, and when one of the slaves broke a crystal vase the order was given by Atedius for him to be seized and thrown to the lampreys. The slave took refuge at the emperor's feet with no other request than that he should die some other way. Moved

\* \* \* \* \*

190 (LVIII) Suetonius *Augustus* 42.1. In margin 'frugal'
  1 Agrippa had restored the existing Roman aqueducts as aedile in 33 BC and added two more, bringing abundant water for baths, fountains, and cisterns.

191 (LXIX) The elder Seneca *Controversiae* 10.5.22 speaks of Timagenes as a dissident Greek historian, repudiated by Augustus and given a home by the elder statesman Asinius Pollio (cf 4.166 above). But the rest of Erasmus' story follows closely the narrative of the younger Seneca *De ira* 3.23.3–5. In margin 'admirable leniency'

192 (LX) Seneca *De ira* 3.40.1–3. Vedius Pollio was one of the wealthiest knights at the time, and an ex-slave himself. In margin 'cruelty censured'

by this unprecedented form of cruelty, Augustus ordered the slave to be let go and all the crystal vases to be broken in front of him, and the fish-pond to be filled with these instead of the slave. Then he rebuked his friend severely: 'Do you order men to be executed and torn apart by a new kind of punishment at a dinner party? If your cup is broken, shall a man's entrails be ripped open? Are you so pleased with yourself that you order a man to be executed in front of the emperor?'

**193** Once in a trial Aemilius Aelianus of Corduba was accused of many charges but especially of speaking ill of Augustus.[1] The emperor turned to the accuser and said, 'Prove it to me. I want Aelianus to know I too have a sharp tongue, and will say worse things about him in return.' Making these threats was enough for him and he made no further investigation of Aelianus.

**194** When Tiberius often complained irritably by letter about those who spoke ill of Augustus he wrote back telling him not to indulge his youth too much in this matter. 'It is enough,' he said, 'if we have a situation such that no man can do us ill.'

**195** He never recommended his sons[1] to the people except with this proviso: 'if they deserve it,' since he wanted honour paid not to his authority but to their merits.

**196** He had sent into exile the two Julias, his daughter and grand-daughter, and later his grandson Agrippa as well, whom he had first adopted then disowned because of his mean and intractable nature.[1] When any of these

\* \* \* \* \*

**193** (LXI) Suetonius *Augustus* 51.2. In margin 'mildness'
  1 This man is otherwise unknown.

**194** (LXII) Suetonius *Augustus* 51.3

**195** (LXIII) Suetonius *Augustus* 56.2. In margin 'modesty'
  1 The traditional practice of leading men 'commending' candidates for office had become more like an automatic command with Julius Caesar's dictatorship. These were Augustus' adopted sons, Gaius and Lucius, sons of his daughter Iulia.

**196** (LXIV) Suetonius *Augustus* 65.4. In margin 'bad children'
  1 Augustus himself was author, through his official denunciation to the Senate, of the general accusations of adultery against his daughter Julia, summarily exiled in 2 BC, and her daughter Julia the younger, exiled in AD 8. Julia's

were mentioned he used to say in the words of Homer 'Would that I had lived unmarried and died childless.'[2] He always called them his three abscesses or cancers.

For he bore the deaths of his children better than their disgrace. Indeed in his will he laid down that if anything befell his daughter Julia and his grandchild, they should not be buried in his tomb.

197 Augustus resented anything being composed about him except in serious vein and by the best writers, and he urged the magistrates not to allow his name to be cheapened in the sketches of mimes and dancers, imitating Alexander the Great in this respect.[1] It is right that the prince's prestige be kept 'windproof and watertight' in all circumstances.[2]

198 There was an island near Capri where his court used to retreat in search of recreation, and he called it *Apragopolis* 'Sans-Souci,' because *apragia* in Greek means 'freedom from business.' [1]

199 When he felt death coming on he called his friends in and asked them whether he seemed to them to have acted the mime of life nicely, meaning that the drama of his life was over, and then he uttered the usual envoi at the end of a comedy: *Dote kroton, kai pantes hēmeis meta charās ktupēsate.*[1]

\* \* \* \* \*

youngest son Agrippa Postumus was first exiled in AD 7 then murdered in AD 14 either by Augustus' orders or by the decision of Tiberius.
2 αἰθ' ὄφελον ἄγαμος τε μένειν, ἄγονος τ'ἀπολέσθαι. Augustus changed the verb in the Homeric verse (*Iliad* 3.40), where Hector reproaches Paris, declaring that '*you* (Paris the adulterer of Helen) should have remained unwed.'

197 (LXV) Suetonius *Augustus* 89.3. In margin 'majesty of the name'
1 See 4.70 above.
2 *Adagia* IV v 37: *Sarta teeta* 'Wind-proof and water tight,' a legal term

198 (LXVI) Suetonius *Augustus* 98.4. In margin 'leisure'
1 Suetonius reports that Augustus took recreation in the coastal resorts of Campania or its islands, mentioning Capri in chapters 72 and 92. His son Tiberius would move to Capri for the last eleven years of his reign as Emperor.

199 (LXVII) Suetonius *Augustus* 99.1
1 Although Augustus did not allow allusions to himself in mimes, he loved to watch them according to Suetonius, and on his deathbed treated his own life as a mime. See 4.181 above. The text of the Greek line appears to be corrupt. Erasmus did not translate it. The general sense is: 'Grant your applause and all

## C. Julius Caesar

**200** When Julius Caesar was fleeing from Sulla as a young man he was taken by Cilician pirates, and when they told him the amount they wanted from him for his ransom, he laughed at the pirates for not knowing whom they had taken and promised them double. Then when he was being kept under guard until the money arrived, he ordered them to keep quiet and not disturb his sleep. He used to recite to them the speeches and poems he composed, and when they did not admire them enough he called them stupid barbarians, and threatened with a laugh to crucify them, as he actually did. For when the money which the pirates had agreed for his release was delivered and he was set free, he hired men and ships in Asia and seized the pirates and nailed them up, but after he had cut their throats,[1] so that his severity should not lack mercy.

Wouldn't you recognize in this the spirit of Alexander the Great, for whom nothing moderate was enough?

**201** He was a candidate for the office of Chief Priest at Rome, and his competitor was Quintus Catulus, a man of the highest rank and power among the Romans. So when Caesar's mother escorted him to the door, he said, 'Today, mother, your son will either be Chief Priest or an exile.'[1]

He had a lofty nature, intolerant of any defeat.

\* \* \* \* \*

beat your hands together with delight.' This is the reading Erasmus adopted in his edition of Suetonius.

**200** (I) Plutarch *Moralia* 205F–206A. Erasmus follows Plutarch *Sayings of the Romans* for 4.200–14 beginning with an anecdote from Julius Caesar's youth. In margin 'a lofty spirit'
The date of this escapade is probably c. 75 BC, when Julius Caesar was about 25 years old. He had incurred the enmity of the dictator Sulla initially by his connection in marriage with Sulla's defeated opponent Gaius Marius, though his life was spared. After failing to make his mark in Roman politics after Sulla's death in 79 BC, he retreated to Asia (ie modern Turkey), ostensibly to study oratory (Suetonius *Julius Caesar* 4.1–2). Cilicia (in southern Turkey) was a notorious hide-out for pirates.
1 This detail added from Suetonius *Julius Caesar* 74.1.

**201** (II) Plutarch *Moralia* 206A. In margin 'self-confidence'
1 This anecdote belongs to 63 or 62 BC. According to Suetonius *Julius Caesar* 13.2 Caesar's debts incurred in bribing the voters (to elect him rather than the obvious candidate) would have forced him into exile, presumably as a bankrupt.

202 He divorced his wife Pompeia because her reputation was damaged by allegations that she had had an affair with Clodius. But when Clodius was prosecuted on these grounds, and Julius Caesar was called as witness he said nothing against his wife. Then when the accuser asked, 'So why did you divorce her?' he replied, 'Because Caesar's wife must be clear even of suspicion.'

Besides the neatness of his reply one must praise its courtesy in sparing the reputation of his divorced wife.

203 When Caesar read the deeds of Alexander the Great he could not hold back his tears and said to his friends, 'At my age now Alexander had defeated Darius, whereas I have done no glorious deed up to this day.'

Suetonius says this happened when he went on assizes as Praetor and saw a statue of Alexander the Great in the temple of Hercules at Gades.[1] If only his temperament had driven him to emulate a moderate rather than a great prince!

204 When he was passing some chilly little town in the Alps[1] and his friends were discussing whether even this place had political troubles and competition for leadership, he paused and thought for a while. 'I would rather be first man here,' he said 'than second in Rome.' This is what the poet Lucan says, that neither could Caesar endure a superior nor Pompey an equal.[2]

*  *  *  *  *

202 (III) Plutarch *Moralia* 206A. In margin 'courteous'
On Caesar's divorce see Suetonius *Julius Caesar* 6.2. Pompeia, granddaughter of Sulla, was Caesar's second wife. The notorious Appius Claudius Pulcher (see 6.208 n1 below) had infiltrated Caesar's official residence as Chief Priest disguised as a woman during the rites of the Good Goddess, restricted to women (see Plutarch *Life of Caesar* 10).

203 (IV) Plutarch *Moralia* 206B. In margin 'ambition'
1 Suetonius *Julius Caesar* 7.1. Caesar was quaestor in Spain in 69–8 BC. He served as praetorian governor of Spain in 62–1 BC, but the earlier date fits better as Caesar was then 31. As the governor's deputy he visited the four main cities of southern Spain to hear Assizes. Gades (Cadiz) had Greeks among its population and this may account for the statue of Alexander so far from the scenes of his exploits.
For Darius III see 4.47 above.

204 (v) Plutarch *Moralia* 206B. In margin 'love of the chief position'
1 Caesar's position as governor of both Northern Italy and Transalpine Gaul (Provence) required him to cross the Alps at the beginning and end of each season.
2 Lucan *Bellum civile* 1.125–6.

**205** He said of actions that are great but dangerous, that 'one should do them and not hesitate about them,' because speed is of the most importance in achieving them. For the weighing up of danger deters a man from boldness.

**206** When he was marching from his province of Gaul against Pompey he crossed the river Rubicon and said, 'Let every die be cast' meaning that he was prepared to risk everything. This is the river dividing Gaul from Italy.[1]

**207** When Pompey had left Rome and was in retreat to the sea, Caesar wanted to take the money in the treasury, but Metellus, the supervisor, resisted and closed it. Then Caesar threatened him with death. When this silenced Metellus with the shock, Caesar said, 'Young man, it was harder for me to say this than it will be to do it.' He meant that he could kill whom he chose with a nod, since he had armed cohorts with him.[1]

**208** Caesar was waiting at Dyrrhachium for soldiers to be sent from Brundisium,[1] and when this was too slow in happening, he took a small boat, unknown to everyone, and tried to cross the sea. But when the boat was sinking in the waves and the helmsman was despairing, he revealed his identity saying, 'Trust in fortune, and know that you are carrying Caesar.'

Such was his presence of mind, as if he had fortune and the gods in his control. But on that occasion the storm got worse and he was prevented from completing his journey. And when his soldiers knew what he had done, they

\* \* \* \* \*

**205** (VI) Plutarch *Moralia* 206B. In margin 'boldness'

**206** (VII) Plutarch *Moralia* 206C
  1 Caesar's unconstitutional invasion of Italy from his province took place in January 49 BC. The province of Nearer Gaul covered Northern Italy; the Rubicon was its boundary. This precipitated the First Civil War which ended with the defeat and death of Pompey, and Caesar's emergence as sole ruler. See *Adagia* I iv 32: *Omnem iacere aleam* 'To cast all the dice.'

**207** (VIII) Plutarch *Moralia* 206C. In margin 'the threats of the powerful'
  1 Plutarch reports this incident also in his *Life of Caesar* 35.6–10. This is Lucius Caecilius Metellus, tribune in 49 BC. Tribunes traditionally defended the rights of the people. See 4.230 below.

**208** (IX) Plutarch *Moralia* 206C–D. In margin 'fearless spirit'
  1 Brundisium in the heel of Italy (Brindisi), Dyrrhachium on the coast of Macedonia. At this stage in the Civil War Caesar had crossed to Macedonia in pursuit of Pompey, his army, and his Republican supporters.

rushed to Caesar and took it badly that he was waiting for other troops as if he had no faith in them.

**209** However when battle was joined, Pompey was victorious, but instead of following up his victory, he retreated towards the main force. Thereupon Caesar said, 'Today the enemy had victory in their grasp, but they do not have a leader who knows how to make use of victory.'

**210** When Pompey drew up his line at Pharsalus and told the men to stay put and wait for the enemy, Caesar said that he had blundered in weakening by delay the force and impact and divine inspiration of spirits ready to charge.

There was rivalry between Caesar and Pompey not just in the fortune of war but in the science of war.

**211** When he defeated Pharnaces at the first encounter, he wrote to his friends, 'I came, I saw, I conquered,'[1] marking the extreme swiftness of the affair.

**212** After the soldiers who followed Scipio into Africa had been put to flight[1] and Cato, defeated, had killed himself at Utica, Caesar said, 'Cato, I begrudge you that death of yours, since you begrudged me your preservation.'

Caesar thought it would contribute greatly to his renown if such a great a man had been defeated by him in war and owed his life to him. But Cato preferred an honourable death to being enslaved to anyone once the nation's freedom had been destroyed. Hence Caesar begrudged the glory

\* \* \* \* \*

**209**  (x) Plutarch *Moralia* 206D. In margin 'make use of victory'

**210**  (xi) Plutarch *Moralia* 206E. The Battle of Pharsalus in which Pompey was defeated decided the outcome of the Civil War. In margin 'delay harmful'

**211**  (xii) Plutarch *Moralia* 206E. In margin 'swift conclusion'
   1 After the murder of Pompey in Egypt (see 4.251 below) Caesar was in 47 BC returning to Rome via Asia Minor (modern Turkey). He conducted a 5-day (but hard-fought) campaign against Pharnaces II, king of Pontus, and his victory occasioned this famous saying. The Latin version (*veni, vidi, vici*) comes from Suetonius *Julius Caesar* 37.2.

**212**  (xiii) Plutarch *Moralia* 206E. In margin 'love of glory'
   1 The last phase of the Civil War was dragged out in the Roman province of north Africa where the remnants of the Republican forces re-assembled. Quintus Caecilius Metellus Scipio became supreme commander and died when fleeing after his defeat in the battle of Thapsus in 46 BC.

of his death to Cato, because the other had begrudged Caesar the credit for saving Cato.

213 Some men suspected Antony and Dolabella and warned him to beware of them. But Caesar said, 'I am not afraid of those red-faced stout men, but of those thin and pale ones,' pointing at Brutus and Cassius.
      And his suspicion was not mistaken, for these men killed him.[1]

214 At dinner, when the conversation turned to the best kind of death, he unhesitatingly replied, 'Sudden,' and what he thought best was indeed the way he died.

215 Once in battle when the standard-bearer of the Martian legion had turned to flee, Caesar seized him by the throat and turned him round, and stretching his right arm towards the enemy said, 'Which way are you going? The men we are fighting are over there.' He set right one soldier with his hands but with his biting words dispelled the fearfulness of all the legions and taught those ready to be conquered how to conquer.

216 After the mime-writer Publius had defeated everyone on stage including Laberius, Caesar declared, 'Though Caesar favoured you Laberius, you're beaten by a Syrian.' For Publius Syrus was a slave and a Syrian in origin.[1] A man is left far behind if he is defeated even when the judge favours him.

217 When Caesar saw rich foreigners at Rome carrying round puppies and monkey whelps in their arms and petting them, he asked whether their

* * * * *

213 (xiv) Plutarch *Moralia* 206F. In margin 'less to fear from fat men'
   1 Cf Plutarch *Life of Caesar* 62 (adapted in Shakespeare *Julius Caesar* Act 1 scene 2). These are Mark Antony, later the Triumvir, and the shady Publius Cornelius Dolabella, at one time Cicero's son-in-law, Tullia's third husband.

214 (xv) Plutarch *Moralia* 206F. He was famously assassinated on the Ides of March 44 BC.

215 (xvi) Valerius Maximus 3.2.19

216 (xvii) Macrobius *Saturnalia* 2.7.7–8
   1 Decimus Laberius was a knight who wrote mimes. See 4.311 below. In a competition in extemporizing, Publius (or Publilius) Syrus (ie Syrian) defeated all comers, including Laberius.

217 (xviii) Plutarch *Life of Pericles* 1.1. In margin 'children as monkeys'

womenfolk bore children. For he felt no puppies were sweeter than children. Plutarch tells the story in his life of Pericles, but he does not say which Caesar said this. I suspect it was Augustus.[1]

218 When he saw his soldiers were terrified as they awaited the enemy, he addressed the assembled troops, saying: 'Know that in a very few days the king will be here with ten legions, 30 squadron of horse, a hundred thousand light infantry and 300 elephants. So let people stop enquiring further or guessing, and believe me who have the facts; or else I will set them on a very old ship and have them carried away by whatever wind blows to whatever shores.'[1]

This was a new method of dispelling panic, not by denying or reducing but by exaggerating the cause for panic, so that they would be sure of the serious danger and get courage worthy of it.

219 When men declared publicly that Sulla had resigned his dictatorship, but Caesar held his for life, which was little short of tyranny, he said, 'Sulla didn't know his alphabet, and so had resigned his dictatorship.'

The grammar teachers dictate to their pupils when they read out or recite what is to be written; it was alluding to this that he said Sulla did not know his alphabet.[1]

220 When Caesar was passing the tribunician benches in his triumph Pontius Aquila alone did not get up, and Caesar resented this so much that he declared, 'Aquila, demand the republic back from me – tribune!'[1] And after that he did not promise anything to anyone for days on end without adding the proviso, 'that is if Pontius Aquila will permit.'

\* \* \* \* \*

1 The sentiment better fits Augustus' views on the importance of child-rearing. See 4.170 n1 above.

218 (xix) Suetonius *Julius Caesar* 66. For 4.218–24 Erasmus uses Suetonius *Divus Iulius* (*Julius Caesar*). In margin 'courage generated by danger'
1 King Juba I of Mauretania supported the Republican side in the Civil War and fought alongside Metellus Scipio (see 212 n1 above) at the battle of Thapsus in 46 BC.

219 (xx) Suetonius *Julius Caesar* 77. In margin 'power resigned'
1 The point surely is that Caesar thought Sulla a fool.

220 (xxi) Suetonius *Julius Caesar* 78. In margin 'honour denied'
1 The tribunes were traditionally defenders of the rights of the people and had the power of veto (see 4.207, 4.222, 4.230). Pontius was later one of Caesar's assassins.

**221** When the people flattered him by hailing him as King, he said, 'I am Caesar, not King.' He preferred his private name, rather than that of king which was seen as hateful.[1]

**222** One of the crowd put a laurel crown bound with a white ribbon on Caesar's statue; but when the tribunes pulled off the ribbon and ordered the man to be taken off to prison, Caesar rebuked them violently and stripped them of their power, and made the excuse, in case he seemed to be aiming at kingship, that they had robbed him of the glory of refusal.[1]

**223** Since Caesar had enrolled many foreigners in the senate a notice was put up saying, 'It is a good deed to show any new senator the way to the Senate house.'

The anonymous writer meant that these foreigners did not even know the way to the senate house unless they were shown it.

**224** Someone wrote under Brutus' statue[1] 'If only you were alive!' because King Tarquin had been driven out thanks to Brutus. And they wrote the following verses on Caesar's statue: 'Brutus drove the kings away and so became the first consul; Caesar drove the consuls out and so became the last king.'

*　*　*　*　*

**221** (xxii) Suetonius *Julius Caesar* 79. This story and 4.222 both come from the episode at the Lupercalia in 44 BC when Antony tried to present Caesar with a diadem. In margin 'modest'
  1 Caesar was originally a family name, like Cicero (see 4.280) eventually adopted by all emperors as a title and it becomes the normal title by which subordinates address the emperor. Since the expulsion of the kings in 510 BC (see 4.224 below) the governing classes had always reacted violently to the very word 'king.'

**222** (xxiii) Suetonius *Julius Caesar* 79.1. In margin 'excuse'
  1 The popular gesture of crowning Caesar's statue employed double symbolism: the laurel marked Caesar as having earned a triumph as commander, but the white ribbon was the diadem associated with Hellenistic kings. Hence the tribunes (who were defenders of the rights of the people against the powerful) pulled it down, and Caesar deposed them from office.

**223** (xxiv) Suetonius *Julius Caesar* 80.2. In margin 'jibe'

**224** (xxv) Suetonius *Julius Caesar* 80.3. In margin 'tyranny'
  1 Brutus' statue was the statue of L. Junius Brutus who drove out the Tarquins, the supposed ancestor of M. Junius Brutus who would kill Caesar. See 4.221 n1 above.

225 When plots seemed to threaten on all sides and Caesar was warned to be on guard for his life, he said, 'It is better to suffer once than always be on guard.'

   He meant that a man who lives in constant fear of death is not really living.

226 After Caesar had reduced the Tigurini and was setting out for an allied city, he heard the Helvetii were approaching on his march and withdrew to a safe place. When he had gathered his forces and drew up a battle line they brought him his usual horse, but he said, 'I'll use him to pursue the enemy rout after the victory,' and attacked the Helvetii on foot.

227 Caesar was now openly enacting many decrees by force and against the law when Considius, who was a very old man, said frankly that the senate was not assembling because it was afraid of Caesar's weapons. When Caesar said to him, 'Then why don't you stay home for the same reason?' Considius said, 'Old age has made me fearless. When there is so little life left I have no reason to trouble myself much.'[1]

228 When the soldier Pomponius was displaying the wound he got in the face during the sedition stirred up by Sulpicius, and boasting that he suffered it fighting for Caesar, Caesar said, 'Take care you don't ever look back when you are running away.' Macrobius credits a similar witticism to Augustus, but Quintilian to Caesar.[1]

       * * * * *

   225 (xxvi) Plutarch *Life of Caesar* 57.7. The remaining stories about Julius Caesar (4.225–35) are drawn from Plutarch's *Lives* and other sources. In margin 'a life of anxiety'

   226 (xxvii) Plutarch *Life of Caesar* 18.2–3. This incident belongs to 59–49 BC, when Caesar held the command of the province of Transalpine Gaul (ie southern France and Switzerland), before he achieved supreme power in 48 BC. In margin 'spirited'

   227 (xxviii) Plutarch *Life of Caesar* 14.13–15. In margin 'the boldness conferred by age'
     1 Quintus Considius, a senator, was praised by Cicero for his integrity as a juryman (*Pro Cluentio* 38.107).

   228 (xxix) Quintilian 6.3.75. In margin 'witty'
     1 Cf 4.151 above, told of Augustus from Macrobius *Saturnalia* 2.4.7; the story in Quintilian, here ascribed to Caesar (reference added in *1535*), is not about

229 Again when a witness, to exaggerate the wrong done to him, said that his thighs had been attacked with a sword by the defendant, Caesar said, 'What else could he do, when you had a helmet and breastplate?'

He was well aware why the man's enemy had chosen to attack that part of his body, but preferred to ignore this and make a joke instead. The breastplate and helmet cover everything except the thighs.

230 When Metellus resisted him to prevent him taking money from the treasury and quoted laws forbidding this, Caesar said, 'The time for arms is not the same as the time for laws. If you can't bear the situation, get away from here now, and when we have made treaties and put down our arms, then if you like you can play protector of the people.'

231 He also used to say that he had the same policy towards the enemy as most doctors towards bodily illnesses, that they should be overcome by hunger rather than steel. For doctors do not resort to surgery until they have tried everything.[1] (This is still the custom with the Italians, who prescribe starvation against every illness.) This is like the remark of Domitius Corbulo, that the enemy should be defeated with a builder's adze.[2]

232 It generated great ill will towards Caesar that one of his envoys to Rome stood in the senate and when he heard the senate would not give Caesar

* * * * *

Julius Caesar but about another member of the *gens*, Gaius Iulius Caesar Strabo, as the reference to (Publius) Sulpicius (Rufus) shows. During his tribunate in 88 BC, there was violence as Sulpicius endeavoured to pass popular measures opposed by this Caesar and other conservatives.

229  (xxx) Quintilian 6.3.91. Cf 6.251 below. In margin 'witty'

230  (xxxI) Plutarch *Life of Caesar* 35.6–7. Cf 4.207 above the same story from a different source. In margin 'weapons pay no attention to laws'

231  (xxxII) Frontinus *Strategemata* 4.7.1–2. In margin 'to win by starvation'
    1 Cf 5.417 below on Scipio Aemilianus. 'For doctors ... everything' was added in 1532.
    2 The 1535 edition drops two sentences explaining the difference between the piecemeal demolition possible with an adze and the immediate impact of the axe (*securis*).

232  (xxxIII) Plutarch *Life of Caesar* 29.7. In margin 'violence in place of legality'

his extension of office, struck his sword hilt and said, 'But this will give it' threatening the republic with violence.[1]

233 When Sulla won the praetorship, he threatened that he would use his office against Caesar. Then Caesar laughed and said, 'You are right to call it your office, since you bought it with your money.'[1]

He was criticizing Sulla for buying that magistracy with bribery.

234 Marcus Tullius in the third book of 'On Obligations' (*De officiis*) writes that Caesar always had lines from Euripides' *Phoenissae* on his lips, which Cicero translates as: 'If we must violate the law, then for monarchy let it be violated; in all else observe piety.'[1]

235 When he sailed for Africa, he fell while disembarking, and turned the bad omen for the better, saying, 'Africa, I hold you!' Frontinus thinks it happened when he was embarking and said, 'Mother Earth, I hold you.'

I suppose he was alluding to the fact that he was distressed by a dream in which he seemed to rape his mother, but the interpreters explained that it denoted rule over all the earth.

* * * * *

1 Caesar wanted his military command in Gaul (see 4.226 above) extended while he manoeuvred for the consulship of 48 BC. The same story is more plausibly told of Octavian's soldier demanding from the senate in 43 BC that Octavian be made consul unconstitutionally and without election. (*Suetonius Augustus* 26.1)

233 (xxxiv) Plutarch *Life of Sulla* 5.5. In margin 'power purchased with money'
  1 Again not about Julius Caesar, but an earlier member of the family, possibly the Caesar of 4.228 n1 above, who supported Sulla's enemy, Gaius Marius. Sulla was praetor in 93 BC when Julius Caesar was seven.

234 (xxxv) Cicero *De officiis* 3.82. In margin 'supreme power does not recognize the rights of piety'
  1 Taken from a speech of the tyrant Eteocles from Euripides *Phoenissae* 524–5:
  Εἴπερ γὰρ ἀδικεῖν χρή, τυραννίδος περὶ / Κάλλιστον ἀδικεῖν, τ' ἄλλα δ' εὐσεβεῖν χρεών.

235 (xxxvi) Suetonius *Julius Caesar* 59. Cf Frontinus 1.12.1 which also quotes the alternative (1.12.2); for the dream, Suetonius *Julius Caesar* 7.2.
  The anecdotes about Pompey are all taken from Plutarch's collection of sayings and his *Life of Pompey* except for 4.252.

## Pompey the Great

236 Gnaeus Pompey, known as Magnus, was as dear to the Roman people as his father had been loathed.[1] While still a young man he devoted himself to the party of Sulla, and although he was not a magistrate or even a senator he drafted a large army from Italy. When Sulla summoned him, he said, 'I shall not present to my commander-in-chief a force unbloodied or without spoils.' And he did not come to him until he had beaten enemy commanders in many engagements.

He already provided the model of an excellent prince born to high achievements. He did not want to contribute mere numbers, but a soldiery tested in valour.

237 When he had been appointed general and was sent by Sulla to Sicily, Pompey began to play the part of a just as well as an efficient leader. For when he found out that his soldiers were deviating from the route on their marches with acts of violence and theft, he executed those wandering and riding around irregularly; and when he sent his own scouts ahead he pressed the seal of his ring on their swords, so that they would not harm anyone on their route.[1]

\* \* \* \* \*

236 (1) Plutarch *Moralia* 203B–C. In margin 'a lofty spirit'
'Pompeius Magnus' (Pompey the Great) was Pompey's preferred title, which he used to assimilate himself to Alexander the Great. (It was first given him by Sulla – Plutarch *Life of Pompey* 13.7 – but Pompey soon used it in his correspondence and orders. See 4.240 below.) He was early given military commands and backed by his successes and his armies held magistracies before the legal age. Between 67 and 63 BC he defeated Rome's great enemy Mithridates and conquered most of the Middle East to add to Rome's imperial revenues, notably clearing the eastern Mediterranean of pirates. Meeting resistance from the traditionalists in the senate he formed an alliance with Caesar and Crassus in 60 BC. He sealed this alliance by his marriage to Caesar's daughter Julia, but after her death he broke with Caesar and accepted a mandate from the Senate to fight against his growing power at the beginning of 49 BC, the beginning of the First Civil War. Pompey was defeated when they met in battle at Pharsalus in 48, and fled to Egypt where he was treacherously murdered
1 For the unpopularity of Pompey's father see Plutarch *Pompey* 1 and for Pompey's early actions *Pompey* 6.

237 (11) Plutarch *Moralia* 203C. In margin 'soldiers doing no harm'
1 Pompey was sent to Sicily in 82 BC to fight Sulla's political opponents, supporters of Marius, who had fled there after losing in battle to Sulla in Italy. See 4.254 below.

238 Pompey ordered the Mamertines to be executed en masse because they had supported the enemy.[1] But the leader of the community, Sthenius, came to Pompey saying, 'You are not acting fairly, Pompey, in preparing to kill many innocent men on account of one guilty person. For I am the one who persuaded my friends and compelled my enemies to support the side of Marius.' At this Pompey felt admiration for the man's courage and said he pardoned the Mamertines, since they had been persuaded by a man who actually put his country's survival before his own; so he set free both the community and Sthenius.

You have in the case of Sthenius an instance of the spirit a leader should have towards the state if danger arises; in Pompey a model of forgiveness: he preferred to honour piety rather than gratify his anger.

239 After he made the sea-crossing to Libya against Domitius and had overcome him in a major battle, his soldiers saluted him as General, but he said he would not accept the honour as long as the enemy palisade stood firm. When they heard this the soldiers charged at the enemy camp, in the face of a heavy rainstorm, and took it by storm.

He rejected an honour he had not fully earned.

240 It was when he returned from that victory that Sulla welcomed him with various honours and first bestowed the name Great upon him. But when Pompey was not content and wanted to hold a triumph, Sulla would not allow it, because Pompey was not yet a senator. However when Pompey remarked to those present that Sulla did not realize that more men reverenced the rising than the setting sun, Sulla cried out, 'Let him triumph.'

* * * * *

238 (III) Plutarch *Moralia* 203D. In margin 'love of country'
  1 The Mamertines were the inhabitants of Messana in north-east Sicily.

239 (IV) Plutarch *Moralia* 203D. In margin 'deserved honours please'
  This is Gnaeus Domitius Ahenobarbus, consul in 87 BC, a supporter of Marius, who fled to Africa after Sulla's victory. Pompey had him killed after the battle. See 8.157 below. It was possibly in this campaign that the title *Magnus* was first used, and later confirmed by Sulla (Plutarch *Life of Pompey* 13.8). See 4.240.

240 (V) Plutarch *Moralia* 203E. The two items 4.240 and 4.241 come from the same context of Pompey's first triumph in 81 BC, in face of Sulla's opposition. Erasmus has expanded the section with material from Plutarch *Pompey* 14.6–8, and Frontinus *Strategemata* 4.5.1. In margin 'the rising sun'

He was afraid of the young man's spirit and his glory which increased every day, and did not hesitate to give way to the man he saw could give way to no other.

241 Meanwhile Servilius, a distinguished conservative leader, was resentful that Pompey had been granted a triumph, and even the soldiers were protesting against the holding of the triumph, not from ill-will towards Pompey but because they wanted donatives, as if the triumph had to be bought from them with bribes. They· said that otherwise they would pillage the money carried in the triumph, and so Servilius and Glaucia tried to persuade him to divide it among the soldiers rather than let it be plundered. But Pompey said he would sooner abandon the triumph than pander to the soldiers, and threw his laurelled fasces in their face, telling them to start plundering with these. Servilius said, 'Now, Pompey, I can see you are truly Great and deserve a triumph.'

Pompey did not think a triumph was splendid unless it was offered for good deeds without canvassing and bribery.

242 It was the practice at Rome for cavalrymen who had served the due period to lead their horse into the Forum before the Board of Two, called censors, and list their campaigns and the generals under whom they had served, receiving praise or blame for their services. So when Pompey was consul he personally led his horse up to the censors Lentulus and Gellius, and when they asked whether he had fulfilled all the military obligations, he answered, 'Yes, all, under my own command.'[1]

He meant that while he had served as commander he had still carried out effectively all the functions of a soldier. He was both a good general and a capable soldier: no higher praise can be given to any prince.

\* \* \* \* \*

241 (VI) Plutarch *Moralia* 203E–F. In margin 'spirited'
Publius Servilius Isauricus was consul at the time, 79 BC. (Servilius) Glaucia (praetor 100 BC) is a mistake (from Frontinus *Strategemata* 4.5.1). The other consul was Appius Claudius Pulcher.

242 (VII) Plutarch *Moralia* 203F–204A. In margin 'soldier and commander both'
1 Pompey's early career had broken the traditional pattern, so that he commanded an army, won triumphs, and was elected consul below the normal age and without ever having been elected to lower magistracies. The episode comes from 70 BC. The two censors were Gnaeus Cornelius Lentulus Clodianus and Lucius Gellius Poplicola.

243 When he obtained possession of Sertorius' dispatches in Spain, which included many letters from leading men inviting Sertorius to Rome to start a
revolution and overthrow the constitution, Pompey burnt them all to give
the disloyal a chance to repent and change their policy for the better.[1]

Now while this should be counted among his wise and moderate actions, I do not see why it is among his apophthegms. But then many such
items occur in Plutarch's collection of sayings.[2] If Pompey had made known
the men's names they would have prepared open violence from fear of being punished. Again in treating the enemy's correspondence with secrecy,
he demonstrated what an offence it is to unseal other men's letters or bring
into the open something entrusted to you under seal.

244 Phraates king of Parthia sent envoys to demand that Pompey accept the Eu-
phrates as the boundary of Roman territory, but he replied, 'On the contrary, we should demand that justice determine the boundaries between the
Romans and Parthians.'[1]

He meant that nobody should prescribe to the Romans how far they
might extend their empire, and that neither mountains nor rivers should
keep them from expansion; instead the only limit of Roman territory would
be where they had no right to proceed further.

245 When Lucius Lucullus abandoned himself to pleasure and lived luxuriously
after fulfilling his military duties,[1] he used to reproach Pompey's desire
to be involved in many enterprises in a way out of keeping with his age.

* * * * *

243 (VIII) Plutarch *Moralia* 204A. In margin 'merciful'
  1 Sertorius (whose life Erasmus would know from Plutarch's *Sertorius*) was a
    Roman supporter of Marius and enemy of Sulla, who broke away and suc-
    cessfully governed his own rebel territory in Spain. Pompey was sent there in
    77 BC to suppress him. Sartorius was betrayed to Pompey by a subordinate
    and assassinated.
  2 See Introduction xix and n11.

244 (IX) Plutarch *Moralia* 204A. In margin 'justice determines boundaries'
  1 Pompey's retort to the Parthian king Phraates III was made probably in 66
    BC after Pompey's defeat of King Mithridates, when he was settling various
    matters in the east of the Roman empire.

245 (X) Plutarch *Moralia* 204B. In margin 'idleness disgraceful'
  1 Lucius Licinius Lucullus had a distinguished military career, especially in the
    east. He was cheated of deserved recognition and retired from public life and
    thereafter became a by-word for luxurious living.

Pompey retaliated that it was more out of keeping with Lucullus' age for an old man to devote himself to indulgence rather than exercising command.

This was a severe criticism of people who think old men should do nothing, whereas it is proper to die either governing the state or on their feet.[2] In young men luxury and idleness are folly; they are an offence in old men.

246 When Pompey fell ill his doctor prescribed a diet of thrushes. But the men commissioned to find them said they could not be obtained, since they were out of season. Then another man said they could be obtained from Lucullus, since he reared thrushes all the year round. 'Do you mean,' said Pompey, 'that Pompey could not live if Lucullus were not addicted to luxury?' And he disregarded the doctor and fed on easily available foods.[1]

What a truly manly spirit! He could not endure even to owe his life to luxuries.

247 When there was a great shortage of grain at Rome, Pompey was given the title of Commissioner of the grain supply but was in reality made master of earth and sea.[1] He sailed to Africa, Sardinia, and Sicily, where he forcibly gathered a large supply of grain and was in a hurry to return to Rome; but when a severe storm arose the captains refused to sail, so he entered the ship ahead of all and ordered the anchors aweigh, saying, 'We have to sail: we do not have to live.'

He meant that one should consider the risk to one's country not one's personal safety. For it is glorious to die out of concern for relieving one's country, but absolutely disgraceful that it should be deserted in time of need because of our cowardice. This reminds us that not only brute animals lose their liberty and are enslaved, but untamed men too can be tamed by hunger. At the same time we learn that personal safety should be second after public welfare.

248 When Pompey's quarrel with Julius Caesar was already public, Marcellinus

* * * * *

2 See 6.83 below on Vespasian.

246 (xi) Plutarch *Moralia* 204B. In margin 'contempt for luxury'
    1 See 4.245 just above for Lucullus' luxury.

247 (xii) Plutarch *Moralia* 204C. In margin 'country dearer than life'
    1 This was in 57 BC, for five years.

248 (xiii) Plutarch *Moralia* 204C–D. This is Gnaeus Cornelius Lentulus Marcellinas, consul in 56 BC. In margin 'ingratitude'

(according to Plutarch, or Marcellus in other sources), one of those whom Pompey was thought to have promoted, transferred his support to Caesar and did not hesitate to make many attacks on Pompey in the senate. Pompey silenced him like this: 'Aren't you ashamed, Marcellinus, to curse the man whose favour turned you from a dumb fellow to an orator, and from a starveling to a glutton who cannot control your vomit?'

He severely reproached the man with ingratitude, for abusing his rank, authority, and eloquence to attack the man he should have thanked. For this is the most disgraceful kind of ingratitude, but only too common, alas!

249  When Cato was inveighing bitterly against Pompey because, while he him-self had repeatedly said that Julius Caesar's growing power would not ben-efit the people's government, but tended towards tyranny, [...] Pompey replied, 'Your words are more prophetic, Cato, but mine are more suited to friendship.'[1]

He meant that what Cato said was not sure to happen, because no man could clearly anticipate the outcome of human events, but he had followed the demands of his friendship with Caesar at that time.[2] He knew what he owed to his friend, but he did not know whether he would be his friend or his enemy in future. However it is more civilized to hope well of a friend than foresee the worst.

250  Pompey would freely admit that he had obtained every magistracy he held before he expected to, and laid it down before others expected him to.

That he won office early was a matter of luck, or youthful excellence, that he laid it down in good time marked his moderation in aiming not at tyranny but the good of the republic.

251  After the battle of Pharsalus he fled to Egypt, and when he was disembark-ing from his trireme into a little fishing boat sent by the Egyptian king, he

* * * * *

249  (XIV) Plutarch *Moralia* 204D. In margin 'prophesying the future'
    1 Erasmus' text seems to have been faulty. The sense requires 'but Pompey had taken a contrary stance,' and in Pompey's reply it should be, 'Your words *were* more prophetic but mine *were* ...' See Plutarch *Pompey* 60.8.
    2 Pompey had been Julius Caesar's son-in-law in 59–54 BC. This exchange took place in 49 BC after Caesar crossed the Rubicon.

250  (XV) Plutarch *Moralia* 204E. In margin 'moderation'

251  (XVI) Plutarch *Moralia* 204E

turned to his wife and son and simply quoted these verses from Sophocles:

> Whoever betakes himself to a tyrant's hall
> becomes his slave, although he freely came.[1]

He seems to have intuited his approaching death. When he climbed into the boat he was struck with a sword, and uttering just one sigh, covered his head and surrendered himself to be killed.

252 Weary of Cicero's wit, Pompey used to say among his friends, 'I wish Cicero would go over to the enemy, so that he would fear us.' He was commenting on Cicero's character which reputedly made him grovelling towards enemies but insolent towards his friends. This is how Quintilian reports Pompey's saying: 'Go over to Caesar and then you will fear me.'[1]

253 After his disastrous defeat fighting Julius Caesar, when he was reduced to extreme despair, Pompey came into his tent as if dazed, and said nothing but 'Right into the very camp, then?,' put on clothing appropriate to his misfortune, and fled in secret.[1]

254 When the uprising had been put down in Sicily and the cities that rebelled had been peacefully reclaimed, only the Mamertines demanded a hearing, citing laws that the Romans had granted them in the past. Pompey said,

* * * * *

1 Sophocles, Nauck fr 789. Pharsalus was the decisive battle in the civil war between Caesar and Pompey. For the Greek words see the anecdote about Aristippus 3.160 above.

252 (xvii) Macrobius *Saturnalia* 2.3.7–8. In margin 'hurtful clever remarks'
After 4.251, which finds Pompey at the moment of his assassination (in 48BC), Erasmus adds chronologically earlier anecdotes from other sources. Cicero was notorious for his wit, not always in the best of taste. See the selection given below at 4.280–320, especially 4.295–6, 4.301–2.
1 Quintilian 6.3.111

253 (xviii) Plutarch *Life of Pompey* 72.5. In margin 'despair'
1 After Pompey's defeat at Pharsalus, he retreated to his camp but Caesar's troops began breaking in in large numbers. See 4.251 above.

254 (xix) Plutarch *Life of Pompey* 10.3. Erasmus has gone back to Pompey's early career under Sulla, the context of 4.236–42 above (see especially 4.238). In margin 'requests backed by weapons'

'Stop quoting laws while you are wearing swords,' meaning that men who wished to negotiate at law did not need swords.[1]

255 When he learnt from a dispatch of the senate that everything that Sulla had taken by force had been put under his official control by the centuriate assembly of the people, Pompey struck his thigh and said, 'Alas, my dangers are never at an end: it would have been so much better to be born humble, if I shall never have a chance to step aside from military responsibilities, escape from this ill will, and live in the country with my wife.'

The inexperienced man seeks great power, but the experienced man shuns it; yet it is not safe to set it aside.

256 When some senators claimed they did not see how he would be able to oppose an attack from Caesar, he cheerfully told them not to be troubled about it, saying: 'As soon as I strike the Italian soil with my foot, cavalry and infantry will spring up in plenty.'[1] A ready reaction, if the outcome had matched it.

Now if you have not had enough of this feast let us add some men of distinction from among the orators too.

**Phocion of Athens**
257 Take Phocion first, an Athenian by race but Spartan in his integrity of char-

* * * * *

1 Erasmus may have misread his text. Pompey says the Mamertines should not hope to negotiate with the Romans who have the swords. This is in line with other 'might is right' sayings (eg 4.207 and 4.232 above).

255 (xx) Plutarch *Life of Pompey* 30.6–7. This belongs to 66 BC, when Pompey was given supreme command in the Third Mithridatic War in Asia (modern Turkey). The dictator Sulla had previously had some military successes there, but much was left unfinished. (See 4.244 n1 above) Pompey had already fought successfully in Sicily (4.238), Africa (4.239), and Spain (4.243). In margin 'weary of glory'

256 (xxi) Plutarch *Life of Pompey* 57.9. In margin 'misplaced confidence'
1 Pompey's confident assertion made shortly before 49 BC proved unwarranted. He had a considerable personal following in Picenum in eastern Italy.

257 (1) Plutarch *Moralia* 187E and 187F (*Sayings of kings and commanders*). In margin 'pithy brevity'
The fourth-century Athenian statesman Phocion, famous for his integrity, defended the interests of Athens as far as he could, and though opposed to Macedonian ambitions, saw that they could not be resisted entirely for practical

acter and concision of speech. He resembled Socrates in this, that he never seemed to weep or laugh, such was his self-control.[1]

Now someone said to him as he sat at an assembly, 'You seem thoughtful, Phocion?' 'You are right,' he said, 'I am working out whether I can subtract anything from what I am going to say to the Athenians.'[2]

Other men are anxious to say as much as possible, so as to seem eloquent: he had a different concern, that is, to express what was relevant in the fewest possible words.

258 When an oracle was given to the Athenians that there was one man in their city who opposed their common will, the assembled people cried out to have the man searched out. But Phocion revealed himself saying, 'I am the man the oracle means. For I alone dislike everything that the crowd does or says.'

What would you admire first in this, his fearless nature, or his generosity, which did not allow suspicion to fall on some innocent man, or his exceptional wisdom, which perceived that the untrained crowd does not do or say anything sensible because it is moved by emotion?

259 One day Phocion was speaking to the Athenian assembly and pleased them all; but when he saw his speech met with general approval he turned to his friends: 'What happened?' he said. 'Did I accidentally say something wrong?'[1]

He was absolutely convinced that nothing which was based on sound judgment pleased the crowd.[2]

\* \* \* \* \*

reasons. He therefore opposed the violently anti-Macedonian policies of the orator Demosthenes, and this often did not please the Athenian crowd. He was condemned to death in 318 BC supposedly for giving Antipater of Macedon access to the Piraeus, although innocent of either conspiracy or corruption. Because he was an austere Stoic later Stoics made him into a kind of hero and Plutarch presents him as a counterpart to Cato of Utica by juxtaposing their lives.

1 This was one of Socrates' most noteworthy characteristics: Cicero *De officiis* 1.90; 3.59 above
2 Phocion's desire to make his speech concise is in the Spartan tradition of brevity (*Laconism*); see General Index: Laconismus, Laconic speech.

258 (II) Plutarch *Moralia* 187A. In margin 'nothing that the crowd does is sensible'

259 (III) Plutarch *Moralia* 188A
1 The same story is told of others in Diogenes Laertius 6.5 and 8 (7.57 and 7.69 below).
2 Cf *Adagia* III i 32: *Panidis suffragium* 'The judgment of Panides.'

260 When the Athenians asked the citizens for the customary contributions for an approaching sacrifice, and everyone else contributed, Phocion was called on repeatedly, but he said, 'I'd be ashamed to add my share to yours and pay nothing back to him,' pointing to his creditor.

Many people think money well spent if it is spent on temples ·and sacrifices and feasts for the gods, but that observant man realized that it was much holier to pay back to your creditors. What would he think of those who cheat their wife and children and heap up royal structures for priests, and spend much of their wealth on feeding such men's idleness?

261 The orator Demosthenes said, 'The Athenians will kill you, Phocion, if ever they go mad.' To which he replied, 'Yes, they'll kill me if they go mad, but you if they return to their right mind.'¹

For Demosthenes usually spoke to win popular favour, with arguments more welcome than salutary.

262 When the informer Aristogeiton had been condemned and was in prison awaiting execution, he asked Phocion to visit him, but his friends would not let him go. Phocion said, 'When else would anyone rather talk to Aristogeiton?'

He wittily reversed his friends' case, meaning that he was not going to play patron to the criminal but to enjoy his well-deserved downfall.

263 The Athenians were angry with the Byzantines for refusing to admit Chares who had been sent with a force to help their city against Philip. Phocion had said they should not get angry with their allies for being mistrustful, but with the leaders for being untrustworthy, and so was himself elected

\* \* \* \* \*

260 (iv) Plutarch *Moralia* 188A. In margin 'use what is left for sacrifices'

261 (v) Plutarch *Moralia* 188A. In margin 'smart retort'
  1 Phocion opposed Demosthenes' anti-Macedonian attitude which he had persuaded the Athenians to support. Plutarch *Moralia* 811A (*Precepts of statecraft*) gives this exchange to the orator Demades (see 4.271 below) who also opposed Demosthenes on this.

262 (vi) Plutarch *Moralia* 188B. In margin 'a pleasure to visit the wicked in prison' Aristogeiton was considered a sycophant and a demagogue, with a coarse vehement style of oratory. He was attacked by Demosthenes in two extant speeches.

263 (vii) Plutarch *Moralia* 188B. In margin 'confidence in a leader'

leader. Because the Byzantines trusted him, he made sure that Philip left without accomplishing his purpose.[1]

He blamed the mistrust of the Byzantines on the leader Chares, because Chares did not seem a man it was safe to trust. It is a mark of proper caution to mistrust an untrustworthy man: but they did not hesitate to trust themselves to Phocion as a man of established good repute.

264 Alexander, king of Macedon, sent a hundred talents to Phocion as a gift, but Phocion asked those who brought it why, when there were so many Athenians, Alexander had sent the gift to him alone? They answered, 'Because he thinks you the only honourable and good man.' 'Then he should let me not only be thought to be such a man, but actually to be one,' he said.[1]

How cleverly he grasped and twisted their argument into grounds for refusing the gift. Who would not be impressed by the integrity of his pure heart? Phocion was poor, but indifferent to the greatness of the gift. At the same time his action shows that statesmen who do not abstain from accepting gifts are not good men and should not be thought such.

265 When Alexander demanded that the Athenians provide him with triremes, and the assembly called on Phocion by name to come and deliver his advice, he rose and said, 'My advice is that you either defeat them in war, or make friends with the victors.'

In brief he urged them to deny nothing to Alexander unless they were sure they could overcome him in war when he was angered with them. But if they thought him superior in fighting power, they should not provoke a spirited young ruler who would be intolerant of a refusal.

266 A rumour of unknown origin had arisen that Alexander was dead, and soon speakers were leaping up to urge the Athenians not to delay but instantly

* * * * *

1 In 339 BC, Philip was blockading Byzantium which had detached itself from Philip and shifted its allegiance to Athens. For Chares see 5.205 n1 below.

264 (VIII) Plutarch *Moralia* 188c. In margin 'corruption by gifts'
1 Phocion had always proposed a conciliatory attitude to both Philip and Alexander. See 4.265 below.

265 (IX) Plutarch *Moralia* 188c. In margin 'the same policy had to be adopted with the Turks'

266 (X) Plutarch *Moralia* 188D. In margin 'precipitate advice'

launch a war. Phocion told them to wait until they had surer information, saying, 'If he is dead today he will still be dead tomorrow and the day after.'

His thoughtful advice restrained the speakers' headlong rashness.

267 When Leosthenes had provoked the Athenian state into war, stirring it up it with grandiose hopes of liberty and pre-eminence,[1] Phocion said his words were like cypresses, which are lofty and beautiful but bear no fruit.

Nothing could be more appropriate to a speech making splendid fancy promises but barren of fruit; just as the cypress with its lofty and pointed top seems from a distance to promise some fine thing, but scarcely any tree is more barren.[2]

268 However when the first phases of the war went well, and the city was thanking the gods for news of success, Phocion was asked whether he regretted what had happened. 'I am indeed glad that this has happened,' he said, 'but I still wish the other decree had been passed.'

He felt that even ill-advised decisions sometimes turn out well, and when this happens the state was to be congratulated, but that did not excuse not making the best decisions on all occasions. Perhaps Phocion also realized that one should not immediately rely on early successes, but the outcome of the whole campaign will reveal the quality of the initial decision.[1]

269 When the Macedonians invaded Attica and ravaged its coastal regions, Phocion led out the young men in their prime. Many of them ran up to him urging him to seize a certain hill and station his force there. 'O Hercules,' he said, 'how many leaders I can see, and how few soldiers.'

Thus he criticized the rashness of youth which tried to dictate to its leader: but the soldier's task is not to give advice but offer good service when it is demanded.

\* \* \* \* \*

267 (xi) Plutarch *Moralia* 188D. In margin 'splendid promises but empty'
  1 Leosthenes urged Athens to join in the wars for Greek liberation after Alexander's death in 323 BC, which they did in spite of the dissuasion of Phocion and Demades.
  2 Cf *Adagia* IV iii 10: *Cyparissi fructus* 'The fruit of the cypress.'

268 (xii) Plutarch *Moralia* 188D. In margin 'the best decisions should be taken'
  1 The war went well at first, but Antipater (see 4.269 n1 just below) and Craterus (another of Alexander's successors) defeated the united Greek forces led by Athens and Aetolia at Crannon in 322 BC.

269 (xiii) Plutarch *Moralia* 188E–F. In margin 'a soldier's duty'

Yet when they engaged in battle he won, and defeated Micion the Macedonian commander. But shortly after, the Athenians were conquered by Antipater, and received a garrison.[1]

270 Later, when Menyllus, the garrison commander, wanted to bribe Phocion, Phocion was indignant and said Menyllus was no better than Alexander; now he had a worse reason to take such a bribe than when he had refused it before.[1]

O what a spirit, which no one's gifts could take by storm!

271 Antipater used to say that of his two friends in Athens, he had never been able to persuade Phocion to take a bribe, nor to satisfy Demades with giving.[1]

This Demades was brilliant in extempore oratory, whereas Demosthenes never spoke except from a written text.[2]

272 Phocion told Antipater when he asked him to do something contrary to justice as a favour to him, 'Antipater, you cannot enjoy Phocion as a friend and as a toady too!'[1]

A friend gives help as far as right and justice allows. Nor should any true friend request something unjust from his friend. But a toady will oblige him in anything.

273 When the Athenian assembly was clamouring for Phocion to lead a force

* * * * *

1 For Antipater see 2.52 n1 above, 4.271–2, 4.274, 5.113–4 below and Index of Classical Persons. The Athenian success against a junior commander was followed by Antipater's own attack and their surrender, resulting in the imposition on Athens of a Macedonian garrison and the exile of Demosthenes and Hyperides, another prominent anti-Macedonian politician.

270 (xiv) Plutarch *Moralia* 188F. In margin 'unbribable character'
1 See 4.264 and 2.69 above.

271 (xv) Plutarch *Moralia* 188F
1 See 4.261 n1 above.
2 See 6.382 below. Plutarch actually says that Demosthenes always prepared very carefully, but was in fact a great extempore speaker (Plutarch *Moralia* 848c).

272 (xvi) Plutarch *Moralia* 188F
1 This is a favourite citation of Plutarch's: *Moralia* 64c (*How to tell a flatterer*), 142B (*Advice to bride and groom*), 533A (*On compliancy*); *Life of Agis and Cleomenes* 2.4.

273 (xvii) Plutarch *Life of Phocion* 24.3–4. See 4.267–8 above.

into Boeotia, and Phocion thought this would not be in the interest of the state, he proposed that everyone in the city from the new recruits to the men of sixty should follow him. When the older men protested and made an excuse of their age he said, 'There is nothing absurd in my proposal, since I myself am eighty and will set out as leader along with them.'

This clever rejoinder quenched the momentary ardour of the crowd.

274 After the death of Antipater,[1] when the Athenian state returned to popular government, Phocion was condemned to death in an assembly. His other friends who were condemned with him, were led off weeping but Phocion went in silence. When one of his enemies met him, he insulted him and spat in his face. Then Phocion looked back at the magistrates and said, 'Will not someone control this man in his indecent behaviour?'

This holy man took thought for public order even on the point of death.

He did not complain of such a savage insult, or demand revenge against the man who illegally assaulted a condemned man, but merely ordered suppression of an example contrary to good manners, and called a disgusting act nothing worse than improper behaviour.

275 One of those condemned to die with Phocion was indignant and lamented his misfortune. Phocion consoled him with these words: 'Isn't it enough, Euippus (or as some read Thoudippus)[1] to die with Phocion?'

Phocion was not only innocent but had served the state well, yet was being led to execution. So it should have been a great comfort to die innocent with this innocent man.

276 Finally when he was offered the cup of blended hemlock, someone asked

\* \* \* \* \*

274 (XVIII) Plutarch *Moralia* 189A. In margin 'acceptance'
   1 After Antipater's death, in the new power struggle between Alexander's generals, Polyperchon, the Macedonian governor, encouraged a democratic revolution at Athens and Phocion (now eighty years old: see 4.273 just above) was condemned by the new popular régime for his past cooperation with Antipater.

275 (XIX) Plutarch *Moralia* 189A
   1 Thoudippos in Plutarch *Phocion* 36.3

276 (XX) Plutarch *Moralia* 189A–B. This is the last saying of Phocion in Plutarch's collection of *Sayings of kings and commanders*. Erasmus now adds some further apophthegms from his *Life of Phocion*. In margin 'rejection of vengeance'

if he wanted to say anything to his son, for his son was present.[1] He said,
'My son, I recommend and even beg you to have no ill feeling towards the
Athenians when you remember this matter.'

The hope of vengeance used to be a particular comfort to others at
their death, but he took thought that his son should not avenge his father's
undeserved death, and preferred him to observe piety towards his country
rather than towards his father.

277 Nicocles begged to be allowed to take the poison before Phocion. 'That is
hard,' said Phocion, 'but I must grant it to one to whom I never denied
anything in life.'

For Phocion loved Nicocles, his most faithful friend, with a special
love, and so it was distressing for him to watch Nicocles die. It was to avoid
this same distress that Nicocles asked to be allowed to drink first. In this
too Phocion obliged his friend.

278 When they had all drunk, and only Phocion was left, the poison had been
used up by his friends and the executioner refused to give him any unless
he paid twelve drachmae, for that was the price of an ounce of hemlock.
So to prevent the man's insistence delaying his death he summoned one of
his friends and said, 'Since we aren't allowed even to die free of charge at
Athens, please give him his price.'

279 When Demosthenes made a savage attack on Alexander who was already
threatening Thebes,[1] Phocion reproved him with a verse of Homer from
book one of the Odyssey:[2] 'you wretch, why do you choose to enrage the
savage man?'

* * * * *

1 Erasmus' text has interpolated, 'for his son was present' but both Plutarch's
  *Sayings of kings and commanders* and his *Life of Phocion* 36.2 imply that the friend
  was offering to take a message.

277 (XXI) Plutarch *Life of Phocion* 36.5. In margin 'friendship'

278 (XXII) Plutarch *Life of Phocion* 36.7. In margin 'dying paid for'

279 (XXIII) Plutarch *Life of Phocion* 17.1. This anecdote was added in 1532.
   1 Erasmus goes back some years, to Phocion's reproach of Demosthenes before
     Alexander attacked Thebes in Boeotia in 335 BC. See 4.57 above.
   2 Not *Odyssey* 1, but from 9.494. Erasmus quotes and translates the Greek:
     σχέτλιε, τίπτ᾽ ἐθέλεις ἐρεθίζεμεν ἄγριον ἄνδρα.

**M. Tullius Cicero**

280 Marcus Tullius was assailed with wisecracks because of his name, Cicero, and was advised by his friends to adopt another name. Instead he replied that he would make the name of Cicero more glorious than that of a Cato, a Catulus, or a Scaurus.

For these were particularly distinguished families among the Romans, whereas Tullius was a new man.[1] And his name was open to jests because it was thought to derive from the chickpea, a very cheap form of pulse. As if the Fabii too didn't apparently get their name from *faba* 'bean' and the Lentuli from *lens* 'lentil.' A man is not very distinguished if he has nothing noble except his name and ancestral images; but the best kind of nobility is won by each man through his own merits. And Cicero was not mistaken. For his name is more celebrated today than three hundred Catuli or Scauri, with all their family trees, statues, and images.

281 When he was dedicating a silver cup to the gods, he marked his name and forename in letters, but instead of Cicero he inscribed the outline of a chickpea, not afraid of the comment of scoffers.

282 Cicero said that orators who shouted when they made a speech were like lame men, since they resorted to shouting as lame men took to horses.

\* \* \* \* \*

280 (I) Plutarch *Moralia* 204E. Erasmus returns to Plutarch's *Moralia* 204E–205F *Sayings of Romans* for 4.280–300. In margin 'nobility won by virtue'
Marcus Tullius Cicero was Rome's greatest orator and an honourable statesman, if ultimately unable to resist the power of the triumvirs and maintain senatorial government by consensus. Cicero recognized the many failings of Pompey and the republican side, but supported them until Caesar's victory forced him to retire from politics, only returning to resist Antony and support Julius Caesar's heir Octavian after Caesar's death. He was assassinated by order of the triumvirs in 43 BC.
1 For Cato, Catulus, and Scaurus, see Index of Classical Persons. Erasmus expands on Plutarch's first saying, adding to the 'chickpea' of Cicero's family *cognomen* parallel cases of aristocratic clans named after beans (the Fabii) and lentils (the Lentuli). The family trees, statues, and images (*imagines*, wax death masks) were all associated with previous members of each clan who had held public office, but Cicero's family had held no office at Rome, which made him a 'new man.' Cf 8.29 below. 'Chickpea' perhaps because the first to be called Cicero had a nick in the end of his nose (Plutarch *Cicero* 1.4).

281 (II) Plutarch *Moralia* 204F. In margin '"chickpea" instead of "Cicero"'

282 (III) Plutarch *Moralia* 204F. In margin 'bawling orator'

You can meet men like this nowadays, who resort to frenzied bawling when they feel weak in their case, so that since they cannot persuade by argument they may extort agreement by shameless browbeating.

283 Verres[1] had a son who abused his youth in perversion, so when Verres assailed Cicero with insults to the effect that he was unmanly and perverted Cicero said, 'You don't seem to know what kind of reproaches should be kept for sons behind the closed doors of the home.'

He meant that this particular taunt did not apply to himself, but to the son of the man who had made it. Now it is the duty of parents to scold their children, but inside the walls of their home, not to take such accusations out of doors. For a man who charges others with what his own sons do at home is bringing his scandals out of doors.

284 Metellus Nepos accused Cicero of causing the deaths of more men by his evidence than he had saved by his advocacy:[1] 'Yes,' said Cicero, 'because I have more credibility than eloquence.'

This was a splendidly clever twist to his own credit. For in a witness his credibility is the issue, in an orator, his eloquence.

285 Again when Metellus kept asking Cicero who his father was (taunting him for his family's lack of distinction), Cicero replied, 'What makes that a rather difficult question to answer is the mother – yours.' For Metellus' mother had a bad reputation. And Metellus himself resembled his mother, fickle and inconstant and a slave to his emotions.

Cicero transferred the insult from father to mother. For the father is unknown when a mother has relations with more than one man.

286 When the same Metellus put a stone crow on the tomb of Diodorus, his

\* \* \* \* \*

283 (IV) Plutarch *Moralia* 204F. In margin 'smart retort'
    1 Verres was the corrupt provincial governor prosecuted in 70 BC by Cicero for extortion from the Sicilians. See 4.290 below.

284 (V) Plutarch *Moralia* 204F–205A. In margin 'insult turned into praise'
    1 This is Quintus Caecilius Metellus Nepos, an aristocrat, who as tribune in 62 BC caused trouble for Cicero and became consul in 57.

285 (VI) Plutarch *Moralia* 205A. In margin 'smart retort'

286 (VII) Plutarch *Moralia* 205A. In margin 'witty'
    Plutarch calls the teacher Diodotus in the *Sayings of Romans*, but, correctly,

former teacher of eloquence, Cicero said, 'He gave him a fair reward. For he taught Metellus to flap about, not to speak,' implying criticism of Metellus' fickle inconsistency.[1] The crow is a bird unblessed by the muses.[2]

287 Cicero had heard that his enemy Vatinius, a most evil fellow, had died, and when he discovered he was still alive he said, 'May the man perish horribly who deceived us so horribly!' meaning that Vatinius did not deserve to go on living.

For every lie is bad, but that lie was twice as bad, because it threw good men into false rejoicing. But his comment was ambiguous, because it could also be said about someone you don't want to die.

288 Cicero was pleading once and a man believed to be of African stock said, 'I don't hear that,' (meaning that he did not approve what was being said). 'That's odd,' said Cicero, 'your ear has a hole in it.'

For that nation usually had ears pierced to hang earrings and jewels, such as we now wear around our neck and on our fingers. Celsus explains how these holes are made.[1]

289 Gaius Popilius wanted to seem a legal expert, although he was ignorant and

* * * * *

Philagrus in his *Life of Cicero* (26.11), which also records Metellus' inability to stick at anything (26.10).
1 See 4.285 just above.
2 Cf *Adagia* I vii 22: *Graculus inter Musas* 'A jackdaw among the Muses.'

287 (VIII) Plutarch *Moralia* 205A–B
Vatinius will be the butt of several more anecdotes below (4.323 and 4.324). As tribune in 59 BC he had proposed several radical bills to the assembly for Caesar, and would later appear as a hostile witness in the prosecution of Cicero's client Sestius in 56. Cicero as defence counsel savaged him verbally and published the proceedings as the 'Interrogation of the Witness Vatinius' (*In Vatinium*). But after being compelled by Caesar, Pompey, and Crassus to defend him on a charge of bribery, Cicero found Vatinius a grateful friend. See 4.338 below.

288 (IX) Plutarch *Moralia* 205B
1 *Afer* 'man of African stock' probably means Carthaginian. See Plautus *Poenulus* 981 for Carthaginians wearing rings in their ears and Celsus 7.8.3–4 for the enormous holes caused by wearing heavy earrings. But pierced ears could also imply a slave origin.

289 (X) Plutarch *Moralia* 205B. In margin 'knowing nothing'

stupid, and once when he was summoned as witness in a case he answered that he didn't know anything. Then Cicero said, 'Perhaps you think I am asking you about the law?'

290 The orator Hortensius was given a silver sphinx as reward for his defence of Verres. So when Cicero was speaking allusively and by implication, Hortensius said, 'I haven't learned to solve riddles.' 'That's odd,' said Cicero, 'you have a sphinx at home.'[1]

Everybody knows the story about the monster called the sphinx, which proposed riddles for a reward, but if men failed to solve them the reward was death.[2]

291 When he happened to meet Voconius, accompanied by his three exceptionally ugly daughters, he surreptitiously muttered a Greek verse to his friends: 'though Phoebus scarce allowed he sowed his brood.'[1]

Cicero meant that he had begotten children against the will of Apollo, either because Apollo is represented as beautiful by poets or because men think luckier children are conceived when the sun is rising.

292 When Sulla's son Faustus put his furniture up for sale because of his enormous debts, Cicero said, 'I think better of this posting than of his father's.'

He was making a pun. For things are posted in an auction, and men were posted, for anyone to kill. This was the cruel way Sulla 'posted' great numbers of citizens.[1]

\* \* \* \* \*

290 (XI) Plutarch *Moralia* 205B–C. In margin 'a sphinx at home'
  1 Cicero's oratorical rival Hortensius received the gift of a (stolen) sphinx from Verres (the rapacious governor of Sicily) in return for his defence of him on charges of extortion. Cicero was speaking for the prosecution.
  2 Oedipus solved the riddle and destroyed the sphinx before his return to Thebes. See Sophocles *Oedipus Tyrannus* 391–8.

291 (XII) Plutarch *Moralia* 205C. In margin 'ugliness disparaged'
  This is possibly Quintus Voconius Naso, mentioned by Cicero at *Pro Cluentio* 53.147; he may have held the office of praetor, but nothing else is known of him.
  1 Φοίβου ποτ' οὐκ ἐῶντος ἔσπειρεν τέκνα. This tragic fragment may come from Euripides' lost *Oedipus* (Nauck *adespota* fr 378 ). Erasmus both quotes the verse in Greek and translates.

292 (XIII) Plutarch *Moralia* 205C. In margin 'joke depending on ambiguity'
  1 *Proscribere* simply meant to post a public notice; Faustus' father, Sulla, the dictator, had used such postings (the infamous 'proscriptions') to put a price on the head of his political enemies. See 8.116 below.

293 When Pompey and Caesar quarrelled, Cicero said, 'I know whom to flee but not whom to follow,' meaning that both leaders were fighting not for the freedom of the republic but for domination.

294 He blamed Pompey for deserting the city in imitation of Themistocles rather than imitating Pericles,[1] although his situation was quite different from Themistocles' and like Pericles'. For Themistocles fled to the Persians, but Pericles stayed in Athens.[2]

295 When he came to join Pompey[1] and regretted coming, he was asked where he had left his son-in-law Piso: 'He is with your father-in-law' he said, meaning Caesar.[2]

Just as Cicero was being criticized for being dissociated from his son-in-law, he retaliated by criticizing Pompey for waging war with his father-in-law.


* * * * *


293 (XIV) Plutarch *Moralia* 205C. In margin 'neither party pleases'

294 (XV) Plutarch *Moralia* 205C
1 When Pompey abandoned first Rome then Italy as Caesar's troops advanced early in 49 BC, Cicero and others saw this as cowardice and betrayal. When Athens was under attack by an overwhelming Persian force, Themistocles persuaded the Athenians to abandon the city in order to man their fleet (cf Herodotus 5.135–59), which then won the battle of Salamis. Pericles too faced a superior force of Spartans and their allies at the beginning of the Peloponnesian war, but persuaded the people of Attica to withdraw within the city walls and stand siege. Pompey, like Themistocles felt that mas- · tery of the sea was decisive, but in Themistocles' case one small city was facing the might of the Persian Empire. The Spartans were a more equal foe, even if having the upper hand at the time. (Cicero *Letters to Atticus* 10.8.4).
2 This is out of place here. It refers to a much later period in Themistocles' life when he was exiled. See 5.149 below.

295 (XVI) Plutarch *Moralia* 205D. In margin 'witty'
1 This and the next witticism are among the bitter remarks made by a disillusioned Cicero when he joined Pompey and the republican nobles in Epirus.
2 Son-in-law ... father-in-law: Pompey had married Caesar's daughter Julia as his fourth wife, and was spoken of as Caesar's son-in-law, even after her death in 54 BC. But both Plutarch and Erasmus have named the wrong son-in-law of Cicero; Piso was already dead, and it was Cicero's third son-in-law, Dolabella, who sided with Caesar in the civil war (correctly named in Macrobius *Saturnalia* 2.3.7).

296 When a deserter from Julius Caesar to Pompey said he had left his horse behind in his haste, Cicero said he had made a better choice for his horse than for himself, meaning he himself would have done far better if he too had stayed with Caesar.

297 Someone reported that Caesar's friends were gloomy.[1] 'Do you mean that they are not on good terms with Caesar?' he said.

   Cicero laughed at the flattering message, which intended to imply that the Caesarians were discouraged and feared Pompey.

298 When Pompey was in flight after the engagement at Pharsalus, Nonius said there were still seven eagles left, and urged them to have confidence. 'You would be quite right,' said Cicero, 'if we were fighting starlings.' But the other man meant eagles in the sense of Roman standards bearing eagle emblems.[1]

299 When Julius Caesar, having gained supreme power, honoured Pompey by restoring the statues that had been pulled down, Cicero said, 'In restoring Pompey's statues, Caesar adds permanence to his own.'

   He meant that Caesar was not doing this for Pompey's sake, but to win good will with his fellow citizens by the pretence of clemency, and so strengthen his domination.

300 Marcus Tullius Cicero was so concerned to speak well, and paid such anxious devotion to this, that when he was going to speak before the Court of a Hundred, and the day was approaching, he set free his slave Eros for announcing that the hearing had been postponed to the next day.

   And someone has put this too among the apophthegms, although it is not one.[1]

       * * * * *

296 (xvii) Plutarch *Moralia* 205D. In margin 'shrewd'

297 (xviii) Plutarch *Moralia* 205D. In margin 'interpretation'
   1 The war was going well for Caesar at the time.

298 (xix) Plutarch *Moralia* 205E. In margin 'fighting starlings'
   1 Again Cicero mocked the republicans who wanted to fight on after the defeat of Pharsalus. Seven eagles implied seven legions.

299 (xx) Plutarch *Moralia* 205E. In margin 'pretended clemency'

300 (xxi) Plutarch *Moralia* 205F. In margin 'concern to speak well'
   1 See Introduction xix n11 above, and dedicatory epistle 8–9 above.

301  When Cicero came to Pompey's camp and they said, 'You have come late,'
     he replied, 'Far from it, for I can see nothing is ready here.'[1]
         This was a reference to those who arrive at a party late. There is word-
     play based on ambiguity, for the man who comes reluctantly is late, and so
     is the man who arrives after the proper time.

302  Pompey gave Roman citizenship to a Gaul who had deserted to him from
     Caesar. Cicero commented, 'A fine fellow, to promise foreign citizenship to
     Gauls, when he can't restore our own citizenship to us.'

303  After Julius Caesar's victory when Cicero was asked why he had misjudged
     his choice of side, he said, 'I was deceived by the way he dressed,' (mean-
     ing that he had not expected victory to side with a namby-pamby effem-
     inate).[1] For Caesar wore his toga trailing one end like effeminate men:
     that is why Sulla used to warn Pompey to beware of the sloppily dressed
     boy.

304  Again when he was dining with Damasippus, his host had served a mediocre
     wine and, wanting to recommend it to the guests for its age, said, 'Drink
     this Falernian, it's forty years old.' Cicero said, 'It carries its age well!'
         This is how we usually talk about a man who has not lost much of his
     good looks and strength with age. But it was absurd to praise wine for its
     excessive age.

305  When Cicero saw Lentulus Dolabella, his son-in-law, wearing a long sword
     although he was a little man, he said, 'Who tied my son-in-law to a sword?'

                 * * * * *

     301  (XXII) Macrobius *Saturnalia* 2.3.7. From here Erasmus starts a run of Cicero's
          witticisms drawn from Macrobius' collection in *Saturnalia* 2.3. In margin 'noth-
          ing ready'
        1 Cicero hesitated a long time before throwing in his lot with Pompey. See 4.293
          above.

     302  (XXIII) Macrobius *Saturnalia* 2.3.8. In margin 'open reproach'

     303  (XXIV) Plutarch *Moralia* 205D. In margin 'witty'
        1 Cf 4.331 below.

     304  (XXV) Macrobius *Saturnalia* 2.3.2. Iunius Damasippus: the bankrupt art con-
          noisseur who appears in Horace *Satires* 2.8. In margin 'old wine'

     305  (XXVI) Macrobius *Saturnalia* 2.3.3. In margin 'disproportionate'

It looked as though the man was attached to the sword, not the sword to the man.[1]

306 He once saw his brother Quintus' likeness depicted on a shield in the province which he had governed, representing his head and shoulders as was customary, but on a huge scale. He said, 'Half of my brother is greater than the whole,' for Quintus was rather short.[1]

307 When Cicero's daughter Tullia walked more briskly than suited a woman, but his son-in-law Piso more casually than became a man, Cicero criticized both of them when he said to his daughter in front of her husband, 'Walk like your man.'[1]

308 Vatinius was consul for a few days[1] and Cicero mocked him by saying, 'There was a great portent in Vatinius' year, for while he was consul there was no winter or spring or summer or autumn.'

For a whole year is defined by these seasons, each of which lasts three months. I don't know if this is the same joke told differently by Pollio in *Marius the Tyrant*.[2] A man who was consul for six hours in the afternoon was also the butt of Cicero's wit: he said, 'We have such a severe and censorious consul that during his consulship nobody lunched or dined or even slept.' But perhaps this refers to Caninius Rebilus.[3]

* * * * *

1 This is Cn. Cornelius Lentulus Dolabella, Cicero's third son-in-law, who went over to Caesar. See 4.295n above.

306 (xxvii) Macrobius *Saturnalia* 2.3.4. In margin 'joke against a short man'
  1 Cicero's brother Quintus governed the province of Asia from 62–60. Magistrates were often honoured with statues and reliefs, in this case his bust (head and shoulders) depicted on an ornamental shield.

307 (xxviii) Macrobius *Saturnalia* 2.3.16. In margin 'walking appropriately'
  1 It is difficult to translate this pun. It means both 'walk like your husband' and 'walk like a man.' Gaius Calpurnius Piso Frugi was Tullia's first husband from 63–57 BC.

308 (xxix) Macrobius *Saturnalia* 2.3.5
  1 On Vatinius see 4.287 above. He was made consul by Caesar's nomination in December 47 BC.
  2 See 6.172 below, from Trebellius Pollio, one of the supposed authors of the *Historia Augusta*. See Introduction xix above.
  3 See 4.310 below.

**309** Again when Vatinius protested that Cicero had been unwilling to visit him when he was sick, Cicero said, 'I wanted to come during your consulship, but night came on too soon.' This may seem a retaliation, for previously when Cicero was boasting that the republic had carried him on her shoulders,[1] Vatinius had asked, 'So how did you get your swollen veins?' For varicose veins trouble the legs of men who stand or walk, not men who sit.

**310** Caninius Rebilus was consul for only one day,[1] and when he went up to the public platform he entered on his office and uttered the oath of departure at the same time.[2] Cicero is supposed to have said of him 'Caninius is a consul *logotheōrētos.*'[3] And he made this other witticism against the same man: 'Rebilus scored a record, that men would ask under which consuls Rebilus was consul.'

For they used to date the years by the names of consuls, and Rebilus was indeed consul, but did not have a year. Again he said, 'We have a very wakeful consul, for he never saw a moment's sleep in his whole consulship.'

**311** Julius Caesar co-opted many senators unworthy of the rank, including Laberius, the Roman knight who became a mime player. So when Laberius passed Cicero looking for a seat in the senate, Cicero said, 'I would have made room for you, if I were not already sitting squeezed up.' Thus he both repulsed Laberius and joked against the new senate, since Caesar had increased its numbers beyond the proper amount.[1] But Laberius did not

\* \* \* \* \*

**309** (xxx) Macrobius *Saturnalia* 2.3.5. In margin 'Vatinius' remark attacking Cicero'
  1 As Macrobius says, this refers to Cicero's triumphant return from exile in 57 BC.

**310** (xxxi) Macrobius *Saturnalia* 2.3.6. In margin 'a brief consulship'
  1 Gaius Caninius Rebilus, was appointed by Caesar for the last day of the old consular year in 45 BC, when one of the consuls died suddenly. Rebilus had held military commands on Caesar's side in the Civil War and this was his reward. See 4.308 above.
  2 Roman consuls swore that they had acted correctly before they stepped down from their office.
  3 Erasmus does not translate the Greek word. Possibly it means 'apprehended by the intellect alone.'

**311** (xxxii) Macrobius *Saturnalia* 2.3.10. In margin 'straddling two seats'
  1 Laberius was never a senator but a knight and composer of stage mimes whom Julius Caesar compelled to appear on stage in his own works. This automatically demoted him from his status as a knight, but Caesar at the end of the performance restored him to his former rank. Laberius immediately made his way through the senators sitting at the front of the theatre to find a seat in the

let this wisecrack pass without retaliation: he said, 'I am surprised you are cramped, for you usually straddle two seats,'[2] reproaching him with fickleness, because he had adhered with slippery loyalty now to one side and now the other.

312 When Cicero's host Titus Manlius asked him to get the position of decurion for his stepson, he said in front of a crowd of citizens, 'If Pompey is in control it will be difficult,' criticizing Caesar's readiness to co-opt new members to the senate.[1]

313 When Cicero was greeted by Andron of Laodicea, he asked why he had come to Rome. Andron said he had been sent as an envoy to Julius Caesar to obtain liberty for his city. Then Cicero said in Greek, making open allusion to the public enslavement: 'If you win your request, be envoy also for us!' or, 'plead for us also.'[1]

314 When Marcus Lepidus said in the senate, 'Conscript, not to say circumscript, fathers,' Cicero said, 'I wouldn't have put such stress on the *homoioptoton.*'[1]

* * * * *

fourteen rows reserved behind them for knights, but they would not let him in because he had been disgraced. Cicero, sitting in the senatorial seats, made this joke at the overcrowding caused by Caesar's new senators. See 4.216 above.
2 Cf *Adagia* I vii 2: *Duabus sedere sellis* 'To sit on two stools'

312 (XXXIII) Macrobius *Saturnalia* 2.3.12. In margin 'joke by implication'
  1 Erasmus it seems had a faulty text. It is not Pompey but the town of Pompeii that is in question. The decurionate was a municipal office and according to Macrobius Cicero replied that, thanks to Caesar's arbitrary treatment of election to office, 'At Rome, if you wish, he will have it; at Pompeii it's difficult.'

313 (XXXIV) Macrobius *Saturnalia* 2.3.12. In margin 'liberty oppressed'
  1 ἐὰν ἐπιτυχῇς, καὶ περὶ ἡμων πρέσβευσον. Cicero's joke points to the request of the Greek envoy for free status for his city of Laodicea as paradoxical, since Caesar has deprived the Romans of the same liberty. Cicero had enjoyed this man's friendship during his pro-consulship in Cilicia (southern Turkey) in 51–50 BC, and no doubt he was hoping for Cicero's support. See Cicero *Ad familiares* 13.67.

314 (XXXV) Macrobius *Saturnalia* 2.3.16. In margin 'unsatisfactory use of figure of speech'
  1 This is ultimately Macrobius 2.3.16, but the text does not make much sense and no satisfactory emendation has been proposed. Erasmus has tried to heal it by introducing a joke based on Quintilian 9.3.72: *ne patres conscripti videantur*

For Lepidus aimed at the figure of words with the same ending, which rhetoricians call *homoioptoton*. But it would have been better to sacrifice the figure rather than offend the senate. However, these words are really less a *homoioptoton* than a *prosonomasia*, 'a play on names'[2] which is more pleasant than the other figure.

315 When a candidate for office who was thought to be a cook's son was asking for another man's vote in front of Cicero, Cicero said, 'I too [*quoque*] will support you.'
   From this we infer that *coce* from *cocus* and the adverb *quoque* have either the same or a similar sound.[1]

316 When Milo's accuser argued on the basis of timing that Milo had planned to assassinate Clodius,[1] and then kept asking when Clodius was killed, Cicero said, 'Late,'[2] indicating by this ambiguous word that it would have benefited the republic if Clodius had been killed much earlier.

317 When Vatinius' death was announced to Cicero, but the source of the rumour was uncertain, Cicero said, 'Meanwhile I will enjoy it on loan,' meaning that

\* \* \* \* \*

*circumscripti*, 'so that the conscript fathers are not circumscript.' 'Conscript fathers' (meaning 'enrolled' or 'registered') was the formal title of the senators and the usual way of addressing the assembled body. Marcus Aemilius Lepidus, the speaker, became one of the Second Triumvirate in 43 BC. As he was the third most powerful man in Rome there would be an edge to such a remark.
 2 The proper term for this kind of wordplay (*adnominatio* in Latin) is *paronomasia*, a frequent error in Erasmus.

315 (xxxvi) Quintilian 6.3.47. Erasmus now cites a number of Cicero's witticism from the collection in Quintilian 6.3. In margin 'joke depending similarity of words'
 1 This pun cannot be reproduced in English. The pronunciation of *quoque* 'also, too' was like *coce* a vocative, 'O cook.'

316 (xxxvii) Quintilian 6.3.49. In margin 'too late'
 1 In this famous case Cicero unsuccessfully defended his friend Milo, whose slaves had killed Cicero's great enemy Clodius after a brawl on the Appian Way. Cicero claimed that Clodius was lying in wait for Milo. Although the encounter was probably accidental, Clodius was wounded and was then carried to safety in a tavern but was then killed, no doubt on Milo's orders.
 2 *Sero* can mean 'too late,' as well as 'late.' Clodius was killed in the evening.

317 (xxxviii) Quintilian 6.3.68. In margin 'temporary enjoyment'

he would enjoy a short term pleasure from Vatinius' death, like a borrower who uses money for a time as if it were his own.[1]

318 He said that Marcus Caelius, who was a better accuser than defending counsel,[1] had a good right hand but a weak left, alluding to the fact that in battle we hold our sword in our right hand but bear our shield on our left; we strike with the sword and defend ourselves with the shield.

319 Cicero refuted Jubius Curtius who kept lying about his age in order to seem younger: 'So when we were declaiming together[1] you had not been born!'

320 When Dolabella's wife Fabia said she was thirty, Cicero said, 'That's true, I have been hearing it for twenty years.' She wanted to seem younger than she was, so Cicero mocked her with a feigned confirmation, implying that she was actually fifty.

321 When they censured him for marrying a young virgin when he was sixty,[1] he said, 'Tomorrow she'll be a woman.' He was joking that this reproach would soon be cancelled, since the next day they would not be able to reproach him as a virgin's husband.

\* \* \* \* \*

1 Another version of the witticism at 4.287 above; see also 4.324 below.

318 (xxxix) Quintilian 6.3.69. In margin 'right hand better'
1 Cicero's former pupil and a distinguished orator, whom Cicero defended in the speech *Pro Caelio*. He made his name by prosecuting a number of distinguished political figures. He was also notoriously part of the Roman social scene.

319 (xl) Quintilian 6.3.73
1 Ie when they were studying oratory and practising techniques. The name could be Vibius Curius, as given in modern texts of Quintilian.

320 (xli) Quintilian 6.3.73. In margin 'pretended agreement'

321 (xlii) Quintilian 6.3.75. In margin 'virgin into woman'
1 On his return to Rome in 47 BC after two years out of Italy Cicero divorced Terentia, his wife of thirty years or more, and quickly married a rich young girl, Publilia, although he was her legal guardian. It was seen as improper on both counts and the marriage quickly broke down.

322 He also made a joke about Curio, who always introduced his speeches with a reference to his age. He said that it was easier every day for him to use this introduction, meaning that his age increased each day.[1]

323 And he made another joke against Vatinius. The man had a foot ailment but wanted to give the impression that he enjoyed better health and said that he now walked two miles. 'Yes,' said Cicero, 'for the days are getting longer.' Fabius ascribes this joke to Cicero but Macrobius to Augustus.[1]

And now too there is a joke just as amusing, if it only had the merit of being ancient. A certain soldier was boasting at a dinner party that he had an arbalest which would shoot a weapon to an unbelievable distance. When all the guests protested, he said his servent had seen it happen. So the servent was fetched in and he asked him whether he had not seen it as his master said. Then the servent said, 'You are telling the truth, master, but on that occasion you shot the arrow with a following wind.'

324 When Cicero heard a false rumour of Vatinius' death, and was questioning his freedman Ovinius, he asked, 'Is everything all right?' and the freedman replied, 'Yes, all right.' Cicero said, 'Is he dead, then?' He meant that everything would not be all right if he was still alive.[1]

325 When a witness called Sextus Annalis had damaged the case of Cicero's client, and the accuser kept insisting: 'Marcus Tullius, say something if you can of Sextus Annalis,'[1] Cicero immediately began to recite the sixth book of Ennius' Annals: 'Thou who canst unravel the mighty causes of the war . . .'

* * * * *

322 (XLIII) Quintilian 6.3.76. In margin 'age as an introductory topic'
1 This is presumably the older Gaius Scribonius Curio, not his son the younger Curio, tribune in 50 BC. In his dialogue *Brutus* 213–6 Cicero offers an unflattering picture of the elder Curio's bad memory and incompetence as a speaker. Erasmus has spoilt the story by not making clear that Curio always started off by making his age an excuse.

323 (XLIV) Quintilian 6.3.77. In margin 'gout'
1 Vatinius (see 4.287, 4.308–309, 4.317, 4.338) was a favourite butt. See 4.162 above where the joke is attributed to Augustus.

324 (XLV) Quintilian 6.3.84. In margin 'against Vatinius'
1 Another version of 4.287 above

325 (XLVI) Quintilian 6.3.86. In margin 'unexpected reply'
1 'Sextus Annalis' could also mean 'the sixth book of annals.' Cicero was defending counsel and had to respond to the incriminating evidence.

For Ennius wrote *Annals* and the accuser was called Sextus Annalis.

326 Again, he misquoted a verse from some old poet against Accius,[1] a clever and tricky man, who had come under suspicion in connection with a court case of some kind, saying, 'Unless indeed Ulysses son of Laertes escaped somehow by ship.'[2]

   The cunning Ulysses escaped both Scylla and Charybdis by ship and so did Accius escape by his trickery from the risk of being brought to court.

327 He also made fun of someone who had once been thought very stupid, but then received an inheritance and began to be asked his opinion before everyone else. 'Who has,' he said, 'the inheritance which they call wisdom?'[1] In the verse he changed 'competence' to 'inheritance,' for the poet wrote 'Who has the competence which they call wisdom?'[2]

   Cicero meant that the man had been endowed with an inheritance instead of wisdom, and now because of it he was called wise.

328 When Marcus Brutus' mother Servilia got hold of a valuable estate from Caesar at a low price when Caesar was auctioning off citizens' confiscated property, Cicero joked, 'and just to show you how good a price she paid for the farm, Servilia got it with a third taken off!' for Servilia's third daughter called Junia Tertia, was the wife of Gaius Considius,[1] and the dictator Caesar had relations as much with the mother as with the daughter.

   Cicero's joke depended on the ambiguity of the words *tertia deducta* which could be construed as 'with a third (of the price) taken off' but a wife or prostitute is also 'taken off.'[2]

          *  *  *  *  *

326 (XLVII) Quintilian 6.3.96. In margin 'a verse misapplied'
   1 Erasmus, using Aldus' 1514 edition of Quintilian, reads *Accius* (a correction of the MS *artium*). The modern emendation *Lartius* gives more point to the quotation: 'Son of Laertes' is in Latin *Laertius*, and Cicero quoted it as *Ulysses Lartius*.
   2 Ulysses' many escapes (from the Laestrygones, from the Cyclops, from Circe, etc) were proverbial. So also were his trickiness and versatility.

327 (XLVIII) Quintilian 6.3.97
   1 Here too Erasmus is following the text of Quintilian in Aldus' 1514 edition.
   2 CRF fr 35.

328 (XLIX) Macrobius *Saturnalia* 2.2.5. In margin 'a third taken off'
   1 'Considius' is a mistake. Tertia was the wife of Brutus' fellow conspirator Gaius Cassius (Longinus) (for whose sayings see 5.457–8 below).
   2 The verb *deducere* was used to signify taking home a new bride, or any woman, with sex to follow.

329 He also mocked the mother of Pletorius who was one of the prosecutors of
Fonteius, with a riddle, saying that she had a school while she lived, but masters when she died; he was implying that while she lived women of ill fame
used to consort at her place, and after her death her goods were sold up.

It seems both an absurd and a preposterous statement, for those who
keep schools are themselves the masters and have the pupils. However,
masters are not only teachers but people in charge.[1]

330 He joked about Verres' name, as if he was so called because he swept everything up, that is, the thieving fellow left nothing behind.[1] In a similar jest
someone called the thief Tullius *Tollius* 'Lifter'[2] and there were even some
who called Tiberius *Biberius* 'Drinker.'[3]

331 He used to say of Julius Caesar, 'Whenever I see his trickery and ambition
lurking under the appearance of human kindness, I fear a tyrant for the
republic; but again when I look at his elegantly flowing locks and see him
scratching his head with one finger,[1] I can hardly persuade myself that he
would conceive such an outrageous deed.'

332 When they reproached Cicero with taking money from a defendant to buy

\* \* \* \* \*

329 (L) Quintilian 6.3.51. In margin 'witty'
Cicero defended Marcus Fonteius in 69 BC on a charge of extorting money
from his province.
1 The joke is that *ludus* 'school' here means 'brothel,' that she was the mistress, and that *magister* 'master' also meant 'receiver,' appointed to sell up a
bankrupt's estate.

330 (LI) Quintilian 6.3.55. In margin 'joking about someone's name'
1 Cicero's prosecution in 70 BC of Verres, rapacious governor of Sicily, is full of
puns on his name, using either the noun 'boar' or the verb *verrere* 'to sweep.'
2 Quintilian 6.3.53, from the verb *tollere* 'to lift.'
3 For Tiberius' punning nickname Biberius Caldius Mero 'the bibulous lover of
hot and strong drink,' see 6.8 below. Tullius might be Lucius Tullius, a friend
of Verres, who was head of the syndicate collecting taxes in Sicily. See Cicero
*Verrines* 3.71.

331 (LII) Plutarch *Life of Caesar* 4.8–9. In margin 'inconsistent character'
1 This gesture was traditionally associated with homosexual practices. Pompey
was similarly accused. *Adagia* I viii 34: *Unico digitudo scalpit caput* 'He scratches
his head with a single finger.'

332 (LIII) Aulus Gellius 12.12.2–4. Erasmus uses Plutarch's *Life of Cicero* for 4.333–
46. In margin 'a charge of lying evaded'

a grand house,[1] he said 'I shall admit accepting it, if I buy it.' And when he bought the house and they reproached him with lying, he said, 'Don't you know it is the mark of a good householder to conceal any plans to purchase?'[2]

333 Cicero had a feud with Crassus.[1] Now one of Crassus' sons rather resembled a man called Dignus 'Worthy,' for which reason suspicion fell on Crassus' wife of having an affair with Dignus. When the son gave a fine speech in the senate and Cicero was asked what he thought of him, he replied, 'A Worthy son for Crassus.'

   He was making a covert illusion to the name Dignus. The joke is smarter if you use the Greek construction and say 'Crassus' Worthy son.'[2] This gives one to understand that there are two Crassuses, the bastard and Crassus' other son, who looks like Crassus.

334 Cicero had been advocate for Munatius when he was on trial, and when after his acquittal Munatius was proceeding against Cicero's friend Sabinus, Cicero angrily reproached him with his own kindness: 'Were you, Munatius, acquitted in that trial by your own effort, or by mine, when I threw a big smokescreen in front of the jury?'[1]

335 When Cicero praised Marcus Crassus on the public platform to great applause from the people, and later attacked him with fierce abuse on the

* * * * *

1  The defendant was Publius Sulla, charged with involvement in the Catilinarian conspiracy. Advocates were not supposed to accept fees or presents.
2  Erasmus' truncated version obscures the story: Cicero when first challenged flatly denied either receiving the money or intending to buy a house, and then later made the quoted remark.

333  (LIV) Plutarch *Life of Cicero* 25.5. In margin 'joke based on a name'
   1  This is Licinius Crassus, the triumvir, with whom Cicero was reconciled on the eve of Crassus' departure for Syria (cf 4.338 below) where he was defeated and killed by the Parthians.
   2  The Greek word for 'worthy' is combined with the genitive case, 'worthy of.'

334  (LV) Plutarch *Life of Cicero* 25.1. In margin 'eloquence triumphs, not the case'
   1  In Roman thinking Munatius Plancus showed ingratitude to his patron, Cicero, in accusing Cicero's client after the orator had secured Munatius' own acquittal. This is possibly Titus Munatius Plancus, tribune 52 BC. It is not known when Cicero defended Plancus. They were usually enemies. See Cicero *Ad familiares* 7.23.

335  (LVI) Plutarch *Life of Cicero* 25.2. In margin 'out of one mouth hot and cold'

same spot, Crassus said, 'What? Didn't you recently praise me in this very place?' 'Yes, I praised you,' Cicero said 'but as an exercise in boosting a contemptible subject.'

For rhetoricians often handle dishonourable themes, such as praising Busiris, or malaria, or ingratitude.[1]

336 When Crassus said, 'None of the Crassi at Rome ever lived beyond sixty' and then regretting his words added, 'What came over me to say that?' Marcus Tullius said, 'You knew the Romans would be glad to hear this, and that is how you came to govern the republic.'

Cicero meant two things: firstly that the name of the Crassi was hateful to the Romans, and secondly that Crassus had been advanced in office by flattery, not by his own merit.

337 When Crassus said, 'There is a Stoic doctrine that the good man is wealthy,' Cicero said, 'Consider the possibility that they really mean that it is the wise man who has everything.'

In this way he covertly criticized Crassus' greed, since nothing was enough for him.[1]

338 Crassus was about to set out for Syria[1] and preferred to leave Cicero as his friend rather than his enemy, so he greeted him very fussily and said he would like to dine with Cicero, and Cicero promptly received him. After a few days some of his friends urged Cicero to be reconciled

* * * * *

1 Cicero's praise of Crassus was insincere, but he turned Crassus' protests by describing it as an exercise. Rhetoricians practised praising paradoxical themes such as fever (malaria), fleas, and baldness; Isocrates' praises of the adulteress Helen and of Busiris, the murderous king of Egypt, survive as examples; also Lucian's praise of Phalaris, a by-word for cruelty. For the marginal comment cf *Adagia* I viii 30.

336 (LVII) Plutarch *Life of Cicero* 25.3. In margin 'acerbic'

337 (LVIII) Plutarch *Life of Cicero* 25.4. In margin 'greed'
1 See Cicero's *Stoic paradoxes* 6, *Only the wise man is rich*, an invective against a wealthy man recognized by everyone as Crassus, the wealthiest man in Rome.

338 (LXIX) Plutarch*Life of Cicero* 26.1. In margin 'reconciliation'
1 Crassus had obtained a command in Syria which he used to mount an ill-conceived expedition against the Parthians, leading to his defeat and death in battle at Carrhae.

with Vatinius as well.[2] 'Does Vatinius want to dine with me, too?' said Cicero.

He meant that Vatinius was looking for dinner rather than friendship.

339 Again when Vatinius, who had boils (a kind of ailment) on his neck, was pleading a case Cicero said, 'We have a swollen orator.'

The speakers called Asiatic are 'swollen' in style.[1]

340 Caesar had decided to share out the Campanian territory among his soldiers, and when many senators were angry at this, Lucius Gellius, a man of great age, said he would not let it happen while he lived. 'Let us wait, then,' said Cicero, 'It doesn't involve a long postponement.' He meant that Gellius was very near death.

341 A certain young man was accused of killing his father with a poisoned cake, and got very angry, threatening to destroy Cicero with abuse: 'I'd rather have that than a cake,' said Cicero, ambiguously imputing parricide to him.

342 Publius Sextius had retained Cicero with several others as advocates in his case, but wanted to handle it all himself and gave the others no chance to speak. When it was clear that Sextius would be acquitted by the jury, and

\* \* \* \* \*

2 Plutarch says the friends told Cicero that Vatinius was seeking reconciliation. See 4.287n above.

339 (LX) Plutarch *Life of Cicero* 26.3. 'a kind of ailment' and the last phrase on the Asiatic style in oratory were added in 1532. In margin 'an ailment taunted'
   1 In rhetoric, the 'Asiatic' style was characterized as flamboyant and showy, 'swollen' by contrast with the plain 'Attic' style.

340 (LXI) Plutarch *Life of Cicero* 26.4. In margin 'against an old man'
   This is Lucius Gellius Poplicola (136–55/52 BC, consul in 72 BC. He was already 77, but lived several more years.

341 (LXII) Plutarch *Life of Cicero* 26.7. In margin 'covert accusation'

342 (LXIII) Plutarch *Life of Cicero* 26.8. Erasmus' P. Sextius is the Sestius mentioned in 4.287n above, and this anecdote probably refers to the same prosecution in 56 BC, in which Sestius is known to have spoken in his own defence. Cicero did not think much of his style (*ad Atticum* 7.17.2). Cf Catullus' complaint, in poem 44, that reading one of Sestius' speeches had made him ill. He was a loyal supporter of Cicero. In margin 'loquacity'

the vote was being cast, Cicero said, 'Make the most of your opportunity today, for tomorrow you'll be a person of no importance,' criticizing the man for pleading the entire brief at his whim.

343 When Marcus Appius said in his introduction that he had been urgently asked by a friend to exercise care, eloquence, and good faith in his client's case, Cicero said, 'Are you so hard-hearted that you satisfy none of your friend's many requests?'

344 Marcus Aquilius had two sons-in-law, both exiled, so Cicero called him Adrastus, because he was the only one to keep his place, referring to the etymology of the Greek name.[1]

345 When Lucius Cotta, who was thought to be extremely fond of his wine, was censor, Cicero was standing for the consulship and feeling thirsty took a drink as his friends crowded round him. Cicero said, 'You are right to be afraid that the censor will take against me, for drinking water.'

Cicero pretended to believe that his friends were standing closely around him so that the censor would not see him drinking water. For like is friend to like.[1]

346 When M. Caelius,[1] who was thought not to be born of free parents, read out a letter to the Senate in a firm loud voice, Cicero said, 'Don't be surprised,

* * * * *

343 (LXIV) Plutarch *Life of Cicero* 26.12. The occasion of this speech by Marcus Appius is unknown. In margin 'mockery'

344 (LXV) Plutarch *Life of Cicero* 27.2
   1 Erasmus' text of Plutarch may have given the name as Aquinius, but Erasmus takes him to be Marcus Aquilius Gallus the jurist. Cicero's joke is based on the mythical King Adrastus of Argos who took as his sons-in-law two exiles, Polynices and Tydeus, but Erasmus' explanation seeks a pun on the Greek adjective *adrastus* 'he who does not run away.'

345 (LXVI) Plutarch *Life of Cicero* 27.3. This comes from an earlier year, 64, when Cicero was a candidate for the consulship. In margin 'bibulous censor'
   1 Cf *Adagia* I ii 21: *Simile gaudet simili* 'Like rejoices in like'

346 (LXVII) Plutarch *Life of Cicero* 27.5. In margin 'a loud clear voice'
   1 This is not Cicero's former pupil, his friend the orator Caelius. Plutarch's text calls the man Gellius, in either case unknown.

for he is one who had to shout.' He meant that Caelius had been an auctioneer or crier, and thus had learned by experience to be clear voiced. On the
other hand, slaves for sale used to be advertised by the crier.[2]

347 A certain Memmius was abusing Cato of Utica, and saying that he was
drunk all night: 'But you don't add the charge that he plays dice all day,'
said Cicero. Thus he courteously exonerated Cato, who devoted the whole
day to the business of the republic and took a few hours at night to relax
his spirit.

348 When Julius Caesar was earnestly defending the case of Nicomedes of Bithynia's daughter in the senate and recalling the king's kindnesses to him, Cicero said, 'Away with that, since we all know what he gave to you and you
to him.' This joke is based on a double meaning, for a man who bestows a
kindness gives, and so does a woman who makes herself available. Hence
Martial's verse: 'to give you wish, but not to give away.'[1]

    Caesar had a bad reputation for being more obliging to King Nico-
medes in Bithynia than the laws of chastity require.

349 Marcus Calidius accused Gallus, whom Marcus Tullius Cicero was defending. And when the accuser declared that he would prove by witnesses, doc-
uments, and cross-examination that the defendant had prepared poison for
him, but enunciated this atrocious charge with a relaxed expression, drawl-
ing voice, and too little emotion in his deportment, Cicero said, 'Would you
plead like that if you were not inventing the charge, Calidius?' He drew the
inference from his delivery that he was not speaking sincerely.

        * * * * *

    2 Erasmus seems to have misunderstood the joke. The meaning probably is 'he
      had to make a claim,' ie to get his freedom. *proclamare* (literally, 'to cry out')
      is in this sense a legal term.

347 (LXVIII) Plutarch *Life of Cato Minor* 6.4. Cf the anecdote about the elder Cato
    5.361 below. In margin 'joke based on adding something'

348 (LXIX) Suetonius *Julius Caesar* 49.3. In margin 'taunt based on double meaning'
    1 Martial 7.75.2, where an old hag wants it, but doesn't want to pay (see *De
      copia* CWE 24 316).

349 (LXX) Valerius Maximus 8.10.3; for Cicero's criticism of the low-key orator
    Marcus Calidius, see *Brutus* 274–8.

350 He also joked against Isauricus when he said, 'I don't understand how it happened that your father, that firm and constant man, left you to us so fickle (*varius*).'

This is another joke depending on a double meaning. For *varius* means 'fickle,' but *varius* also means a man 'marked by bruises.' Now it was common talk that this Isauricus had once been beaten by his father with straps, which explains not a saying but an action of the praetor M. Caelius: when Isauricus as consul broke Caelius' curule chair of office, Caelius set out another chair with a seat of leather straps, silently threatening and reproaching him for being beaten with thongs by his father.

### The orator Demosthenes

351 Pytheas reproached Demosthenes[1] because his arguments 'smelled of the lamp'[2] (meaning that he never spoke except from a written text, and with material he had worked on by night). But Demosthenes turned this criticism against him, by commenting that his lamp and Pytheas' lamp did not cost the same.[3]

He meant that the other man indulged in feasts all night, spending more on luxury than Demosthenes did on his profession.

\* \* \* \* \*

350 (LXXI) Quintilian 6.3.25 and 6.3.48. Publius Servilius Isauricus was a distinguished Roman politician and general, being consul, proconsul and censor. Quintilian thinks Cicero's jibe inappropriate and in poor taste. In margin 'taunt based on double meaning'

351 (1) Plutarch *Life of Demosthenes* 8.4–5. In margin 'smells of the lamp'
Erasmus has saved to the end of the book the Athenian orator Demosthenes (384–322 BC), who led the opposition first to Philip of Macedon then to Alexander and Alexander's regent, Antipater, and, as the fickle Athenian assembly shifted its allegiance, was subsequently exiled from Athens (see 4.358–4.368 below). Plutarch did not include sayings of Demosthenes among those of his other Athenian generals and statesmen, so Erasmus depends on Plutarch's *Life of Demosthenes* and other sources.
   1 Pytheas was an Athenian orator of disreputable character and shifting political alliances, but his animosity towards Demosthenes was unceasing. He opposed the Athenians' proposal that Alexander be offered divine honours (Plutarch *Moralia* 804B [*Precepts of statecraft*]) but later supported Macedonian interests. See 5.212 below.
   2 *Adagia* I vii 71: *Olet lucernam* 'It smells of the lamp'
   3 Possibly Erasmus' text was faulty. The Greek says, 'His lamp and Pytheas' lamp were not privy to the same activities.'

352 When others held his excessive practice for speaking in public against him, he answered that preparation for public speaking showed a man to be a lover of the people, whereas those who neglected it belonged to the party seeking tyranny over the people, since they did not aim to persuade by words but to compel by force.

353 Whenever Phocion got up to speak in the assembly Demosthenes used to say to the friends around him that a hatchet was being lifted to chop his arguments.
    For Phocion was a concise but sharp speaker, and he usually disagreed with Demosthenes.

354 The Athenian assembly was pressing Demosthenes to accuse a certain person, and when he refused they began to shout at him, as they do. Then he got up and said, 'Athenians, you have me as your adviser whether you like it or not, but you will never have me as your slanderer, even if you want.'

355 Demosthenes was one of the ten envoys sent by the Athenians to Philip of Macedon. So when Aeschines and Philocrates, whom Philip had treated with special warmth, returned from the embassy they praised the king for many reasons and especially for his good looks, eloquence, and hard drinking. Demosthenes made fun of them, saying none of the qualities they praised were worthy of a king; for the first was a merit in women, the second in sophists, and the third in sponges.[1]

* * * * *

352 (II) Plutarch *Life of Demosthenes* 8.6. In margin 'popular eloquence'

353 (III) Plutarch *Life of Demosthenes* 10.4. For Phocion, whose policies in opposition to Demosthenes were for conciliating the Macedonian king, see 4.257–79 above. He was considered a more effective speaker than Demosthenes even if less eloquent (Plutarch *Moralia* 803E [*Precepts of statecraft*]. In margin 'concise and effective speech'

354 (IV) Plutarch *Life of Demosthenes* 14.4. In margin 'adviser, not a slanderer'

355 (V) Plutarch *Life of Demosthenes* 16.2–4
  1 The Athenians sent this embassy to Philip II in 346 BC to negotiate peace. Philocrates was the chief architect of the settlement, which the Athenians later rejected. The orator Aeschines was another opponent of Demosthenes.

**356** Demosthenes had written in gold letters in Greek on his shield 'For good luck.' But when it came to fighting, he immediately threw away his shield and ran. When men insulted him as a 'shield-ditcher,'[1] he dismissed it with this well-known saying: 'a man who flees and runs away will live to fight another day.'[2]

He thought it more service to his country to run away than to die in battle. For a dead man cannot fight, but the man who seeks safety in flight can be useful to his country in many battles.[3]

**357** When Alexander offered peace to the Athenians on condition they handed over to him eight citizens, among them Demosthenes, Demosthenes told them the fable of the wolf who offered the sheep peace on condition they surrendered the sheepdogs: he meant that Alexander was the wolf, the dogs were those guarding people's interests, while the sheep were the Athenian masses. Then he added, 'As merchants present a small quantity of grain as a sample in a side dish, as a means of selling vast heaps of grain, so if you now offer the eight citizens he demands, you will be surrendering the entire people.'

**358** When he was condemned by the council of the Areopagus and was making his escape from prison, he met a number of men from the opposite party

* * * * *

**356** (VI) Aulus Gellius 17.21.31; Plutarch *Life of Demosthenes* 20.2. Erasmus is combining sources here. See also Plutarch *Moralia* 845 F (*Lives of the ten orators*). In margin 'flight excused'
  1 For the disgrace of ditching one's shield see 1.168 and 2.110 above. He threw away his shield at the battle of Chaeronea (338 BC) when Philip of Macedon defeated the Athenians. See *Adagia* II ii 97: *Abiecit hastam. Rhipsaspis* 'He threw away his spear.'
  2 Erasmus quotes and translates the Greek: Ἀνὴρ δὲ φεύγων καὶ πάλιν μαχήσεται. The line is from Menander *Sententiae* 45 (56 Jäkel). See also the proverb collection CPG 2 Apostolius 3.19a; *Adagia* I x 40.
  3 The words 'He thought ... in many battles' were added in 1532.

**357** (VII) Plutarch *Life of Demosthenes* 23.4–5. This was after the defeat of the allied Greek states at the battle of Chaeronea in 338 BC and the destruction of Thebes in 336 BC. See 4.57 n1 above. In margin 'a few on behalf of all'

**358** (VIII) Plutarch *Life of Demosthenes* 26.3. Demosthenes was found guilty of taking bribes from Harpalus (see 3.370 n1 below) in 323 BC, but the charge may have been politically motivated. He fled to Arcadia. In margin 'desire for one's homeland'

a little distance from the city, and at first wanted to hide, then when they called him by name and told him to cheer up and offered him some travelling money as well, he groaned deeply, saying, 'How can I leave this city, where I have better enemies than I would have friends in another city?'

**359** They say that on his flight he kept looking back at the Acropolis and stretched out his arms to Pallas, saying, 'Pallas, mistress of cities, why do you delight in three ill-omened beasts, the night owl, the serpent, and the common people?'

For the night owl is the most unlucky of birds, but sacred to Pallas, and she wears serpents on her breastplate, and the people is a beast with many heads, accustomed to give the worst thanks to those who serve it best like Socrates, Phocion, Scipio, and many others.[1]

**360** He used to say to the young men associated with him that he now knew how much ill will, fear, slander, and danger was to be expected by a politician, and if he had to choose between the two, he would sooner face death than go on the platform or rostrum.

**361** When Demosthenes was an exile in Arcadia, Pytheas was speaking in support of the Macedonians,[1] and said, 'As we suspect that a house in which

\* \* \* \* \*

**359** (IX) Plutarch *Life of Demosthenes* 26.6. See 358 immediately above. In margin 'the people a deadly creature'
  1 Erasmus explains Demosthenes' prayer: Athens' tutelary goddess Athena has as her sacred bird the ill-omened owl, and she bears the Aegis, a shield adorned with the head of Medusa, which he interprets as symbolic of the many-headed and bestial nature of the common people whom she protects. He then cites the ingratitude with which the Athenians condemned Socrates and Phocion to death; See 3.73–5 and 3.89 above for Socrates, and 4.274–8 above for Phocion. The snake is, however, the sacred snake which lived on the Acropolis. The Scipio mentioned here is the elder Scipio (Africanus Major), the conqueror of Hannibal, who amid increasing hostility was involved in his brother Lucius' conviction (183 BC) and, being accused himself, retired from political life, complaining of the nation's ingratitude.

**360** (X) Plutarch *Life of Demosthenes* 26.7. In margin 'avoid politics'

**361** (XI) Plutarch *Life of Demosthenes* 27.5–6. In margin 'an exile loyal to his country'
  1 See 4.358 above for Demosthenes' exile. The slanging match between Demosthenes and his enemy Pytheas occurred in the Arcadian assembly, when an embassy had arrived from Athens. This was after the death of Alexander. Athens

milk has to be purchased[2] and brought in, is suffering some misfortune, so a state must be sick when an Athenian embassy comes to it.' Then Demosthenes retorted, 'As milk is brought in to restore the sick to health, so the Athenians are here for the health of the cities.' When the Athenian people heard of this they immediately recalled him from exile.

362 A ship was sent for him when he came back from exile and many magistrates and citizens came to meet him. Then he stretched his arms to the sky and said that his return to his country did him more honour than that of Alcibiades, because Alcibiades returned when his fellow citizens were forced into it,[1] but he had returned because they were convinced it was right.

363 After Demosthenes fled to the island of Calauria for fear of Antipater, he kept to the temple of Neptune as sanctuary. Then Archias, who had risen to power from being a tragic actor, tried to persuade him with soft words to trust himself to Antipater, saying that he would not suffer any ill but would be honoured with lavish gifts. Demosthenes said, 'I never fancied you as an actor on stage, and you will not persuade me now as an orator.' But when Archias grew angry and threatened to drag him from the temple, he said, 'At last you have spoken the true oracular response of the Macedonians; before you were pretending like an actor.'

* * * * *

wanted to set up a coalition of Greek states to attack Alexander's successor, the Macedonian ruler Antipater (see 2.51 n1 above, 4.363 below). Demosthenes even in exile continued his anti-Macedonian policies and supported the embassy, whereas Pytheas was at this time pro-Macedonian.
2 Erasmus seems to have confused two Greek words. This should be 'asses' milk,' used as a medicine.

362 (XII) Plutarch *Life of Demosthenes* 27.7–8. In margin 'things freely offered give pleasure'
1 After many ups and downs in his career, Alcibiades had once again been a successful commander. The political situation at Athens had made his return from exile necessary. See 5.184 n1 below.

363 (XIII) Plutarch *Life of Demosthenes* 29.1–3. Cf *Moralia* 846F (*Lives of the ten orators*). In margin 'acerbic'
Antipater and Craterus had just defeated the coalition of Greek cities at the battle of Crannon, 322 BC. The one-time tragic actor Archias was known as *phugadotheras*, 'the exile hunter,' and was responsible for the deaths of several other distinguished exiles, whom he dragged from sanctuary (*Demosthenes* 28.4).

364 Demosthenes is supposed to have been enticed by the reputation of the famous harlot Lais to sail to Corinth so as to experience her notorious lovemak-
ing. But when she demanded ten thousand drachmae for a night, he changed
his mind, put off by the enormous fee, and said 'I don't pay that much for
something I'll regret.'[1] He meant that regret was the sure consequence of
shameful pleasure.

365 There is a famous saying of Pytheas, that 'Demosthenes' speech smells of
the lamp'[1] because he composed and wrote out by night what he was intending to say. Then when another man who had a bad reputation for thieving was attacking him on the same grounds, Demosthenes said, 'I know
we are a nuisance to you for lighting a lamp at night.' For thieves prefer
darkness.

366 Again when Demades cried out, 'Demosthenes wants to set me straight, like
a pig teaching Minerva,'[1] Demosthenes said, 'But that Minerva got caught
in adultery a year ago.'
    He turned Demades' adultery against him, while the poets make Min-
erva a virgin.

367 Again when the Athenians demanded his advice, he said, 'I have not been
brought into line.'
    He meant that he was not a slave to the people's desires, but made his
own decision what he thought he should do.[1]

*  *  *  *  *

364 (xiv) Macrobius *Saturnalia* 2.2.11; Aulus Gellius 1.8.3. In margin 'pleasure cost-
ing much'
    1 See *Adagia* I iv 1: *Non est cuiuslibet Corinthum appellere* 'It is not given to every-
    one to land at Corinth.'

365 (xv) Plutarch *Life of Demosthenes* 11.6). In margin 'witty'
    1 See 4.351 above. Whereas Demosthenes prepared his speeches carefully, his
    enemy Demades (see 4.366 just below) was highly esteemed for his extempore
    eloquence; see also 6.382 below.

366 (xvi) Plutarch *Moralia* 803D (*Precepts of statecraft*). In margin 'acerbic'
    1 *Adagia* I i 40: *Sus Minervam* 'The sow (teaches) Minerva'

367 (xvii) Plutarch *Moralia* 6D (*The education of children*). In margin 'resolute'
    1 Erasmus quotes the Greek words οὐ συντέταγμαι. A similar anecdote and retort
    are attributed to Pericles in 5.183 below, which is drawn from the same section
    in Plutarch. The context is the dangers of lack of preparation. Both Pericles

**368** A maidservant received money as a deposit from two guests on condition that she returned it to them both at the same time. After a while one of them came in mourning clothes, pretending that his friend had died, tricked the woman and took away the cash. After this, the other one returned and began to ask for his deposit back. When the woman became panic-stricken and thought about hanging herself, Demosthenes took up her defence. Entering to plead her case, he challenged the claimant like this: 'The woman is ready to keep the agreement, but if you do not bring your friend, she can not do so, because, as you say, the terms were that she should not pay over the money to one without the other.'

By this clever argument he saved the poor woman and frustrated the conspiracy of the two wastrels who had done this to get the same money twice over.

**369** When someone asked Demosthenes what was most important in oratory, he answered 'performance' (*hypocrisis*). When asked what came next, he said, 'performance' and when asked what came in third place, he said nothing except 'performance.'

He thought delivery was so important that the whole art depended on it. For delivery includes many things, control of the voice, power of the eyes, expression of face, and the movement of the whole body.[1]

**370** When the Athenians were eager to aid Harpalus,[1] and were already arming against Alexander, Philoxenus, whom Alexander had put in charge of his naval campaigns, made a sudden appearance. The people were astounded and fell silent in fear. Demosthenes asked what they would do if they saw the sun, since they could not face a lantern?

This is how he condemned the people's ill-considered reactions.

\* \* \* \* \*

and Demosthenes prepared carefully. Erasmus interprets both remarks in the same way; the words probably mean 'I am not prepared.'

368   (xviii) Valerius Maximus 7.3 ext. 5. In margin 'cunning'

369   (xix) Plutarch *Moralia* 845B (*Lives of the ten orators*). In margin 'delivery is all'
    1 See also Cicero *De oratore* 3.213 and Quintilian 11.3.6.

370   (xx) Plutarch *Moralia* 531A (*On false shame*). In margin 'rashness'
    1 Harpalus was a friend of Alexander who had defected to the Athenians. See
    4.26 above (on Philip).

**371** When some people thought Demades had ceased his knavery, Demosthenes said, 'Yes, for now you see him well fed, like lions.'[1]

Demades was greedy for money, and lions are milder when they are well fed.

**372** When he was being provoked by some abusive fellow, Demosthenes said, 'I am being challenged to a combat in which the one who emerges superior will be the worse man, and the loser will be the victor.'

**373** On another occasion, when he heard an orator shouting excessively, Demosthenes said, 'What is great need not be good, but what is good is great.'

This is also credited to others.[1] Some people even think dinners are smart if they are prolonged and furnished with many courses.

\* \* \* \* \*

**371**  (xxi) Plutarch *Moralia* 526A (*On love of wealth*)
  1 See 4.271 above (on Antipater).

**372**  (xxii) Stobaeus 18.4 (Meineke I 300). In margin 'weighty'

**373**  (xxiii) Stobaeus 4.51 (Meineke I 102). In margin 'shouting'
  1 Cf Zeno at 7.310 below.